TRAVEL LAW AND LITIGATION

Fourth Edition

In memory of Alan Graeme Saggerson

TRAVEL LAW AND LITIGATION

Fourth Edition

Alan Saggerson
BCL MA (Oxon) Barrister
Bencher of Lincoln's Inn
A Recorder

© Alan Saggerson 2008

Published by
XPL
99 Hatfield Road,
St Albans, UK
AL1 4JL

www.xplpublishing.com

ISBN 978 1 85811

Printed and bound in the UK.

Contents

Table of Cases

Martens v Thomson Tour Operations Limited Unreported – Mayor's & City of London County Court May 2000, 166,375
Martin v Thomson Tour Operations Ltd. [1999] CLY 3831, 267
Martin v Travel Promotions Limited [1999] CLY 3821, 232
Mason v Titan Travel Ltd. 17 June 2005 Grimsby CC (Unreported) TATLA Newsletter Autumn 2005, 29,263,264
Mauro Tarantini di Maggio v Lunn Poly Unreported – 2 May 2003 – Woolwich County Court, 216
Mawdsley v Cosmosair Plc [2002] EWCA Civ 587; [2003] ITLJ 23, 126
MFI Warehouses Ltd v Nattrass [1973] 1 WLR 30, 551,580
Millensted v Grosvenor House (Park Lane) Ltd [1937] 1 K.B. 717, 648
Milar SrL v British Airways [1996] QB 702, 456
Minhas v Imperial Travel Limited [2003] CL February 263, 223
Moncrieff v Cosmos 6 October 2006 (Swansea CC) Unreported, 163
The Moorcock (1889) 14 PD, 25
Moran v First Choice Holidays and Flights Ltd. [2005] EWHC 2478 (QB), 64
Morris v KLM Royal Dutch Airlines [2002] 2 WLR 578, 38,50
Morris v West Hartlepool Steam Navigation C. Ltd. [1956] AC 552, 180
Murphy v Culhane [1977] Q.B. 94), 628
Murphy v First Choice Holidays 22 February 2007 (Birmingham CC) Unreported, 173
Murphy v JMC Holidays Limited [2003] ITLJ 16, 216

Nanuwa v Lufthansa (1999) CLY 4885, 493
Ng Cbun Pui v Lee Cheun Tat [1988] RTR 298, 527
Nikitin v Butler [2007] EWHC 173 (QB), 624
Norfolk v MyTravel Tour Operations Limited [2003] Unreported – Plymouth County Court 21 August 2003, 85
Norman v Bennett [1974] 3 All ER 351, 611
Numan v Southern Railway [1923] 2 KB 703, 528

Nugent v Michael Goss Aviation Limited [2000] Lloyds LR 222, 479

O'Brien v TUI UK Ltd 17 January 2006 (Bury CC) Unreported., 175
O'Connor v British Transport Commission [1958] 1 WLR 346, 526
O'Grady v Cresta Holidays Ltd 18 October 2007 (Liverpool CC) Unreported, 174
Office of Fair Trading v Lloyds TSB Bank plc and others, 535
Old Barn Nurseries v West Sussex County Council 5 December 1994, 561
Olley v Marlborough Court Hotel [1949] 1 KB 532, 251

Painting v Oxford University Press [2005] P.I.Q.R. Q5, 652
Parker v Flint [1699] 12 Mod Rep 254, 409
Helen Parker v TUI UK Limited (T/A AusTravel) Central London County Court 30th October 2006, 492
Parr [1996] CL Oct 131, 360
Parrott v Jackson [1996] P.I.Q.R. P394, 629
Partridge v Crittenden [1968] 1 WLR 1204, 244
Patel v India Air (1999) CLY 4904, 493
Patrick v Cosmosair Plc, 5 March 2001, Manchester County Court, 83
Patschieder v Great Western Railway Company [1878] 3 LR Exch 153, 528
Perry v Butlins Holiday World [1998] Ed. CR 39, 417
Perry v TUI (UK) Limited 13 April 2005 Bromley CC Unreported, 237,279
Philips v Air New Zealand Limited [2002] EWHC 800, 466
Phillips v First Choice Holidays and Flights Ltd Medway County Court 7 February 2007 DDJ Beech (Unreported), 275,474
Phipps v Rochester Corporation [1955] 1 QB 450, 418
Potter v TUI UK Ltd.26 March 2006 (Mayor's Court) Unreported, 174
Powell v Thomson Holidays Ltd 28 April 2005 (Exeter CC) Unreported, 351,406
Power v Panasonic UK Ltd [2003] IRLR 151 EAT, 42-
Priddle v TUI UK Limited 19th November 2004 (Taunton CC) Unreported, 207
Prince v Prince 22nd June 2007 (Lincoln County Court) Unreported, 325,328

Table of Statutes

Conventions

Athens Convention
a1, 99
a1.1, 85
a1.2, 85
a1.5, 508
a2, 92
a3, 92,97
a5, 90,97,101
a6, 512
a7, 86,93.97
a8, 86,93.97,102
a10, 86,94
a11, 513
a13, 94
a14, 86,89,93
a15, 516
a15(3), 97
a16, 86,89,103,105
a17, 507
a18, 513

Berne Convention, 518
a26, 518
a27, 520
a29, 521
a30, 521
a31, 522
a38, 523
a39, 523
a40, 523
a42, 523
a55, 523

Brussels Convention
aa5-6, 20
a16, 20
a17, 20

Montreal Convention 1999, 7,445-480
a1, 448
a3, 453
a17(1), 456
a17(2), 468
a17(3), 468
a19, 471
a20, 477
a21, 467,477
a22(1), 471
a22(2), 470
a22(5), 470,479
a22(6), 469,470
a25, 470
a29, 475
a31, 478
a33, 454
a35, 473

Warsaw Convention 1929
a17, 38,39

Table of Regulations and Directives

Preface

"The miserable have no other medicine but only hope."
Shakespeare: *Measure for Measure*

On 12 August 1873 the Hobbs family – Samuel Hobbs, his wife Elizabeth, and two children (5 and 7 years old) – took the train from Wimbledon to Hampton Court. Alas, the train did not go to Hampton Court. Instead, unannounced, it ventured down a branch line to Esher where it deposited the Hobbs family at about midnight. Neither alternative transport nor any accommodation was available at Esher at midnight in 1873 and there were no more trains until the next day. The family was forced to walk five miles home in the rain where they arrived at 3 o'clock in the morning. Mrs. Hobbs in particular suffered "*much in mind and body*" and as a result of catching a bad cold she was unable to attend to her domestic affairs, business and children. Samuel and Elizabeth Hobbs claimed £400.00 in damages from the railway company at a trial before Chief Baron Kelly and a jury at Kingston-Upon-Thames Assizes. The railway company paid £2.00 into court. The plaintiffs were awarded £28.00 comprising £8.00 for their inconvenience and £20.00 in respect of Mrs. Hobbs' cold.

The railway company appealed and the appeal, presided over by Lord Chief Justice Cockburn and three Justices of the High Court, occupied a Serjeant, two Queen's Counsel and two Juniors. The railway company's appealed was allowed.[1] Although entitled to the £8.00 for inconvenience, the £20.00 allowed for the vexation caused by Mrs. Hobbs illness was "*purely sentimental*" and the jury's award was reduced accordingly.[2] The jury's refusal to award any sum for consequential losses arising out of Elizabeth's illness was upheld on the grounds (no doubt compelling in the 1870s) that "*A person might walk a hundred times from Esher to Hampton without falling down and breaking a limb.*"

By the time a Mrs. Kemp reached the Court of Appeal 100 years later (*Kemp v Intasun Holidays*[3]) Kerr LJ thought it perfectly obvious that if, due to overbooking, a hotel condemned a family to sleep a night on the beach, as a

---

[1] *Hobbs v London & South Western Railway Co* [1875] 10 LRQB 111.
[2] See e.g. Mellor J at 12   2.
[3] [1987] CLY 1130; [1987] 2 FTLR 234.

result of which they caught colds or even pneumonia, they should recover damages. However, Mrs. Kemp's *asthma attack* was not foreseeable. Even now, it seems, the Court of Appeal's sentiment will only stretch so far.

The large volume of "railway" cases from the last quarter of the 19th century – such as the Hobbs' case above – illustrates that there is nothing new about travel related litigation. As cheaper transport became more easily accessible to the general population it was perhaps inevitable that disputes would arise between the consumer and transport providers. Litigation involving carriage contracts resulted, and as different means of transport extending over ever greater distances developed in the first half of the 20th century, so the scope for dispute increased.[4] However, it was the social phenomenon of mass tourism, and particularly the package holiday, which made the most profound difference, and the growth of the package holiday industry since the middle of the 1960s has created in its wake a new sub-species of litigation – Holiday Law.[5] Since then travel related disputes have not been confined to contracts of carriage or the rights and obligations of innkeepers (though such actions still abound). The law has recognised that the provision of an environment free from vexation and the right to recover damages for what the Court of Appeal in *Hobbs* described as "purely sentimental" factors (loss of enjoyment as we might now describe them) lies right at the heart of cases generated by alleged breaches of *holiday* contracts. This was the position recognised by the Court of Appeal in the now infamous case of *Jarvis v Swan Tours*[6] a case which forms part of the legal vocabulary of every student.

The fact that the family holiday abroad is regarded by many as an annual necessity (not just an occasional luxury) and the provision of economically accessible packages to the mass market by tour operators do not themselves fully explain the enormous growth in holiday and travel related litigation in recent years. No doubt this growth is partly accounted for by increased public awareness of consumer rights and a degree of consumer militancy which no longer tolerates sub-standard services with the equanimity of yesteryear – but the combination of package travel availability and consumer militancy is only part of the picture. The modest increase in travel related litigation in the 1970s and 1980s owes much to these changed social conditions. Modesty, however, was cast aside with the introduction of the *Package Travel, Package Holidays and Package Tours Regulations 1992*. It is

---

[4] And with the growth of international travel by difference means so regulators increasingly intervened by means of devices such as the Warsaw Convention in 1929.
[5] Other relevant texts on the subject include Grant and Mason *Holiday Law*, 4th edition which bears witness to the growing importance of travel law as an independent discipline.
[6] [1973] All ER 71.

these Regulations more than anything else which have instilled real vigour into consumer *Holiday Law* – not only in terms of the volume of cases being conducted in county courts throughout the land – but in respect of the independence of Travel Law as a legal discipline. The identification of this discipline in the 1990s must be akin to the growth and development of "motor claims" in the 1930s. Both in their time have reflected radical, social and economic change and like motor claims, Travel Law is likely to remain a permanent fixture on the legal landscape.

The first edition of this book was born of lectures and seminars given by the author at the invitation of Central Law Training and at Barnard's Inn Chambers in London. The second edition was a complete revision, less closely tied than the first to the original presentations on which the third was a further improvement. This fourth edition revises again the original scheme and includes some new sections on, for example, Hotels; Discrimination and the Montreal Convention as well as commentary on the effect of a wide range of cases decided in the higher courts[7] and about *one hundred* new cases decided in the lower courts since the last edition was published in 2004 not only under the *Package Travel [Etc.] Regulations 1992* but in the related areas of international transport, timeshare and the conflict of laws. Some significant areas of uncertainty have been resolved; many uncertainties remain; a few have been compounded. Such is the common law.

I have tried to reflect the law as of 29th. February 2008.

I am grateful to *xpl publishing* for their encouragement and patience in the preparation of this edition, as I am to all the members of the International Travel Law team at what is now *1 Chancery Lane* (formerly No 1 Serjeants' Inn). More than previously, this edition is a collaboration. I am especially indebted to *Matthew Chapman* (liability cases and consumer credit); *Sarah Prager* (liability cases, the relevant criminal law and civil procedure); *Ian Miller* (discrimination) and *Jack Harding* for his unparalleled attention to detail in matters regulatory.[8] Each of the above has contributed to the text and participated in discussions and seminars on many related issues. All have been able to produce reliable case notes on literally hundreds of decisions in the County Court which would otherwise be unreported; some of which shed at least some watery light on travel law as she is practised on a day to day basis. The errors that undoubtedly remain, as they say, are mine. Those looking for more information on the many unreported decisions used to illustrate the text in this edition will find digests of many such cases in the

---

[7] Including the European Court of Justice.
[8] Denied Boarding in particular.

Newsletters of the *Travel and Tourism Lawyers' Association* available at www.1chancerylane.com and in the *International Travel Law Journal*.[9]

Despite the many recent legal developments covered in this edition and to both appropriate and misquote a phrase that is all too familiar; *reports of the death of the package holiday have been much exaggerated.*

Alan Saggerson
1 Chancery Lane
London
WC2A 1LF

29th February 2008

---

[9] University of Northumbria – 1994-2008.

Introduction

> To travel hopefully is a better thing than to arrive, and the true
> success is to labour.

> **RL Stevenson, *El Dorado***

This book is about the law relating to travel and tourism. Its intended
audience is the busy practitioner and for that reason includes not only
discussion about the substantive law, but a number of precedents and
appendices to which those engaged in travel related litigation may need to
have frequent recourse. It is assumed that the reader will know the basics of
the English legal system as well as the law of contract and tort. Much of the
contents of this book will be of interest to those concerned with *holiday*
litigation but it is hoped that the scope and interest is much broader than
that. By no means does all travel related litigation arise out of holiday and
leisure disputes and increasingly the line between business and leisure travel
has become blurred. This edition, like its forerunners is not devoted
exclusively or even mainly to the law relating to *package holidays* though
inevitably package holidays make up a significant proportion of its
components. One of the (many) curiosities that will be discussed in detail in
the course of the following chapters is the fact that whilst in recent years the
travel industry has worked long and hard to distance itself from the grasp of
package holiday law by mechanisms variously known as "split-contracting";
"dynamic packaging"; "off-package sales" and even "unpacked packages",
the law has been sprightly in keeping up with such commercial
developments[1] to the extent that one might conclude that the Package Travel,
Package Holidays and Package Tours Regulations 1992[2] have now been
construed as having a wider application than may have been thought
possible in the recent hey-day of the regulated package holiday. In other
words the industry's valiant efforts at legitimate regulatory (PTR 1992)
avoidance have led to (or at least have coincided with) the widening of the
regulatory net. Thus, even though the traditional off-the-shelf package
holiday may have been in decline, reports of the death of the package holiday

---

[1] *ABTA v CAA* [2006] EWCA Civ 1356.
[2] See in particular Chapters 1-4.

and in particular reports of the death of the PTR 1992 have both been much exaggerated.[3]

Travel Trends

Approximately 30% of the adult population of the United Kingdom has yet to make a visit abroad for any reason. Nonetheless, the European Council Directive on Package Travel[4] expressly recognises package holidays as an essential part of the internal market and notes the increasingly important role of tourism in the economies of Member States. This was undoubtedly true in 1990 and remains every bit as true today. The statistics (at least in this instance) do not lie. Visits abroad by UK residents increased from 50.9 million in 1998 to 59.4 million in 2002[5] and spending increased in the same period by an impressive £7.5 billion to £27.0 billion. Included in these figures is a staggering increase in the volume of holiday travel of 25% in the 5 years to 2002 in which year 39.9 million foreign holidays were taken. Of these 20.6 million were inclusive tours.[6] Given the significant proportion of the population yet to travel abroad for any reason it is clear that a large minority of UK residents are travelling on holiday abroad more than once a year.

More recently,[7] during the 12 months to September 2007, visits abroad by UK residents increased by 1 per cent, from 68.7 million to 69.6 million. Over this period, visits to North America increased 3 per cent (to 4.8 million), visits to Europe remained broadly the same (at 54.6million) and visits to other parts of the world rose by 10 per cent (to 10.2 million). Spending on visits abroad by UK residents increased to a record £32.2 billion, a fourfold increase between 1985 and 2005 in real terms, and a 6 per cent increase between 2004 and 2005. During July to September 2007, the seasonally adjusted number of visits overseas by UK residents remained broadly the same at 17.2 million when compared with the previous three months, while the associated spending decreased by 1 per cent to £8.8 billion. Europe remained the most popular destination for UK residents, accounting for 80 per cent of visits abroad. Spain continued to be the most popular country to visit, with 13.8 million visits in 2005. Spain has been UK residents' favourite holiday destination since 1994. This has continued and in 2003 Spain hosted 30 per cent of all holidays abroad, followed by France (18 per cent - 11.1 million visits).

---

[3] The European Commission is consulting on the ambit of the 1990 Directive which gave rise to the PTR 1992.
[4] 90/314 EEC – Reproduced as Appendix 1. [In this book "the PTR 1992".]
[5] Statistical source: *Travel Trends: The Office of National Statistics,* 2002.
[6] So it seems about 50% of those travelling on holiday abroad do so on package holidays.
[7] Travel Trends on the web site of the Office of National Statistics 2007.

The number of visits abroad made by UK residents has more than tripled since 1985, to a record 66.4 million visits in 2005 and 69.6 million to September 2007 (seasonally adjusted). Two-thirds of these visits abroad were holidays, just under half of which were package holidays. Although the number of holidays overall has continued to increase year-on-year, there has been a fall in the number of package holidays in the last five years. UK residents made a record 41.2 million holiday trips in 2003. This was 3 per cent more than in 2002 and was a continuation of the rise in overseas holidays over the last three decades from 6.7 million in 1971. About half (47 per cent) of the holiday trips abroad in 2003 were package holidays. As in previous years, nine out of the ten most popular countries UK residents visited in 2003 were in EU Europe. The exception was the USA. After two years of decline in the number of holidays, the USA experienced a small increase in 2003, when it accounted for 5 per cent of all holidays.

Visits by overseas residents to the UK increased by 1 per cent, from 32.2 million to 32.4 million. Visits from residents of Europe increased 1 per cent (to 23.3 million), from North America decreased by 1 per cent (to 4.6 million) and from other parts of the world rose 1 per cent (to 4.5 million). The seasonally adjusted number of visits to the UK by overseas residents dropped 6 per cent when compared with the previous three months, to 7.8 million. Spending by overseas residents on visits to the UK decreased by 1 per cent to £4.0 billion.

Package Holidays

The *package* holiday has been particularly beloved of UK residents. The statistics reveal that whatever the decline from its hey-day, the traditional package holiday still retains a place close to the heart of the UK traveller. A far higher proportion of UK residents' visits overseas are as part of a package holiday (29 per cent in 2005) than of overseas residents' visits to the UK (6.3 per cent in 2005). UK residents make approximately 10 times as many package holiday visits abroad as overseas residents make to the UK. The number of package holidays made by UK residents travelling abroad declined by 7.9 per cent from 20.6 million in 2001 to 19.0 million in 2005 although there were rises and falls over this period. Overseas residents made 2.0 million package holiday visits to the UK in 2001 and although these also fluctuated over the five year period they remained almost unchanged at 1.9 million in 2005. As a proportion of all holidays, package holidays fell for both overseas residents visiting the UK and UK residents travelling abroad over the 5 years from 2001 to 2005. For overseas residents, package holidays fell from 26 per cent of all holidays in 2001 to 19 per cent in 2005 but for UK residents the fall in the proportion of holiday trips which were package holidays was even greater, dropping from 53 per cent in 2001 to 43 per cent in 2005.

For air travel, the changes in the proportion of package holidays is similar for both UK residents and overseas residents but for sea and the Channel Tunnel they differ. For trips made by air by overseas residents there was a gradual decrease in the proportion of package holidays from 19 per cent of all holiday trips by air in 2001 to 11 per cent in 2005. The opposite was true for visits to the UK via the Channel Tunnel, with the proportion of holiday visits being package holidays rising from 24 per cent of all holiday visits in 2001 to 34 per cent in 2005. Package holidays to the UK by sea showed no clear trend. For UK residents travelling abroad by air there was a downward trend in the proportion of holiday visits which were package holidays from 57 per cent in 2001 to 44 per cent in 2005. Although by sea the equivalent proportion of package holidays abroad rose and fell over the years there was an overall decrease from 42 per cent in 2001 to 36 per cent in 2005. The proportion of all holiday visits on packages via the tunnel for UK residents travelling abroad fell from 42 per cent in 2001 to 33 per cent in 2003 before rising again to 39 per cent in 2005, still lower than the level in 2001.

Social Trends

The statistics do not reveal the increased importance of travel and tourism as part of the social fabric of a country and its population. Departmental graphs and pie charts tell us nothing about the *qualitative* importance of both leisure and business travel abroad, and they say little about the *diversity* of travel options available both at home and abroad or the *comparative* increase in expenditure by UK residents on travel as a proportion of annual income. National newspapers and magazines devote entire sections to the travelling consumer; travel agents offer a bewildering array of options for pockets of all shapes and sizes, and indeed for those with no pockets at all[8]. University departments, legal texts, journals and a growing number of legal and industry conferences, specialise in the complexities of travel and holiday law to help sort out the mess when something goes badly (and often not quite so badly) wrong as it invariably will. Consumers associations have departments specialising in the consumer traveller. Even standard texts such as *Chitty on Contracts* now give nodding recognition to the travel litigator. Those accustomed to scanning the *Current Law* service for cases on broken heads and bruised legs will now invariably stumble on comparative quantums for broken holiday promises and bruised travellers' egos. Indeed since the first edition of this book, *Current Law* has devoted a separate

---

[8] Students in 1998 were offered a "package" in Eastern Europe helping to clean sewerage from disused canals – not surprisingly at no cost.

leisure section to which such cases (and an increasing number of self-reported cases on matters of substantive law) are now consigned.[9]

Another continuing development since previous editions is the proliferation of "fly-on-the-wall" travel television. Programmes are no longer just designed to tempt the population to travel abroad, but in some cases appear positively to luxuriate in the travelling misfortunes of fellow consumers and those retained to look after them. Autumn and winter broadcast schedules are bursting with drama-documentaries about holidays from hell, holiday swaps, or behind-the-scenes shenanigans at some holiday resort, representative or airport as well as broadcast consumer magazines which often appear to engage in breathless hyperbole about travellers' agonies. Programme planners have hit a rich vein of relatively cheap television, but the vein is only so rich because the results captivate audiences in large numbers representing at least some anecdotal evidence of the importance attached to travelling by a significant sector of the population. Travel items are seldom long out of the news headlines either. We read not only about rail catastrophes in India as well as at home, adventure holidays in Switzerland involving "canyoning" and the resulting 21 deaths; sinking cruise liners; but also about a British man allegedly consumed by lions whilst on safari in Zimbabwe. On a more prosaic level when a holidaymaker is hit on the head by a falling coconut her resulting successful claim is hailed as an example of the worst excesses of the "compensation culture". What's more a tourist has been imprisoned for 12 months for refusing to turn off his mobile telephone whilst on board an aircraft. As more consumers search for ever more adventurous travel options, so the potential liabilities of those responsible for their arrangements escalate. Even the less adventurous taking package holidays in Europe are just as susceptible - perhaps more susceptible - to accident and illness than they are at home due to the fact that holidaymakers are inclined to indulge in escapades they would not countenance at home.[10]

Risks arising out of badly managed or cheaply maintained accommodation designed for the mass tourist market are legion and the travelling consumer from the UK is not always best placed to bear such hazards in mind especially when the standards of safety and hygiene encountered abroad are often *different*[11] to those that are likely to be encountered at home. No statistical analysis has been published, but certain types of accident are commonplace. British tourists frequently walk through the glass of unmarked patio or balcony doors. This is not, one hopes, because British tourists are particularly stupid, but because they are unaccustomed to the

---

[9] Now to found in the section "Hospitality and Leisure".
[10] Alcohol is also frequently implicated.
[11] But not necessarily worse.

facility. Local residents can be mystified at the frequency of such accidents simply because they themselves are accustomed to living a greater part of their lives *al fresco*. This clash of cultures is itself part of the reason local property managers neglect to put in place safety procedures which might help visitors remember where they are, and that a sheet of non-laminated glass stands between them and relaxation on their patio or balcony. Tourists from all over the world happily mount, and allow their children to ride, jet-skis without any form of training or instruction and without appreciating that they are every bit as dangerous as all other forms of motorised transport when they would not even consider the possibility of their off-spring driving a car or a motorcycle. People who have never so much as been on a horse, gamely jump aboard barely supervised camels in the middle of nowhere, and when they fall off, look to blame someone else for their misfortune, sometimes with abundant justification.

It is not only in respect of injury and illness that travel organisers need to beware of their potential liabilities. In *Heald & Heald v Thomson Tour Operations Ltd*,[12] two ladies travelling alone successfully sued their tour operator for damages for sexual harassment. Not harassment engaged in by the tour operator or those employees for whom it was vicariously liable, but harassment undertaken by hotel staff in a Tunisian hotel. The allegations were of lewd and disgusting suggestions made by restaurant waiters and offers of extra food and pots of tea.[13] The court appears to have been perfectly prepared to imply a term into the holiday contract to the effect that consumers would be accommodated in hotels where they would be reasonably free from the sort of behaviour engaged in by the hotel staff in question — and for breach of that implied term the tour operator was liable. However, whilst package holiday cases predominate in some parts of the text, the general principles discussed apply to travellers be they undertaking business or leisure. Many parts of the text are of general application, and whilst they may apply to the package tourist, they apply with equal force to the non-package traveller.

Despite the size of the travel industry in the UK and the increasing importance of travel to ordinary households, it is often overlooked that the profit margins for organisers can be extremely small; so small that the offer of even the smallest *ex gratia* payment can easily outweigh the notional profit the organiser expected to make.

---

[12] Reported only in the *Daily Mail* – August 1996.
[13] Neither the Particulars of Claim nor the judgment revealed what form these lewd suggestions took.

Statutory regulation

As travel has become a growth industry in economic terms, so travel *law* has become a growth legal industry in turn, servicing not only the requirements of the disgruntled consumer after the event, but by *regulating* in advance the manner in which many travel services should be provided. At the end of 1992 The Package Travel, Package Holidays and Package Tours Regulations[14] came into force. By these Regulations Parliament has for the first time imposed a regulatory framework designed to govern the relationship between consumers and the suppliers of travel services. The regulations, as their title suggests, are by no means limited to the standard "package holiday" but have a radical impact on all aspects of the travel industry and affect the business traveller as much as the holiday-maker. Much of the following text, and many of the cited materials and precedents are concerned with these Regulations. Perhaps more than any other single influence, the PTR 1992 have been responsible for identifying travel law as an independent legal discipline. In the years since the introduction of this legislative framework we have seen the development of a body of case law quite distinct from the travel cases hitherto found scattered around the general law of contract and tort. As with much new legislation — particularly in spheres largely left to the piecemeal treatment of the common law - the PTR 1992 themselves create new ambiguities and uncertainties which only authoritative judicial interpretation will resolve. The effect and interpretation of these regulations are given extensive treatment throughout the course of this book.

The PTR 1992 may be by far the most radical in scope to affect the travel industry in the UK, but they do not, by any stretch of the imagination, represent the first or only example of domestic legislative activity produced as a result of international initiative. The Warsaw Convention (1929), as subsequently amended by the Hague Protocol (1955), was introduced into domestic law by the Carriage By Air Acts of 1931 and 1961 (now all appearing under the gleaming livery of the Montreal Convention 1999[15]) respectively, and what Warsaw achieved in the air, Athens introduced for the sea[16]. However, there is a material difference in the ambitions of earlier international conventions and those of the European Directives of the 1990s. The latter are unashamedly designed to ensure greater consumer protection — the same could not be claimed for the international conventions.

> *"The aim of the Warsaw Convention is to*
> *protect those users of aircraft (passengers) while*

---

[14] 1992 SI 3288 – Appendix 2 – PTR 1992.
[15] See Chapter 10.
[16] Schedule 6 of the Merchant Shipping Act 1995.

> *not endangering the financial rewards for carriers which result from the carriage of passengers and their luggage.* "[17]

It should not come as a surprise to anyone to learn that the protection of the carriers' financial rewards was uppermost in the minds of the negotiating governments at times (both in 1929 and 1955) when international airlines were commonly nationalised, administered and managed by the very governments who negotiated the Conventions. No-fault liability for injury, loss and damage was imposed on the carrier in exchange for miserly limits[18] on the amount of compensation recoverable by the victimised passenger: even today the upper limit of compensation stands at the sterling equivalent of £13.00 per kilo for hold baggage, and £13,000.00 in respect of death or personal injury, unless the damage can be proved by the passenger to have been caused intentionally or recklessly The original limits have been revised many times and by many different regimes in recent years, the details of which have largely been overtaken by the Montreal Convention but as will be seen, the ghost of these international restrictions continues to haunt the PTR 1992 and in some limited respects confine their effectiveness as a tool of consumer protection.[19]

Since 1972, consumers travelling on package holidays by air have also enjoyed additional statutory protection through the ATOL system administered by the Civil Aviation Authority (CAA). This system makes it compulsory for tour operators selling package holidays involving air travel to be in possession of an "ATOL" (air travel organiser's licence) — pursuant to The Civil Aviation (Air Travel Organiser's Licensing) Regulations. Basically, to obtain an ATOL, the organiser must satisfy the CAA of its financial standing, and purchase a bond which can be called upon to assist consumers in the event of the organiser's insolvency. ATOLs continue to be administered in tandem with the new security provisions applicable to *all* tour operators in the PTR 1992 and it is in the context of the 2003 amendments to the ATOL Regulations that the Court of Appeal has most recently engaged in a discussion as to the scope and reach of the PTR 1992[20] as regards the meaning of terms such as "*pre-arranged*" and "*inclusive price*".

---

[17] Downes & Paton: *Law for the Travel Industry* – page 197.
[18] Although in the context of the value of money at the time the limits may not have appeared so draconian.
[19] Usually where a tour operator incorporates the provisions of an international convention (Montreal or Athens) into its standard consumer conditions of contract as permitted by PTR 1992 regulation 15(3).
[20] *ABTA v CAA* [2006] EWCA Civ 1356.

Intervention from Europe is far from complete. In October 1994 the Official Journal of the European Communities published Directive 94/47 requiring Member States to introduce legislation by April 1997 regulating the sale of "timeshare" properties. To a modest extent the UK was ahead of the game in this context. The Timeshare Act 1992 and associated statutory instruments already provided for a 14-day compulsory "cooling off" period following the conclusion of a timeshare purchase agreement. Further subordinate legislation has been enacted.[21] A revised version of the PTR 1992 was expected at the time of the second edition in 1999 and although we are still waiting, DBERR[22] has recently issued fresh guidance on what *it* (now) contends is the meaning of a regulated package whilst the European Commission has also recently issued a public consultation document[23] seeking views on future redrafts of the PTR 1992 the implications of which will be discussed in more detail in the appropriate chapters to follow.

Some initiatives for travel regulation are home-grown. Increasing concern about the quality of supervision offered by sports and activity centres in the UK has led to calls for a system of compulsory registration and licensing in the interests of ensuring higher standards of health and safety. In particular safeguards are sought to provide parents, schools and social organizations with some means of verifying the quality of training, services and facilities offered to those consumers (often, but not always, children and young persons) looking for a taste of excitement or even danger in their leisure and educational activities. A period of intense activity led by the Department for Education in this context in the aftermath of the Lyme Regis canoeing tragedy in March 1993 has produced the Outdoor Activities (Safety of Young Persons) Act 1996 together with associated regulations.[24] However, even in the absence of specific regulation in this field, activity holidays and the potential they have for accident, injury and worse, helps to underline the fact that existing criminal law legislation (*e.g.* the Health and Safety at Work Act 1974) has an important role to play in the regulation of the travel industry in the United Kingdom. Whilst this text is mainly concerned with those criminal offences created by the PTR 1992 and those already to be found in statutes such as the Trade Descriptions Act 1968, the Consumer Protection Act 1987, the Timeshare Act 1992 (as amended) which have particular application to the travel industry and its contractual relationships with consumers (enforced through local authority weights and measures or trading standards departments). The Unfair Commercial Practices Directive,

---

[21] The Timeshare Regulations 1997 SI 1081.
[22] The DTI renamed as the Department for Business, Enterprise and Regulatory Reform in 2007.
[23] See [2007] ITLJ 155.
[24] Trotter: *Activity Holidays and the Law* [1994] NLJ 454.

is a major reform of the law concerning unfair business practices in the European Union which is to come on stream by April 2008.[25]

It is worth noting more generally, that the call for the statutory creation[26] of the offence of "corporate manslaughter" was generated in no small part by travel and leisure disasters such as the ferry catastrophe at Zebrugge, railway accidents, or as a result of fatalities suffered on outward-bound courses, or at fairgrounds.

Voluntary regulation

Through the Association of British Travel Agents (ABTA) the travel industry has endeavoured to provide a framework of self-regulation. ABTA is a trade organisation that represents both tour operators and travel agents. For decades membership of ABTA has been seen by the travel industry and public alike as a badge of respectability: a club from which tour operators and travel agents would wish to avoid expulsion. The prestige of the organization has enabled ABTA to impose and enforce measures designed to protect the consumer against the worst excesses of the travel industry "cowboys" in a number of respects, by creating for its members rules governing:

- the provision of reserve or security funds for the repatriation of passengers stranded as a result of a tour operator's demise;

- the compulsory imposition of financial bonds (representing a proportion of a tour operator's turnover), from which bonded funds consumers can be compensated for losses sustained following an operator's insolvency;

- Codes of Conduct (drafted in consultation with the Office of Fair Trading under the Fair Trading Act 1973), governing the relationships between the professional service providers and the public, and imposing on ABTA members the requirement to include in their contracts with consumers certain specified terms and conditions (which in a number of respects foreshadow those now imposed on members and non-members alike by the PTR 1992);

---

[25] Directive 2005/29/EC, (Article 1 of which provides that *Unfair commercial practices shall be prohibited!*) see Chapter 12.
[26] Corporate Manslaughter and Corporate Homicide Act 2007. Although the offence of corporate manslaughter was the subject of a frenzy of speculation and concern in the travel industry and particularly amongst tour operators before 2007, the Act only applies [see section 28] where the harm resulting in death to which the Act applies occurs in the United Kingdom or its territorial waters, some off-shore installations, British registered ships and British operated aircraft. Individuals cannot be made liable under the Act either as principals or accessories.

- access to the independent and informal arbitration scheme administered by the Chartered Institute of Arbitrators for small claims.

The current edition of the ABTA Code of Conduct is on the ABTA website.

Until the introduction of the PTR 1992 the protective framework administered by ABTA on behalf of its members could be justly regarded as ahead of its time. The general application of the PTR 1992 to ABTA members and non-members alike, may however reduce the importance of self-regulation of this type, and following their introduction ABTA abandoned the long-standing "stabiliser" — the arrangement whereby ABTA tour operators could only sell products through ABTA travel agencies, and ABTA agencies could only promote and sell the services of ABTA tour operators (a cartel that was sanctioned in the public interest (the Restrictive Practices Act 1976 notwithstanding) by Anthony Lincoln J in *Re: Association o f British Travel Agents Ltd's Agreement.*[27]

Smaller and independent tour operators (*i.e.* those who fall outside the classification of "package giants") often belong to the Association of Independent Tour Operators (AITO), and their travel agent counterparts to the National Association of Independent Travel Agents (NAITA). In the services they provide to, and require of, their independent members, both organizations mirror the sort of voluntary discipline imposed by ABTA on their big brothers.

Consumer Independence

Despite statutory and voluntary regulation of the travel industry and in particular the holiday travel industry the consumer appears to remain oblivious to the cost-benefits of buying protected products – such as regulated package holidays where a tour operator is deemed to be liable for *any* improper performance of the holiday contract however serious the consequences. Instead the consumer searches for the cheapest deals often putting together individual travel arrangements for himself on-line. When something goes wrong, this same consumer can be left without any domestic remedy. The problems created by this absence of a local remedy have been and will continue to be responsible for generating much of the case law on issues such as the scope and content of the duties created and imposed on travel providers under the PTR 1992 and the same issue is likely to be the driving force behind any broadening of their scope should they be revised in the near future as a result of current EU consultation.

---

[27] [1984] ICR 12.

The Pope

Package travel is a serious business indeed. As reported by Bruce Johnstone of the *Daily Telegraph* on 21 June 2001 even the late Pope John Paul II had cause to slam *"package holidays; packed lunches & pizzerias"*.

> The Pope savaged the package tourism industry, accusing it of trivialising or ignoring other cultures and humiliating travellers and their host countries. In a message for World Tourism Day, the 81-year-old Pope said that travel was supposed to be about people experiencing "other ways of life, other religions, and other ways of looking at the world and history". This allowed them to "discover themselves and others" and freed from them from being "bound up with themselves". He said mass tourism was hawking a "superficial exoticism" which ignored the true culture of holiday destinations. He claimed that "sophisticated holiday centres" offered a "reconstructed ethnicity" to satisfy a "thirst for new thrills". This transformed cultures, religious ceremonies and ethnic feasts into consumer products. In some instances tourism had "generated a form of sub-culture that humiliates both the tourist and his host community". In his message, the Pope reserved particular criticism for sex tourism. He said: "Sadly, unchecked desire leads at times to humiliating aberrations, such as the exploitation of women and children in an unscrupulous sex trade which is an intolerable scandal. Let no one succumb to the temptation of making free time a period of rest from values." He also lamented the way that the tourism industry was "revealing itself to be like the world", meaning that it was "ever more globalised, and inter-dependent". While a common "conscience of the importance of the great works of art" existed, this was not true for foreign cultures, where the vestiges of primitive civilisation and rites of initiation still existed. The Pope is the most travelled pontiff in history and earlier this year the Church boasted that it had attracted an estimated 23 million pilgrims to Rome for its Millennium Jubilee celebrations. Many visitors travelled on package tours and some were criticised for living cheaply and sightseeing en masse with packed lunches. Italian tour operators objected to the Pope's criticisms, which they insisted were out of date because they applied to an "old form of tourist village"... Armando Peres, director-general of the Italian Touring Club, defended the Pope's comments, saying that tourist villages "committed the serious error of presenting life as a soap bubble, that doesn't exist". He said: "Tourism organisations are simplifying our lives. They recreate a life just like our own, and they surround us with interpreters who speak our language. But this is a diabolic road to follow. Because it means that in the end, all of the Italians who go to the Caribbean find themselves together in the same pizzerias, where the only thing local is the black dancing girls."

Trivialisation, superficial exoticism *and* diabolic; a mix that has entertained millions over the last 40 years or more. Long may it continue.

Chapter 1

REGULATED PACKAGE CONTRACTS

Introduction

The Package Travel, Package Holidays and Package Tours Regulations 1992[1] (referred to throughout the text as "the PTR 1992" or simply "the regulations") came into force on 23 December 1992 and apply to all regulated travel packages sold or offered for sale on or after 30 December 1992. The 1992 Regulations implement in the United Kingdom, European Directive 90/314 of June 1990.[2] The purpose of the Directive was to achieve harmonisation of the laws relating to consumer protection within the European Union and the Single Market in the context of package tourism; to equalise the competitive position of tour operators within the Union and for the purposes of consumer protection.[3] The regulators acknowledge the increasingly important economic role played by the travel industry in the economies of Member States[4] and clearly believe that the creation of uniform rules regulating package travel is likely to produce benefits not only for the consumer but for the travel industry throughout the Union by attracting customers from outside the Community seeking the advantages of guaranteed standards in packages the regulatory framework provides.[5] The Directive and the PTR 1992 do not, however, guarantee the standards of the packages supplied to consumers by the industry. It is impossible for the regulators to regulate in such a way as guarantees a perfect or even a satisfactory package every time. Rather, by regulating, the Community has provided uniform standards in respect of the remedies that should be available to consumers in the event that something goes wrong. This harmonisation of *remedies* does ensure that service providers throughout the Union operate on a reasonably equal footing, and it could be argued that the provision of harmonised remedies in Member States, which make it easier for the consumer to take action in respect of poor services, is itself likely to lead indirectly to a reduction in the number of occasions on which the consumer

---

[1] SI 1992 No 3288 reproduced in full as Appendix 2.
[2] The Directive is reproduced in full as Appendix 1.
[3] See Appendix 1 — preamble.
[4] Now 27 in number.
[5] Council Dir 90/314 — preamble para. 12.

will have cause to complain against the tour operator. Putting it bluntly, the easier it is for the consumer to take action and succeed against a tour operator in respect of travel related service complaints, the more likely it is that the tour operators or organisers will themselves exert pressure on *their* subcontractors to deliver a reasonable product.

It would be difficult to overstate the impact of the PTR 1992 on the law affecting package travel contracts in England and Wales. The PTR 1992 have in practice transformed the relationship between the consumer and tour operator. The transformation affects holiday consumers in the greatest number, but the impact of the PTR 1992 is not expressly limited to holiday contracts. The reach of the PTR 1992 apparently extends to business travel. Compliance with the rules is not limited to those who sell regulated packages or travel services in the course of a business. The impact of the PTR 1992 has been greatest on the traditional holiday-maker who has purchased a package holiday from a brochure produced by a tour operator and circulated either by travel agents or through general advertising, but the scope of the PTR 1992 is not limited to holiday consumers.[6] Whether the PTR 1992 in an amended form *should* be limited to holiday consumers or natural persons contracting other than in the course of their trade or business is currently under consultation with the Director-General for Health and Consumer Protection at the European Commission.

The PTR 1992 do not supplant common law principles of contract[7] and tort,[8] but they certainly deploy them in a way that has at least created the impression that new consumer rights exist where none did before. It may well be that a cogent argument could be made to the effect that the regulations have altered the common law framework very little, putting the consumer in a contractual position that is no different to that which existed

---

[6] "*The scope of the Directive's application cannot ... be defined by reference to the purpose of the travel. There is nothing, either in the wording of the Directive or related to its objectives, that can be prayed in aid to support the conclusion that only "recreational" travel is protected under the substantive rules of the Directive and that travel for other purposes (business, conferences, family visits, study, to name but a few) is by definition excluded and therefore not subject to the consumer protection provisions ... *" [Opinion of the Advocate-General in *AFS Finland v Kullutajavirasto* –ECJ C-237/97].
[7] In *ABTA v CAA* [2006] EWHC 13 (Admin) Goldring J said at paragraph 161: "*In my view, whether the agreement links the consumer to the organiser or retailer or both depends upon the application of the English law of contract, in particular the law of agency. So too do decisions as to whether the organiser or retailer or both are parties to the contract or whether under Regulation 15, the organiser or retailer or both are liable under it. If by application of the English law of contract the retailer is liable under the contract between him and the consumer, he cannot escape his liability by blaming the lack of proper performance of the obligations under it on someone else.*"
[8] See Mason: *Apocalypse Now* [2006] ITLJ 90 at 93.

before the regulators intervened. Nonetheless, however cogent such an argument might be, the *perception* that has taken root is that the PTR 1992 have themselves created a landscape altogether more favourable to the consumer, to the extent that it is now commonplace to find travel cases litigated with reference *only* to the PTR 1992 even though much of what the regulations contain might be found in general common law principles of contract and tort. The travel *contract* is ignored with startling frequency at the expense of the PTR 1992. Increasingly consumers and claimants neglect to look at or rely on the express terms of their contracts usually to be found in the "small print" at the back of a holiday brochure described as a Fair Trading Charter, a Code of Practice, or more prosaically as Standard Terms and Conditions. Many consumers would be surprised to find that this "small print" is often more favourable to them than the PTR 1992. More importantly, however, whatever benefits the regulations bring to the consumer, the contents of the travel contract — the terms of the contract — remain central to the question of both liability and remedies. The regulations do *not* create a regime of absolute liability in respect of which the party supplying the package is rendered responsible come what may to a dissatisfied or injured consumer. The Regulations create a new framework within which liability for breaches of regulated contracts is distributed.

Broadly speaking, the PTR 1992 cover six areas:

(i)   information to which the consumer is entitled before entering into a contract;[9]
(ii) the form that a regulated package must take;[10]
(iii) the content of regulated packages;[11]
(iv) the parties on whom regulatory obligations are imposed and in whom enforcement rights are vested;[12]
(v)   remedies for consumers in both civil and criminal courts;[13]
(vi) rules governing the security in respect money paid by consumers in anticipation of the provision of the travel service provided for in the contract to cover events such as repatriation in the event of a tour operator's insolvency.[14]

This chapter is mainly concerned with the application and definition of regulated package travel arrangements.

---

[9] Regulation 7 and Schedule 2.
[10] Regulation 9.
[11] Regulation 6 and Schedule 2.
[12] Regulation 2.
[13] Regulations 4, 5, 14, 15, 22 and 24.
[14] Regulations 16-22.

Application of the PTR1992

The PTR 1992 apply to packages sold or offered for sale in the United Kingdom.[15] The scope of the regulations extends beyond those instances where a package *contract* is actually concluded. Suppliers will find themselves subject to the regulations even if a holiday is never sold.[16] Those who merely *offer* packages for sale in the United Kingdom must abide by the regulatory requirements on the form and content of promotional literature, and must have in place the necessary safeguards for consumers' money irrespective of whether a sale is ultimately made. Any party intending to enter into the package travel sales market in the United Kingdom must comply with the PTR 1992 before a single sale is made. Furthermore, the application of the regulations is *not* limited to those who are in business selling travel arrangements to consumers — and the application of the regulations is certainly not limited to those in the business of supplying *holidays.*[17]

It is clear that the regulations apply irrespective of the domicile, seat or residence of either the vendor or purchaser — provided the sale or offer for sale takes place in the United Kingdom. So, the PTR 1992 are not limited to:

- holidays;
- "foreign" travel; the PTR 1992 applies in appropriate circumstances to regulated packages to be performed in the United Kingdom;
- business or commercial suppliers or organisers but extend to all those offering packages otherwise than occasionally;
- organisers who are in any way based in the United Kingdom or anywhere in the European Union.

The important point is that the PTR 1992 are not limited in their application to tour operators selling foreign package holidays to British consumers. An extreme example may illustrate the breadth of the regulations' potential reach. Any travel organiser based in the United States, advertising regulated packages in the British press, will be subject to the regulations even though the travel contract made as a result of the advertisement is concluded in New York, and even though the consumer may be resident outside the European Union. The advertiser's invitation to treat in respect of the regulated package constitutes an "offer" for sale within the territory of the United Kingdom and is subject to the PTR 1992. The terms implied into the travel contract by reason of the regulations are imposed irrespective of which law governs the

---

[15] Regulation 3(1).
[16] Regulation 5 applies to *possible consumers.*
[17] See above.

contract.[18] Even if the American advertiser is relaxed about the prospects of having the contract enforced in the civil courts, the application of the regulations will make that organiser subject to criminal sanctions in respect of the package offered and in particular the form and content of the advertising leading up to the conclusion of the travel contract. Indeed as noted above some parts of the regulations apply even though no travel contract results at all.

It probably goes without saying that it is not every type of "package" that is covered by the PTR 1992, only *regulated* packages. That is, those combinations of services and facilities that satisfy the regulators definition of a package. So, the first two questions for any party are these.

1. Do the express provisions of the contract (to be found in the "small print") provide this consumer with equal or greater protection than the PTR 1992?[19]
2. Do the services provided to this consumer satisfy the statutory definition of a package? In other words, is this package *regulated*?

The rest of this chapter is concerned with the definition of regulated packages.

Regulated Packages Defined

What limits the reach of the PTR 1992 is the definition of package travel. Unless the arrangements sold or offered for sale fall within the statutory definition there is no regulated package and self-evidently the PTR 1992 cannot apply to those arrangements. This important qualification to the application of the regulations is, surprisingly, often overlooked. If travel arrangements cannot be brought within the regulations then parties will have to look to the general law to resolve their differences.

By Regulation 2(1) a package means:

> *"the pre-arranged combination of at least two of the following components when sold or offered for sale at an inclusive price and when the service covers a period of more than twenty-four hours or includes overnight accommodation —*
> *(a) transport*
> *(b) accommodation*
> *(c) other tourist services not ancillary to transport or accommodation and accounting for a significant proportion of the package ..."*

---

[18] Regulation 28.
[19] And of so is it necessary to rely on the regulations?

Throughout this text any package which satisfies this definition is referred to as a "regulated package". There are many possible combinations of travel arrangements sold or offered in a variety of ways which do not satisfy the regulators' definition. These will be referred to where necessary as "non-regulated packages".

A regulated package must have at least five ingredients:

1. The package must comprise a combination of two out of the three listed qualifying components.
2. The combination must be pre-arranged.
3. The combination must be sold or offered for sale at an inclusive price.
4. The arrangements must extend over a period exceeding 24 hours, or involve overnight accommodation.
5. The package must be sold or offered for sale in the United Kingdom.

If any one or more of the five ingredients is missing the arrangements are not a regulated package. The chances are that a considerable proportion (but by no means all) of the holidays sold off the shelf from brochures by travel agents will qualify as regulated packages. However, because there are exceptions to this general principle and because the grasp of the PTR 1992 extends well beyond the scope of holiday contracts as commonly understood, it is worth looking at the regulated ingredients in more detail. In doing so it should be noted that even fifteen years after the implementation of the PTR 1992, there remains only limited authoritative judicial guidance as to a number of important ambiguities in the regulations themselves. Guidance has been forthcoming on a case-by-case basis but ambiguities remain. Sometimes because of the fact sensitive nature of English case law the "guidance" raises as many questions as it answers.[20] Where authoritative guidance has been given to date it has often been in the context of personal injury actions of significant value, or claims brought on behalf of large groups of claimants where the value of the actions is also more likely to lead to the litigation being conducted in the High Court, or where appeals from county court decisions are more likely to be economically viable. Nonetheless, the cases reported from the higher courts are of general application in so far as they deal with matters of principal.

A large number of cases have been reported in the journals[21] from county courts up and down the country, but the decisions on liability are reported in much the same way as decisions on quantum — on a voluntary basis by

---

[20] *ABTA v CAA* [2006] EWHC 13 (Admin) Goldring J; [2006] EWCA Civ 1356 Chadwick LJ and *Evans v Kosmar Villa Holidays* [2007] EWCA Civ 1003 Richards LJ.
[21] Such as *Current Law* and the *International Travel Law Journal* and the Newsletter of the Travel and Tourism Lawyers' Association available at www.1chancerylane.com (resources).

advocates involved in the cases — or even by journalists who have taken an interest in litigation that has, for them, an attractive human angle. Such reporting is necessarily cryptic and truncated and must be approached cautiously. Much of the reasoning of the judges and all of the arguments projected on all sides is omitted from such reports, and it can be dangerous to assume that the decision is necessarily unambiguously authoritative for the bald proposition of law cited unless a transcript of the decision is available.

In order to understand how some of the most recent judicial guidance on the construction of the PTR 1992 has come about it is necessary to take a short diversion into the world of the Civil Aviation Authority and the ATOL[22] Regulations – regulations which adopt for some purposes the definition of a regulated package from the PTR 1992.

The CAA and ATOL Regulations

The CAA was conceived (amongst other things) as the licensing authority concerned with the *financial* protection of consumers following a number of high-profile tour operator failures which left holidaymakers stranded abroad or abandoned at home without holidays for which they had paid.[23] Licensing provisions were introduced with regard to the provision of flight accommodation. By means of the ATOL Regulations 1995 introduced under the Civil Aviation Act 1982 as subsequently amended in 2003 the consumer was supposedly protected against tour operator business failures by means of the fact that any flight accommodation provided had to be directly traceable back to an ATOL holder, and the holding of an ATOL would itself be a badge of security protecting the consumer effectively guaranteeing repatriation and/or compensation in the event of insolvency. The relevant 2003 amendment to the ATOL Regulations provided that "*A person shall not make available flight accommodation which constitutes a component of a package in the capacity of an agent for a licence holder except where all the components of the package are made available under a single contract between the licence holder and the consumer.*"

The apparent objective of this amendment was to cure the perceived mischief of contract splitting - to put a stop to "unscrupulous" travel agents hiving off air transport from hotel services, and making each the subject of *separate* contracts so that only the air transport element was protected under the ATOL. The consumer, it was thought, was likely to believe that they were purchasing a

---

[22] All travel organisers selling package holidays including air transport must have an ATOL – an Air Travel Organiser's Licence.

[23] Remember "Court Line" or as Professor Grant describes it at [2005] ITLJ 165, "the Court Line *disaster*".

package holiday (hotel and flights) whereas they were not, due to the separate contracts. The 2003 amendment to the ATOL Regulations simply provided that if the seller was acting as an agent for an ATOL holder, the flights sold to a consumer as part of a package had to be sold as part of a *single contract* between the ATOL holder and consumer encompassing all package elements. The amended regulations did *not* say that wherever split contracting was attempted by the travel agent the travel agent should be deemed to have entered into a package contract with the consumer. The ATOL Regulations as amended in 2003 adopted the same definition of a "package" as the PTR 1992 - but it was not the 2003 amendment to the ATOL Regulations that was open to challenge but CAA Guidance issued pursuant to it.

Guidance Note 26

By Guidance Note 26[24] the CAA advised (in short)[25] that a number of contract-splitting arrangements were likely to constitute *regulated packages* requiring travel agents (assuming the provision of flight accommodation) to have ATOLs. Examples were given in the Guidance Note of which the following 3 will suffice by way of illustration as to how the travel agent was to be required to have an ATOL:

> Where a travel agent advertised a number of travel facilities that were mixed-and-matched or put together by the consumer from different providers to form a single holiday.
>
> Where a travel agent offered the consumer a choice of facilities from different providers and that choice resulted in the sale of a holiday.
>
> Where a travel agent advertised his services as including the provision of "dynamic" packages or tailor-made holidays and an arrangement with more than one supplier resulted.

The common thread in these 3 examples is not simply that they purported to extend the occasions on which a travel agent would need an ATOL (an expensive business) but that the examples applied *regardless* of whether the holiday components were supplied as part of *one* contract with *one* ultimate supplier at an "inclusive price" or several separate contracts with several

---

[24] Guidance Note 26: "Sale of Air Package Arrangements: Advice on the need to provide consumer protection".

[25] Paragraph 1.2 of the Guidance Note is in these terms:
"This Guidance Note explains the types of air package business which a travel company is required to protect under an Air Travel Organiser's Licence (ATOL). The Note should be read in conjunction with the Regulations. The purpose of this Guidance Note is to explain the background to the Regulations and to offer an interpretation of certain provisions. Only the courts can give a determinative view on the law."

suppliers at a "total (or aggregate) price". The total price at the bottom of the list of separately purchased facilities from separate providers *was* the necessary "inclusive price" as required to constitute a regulated "package" maintained the CAA. In other words a travel agent was likely to need an ATOL wherever the travel agent actively interposed himself between consumer and holiday service providers. So, travel agents were in need of ATOLs not because Parliament expressly said so and not because the courts have so construed the definition of a "package" or interpreted the words "inclusive price" but because an autonomous public (but non-governmental) organisation *said* it was necessary in the interests of consumer protection. The Guidance was challenged and quashed in the Administrative Court at first instance,[26] which decision was upheld for different reasons in the Court of Appeal.[27] The challenge was mounted by ABTA not least of all because it was travel agents who were considered most likely to be subject to a new requirement emanating from Guidance Note 26 to secure ATOLs – a considerable financial burden. The essence of the ABTA challenge was that the CAA was not empowered to impose its own interpretation of what constituted a regulated package on the industry and that the CAA had unilaterally broadened and misinterpreted the definition of a regulated package particularly in the context of the expressions *"pre-arranged combination"* and *"inclusive price"*.

Pre-arranged combination

To be a regulated package there must be a pre-arranged combination of at least at least two of the *qualifying components* identified in regulation 2. What constitutes a qualifying component is dealt with in detail below. Two such components must be combined in order for the resulting package to fall within the scope of the regulations.

The combination — or putting together — of the qualifying components is what must be pre-arranged. The regulations are silent as to the point in time when one judges whether there has been a pre-arrangement or not. It must be possible to draw an imaginary line somewhere and say that the combination of the qualifying components must be pre-arranged at such and such a time. This issue is one of some importance. For many consumers, the holiday services that are purchased from a brochure circulated by a travel agent on behalf of a tour operator, are combined in advance of the publicity and purchased by the consumer as offered in the brochure without revision "off the peg". In other cases however, when is pre-arrangement complete? Is "pre-arrangement":

---

[26] *R. (ABTA) v CAA v* (DTI Interested Party) [2006] EWHC 13 (Admin) Goldring J.
[27] [2006] EWCA Civ 1356 Chadwick LJ.

- before the combination is made available to the public (*e.g.* in the form of a brochure of advertising material)?
- at the time the contract is concluded?[28]
- anytime before the consumer departs?[29]

Furthermore, by *whom* does the pre-arrangement have to be organised? Does the pre-arrangement have to be organised by a tour operator, or can the retailer put together the necessary components to constitute a regulated package? If a consumer arranges a tailor-made holiday with the help of his high street travel agent, will the travel agent be bound by the requirements of the PTR 1992?

Pre-arranged before offered to public?

If, for example, the combination of qualifying services must be pre-arranged at the time the services are offered to the public by a tour operator (in a brochure, for example) in order for a package to be a regulated package, it would seem that most if not all tailor-made holidays would be excluded from the statutory definition. The same reasoning might exclude from the realms of regulation such travel arrangements as fly-drive holidays where the customer chooses his own itinerary from an array of options advertised in the brochure. In tailor-made holiday cases the consumer conventionally chooses between components which are made available *for the purposes of combination* which is not at all the same thing as pre-arrangement at the point of offer. The rigid approach to pre-arrangement — *i.e.* that the pre-arrangement must have occurred before the services are offered to the public — excludes so many arrangements that are conventionally regarded as "package holidays" as to make it unlikely that regulators intended the expression "pre-arranged" to be taken so literally or to be judged at such an early stage of the contractual chain. Indeed, such a narrow construction of the expression "pre-arranged" would also exclude those many "mix-and-match" holidays where the tour operator offers through its brochure a number of alternative standards of accommodation at the same destination. In such cases, as with fly-drive and tailor-made itineraries, the arrangements are put together by the *consumer* through the exercise of the consumer's choice, the services and accommodation (as a combination) are not pre-arranged by the tour operator and then offered to the public. In other words, it is thought unlikely that the expression "pre-arranged" is intended to restrict the application of the PTR 1992 to those unchangeable take-it-or-leave-it arrangements devised by the organiser in advance of any promotional activity.

---

[28] Which would bring tailor-made arrangements easily within the scope of the PTR 1992.
[29] Which would bring within the scope of the PTR 1992 all travel components including those added-on after the initial purchase of and original facility was concluded.

The fact that a strict, pre-offer interpretation of the expression "pre-arranged" might exclude large numbers of holidays from the regulations which are commonly regarded in popular parlance as being "package holidays", does not necessarily mean that such a narrow interpretation should not be adopted. However, the exclusion of so many tailor-made or quasi-tailor-made arrangements from a system of regulation explicitly designed for the purposes of consumer protection would probably be regarded as regrettable. It is unlikely, therefore, that such a narrow interpretation would be imposed the expression "pre-arranged" unless such a construction was unavoidable. In the interests of consumer protection it is just as well, as will be seen below, that such a narrow interpretation is far from unavoidable. It is also worth noting that in practice few, if any, tour operators have sought to argue that the PTR 1992 do not apply to tailor-made or mix-and-match holidays, or that the Regulations only apply to those combinations of qualifying components as have been pre-arranged before the services are offered to the public at large in the form of a brochure of other promotional literature. In short there has been little enthusiasm in practice for the contention that the expression "pre-arranged combination" means *only* such combinations as are arranged or put together before the product is advertised or promoted. Neither has there been any apparent enthusiasm for the contention that any pre-contract deviation[30] from an advertised combination of services would of itself take the final contractual arrangements outside the scope of the regulations. Finally, against this strict interpretation of "pre-arrangement" is that part of regulation 2(1)(c)(ii) which provides:

> "*the fact that a combination is arranged at the request of the consumer ...
> shall not of itself cause it to be treated as other than pre-arranged.*"

At first blush this provision seems to confirm that tailor-made arrangements put together at the request of the consumer, and "mix-and-match" holidays selected from a choice provided by the supplier in the form of alternative recipes involving the same destination from which the consumer can make a choice, are to be regarded as regulated packages. In fact regulation 2(1)(c)(ii) does not quite say as much. It says merely that such an arrangement does not *of itself* indicate that the holiday is *not* a package. Plainly, arrangements that are combined at the request of the consumer *cannot possibly* be pre-arranged before the point in time when the services are offered through a brochure or other promotional material to the public, so because do-it-yourself combination may still be "pre-arranged" it is to be inferred that "pre-arrangement" must mean pre-arrangement before some other event.

---

[30] E.g. the substitution of the advertised accommodation for an alternative more to the consumer's liking.

The issue of pre-arrangement is one of some importance because on the answer given depends the number of traditional types of travel arrangements that could properly be described as regulated packages, and the class of persons who might wittingly or otherwise make themselves liable to the regulatory regime of liability. Following the decision of the Court of Appeal in *ABTA v CAA*[31] the position is somewhat clearer than it was. Chadwick LJ at paragraph 20 said:

> The requirement that the components of the package must be sold or offered for sale as a "pre-arranged combination" is met not only where the components are put together by the organiser without input from the customer (typically, the brochure holiday) but also where the components are put together by the organiser in accordance with the specifications of the individual customer (or consumer) or group of customers (typically, the 'customised' holiday)[32]... And the requirement is satisfied not only in cases where the components have been put together and offered for sale by the organiser in advance of any contact with the individual customer but also in cases "where the combination of tourist services is the result of the wishes expressed by the customer up to the moment when the parties reach an agreement and conclude the contract"[33]. It can be seen, of course, that the principle is expressly stated, as proviso (ii), in the definition of "package" in both the Package Travel Regulations and the ATOL Regulations (as amended in 2003).

He continued later in the judgment in the context of paragraph 4.7 of CAA Guidance Note 26 which provided: *Paragraph 4.7:*

> "If an agent advertises that he can provide tailor-made holiday arrangements or he can provide dynamic packages, then he will need an ATOL to cover the majority of such sales. However if all facilities were offered and sold by the agent on behalf of a single ATOL holder, an ATOL would not be required."

> The first sentence is a correct statement of the law in so far as it relates to "dynamic packages" – provided, of course, that the package includes flight accommodation. On the other hand, "tailor-made holiday arrangements" are not necessarily within the definition of "package"; although some (indeed, perhaps, the majority) will be. That issue will turn on the facts of the particular case: is the advertisement to be seen as an offer to sell a pre-arranged combination of travel services (including flight accommodation) or as an offer to sell a number of separate services, each at its own price. If the

---

[31] [2006] EWCA Civ 1356.
[32] *Club-Tour, Viagrens e Turismo SA v Alberto Carlos Lobo Gonçalves Garrido* (Case C-400/00) [2002] ECR I-4051.
[33] *Club-Tour.*

latter, the agent will not need to hold an ATOL. The second sentence is plainly correct.

In the *Club-Tour* case[34] Mr. Lobo Goncalves Garrido purchased from *Club-Tour*, a holiday consisting of air tickets and accommodation for two weeks, full board, in the holiday village of Gregolimano (Greece). For that purpose, Club-Tour bought a holiday from the travel agency Club Med Viagens Ld. ('Club Med). It was thus Club Med which undertook to make the necessary reservations at the holiday village of Gregolimano for accommodation, meals and transfers, organised and published the holiday programme, and fixed the overall price. On their arrival at the holiday village, Mr. Lobo Goncalves Garrido and his family noticed that it was infested by thousands of wasps, which prevented them from fully enjoying their holiday. For that reason, on his return home, Mr. Lobo Goncalves Garrido refused to pay the price of the holiday agreed with Club-Tour. The latter thereupon sought an order from the Portuguese court that the price of the holiday be paid. Before that court, Club-Tour denied that the Directive applied to the present proceedings, arguing that the holiday sold was outside its scope. The ECJ[35] ruled:

> Taking the view that the Directive aims to protect consumers of holiday services by making tour operators and travel agents liable for loss caused to consumers as a result of the improper execution of a contract, and that national law must be interpreted and applied in accordance with the Directive...
>
> 11. By the first question, the court of reference essentially asks whether the word 'package used in Article 2(1) of the Directive must be interpreted as including holidays organised by a travel agency at the request of and according to the specifications of a consumer or a defined group of consumers.
>
> 12. ... the answer to that question must be in the affirmative.
>
> 13. The Directive, which is designed amongst other things to protect consumers who buy 'package holidays, gives a definition of that term in Article 2(1) whereby it is enough, for a service to qualify as a 'package, if, first, the combination of tourist services sold by a travel agency at an inclusive price includes two of the three services referred to in that paragraph (namely transport, accommodation and other tourist services not ancillary to transport or accommodation and accounting for a significant

---

[34] See footnote 31.
[35] Alarmingly, the Advocate-General had suggested in his Opinion for the Court that the expression "pre-arranged" was "superfluous".

proportion of the package), and, second, that service covers a period of more than 24 hours or includes overnight accommodation.

14. There is nothing in that definition to suggest that holidays organised at the request and in accordance with the specifications of a consumer or a defined group of consumers cannot be considered as 'package holidays within the meaning of the Directive.

...

16. ... the term package used in Article 2(1) of the Directive must be interpreted as including holidays organised by a travel agency at the request of and according to the specifications of a consumer or a defined group of consumers.

So we can be confident that "tailor-made" holidays (whether put together by tour operators or travel agents) *can* and *often will* be regulated packages, subject always to Chadwick LJ's warning that whether or not any given travel arrangements are a regulated package will invariably turn on the *facts* of the case. The PTR 1992 clearly, therefore, extends beyond the scope of the "pre-brochured" or pre-selected package holiday.

Pre-arranged before contract?

A second alternative is that the regulators intended to regulate all combinations of qualifying components that are pre-arranged at the time the supplier agrees to accept the consumer's offer to purchase a selected holiday. This construction of the phrase "pre-arranged" provides a more promising possibility.

If the consumer's order is regarded as an offer to purchase — which is accepted in due course by the supplier or tour operator, most mix-and-match and tailor-made holidays (as well as the traditional and conventional brochure holidays) would be packages covered by the regulations. The consumer's choices (constituting the pre-arrangement) are made before the point at which the supplier concludes the contract with the consumer by accepting the consumer's offer to purchase and so the ordinary sense of the expression "pre-arrangement" is not offended. Furthermore, this construction allows most of those arrangements which would colloquially be regarded as packages to be *regulated packages*. Whilst neither of these reasons is of itself conclusive, consistency of this interpretation with ordinary language and with what the consumer would usually understand by the expression "package" is a reasonable working basis for any definition. It also means that the "pre-arrangement" can be brought about by the consumer; the travel agent, organiser or the supplier — or all of them — and retain its regulated status. If the tour operator or organiser agrees to accept the consumer's offer (whoever put the combination of components together), that party can still properly be regarded as the party responsible for selling the package even though responsibility for putting the package together is the consumer's or the retailer's.

Given that a line must be drawn somewhere, it is submitted that pre-arrangement before the supplier agrees to accept the consumer's offer and thereby concludes a contract, is the most appropriate of the several possibilities. Such a construction also means that the travel agent or other retailer should not be contractually responsible for the tailor-made package he has put together in consultation with the consumer, but which is actually supplied as a result of a tour operator's acceptance of the offer to purchase made by the consumer. Some support for this construction of "*pre-arranged*" comes from *Club-Tour*.[36] The decision is also important for another reason. Because it was the travel agent who combined the services for this tourist, it was the travel agent who was the organiser of the package as well as the retailer and liable for the improper performance of the package contract[37]. It also highlights the possibility that there may be different packages involving different services and facilities for which different people are liable. Imagine that the Club-Med part of the holiday was itself a regulated package due to the inclusive facilities offered as part of the Club-Med deal. Superimposed on that package would be the second regulated package with the air travel grafted on to the Club-Med arrangements. In this situation would the retailer still be liable for the proper performance of the lesser package (the Club-Med wasps) when all he had done was add on the flights to create a sort of outer-package? The *result* in *Club Tour* might suggest that the retailer would be liable for both the lesser (Club-Med) and outer packages even though the improper performance did not arise out of the outer package that the retailer had pre-arranged, but would this necessarily be so if the "lesser" part of the holiday was also in its own right a regulated package?

Pre-arrangement before departure?

In most cases, even where the arrangements are tailor-made or *à la carte*, any pre-contract pre-arrangement will also be pre-departure pre-arrangement. That is, the consumer embarks on the travel arrangements agreed in the contract with the supplier. There may, however, be cases where a combination could come into existence before the consumer travels even though there was no combination of components at the time the travel contract was originally made.

It is possible that in some cases where, for example, a flight only or accommodation only arrangement is made, the supplier may later agree to

---

[36] See above.
[37] As to which see further in Chapter 2.

supply (without charging a separate price) some additional transport, accommodation or other tourist service as part of the deal. Instead of the originally envisaged single service, a combination of two is provided. (Accommodation may be supplied with a free excursion, or a flight only arrangement may be altered to include some basic accommodation.) Would such combinations fall outside the PTR 1992 because they were not pre-arranged before the contract for the original service was made?

There are two ways of approaching this. The first is to say that such circumstances are so theoretical or will be so rare as not to cause a significant practical problem. The second, and preferred approach, is to say that such rare cases would in fact be examples of pre-arrangement *before contract*. The only difference is that the contract in question has been *amended, varied* or *substituted* so as to add the second facility or component. The element of pre-arrangement occurs before the amended contract (pursuant to which the consumer travels) is concluded.

It is suggested, therefore, that in order to constitute a regulated package, the qualifying components must be pre-arranged before the contract *pursuant to which the consumer travels* is concluded. As a result, it does not matter who does the arranging or selects the components of which the arrangements are comprised, neither does it expose retailers to potential liability where they assist a consumer to select appropriate components. In practice, however, pre-arrangement before contract, and pre-arrangement before travel or departure will amount to the same thing.

Pre-arrangement: Does it matter?

As originally proposed the draft directive on package travel would not have referred to "pre-arranged" combinations, but rather to packages offered by means of "*brochures or other forms of advertising*". The Advocate-General in *Club Tour* felt the expression was superfluous and the European Commission in a report on national legislation implementing the Directive[38] considered it "artificial". As things stand, however, the expression is of some importance when taken in conjunction with other parts of the definition of a package such as "inclusive price". Cases such as *Gallager v Airtours Holidays Limited;*[39] *Rochead v Airtours Holidays Limited*[40] and *Mason v Titan Travel Ltd.*[41] illustrate why.[42] In supplying skiing holidays to consumers, Airtours operated a system of selling ski-packs to customers

---

[38] Report on the Implementation of Directive 90/314 EC – SEC (1999) 1800 Final.
[39] [2001] CLY 4280.
[40] Unreported – Central London County Court – June 2001.
[41] 17 June 2005 Grimsby CC (Unreported) TATLA Newsletter Autumn 2005.
[42] These cases are discussed further in Chapter 4.

whilst they were on board their transfer buses from airport to ski-resort. Accordingly, liability for anything that went wrong as a result of the supply of services pursuant to the *ski-packs* did not fall to be considered under the PTR 1992 because the ski-packs did not form part of a pre-arranged combination of services and facilities sold at an inclusive price. The ski-packs were voluntary add-ons selected by the consumers long after the holiday contract had been bought and paid for by the consumer.[43] This is also why the other party to the package holiday contract will not be liable pursuant to the PTR 1992[44] for quality complaints or accidents arising out of the provision of excursions bought by consumers after their arrival at their destination.[45] It is also likely that where the element of pre-arrangement is missing, there will also be an absence of an *inclusive price*[46] as was the case in the two Airtours cases and *Mason* mentioned above.

The expression "pre-arranged" helps to reinforce the attitude that it is only those services and facilities purchased before departure that form part of the regulated package for which the other party to the contract is liable, just as it helps to reinforce the impression in "split contracting" cases that the consumer is not buying a package at all. So, pre-arrangement is an important requirement in considering three distinct, but similar, types of purchasing. The first is the tailor-made arrangement[47] where the consumer mixes and matches a number of components usually made available by the same retailer to be delivered by the same tour operator, secondly where the consumer purchases through the same retailer but for services to be delivered by *different* and tour operators and thirdly, *split contracting*[48] cases where a consumer purchases distinct travel components from different retailers or promoters but by using the same purchasing resource. These resources now include travel web-sites.[49] If a consumer purchases a flight using an airline's web-site and then is invited to link up with another site offering hotel accommodation, and then a third site offering car rental or other travel services, provided the consumer concludes a contract at each site as a result of making a free choice of the services and facilities offered on each, it is difficult to see how the combination the consumer comes up with could be regarded as "*pre-arranged*" in any sense, or pre-arranged before "the

---

[43] See further *Excursions: Tour Operators and the Negligence of Local Suppliers* – Chapman [2002] ITLJ 123.
[44] But may be liable for other reasons – see above.
[45] *Mason* above being a classic example.
[46] The relationship between *pre-arranged combination* and *inclusive price* was discussed by Chadwick LJ in *ABTA v CAA* as to which see "*Inclusive price*" below.
[47] Sometimes described as *a la carte* or *bespoke* holidays.
[48] A number of euphemisms have been adopted to describe this situation, one of the more recent being *dynamic packaging*.
[49] See: *Chapman: What does the ABTA Judgment mean for Internet sales?* [2006] ITLJ 85.

contract" is concluded because each facility is provided pursuant to a separate contract with a separate provider. Whether such web-site hosts are held to be organisers of regulated packages within the PTR 1992 will often depend on the transparency with which the sites make it clear that each time the consumer "links" he is visiting a new provider and making a separate contract. This does not mean, however, that a web-site host[50] might not be a "*retailer*" and liable in the event that misleading information is disseminated, neither does it mean that the web-site host may not be selling or offering for sale regulated packages already "pre-arranged" and available as such on-line.

The following guidance is offered:

1. Where the consumer purchases a holiday comprising components promoted in a single brochure[51] this will be regarded as *pre-arranged*[52] and the tour operator is likely to be *the other party to the* (resulting) *contract.*
2. Where the purchase is of several components from different promotional resources that emanate from the same tour operator or supplier the tour operator is likely to regarded as an organiser and the selling agent is likely to be regarded as at least a retailer (if not also an organiser) of a pre-arranged combination of components within the meaning of the PTR 1992. The tour operator is likely to be regarded as *the other party to the contract* that results.
3. Where the consumer purchases several components from separate promotional material and the components are to be delivered by *different* tour operators or suppliers the tour operators or suppliers are not likely to be regarded as selling a pre-arranged combination but the retailer may be regarded as a retailer if not also an organiser of a pre-arranged combination, as well as being *the other party to the contract.*
4. In split-contracting cases neither the retailer nor the suppliers should be regarded as selling pre-arranged combinations but the retailer must take care that the distinctiveness of each contract for each separate component is transparent.

The qualifying components

Only pre-arranged components that are qualifying components under the PTR 1992 are good enough to make up a regulated package. Two out of three specified components must be present for the purposes of the PTR 1992. They are: "transport", "accommodation" and "other tourist services".

---

[50] A split-contracting seller.
[51] Or leaflet or web display.
[52] The standard off the shelf sort of package holiday.

It probably goes without saying that arrangements for "flight only" deals, or occasions on which the consumer simply books a room in a hotel, would not satisfy the regulatory definition of a package. Each of the qualifying components is worth considering in turn.

Transport

This includes any mode of transportation to the consumer's destination. It plainly covers airline flights, ferries, coaches and any other means by which the consumer is transported to the holiday or other ultimate resort. However, in the absence of any regulatory definition or restriction, "transport" also covers things like:

- bus and taxi transfers from airport to city centre;
- transfers between different destinations on a twin centre holiday or between the business and leisure parts of an hybrid package;
- the transport element of any pre-arranged and inclusive excursion (*e.g.* a city coach tour thrown in as part of the price of accommodation supplied for a city break);
- means of transport which the consumer is to use — such as hire cars.

There is no apparent reason why "transport" should not also include those free shopping or city centre shuttle buses so beloved of suburban hotels, or the beach shuttles run by seaside hotels whose sea views require agility and an iron nerve on the part of residents. It must be remembered that in the context of "transport" and "accommodation" the PTR 1992 do not expressly impose any quantative threshold. To qualify as "transport" the service may only be ancillary to the "accommodation". Conversely, accommodation might only be ancillary to transport, and yet be a qualifying component within the 1992 Regulations. This should be compared with the third component — "other tourist services" which alone must be *more than ancillary* to other components *and* account for a significant proportion of the package.[53]

Transport of any kind qualifies as a package component however insignificant it is in proportion to the package services as a whole and however ancillary it may be to the provision of accommodation. Even so,

---

[53] This paragraph and the following must now be viewed in the light of the dictum of Gage J. in *Keppel-Palmer v Exsus Travel Limited and Others* [2003] QBD All ER (D) 183 June. The transport in question was a transfer by limousine from the airport in Barbados to a holiday villa. Gage J. considered that in the context of a month's villa rental and separately paid for return flights on Concorde, the limousine element was *de minimus* and did not qualify as "transport" within the meaning of the regulations to make the arrangements with the Defendant a regulated package holiday.

one suspects that in practice many courts would flinch before allowing the golf buggies at a country house hotel, or a free ski-lift at a winter resort to qualify as separate "transport" package components — even though on a literal reading of the regulations there is no apparent reason why they should not be.

In the few examples given — such as the beach and city shuttles — the fact that the service comprises only a tiny proportion of the contract as a whole should be immaterial if one reads the words of regulation 2 literally. In the case of the country house golf hotel, the inclusive provision of buggies may make the difference between a weekend break qualifying as a regulated package and its not qualifying. The consumer who buys an apparently "accommodation only" golfing weekend may need to argue that what was provided was actually a regulated package due to the provision of free transportation around the hotel's golf course in order to gain the additional protection of the PTR 1992.

"Transport" should also cover those instances where the consumer is provided with a vehicle of transportation to use at the consumer's discretion. In other words, the regulations are drafted widely enough to cover not only transportation which the consumer is provided as a means of reaching a destination, but means of transport assigned to the consumer for use whilst *at* the destination. The provision of bicycles or horses at country resorts should fall within this second part of the "transport". More obviously, the provision of a car in a fly-drive holiday[54] would almost certainly be regarded as "transport".[55] The *easyCar* case was concerned with whether car rental arrangements were exempt (as "transport services") from certain consumer rights under the Consumer Protection (Distance Selling) Regulations 2000. The ECJ concluded that car rentals were indeed "transport services" and thus exempt from the relevant consumer protection requirements. One might use this conclusion to bolster the proposition that what constitutes "transport services" in one directive[56] should also constitute "transport" *or* "other tourist *services*" for the purposes of another[57] further underpinning the conclusion that fly-drive car hire is "transport" for the purposes of the PTR 1992.

---

[54] *easyCar(UK) Ltd v OFT* [2005] ECJ – C-336/03.
[55] In the case of most fly-drive holidays the consumer is provided either with some accommodation, or the service of an accommodation voucher system through which accommodation may be selected. Therefore, either the accommodation itself constitutes the second qualifying component, or the voucher system service is another significant tourist service for the purposes making the fly-drive a regulated package.
[56] The Distance Selling Directive.
[57] I.e. the Package Travel Directive.

What is apparent from the reasoning of the ECJ in *easyCar* is that the court felt that car rentals were *intended* by the regulators to be exempt from the rights to cancel that consumers would otherwise have had. This "purposive" approach is perhaps inevitable in the absence of stricter (or indeed any) statutory definitions in some directives, and one gets more than a hint of such a purposive approach being adopted in cases like *Keppel-Palmer*.[58] No doubt the same fate would also befall some of the more extreme or unlikely "transport" examples given above which would be purposively excluded from the reach of the PTR 1992 as has happened in at least one instance relating to "accommodation".[59]

Accommodation
"Accommodation" is not defined by the PTR 1992. In the majority of cases the provision of a hotel room, villa or apartment (with inclusive transport) will render further discussion of the meaning and limits of the word "accommodation" unnecessary. Neither the duration nor the quality of the accommodation is mentioned in the PTR 1992 as limiting the scope of this component. In *AFS Intercultural Programs Finland v Kulluttajavirasto*[60] the Advocate-General gave an opinion for the court stating that *"...accommodation...clearly covers any kind of accommodation...The duration of the accommodation is of no importance in the scheme of the directive."* However, the court disagreed. For reasons that remain opaque the ECJ decided that accommodation over an extended period of time with host families as part of a student exchange scheme *"...cannot be described as accommodation within the meaning of the Directive."* Unhelpfully the ECJ did not say what accommodation *was* intended to be within the meaning of the Directive.[61] This decision is probably better regarded as limiting the *types* of accommodation considered as a qualifying component rather than a decision about the *duration* over which the accommodation is available to the consumer.

There will be other cases where the definition and extent of the word "accommodation" assumes considerable importance. There are at least two problems that arise out of determining the precise scope of "accommodation". The first is simply the problem of knowing what constitutes accommodation and what does not. Is a consumer accommodated in a tent at the camp site, or on the camp site itself? Does it make any difference that the consumer brings his own tent or caravan, which

---

[58] See footnote 51.
[59] *AFS – See further below.*
[60] ECJ – Case C-237/97/
[61] Frankly, the opinion of the Advocate-General is to be preferred.

is accommodated by the tour operator on space at a site provided for the purpose? The second problem involves fixing the appropriate boundaries of the meaning of "accommodation" in order to determine whether *other* services provided might be separate qualifying components - namely "*other tourist services*". Plainly those facilities and services that form part of the "accommodation" cannot also be deployed as "other tourist services". Similarly, those services which are part of the "transport" cannot also be "accommodation". These difficulties are addressed in more detail below.

The two problems might be summarised in this way. First, what facilities qualify as "accommodation". Secondly, what services or facilities form an integral part of the "accommodation" itself. In other words what does the accommodation include? On the answer to this question may depend whether "other tourist services" are provided, because if the facility is part of the accommodation it cannot also be another tourist service.

Before turning to face these problems it is worth noting that some species of accommodation are easily identifiable within the regulatory definition. There is no room for argument that hotel rooms, villas, apartments, mountain huts, cottages, caravans and tents would all be regarded as "accommodation" within the meaning of regulation 2 and the provision of any of them would amount to one of the two necessary qualifying components of a regulated package.

Some cases are more difficult. Is a sleeper berth on a trans-continental rail journey "accommodation"? Or a compartment on a ferry? If a rail sleeper berth[62] is "accommodation", why not an overhead bunk in the main carriage, or even a seat in which perforce the standard class passenger may have to be accommodated overnight on a long rail journey? As with "transport" when taken as a qualifying regulatory component, there is no requirement that the accommodation should make up a significant proportion of the package services. The qualification of "*significant proportion*" only applies to "other tourist services".[63]

What facilities qualify as accommodation?
It should be noted at the outset that there is no authority on the PTR 1992 that makes it easy to answer this question.[64] The value of claims brought in

---

[62] The DTI advises that it is *not* in Guidance Note URN 06/1640 of November 2006.

[63] In the same Guidance note, however, the DTI suggests that a "facility" that is merely ancillary to another qualifying component is not sufficient to constitute a qualifying component in its own right.

[64] Neither does the decision in *AFS Finland* above although the Court appears to have been swayed by a combination of factors such as the long duration of the stay, the fact that the

small cases will often prohibit the seeking of authoritative guidance from the higher courts. Some obvious examples of accommodation have been suggested above. Even in these obvious examples (such as villas and hotels), what actually forms part and parcel of the accommodation may be subject to heated debate. This will be dealt with in due course.

First, an illustration may highlight some interesting difficulties that could arise. Assume that four passengers are booked on a three night intercontinental rail journey. Each travels in a different class. The first in "luxury", has a compartment of her own, but for the second night (a long maintenance and cleaning stop) is put up in a hotel. The second, travelling "first" class has a compartment to himself (like a miniature hotel room). The third travels "standard", where the seats and overhead racks are converted into a dormitory style sleeping unit for everybody in the carriage. The fourth — a student — travels in the back of the train with local traffic and has to sleep on the bench where she would sit during the day.

Which of the consumers has "accommodation" within the meaning of the PTR 1992? There is no doubt about the first. The hotel on the second night clearly distinguishes her case from the others. It is tentatively suggested that *none* of the others enjoys the benefit of "accommodation" within the meaning of the regulations even though a cogent case could be made out for each of them in descending order.

The reason why the other three travellers probably do not have "accommodation" is as follows. Whilst there is no provision in the PTR 1992 to the effect that the accommodation has to be *more than ancillary* to the transport, or indeed that it must necessarily be overnight accommodation (neither is there any provision to the effect that accommodation has to comprise a significant proportion of the package) it is submitted that for the purposes of identifying a qualifying package component, that component must be reasonably divisible, or separate, or severable from any other qualifying component. *Severability* or perhaps *independence* it is suggested is the key to determining whether certain arrangements can themselves be regarded as a qualifying *component* in its own right as opposed to a part of another component. A "component" is something which forms a *constituent part* of something else. This at least conveys the impression that the constituent parts should have a measure of individuality or separate identity. In addition, one cannot but suspect that to most people the provision of a long railway journey (whatever the passenger's sleeping arrangements) does

---

accommodation was free and not in a hotel or similar establishment to reach the view that the hosting arrangements were not covered by the Directive.

not in itself look like what most would consider a "package" arrangement.[65] Similar marginal examples could be given covering coach travel and ferry journeys. For the same reasons it is submitted that it would be dangerous to assume that by mere dint of the fact that provision was made for the consumer to sleep — either in a seat or a berth — that "accommodation" had been provided. What constitutes a sufficient degree of severability can only be a matter of fact and degree dependent on the peculiar facts of individual cases.

It cannot, however, be assumed that the severability test[66] on its own will provide a clear-cut answer in every case. In the trans-continental rail example given above, it may be plausibly argued that in the case of the first class traveller, the accommodation facilities provided were of sufficient substance as to make them distinct from the carriage part of the services, and that whilst total severance between transport and accommodation could not be achieved where the provision of the facilities was so intertwined, the accommodation was sufficiently distinct from the transport and of sufficient substance as to constitute a separate qualifying component within the meaning of the PTR 1992. Naturally, the fact that in the example given it is the "luxury" and "first" class travellers who might enjoy the protection of the PTR 1992 is purely coincidental. There is no reason in principle why, on appropriate facts, the budget traveller could not have the advantage of regulatory protection. It seems, therefore, that any judgment on the *separateness* of different facilities or services might in part depend on the *substance* of those facilities or services, even though the regulations themselves do not require either transport or accommodation to comprise a significant *proportion* of the resulting package.

The scope of the accommodation
Even where the facility is clearly "accommodation", it is necessary in some cases to determine what precisely the accommodation comprises. That is, what does the accommodation include? For example, is a consumer accommodated in a hotel room, or in the hotel (as a whole) itself? What comprises the hotel when taken "as a whole"? Does the "accommodation" extend to all facilities such as restaurants, health club, golf course and

---

[65] It is also difficult to escape the conclusion that Gage J. in *Keppel-Palmer* (above) instinctively felt that a "package" was more than simply a literal count of its various parts. A similar instinctive approach might be discerned in the response of the DTI in Guidelines issued relating to the PTR 1992 in which the view was expressed that "accommodation" would have to be more than ancillary to another service to qualify as a component under the regulations. Furthermore, the view was expressed that a cross channel ferry berth would not be qualifying accommodation whereas a berth on a cruise vessel would be.
[66] See "Cruises" further below.

business centres, or can these other services be regarded as "other tourist services" sufficient to amount to a second independent qualifying component as part of a regulated package? An example already ventilated above concerned a camp site. Is the consumer accommodated on the camp site, or in the tent or caravan situated there? If it is the tent or caravan that constitutes the "accommodation" can the other facilities[67] on site be regarded as "other tourist services" for the purposes the PTR 1992?

The question as to what "accommodation" includes, or the scope of the "accommodation" as defined by the regulations is of some considerable importance to hoteliers. If some services and facilities provided at an hotel can properly be regarded as severable from or independent of the "accommodation" and those services themselves can be taken as "other tourist services", then many hotels on taking a direct booking from a member of the public could be supplying a regulated package. If so, these hotels would have to comply with all the contractual and security requirements set out in the regulations. The linked problem with the definition (or lack of definition) in respect of the qualifying components necessary for the purposes of establishing a regulated package, is that it may be necessary to know the scope of *"other tourist services"* before one can state with any degree of confidence what "accommodation" should be taken to include. For example, if a health club facility is regarded as being an integral part of a hotel *and* part of the accommodation for the purposes of the regulations, that facility cannot be "other tourist services". If, on the other hand, the health club is not part of the "accommodation" (even though it may be part of the hotel) it *might* be capable of being "other tourist services" and the hotelier itself could find that it is subject to the regulatory regime as the supplier of a qualifying combination of services. It is safe to say that most hotels — even those offering the most extensive range of facilities — would not regard themselves as being the organisers of package contracts. Where hotels really need to beware, however, is where they provide free transport shuttle services to residents. It is difficult to avoid the conclusion that in these instances, the hotel is providing not only "accommodation", but "transport", to which the PTR 1992 must surely apply. This same issue has an impact on other service providers. The railway and ferry companies supplying transport and berths, or even just transport and other additional facilities[68] could find themselves unwittingly subject to the PTR 1992.

The fact that hotels, rail and ferry operators do not look like package travel suppliers does not mean that they are not. However, it is likely that such

---

[67] Washrooms, shops, sports facilities, restaurants and play areas.
[68] Shops, fitness centres and cinemas being some of the more obvious examples.

suppliers will be spared the implications of being subject to the regulations by careful judicial scrutiny on the facts of individual cases as to the scope of their most obvious travel service (*i.e.* transport or accommodation) in order to avoid the conclusion that what does not look very much like a package is not transformed into one. If in the ferry example, where an overnight berth is provided as part of the price of a ticket, the court concludes that this is just "transport" albeit of a particular type and class, it is at the end of the day unlikely that the court would be easily persuaded that additional facilities provided on board could properly be classified as "other tourist services". Closer consideration of "other tourist services" will help to put these problems into perspective.

Other tourist services

The third potential qualifying component is itself worth subdividing as a reminder that it includes distinct elements. In order for "other tourist services" to be an independent qualifying component there must be:

- tourist services available for users;
- that are merely not ancillary to transport or accommodation;
- and which account for a significant proportion of the package.

Once again the PTR 1992 provide no assistance with a more detailed definition of this component. Neither do we find any assistance as to who qualifies as a *tourist*.[69] Whilst a tourist is usually taken to be someone who is travelling for leisure, a "tourist" *need* not be a leisure traveller, but merely *one who tours*. The expression "tourist" and thus "other tourist services" could, therefore, extend to business travellers, and certainly those who are travelling with a mixed agenda. It might be dangerous, therefore, to assume that these other services were limited to those that are offered to holidaymakers. The regulations place no such express limit on this third qualifying component.

(a) What services?

"Other tourist services" probably means no more than services "other" than transport and accommodation that are offered to the consumer as part of the prearranged parcel of travel services sold at an inclusive price. It is doubtful whether the phrase "other tourist services" is intended to convey the impression that there must be some special tourist hallmark before the service could fall within the definition. It would be very difficult to identify such a hallmark. Perhaps one could try by stating that the service should include the "sort of thing a tourist might reasonably be expected to do". This

---

[69] See Robinson: *Who is a Tourist?* [1995] ITLJ 77.

is not particularly helpful. What sorts of things *are* tourists reasonably expected to do? Tourists do not fit neatly into predictable categories. If one tries to address the difficulty in another way by stating that "other tourist services" must mean those things that are actually included in the consumer's travel contract apart from transport and accommodation, one could be accused of putting the cart before the horse. This latter attempt to define the services would mean that *anything* in the contract other than accommodation and transport that was not merely ancillary to those two components would fall within the meaning of "other tourist services". However, it is submitted that this is the best available option. "Other tourist services" are all those services in the consumer's contract which are not ancillary to transport or accommodation. These services — whatever they may be — become tourist services by reason of the fact that they are included in the consumer's inclusive arrangements. The fact that such services might also be available to non-tourists does not deprive them of their qualifying nature for the purposes of the PTR 1992. For example, a winter holiday may provide accommodation (but no transport) and inclusive daily skiing lessons from an accredited instructor. It would be ludicrous to think that this inclusive service was disqualified for the purposes of calculating whether the consumer had purchased a regulated package simply because the instructor was also available and providing assistance and support to local residents.

The problem with this suggested approach to the *other tourist services* is that if anything which is more than ancillary to transport or accommodation is included in the consumer's contract can count as a qualifying component, the definition could include a whole range of facilities that do not have a very "touristy" image. The hotel business centre is a tolerable example. If this is not merely ancillary to the "accommodation"[70] but is available for the consumer's use as part of the travel contract, the business centre will be another *tourist* service. On reflection, however, perhaps the modern tourist, even some modern holiday-makers, would regard the provision of such a service as a reasonable facility to provide for holiday consumers even if its purpose was not typically "touristy". The travelling businessman when regarded as a tourist, or the hybrid traveller on mixed business and leisure may regard such a facility as absolutely essential. What about educational services? If a music school offers adult residential refresher courses including accommodation, expert tuition, practice facilities and instruments, are these additional services "other tourist services" despite their educational purpose?[71] It is suggested that the residential music school is likely to feel the

---

[70] And this would depend on how one defined the scope of the accommodation.

[71] The DTI (DBERR) has suggested that educational services are outside the scope of "other tourist services" provided the education is undertaken with a view to obtaining a recognised qualification. This is an improbable solution to the problem. Does it mean that any educational

full force of the PTR 1992. The fact that the residents have chosen a particular activity with which to fill their leisure hours is immaterial — they are merely tourists of a particular type. The tourist service represents tourism of a specific character. If the music school is not providing "other tourist services", what distinguishes such services from those of the expert on a wine-tasting tour of southern France? Limiting the potentially wide scope of "other tourist services" almost certainly has to be approached by means of the other two elements within this particular component.

It is, however, possible to identify some services that, all other things being equal, would be likely to count as *"other tourist services"* if the suggested approach to this topic is adopted. For example:

- pre-booked, inclusive excursions;
- a lecturer or guide;
- a health club and spa;
- instructors;
- food and wine tasting as part of a gourmet tour;
- the provision of "facilitators" on themed trips.

One attempt to limit the wide scope of "other tourist services" has been to draw a distinction between "services" on the one hand, and "facilities" on the other. If what is offered is a "facility" it is not a "service" and furthermore, it is likely to be regarded as ancillary to transport or accommodation. If a "facility" is provided, the tourist is given the resources with which something might be done. A "service" when distinguished from a "facility" probably means the act of assisting a consumer to do something or actually doing something for someone else. If this distinction is workable, then the availability of resources provided by a resort would not be enough to constitute *"other tourist services"*. At a stroke, therefore, one can exclude the provision of hotel spa or sports facilities and equipment and business centre facilities from the scope of "other tourist services". Although in the past, guidance from the Department of Trade and Industry has suggested that this distinction between "services" and facilities" is a proper one, it is not thought at the end of the day that it is workable. The provision of facilities will more often than not involve the provision of an underlying service, even if the service is passive at the point of use. A facility may often be no more than the result of the provision of a number of behind the scenes services. Some facilities will have services attached to them. A spa, for example, may include the availability of instructors and attendants. Should it

residential course must "vet" its applicants to ensure that they are not only serious but vocational in their ambitions?

make any difference that some consumers might not use the attendants or instructors? Is the *availability* of instructors and attendants not all part of the service, even if they are not used? The DTI had suggested as an example that a hotel swimming pool, being a *facility*, would not count as a service. This suggestion overlooks the extent to which such a facility has to be *serviced* in order to be of use to the consumer. The *facility* it is suggested is only a part of the *service* offered by the resort in question. It is submitted that there is no workable or useful distinction to be drawn between *services* and *facilities* and that in practice, in order to avoid the application of the PTR 1992 to the likes of resort hotels, the service provider will concentrate on the argument that whether they be described as services or facilities or both, the swimming pool, the spa or the business centre is not sufficiently independent or distinctive enough to be regarded as anything but merely *ancillary* to the accommodation, or that the facility does not account for a *significant proportion of the package* or both.

In more recent[72] Guidance[73] the DTI[74] unwittingly illustrates the difficulty of laying down hard and fast rules about what does and does not constitute a package component. It advises apparently that if one hires out a canal barge with which maps are also provided, there *is* a regulated package[75] as is the holiday where the hirer of a private yacht provides skippering services. However, putting on Christmas entertainment at a hotel for *all* guests does not, apparently, turn an accommodation only contract into a regulated package because the entertainment would be a "*facility for all guests and not a tourist service*". It remains something of a mystery why something that is available to all cannot be a tourist service.

(b) Not ancillary to transport or accommodation
The "other tourist services" must be more than merely accessories to transport or accommodation before they can be counted as an alternative and independent qualifying component. If something merely supplements or is an accessory to accommodation, it cannot be a qualifying component in its own right. If something is "ancillary" it provides essential support to the principal service. It is always dangerous to put a gloss on the words of a regulatory provision, but in the absence of further assistance from the

[72] But not the most recent – DBERR has subsequently offered Guidance of January 2008 anchored firmly in the Court of Appeal's decision in *ABTA v CAA* and quoting extensively from the examples given in the judgment of Chadwick LJ.
[73] November 2006 – URN 06/1640.
[74] Now DBERR.
[75] The DTI does not condescend to explain how maps would come to be regarded as a significant proportion of the services provided. Or why the maps would not be regarded as merely ancillary to the transport.

regulations themselves, it could be said that in order for a service to be "*not ancillary*" to transport or accommodation, it should be free-standing, independent, severable or clearly distinguishable from transport and accommodation. If a service simply provides essential support to transport or accommodation or is merely an accessory, it lacks the necessary element of independence which would justify its identification as a qualifying component within a regulated package. Ultimately, what is "*not ancillary*" must be a matter of fact and degree in each case.

Some suggestions as to what are likely to be regarded as ancillary services would be:

- *ancillary to transport*:
    - refreshments;
    - duty free facilities;
    - in-transit entertainment;
    - stewarding services;
    - breakdown services;
    - en route courtesy rooms during a long haul coach trip;

- *ancillary to accommodation*:
    - chambermaid, laundry and concierge services;
    - security;
    - room service;
    - portering;
    - foyer shops;
    - swimming pools;
    - communications centres.

All the above examples, it is submitted, are likely to be held to be ancillary to the principal service (or facility), and thus incapable of being regarded as free-standing "*other tourist services*" to count as an independent qualifying component.

It is worth emphasising that in the accommodation examples given it is assumed that the consumer is accommodated in the hotel, not just in a room. The need to define the scope of the principal services remains an essential prerequisite to discovering whether some other facility can be identified as "*other tourist services*". Care, for example, needs to be taken when considering the cases of consumers accommodated in hotels but permitted as part of their deal to utilise facilities in neighbouring resorts, or where the health and sports facilities within their own resort are extensive. Such facilities, or their availability, may be adequately independent and significant to be regarded as "not ancillary" to the accommodation.

One possible quirk in the PTR 1992 has already been noted above in considering "transport" and "accommodation". Shuttle buses and courtesy limousines may be regarded by many as auxiliary services offered at an hotel. Looked at as "auxiliary" services they can be dismissed as possible "*other tourist" services*". However, when looked at in conjunction with the accommodation provided, such services are almost certainly "transport" and count in their own right as a qualifying component regardless of the significance they place in the overall package, and regardless of whether their provision is merely ancillary to the accommodation.

(c) Accounting for a significant proportion of the package
A number of linked factors come into play when judging whether something accounts for a significant proportion of the package. They are:

* the time taken to deliver the service;
* the relative importance of the service in the context of the individual package;
* the cost of the service relative to the cost of the package;
* the independent identification of the service by the supplier.

It should also be remembered that "other tourist services" appears in the plural, and that, therefore, it should be possible in marginal cases to take a number of such services together in order to determine when as a group the services account for the necessary significant proportion of the whole.

What constitutes a significant proportion of the package is not defined in the PTR 1992. At first glance it may appear that a *significant proportion* should be measured in *time*. However, this would probably be too restrictive. Part of the process in judging whether a service constitutes a "significant proportion" of the package involves consideration of the type of package that is being supplied, its purpose and the *qualitative* significance of a service within the general framework. Travel package obviously extends over a certain period of time, but something of qualitative significance might in actual fact take up a relatively modest proportion of the time taken for the whole package. For example:

* the historical tour of Egypt might be blighted without the introductory course of lectures;
* the arduous six-week cruise to the Antarctic may be ruined if the promised landing at Shackleton's base camp is aborted;
* the African safari could be compromised without the dawn balloon trip;
* a Caribbean holiday may be undermined if the water sports centre is closed.

"*Significant proportion*" should be judged as much by the nature and quality of the service as by the quantity of time it would take to perform. It refers to services which are of more than minimal or incidental or casual importance to the purpose of the trip *and* to those services which might extend over an identifiable period. In this context, *significant* it is submitted does not mean *substantial*. The judgment should involve both the time the service takes in the context of the package as a whole, and the relative importance of that service when set in the context of the particular package under discussion.

The test as to what accounts for a significant proportion of the package should be an objective one. The fact that a particular consumer may personally regard a given feature as vitally important may be of some *evidential* importance, but is unlikely to be conclusive. The issue is whether that consumer's assertion is *reasonable*. However, from an evidential point of view, if a supplier specifically promotes a service in the pre-contract advertising material or even identifies the service in the pre-contract promotional literature it is going to be difficult for that supplier to persuade a court that the service did not account for a significant (as opposed to substantial) proportion of the package. If the service was not significant, why promote it? Anything specifically promoted is likely to be promoted in order to induce or entice consumers to purchase the package, or at least to provide an identifiable good reason for choosing that package rather than another.

Accordingly, a further way of identifying services which account for a significant proportion of the package is to see if the service has been individually identified, promoted or advertised by the supplier. Is the service in question a specified *unit* or *item* within the package that the supplier has identified? If the service (*e.g.* the introductory historical lectures on ancient Egypt in one of the instances given above) is identified and promoted by the supplier and appears in the brochure or advertisement as a separate item within the services forming part of the package, even though the lecture may be of relatively modest duration, it is likely to be regarded as qualitatively significant, particularly if it appears alongside other services designed to project the package as educational, or at least more informative than others to the same destination.

If the prospect of describing accommodation plus an introductory historical lecture as a regulated package seems alarming,[76] it should be remembered

---

[76] The current EC consultation on the revision of the Package Travel Directive asks whether the scope of the regulations should be extended further to include day trips, sporting and concert events.

that in many instances there will be more than one additional service to be placed in the equation. Judging whether this possible component of a regulated package is indeed an independent component in its own right will often involve taking into account a number of "other tourist services" (in the plural). In practice, the introductory lecture is likely to be one of several "other services" of an educational, informative or any other character which should be looked at in the round and where, if they are provided in addition to accommodation, the question will be whether when taken *together* these "other services" (even if modest when looked at individually) account for a significant proportion of the package. In order to count as a separate qualifying component, these "other services" do not necessarily have to enjoy any feature linking them together (apart from the fact that they are supplied pursuant to the same contract with the consumer). A basket of disparate services when taken together might comprise a significant proportion of the package when judged on any of the tests canvassed above, even though as individual services the threshold of significance is not crossed. If a number of services are to be combined in this way for the purposes of making up a significant proportion of the package, care must be taken to ensure that none of the individual elements is merely ancillary to either "transport" of "accommodation". An example of this approach might be a vacation in the south of France where accommodation is provided in addition to a wide range of social and educational activities — including perhaps things like historical lectures, wine-tasting and an art appreciation course.

Qualifying components — a summary
In the absence of any authoritative decision from the courts the following conclusions are offered as to some of the difficulties canvassed in respect of the meaning of the three qualifying components.
1. Consumers are likely to be regarded as being accommodated in their hotels, apartment blocks, villas and camping sites rather than merely in their rooms, caravans or tents.
2. Services and facilities that are available to consumers in their hotels (such as pools, sports and communications services) will, therefore, form part of the consumer's "accommodation" and are not likely to qualify as "other tourist services". Alternatively, such services will be regarded as merely ancillary to the accommodation and not capable of qualifying as regulated components in their own right.
3. Hotels are not likely to be regarded as peddlers of regulated packages unless they provide free limousine or shuttle transfer services.[77]

---

[77] Query *Keppel-Palmer v Exus Travel* (above).

4. Where such transfer services *are* provided there is a risk that hotels could be regarded as offering transport inclusive with the cost of the accommodation, and hotels would be best advised to impose a small additional charge to avoid this risk.
5. Transport providers will only be regarded as supplying "accommodation" as a *separate* component, where the berth is private and is designed for the purpose of providing more than merely a means of transporting the consumer to a destination or giving sleeping space whilst that transportation is underway (*i.e.* where there is some *purpose* in the journey other than merely the means of getting from A to B such as a cruise[78]).
6. "Other tourist services" will be judged *qualitatively* as well as quantatively as to whether they form when taken together a "*significant proportion of the package*".

Inclusive price

The nature of an "inclusive price" was at the very heart of the litigation between ABTA and the CAA in 2006.[79] Chadwick LJ at paragraph 23 of his judgment said:

> The CAA does not challenge the judge's conclusion that: "For the sale of a package at an inclusive price the relationship between the component parts of that package must be such as to mean that the consumer is buying and paying for them as a whole"... It is said that it did not dispute that proposition in the Administrative Court: "nor is it inconsistent with the Guidance". It submits that the proposition "is an echo of the CAA's argument that the concept of 'inclusive price' taken in conjunction with that of 'pre-arranged combination' focuses on whether the different components are sold or offered for sale together, on a composite basis".

If the price of the package is not "inclusive" it does not matter how many qualifying components there may be.[80] The PTR 1992 will not apply. But what constitutes an "*inclusive price*"? In many instances the answer will be obvious:

---

[78] But even here the impact of the PTR 1992 is likely to be overridden by any International Convention applicable to the carrier – *Norfolk v MyTravel Tour Operations Limited* [2003] Unreported – Plymouth County Court 21 August 2003.

[79] [2006] EWCA Civ 1356 Chadwick LJ.

[80] ABTA v CAA (CA) [2006] EWCA Civ 1356 Chadwick LJ paragraph 24: The requirement that the components be sold or offered for sale "at an inclusive price" must be read in conjunction with the requirement that the components be sold or offered for sale as a pre-arranged combination. The price is the price of the combination.

In many cases – indeed, I suspect, in the majority of cases – the price of the combination will not be the aggregate of the prices for which the components within the combination would have been sold or offered for sale if each component had been sold or offered for sale as a separate service outside the combination. That may be because some of the components (for example, the services of the organiser's local representative) would not be available as a separate service outside the combination. Or it may be because some of the components can be provided more cheaply if provided in conjunction with other components - the hotel may provide a courtesy airport transfer service. Or it may be that, in order to sell the package, the organiser will price attractively: the organiser will offer the package of services at a price which is below the aggregate of the prices which would be charged if the components had been sold separately. In those cases there is unlikely to be difficulty in reaching the conclusion, on the facts, that the components (including flight accommodation) are being sold as a pre-arranged combination and at an inclusive price. The same could be said of cases – which, I suspect, are likely to be rare indeed – in which the price of the combination exceeds the aggregate of the prices for which the components would have been sold or offered for sale separately.[81]

The regulators injected an anti-avoidance provision in the definition:

> the submission of separate accounts for different components shall not cause the arrangements to be other than a package".[82]

This does not mean that where separate accounts *are* rendered the arrangements will nevertheless always be a package; far from it. By the same token, this does not necessarily mean that where separate arrangements are invoiced on the same account they must be regarded as having been provided at an "inclusive price". Therefore, apart from representing a warning to clumsy suppliers who might artificially divide an account into two parts in order to avoid the application of the regulations, it is difficult to see what this part of the definition achieves. Nonetheless, where components are sold at different times, or where they are co-ordinated from a range of different suppliers or by the same supplier in a different capacity, the rendering of separate accounts may be very good *evidence* that the price charged for the arrangements as a whole should not be regarded as "inclusive".[83]

---

[81] *ABTA v CAA (above)* paragraph 25 Chadwick LJ.
[82] Regulation 2(1)(i).
[83] At first instance in *ABTA v CAA* Goldring J said: *if the arrangements would otherwise be a "package" – because the services are sold or offered for sale as components of a pre-arranged combination and at an inclusive price – the substance of the arrangements is not altered by invoicing the components separately. But, if the arrangements would not otherwise be a "package" – because the services are, in fact, sold or offered for sale separately – separate billing merely reflects the substance of the arrangements. The most that could be said is that composite billing might be evidence (in the particular case) that the services had been sold as a package.*

However, what constitutes an "inclusive price"[84] is still surrounded by a shadow of grey.

> The more difficult cases are those in which the price for the whole is equal to the aggregate of the prices for which the components would have been sold or offered for sale separately. The principle is, perhaps, easier to state than to apply in practice. If the components are offered for sale as a pre-arranged combination – albeit that the components are not combined (and, perhaps, not all identified) until "the moment when the parties reach an agreement and conclude the contract" (to adopt the language of the Court of Justice in the Garrido case) – then the price for the combination will be "an inclusive price" notwithstanding that it may have been calculated, arithmetically, by aggregating the prices of the components: that is to say, notwithstanding that the price for the combination is the aggregate of the prices for which each component would have been sold or offered for sale if it had been sold or offered for sale as a separate service outside the combination. The factual question to be resolved – on a case by case basis – is whether the services are being sold or offered for sale as components of a combination; or whether they are being sold or offered for sale separately, but at the same time.[85]

Important conclusions can be drawn from this. *First,* whether one has an "inclusive price" is a fact sensitive matter to be determined according to the facts proved in a given case.

> "...difficult questions of fact are likely to arise if the customer chooses and contracts for two or more of the services on the same occasion. The principle is not in doubt. If the services are sold or offered for sale as components of a combination, there is a package: if they are sold or offered for sale separately but at the same time, there is no package. The question whether they are sold as components of a combination - or separately but at the same time - is a question of fact. That question may not be easy to resolve in the particular case."[86]

There are no stock, all-purpose answers. *Secondly,* an "inclusive price" is achieved even though the price of each component may be merely added-up to reach the total (and one might have bought each of the components for the same price individually). *Thirdly,* the key issue in determining whether there is an "inclusive price" is not to be approached by pouring over the invoice or invoices but by answering a factual question: were the components

---

[84] For a variety of detailed discussions about the *ABTA* litigation see generally: [2006] ITLJ Volumes 2 & 4.
[85] [2006] EWCA Civ 1356 Chadwick LJ at paragraph 26.
[86] Above: Chadwick LJ at paragraph 31.

sold in combination or were they conscientiously sold separately (whether at the same time or different times)? It will be seen that the answer to this question depends on traditional principles of English contract law and it must be said on the *evidence*. The fact specific nature of case law in the English legal system is underlined by this further extract from the judgment of Chadwick LJ:[87]

> If the customer approaches an agent "to buy a holiday", it is likely that what will be sold or offered for sale will be a pre-arranged combination of services at an inclusive price: that is to say, "a package". If the customer wants to buy "a flight and accommodation and/or other services", then (as I have explained) it will not necessarily follow that the services sold or offered for sale will be sold or offered as a package: but they may be.

Retailers and travel agents beware. Perhaps the real question is: is there one contract or more than one? This is an example given by Chadwick LJ:[88]

> Suppose a customer, in London, who wishes to spend a week at a named hotel in, say, Rome. He asks his travel agent what the trip will cost him. The agent ascertains that the cost of the return flight will be £X, the cost of accommodation will be £Y and the cost of the airport transfers will be £Z. Without disclosing the individual cost of each service, the agent offers the customer flights, accommodation and transfers at a price of £(X+Y+Z). The customer accepts without further inquiry. In that case there would be little doubt – as it seems to me – that the services were sold as a pre-arranged combination and at an inclusive price.

By way of further illustration, the consumer who purchases an off-the-peg holiday from a brochure expecting to pay the price for flights and accommodation set out in the price panel at the bottom of the page, will not be deprived of the protection of the PTR 1992 simply because the supplier artificially divides the total price into two parts and renders separate invoices: that reflecting the price of the flights and the second reflecting the cost of the accommodation. On the other hand, simply because the supplier also sells travel insurance to the consumer with a "flights only" contract and includes the insurance premium in the same invoice, will not of itself render the supplier subject to the Regulations. The insurance example may be the most accessible illustration of how a separate and severable item can be offered to the consumer by the same supplier and charged for in the same invoice as other services, without the cost of the insurance being regarded as part of an "inclusive price".

---

[87] At paragraph 49. It should be borne in mind that *ABTA v CAA* itself "only" involved the accuracy and legality of certain Guidance Notes issued by the CAA and whether such Guidance should be ordered to be quashed or withdrawn – the decision was that the Guidance should be withdrawn. All the examples offered at first instance and on appeal are simply examples illustrating why the Guidance was inaccurate.
[88] At paragraph 27.

Chadwick LJ gave further examples:[89]

> Now suppose that the agent has informed the customer that the cost of flights will be £X, the cost of accommodation will be £Y and the cost of transfers will be £Z; and has explained to the customer that he can purchase any one or more of those services, as he chooses, without any need to purchase the others. He has explained, in effect, that the customer can choose to purchase the other services elsewhere; or to make other arrangements. In that case – as it seems to me – there would be little doubt that the services are not offered for sale as a pre-arranged combination and at an inclusive price.

> What, then, if the customer chooses, and contracts for, one of those services. It is plain that that service would not be sold as a pre-arranged combination: it is not sold in combination with any other service. And it is plain that that position would not alter, if having paid for one of those services, the customer subsequently decides to take, and contracts for, another of the services. Nor would the position alter if, after paying for the second service, the customer later decides to take, and contracts for, the third service. And it would make no difference if, having entered into three separate contracts and received three separate invoices, the customer were to pay the three invoices with a single cheque. The position would be the same. There would have been no sale of a pre-arranged combination of components at a single inclusive price. Rather, there would have been three separate sales of independent services, the aggregate of the prices payable for the three separate services being satisfied by a single payment.

In the examples given by Chadwick LJ there is a lesson for those engaged in dynamic packaging or split contracting – or who *think* that they are so engaged. Legitimate avoidance of the PTR 1992 on the basis of dynamic packaging must pay attention to the contracting procedures in place with their consumers and must be able to adduce evidence of those procedures. The contracting procedures are important because to stay outside the reach of the PTR 1992 it will be necessary to demonstrate by admissible evidence[90] that the consumer has entered into two or more separate contracts even if these contracts are close to each other in time and paid for by a single payment. In having contracting procedures in place to demonstrate the separateness of the sale of each element of the travel arrangements the provider may lose the appearance of a "one-stop-shop" that many correctly perceive as important to the travelling public. Herein lies the heart of the matter. Many organisers want to retain the appearance and marketing benefits of the "one-stop-shop" creating the impression that regulated

---

[89] Paragraphs 28 and 29.
[90] Which is quite different from a mere assertion.

packages are on offer whilst simultaneously retaining the benefits of split-contracting or dynamic packaging. One cannot have it both ways and organisers are badly placed to complain when courts and consumers conclude that what has in fact been offered *is* a regulated package hiding behind the cosmetics of a dynamic package.

Free services and facilities

Some organisers have taken to supplying flights or other means of transport and offering to throw-in accommodation or any number of other services and facilities free of charge. This is particularly common amongst some time-share operators. The flights are sold in the conventional way, but the consumer is rewarded with accommodation for which no charge is apparently made, usually in empty or under-used timeshare facilities. Sometimes it works the other way round – a free flight is added on to costed accommodation. This sort of arrangement often occurs in the course of promotional activities or as prizes. The combination of transport and accommodation is without doubt a qualifying combination within the PTR 1992. However, is the combination (as opposed to just one component within the combination) *sold* and is the resulting price paid by the consumer for the transport or the accommodation an *inclusive price*? The same problem might rear its head in those situations where a villa is rented with the "free" use of a car for the duration of the rental.

Organisers of time-share arrangements need to be particularly careful. Courts may take little persuading that the arrangements are a sham designed to avoid the application of the PTR 1992. Where the organiser insists that the flight to the time-share resort is purchased from the organiser's own selection of available flights, it is likely that the cost of the flight would be regarded as *the* "inclusive price" of the entire package, and loading the cost entirely onto the transport element of the arrangements is nothing more than a device to avoid regulatory control. The organiser would be in a much stronger position if it were made clear to the consumer that the flight could be purchased from *any* supplier — linked with the organiser or not — or if the organiser could demonstrate that the cost of the flight was the genuine market price for seats on the flight chosen.

Neither the time-share owner nor the organiser offering the free use of a car at the holiday villa would be able to escape the grip of the PTR 1992 on the grounds that the free element of the arrangements was not "sold or offered for sale". This is because it is only the *combination* of components that has to be "sold or offered for sale". If the combination of components taken together can properly be described as being offered for sale, it hardly matters that some of the components within the combination have no separate price assigned to them. *Rechberger v Austria*[91] was a case of a promotional newspaper offer that proved so popular that the organiser went bankrupt. Many of the complainants had been provided free travel components as part of the promotion or paid for only some of the components getting others free of charge. This made no difference according to the ECJ. It was not necessary that the cost should cover all the components, the components as a whole were provided for an inclusive price even though that price was related only to a limited number of components sold to the consumers. The Austrian Government argued that there can be said to be a package only where the consumer is required to pay, as consideration for all the services stipulated in the contract, a price which *corresponds to the value*, and is calculated on the basis, of all the travel services. If the person travelling is only required to pay a single-room supplement instead of a global price for a trip which is essentially offered free of charge (apart from minor ancillary costs) then it is not a package within the meaning of the Directive. Moreover, so Austria argued, the scope of the Directive does not extend to trips which are neither sold nor offered for sale on the market to an unlimited number of potential customers but are instead offered as a gift only to a predetermined class of persons. The ECJ disagreed:

> ...the Directive applies to trips which are offered by a daily newspaper as a gift exclusively to its subscribers as part of an advertising campaign ... for which the principal contractor, if he travels alone, pays airport taxes and a single-room supplement or, if he is accompanied by one or more persons paying the full rate, airport taxes only.

In this respect a time-share operator or villa owner faces a problem similar to that of the hotel offering free shuttle services as part of the facilities available at the hotel; or indeed any organiser or provider who decides by way of incentive to throw in a few "free" extras. If a component is thrown-in without a charge being levied at the point of use, the cost of that component has almost certainly been taken into account in determining the cost of the components for which a charge *is* made. This makes the price for all the components look all the more *inclusive*. The shuttle in the case of the hotel[92], the accommodation in the case of the time-share organiser and the car in the case of the villa owner are likely to be taken as "included" in the price paid for the flight or the accommodation, as the case may be. The problem posed by apparently free services or facilities is that they begin to make the arrangements look even more like a package than they would if separate charges were levied. The combination is sold, even though one element within the combination carries no obvious charge. The best way of avoiding

---

[91] [ECJ – C-364/96].
[92] Bear in mind that to be a regulated package.

this difficulty is for organisers to show that the charge for the component that is actually priced would be the same irrespective of whether the other "free" service was provided. In this way it may be possible to argue that the "combination" was not sold, merely one aspect of the combination and that the other was genuinely provided free of charge. This is likely to be evidentially difficult. If it cannot be done the price paid by the consumer for the combination of priced and "free" services is in danger of being regarded as an "inclusive price". Providers may, as a result, find it more efficient to make small (even nominal), additional but locally levied charges for what would otherwise have been "inclusive" ancillary services.

Twenty-four hours or overnight accommodation

The service supplied pursuant to the package contract must cover:

- a period of *more* than 24 hours; *or*
- overnight accommodation.

The two elements are alternatives, although it is difficult to imagine many "packages" of more than 24 hours which would not involve the provision of overnight accommodation. One example might be where a transport provider carries passengers without providing separate accommodation, but where other qualifying package services *are* provided. This might happen where on a long distance, trans-continental coach journey it is taken for granted that passengers will sleep in their seats, but where other comfort, and rest services (day time courtesy rooms) are provided as part of the inclusive ticket price.[93]

It is the service set out in the contract that is important. If the service *contracted for* is intended to cover more than 24 hours or overnight accommodation, then the result will be a regulated package. If for some reason the service is curtailed and the intended 24 hour-service is aborted or reduced in time, the combination of components remains a regulated package regardless of the actual time taken. What is a regulated package by reason of the contractual services remains a regulated package thereafter, whatever unusual or curtailing events might intervene. Similarly, if a day trip is unavoidably prolonged it does not become a regulated package merely by dint of the fact that some unforeseeable event has delayed the party's return journey. A 16-hour ferry crossing that is delayed 10 hours due to adverse weather conditions is not transformed into a regulated package merely by

---

[93] But query whether such services would be more than ancillary to the transport – it will as ever be a question of fact and degree.

reason of the delay. The *pre-arranged* combination of components did not envisage a journey of such duration.

In the context of this requirement, "accommodation" as in "overnight accommodation" must mean something more than simply a place where the passenger is allowed or constrained to spend the night. A coach passenger on a long distance journey will often spend the night or several nights in a seat. This is not overnight accommodation. A long distance ferry passenger who uses the lounge is unlikely to be regarded as having overnight accommodation as distinct from the transport facility but the passenger who has a cabin is a more marginal creature. Plainly, the same problems arise in the context of "overnight accommodation" as were identified in the discussion of "accommodation" as a qualifying component of regulated packages above.

For the purposes of the present requirement it suffices to look at the additional "overnight" factor. This is not as obvious as it may seem. If a passenger on a ferry is allocated a cabin, would that accommodation (if accommodation it is) be *overnight* accommodation if the contractual time of arrival was 2 o'clock in the morning? If not, at what point on the clock can one legitimately say that the passenger has had overnight accommodation? Could it be argued that a cabin passenger whose ferry journey commences at 4.30 in the morning had the use of overnight accommodation? If so, how late does the journey have to start before such a classification becomes unrealistic? Most cases will be decided on the basis of whether accommodation, on the one hand, and transport, on the other, are separate qualifying components, but there may yet be grounds for dispute where accommodation and transport plainly are separate, but the period over which the accommodation is offered is less than 24 hours and only arguably "overnight".

The regulators' ambition was clearly to keep *day trips* out of the frame as far as the PTR 1992 are concerned, no doubt to prevent overburdening the administration and financial abilities of many thousands of small organisers of such events. By imposing the need to have overnight accommodation or a tour of at least 24 hours' duration, the regulators have undoubtedly succeeded. It will only be in exceptional cases (probably accident cases or cases involving extensive consequential loss) where it would be worth the passenger's while arguing that his ferry or rail journey constituted a regulated package on the basis that overnight accommodation was part of the contract. Even then — regulated package or not — in many cases, the *carrier* is likely to be liable pursuant the provisions of international transport conventions even if that liability is limited.

Cruises

Cruise holidays are sometimes regarded as being in a category all of their own. In many cases, where the cruise is supplied with return flights to the point of embarkation as part of the inclusive price there will be no problem. These arrangements are clearly regulated package holidays. But what is the position where the passengers make their own way to the point of embarkation and all that is supplied is the cruise itself. Is the stand-alone cruise a regulated package holiday? Whether it is or not, it is always worth checking first the terms and conditions of the cruise company supplying the cruise. In many cases the supplier will draw no distinction between those travelling on stand-alone cruise holidays and those to whom air transport has been provided as part of the deal. As a result, the same terms and conditions will apply to all passengers and if some of them are travelling as part of a regulated package the terms and conditions will almost inevitably apply the same liability provisions to both package and non-package customers. Given that regulated package consumers will, as a rule, have the PTR 1992 mirrored in the terms and conditions offered by the supplier[94]. Thus, the non-package consumers will have the same protection as the packager travellers and the question of whether the stand-alone cruise is a regulated package becomes of much lesser significance.

It is tentatively submitted[95] that where a cruise company offers (whether free or for payment as part of an inclusive price[96]) transport[97] to the place of embarkation or disembarkation to or from an airport or other point of arrival, there will be a transport component in the arrangements sufficient to make the cruise holiday a regulated package. Even if the transport element is modest in comparison to the whole package, it is likely to play an essential, or alternatively a significant role in the holiday looked at in the round and is likely to have been one of the factors that induced the consumer to choose the supplier offering that cruise holiday.

Potentially more problematical are stand-alone cruises where literally all that is provided is the cruise holiday itself.[98]

---

[94] Particularly is the supplier is a member of ABTA or one of the other main trade associations.

[95] Tentatively because of the decision in *Keppel-Palmer v Exsus Travel* [2003] All ER (D) 183 which is at present binding authority for the proposition that *de minimis* transport can be ignored for the purposes of determining whether there is a transport component in what would otherwise be a regulated package.

[96] *Rechberger* above.

[97] Buses, limousines, rail links.

[98] Assuming shore excursions are booked on board the vessel after arrival so that such additional services are not part of the pre-arranged combination of services offered at an inclusive price in the UK.

a. Does a cruise vessel provide both accommodation *and* transport thus supplying at the same time two necessary qualifying components for the purposes of being a regulated package?
b. If the vessel itself can only be regarded as *either* accommodation *or* transport (and so only one component) are other facilities and services on board sufficient to constitute *other tourist services* in order to secure the necessary second component to make the whole thing a regulated package?

The short answer is that it is overwhelmingly probable that most courts *would* regard the stand-alone cruise as a regulated package whichever route is taken to get such an answer. To repeat a frequent refrain: it is all a matter of fact and degree. A cruise vessel is certainly "transport", but it is much more than merely transport. It offers "accommodation" that goes beyond being merely an accessory to the transport and whilst it may be difficult to unpick the accommodation from the transport and *vice versa* one gets a strong sense that both are essential features of an undivided whole. Added to this whilst some of the facilities and services offered on board most modern cruise vessels could be regarded a merely adjuncts to the accommodation (e.g. the restaurant, bar and spa facilities) there are likely to be many others[99] these days that, when taken together, can be regarded as "other tourist services" not ancillary to transport and accommodation and accounting for a significant proportion of the package within the meaning of the PTR 1992.

So, assuming this purposive approach to the PTR 1992 and stand-alone cruises prevails, where is the line to be drawn? Is a ferry crossing to be regarded as regulated package because it comes with berth accommodation or lasts for more than 24 hours? If the cruise has both transport and accommodation components why not a ferry crossing? Many consumers would not describe or regard such ferry journeys as "packages" – one does not say "I am taking a package ferry crossing to Spain".[100] Perhaps the answer lies partly in the full title of the Directive – Council Directive on Package Travel, Package Holidays and Package Tours – reinforcing the fact that we are not concerned only with holidays or leisure activities but with package *travel*. Looked at simply as a species of travel there is no obvious reason why an overnight ferry crossing should not be regarded as a regulated package. The DTI in its Guidance Note[101] thought otherwise saying in answer

---

[99] Guides, lecturers, trainers, cinemas, casinos and theatres.
[100] The CAA advised in its Guidance Note 26 that what the consumer *thought* he was getting was an important factor in determining whether what was sold was a regulated package. That did not find favour with the courts, but it is interesting to see the same proposition potentially working in the opposite way.
[101] November 2006 URN 06/1640.

to the self-posed question *"Is a berth on a cross-channel ferry accommodation?: No. The berth ... or sleeping accommodation on an overnight train is a facility. For "accommodation to be an element in the creation of a package it needs to represent more than a facility which is ancillary to other aspects of an arrangement."* One does not find any support in the PTR 1992 themselves for the proposition that an accommodation "facility" has to be more than ancillary to the transport element of a package in order for it constitute a qualifying component in its own right, but on an emotional level and wielding a purposive broad brush one suspects that the DTI's reaction is one that most people are likely to share.

Sold or offered for sale in the United Kingdom

It was noted in the introduction to this chapter that the scope of the 1992 Regulations[38] was wide enough to cover occasions where a foreign organiser offers packages for sale abroad, where the offer is presented in the United Kingdom, but the contract is made elsewhere. In short, all those who offer packages to the public in any part of the United Kingdom must comply with the 1992 Regulations irrespective of where the package is to be performed, where the package contract is made and where the organiser happens to have its principal place of business.

It is worth emphasising that whereas the point of sale, or offer for sale is of crucial importance, the location or destination of the travel contract is immaterial. The Regulations apply as much to packages performed in Africa and Asia as they do to those the performance of which is undertaken in the European Union. So, by way of extreme, but not preposterous example, an Australian company offering packages to Antarctica via Australia through advertising agencies in the United Kingdom, will be subject to the PTR 1992 even if the contract is made in Australia and purports to be subject to the laws of the Commonwealth of Australia. Those who protest the exorbitant effect of this should be alert to the fact that the *application* and *enforceability* of the PTR 1992 are two distinct issues. Nonetheless, those promoting package travel arrangements on the internet, for example, despite having no other connection with this jurisdiction, are subject to the theoretical reach of the regulations, even if enforcing a remedy for improper performance would be difficult.

An offer for sale includes an invitation to treat.[102] "Offer" therefore bears a wide meaning. The circulation or display of travel brochures and leaflets, the placing on inserts and advertisements in newspapers and magazines would all be regarded as invitations to treat at common law. Under the PTR 1992,

---

[102] PTR 1992 regulation 2(1).

they are "offers". It was important that organisers and retailers should not be able to avoid the application of the PTR 1992 merely on the basis of the technical argument that it was the *consumer* who offered to *buy* the package and not the organiser who offered to sell it. Plainly, if retailers or organisers were able to avoid the application of the PTR 1992 merely by reason of the fact that they were engaged in inviting the public to treat, the effect of the regulatory framework would be seriously undermined.

The concept of an invitation to treat is a familiar one in English law. In *Fisher v Bell*[103] a shop keeper was acquitted of making an offer to sell a flick-knife by displaying it in his shop window with a price ticket attached. This was not an offer to sell but only an "invitation to treat" and did not offend against the section 1(1) of the Restriction of Offensive Weapons Act 1959 which prohibited "offers for sale" but not invitations to treat. The position was corrected by Parliament with the Restriction of Offensive Weapons Act 1961 which created the offence of "exposing or possessing" such weapons for the purposes of sale or hire. Avoiding a narrow interpretation of "offer" is commonplace in English law due to the distinction between offers and invitations; another example of Parliament being careful to give an extended meaning to the word "offer" can be found in section 10 of the Consumer Protection Act 1987 — and of course now, the PTR 1992.

The fact that "offer" has this extended statutory meaning for the purposes of applying the PTR 1992 does not mean that the process by which the package contract is made differs in any respect from the common law rules. The traditional rules of offer, acceptance and consideration apply. The travel agent may well be *offering* a package for sale by displaying a brochure on its shelves for the purposes of the Regulations, but that does not mean that the agent is making an offer to sell in the contractual sense. The extended meaning assigned to the expression "*offer to sell*" applies for the purposes of determining whether the PTR 1992 are engaged. The common law rules of contract-making still prevail. The party who displays a brochure may well be caught by the regulations as an offeror, but a consumer cannot usually go into a travel shop and say "I accept your offer to sell that package". As a matter of contract-making, the organiser is still inviting the *consumer* to treat, and it is the consumer who offers to *buy* the package promoted in, for example, the brochure. Ultimately it is the organiser who accepts the consumer's offer to *buy*. For commercial reasons this rule is important. It would create enormous difficulties for both organiser and consumer if at the moment a consumer purported to "accept" an offer to sell on the part of the organiser a binding contract came into effect.

---

[103] [1961] 1 QB 394.

Chapter 2

PARTIES

This chapter considers the parties who are affected by the PTR 1992. First of all the regulations create a framework of civil liability whereby the "*other party to contract*" is rendered liable for the proper performance of the package contract irrespective of whether the performance of the package services is undertaken by the "*other party*" or some other supplier of services.[1] In other regulations[2] liability is imposed on the "organiser" or the "retailer" of the package — or both – sometimes regardless of whether a package contract comes into existence.[3] However, before looking at issues of civil liability imposed on different people under different regulations in the PTR 1992[4] it is necessary to consider:

- how the regulatory liabilities arise;
- the parties who can enforce the regulatory liabilities;
- the parties on whom the PTR 1992 impose such liabilities.

The Contract

The PTR 1992 might be regarded as being mainly concerned with civil liability under package travel contracts. As we have already seen for there to be a *regulated* package the arrangements which constitute the package have to satisfy certain specified conditions.[5] Regulation 2(1) defines the "contract" as "*the agreement linking the consumer to the organiser or to the retailer, or both, as the case may be.*" As with other parts of the regulations it is important to remember that the provisions need to be looked at as a whole. It is impossible to understand the full significance of this definition of "the contract" without some insight into the nature of the parties that are subject to the PTR 1992's reach.

It will be noted immediately that "the contract" is that agreement which *links* the consumer with an organiser or a retailer (or both as the case may be). It is

---

[1] Regulation 15 in particular is considered in detail in Chapter 4.
[2] For example regulation 4 – see Chapter 3.
[3] See regulation 5 and the imposition of criminal liabilities – Chapter 12.
[4] See Chapters 3 and 4.
[5] See Chapter 1.

not necessary that the consumer be a *party* to the package contract provided the contract in place provides this *link*. Accordingly, where later regulations make reference to the [package] contract, and the "other party to the contract", one should bear in mind that persons can be brought under the umbrella of the contract who would not be considered parties to that contract at common law. To this extent the Regulations cut across the common law notion of privity of contract, and, at a stroke, give certain classes of person access to remedies under the Regulations that they may not otherwise have had.

The closest we have come to an understanding[6] of the use of the expression "*links*" comes from some passing remarks by Douglas Brown J. in *Hone v Going Places Leisure Travel Plc:*[7]

> [It was] accepted that the word "link" was a difficult word to give meaning to. It certainly could not be construed as to mean that the retailer should be generally liable under the regulations for the way in which a tour operator or its carrier provided the package holiday. ... a number of reasons [were advanced] of which I need only mention two. Firstly, there are statutory schemes compensating those who fall victim to insolvent airlines and tour operators e.g. the Air Travel Trust and the ATOL scheme itself run by the Civil Aviation Authority, and these are not applicable to retailers, unless the retailers are themselves actually providing the package holidays. Secondly, a travel agent does not have direct control over the services delivered as part of the package holiday. It has no control over, and cannot influence, standards of service or facilities provided during the holiday. Regulation 15 (1) does reserve rights of indemnity, but a travel agent would not be able to take advantage of those rights.

The implications of this distraction from the common law principles of privity will become clearer in the context of the following discussion on the parties affected by the PTR 1992. However, a single example at this stage may illustrate the point. An individual books and pays for a regulated package holiday for himself and his partner. The contract is made between the individual and the tour operator and is essentially just a package holiday sold to the individual "for two". In the course of the holiday the *partner* sustains injury caused by the improper performance of the package contract by the tour operator. The partner has a good claim and a direct claim under the regulations. The contract is an agreement that links or connects the partner with the tour operator even though the partner was not himself a party to the contract[8] and did not pay for the holiday. References to "the contract" and liability for improper performance of the contract in the Regulations is broad

---

[6] Assuming it to be a material expression.
[7] As to which see further below.
[8] Subject to arguments about a relation ship of principal and agent between the two holidaymakers.

enough to include the partner because he is linked to the tour operator by the agreement made between the individual and the company. Looked at in reverse, the party liable for the damage caused by the injury cannot avoid liability on the grounds that the partner was not a *party* to the contract. The partner may sue in his own right, whilst the individual who *was* a party to the contract need not participate in proceedings that are of little or no personal interest to him.

The same result might sometimes be achieved at common law by adopting and deploying agency principles.[9] The contracting individual could often be regarded as the contracting agent for his friend's half of the holiday. However, where the sole contracting individual paid the price of the holiday without charging his partner for a half share, such agency arguments could often assume a contorted look. The contracting individual was not really buying half the holiday as his partner's agent he was buying for himself a holiday for two persons. The problem without the intervention of the PTR 1992 might be that the contracting individual at common law had not suffered an accident and did not sustain a material loss whereas the partner who did not pay, suffered loss and damage but was not a contracting party. However much the principles of agency might be implemented to come to the assistance of the injured partner in order to allow an action for damages to proceed in his own name, such an artificial approach is completely avoided by the manner in which the PTR 1992 have been formulated. By reason of regulation 2 the injured partner in the example given above has a direct cause of action in his own right and it matters not that he was not a party to the contract, nor does it matter that he cannot show that his partner contracted on his behalf as an agent.

The Consumer

The "*other party to the contract*" is liable to the *consumer* for any failure to perform or improper performance of the package contract.[10] Regulation 2(2) provides as follows:

> In the definition of 'contract' … 'consumer' means the person who takes or agrees to take the package ['the principal contractor'] and elsewhere in these Regulations 'consumer' means, as the context requires, the principal contractor, any person on whose behalf the principal contractor agrees to purchase the package ['the other beneficiaries'] or any person to whom the principal contractor or any of the other beneficiaries transfers the package ['the transferees'].

---

[9] And also now by using the Contracts (Rights of Third Parties) Act 1999.
[10] As we shall see in under regulation 15 in Chapter 4.

The party liable for improper performance under the PTR 1992 is liable to four classes of persons all of whom are classified as "the consumer"[11] under regulation 2(2).

1. *The person who takes the package.*

2. *The person who agrees to take the package.*

3. *The other beneficiaries.*

4. *The transferee.*[12]

The principal contractor

The expression "principal contractor" covers the first two of the above classes of person who are deemed to be consumers under the PTR 1992, *i.e.* those who *take* or *agree to take* the package. The regulations plainly envisage circumstances in which one can *agree* to take a package without *actually* taking it, and agree to take it or take it without actually *buying* it. So although it is tempting to conclude that only a person[13] who *purchases* a package, or agrees to purchase a package (whether for himself or others) is a "principal contractor", this is not the case. A volunteer may be a "principal contractor". If the regulators meant to define a principal contractor as a purchaser, they could easily have said so. Because they did not say so, the reader of the PTR 1992 is left with the strong impression that the regulators intended to extend the meaning of "principal contractor" to cover more than purchasers or intending purchasers.

The regulators distinctly avoided the use of the expressions "purchase", or "buys" or similar, so the "principal contractor" (it can safely be assumed) is not necessarily linked personally with the money paid for the travel services. The words used in the definition of "consumer" are "takes or agrees to take". One question that arises, therefore, is: *take* [the package] *in what respect?* Colloquially, a person might be regarded as "taking" a package if she "goes" or embarks on one. But the regulators cannot surely have intended that "principal contractors" be *all* those who "take" a package in this colloquial or "embarking" sense. First, because this would mean that a corporation[14] could not benefit from the Regulations in circumstances where it made a block hospitality package contract with a tour operator: a

---

[11] Note that in respect of criminal liabilities imposed by regulation 5 the regulators speak of *"a possible consumer"* which appears to be the world at large.

[12] See also Chapter 3 and PTR 1992 regulation 10.

[13] And this will include corporations.

[14] Whether the option of a corporation being regarded as a consumer within the PTR 1992 should continue to be even an arguable possibility is the subject of the current European Commission consultation on the future of the Package Travel Directive 1990.

corporation cannot "go" on a package tour. (It would be left to the individual travellers to take action in respect of any failure in the performance of the corporate hospitality package). Secondly, because both "other beneficiaries" and "transferees" are all likely to "go" or "embark" on the package, so they too would be *principal contractors*, and further references and sub-definitions regarding them as separate species would be wholly unnecessary. If the "principal contractor" could be *anybody* who actually went on the package holiday there would be no need to define "transferees" and "other beneficiaries" separately.

Neither of the two most obvious constructions of the term "*takes or agrees to take the package*" fits very neatly. The words are unlikely to be limited to those who purchase or agree to purchase the package (otherwise the regulators would have said so), and it is unlikely to be taken to be only or even those who "go on" or merely agree to "go on" the package tour because this could exclude some purchasers (such as corporations).

Who then is a "principal contractor"? The answer is probably a simple one: all of the above. Those who purchase, agree to purchase and those who go on a package or *get* the package in some other way may all be regarded as "principal contractors". The regulators have outwitted the textual critics. The Regulations are deliberately drafted widely in the interest of consumer protection. The expressions "principal contractor", "other beneficiary" and "transferee" need not be mutually exclusive. The definition is designed to cover a host of eventualities *including those circumstances where the package is provided free of charge*. So, the "principal contractor" is *any* party who:

- purchases the package *and* goes on it;

- purchases the package but does *not* go on it (*e.g.* corporate buyers, generous gift donors, and transferors);

- agrees to purchase the package, but does not personally pay the bill (*e.g.* it goes on a business or family member's credit card);

- goes on the package without buying it because it has been won in a prize draw or as a rewards bonus;

- is the winner of a competition but donates the prize to family or friends;

- is, perhaps, any other person named on the travel itinerary or invoice.

Other beneficiaries

"Other beneficiaries" is an expression that includes *any person on whose behalf the principal contractor agrees to purchase the package*. Note, in this instance, the principal contractor must be a person who agrees to *purchase*. So to qualify as "other beneficiaries", there must be a principal contractor who has agreed to purchase the package. This leaves open the position of those additional travellers who take advantage of a holiday won by someone else, or otherwise provide, free of charge. Nonetheless, the intention of the PTR 1992 is to short-circuit common law rules of privity of contract. Because "other beneficiaries" fall within the definition of "consumer" and because it is the "consumer" who is given rights under the PTR 1992, persons who are not necessarily parties to the contract or buyers of the travel services are given rights and remedies of their own. The "other beneficiaries", in other words, can enforce the regulations without invoking the support of the principal contractor. Similarly, any party, such as a tour operator liable under the PTR 1992, cannot avoid their enforcement on the grounds that the "other beneficiaries" were not privy to the package contract.

The expression "other beneficiaries"[15] is clearly designed to include:

- members of a family or group of friends travelling together on a contract made by only one of them;

- employees travelling on package contracts made by their employers;

- social groups travelling under the umbrella of an organisation or club.

In the last two examples there would be no question of the "principal contractor" travelling with the group, and there may be many circumstances in which the principal contractor would not sustain any loss in the event that there was a failure to perform the contract on the part of a supplier. The direct remedies for the "other beneficiaries" created by the PTR 1992 helps to avoid the need to adopt sometimes contorted arguments of agency in order to justify proceedings on the part of those who have no direct contractual relationship with the supplier.

Lord Denning MR in *Jackson v Horizon Holidays*[16] gave three examples (not all package holiday examples) that are worth poaching here. Each was an example where the court felt that it was difficult to maintain the argument that the contracting party was contracting as an *agent*. There were:

- a host who makes a party booking at a restaurant;

- a vicar who arranges a trip for the choir;

- a husband who makes a holiday contract for himself, his wife and family.

---

[15] The preamble to the Council Directive on Package Travel (Etc.) (90/314/EC – Appendix 1) sets out the regulators' ambition in respect of the broadening of the direct remedial scope of regulations enacted by Member States. Persons are supposed to be given the benefit of regulatory protection and remedies irrespective of whether they are direct contacting parties.
[16] [1975] 1 WLR 1468.

Each of the above was an example of the contracting party making a contract *for his own benefit* as well as for the benefit of others. The contracting party could of course sue in the event of a breach of contract, but would be suing for damage affecting *him* even though that might arise out of defective contractual performance which compromised the enjoyment of the others. The added difficulty was that the "others" would not have any direct right of action themselves, so that the vicar would have to be the claimant even if he himself did not go on the trip; or the husband would be the claimant even though he booked the family holiday to compensate for the fact that he was travelling elsewhere on a business trip. All this had an air of unreality. The persons most directly affected and damaged could pursue a remedy only through the conduit of a person not personally affected by the defective performance. The PTR 1992, through the mechanism of the extended meaning to "consumer" by the inclusion of "other beneficiaries", puts a stop to such artifice. From 1993 onwards, these "other beneficiaries" have direct rights on which they can sue, and direct remedies to which they are personally entitled. The "principal contractor" need not even be a party to the action. In the examples given by Lord Denning, the members of the travel parties concerned[17] would enjoy an independent regulatory status that is not otherwise recognised by the common law. Each of the "others" is a "consumer" within the extended definition provided.

One more point should be made in this context. Simply because these "other beneficiaries" now enjoy an independent regulatory status, it does not mean that there are no circumstances in which a "principal contractor" cannot make or take the package contract through the agency of another. The common law is not supplanted, merely supplemented. Just because an agent makes or takes the contract on your behalf does not in itself mean that you are not the principal contractor within he meaning of regulation 2(2). A person may "agree [through an agent] to take" a package, and thus still be the principal contractor. The important point is, that whilst when one comes to consider the express and implied terms of the travel contract (outside the four corners of the PTR 1992) privity will still have its part to play but under the PTR 1992, the contractual position of the complainant is of less significance.

The contractual position of the complainant may be of *less* significance but it is not *without* significance. Where someone who sues as an *"other beneficiary"* that other beneficiary can sue only in respect of their own losses. To take an example; suppose a member of a package holiday party sues in respect of personal injury damages sustained as a result of defective facility supplied in the course of a regulated package and adds a claim for loss of bargain and loss of enjoyment. That party is not self-evidently entitled to include a claim for

---

[17] Provided the arrangements constituted a regulated package.

loss of bargain and/or enjoyment for the other members of the travelling party whose holiday has been compromised by the accident befalling the injured party. This is simply because such losses are not the losses of the injured person. The position is different where the injured person is also the person who made the holiday contract (the principal contractor). The principal contractor can sue for loss of bargain and loss of enjoyment on behalf of all the travelling members of the package holiday party[18] but this principle would not apply to someone who was simply one *"other beneficiary"* – or at least there is no authority to support such a proposition. Technical though it may be, if the accident affecting the injured party has affected the bargain or enjoyment of fellow travellers, or if those fellow travellers have quality complaints of their own whether related to the injured person's accident or not, then the principal contractor should be joined in the proceedings as a co-claimant ion order to justify a remedy being awarded.

Transferees

The third category of "consumer" is the transferee. That is a person to whom the package is transferred pursuant to regulation 10[19]. In brief, the "consumer" is entitled in certain prescribed circumstances, to transfer his booking to someone else. This means that *either* a principal contractor *or* other beneficiaries are permitted to be transferors under the regulatory scheme. The transferee is then regarded as a "consumer" and enjoys all the direct rights and remedies of other consumers under the PTR 1992. As the terms transferor and transferee suggest, the transferee is in no better position than the principal contractor or other beneficiaries, and enjoys rights and remedies derivative from those initially vested in either the principal contractor or the other beneficiaries. In other words, there cannot be a transferee without there first being a principal contractor or other beneficiaries — although it is extremely difficult to imagine circumstances in which anyone could canvass the possibility of there being a transferee or indeed other beneficiaries without there being a principal contractor somewhere in the contractual matrix.

The PTR 1992 do not expressly appear to tolerate the idea of a sub-transfer. That is, a transferee is not apparently permitted by the Regulations to transfer the package to a second alternative passenger. Neither do the PTR 1992 appear to sanction the notion of re-transfer — that is, the transferring of the benefit of package from the transferee back to the transferor. The importance of this arises in circumstances where there may be an unusually fluid group of intending travellers. The supplier of the package (subject to the rules laid out in regulation 10) must permit one traveller to transfer the benefit of the package

---

[18] See *Jackson v Horizon Holidays* [1975] 1 WLR 1468 – Damages & Other Remedies Chapter 7.
[19] See further Chapter 3.

to another individual. This may cause some modest inconvenience to the supplier. If that transferee himself cannot travel after all, the is the supplier permitted to refuse to sanction any such sub-transfer? In practice on the rare occasion when these sorts of multiple transfers are requested, the tour operator will probably not raise any objection. However, it may well be that because the *transferee* after the transfer has occurred himself becomes a *consumer*[20] the transferee may then engage in a further sequential transfer to an alternative transferee provided the other conditions of regulation 10 are met.

The Other Party to the Contract

Under the PTR 1992 some liabilities are imposed on "*the other party to the contract*",[21] and some on the "*organiser*" or "*retailer*" or "*both as the case may be*".[22] It is important to distinguish between these various species throughout the regulations. "*The other party to the contract*", however, must be either the *organiser* of the package, the *retailer* of the package or both (if indeed they are different persons). So, one might be an *organiser* or a *retailer* without being *the other party to the contract* but one cannot be *the other party* without being either an *organiser* or a *retailer*.

"*The other party to the contract*" means "*the party, other than the consumer, to the contract, that is, the organiser or the retailer or both as the case may be*".[23] One immediate difficulty with this definition of the party on whom important civil liabilities and obligations of the PTR 1992 are imposed, is that (as we have just seen) "*the consumer*" does not have to be a party to the contract at all. However, it cannot possibly be the case that where the consumer is *not* a *party* to the contract, for example, because the consumer is a transferee or one of the other beneficiaries, that the obligations imposed by the PTR 1992 do not fall on the party supplying the package. What is clearly intended is that the "*other party to the contract*" on whom the obligations are imposed, should be the party *other than the principal contractor, other beneficiaries or transferees*, that is, the organiser or the retailer or both as the case may be.

Organiser

An organiser means:

> the person who otherwise than occasionally, organises packages and sells or offers them for sale, whether directly or through a retailer.[24]

---

[20] By virtue of regulation 2(2).
[21] Regulation 15.
[22] Regulations 4 and 5.
[23] Regulation 2(1).
[24] Regulation 2(1).

To define an "organiser" as one who organises is perhaps not as helpful a definition as it might have been. The "organiser" in the overwhelming majority of cases will be a tour operator — but *organiser* is not limited to tour operators. It is worth underlining the fact that an organiser does not have to be acting in the course of a trade or business. There are many instances where someone might be the organiser of a regulated package even though they do not operate commercially or for profit. A gratuitous organiser can still be a regulated organiser within the meaning of the PTR 1992. Conversely, a commercial organiser who organises only occasionally is outside the regulations. There are three requirements of an organiser under the Regulations.

1.   The organiser must *organise*.

2.   Organising must occur *otherwise than occasionally*.

3.   The organiser must *sell or offer for sale*[25] the packages directly or through a retailer.

Of course what has to be organised is a *regulated* package.[26] If as a result of the organisation there is no regulated package,[27] the party responsible for the organising is not caught by the Regulations. If, on the other hand, the arrangements constitute a regulated package, the consumer does not have a remedy if the party responsible for the organisation does not do so *otherwise than occasionally*. Only if the organiser does so otherwise than occasionally do the regulatory obligations and liabilities arise. Unfortunately, the PTR 1992 give no guidance as to what constitutes regulated organisation or when such organisation is to be regarded as being done otherwise than occasionally. Whether or not there has been organisation other than occasionally will be a matter of fact and degree.

Organisation

An organiser, it is submitted, is one who puts together or arranges the component parts of the package. It is the organising or putting together of the component parts of the package that matters, not the arrangement or provision of the services lying behind the component parts of the package themselves. Accordingly, a party who arranges to link accommodation and transport facilities already in place is still likely to be an organiser. The two most obvious examples of "organisers" are tour operators and travel agents — though the latter seldom recognise themselves as such.

---

[25] Offers for sale include invitations to treat.
[26] See Chapter 1 and the *ABTA v CAA* litigation with regard to the potential problems this gives rise to for travel agents.
[27] Such as accommodation only or a group of services sold separately not forming part of an inclusive price.

The tour operator who pre-arranges components and promotes them in the form of brochures circulated through, amongst others, travel agents is the classic "organiser" within the meaning of the PTR 1992. The tour operator will often still be an organiser of package travel arrangements where it assists a consumer to put together tailor-made options comprising the final travel contract. In both instances the tour operator is putting together or co-ordinating the purchase of travel components that then form part of one supply contract sold at an inclusive price.

However, travel agents too may be within the definition of "organiser" under the PTR 1992. There are many instances where it is the travel agent, acting as a travel consultant, who mixes-and-matches the component parts of a holiday for the consumer or "puts together" individual arrangements on behalf of the consumer. It hardly matters that the arrangements that are compiled in this way are from different parts of the same brochure or from different brochures promoted by different tour operators. One must not lose sight of the fact that an organiser is described in the PTR 1992 in order for the consumer to identify "*the other party to the contract*". It is on the "*other party to the [package] contract*" that most of the civil liabilities imposed by the 1992 Regulations fall. Therefore, in many instances (although certainly not all), even if the travel agent *has* organised the package components or put them together for the consumer, the travel agent will not *necessarily* be the party linked with the consumer under the package contract. The principal civil liabilities[28] created by the PTR 1992 do not land on the *organiser*, as such, but do so only if that organiser happens also to be the "*other party to the contract*". However, where it is shown that the travel agent *is* the other party to the contract, there is every reason why the principal civil liabilities in the PTR 1992 should apply to him.

The fundamental problem for travel agents is that *the other party to the contract* must be either the *organiser* or the *retailer;* or it may be *both as the case may be.* Where the travel agent is the retailer but not the organiser it becomes a question of fact as to whether the travel agent is in reality the *other party to the contract* or one of the other parties to the contract or whether in fact it is, say, the tour operator as *organiser* that is the *other party to the contract.* However, where the travel agent is the *organiser* it will almost invariably also be the retailer and consequently also *the other party to the contract* on whom the civil liabilities under regulation 15 are imposed.[29] The position of travel agents is further complicated due to the fact that simply because the tour operator as *organiser* is *the other party to the contract* does not necessarily mean that the travel agent as *retailer* is not also *the other party*

---

[28] That is, the regulation 15 liabilities.
[29] See the discussion of the *Club Tours* case [C-400/00 ECJ] in Chapter 1.

to the contract because regulation 2(1) appears to envisage that both organiser and retailer may be *other (parties) to the contract.* It is worth noting that just because a retailer or travel agent may in certain circumstances be regarded as requiring an ATOL because an air transport package has been sold by that travel agent it does not *necessarily* follow (though it might) that the travel agent is *the other party to the contract* and so liable for quality complaints or accidents under regulation 15 of the PTR 1992.

The civil liability of travel agents under regulation 15 of the PTR 1992 was discussed at first instance in *Hone v Going Places Leisure Travel Limited.*[30] This was a case where the claimant was injured during the course of the emergency evacuation of an aircraft at Istanbul airport at the conclusion of a package holiday. The claimant sued the travel agent, *Going Places* because both tour operator and airline had ceased trading. He had booked his holiday using Teletext and had not been informed of the fact that the holiday was to be supplied and had been organised by a tour operator rather than *Going Places* itself until after the contract had been made and the tickets arrived at his home address naming the relevant tour operator. Douglas Brown J. considered the extent to which retailers were liable under regulation 15 of the PTR 1992.[31] The trial judge concluded that retailers would only be characterised as *the other party to the contract* in 2 situations. First where the retailer had organised or been one of several organisers responsible for putting together the package arrangements, or secondly, where as in the present case, the retailer was acting as agent for an undisclosed organiser-principal.[32] Thus it would seem that the retailer travel agent is not concurrently liable with the organiser tour operator in regulation 15 cases unless the retailer has also been an organiser of the package. The retailer is unlikely to be a joint organiser in cases where a package is simply selected from a tour operator's brochure. Douglas Brown J said at first instance in *Hone* (albeit following a concession made on behalf of the claimant):

> [It was] accepted that a wider construction of the regulations putting liability on retailers who had made it clear they acted as agents for operators, was probably not permissible. This was because such a construction would represent such a substantial extension of liability for travel agents that much plainer words would be required to bring such liability about. For the purposes of [this] case [it was] contended on the perhaps unusual facts of this case the retailer was liable as the other party to the contract."[33]

[30] [2001] EWCA Civ 947 – first instance decision discussed at [2001] ITLJ 153.
[31] Although this was strictly unnecessary because the Claimant lost his action on the "merits".
[32] This part of the decision was not the subject of the subsequent appeal which was concerned with whether PTR 1992 regulation imposed strict or fault-based liability – see further Chapter 4.
[33] QBD 16 November 2000.

Judicial opinion on the extent of a retailer's regulation 15 liability has not, however, been unanimous. In *Minhas v Imperial Travel Limited*[34] the consumers sued their travel agent for damages for a variety of quality complaints pursuant to regulation 15 and a district judge concluded that because the consumers had paid the price of the holiday directly to the travel agent, the travel agent was not only a retailer but also *the other party to the contract.* The consumers had also sued under regulation 4[35] so the reasoning that justified a conclusion under regulation 15 may not have been an essential part of the decision. Nonetheless, the fact that the money for the holiday had been paid to the travel agent (directly or otherwise) is surely neither here nor there. If the money was paid to the travel agent in the capacity of *booking agent* for the tour operator (presumably a disclosed principal) it is difficult to see why this factor should transform the agent into *the other party to the contract.* The question of the capacity of the travel agent in receiving the money from the consumers does not seem to have been discussed in *Minhas.* Consumers will invariably pay money to the travel agent, which will then be transmitted to the tour operator with or without a deduction for the agent's commission. Why this should make the agent the *other party to the contract* is difficult to understand.

It is submitted that the dictum of Douglas Brown J. is to be preferred. The retailer is liable under regulation 15 where it has acted as an agent for an undisclosed principal or where it is also an organiser – not otherwise. *Hone* does not appear to have been cited in *Minhas. Hone* is to be preferred because it gives effect to the provisions of the PTR 1992[36] that recognise that the *other party to the contract* will not always and in all circumstances be the retailer and the organiser concurrently. Had the regulators intended to make the retailer concurrently liable with the organiser in all regulation 15 cases for the improper performance of the holiday contract[37] they would surely have said so by providing that the consumer could pursue a claim for improper performance against either the retailer or the organiser. There would have been no need to complicate matters by reference in regulation 15 to *the other party to the contract.* It follows that regulation 15 and other references to *the other party to the contract* in the PTR 1992 cannot be intended to mean that the consumer can elect which of the organiser or retailer to sue.[38]

---

[34] [2003] CL February 263.
[35] The provision of misleading descriptive matter, liability for which undoubtedly lies on the retailer under regulation 4.
[36] The definition of *other party to the contract* in regulation 2.
[37] Which would be the case if simple receipt of the purchase price was the test.
[38] But the consumer may plainly elect under regulation 4 – see Chapter 3.

The duty to ensure that proper financial security arrangements are made[39] to safeguard consumers' purchase money is also a duty that is imposed on the "*other party to the contract*". Therefore, travel agents will only need to heed such security requirements in those cases where they are not only organisers or retailers, but also the "*other party to the contract*".

Otherwise than occasionally

To be an organiser one does not need to be either a travel or a tour operator — both of whom self-evidently undertake their roles otherwise than occasionally. There are many other potential "organisers", and as regulated organisers these other potential organisers may well be the "other party to the contract" and liable to both the criminal and civil sanctions imposed by the 1992 Regulations.

Who are these other potential organisers? Any list would include:

- employers arranging packages for employees and their families;

- social organisations arranging packages for their members;

- schools and school governors arranging school trips;

- educational institutions arranging packages for vacation courses;

- churches and charities putting together packages for members, guests and beneficiaries;

- an individual who puts together a package for a group of friends.

If an organiser in this additional list puts together package travel arrangements the PTR 1992 imposes both criminal and civil sanctions so the responsibilities should not be underestimated. Non-commercial organisers such as those listed above need to beware — not only because civil and criminal sanctions are potentially imposed directly on them whether they are the "*other party to the contract*" or not, but because there will be certain instances where there is no intervening tour operator or travel agent, or where the commercial supplier has become insolvent when the non-commercial organiser may find itself the *only* target for litigation in the event that something goes wrong.

The social co-ordinator is not likely to be regarded as an organiser where the role played is simply that of inviting other participants to engage in the choice of pre-arranged packages put together by others. However, the social organiser is likely to be a regulated organiser where the components of the package are

---

[39] Regulations 16-20.

sourced, combined, priced and co-ordinated *by that organiser* before they are offered to, for example, the members of a club or other social organisation.

The principle get-out for the non-commercial or social organiser will usually be to maintain that he is not an organiser otherwise than occasionally — or to remove the double negative, he is only an occasional organiser.[40]

So, when does one organise "*otherwise than occasionally*" in a way that is likely to be caught by the PTR 1992? This is clearly intended to be a matter of fact and degree to be judged in the light of individual cases. In the majority of instances the answer may be perfectly obvious — irrespective of whether the organiser is commercial. The existence of a commercial element is likely to be of some evidential importance as to whether the organiser was "occasional" or not but cannot be regarded as conclusive Otherwise, the regulators would have limited the scope of the 1992 Regulations to *commercial* organisers in the course of their trade or business.

For those that are described above as the social or non-commercial organisers defining "*otherwise than occasionally*" it is submitted is a matter of *frequency* as opposed to *regularity*. So, whilst a specialist climbing association might *frequently* organise packages for its members and thus be a regulated organiser, the *regular* organisation of the annual school field trip would not necessarily be regarded as something done "otherwise than occasionally". Something can be done *occasionally* (once or even twice a year), yet with monotonous regularity. It is unlikely that the substitution of the term "otherwise than occasionally" for others such as *casually*, *incidentally*, or *now and then* substantially illuminates the expression used in the PTR 1992 to describe a regulated organiser.

It will be born in mind that there is no logical or practical reason why in respect of a single package there cannot be more than one organiser. There may be several organisers, one of whom is commercial and another social. Where there is a group of organisers or at least more than one, the key issue in most cases will be: which organiser (or retailer) is "the other party to the contract"? With some important exceptions outlined above, it is on this "other party" that most of the burdens of the PTR 1992 fall.

Sells or offers for sale

In order to be a regulated "organiser" the organiser must not only organise otherwise than occasionally, but also *sell or offer for sale* the package in question. This does not necessarily excuse the social organiser. Schools, clubs or associations may offer for sale a package put together by another supplier,

---

[40] See also the need for the organiser to sell or offer for sale the package arrangements (below).

even though the actual sale is affected directly between the supplier (*e.g.* a tour operator or travel agent) and the ultimate consumer. If such social organisers are offering packages to their members and guests they need to be aware that they are subject (as organisers) to the criminal sanctions applicable to those organisers who pedal misleading promotional material[41] even if the travellers make their contracts directly with a tour operator.

However, there is also a risk that such social organisers will themselves (as organisers) also be "*the other party to the* [package] *contract*" where the members of the club or association pay money directly to the co-ordinator who may already have purchased either a package or an option on a certain number of packages or components from the ultimate suppliers[42]. Although there is no authority on the matter to date, it is anticipated that the courts are likely to be fairly tender in their attitude towards social or non-commercial organisers. There will be many instances where the co-ordinating role (even a role that involves pre-purchasing options or packages for onward transmission to members) is regarded as an agency role. Whilst the organiser's status as an agent does not necessarily prevent it from being a regulated organiser (an agent can be just as much a regulated organiser as a principal), it will often prevent that social organiser from being "*the other party to the* [package] *contract*" as a result of which the main civil and security provisions of the PTR 1992 will not apply. Nonetheless, the potential criminal liability for pedalling misleading promotional material may still be a daunting prospect for many volunteer organisations — and this is a liability that attaches to organisers whether or not they are also "the other party to the contract".

Those responsible for arranging or putting together social travel programmes for schools, churches, charities and sports organisations can be seen as regulated organisers if they are other than occasionally offering for sale the packages that their members subsequently purchase even though the travel contracts might be made by the consumers with a tour operator or a primary service provider once the "organiser" has pointed the consumers in the right direction.

Retailer

The other class of person capable of being "*the other party to the contract*" and subject to a variety of sanctions in the PTR 1992 is the retailer. A "retailer" is "*the person who sells or offers for sale the package put together by the organiser.*[43]" The clearest example of a "retailer" is the travel agent.

---

[41] Regulation 5.
[42] It will be recalled that the effect of accepting a payment from the consumers in *Minhas v Imperial Travel* (above) was to make the recipient the *other party to the contract.*
[43] Regulation 2(1).

However, it will be apparent from the definition quoted that the social organisations discussed above, will sometimes be retailers even if they are not organisers. Accordingly, the PTR 1992 get social co-ordinators one way or the other. The regulations are not limited in their scope to those operating in the course of a trade or business or for profit.

Apart from travel agents there are other examples of persons who are vulnerable to being regarded as regulated retailers:

- magazines and newspapers promoting or advertising holidays;

- internet site hosts;

- credit and charge card companies promoting travel offers;

- any social group which promotes travel arrangements to its members;

- an individual who persuades a group of friends to embark on, or even to consider, a package tour selected by that individual.

Whether persons identified on this list or others are classified as retailers will invariably turn on the facts of a given case and the terms in which the package arrangements are advertised or described. It was necessary for the regulators to extend the meaning of "retailer" beyond those who actually *sell* packages, to include those who *offer* to sell or invite to treat. If there was not such an extended meaning ascribed to "retailer" then travel agents would often be excluded from the ambit of the 1992 Regulations on the grounds that it is (usually) the tour operator who actually makes the contract with the consumer. Again it is worth bearing in mind that the "offer for sale" can be an offer by an agent acting for a retailing principal.

One possible get-out for the social or non-commercial "offeror" is that he is not offering to *sell* the package at all. He is merely placing before the consumer an option which is being offered by another party (*e.g.* a tour operator). The problem with this get-out is that it would probably come to the rescue of travel agents as well as the so-called social organisers, given that travel agents often merely place before their customers the packages "on offer" from tour operators. Furthermore, it needs to be re-iterated that the PTR 1992 draw no distinction between retailing or organising as a principal or as an agent, and draw no distinction between commercial agents and non-commercial agents. Any such limitation on the scope of the PTR 1992 awaits a judicial gloss based on perceived regulatory intention. As Goldring J. noted at first instance in *ABTA v CAA*[44] the PTR 1992 do not alter the common

---

[44] [2006] EWHC 13 (Admin).

principles of agency. At the end of the day who contracts as a principal and who as an agent remains one of fact and degree.

There is no reason to suppose that the expression "retailer" is exclusive of the term "organiser". It is perfectly feasible that the organiser will also be the "retailer" and vice versa. Indeed, it will often be the case that the tour operator is both retailer and organiser. In the modern travel market one may wonder what useful function travel agents serve, given the preponderance of direct selling undertaken by tour operators and other service providers.

The important point for any potential "retailer" to bear in mind is the strict liability imposed by regulation 4 not to disseminate misleading promotional material.

Or both as the case may be

The 1992 Regulations impose regulatory responsibility for non-performance of the package contract or failures in the performance thereof (as well as a range of other civil and criminal liabilities) on the "*other party to the contract*". This must be either the organiser or the retailer or both *as the case may be* because in the definition of "contract" in regulation 2(1) it is only the organiser or the retailer (or both) who can make an agreement that links with the consumer.

What the consumer must do is discern with whom the package contract was made. In doing so the consumer has three choices. The contract will be deemed to have been made with:

1.   The organiser, or

2.   The retailer, or

3.   Both organiser and retailer.

The danger for the travel agent and other retailers is that regulation 2(1) does not absolve *agents* as such. The retailer may be subject to an agreement which *links* the travel agent (*as an agent*) to the consumer even though the tour operator is the other principal contracting party. Accordingly, for tailor made or mix-and-match "packages" the consumer is given a choice. The "*other party to the contract*" may be both the tour operator (as principal) and the travel agent (as agent) and the consumer has a choice of targets for his action — he may sue either the principal or the agent in the absence of any judicial authority to the contrary. Fortunately for retailers as a whole, and travel agents in particular, the present culture appears to be firmly biased in favour of legal action against solvent or insured tour operators whenever a package goes wrong.

Chapter 3

INFORMATION, FORM AND CONTENT

The PTR 1992 specify in some detail the information which must he transmitted to the consumer, and make provision for certain matters relating to the form and content of package travel contracts. This chapter is concerned with the information that is prescribed, and the required form and content of contracts governed by the Regulations. Both criminal and civil liabilities are imposed as the mechanism for enforcing these regulatory requirements within a varied framework of:

*   statutory duties;

*   implied contractual terms;

*   implied warranties and conditions.

Some of the obligations imposed by the Regulations are negative: things the promoter must not do. Others impose positive requirements. The simplest approach is to look at the most important of these regulations in turn.

Regulation 4

Regulation 4 is a classic example of a negative obligation breach of which gives rise to a statutory civil liability. It is couched in wide terms.

> 4.-(1) No organiser or retailer shall supply to a consumer any descriptive matter concerning a package, the price of a package or any other conditions applying to the contract which contains any misleading information.
>
> (2) If an organiser or retailer is in breach of paragraph (1) he shall be liable to compensate the consumer for any loss which the consumer suffers in consequence.

The terms, "organiser", "retailer" and "consumer" have already been discussed in chapter 2. It should be noted, however, that regulation 4 imposes liability on whichever is the "supplier" of the descriptive matter, or both if both are suppliers of the information. Regulation 4 applies to the organiser's or retailer's obligations in respect of descriptive matter to "*a* consumer" and in this respect it should be compared with regulation 5 which imposes obligations in respect brochures made available to "a *possible* consumer". The likelihood is, therefore, that regulation 4 is intended to apply only to descriptive matter containing information supplied to those who actually enter into or benefit from package travel contracts made with an organiser or retailer, whereas regulation 5 is designed to apply to brochures made available to the public at large irrespective of whether any package travel contract is made on the strength of the offending brochure.

Organiser or retailer

The liability created by regulation 4 is imposed on whichever of the "organiser" and the "retailer" is responsible for the supply to the consumer of the misleading information in descriptive matter. The consumer may have a choice of target in the event that misleading information has been supplied. The scope of this liability particularly for retailers is potentially wide-ranging — but hitherto largely untapped. Liability under regulation 4 is not limited to the party that qualifies as "the other party to contract" under regulation 15. Because "the other party to the contract" will be liable for the improper performance of the contract under regulation 15, regulation 4 may not add significantly to that other party's liabilities. However, where the supplier of the descriptive matter is not the "other party to the contract" (usually the retailer or travel agent) the effect of regulation 4 will, in many cases, lead to that supplier of information being liable for damages in respect of a contract which it was not intended to perform and over the performance of which and description it had no control or influence.

The potential importance of this liability arises in at least two ways. First, travel agents (the classic retailers) do not appear to appreciate that they are potentially responsible for all sorts of promotional material which they supply to the public.[1] Secondly, regulation 4 is not qualified by any statutory defences which might avail either the retailer or travel agent or for that matter the tour operator. It is entirely possible, at least in theory, for a consumer to sue the retailer under regulation 4, and the tour operator under regulation 15 in respect of the same complaint, only to find that the tour operator can successfully deploy one of the statutory defences,[2] but the travel agent (the mere retailer of the package) cannot, and is strictly liable for supplying the tour operator's literature. Travel agents are potentially subject to the strict obligations of regulation 4 when they can realistically have had little control over and no input into the contents of the promotional material or "matter" with which they are provided by tour operators but, at least arguably, supply to consumers.

---

[1] Although the liability of travel agents arising out of the display of package brochures may be more limited than at first appears.
[2] Regulation 15(2)(a), (b) and (c).

An example will illustrate the retailer's difficulty. In the classic off-the-shelf package, the consumer may be beguiled by the pictures of the nearby mountains taken from the balcony of the hotel. However, the pictures give no hint of the presence of an urban motorway under construction immediately beneath the balcony. The pictorial information may reasonably be considered misleading within the meaning of regulation 4. The consumer decides not to sue the tour operator because the tour operator is a foreign company with a questionable attitude, and unknown resources and against whom enforcement of a judgment could prove awkward and expensive. Instead the local travel agent is the target. It was the travel agent who arguably "supplied" from the shelf a copy of the brochure in question which created such a misleading impression of the consumer's intended location. It is difficult to see what defence the travel agent would have to this action under regulation 4 — and protestations that it was not their "fault", or that they had no reasonable cause to believe that any misleading information was being supplied would be useless. The tour operator can be said to have supplied the brochure as well (indirectly through the retailer), but the fact that the tour operator may *also* be liable under regulation 4 or regulation 15 does not provide the travel agent or other retailer with a defence. The retailer will have to undertake the burden of trying to seek an indemnity from the person actually at fault for the provision of the descriptive matter in question.

Significantly, in many cases where there has been an improper performance of the package contract or a failure to perform the package contract[3] it will be possible to identify some respects in which the descriptive matter supplied to the consumer was misleading. This is particularly likely in cases of so-called "quality" complaints. For example, if a consumer purchases a package holiday based at a hotel advertised in a brochure as being of "5-star" standard and arrives to find the property is "3-star" self-catering apartments, causes of action will arise under both regulation 4 (potentially against both retailer and tour operator) and regulation 15 (only against the other party to the contract). *Keppel-Palmer v Exsus Travel Ltd & Royal Westmorland Villas Ltd*[4] was just such a case. The claimant booked a month's holiday in a luxury villa in Barbados for US$140,000. In several important respects it did not match the description in the leaflets promoting it. She sued both the booking agent (Exsus Travel) and the principal responsible for renting her the villa (Royal Westmorland), the former on the basis that it had supplied descriptive matter about the villa that was misleading and the latter on the grounds that she had not been supplied the standard of villa she had been contractually promised. In the event the trial judge was not satisfied that the

---

[3] Giving rise to liability imposed on "the other party to the contract" under regulation 15.
[4] [2003] All ER Digest 183 (June) - [2003] ITLJ 185 – discussed in Chapter 2 in respect of the definition of regulated package travel arrangements.

contract was for the provision of a regulated package holiday, so regulation 4 did not apply, neither was the judge satisfied on the facts that the booking agent (the retailer) had actually supplied the descriptive matter concerning the villa, and so the Claimant was unsuccessful against the retailer. Nonetheless, the case illustrates how the same facts can give rise to a potential liability under both regulations 4 and 15, and it also illustrates a good reason why consumers may wish to pursue the retailer: Exsus Travel (the retailer) was a company registered in England and Wales whereas Royal Westmorland (the principal to the rental contract) was not.

Supply

In *Keppel-Palmer*[5] Gage J. was not satisfied that the retailer had supplied the descriptive matter (leaflets) about which complaint was made. This was a decision based on the facts of the case and it is submitted that whether or not a supply (by a retailer or organiser or both) has occurred is likely to be a fact sensitive issue. The Claimant received leaflets by fax transmitted from the booking agent. The leaflets were no more than the documents that had been faxed to the booking agent by the principal in Barbados. The booking agent had acted only as a conduit and had not in any real sense supplied the leaflets to the Claimant. The agent had been little more than a posting stage. It will be remembered that the judge decided that the holiday was not a regulated package in the first place, so his decision that there had been no supply by the agent under regulation 4 was *obiter* and the reasons were given shortly. Even so the decision indicates that the courts are likely to approach "supply" pragmatically so that not every passing-on of descriptive matter to a consumer will be regarded as a supply within the meaning of regulation 4. The difficulty is to know where to draw the line.

A travel agent displaying tour operators' brochures is certainly making those brochures available to a consumer who visits the shop. When the consumer picks one up has the travel agent supplied the brochure to the consumer or has the tour operator supplied it through the agency of the travel agent, or merely by using the travel agent as a conduit or both? Although it is tempting to conclude that in this situation both tour operator and travel agent are suppliers of the brochure in different ways to the consumer, the answer is not free from doubt. Suppose the consumer picks up a brochure from the travel agent and takes it home, from where he makes a direct booking with the tour operator. Is the travel agent to be regarded as liable for any misleading information in the brochure under regulation 4 as would probably be the case if the consumer booked the holiday with the agent from where he got the brochure? If the making available of brochures in travel

---

[5] Above.

agencies is regarded as a supply under regulation 4 when the consumer picks one up it is difficult to see why the travel agent should not be liable under regulation 4 even though the travel agent is excluded from the subsequent booking process. Conversely, if the travel agent is *not* liable to the direct-booking consumer because there has been no supply of the brochure it is difficult to see how what is not then regarded as a "supply" becomes one simply because the consumer makes a booking through the agent on the spot. What if a person selects a brochure from the shelves of a travel agent, takes it home, whereupon a spouse books a package using the brochure, but with another travel agent? Does the host of an internet site supply descriptive matter to a visitor simply by giving access to electronic brochures and leaflets by means of on-line links to other sites?

It has been suggested[6] that the answer lies in a close construction of regulation 4 itself. The suggestion is that because the descriptive matter supplied must concern "*a package, the price of a package or any other conditions applying to the contract*", and the contract[7] is the "*agreement linking the consumer to the organiser or the retailer or both as the case may be*" then the retailer's liability under regulation 4 only arises where the consumer makes a contract using the travel agency that made the brochure available. Thus, where the consumer books directly with the organiser or uses a second agent there is no "supply" under regulation 4 because the supply of the misleading brochure would not concern a contract linking the consumer to the organiser or to the retailer or both, as the case may be. This attempt to distinguish the case where a consumer takes a brochure from an agent's shelves and books on the spot, from the case where the brochure is taken away and an alternative agent is subsequently used or direct booking with the organiser is placed, is questionable. Regulation 4 contains 3 prohibitions with regard to the supply of any descriptive matter to a consumer which contains misleading information, namely descriptive matter:

- concerning a package;

- concerning the price of a package; and

- concerning any other conditions applying to the contract.

The attempt to distinguish "on the spot" purchases from travel agents on the basis that there must be a "contract" ("*the agreement linking the consumer to the organiser or to the retailer or both, as the case may be*") can only work, if it works at all, in respect of the third prohibition set out above. Even then it is submitted the attempt is unsatisfying. There is no apparent reason why the agent from whose shelves the brochure is taken should not be

---

[6] Grant & Mason *Holiday Law* (3rd. edition - Thomson Sweet & Maxwell).
[7] Regulation 2(1).

supplying descriptive matter that includes information *concerning* the conditions of an agreement made subsequently linking the consumer with another agent or with the organiser directly (or both as the case may be). If the brochure sets out the terms and conditions of the organiser (as it invariably will) it is inevitable that the brochure contains information concerning conditions applying to the contract that the consumer enters into – which is an agreement linking him to the organiser. As regards the price of the package and any descriptive matter concerning the package it is not obvious from the wording of regulation 4 that as a matter of construction these are limited in application to the retailer through whom or with whom the package contract is made. However, the attempted distinction may well be a mechanism adopted to limit the otherwise even more wide-ranging (and in many respects some might think unfair) liabilities imposed on retailers by regulation 4.

One should not overlook the fact that travel agents have no control over the content of brochures and cannot sensibly be expected to examine every item in every brochure to check for accuracy. Even if time permitted such examination, travel agents do not have the wherewithal to cross-check information about facilities and services that are invariably to be provided abroad. In this context one must bear in mind that there is no defence provided to regulation 4 liability whether by means of an express defence such as due diligence or the reversal of the onus of proof.[8] Finally, even assuming the tour operator responsible for the production of the brochure remains solvent, it is not obvious in the absence of an express contract term as between travel agent and tour operator that the travel agent would be able to secure an indemnity from the tour operator in the event that the consumer sued the agent for loss arising out of misleading information contained in a brochure displayed by the agent.[9]

Given these factors, it is submitted that the mere fact that travel agents are used as a distributing point for tour operators' brochures does not make them suppliers of the brochures within the meaning of regulation 4. *Keppel-Palmer* provides some indirect support for this proposition. It is further suggested that something more active than mere display of a brochure or onward transmission of pre-prepared information from the organiser is necessary in order to establish a "supply" of matter by a retailer within regulation 4. This does not mean that retailers have no potential liabilities under regulation 4.

---

[8] Such as one finds under the Trade Descriptions Act 1968 and in other parts of the PTR 1992.
[9] Part I of the Civil Liability (Contribution) Act 1978 may provide the most straightforward route to such an indemnity.

Retailers in general and travel agents in particular will often be involved in the production of itineraries, dossiers, holiday-packs and other material containing descriptive matter about a package. Retailers in some instances will be "the other party to the contract"[10] or one of several other parties to the package contract. Retailers also engage in promotional activities that involve disseminating descriptive matter about packages. In each of these instances the retailer is more likely to be a source of supply of the descriptive matter to the consumer and subject to the restraints of regulation 4. There is nothing in this regulation from which it might be inferred that the descriptive matter must be supplied before a contract is made, or even before the travel arrangements commence. Provided it is descriptive matter concerning the package a supply at any time is likely to fall within the prohibition of regulation 4. Where the descriptive matter concerning a package is supplied after the contract is made, however, arguments are likely to arise as to whether the misleading content has been the cause of any loss.

Descriptive matter

This, it is submitted, is a deliberately wide expression intended to cover all categories of written and pictorial representations of the package services and facilities in any tangible form. "Descriptive matter" is plainly not limited to brochures, otherwise the regulators would have used the term "brochure", the expression that is used elsewhere in the PTR 1992.[11] "Descriptive matter" will include:

- advertisements, whether in newspapers or hand-outs;

- brochures, leaflets and timetables;

- letters;

- photographs;

- confirmation invoices and itineraries.

All of the above examples are of tangible "matter" with which the consumer can be supplied under regulation 4. But is "matter" limited to such tangibles? One definition of "matter" extends the meaning to material of "thought, speech or action".[12] If such an extended meaning of "matter" were to be adopted it would cover the spoken word, oral descriptions of the package given by tour operator or travel agents' representative, as well as "matter" publicised on the internet or transmitted by e-mail. Consumers *can* be "supplied" with *information* in these forms, and if that information is

---

[10] E.g. some tailor-made arrangements.
[11] E.g. the subheading of regulation 5 and regulation 6(1).
[12] *Oxford English Dictionary.*

classified as "matter" under regulation 4, then many forms of publicity by means of the spoken word, in radio advertisements or presentations, or in any form of electronic transmission would be subject to the prohibition imposed by regulation 4. It might at first blush be thought to be stretching a point to say that e-mail transmissions, internet sites or radio advertisements were "matter" supplied to the consumer, but in respect of internet pages or e-mails the information can be down-loaded by the consumer into a printed form that would certainly be "matter" within regulation 4 and it is difficult to see why an organiser or retailer should be subject to regulatory control for handing out a copy of its brochure or a leaflet, but not for making the same things available on-line. In other areas the law has been willing to classify information transmitted by electronic means as "documents" in the context of legislation such as the Civil Evidence Acts[13] for many years, and it is unlikely that it would fail to recognise modern communication systems in the context of the promotion and supply of package travel services for the purpose of regulating the content of material supplied in order to induce consumers to purchase or provide consumers with information about their travel arrangements.

Regulation 4 provides that the descriptive *matter* should not contain any misleading *information* so it is unlikely that "matter" is the same as "information". It is submitted that the most pragmatic and logical construction of regulation 4 is that it was intended to draw a distinction between spoken representations and other forms of material. Despite the dictionary definition of "matter" offered above it is submitted that regulation 4 does not concern itself with the spoken word but that it will bite on all other forms of communication whether in hard copy of on-line. It is suggested that "matter" means "material". Had the regulators decided to adopt a prohibition in regulation 4 regarding the supply of any descriptive information, then (but only then) would it have been logical to conclude that the spoken word was included in *this* prohibition.[14]

Concerning the package

The "matter" that is supplied by the organiser or retailer must be "concerning a package". This expression goes beyond merely the package contract or its terms. The regulators probably had in mind "matter" that

---

[13] Section 13 of the Civil Evidence Act 1995.
[14] One should never overlook the fact that there are many other potential causes of action and criminal offences to which the travel promoter may be vulnerable in addition to the cause of action created by regulation 4 and in cases of any doubt enforcing authorities and litigants will no doubt have recourse to such alternatives as the Misrepresentation Act 1967, the Trade Descriptions Act 1968 or the Control of Misleading Advertisement Regulations 1988 (to name but three).

described not only the travel arrangements that are on offer, but also the nature of the location, region and ancillary facilities, events or even geographical attractions that may be canvassed in the promotional material. This is reinforced by the fact that regulation 4 specifically states that in addition to descriptive matter concerning the package no organiser or retailer should supply misleading descriptive matter concerning: *"the price or any other conditions applying to the contract"*. Had the regulators intended to limit the reach of the sanctions imposed by regulation 4 to the terms of the package contract itself and the facilities and services set out therein, it would have been relatively easy for them to have said so.

Accordingly, regulation 4(1) covers:

- the price of a package;

- the terms and conditions of a package contract;

- the contents of a package contract (the services and facilities to be provided as part of the price);

- *and* descriptions about anything else concerning a package.

Misleading information

Regulation 4 certainly covers information that is simply false or in some respect plainly inaccurate. However, it also covers information that may be literally true but where the truth gives rise to a reasonable but false impression in the mind of the consumer. Between false and misleadingly true information there might be a third category – those instances where the truth, accuracy or otherwise of the information supplied falls to be assessed as a matter of fact and degree.

False, and thus misleading, information should be easy enough to identify in its worst form. The price quoted; the timetable; the itinerary or the rating of the accommodation supplied may simply be wrong.

However, a truthful statement can still be a misleading one. Indeed in some instances one might say the greater the truth the greater the potential for misleading the uninitiated. The picture of a sumptuous art deco entrance hall at a city centre hotel, particularly if it is combined with eulogistic descriptions in writing, may disguise a singularly dingy and unprepossessing establishment. The sea view photographed from the hotel terrace may be *exactly* what can be seen — provided the viewer is prepared to tolerate the noise and filth generated by two arterial roads between the terrace and sea front and ignore the industrial site next door. The luxury rooms represented in the literature may give no hint of the deafening disco which thunders nightly below. Misleading information is not necessarily false either in whole or in part. It can be true — but if it promotes in the mind of the reasonable consumer a false or unrealistic *impression* it is likely to be regarded as misleading.

There are many other plausible examples of misleading information masquerading as the truth:

- a shuttle bus service may operate *regularly* (as advertised) but only twice a week;

- the yacht may have a resplendent sailing capacity, but be unable to keep to its itinerary without constant recourse to its engines;[15]

- sports facilities may indeed be free to residents, but of little use if they are so over-booked or over-used as to be pragmatically unavailable for significant portions of the package.

The concept of the misleading truth or half-truth is well recognised in other contexts. A misleading indication as to price[16] is also covered by section 21 of the Consumer Protection Act 1987 in which we are told that "*an indication given to any consumers is misleading as to price if what is conveyed by the indication, or what those consumers might reasonably be expected to infer from the indication or any omission from it includes any of the following,...* " and a list is given. The point is that what is or is not misleading is judged by what the *consumer* might reasonably infer from that which is indicated as to price. The same is undoubtedly true of other descriptions in that what a consumer would reasonably infer from the description supplied will be the test for regulation 4 liability.[17] This is dangerous territory for both organisers and retailers in an industry where it is necessary for them to produce a positive impression of the packages available (even, or *particularly*, at the budget end of the market) *and* where consumers' expectations are invariably high (often unrealistically high) and straight-laced.[18]

The third main category of misleading information identified above may give rise to more difficulty. This is where a judgment on whether or not the information supplied is misleading is itself a matter of fact and degree. Much here depends on context and the totality of the information supplied. If the consumer is supplied with information to the effect that holiday accommodation will be in "villas" is

---

[15] See *Yugotours v Wadsley* below which also indicates albeit in another context that the information need not be conveyed in words.
[16] One of the specific prohibitions under regulation 4.
[17] See e.g. *Thomson Travel Ltd. v Roberts* [1984] 148 JP 666 - a case under the Trade Descriptions Act 1968.
[18] The public is not always as quick to spot an amusing advertising gimmick as one might think. No fewer than 186 members of the public (unsuccessfully) complained to the Advertising Standards Authority about Easyjet's advertising campaign depicting well-endowed bikini-clad women under the banner "Weapons of mass distraction". [2003] ITLJ Bulletin xxi.

this information misleading where the accommodation is in fact detached, self-contained bungalows? Would the answer be any different if the bungalows were semi-detached or terraced[19]? The answer almost certainly depends on what other information is supplied in writing or in pictures that might reasonably be taken to qualify or explain the word "villa". Even more problematic will be information supplied that includes adjectives or opinions. If a bungalow might be a "villa" how comfortable does it have to be to warrant the description "luxury villa"? How user friendly does a resort have to be to be deserving of the opinion that it is "family friendly"? Context and reasonableness (when viewed from the perspective of the reasonable consumer) will provide the answers to these questions.

Mawdsley v Cosmosair Plc[20] illustrates two categories of potentially misleading information. The tour operator's brochure advertised a hotel in Turkey and included information that it had a "*Lift (in main building)*" and was "*suitable for parents with young children*". The Claimant booked a half-board holiday for herself and her young family at the hotel and was injured when she fell down a set of 39 steps[21] leading to the hotel restaurant which was on a mezzanine floor not served by the lift that stopped on all the other floors in the main building. At the time of her fall she was manhandling two toddlers and a pushchair down the stairs. She brought a claim based in part on regulation 4[22] of the PTR 1992 alleging that the information in the brochure was misleading. The trial judge and the Court of Appeal agreed that it was. The trial judge said with regard to the lift:

> ...if you say there are lifts in the main building, it clearly implies that that will provide access to everything... It was misleading to say that there was a lift in the main building because the lift only gave access to all the floors bar the restaurant.

He said with regard to the suitability of the premises for parents with young children:

> In my judgment, it was unsuitable for children, because for an hotel to provide the only available access to the restaurant which holiday makers had to use together with their children, via 24 or 39 steps, is not providing a hotel which is suitable.[23]

---

[19] Terraced accommodation it seems is not a "villa" – see *Josephs v Sunworld Limited* [1998] CLY 3734.
[20] [2002] EWCA Civ 587; [2003] ITLJ 23.
[21] There was nothing structurally wrong with the steps and they were properly maintained.
[22] The claim was also brought under regulation 15(2) of the PTR 1992.
[23] The logic of this conclusion is circular.

Jonathan Parker LJ (with whom Dyson LJ agreed) upheld the judge's conclusion in respect of the lift but not with regard to the hotel's suitability for children. He said:[24]

> ...I would agree that the description "Lift (in main building)" is a misrepresentation.[25] On the other hand I am unable to agree with the judge's further conclusion that the fact that there is no direct access to the restaurant by lift rendered the hotel unsuitable for young children... It is unrealistic to conclude that the mere fact that access to the hotel restaurant involves negotiating stairs renders the hotel unsuitable for young children; the more so when one looks at the nature of the hotel complex as shown in the photographs ...

The Court of Appeal also differed modestly from the trial judge in concluding that the misleading nature of the description *"Lift (in main building)"* was that it implied that the lift would give access to all floors in the main building, not (as the trial judge had concluded) that it would give access to "everything". Nonetheless, the claim succeeded and the Defendant's appeal[26] was dismissed.

The description of the hotel as having a lift in the main building is clearly an example of a description that was literally true. The hotel did indeed have a lift and the lift served all floors in the main building except the mezzanine, restaurant floor. It is debateable whether the description could also accurately be described as a misrepresentation because as a statement of fact it was substantially true.[27] That it was substantially true and arguably not a misrepresentation did not prevent the description from being *misleading* because the consumer might reasonably expect the lift to visit each floor in the main building of the hotel or at least each of the main facilities in the main building, particularly those facilities that would inevitably be used by a family on a half-board regime.[28]

The description of the hotel as being suitable for parents with young children is different. It is submitted that in approaching a description such as this; one that involves an assessment of suitability, standard or style of accommodation or other facilities and services, a balance has to be struck between what the author of the description might reasonably conclude and what the consumer would reasonably expect in the context of the totality of information made available. The Court of Appeal in *Mawdsley* considered

---

[24] [2003] ITLJ at page 30 – judgment paragraph 41.
[25] It is respectfully submitted that he meant that the information about the lift was misleading.
[26] The appeal focused largely on causation and the absence of any structural or maintenance problem with the steps.
[27] *Yorkshire Insurance Company v Crane* [1922] 2 AC 541.
[28] In fact the tour operator in *Mawdsley* had never stated whether the restaurant was in the main building or somewhere else.

that the mere fact that a family with young children had to negotiate stairs (39 of them) to reach a restaurant did not render the hotel unsuitable. Presumably the need to negotiate large numbers of steps would only be one factor among many determining whether a hotel was or was not suitable for young children. The presence of a large number of steps might be significantly counter-balanced and outweighed by a range of other facilities and services eminently suitable for young families.

Becoming misleading after supply

The critical time for the purposes of regulation 4 is the time at which the supply of the descriptive matter to the consumer takes place. However, in practice one has to recognise that if information given turns out to be wrong in practice there will be an evidential burden on the supplier of the descriptive matter to show that circumstances have changed since the material was supplied. If descriptive matter is not only accurate but gives a true impression of the services or facilities at the time the material is *supplied* to the consumer, the organiser or retailer cannot be rendered liable if the material *becomes* misleading at a later date. To adopt one of the examples given above, will the organiser and retailer be liable under regulation 4 if construction of the urban motorway below the balcony at the Alpine hotel only commences after the brochure with its glorious photographs have been supplied to the consumer? At the time the supply took place the photographs were not misleading of circumstances as they then were. The pictures have only *become* misleading later. Another example may be along these lines. A picture of a resort may become misleading after it is supplied to the consumer due to adverse climatic conditions such as a hurricane. The resort may have re-opened and be fully functioning, but is likely to be tired and jaded as a result of the climatic onslaught. Has misleading matter been supplied to the consumer in the form of the pre-hurricane photographs? The answer is probably "no" but the organiser or retailer would be wise to be able to demonstrate that circumstances had radically changed since the material was supplied.

The prohibition imposed by regulation 4 is against the *supply* of matter *which contains misleading information*. That is, at least implicitly, the information should be misleading at the time of the supply. If it is not there is no realistic sense in which something misleading has been supplied. On the contrary, something accurate has been supplied, the accuracy of which has subsequently been compromised. Another reason why regulation 4 liability is likely to be limited to those instances where the information is misleading *at the time of its supply* to the consumer, is that it is unlikely that a consumer could show that he had suffered any loss as a result where the information subsequently became misleading. After all, by the time the circumstances change the contract has been made and any disappointment to the consumer results from the change in circumstances, not by reason of the supply of the information.

There is no need to devise a construction of regulation 4 that would permit a consumer to recover damages where circumstances had significantly changed since the supply of the descriptive matter (on the basis of some implicit obligation to ensure that consumers were informed if and when an accurate representation became a misleading one). Other parts of the PTR 1992, such as regulation 12, deal with the consumer's rights where the organiser is constrained before departure to alter an essential term of the contract. Whilst the rights that arise where essential *terms* of the contract have to be altered[29] are narrower in scope than the prohibition against supplying misleading descriptive matter *concerning a package*, the cases where descriptive matter becomes misleading after supply to the consumer which concern a package but do not constrain the organiser to alter significantly and essential term of the contract will be few and far between.

Reliance and causation

No compensation is payable to the consumer unless it can be shown that the misleading information supplied caused a loss. The supplier of the information is liable to compensate the consumer *"for any loss that the consumer suffers in consequence"*. That is, unless the consumer can establish that reliance was placed on the material supplied (which necessarily implies that it was read and understood), it is unlikely in the extreme that he could demonstrate that its misleading nature was responsible for some diminution in his enjoyment, loss of bargain or some consequential expense.[30] Reliance on the misleading information does not have to amount to a primary or even a significant reason for the package being booked. It is submitted that reliance will be established where the consumer satisfies the court that the information was simply *one* reason (even a minor reason) why the package was selected. Accordingly, even if the balance of a holiday is satisfactory, a loss will have been sustained if as a result of misleading information the consumer reasonably thought there would be an additional facility which in fact was not available. The loss contemplated by regulation 4 would encompass loss of enjoyment, diminution in value and any expenses incurred as a result of making-do. The evidential problem for organisers and retailers is that any discrepancy between the package as described and that actually delivered (however inconsequential it may appear) can be latched onto by

[29] Regulation 12.
[30] The expression "any" loss is certainly wide enough to cover all these conventional heads of damage in travel cases.

consumers claiming that the information originally supplied was indeed one of the reasons that a particular package was selected.

Would reliance on misleading information entitle a Claimant to recover damages for personal injury? Assume that a wheelchair-bound consumer books a package that has been advertised as being "suitable for the disabled". The description is in all material respects, save (arguably) one, accurate. Access to the sun terrace is only by means of a steep sloping, unguarded path. The consumer attempts to wheel herself to the terrace but loses control of the wheelchair and an accident results. The consumer maintains that had she known that access to the terrace was so limited she would have booked a different hotel or a different package altogether. Does the injury sustained constitute a loss that the consumer has suffered in consequence of the arguably misleading information supplied to her? It might be thought that *Mawdsley v Cosmosair PLC*[31] provides an answer. The presence of many stairs to the restaurant did not render the hotel unsuitable for families with young children, so it might be thought that difficulty with access to *one* facility[32] did not render a hotel unsuitable for the disabled. However, this part of the decision in *Mawdsley* was on the issue of whether the information supplied was *misleading*, not on whether the injury sustained was a consequential loss. What *was* misleading in *Mawdsley* was the indication that there was a lift in the main building. It would appear that Mrs. Mawdsley's injuries *were* considered to be a loss suffered *in consequence* of that misleading information. It is not so much that in consequence of reading the brochure Mrs. Mawdsley fell down the stairs, but that in consequence of reading the brochure she booked a holiday to a hotel which included a hazard she would not otherwise have encountered and that hazard caused her injuries. It is submitted that this stretches causation about as far as one can legitimately go. If causation is to be stretched in this way one must take care to avoid offending against the rules of recovery limited by remoteness. To take an imaginary example, if Mrs. Mawdsley had been given accurate information about the hotel lift she would not have booked this package, and so would not have been visiting the local town and injured when it was subjected to a terrorist attack. The result in *Mawdsley* is understandable only when one considers that it was the very feature of the hotel she was concerned about and about which she was misled (i.e. the existence of lots of stairs to the restaurant) that led to her accident.

---

[31] See above.
[32] It may depend on how important the facility was.

Qualifying descriptions

A truthful but nonetheless misleading statement (for example, the picture of the Alpine mountains from the hotel balcony compromised by a dual carriageway unseen in the foreground) may have the sting of any misleading interpretation neutralised if accompanied by adequate disclaimers or other appropriate forms of words which supply the consumer with comprehensive information about the hotel or resort. To enlarge on two examples already used:

- if the mountain picture has in close proximity a written description of busy main roads, the misleading effect of the picture may be reduced or eradicated provided the written description is in appropriately bold or prominent form;

- if the resort is suitably described as lively and noisy at night, with many discos and night clubs in close proximity, the consumer will not be well placed to complain that the picture of the luxurious and relaxing rooms was apt to mislead, when taken in the context of the descriptive matter as a whole.

This last point cannot be emphasised too much. As already noted it is likely that the courts will want to look at the entirety of the "matter" supplied and judge the whole and its likely overall effect on the mind of the reasonable consumer.

Regulation 5

This regulation imposes criminal sanctions and is, therefore, discussed in detail in Chapter 13 on criminal offences. It is concerned with form and contents of brochures with which regulation 6 also deals in a civil context.

Regulation 6

Regulation 6 in conjunction with regulation 15[33] is one of the more important provisions of the PTR 1992.

> 6-(1) Subject to paragraphs (2) and (3) of this regulation, the particulars in the brochure (whether or not they are required by regulation 5(1) above to be included in the brochure) shall constitute implied warranties ... for the purposes of any contract to which the particulars relate.
>
> (2) Paragraph (1) of this regulation does not apply -

---

[33] As to which see Chapter 4.

(a) in relation to information required to be included by virtue of paragraph 9 of Schedule 1 to these regulations; or

(b) where the brochure contains an express statement that changes may be made in the particulars contained in it before a contract is concluded and changes in the particulars so contained are clearly communicated to the consumer before a contract is concluded.

(3) Paragraph (1) of this regulation does not apply when the consumer and the other party to the contract agree after the contract has been made that the particulars in the brochure, or some of those particulars, should not form part of the contract.

Brochures

Regulation 6 is directed at brochures. The expression "brochure" is not usefully defined in the PTR 1992. In common usage a brochure is nothing more than a short printed work, pamphlet or leaflet.[34] In regulation 2 there is an attempt to describe brochures, but it merely provides that "*brochure means any brochure in which packages are offered for sale*". This is a singularly unhelpful attempt on the part of the regulators, save to the extent that it conveys the impression that the term was intended to be far-reaching. If brochure is *any* brochure in which packages are offered for sale one can draw the conclusion that the term is not supposed to be limited to those publications that appear on the travel agents' shelves that contain package travel arrangements and nothing else. The purpose, therefore, of the regulatory definition is probably not to limit or confine the meaning of the word "brochure" but to make it clear that the 1992 Regulations extend in their reach to all sorts of publications and pamphlets *part of which* are used to offer packages for sale.[35]

Apart from the standard form brochure which appears on the shelves of the travel agent's shop the term "brochure" probably extends to advertising, promotional and informative literature of a wide variety, including:

- handouts and circulars;
- mailshots;
- travel and life-style magazines;
- hotel and group booklets.

Whether it also covers material such as newspapers or their associated magazines is a moot point. The Sunday supplement may not be instantly recognised as a "brochure" or even a pamphlet — but it is a printed work

---

[34] *Concise Oxford Dictionary.*
[35] An offer includes an invitation to treat.

which is likely on any average Sunday to include a wide variety of packages being offered by tour operators directly to the general public.

Particulars

No definition of "particulars" is provided. Again, one suspects that its meaning is left open deliberately so as not unduly to confine the application of the regulation. "Particulars" will no doubt come in many forms and the term certainly includes the words, phrases and symbols in the brochure that are associated with a *particular* package, hotel, resort, transport and all other arrangements concerning the package. It would also clearly include all such words and phrases of *general* application to all of the packages promoted in the brochure as a whole such as one usually finds in the front pages — for example, brochures that are aimed at a particular market, be it the elderly, those with young children or those interested in adventure travel. Therefore, "particulars" might be found either in the descriptions of individual packages or in the general "blurb" describing the nature of the services and facilities available in respect of the brochure as a whole or certain identifiable species of travel arrangements included within the brochure. For example, where a tour operator is promoting fully accompanied tours, much may be said about the nature and quality of the escorts to be provided in the general information at the front of the brochure rather than on the pages devoted to the individual packages themselves. The same might apply to arrangements for the entertainment and supervision of children.

It is submitted, however, that "particulars" is a term intended to go beyond words and phrases and extends to symbols, artists impressions and photographs where such representations are likely to be associated by the reasonable reader to the package in question. Sometimes these pictorials may be associated with a package or a group of packages without any words or symbols of direct association. A good example can be found in the facts of *Yugotours* v *Wadsley*.[36] In this case the tour operator offered a wide variety of Adriatic island adventure cruises amongst its extensive holiday options. At the beginning of the section of the brochure advertising these cruises there appeared a full page photograph of a majestic schooner in full sail. Consumers were understandably angry and bewildered when it emerged that the cruises which they undertook were aboard petrol-engined barges with little or no sailing capacity at all. This case was decided long before the 1992 Regulations came into force and the outcome (unfavourable to the tour operator) did not turn on the meaning of "particulars"[37] but there is no

---

[36] [1988] Crim. LR 623.
[37] It was a case on recklessness within the meaning of the Trade Descriptions Act 1968 and is dealt with further in Chapter 13.

reason why, with the assistance of regulation 6, the consumer could not succeed on the basis that the photograph of the schooner (which was plainly intended to convey the impression that cruises would be undertaken on that or a similar vessel) was part of the "particulars" in the brochure associated with the package sold by the tour operator. Similarly, it is submitted, there is no reason why a consumer could not successfully maintain that a picture of rolling Cotswold countryside, if reasonably attributable to the holiday cottages advertised on the facing page, amounted to "particulars" within the meaning of regulation 6.

Even where the pictures are presented without being expressly associated with a particular package, it may be perfectly reasonable for the consumer — bringing everyday common sense to bear on the interpretation of the material in the brochure as a whole — to conclude that a symbol or pictures are intended to convey the impression of the location or amenities available at a given location. Essentially, by means of the picture or symbol the brochure is *particularising* the type of accommodation, facilities, the location or the resort at the centre of the package on offer. For example, a touring package may say nothing at all about the quality of the coach on which the consumer is to be transported, but if the brochure contains a photograph of a luxury air-conditioned vehicle, the picture is as good as telling the consumer that this is the sort of vehicular transportation you can expect on one of the advertised coach tours. The association with the package is all the easier to make if the picture is in close proximity to the details of the package on offer, but proximity in terms of brochure space is not essential. A coach tour brochure may just have one luxury coach on the front cover and say nothing more about the standard of transport inside. The consumer's association between the picture and type of transport likely to be made available by the tour operator is understandable. There is no reason in logic or principle why something described in words should be capable of being "particulars" but something represented in pictures should not. In the modern package market, those selling packages are extremely skilled at conveying an impression without stating in so many words what is actually available. It is unlikely that regulators whose primary purpose was the protection of consumers would have intended to exclude from the term "particulars" anything that was not in writing.

"Particulars" will also include prices.

Implied warranties

The particulars in the brochure constitute implied warranties for the purposes of any contract to which the particulars relate. In this way the PTR 1992 cuts across a debate that had affected package travel contracts at common law for many years. Before the PTR 1992 were enacted it was a matter of some debate whether the contents of the package brochure could be deployed as terms of the package contract. That is, if the brochure described the hotel as being "walking distance from the beach", was this statement a term of the package contract or not? Did the tour operator contract with the consumer for the provision of all the matters promoted in the brochure, or was the tour operator merely a facilitating organiser liable only if an actionable misrepresentation could be proved? What if the matters described in the brochure were true at the time the contract was made, but rendered inaccurate by subsequent events?

Pre-1992 cases were pleaded as a matter or routine in both breach of contract and misrepresentation to maximise the consumer's prospects of success.

The PTR 1992 effectively do away with the need for this. Regulation 6 when taken in conjunction with regulation 15 creates a free-standing regulatory framework within which a consumer can identify causes of action which can be directly targeted at the tour operator or "*the other party to the contract*". If something can properly be regarded as "particulars" under regulation 6, it is a term of the contract. The failure to provide the facility or service, or an improper performance of the "particulars" in the brochure is actionable under regulation 15 against "the other party to the contract" — usually the tour operator. Accordingly, despite the burgeoning volume of travel related litigation in recent years it is now not common to see consumers' cases pleaded in misrepresentation. Breach of contract based on the PTR 1992 is all that is required. Those who before the advent of the PTR 1992 believed that the contents of the brochure could be properly identified as terms of the contract, in respect of which there was, in any event, a direct contractual cause of action against "the other party to the contract" (the tour operator) need no longer worry about whether they were right. This argument is now only necessary in those marginal circumstances where the package is not, or may not be, a *regulated* package or where "the other party to the contract" does not supply a package at all, but merely one service or facility.[38]

Breach of warranty sounds in damages. Breach of any term of the contract based on "particulars" in the brochure would not allow the consumer to treat himself as discharged from further performance of the contract. Subject to other provisions in the 1992 Regulations[39] the consumer must pay for the package and persevere with its performance, even if a breach of warranty has occurred. The consumer's remedy is an action for damages, not the abandonment of the contractual arrangements.

---

[38] Even at common law, however, things have moved on as a result of *Wong Mee Wan v Kwan Kim Travel* [1998] 1 WLR 38 which is discussed in Chapter 6.
[39] For example, Regulations 12 and 14 below.

For the purposes of any contract to which the particulars relate

The particulars in the brochure constitute implied warranties for the purposes of *any* contract to which the particulars relate. Particulars in the brochure can *relate* to any number of contracts even though the consumer has not relied on the brochure or made a booking based on the brochure. This would appear to mean that a consumer who has not even seen the brochure can *ex post facto* rely on its particulars to maintain a breach of contract claim. For example, two consumers purchase the same holiday from the same tour operator. One uses the *brochure*, the other books a holiday having seen an advertisement in a newspaper in which the particulars are radically edited. Both are transported to their destination on a small turbo-prop aeroplane which stops for refuelling twice en route to the final destination. The *brochure* described transportation as non-stop in modern wide-bodied jets, the newspaper advertisement said nothing about the means of transportation.

The particulars in the brochure *relate* to both consumers' holidays. It was precisely the same holiday. The only difference is that one consumer saw the brochure and the other did not. Is it only the consumer who saw and relied on the brochure who has a cause of action for breach of contract against the defaulting tour operator? The answer to this question it is suggested is "yes".

The relationship demanded by regulation 6 is between the *contract* and the *particulars* in the brochure, not the *package holiday* and the particulars in the brochure. It is thought likely, therefore, that regulation 6 would be interpreted as being of use only to those whose contracts were related to the brochure because they were in some sense based upon it. It would be extraordinary if a consumer who had never relied on, or never even seen the brochure could invoke its particulars as the basis for a breach of contract action against the supplier. This conclusion, it is submitted, accords with how most English courts would view the contractual relationship between the brochure and the services offered to a consumer. That is, reliance on the particulars in the brochure is surely an essential prerequisite for a consumer to succeed.

Exceptions

Not all the material in a brochure qualifies as an implied warranty under regulation 6. For example, the particulars required to be in the brochure about security for consumers' money in the event of insolvency[40] is not classified as an implied warranty.[41] There are two further exceptions.

---

[40] Schedule 1 paragraph 9 of the PTR 1992.
[41] Regulation 6(2)(a).

Unilateral pre-contract changes

Where the brochure contains an express statement to the effect that changes may be made in the particulars before the contract is concluded *and any changes are clearly communicated to the consumer before the contract is made* the particulars which have been changed will not constitute implied warranties in the package contract. This allows the supplier to make unilateral changes in the services or facilities on offer *provided* he has clearly announced in the brochure that changes might occur. Where changes do occur, they must be communicated to the consumer clearly (writing is surely preferable for evidential reasons if not in the interests of clarity) before any contract is made.

It is commonplace to see tour operators make provision for this in their trading terms — usually to be found at the back of their brochures, and sometimes even in the introductory pages of their publications. They are invariably prefaced with an observation to the effect that "*This brochure is published many months in advance ... sometimes changes are made ...*"

So, for example, where a resort hotel is promoted as offering beach-front refreshment facilities, but these are closed for renovation, the particulars in respect of this are not to be regarded as implied warranties on which the consumer can sue, if, but only if, the supplier has stated in the brochure that pre-contract changes to the advertised facilities might occur, and before a contract is concluded the consumer is alerted to the fact that the beach-front facilities have been closed and will not be available after all. If the consumer proceeds with the package nonetheless, there will be no cause for complaint on the basis of the warranties to be implied by regulation 6.

Exclusion by agreement

After the contract is made the parties to the contract may agree between themselves that certain particulars in the brochure should not constitute implied warranties. This may arise where after the contract is made the supplier learns that a certain advertised facility is no longer going to be available. In order for agreement to be reached with the consumer, the consumer obviously has to be notified of this change, and may well agree that the change is modest or of such a character as not to interfere with his enjoyment of the package. Such a consensual *variation* of the package contract is authorised by regulation 6 and the consumer cannot subsequently complain if, on reflection, it would have been preferable had the facility been available.

As a result it is common to find suppliers writing to consumers notifying them of changes after the contract is in place. This notification is only effective if the consumer agrees that the facility should not be regarded as an implied warranty. It is doubtful whether the consumer's *silence* in this context could properly be regarded as agreement. Under regulation 12 the consumer is given the right to withdraw from the contract if an *essential term* is altered *significantly* prior to departure. The consumer is afforded no such right if the change is not to an essential term and is not significant. Therefore, there will be many instances where the post contract change notified by the supplier is not to an essential term and is not significant in the context of the package as a whole, and where the consumer has little option but to tolerate the change. In these circumstances, the consumer must proceed with the package, but can and should reserve his rights in respect of an action for breach of warranty on his return. Because in the event of minor changes the consumer has no option but to continue with the package it would be harsh to conclude that silence and continuation with the holiday in the face of notified minor changes constituted a consensual variation of the terms of the holiday contract.

Accordingly, it is a little difficult to see (in the absence of cash consideration or some other inducement) why the consumer should ever agree that particulars in the brochure that are changed (which are not in respect of essential terms and significant) should not thereafter be regarded as implied warranties. It would be a redundant exercise for the consumer to write to the supplier saying "I do not agree that the particulars in respect of the beach-front bar should not be regarded as implied warranties" when there is absolutely nothing the consumer can do about it, save to complain and claim compensation *on his return*. It is submitted, therefore, that unless the supplier secures the *express* consent of the consumer to the effect that the brochure particulars (or some of them) should not form part of the contract, no amount of notification by the supplier to the consumer should deprive the consumer of the right to complain if an advertised facility or service is withdrawn, and no amount of resigned silence on the part of the consumer should deprive the consumer of a claim for breach of warranty.

As will be seen in the context of the discussion of regulation 12, it is likely that any changes to accommodation or transportation or anything that affects another material purpose of the package should be regarded as changes to an "essential" term, and they are likely to be "significant" if the changes are anything more than minimal. In these situations, therefore, the consumer should always be offered the opportunity to withdraw from the contract as permitted by regulations 12 and 13.

Regulations 7 and 8

Regulation 7 sets out the information which must be supplied by "the other party to the contract" to any intending consumer before a contract is made. Regulation 8 deals with the information that "the other party to the contract" must send to the consumer *after* the contract is made but in "good time" before the start of the journey.

Both regulations 7 and 8 impose criminal sanctions on "the other party to the contract"[19] for failure to comply. They are dealt with in detail in Chapter 13 on criminal offences.

Regulation 9

Regulation 9 and Schedule 2 of the PTR 1992 deals with the minimum content of the any regulated package contract, the form of the contract and the communication of such content to the consumer.

> 9.-(1) The other party to the contract shall ensure that -
>
> (a) depending on the nature of the package being purchased, the contract contains at least the elements specified in Schedule 2 ...
>
> (b) subject to paragraph (2) below, all the terms of the contract are set out in writing or such other form as is comprehensible and accessible to the consumer and are communicated to the consumer before the contract is made; and
>
> (c) a written copy of these terms is supplied to the consumer.
>
> (2) Paragraph 1(b) above does not apply when the interval between the time when the consumer approaches the other party to the contract with a view to entering into a contract and the time of departure under the proposed contract is so short that it is impracticable to comply ...
>
> (3) It is an implied condition ... of the contract that the other party complies with the provision of paragraph (1).

The intention of the regulators is clear enough in this provision. The terms of the contract should be reduced to writing and supplied to the consumer and those terms should include at least those provisions which are required by Schedule 2. The requirement is two-fold. First, to communicate the terms to the consumer in writing or some other comprehensible form *before* the contract is made, and secondly to supply the consumer with a written copy of the contract. There is no reason why the two obligations cannot be satisfied at the same time by the provision of a complete draft contract. Usually the other party to the contract complies with this provision by means of obtaining the consumer's signature confirming that the booking conditions have been read and by supplying a pre-contract itinerary which later forms the basis of the confirmation invoice. Late deals may be an exception to the regulation 9 requirements but only it is submitted in exceptional circumstances. The "other party to the contract" is excused from the pre-contractual obligation to communicate all the terms where the consumer makes such a last minute booking that it is *impracticable* to comply with this requirement. In these days of word processors, faxes and e-mails it will be a rare package where the "other party" finds it impracticable to set the terms of the contract down in writing and cannot transmit those terms to the consumer. Even where time makes it impracticable for the terms to be reduced to writing *before* the contract is made, the "other party to the contract" is still obliged to supply to the consumer in writing the terms on which the contract has been made (including of course the particulars demanded by Schedule 2). However, where the parties are extremely pressed for time, it should be noted that there is no requirement imposed by regulation 9 that a copy of the terms should be supplied to the consumer before departure.

Schedule 2 — minimum content

The information required by Regulation 9 is mandatory. At least (where relevant) the details canvassed by Schedule 2 must find their way into the written contract. They are:

- the travel destinations, periods of stay and dates;

- the means, characteristics and categories of transport;

- the location of any accommodation, its category, degree of comfort, main features and where it is situated in a Member State, its compliance with the rules of that state;

- the meal plan;

- whether a minimum number of passengers is required for the package to be supplied;

- the itinerary;

- visits and excursions that form part of the package;

- the name and address of the organiser, the retailer and the insurer;

- the price of the package and the mechanism by which that price may be varied (if any);

- a payment schedule and methods of payments;

- any special requirements the consumer has communicated to the organiser or retailer which have been accepted;

- the periods within which the consumer must make a complaint about any failure to perform or inadequate performance of the package contract.

All the terms

Compliance with the particulars set out in Schedule 2 is not the end of the matter as far as "the other party to the contract" is concerned. *All* the terms must be set out in writing unless time makes this impracticable according to regulation 9(1)(b). This is a curious insistence on the part of the regulators — or at least curiously phrased. The package contract is likely to contain a number of implied terms. Indeed the 1992 Regulations themselves insert a number of implied warranties, and regulation 9 itself creates an implied *condition*. It would appear, therefore, that any failing on the part of "the other party to the contract" to itemise in writing the implied warranties, conditions and other terms including the implied condition created by regulation 9, will be a breach of the 1992 Regulations. However, once set out in a set of booking conditions the "implied warranties" surely become express terms of the contract.

Tour operators and travel agents go to some lengths to ensure that a contract with the consumer is not concluded until such time as the consumer has signified in writing that the company's written terms and conditions have been read and understood by or on behalf of all those to be named in the booking form.[42] The confirmation invoice and itinerary (often a combined document) will then be despatched in compliance with regulation 9(1)(c). Even so, regulation 9 is not taken literally. Not *all* the terms are either communicated to the consumer or reduced to writing. For example, in order to give effect to the presumed common intention of the parties, there will often be a term implied into a package contract to the effect that the food served at a resort will be reasonably fit for human consumption. It would be expecting too much for tour operators to include such a provision explicitly in their written terms and contractual documents. It would look bizarre, and is not likely to fill their customers with confidence. In practice, tour operators approach this issue in a more general fashion. Pragmatically, tour operators usually include a provision in their booking conditions to the effect that the services included in the package will be carried out "properly" or "to a reasonable standard", or some other generalisation which covers many, if not all, eventualities. It is also commonplace to see tour operators' terms and conditions which appear to mimic large portions of the PTR 1992. No doubt the reason this is done is to comply with regulation 9.

---

[42] In *Desmond Gow v TUI UK Ltd t/a Crystal Holidays*: 27th April 2006, DJ Perusko.(Watford County Court) concluded that it was common knowledge amongst consumers making travel arrangements that a contract would not be completed until the terms and conditions and arrived and been sign on the consumer's behalf.

In writing or such other form as is comprehensible and accessible

Before the contract is made the communication of the terms does not have to be in writing. A written copy of the terms may be supplied to the consumer after the contract is made. However, if at the pre-contract stage, the terms are not communicated in writing they must be communicated in some *other* comprehensible and accessible form. It is difficult to know what would be permitted by this alternative. Would a clear oral précis of the terms be adequate? What other form of communication could there possibly be that was not in writing? Did the regulators intend to say that at the pre-contract stage the written information did not all have to be from the same source (*e.g.* it could be taken for a number of different brochures, leaflets and letters)? Were they intending to cater for consumers who couldn't read? Surely not, because the provision of the terms in writing to the illiterate would still satisfy the requirements of regulation 9(1)(b). In all probability, the alternative "comprehensible and accessible form" in which the terms can be conveyed, would be a full and clear oral explanation of the terms followed up by the written contract pursuant to regulation 9(1)(c). The communication of course must be comprehensible and accessible to the consumer[43]. The test must be objective at least for those packages offered to the public as a whole, the benchmark being the reasonable consumer exercising a reasonable degree of intelligence and care. It cannot have been the regulators' intention to require the production of contract terms in Braille, or in some other form accessible to the retarded, impatient or dyslexic.

Implied condition

Regulation 9 does not in itself provide for a remedy in the event of breach. The provision of the information required by regulation 9 will, of course, make it easier for the consumer to compare what was bought with what was actually delivered and reduce the scope for dispute about precisely what "the other party to the contract" promised. However, regulation 9 does not provide for damages to be recovered in the event of breach.

The remedy implied by regulation 9 is the withdrawal of the consumer from the contract in the event that the mandatory information is not supplied or a copy of the written terms is not forthcoming. By making the requirements of regulation 9 an implied *condition* the consumer may terminate the contract in the event of "the other party's" failure to comply. So, where the consumer makes a contract, but is not supplied with the terms of the contract in writing, that consumer is entitled to have second thoughts about the

---

[43] See *Akehurst v Thomson Holidays Limited* (below).

reliability or even honesty of "the other party"; the consumer may treat the other party's failure as a repudiatory breach of contract, accept that breach and terminate the contract. If all goes well with the package travel arrangements it is difficult to see how a consumer could be entitled to anything more than nominal damages for any failure on the part of the other party to comply with the requirements of regulation 9.

In order for this remedy to have any significant force it is necessary to read into regulation 9 a requirement that the terms of the contract should be communicated and provide in writing *a reasonable time before the intended date of departure*. If this is not implied into regulation 9 the consumer's right to "rescind" the contract is seriously diluted. The whole point of regulation 9 is to provide the consumer with documentation against which his arrangements can be measured. Is that what was agreed in the pre-contract negotiations? Are all the services and facilities included? Have there been any mistakes? The intention to provide consumers with this sort of reference point is completely negated if there is no obligation to provide the consumer with the written contract a reasonable time before departure. It is thought likely that if this was ever put to the judicial test, a tour operator would not be allowed to succeed on the basis that a written contract was to be supplied at the time of departure or even after departure, unless the booking was one of considerable lateness as to make earlier communication of the contract terms impracticable in the circumstances envisaged by regulation 9(2).

There is a further quirk in the drafting of regulation 9. It is an implied condition of the contract that "*the other party to the contract*" complies with regulation 9(1). A literal reader might be inclined to suggest that this completely undermines the late bookings exception in regulation 9(2). If this literal interpretation were to be correct, then the late bookings exception would be of no effect. Obviously, the implied condition created by regulation 9(3) must, therefore, be a condition that imports both 9(1) and (2). That is, the implied condition is contained in regulation 9(1) as qualified by regulation 9(2).

The importance of the pre-contractual need for comprehensible communication of terms is reduced, and the room for factual arguments as to when time might make such communication impracticable, is very much reduced if the written terms of the contract demanded by regulation 9(1)(c) have to be supplied before departure *in all cases* including those of last minute bookings. No doubt the regulators were anxious to ensure that consumers had comprehensive and comprehensible information so far as practicable before making their *choice* of package.

Regulation 9 plainly has implications for tour operators where the incorporation of terms into a contract is at the heart of any dispute. In *Akehurst and Others v Thomson Holidays Limited and Others*[44] the claimants were passengers on board a Britannia aircraft that crash-landed at Gerona airport. Their claims included claims for psychological injury which could not be pursued against the carrier.[45] The claims for psychological injury were brought against the tour operator under regulation 15 of the PTR 1992. Clauses 6 and 7 of the tour operator's written conditions of contract provided that the tour operator would accept liability for personal injury[46] where there had been a failure on the part of a supplier to perform its duties properly. The written contract conditions also included the following: *When you travel by air or on water, the transport company's Conditions of Carriage will apply to your journey. You can ask the travel agent booking your holiday to get you a copy of any conditions that apply to your journey if he has not already got them.*" The tour operator argued that it had thus incorporated into the package holiday contracts Britannia's conditions of carriage which themselves incorporated by reference the provision and limitations under the Warsaw Convention. Thus, it was argued, the tour operator (like the carrier) was not liable for the passengers' psychological injuries. In the context of regulation 9 the trial judge said this:

> The purpose of these regulations, and in particular regulation 9, is to protect the consumer. All the terms of the contract must be brought reasonably and fairly to his notice, particularly where terms are onerous or exclude or limit liability. I agree with the claimants that the object is to avoid the manifestly unjust situation in which a consumer is said to be bound by terms to which he had no idea he had "agreed".... Thomson's obligation was to ensure ("shall ensure") that all the terms of the contract set out in writing were communicated to the consumer before the contract was made. The obligation was not discharged by attempting to place the onus on the consumer to ask the travel agent to get him a copy of "any" conditions (not even "the" conditions) that applied to his journey. Secondly, it was not clearly set out in writing or in any other form comprehensible and accessible to the consumer that it was a term of the contract that the benefits conveyed by clauses 6 and 7 were being substantially cut down by the air carrier's Conditions of Carriage.

He concluded:

> Thomson certainly is seeking to take advantage of its own wrong. It is seeking to hold the consumer to an alleged term of which he was unaware

---

[44] Cardiff County Court – HHJ Graham Jones 6 May 2003 (Unreported).
[45] Under article 17 of the Warsaw Convention only claims for bodily injury could be brought against Britannia Airways.
[46] Not limited to bodily injury.

because it, Thomson, failed to communicate the term to him when it was under an express statutory duty to do so.

The judge was unimpressed by the submission that regulation 9 was just about the communication of contractual terms to the consumer *not* about the substance of those contractual terms and held (amongst other things) that if the tour operator was allowed to rely on its purported incorporation of the Britannia conditions of carriage it would be taking advantage of its own failure to comply with the statutory duties regarding comprehensible and accessible communication under regulation 9(1)(b). It seems to follow, therefore, that even where the other party to the contract has sufficiently complied with the common law rules regarding the incorporation of contractual terms by reference, where there has been a breach of regulation 9, the other party will not be permitted to rely on that incorporation because to do so would have the result that the other party would be able to take advantage of its own wrong in failing to comply with regulation 9.

Regulation 10 — Transfers

10.-(1) In every contract there is an implied term that where the consumer is prevented from proceeding with the package the consumer may transfer his booking to a person who satisfies all the conditions applicable to the package, provided that the consumer gives reasonable notice to the other party to the contract of his intention to transfer before the date when departure is due to take place.

(2) Where a transfer is made in accordance with the implied term set out in paragraph (1) above, the transferor and the transferee shall be jointly and severally liable to the other party to the contract for payment of the price of the package (or, if part of the price has been paid, for payment of the balance) and for any additional costs arising from such transfer.

Prevented

The consumer's right to transfer the benefit of the package contract is not absolute. It arises only in limited circumstances. The most important limitation is that the consumer must be *prevented* from proceeding with the package. There is no reason to suppose that this expression should be given an unduly restricted interpretation. A consumer is likely to be regarded as having been "prevented" from proceeding with the package in circumstances where by personal accident or illness, or serious ill-health affecting a close member of the family, the consumer cannot reasonably be expected to proceed with the package arrangements. Whilst medical emergencies to members of the family, or some personal illnesses might not *physically* prevent a consumer from proceeding, it is not considered probable that the courts will place such a literal construction on this provision. One can be *reasonably* prevented from travelling for any number of good social reasons that do not actually stop the consumer from getting on the aeroplane. Regulation 10 is also likely to apply in situations apart from accident or illness. A consumer could be prevented from proceeding by reason of intervening work commitments, or altered working shifts affecting an intended member of the travelling party (a spouse for example). No doubt the wording of the regulation is left intentionally wide and undefined to allow the courts to approach any given case on its own peculiar facts. Had the regulators intended the act preventing the consumer from proceeding with the package to be limited to *personal* problems (as opposed to problems affecting work or family), or that they should be health related, they could easily have made narrower provision to this effect.

However, it is thought that a consumer will never be regarded as being "prevented" from proceeding with a package simply because there is a change of heart, or where, for example, one member of the party decides to sacrifice their place to another friend or family member who might not originally have been able to go on the package.

Where the consumer is prevented from travelling, regulation 10 allows for the transfer of the benefit of the arrangements to another without the consumer incurring cancellation charges (up to 100% of the cost of the package if the cancellation is very near in time to the date of departure). In practice the larger tour operators have often been fairly relaxed about the substitution of named travellers within a family or group party provided ample time is given for the necessary administrative arrangements to me made. Regulation 10 makes it possible for the consumer to substitute one or members of a party for others, without the consent of "the other party to the contract".

Satisfies all the conditions

The transferee must satisfy all the conditions (if any) that apply to the package. The substituted consumer must qualify for the package under any age or health restrictions, and possess any skill or ability necessary for the purposes of the activities which form part of the package. Obvious examples are holidays for the over 50s, or those up to the age of 30. Less common examples might be packages where a minimum level of diving or climbing skill is an essential qualifying condition.

Notice to the other party

The consumer must give reasonable notice of the intention to transfer to the other party to the contract. What constitutes reasonable notice will depend on all the circumstances. For the common or garden package for a fortnight in the sun, the period of notice might be fairly modest — enough time to allow the other party to the contract to arrange for name changes on the tickets. Other packages where, for example, group visas have been obtained or involving a complicated itinerary with many incidental ticketing changes may require longer notice. Tour operators can and do attempt to pre-judge what is and what is not reasonable by stipulating in their terms and conditions that the minimum reasonable period of notice of transfer should be, for example, one month. By inserting such a provision in their conditions the agreed minimum period of notice becomes a term of the package contract. Whilst it is most unlikely that such a term would oust the more general principle under regulation 10, it is submitted that a stipulation agreed between the parties as to what would be the minimum period of notice considered reasonable, would be good evidence, or at least some evidence, on which a court might subsequently act. Nonetheless, tour operators should be aware that they might be called upon to explain why even a month's notice is necessary for many European standard form packages. Pre-determination as to what the parties agree to call "reasonable notice" is not necessarily going to work in all cases. Tour operators are likely to be subject to at least an evidential burden for the purposes of explaining why such notice as a consumer has given is not reasonable in the circumstances of the particular package.

Joint and several liability

Both the original consumer and the transferee are jointly and severally liable for the price of the package or any outstanding balance. If the price is not paid the tour operator would no doubt refuse to allow either party to travel at all, but before things reach such a stage, demand for the price or the balance can be made of either. If consumer and transferee squabble about the liability to pay, and the other party to the contract is not paid; the transferor and transferee must sort it out between themselves.

This joint and several liability extends to any "additional costs arising from [the] transfer". The cost of reissuing tickets and visas, changing names on itineraries and records and communicating the changes to local representatives and suppliers are all chargeable by the other party to the contract. These charges can be passed on to either the original consumer or the transferee or both. It is common for tour operators to stipulate a standard "administrative" charge for such changes. The transferee will usually pay such an administration charge in order to obtain the benefit of the package. Standard charges, by very dint of the fact that they *are* standard, often smack of a *penalty* and once again it would be advisable for tour operators to be able to explain how the standard transfer cost is arrived at if one is imposed. There is no reason in principle why a standard charge could not be imposed in instances of transfer, provided there is some sensible underlying logic explaining the final figure which is proportionate to any work actually undertaken by the tour operator in administering the change.

It is worth noting that it is the *arranged package* that is the subject of the transfer and governed by regulation 10. The transferee is not entitled to insist on additional facilities that formed no part of the transferor's contract. For example, otherwise than with the goodwill of the tour operator and suppliers, the transferee cannot demand a twin room where the contract provides for a double; or accommodation for a man where the original accommodation was in women's quarters. The transferee is not entitled to demand Club Class flights (even at an additional cost) where economy travel was part of the original deal. No doubt alterations can always be agreed where the other party to the contract is willing and able to oblige — but the subject of the transfer is the original contract made between the transferor and the other party to the contract.

Regulation 11 — Price Revision

Rather like regulations 4 and 5, regulation 11 concerns itself with matters which should *not* find their way into the package contract.

> 11.-(1) Any term in a contract to the effect that the prices laid down in the contract may be revised shall be void and of no effect unless the contract provides for the possibility of upward or downward revision and satisfies the conditions laid down in paragraph (2) below.
>
> (2) The conditions mentioned in paragraph (1) are that:
>
> (a) the contract states precisely how the revise price is to be calculated;
>
> (b) the contract provides that the price revisions are to be made solely to allow for variations in: -
>
> (i) transportation costs, including the cost of fuel;
>
> (ii) dues, taxes or fees chargeable for services such as landing taxes or embarkation or disembarkation fees at ports and airports; or
>
> (iii) the exchange rates applied to the particular package; and
>
> (3) Notwithstanding any terms of the contract:
>
> (i) no price increase may be made in a specified period which may not be less than 30 days before the departure date stipulated; and
>
> (ii) as against an individual consumer liable under the contract, no price increase may be made in respect of variations which would produce an increase of less than 2% or such greater percentage as the contract may specify ('non-eligible variations') and that non-eligible variations shall be left out of account in the calculation.

As a "no surcharges" clause, regulation 11 is somewhat cumbersome. In fact regulation 11 *does* permit increases in price after the contract is made (i.e.

surcharges) with stringent qualifications. Permitted price increases must satisfy four conditions.

1. The price change mechanism must provide for changes in either direction — both up and down.

2. The revision mechanism can only be applied to certain qualifying elements.

3. The revision must not be made less than 30 days before departure.

4. Any price revision must not be less than 2% of the net price.

Increases and reductions

Any term in the contract to the effect that prices in the contract may be revised are void and of no effect[47] unless the contract itself provides for the possibility of both upwards and downwards revisions. The contract must state:[21]

- precisely how the revised prices are to be calculated; and

- changes to the price can only be made if they concern a qualifying element.

Regulation 11 probably represents a regulatory compromise. A complete ban on surcharges could work unfavourably on tour operators particularly where fuel crises intervene or where governments unilaterally change landing charges or airport taxes. Multiplied across a season's package holidays such price fluctuations could seriously compromise the financial well-being of a significant part of the industry. On the other hand, the regulators were clearly determined that suppliers should not have *carte blanche* to impose surcharges at will (although competition in the industry would surely minimise the risk of this). Accordingly, surcharges are permitted by the regulations provided they arise only in respect of the qualifying elements and are strictly limited in scope as set out in regulation 11.

Upward or downward

The way regulation 11 is phrased, the provision in the contract for upward or downward price movement might be considered an *alternative*, that is, a tour operator who made provision only for upward movement would have complied with one of the stipulated alternatives. Conversely (although it is unlikely that there would be any fuss about it) a tour operator could make provision for only downward movement of prices in the contract. However,

---

[47] Regulation 11(1).

it is thought that upward or downward revision is *not* intended to provide an alternative, and that any tour operator only making provision for upward movement would fall foul of regulation 11(1). It is the *formula* in the *contract* for price revision which must provide the alternative upward or downward possibilities. It is most unlikely that the regulators would have considered it necessary or appropriate to regulate against price *reductions* unless stringent pre-conditions were first set out in the contract.

Therefore, the price revision *formula* must be specified in the contract and that formula has, at least in theory, to account for the possibility that the qualifying elements could drive prices down as well as up. The formula must be "precisely" set out in the contract.[48]

Qualifying elements

The contract itself must make clear that the price revision formula can only be applied in order to make provision for variations in:

- transportation costs, including the cost of fuel;
- dues, taxes or fees chargeable for services, such as landing taxes or embarkation or disembarkation fees at ports or airports;
- the exchange rates applied to the particular package.

Transportation

Fuel costs are the most obvious example where transportation costs may vary between the time the contract is made and the time of departure, and fuel is the example given by the regulators. However, transportation costs potentially covers a multitude of sins. Increased costs brought about by staff wage increases or government regulation (such as the Working Time Directive); the cost of up-grading of vehicular transport to provide enhanced facilities and comfort, administrative as well as extra fuel costs incurred as a result of transport having to be re-routed to avoid dangerous war zones or areas of civil disturbance — could all be examples giving rise to varied transportation costs that are not necessarily directly related to fuel charges.

Dues, taxes and fees

The regulators had in mind sea port and airport charges in particular, but again the regulation is not limited to these. The regulators have chosen to given sea and airport charges as examples of what they had in mind: "*such as landing taxes ... (etc)*".[49] So, the change in price must be to allow for

---

[48] Regulation 11(2)(a).
[49] Regulation 11(2)(b)(ii).

variations in "dues, taxes or fees chargeable for services" but port charges are merely an example of the matters to which regulation 11(2)(b)(ii) applies. The examples given must in some way govern the interpretation of the sorts of services in respect of which an increase (or decrease) in price can lead to a revision of the contract price. In the broadest (and it is submitted least probable) sense, regulation 11(2)(b)(ii) could be interpreted as allowing for price revision where a hotel decides to charge an additional premium on its rooms after contracts have been made. This would be a fee payable for the hotel services and arguably within the terms of permissible price revision. However, it is thought that this is not likely to be the way in which regulation 11(2)(b)(ii) will be construed.

The words *dues, taxes or fees* implicitly suggests that the charges covered by regulation 11(2)(b)(ii) are those that are levied by some official[50] organisation or corporation in respect of public services provided outwith the scope of the services and facilities that are at the core of the contract between the organiser and the consumer. It must be admitted that there is nothing expressed in the regulation itself which necessarily limits its construction in this way, but the whole tenor of the provision appears to be to the effect that where the organiser or supplier is met with unilateral price increases for services which are collateral to the package contract, but essential nonetheless for the performance of the package contract, the organiser should be permitted to pass on any such increases — subject to the other rules in regulation 11. Apart from the examples given one might envisage others such as tolls for roads, bridges and tunnels; visitors taxes; increases in purchase, sales environmental or local value added taxes; licence fees for free-way transport, sporting facilities or district government licence fees or charges for access to beaches or other facilities previously provided free of charge.

However, it is thought that because of the restrictions imposed by regulation 11(3)(ii), this regulation is unlikely to be the subject of much litigation.

Exchange rates

Price variations are permissible where needed to allow for variations in exchange rates *applied to the particular package*. This probably means that where the organiser is faced with payment for package services in a sharply rising currency, this can be taken into account in determining whether or not a permissible surcharge is triggered by regulation 11(2)(b)(iii).

---

[50] Not necessarily governmental.

30 days before departure

Regardless of the terms of the contract no price increase may be made less than 30 days before the departure date stipulated in the contract.[51] The contract may specify a longer period than 30 days, in which case the agreed period is the latest at which a price increase may be made. No civil or criminal remedy for breach of this prohibition is specified in the Regulations. One assumes that if an organiser demands payment of a surcharge the consumer can refuse to pay. If the supplier is insistent it would seem that the consumer has two choices. Either pay and recover the price increase later by civil proceedings if necessary, or alternatively, refuse to pay and run the risk of being prevented from travelling, in which case the consumer would be able to pursue the supplier for damages in respect of the non performance of the entire travel contract.

Not less than 2%

Regulation 11(3)(ii) prohibits any price *increase* which has the effect of increasing the package price less than 2%. If the package contract stipulates a higher minimum percentage, then that higher figure applies. The purpose of this is to prevent price "tinkering". Modest increases in the cost of qualifying elements of less than 2% are to be covered by the organiser. No doubt, more often than not, minor price variations of at least up to 2% are catered for in suppliers' original pricing policies. The objective which regulation 11(3) (ii) seeks to attain, is to allow the transmission of price increases only where they are significant. Anything other than significant variations is at the risk of the other party to the contract.

Whether a price variation is less than 2% is calculated *as against an individual consumer liable under the contract* and judged against the original contract price. Any variations in price that have affected the supplier but which cannot be relied on for the purposes of varying the contract price under the Regulations[52] are left out of account in calculating whether the price revision proposed is more or less than 2%. Although the Regulations make no provision for this, it must be the case that the variations in the price of services with which the organiser is faced have to be divided proportionally between each traveller in respect of which the service would be charged in those circumstances where a single licence fee or charge was levied for the use of a facility which was not levied per passenger (*e.g.* a road fund tax for free-way usage). The consumer who is *liable* (presumably this means liable to pay) under the contract is the *principal contractor.* If the variation is 2% or more of the price payable by the principal contractor

---

[51] Regulation 11(3)(i).
[52] The so-called "non-eligible variations".

(however many travellers are covered by the contract), then a permissible surcharge can be made. 2% of the principal contractor's liability is the threshold for a permissible surcharge. Therefore, in marginal cases, it will be important to identify those travellers on any invoice or itinerary who are the principal contractors (whether or not their contracts are made through another's agency) and who are the other *beneficiaries*.[53] Whether a mother travelling with three children who have benefited from junior discounts reaches the 2% threshold before or after the party of four adults on the same holiday, depends entirely on whether each of the four adults fall on the facts of the case to be treated as a principal contractor. If mother pays £250.00 for herself and £250.00 for the three children, the trigger for permissible surcharging[32] under regulation 11(3)(ii) will be £10.00. If each of the four adults pays the same £250.00, but only the lead name on the contract is regarded as the principal contractor, then the relevant figure for permissible surcharging is £20.00. However, if each of the adults is regarded as a principal contractor and thus liable under the contract, the surcharge threshold is only £5.00. Perhaps it is just as well that market forces, and the intervention of voluntary regulatory bodies has made surcharging a minority interest amongst tour operators in recent years.

General application

If an organiser includes a price variation formula in the contract by which it is entitled to revise a price upwards or downwards, is that organiser *obliged* to invoke the price variation mechanism if the circumstances arise? The answer to this is "no". Just because the revision is permissible does not make it compulsory. However, this leaves us with one more quirk in the framework of regulation 11. Whilst it is compulsory to provide a formula by which the price may go up or down if any increases are to be permitted at all (within the rules of regulation 11), there is nothing to stop organisers *invoking* that mechanism only when the price goes *up*. The same formula may apply to price movements in both directions, but using that formula to reduce package prices already paid is entirely at the suppliers' discretion. It is a discretion that is seldom exercised. The consumer has no remedy if the mechanism is not deployed to reflect savings made by a supplier who has profited from the advantageous value of sterling for example, and the consumer has no redress if, in respect of the *same contract*, the supplier chooses to use the contractual price variation formula to increase the price to

---

[53] As to which see regulation 2.

reflect new airport landing charges. Therefore, the consumer still potentially loses both ways despite the best efforts of the regulators.[54]

Regulation 12

Regulation 12 concerns those occasions where an organiser has to make changes to the contract before departure.

> 12. In every contract there are implied terms to the effect that: -
>
> (a) where the organiser is constrained before departure to alter significantly an essential term of the contract, such as the price ... he will notify the consumer as quickly as possible in order to enable him to take appropriate decisions and in particular to withdraw from the contract without penalty or to accept a rider to the contract specifying the alterations made and their impact on the price; and
>
> (b) the consumer will inform the organiser or the retailer of his decision as soon as possible.

This regulation should be looked at in conjunction with regulation 13. The object of both regulations taken together is generally to allow an organiser to make certain changes to a concluded contract, but to provide the consumer with the protection of the right to cancel the package in the light of those alterations.

Regulation 12 applies where two conditions are satisfied. First, where there is an alteration to an *essential term* and secondly, where that alteration is *significant*. Neither of these expressions is defined further in the PTR 1992, save that an example of an essential term (the price) is given. What is "essential" and what is "significant" will be matters of fact and degree to be decided in the context of individual package contracts[55]. However, it is submitted that the test for both "essential terms" and "significant" changes must have an objective element. Given that the organiser cannot reasonably be expected to react to the individual whims and fancies of every traveller who is booked on a regulated package. This element of objectivity would be recognised if the test were to be those terms which would reasonably be regarded as essential (as opposed to inessential) by a consumer considering the package at the time of booking, and a "significant" change would be a change reasonably regarded by a consumer as more than incidental at the time the booking was made. Accordingly, *any* change in accommodation, or

---

[54] Tour operator members of the Association of British Travel Agents (ABTA) however must comply with the ABTA code of practice on surcharges which is in many respects more demanding than regulation 11 of the PTR 1992. Members are obliged to keep ABTA informed of their surcharge protocol and obtain the consent of ABTA before any surcharge is levied.

[55] Essential terms will surely include anything prescribed in Schedule 2.

alteration of itinerary by more than eight hours should be regarded as a change to an essential term (place and time both being at the heart of any travel contract) and likewise, any alteration in the facilities which were advertised or promoted by the organiser which originally formed part of the accommodation or transport arrangements in the contract should be regarded as significant. If these were not significant there would have been little point in promoting the services or facilities in the promotional material.

Essential terms and significant alterations

So an "essential" term is likely to be taken to include or should include the following:

- the price;

- the precise accommodation, standard of accommodation and accommodation facilities booked (in particular whether building works at or in the vicinity of the accommodation have been commenced or enlarged since the time the contract was made);

- the type and standard of transport;

- the place of departure and destination;

- any facility or service advertised or promoted as forming a part of the package,[56] or something which a consumer may purchase as part of a pre-arranged combination of components (even though an individual consumer may subjectively not wish to make use of that facility or service[57]);

- any term required by the PTR 1992 or the ABTA Code of Conduct to be included as part of the contract."

A "significant" alteration in one of these essential terms must be an alteration that is more than trivial, incidental or wholly collateral to the package booked by the consumer.

This is a stiff test for organisers and suppliers and few at present appear to pay more than lip service to it. There are two related issues worth considering in more detail. First, it is commonplace to find tour operators and other organisers classifying in the contract terms those changes that are to be regarded as "significant" and those that are only "minor". Despite the common confusion between the "essential" term and the "significant" alteration to it, organisers argue that where the parties have "agreed" in

---

[56] But see *Jervis v Kuoni Travel Limited* (below) where a change of Thai resort island does not seem to have been regarded as significant in all the circumstances.
[57] Such as sports facilities.

advance by way of the organiser's terms and conditions what is and what is not to be regarded as a "significant" change, the consumer should not be allowed to go behind that "agreement". So, where the organiser states that only itinerary changes of more than 24 hours are to be regarded as "significant", the consumer cannot complain if a change of 18 hours has to be made. If the change is *not* "significant" the argument goes, it does not matter whether the term is an essential one or not. If this argument of the tour operators were to prevail, the number of possible "significant" changes would be very small indeed and the consumer would be left having to put up with all sorts of changes that had been "agreed" were not significant.

The second and potentially more damaging issue for consumers is that before any decision can be made as to whether a change has been made in any term of the contract (essential or otherwise; significant or not) one first has to determine precisely what the original term of the contract provides for[58]. If the original contract is loosely configured, no change may arise even if the consumer ends up getting something different from that which they thought was being offered. An example may illustrate this. A tour operator might sell a regulated package promoting with pictures a particularly famous and well appointed hotel. The accommodation panel and price of the package may provide for accommodation at that pictured hotel "or similar standard". If the consumer is actually accommodated in the "similar" hotel, she need not be notified of the "change" because strictly speaking there has been no change in the contract terms. The consumer may well have an action for breach of contract if it can be shown that the "similar standard" accommodation was not at all of a "similar standard", but the consumer who harboured an ambition to stay at Raffles in Singapore who is accommodated in the "similar standard" but ultra-modern Marina Hyatt will not necessarily have a remedy, and furthermore, will have been deprived of the opportunity to satisfy the ambition that the consumer almost certainly thought was being paid for. If the alternative is indeed of a similar standard, there has been no breach of contract because the organiser did not agree to provide anything other than Raffles or a hotel of similar *standard*. In these circumstances organisers would have to be careful to ensure that the contractual documentation did not specify a particular hotel as this would be

---

[58] This is the familiar contractual issue of distinguishing terms that define the scope of the contract from those that limit or exclude liabilities under the agreed contractual scope. A good example of this issue is found in *Cooper v Princess Cruises Limited* Chester County Court 29 January 2002 (Unreported) where the cruise contract reserved to the captain of the vessel the right to change the itinerary. When the vessel's intended route was severely compromised by a hurricane, the captain exercised his discretion and radically altered the itinerary. The judge held that there was no breach of contract because it was a term of the contract that changes of this sort could be made. The scope of the original agreement between the parties entertained such radical changes.

good evidence for the consumer that there had been an agreement for the specific accommodation in question — but careful phrasing of the brochure and conditions and confirmation invoice can provide the organiser with a degree of latitude that would come as a surprise to many consumers.

Does an organiser agree to provide as a term of the contract those facilities which are described in a brochure as being "subject to availability", or those which are encompassed in the conventional panel warning tourists that certain facilities may not be available due to excess or lack of demand? If these facilities are not in fact available, is there *any* "change" to a term of the contract (essential or not) let alone a "significant change"?

In practice some organisers define "significant changes" in their brochure conditions in a very restrictive way.[59] This purports to limit their obligation to notify the consumer in the event that alterations are made after booking but before departure in respect of alterations other than those contractually stipulated to qualify as significant alterations to essential terms. Additionally, some organisers define *what it is* they agree to provide in the contract in such a way as to ensure so far as possible that re-organising of services and facilities does not amount to a "change" in the agreed terms at all.

Whilst this may not matter where the promotional material is misleading or where it can be shown that the alternatives provided do not actually comply with the stipulations in the contract (*e.g.* the hotel was not only *not* the one pictured in the brochure but was not even five star) so that the consumer has a civil remedy on her return; not only will such a remedy not always be available, but the consumer may find herself facing unexpected but important "changes" without ever having been notified of them and without ever having been given the option of cancellation provided by regulation 13.

Constrained

One possible brake on the organiser is that he must be "constrained" to alter significantly an essential term before regulations 12 and 13 take effect. The PTR 1992 give no help as to what sort of constraints should apply before the organiser is entitled to invoke regulation 12 alterations in essential terms. To be "constrained" is to have one's freedom of action somehow limited. These limitations may arise in any number of ways, including as a result of economic, political or social factors, matters which apply to the package

---

[59] But if an attempt is made the tour operator must get it right. See e.g. *Williams v Travel Promotions Limited* [1998] CLY 3742; *The Times* March 9 1998 where the tour operator specified that it was entitled to make "necessary" changes rather than desirable or sensible ones should circumstances demand. The tour operator in this case had changed a hotel for the last night of a package based at Victoria Falls because it considered it sensible to have the tourists nearer their departure airport on the last night.

itself, or to the destination where the package is to be performed. The organiser may find himself constrained by industrial action at home or abroad, by local disease, or even by breaches of contract on the part of his own suppliers. There is nothing in the PTR 1992 to suggest that the constraint must be formidable, but it is submitted that in practice a court is likely to construe a regulation 12 constraint as an impediment which the organiser could not overcome by exercising reasonable care or adopting reasonably accessible measures.

There has been some case law since the above paragraph first appeared in the 3rd. edition. The *constraint* referred to above was surely originally designed to prevent the organiser from making undue changes in published itineraries but in practice it has been deployed *by organisers* to keep consumers to their holiday contracts. Cases arising out of the SARS[60] health scare in Asia in 2003 illustrate the point.

Lambert v Travelsphere Limited[61] was the first. In January 2003 Mr. and Mrs. Lambert booked a package tour with Travelsphere, a tour operator, for the 23 day period between 27th April and 19th May 2003. The package included flights to Beijing, a tour of China, and, at the end of the holiday, 3 days in Hong Kong. In March 2003 as a result of the SARS epidemic the World Health Organisation issued warnings to international travellers intending to travel to Hong Kong. On 2nd April 2003 the World Health Organisation and the Department of Health strongly advised holidaymakers not to travel to Hong Kong. On 8th April 2003 T wrote to the Claimants notifying them that they were rearranging some travel itineraries but that they might be able to visit Hong Kong at the end of the holiday. On 12th April 2003 the Claimants cancelled the holiday but reserved their rights as to the cancellation fee charged by the tour operator pursuant to their standard terms and conditions. On 23rd April 2003 the tout operator cancelled the holiday and provided *all the other* holidaymakers with a full refund in accordance with Regulations 12 and 13 of the PTR 1992. The Claimants brought an action for a refund of the cancellation fee on the basis that they were entitled to cancel the holiday without fee pursuant to Regulations 12 and 13, because the tour operator had been constrained to alter the itinerary before departure. The tour operator argued that their notification did not constitute an alteration, because it was still possible that the group might be able to travel to Hong Kong and at the time the Lamberts cancelled it was still possible that the full trip could go ahead. On appeal the judge concluded that although as at 8th April 2003 the tour operator was constrained *to consider* altering the itinerary, they were not

---

[60] Severe Acute Respiratory Syndrome.
[61] September 1st, 2004, Circuit Judge Darrock(Peterborough) – unreported.

constrained actually *to alter* it. Any uncertainty travellers' minds as to whether or not they would be able to go to Hong Kong was a product of the SARS epidemic and not of the letter. In the circumstances, Regulation 12 was not even engaged. Furthermore, whilst a tour operator cannot shut its eyes to an obvious danger so as to deny that it is constrained to alter an essential term, it was permissible for it not to alter the term until there is not *a flicker of hope* that the contract could be performed in accordance with the original term. In order for a tour operator to be constrained to alter a term, it must be *absolutely inevitable* and *unavoidable* for it to be altered. Accordingly, the Lamberts lost their claim.

Clark and others v Travelsphere Limited[62] is another example. The Claimants, two couples, had booked package holidays with the Defendant tour operator to travel to China and Hong Kong between the 12th and 27th April 2003. The holidays were to consist of an 11-day tour of China and a 3-day add-on trip to Hong Kong and Guangdong province. Both couples paid the full cost of the holiday in advance but became concerned about the SRAS epidemic. They were told by the tour operator (based on evidence from local sources about the monitoring of the situation on an hourly basis) that the planned trip including the Hong Kong element would go ahead subject to the proviso that if FCO guidance on Hong Kong remained the same at the end of the 11-day tour of China, holidaymakers would be flown home. The Clarks simply did not turn up at their departure airport sending an email the next day purporting to cancel the holiday on the grounds that they were fearful of the SARS outbreak and despite the fact that the holiday contract made plain that no refunds would be given in the event of consumer cancellation 72 hours or less before departure, they sued for damages. In part they relied on the fact that the Hong Kong element of the trip *had* indeed been abandoned for all the other travelling passengers all of whom had received a refund of that element of the holiday cost. Their claim was unsuccessful and the Defendant's argument mirroring that deployed in *Lambert* to the effect that *at the time the itinerary commenced* it remained a plausible possibility that the Hong Kong trip would go ahead, prevailed.

Notification

Notification is a two-way street under regulation 12. The organiser must notify the consumer of significant alterations to essential terms *"as quickly as possible"* whilst in turn the consumer must notify the organiser or retailer of any decision she makes as a result of being told of the alterations *"as soon as possible"*. No doubt satisfaction of these requirements is to be judged on the

---

[62] [2004] 22nd October, Leeds County Court (Unreported).

particular facts pertaining to individual packages and consumers in accordance with what can reasonably be expected of a particular organiser and a particular consumer in all the circumstances of the case. In *Jervis v Kuoni Travel Limited*[63] the consumers were notified only 5 days before departure on their honeymoon that the resort island off the coast of Thailand which they had booked was closed for refurbishment and they were offered an alternative, smaller island which alternative they felt they had to accept. Notwithstanding the lateness of the notification (the letter of notification was dated some 16 days before it was received by the consumers) and the fact that it is difficult to believe that the tour operator would not have known of the closure of an entire island resort a long time in advance of the holiday season, the circumstances in which the consumers were notified does not seem to have been the subject of any criticism by the trial judge.[64] However, the absence of any criticism regarding the lateness of notification is probably closely linked to the judge's conclusion that (sports facilities apart) the differences between the two island resorts was minimal.[65]

For organisers, it is submitted, the following factors will have an impact on whether the consumer has been notified as quickly as possible.

- the date on which the organiser first learnt that significant alterations to an essential term would be necessary;[66]

- the date on which the organiser first knew that such alteration would be necessary;

- the nature and complexity of the alterations of which notification is required;

- the proximity of the date of departure;

- the identity of the consumer and the ease with which communications can be transmitted to that consumer (*e.g.* has the consumer got access to a fax machine or e-mail; or is all communication by post through a small local travel agency).

---

[63] [1998] CLY 3733.
[64] The consumers won in part for other reasons, namely the lack of sports facilities on the alternative resort island.
[65] And therefore the change did not represent a significant alteration in an essential term.
[66] The fact that significant alterations to an essential term might become necessary does not seem to trigger any obligation to warn consumers. See e.g. *Hayes v Airtours PLC* [2001] CLY 4283 a case where 2 days before departure to the Caribbean Airtours had information that hurricane Georges was devastating parts of the region but were unable reasonably to predict that it would hit the Dominican Republic where the consumers were destined.

For consumers the following factors are likely to play a part in any decision on whether notification of their decision to the organiser has been made as soon as possible.

- the nature of the alterations made and their relative significance to the package as a whole taking into account the requirements of that consumer;

- the number of other beneficiaries of the contract who may have to be contacted and consulted;

- the proximity of the date of departure; the diligence with which the organiser has acted when constrained to make the alterations;

- the means of communication available to the consumer;

- any commercial, travel or business experience of the consumer which may make decision-making more straightforward and communication easier.

Consumer Choice

The purpose of notification is so that the consumer may make an informed choice as to whether to withdraw from the contract without penalty or accept (or one might add negotiate) variations to the original contract. In *Crump v Inspirations East Limited*[67] the consumers were despatched to an unfinished 5-star hotel in Goa that was subject to 24 hour-a-day building works. The tour operator knew perfectly well of this problem before the consumers departed but apparently gave no notification of such a significant alteration to an essential term of the holiday contract.[68] The failure to give notification is a breach of regulation 12.[69] Reference might also be made to *Hook v First Choice Holidays and Flights Limited* and *Graham v First Choice Holidays and Flights Limited*[70] similar cases where the tour operator was aware before departure that the hotel booked by the consumers was not available and they had to be accommodated in alternatives of inferior quality.[71] In *Josephs v Sunworld Limited*[72] the tour operator was found to be

---

[67] [1998] CLY 1427.

[68] Namely an implied term to the effect that the facilities would be of a reasonable standard commensurate with the hotel's rating.

[69] The conditions at the hotel would also constitute an improper performance of the contract pursuant to regulation 15.

[70] [1998] CLY 1426 and 1771 respectively.

[71] See Grant & Mason page 330 where it is suggested that the trial judge in *Hook* stated that the consumers had been entitled to be properly informed of their choices under regulation 12 and that this should entail the tour operator setting out the regulation 12 rights in writing when such significant changes had to be made.

[72] [1998] CLY 3734.

in breach of several obligations arising under the PTR 1992. The consumers booked a villa holiday in the Algarve only to find on arrival they had been allocated terraced accommodation in a different resort a 15 minute drive from where they had booked. The facilities they discovered on arrival were cramped and broken-down. It was held that there had been a significant alteration to an essential term of the contract in moving the family to another resort and that no regulation 12 notice had been given, which amongst other reasons entitled the family to compensation.

Once given the necessary notice under regulation 12(a) the consumer is obliged to inform the organiser or the retailer of his decision "as soon as possible". Presumably a failure to inform the organiser or retailer as soon as possible (in all the circumstances) would deprive the consumer of the right to withdraw from the contract or demand alternative options pursuant to regulation 13.

Regulation 13

This is twinned with regulation 12.

> "13.-(1) The terms set out in paragraphs (2) and (3) below are implied in every contract and apply where the consumer withdraws from the contract pursuant to the term implied in it by virtue of regulation 12(a), or where the organiser, for any reason other than the fault of the consumer, cancels the package before the agreed date of departure.
>
> (2) The consumer is entitled —
>
> (a) to take a substitute package of equivalent or superior quality if the other party to the contract is able to offer such a substitute; or
>
> (b) to take a substitute package of lower quality if the other party to the contract is able to offer him one and to recover from the organiser the difference in price between the price of the package purchased and that of the substitute package; or
>
> (c) to have repaid to him as soon as possible all the monies paid by him under the contract.
>
> (3) The consumer is entitled, if appropriate, to be compensated by the organiser for non-performance of the contract except where —
>
> (a) the package is cancelled because the number of persons who agree to take it is less than the minimum number required and the consumer is informed of the cancellation, in writing, within the period indicated in the description of the package; or
>
> (b) the package is cancelled by reason of unusual and unforeseeable circumstances beyond the control of the party by whom this exception is pleaded, the consequences of which could not have been avoided even if all due care had been exercised.

(4) Overbooking shall not be regarded as a circumstance falling within the provisions of sub-paragraph (b) of paragraph (3) above."

The remedies available to the consumer under regulation 13 apply *only* when the organiser has been constrained to alter significantly an essential term of the contract within the meaning of regulation 12. It is not every alteration in the minutiae of the contract that entitles the consumer to withdraw from the contract or deploy the regulation 13 alternatives.

First and foremost regulation 13 applies where an *essential* term of the contract has been altered *significantly* and that the organiser has been constrained to make the alteration within the meaning of regulation 12. However, the compulsory options to be given to the consumer apply whenever the organiser cancels the package before the agreed date of departure (unless sit be the consumer's fault). Where these conditions are satisfied the consumer has choices as a result of the terms implied by regulation 13(2). Where the regulation 12 conditions are satisfied and the consumer withdraws from the original contract or the organiser cancels the package the consumer has three choices.

1. To take an equal or better package (and if either is more expensive then the consumer is likely to have to pay the balance).

2. To take a substitute of a lower standard and recover from the organiser the difference in the price.

3. Claim a full refund of the price paid for the original package.

Much of the consumer's theoretical choice or options depend on timely notice by the organiser that an essential term is to be altered significantly or the package otherwise cancelled. If the notification is not timely, there is a grave risk that the consumer will feel obliged to take the first and only alternative offer the organiser proposes.[73] Few consumers on the eve of a holiday would resist the first "equivalent" or roughly equivalent offer that came along. Whilst some consumers in these circumstances would be minded to submit a claim on their return if the equivalent package was questionable, many would not. The choices provided by regulation 13 are, therefore, to some extent illusory. The consumer's rights of action are also limited by the fact, as discussed above, that there is room for debate as to what will constitute a significant alteration and an essential term.

Equivalent or superior quality

Whether the alternative offered to the consumer is of equivalent or superior value must be a question of fact and degree to be judged on the particular

---

[73] As in *Jervis* and *Hook* (above).

facts of individual cases. Factors that should be taken into account, however, would include the following:

- the brochure price;

- the official standard of the accommodation and transport facilities;

- the destination or the type of destination (*e.g.* beach resort or city centre);[74]

- where the original package or destination offered unique opportunities for sight-seeing, and whether the alternative offers similar opportunities both in terms of quality and type.

This part of regulation 13 is most likely to give rise to problems in "quality" cases, where a superior graded hotel is substituted for one that turns out to be decidedly mundane, because it will be borne in mind that the options available to the consumer under regulation 13(2) are entirely the consumer's. If an alternative is offered by the organiser, but the alternative involves another destination, it is always open to the consumer to refuse the offer and claim a refund instead. Where, for example, an historical tour of Egypt is substituted for an historical tour of the sites of ancient Greece, the consumer will be poorly placed to argue that there was inadequate equivalence (all other things being equal) because that is the sort of decision that could easily have been taken at the time the offer of the substitute was made. Once the consumer has elected to take the substitute offered, it is unlikely that the same consumer could cogently maintain that the substitute was not "equivalent" at least in terms of destination. As already noted, quality complaints about the standard of substitute accommodation, are a different matter altogether. Even in terms of quality, however, there are problems in judging the equivalence of the substitute offered to the consumer. Is a five-star modern tower-block hotel in the same city "equivalent" to or superior to a four-star deluxe hotel of traditional character in the same city? It is suggested that in this example the consumer is faced with a similar difficulty. If it was thought the substitute was not "equivalent" or "superior", why would the consumer have accepted the offer? It is only when the alternative supplied is not a five-star standard hotel at all, or where the alternative is promoted as "traditional" whereas it is actually modern, that the consumer is reasonably placed to complain about the equivalence of the accommodation supplied. However, in these last situations, the consumer probably does not need the intervention of regulation 13 at all. The choice

---

[74] Comparison, however, above of Jervis (no significant alteration on a change between 2 Thai resort islands with similar characteristics) and Graham (significant alteration where a business hotel 80km distant from the substituted holiday hotel) illustrates the danger of being too prescriptive in listing factors that are considered likely to be determinative.

has been made; the description is either misleading, or there has been a breach on the part of the other party to the contract to supply a five-star or traditional type hotel-in which case the consumer has a direct right of action against the other party to the contract without troubling with regulation 13.

If the other party ... is able to offer

The consumer's right to take an equivalent or superior package can only be exercised where the organiser is able to offer one. Does this mean that the organiser *must* make an equivalent offer where an alternative package is available? In practice most *would* make such an offer because it is not in most commercial organisers' interests to disappoint their consumers. Packages of equivalent or superior quality will probably be easier to spot in practice than they are to define with precision in the abstract.

Payment for superior quality

Regulation 13(2)(a) is silent as to whether the organiser is entitled to charge for a package of superior quality when it is offered to the consumer as a substitute. There are respectable arguments both ways. The fact that the regulation itself makes no provision for extra payment by the consumer indicates that no charge for superior quality can be levied by the organiser. On the other hand, may it not be that an organiser is not "able" to offer a superior quality package unless the consumer is prepared to pay for the superior element? It is suggested that the "no payment" construction is the more likely because the same form of words is used in regulation 13(2)(b) where the organiser is "able" to offer a package of inferior quality. In this situation, the organiser can hardly maintain that he is *economically* unable to offer the substitute. In the interests of consistency between subparagraphs (1) and (2) of Regulation 13 it is thought likely that the organiser's "ability" will be judged in terms of what is practicable, not what is economic or profitable. If this is right and the organiser is not *entitled* to charge a supplement for a superior package under regulation 13(2)(a) it seems likely that whether a substitute package of "equivalent ... quality" will invariably be judged by the price. No doubt in circumstances where the organiser indicates that there is a supplement for a package of superior quality, the consumer will either pay the supplement[75] or simply exercise the right to a refund and compensation under regulation 13(2)(c) and 13(3).

---

[75] And in so doing effectively make a new contract with the organiser.

Lower quality

Where the organiser is practically "able" to offer a substitute package of lower quality, then the consumer is entitled to a refund of the difference in price between the original contract and the substitute. This price difference is likely to be judged on brochure prices.

Is there a hierarchy of offers?

Where there are available alternatives of superior, equivalent and lower quality, does the organiser have to offer the superior package before or simultaneously with the equivalent or lower quality substitute? The answer to this must be that if the construction of regulation 13(2)(a) suggested above is correct, the alternatives must either be offered simultaneously if the organiser is "able" to offer them, or the superior alternative must be offered first before the equivalent or lower quality package. This is because if the superior package is available, the organiser is "able" to offer it, and as has been seen it is likely that the requirement to make the offer of something that is available, is compulsory.

Compensation

The last option available to the consumer is simply to accept a refund of the package price irrespective of whether substitute packages of superior, equivalent or lower quality are offered. Is the holiday consumer entitled to additional compensation for example for loss of enjoyment?

The wording of regulation 13(3) opens up the possibility of compensation *additional* to the provision of an alternative (even a superior or equivalent alternative) package. It certainly gives rise to scope for argument that the consumer who takes a lower quality package or accepts a refund under regulation 13(2)(c) is entitled to more than just a refund. Regulation 13 (3) provides that the consumer is entitled to compensation *if appropriate*. That is, the consumer can additionally claim compensation on top of a complete or partial refund where a loss is proved to have arisen as a result of the organiser's alteration of an essential term in the original contract. This could arise where, for example, the consumer had notified the organiser in advance of a particular feature of the original package that was of importance, but that feature was missing from the alternative package accepted by the consumer under regulation 13(2)(a) or (b). The consumer's enjoyment of the package may be compromised to a more radical extent than can be measured by package price comparisons: to take a mundane example, the consumer who books a sea view may be offered and may accept equivalent accommodation in a hotel of equal quality very nearby with views over the street. The price difference (if any) should be refunded to him, but in addition that consumer has lost the additional benefit of the sea view he had

booked and should be compensated for that loss. Another example might be
this. An elderly consumer agrees to accept an alternative package of
equivalent quality at the same price that involves an escorted tour of the
Republic of China. The alternative tour, however, omits the Great Wall and
the terracotta warriors at Xian. It may have been a lifelong ambition of the
consumer to visit such sites, and he may reasonably conclude that he is
unlikely to revisit this part of the world again. Despite the equivalence of the
alternative package in price, standard and all other places visited the
consumer has lost something significant that should be the subject of
compensation under regulation 13(3).

A consumer's loss of enjoyment may not be regarded as significant however,
or he may fail reasonably to mitigate that loss of enjoyment, if a reasonably
suitable substitute package is offered but refused.

Robson v Thomson Holidays Limited[76] illustrates how regulations 12 and 13
can operate in the consumer's favour. In May 2000 the claimant booked a
package skiing holiday to Colorado, USA for herself and a small party of
family and friends (5 persons in total). She was adamant that direct flights to
and from Denver airport should be provided and this was a component of
the holiday that she booked. The tour operator confirmed on more than one
occasion, in response to the claimant's enquiries, that direct flights to and
from Denver had been booked. Shortly before the holiday was scheduled to
commence the defendant informed the claimant that there had been a
mistake and that the flights to and from Denver would be *indirect*
(necessitating a change of aircraft at an intermediate US airport). Direct
flights were not available as a result of a straightforward administrative error
on the part of the defendant. The change of plane would not have any
appreciable impact upon the skiing time in resort or on the length of the
holiday. The claimant treated the breach of contract (admitted by the
defendant) as a repudiatory breach. She received a full refund of the cost of
the holiday (being over £5,000). She then went ahead and reserved club class
seats for herself and her party on a BA flight direct to Denver. She gave the
defendant the option of paying for these seats for herself and the party. The
defendant refused so the claimant then booked the seats, paid for them and,
on her return from holiday, sued for the cost of the seats and ancillary
expenses (an additional sum of £10,000 above and beyond the refund). The
undisputed evidence was that the club class seats were the only seats
available on a direct flight to and from Denver that conformed to the
claimant's existing holiday dates.

---

[76] Unreported – 5 April 2002 Luton County Court.

The claimant was awarded the sum of £10,000 odd at first instance. The defendant appealed. The grounds of appeal were based, among other things, on the following. First, the District Judge's error in holding that the claimant had mitigated her loss. Secondly, the District Judge's identification of a direct flight to the United States of America as the loss to be mitigated. Third, and by extension, the District Judge's decision that the claimant had acted reasonably and proportionately in purchasing club class seats to the USA and in, effectively, assembling her own holiday.

On appeal it was held that the District Judge had correctly identified one stop (direct) flights to Denver, USA as the loss to be mitigated. It was held that there was no alternative solution available to the claimant for mitigation of this loss, save for the self-help remedy adopted by her. On acceptance of a repudiatory breach the claimant was entitled to a refund and compensation or to reinstatement of the holiday which the defendant was unable to provide. If the claimant had settled for the first option then the compensation for loss of enjoyment would, the Judge stated, have approached £10,000 in any event. The claimant chose to accept the refund and to reinstate the holiday. The cost of doing so was, it was held on appeal, reasonably recoverable. The learned Judge tested his conclusions by reference to regulation 13 of the PTR 1992. If regulation 12(a) of the regulations had permitted reference to regulation 13 (there was no evidence at first instance on which this conclusion might be based in the present case) then regulation 13(2)(a) entitled the claimant to choose a substitute package of equivalent or superior quality. The judge concluded that the claimant had put together a substitute package of superior quality which could have been offered to her by the defendant and for which she was entitled to be compensated.

Exceptions to additional compensation

The consumer's right to compensation over and above the right to a complete or partial refund does not arise where the original package is cancelled due to lack of support, where a minimum number of bookings is a pre-condition of the package taking place. In this situation, a refund in whole or in part (depending on whether a substitute is offered and accepted), is all the consumer can hope for.

Similarly, where the package is called off due to unusual and unforeseeable circumstances beyond the control of the [organiser] the consequences of which could not have been avoided even if all due care had been taken no right to *additional* compensation arises.[77] This phrase will be considered in detail in the context of regulation 15. Suffice it to say for the time being that

---

[77] This may have implications for Regulation 14 – as to which see further below.

it presents the organiser or the other party to the contract with a high threshold to cross. Regulation 13(3)(b) is likely to apply most often where the organiser has to call-off a package due to some natural or manmade disaster or civil unrest. Regulation 13(4) makes it clear that overbooking shall not be regarded as an unusual and unforeseeable circumstance. Accordingly, where the changes in the package are made by the organiser because of overbooking at package accommodation (whoever may be responsible for the overbooking), the consumer not only has the choice of options listed in subparagraph (2), but is also entitled (if appropriate) to compensation under regulation 13(3) where a loss arising from the change in plans can be demonstrated — whether that be a loss of bargain, loss of enjoyment or the incurring of additional expenses.

Regulation 14

Regulations 12 and 13 are concerned with significant alterations to essential terms before departure. Regulation 14 is concerned with changes that arise *after* departure. There is a significant degree of overlap, however, between regulations 12, 13, 15 and regulation 14. The "changes" after departure include those circumstances where a significant proportion of the package services is simply *not provided* which is likely to give rise to a regulation 15 liability in any event.[78]

> 14(1) The terms set out in paragraphs (2) and (3) below are implied in every contract and apply where, after departure, a significant proportion of the services contracted for is not provided, or the organiser becomes aware that he will be unable to procure a significant proportion of the services to be provided.
>
> (2) The organiser will make suitable alternative arrangements, at no extra cost to the consumer, for the continuation of the package and will, where appropriate, compensate the consumer for the difference between the services to be supplied under the contract and those supplied.
>
> (3) If it is impossible to make arrangements as described in paragraph (2), or these are not accepted by the consumer for good reasons, the organiser will, where appropriate, provide the consumer with equivalent transport back to the place of departure or to another place to which the consumer has agreed and will, where appropriate, compensate the consumer.

Regulation 14 again employs the device of implying terms into the package contract, this time to cover those occasions where the organiser fails to or is unable to provide or procure a significant proportion of the package services

---

[78] See in particular cases like *Josephs v Sunworld Limited* [1998] CLY 3734 where the court treated regulations 14 and 15 as interchangeable where the standard of villa provided fell lamentably short of that advertised.

once the package is already underway. However, regulation 14 is not limited in any way to "essential" terms but rather concerns itself with the measurement of "significant" proportions of the package. Two things are worthy of note by way of introduction to regulation 14. The first is that it applies irrespective, of the cause of the inability to provide the services. The second is that it does not in itself provide the organiser with any *force majeure* defences.[79] *Whatever* the circumstances giving rise to it, wherever the organiser cannot provide or becomes aware that it cannot procure package services (once the consumer has departed) the action demanded by regulation 14 is mandatory – but the paying of *compensation* is not. The point underpinning regulation 14 (compared with the right of action for damages created by regulation 15 where there has been a failure to perform the contract, or an improper performance of the contract) is that the organiser must do something about the lack of services whilst the consumer is travelling. The intention is plainly to compel organisers to react to problems on the spot (and bring them home if necessary) rather than cross their fingers and hope that only a small proportion of their consumers will sue. In some respects it might be thought that the object of regulation 14 was to instil in organisers a proactive culture where problems arise and thus limit their exposure to non-performance damages under regulation 15.[80]

Significant proportion of the services

Before the remedies created by regulation 14 crystallise, there must be a failure or anticipated failure in respect of a *significant proportion* of the package services. What constitutes a significant proportion of the services depends on the particular facts of individual packages. It is submitted that the measure of significance is as much a matter of quality as it is quantity. An historical Nile cruise may be missing a significant proportion of the package services if the lecturer is unable to attend just as much as where the cruise boat gets stuck on the wrong side of the Esna Lock, miles north of Luxor. A Caribbean beach resort may be missing a significant proportion of services where the sea is unexpectedly infested with jelly fish. A city centre hotel may be short of a significant proportion of its services if the business centre is closed for refurbishment without prior announcement. A resort hotel may be lacking a significant proportion of its services if its swimming and leisure pools are closed due to an outbreak of cryptosporidiosis.

An example of a decision where a significant proportion of the services contracted for was not provided, is *Martin v Travel Promotions Limited*.[81]

---

[79] As compared with regulation 15(2).
[80] See also regulation 15(8).
[81] [1999] CLY 3821.

The trial judge concluded that the tour operator's inability to fly the consumers home from India on the date specified in their itinerary constituted a failure to provide a significant proportion of the contract services. The tour operator had made arrangements to fly the consumers home the following day (suitable alternative arrangements) but was obliged under regulation 14(2) to compensate them for the delay and inconvenience. What the tour operator was *not* liable for was the cost of the *first class* flights bought by the consumers for their intended date of return. Such an expense had been incurred hastily and was disproportionate to the breach of contract and was not caused by the breach. So, whilst there had been a failure to provide a significant proportion of the services, the alternative arrangements made were "suitable" and only modest compensation flowed as a result – paying for first class flights was not "appropriate".

Suitable alternative arrangements

The first demand made of the organiser under regulation 14 is that it *will* make suitable alternative arrangements. There is nothing discretionary about this. Suitable alternative arrangements *will* be made. No charge can be levied for these alternative arrangements. This begs the question as to what should be considered as "suitable" by way of the alternative arrangements — but the intention is that *something* should be done. If the alternative arrangements are not "suitable" — that is, would not be regarded as suitable by the reasonable consumer — the consumer can be transported home (but only if this is *appropriate*). In practice, if the consumer is dissatisfied with the alternative arrangements made by the organiser, and the organiser does not feel it appropriate to bring the consumer home, the consumer has two options:

- to return home under his own steam, and attempt to recover the cost afterwards; and/or

- seek compensation from the organiser under regulation 15.

To use an example given above: suppose the organiser of the Nile cruise stuck on the wrong side of the Esna Lock cannot commission an alternative boat on the right side of the lock, but instead arranges for the balance of the tour to Luxor to take place by coach. This may be the best available option for the organiser in the circumstances, but it is hardly a "suitable" alternative for the cruise. There is a world of difference between cruising the Nile to Luxor and embarking on a prolonged desert coach trip. If the organiser refuses to return the consumers to their destination, the consumers will have to seek appropriate compensation on their return home. The consumer can claim compensation under regulation 14(2) on the grounds that the alternative arrangements made were not suitable; or claim under regulation 15 on the basis that the other party to the contract has failed to perform its obligation under the regulation to provide suitable alternative arrangements or return the consumers to their point of departure. The benefit of making a claim based on regulation 14 is that unlike regulation 15, no provision is made to excuse the organiser from its obligations on the grounds that the contract services were compromised for unforeseeable or unavoidable reasons. To this extent, regulation 14 is a weapon in the consumer's armoury that appears to be underused. An example of its use can be found in *Buhus-Orwin v Costa Smerelda Holidays Limited*.[82] The consumer was promised a villa of "opulent luxury" in Sardinia. It was rat-infested. An alternative was offered but the consumer thought it unsuitable compared to what he had been promised given that the alternative had no private pool and no garden. The family returned home at their own expense. The judge found that the tour operator was in breach of its obligations under regulation 14(2) and 14(3) and awarded the family a full refund of the holiday price plus £2,000.00 in additional compensation. An unusual decision on the obligations imposed by regulation 14 arose in *Hibbs v Thomas Cook Group Limited*.[83] Following a ferry breakdown the organiser had to change the itinerary for the last third of a 15 day tour of the Canadian Rockies. The consumer complained that the alternative arrangements were inappropriate and sued for the return of one third of the holiday price. It was held that the ferry breakdown was a *force majeure* event and that the tour operator could simply have flown the tourists home from the point at which the itinerary as originally planned became impossible. The tour operator was, apparently, under no obligation in these circumstances to put alternative arrangements in place. This decision (as reported) should be treated with caution and might be considered a lucky win for the tour operator. Alternatively, it may well be that it is best approached as a decision to the effect that the alternative arrangements made for the itinerary (under regulation 14(2)) *were* suitable and that the difference in the consumers' enjoyment of the holiday was not significant enough to warrant any additional compensation.

Where appropriate, compensate the consumer

The compensation envisaged by regulation 14(2) where suitable alternative arrangements are provided, it might be thought, is the difference between the contract price and the value of what is actually provided. Two things are worthy of note in this regard. The first is that this "difference in value" measure of damages appears, at least implicitly, to exclude the recovery of damages for disappointment and loss of enjoyment. The second is that the regulation assumes that there will be occasions when alternative arrangements are "suitable" but nonetheless of less value. It may well be,

---

[82] [2001] CLY 4279.
[83] [1999] CLY 3829.

therefore, that "suitable" in regulation 14 implies the possibility of an imperfect match between the contract services and the alternatives. This is an important point of warning for consumers inclined to take unilateral action to pay for their own return home instead of taking up the alternative offered. If the four-star hotel booked as part of the package is not available after the first night of a holiday due to a catastrophic electricity supply failure and the organiser offers a three-star hotel down the road, it is submitted that this likely to be regarded as a "suitable" if imperfect alternative.

Does regulation 14(2) envisage compensation for loss of enjoyment? The case of *Lara Tanner & Others v TUI UK Limited*[84] is illuminating. On 9 November 2001, SS *The Topaz*, a cruise liner, sailed out of Palma Majorca. The charterers were Thomson Holidays and 1,000 passengers were on board. The vessel was scheduled to visit 5 ports in the course of a cruise that would end at Palma, Majorca on 16 November 2001. The contracted amenities and services, scheduled to be available on board, were set out in the Defendant's brochure and included, among other things, open meal sittings, entertainment, 24 hour dining, table wines/draught lager/cocktails/brand name spirits, gala nights and the like. A variety of facilities were also scheduled to be available on board (eg. 3 restaurants, 4 bars, 2 lounges, discotheque, whirlpool, swimming pool, hairdresser and massage and so forth). The Claimants' enjoyment of their holidays was severely curtailed; the reason was some extremely rough weather conditions. A number of changes had to be made to the itinerary and 3 out of 5 scheduled ports of call were missed. The *Topaz* sailed through winds of force 8/9 and upwards (including some Beaufort force 12 weather off Barcelona). The Claimants were on board the *Topaz* uninterruptedly for a period of 56 hours after missing ports of call through rough weather. The rough weather also affected the amenities/services on board. A large number of passengers were violently seasick and unable to leave their berths and, during the especially rough weather, announcements were made to passengers that they should not leave their cabins unless they had a good reason for doing so.

The Lara Tanner passengers sued the tour operator for their spoilt holidays (or, at least, around 240 of them did so). The Claimants relied on two causes of action (both framed in contract): (a) the mandatory implied contractual term contained in regulation 14 of the Package Travel etc. Regulations 1992; and, alternatively, (b) breach of the implied term to exercise reasonable care and skill (derived from section 13 of the Supply of Goods and Services Act 1982) giving rise to liability on the part of the Defendant tour operator for the negligence of its suppliers, their sub-contractors, servants or agents (regulation 15(1) and (2) of the 1992 Regulations): the "*negligence*" cause of

---

[84] 18 October 2005. HHJ Karsten QC, Central London County Court – Unreported.

action. Both parties relied on expert evidence with respect to the negligence cause of action. The Claimants' case on this issue was that the severe weather conditions were clearly forecast and that the Master of the *Topaz* was negligent in sailing into a forecast force 10/11 storm on route to Barcelona. There was an additional, subsidiary, allegation that the Master had failed to make sufficient use of the vessel's stabilizers while on route to Italy at the start of the cruise. These issues were resolved in the Defendant's favour at trial (on the basis that the trial Judge was reluctant to second guess the decisions made by the Master and on the basis that he preferred the Defendant's expert evidence in any event). The Judge concluded that the Defendant had successfully drafted its booking conditions so as to reserve the right to alter the scheduled itinerary of the cruise holiday in the event of adverse weather, but had not succeeded in achieving the same result with respect to alterations made to the services/amenities on board. The judge concluded that it made no difference to the application of regulation 14 that the Defendant sought, in its booking conditions, to qualify its performance/provision of these services. Defining the circumstances in which services were to be provided did not, on a fair construction of regulation 14(1), prevent these from being *"services contracted for"*. It was accepted that regulation 14 does not require there to have been any breach of contract before its provisions take effect (it was conceded by the Defendant that regulation 15(2) had no application in the context of a case brought under regulation 14). Having reached this conclusion, the Judge decided that the cumulative effect of failing to visit 3 out 5 scheduled ports and the loss of amenities/services on board constituted a failure to provide a significant proportion of services. The Judge went on to find that, in the circumstances, the Defendant had made suitable alternative arrangements, at no extra cost to the consumer, for the continuation of the package. This left a final issue: namely, whether it was *"appropriate"*, within the meaning of regulation 14(2), to *"compensate the consumer for the difference between the services to be supplied under the contract and those supplied."* The Judge's conclusions on this issue were that it was necessary to consider the circumstances leading to the need to make suitable alternative arrangements. Here, it was adverse weather that caused the shortfall in what was promised and it was weather which occurred through no fault of the organiser of the holiday. It would be quite wrong to expect the tour operator to provide compensation in those circumstances. A person taking a cruise holiday, the Judge concluded, takes the risk of the weather conditions. The Claimants' claims were, accordingly, dismissed.

A similar result was obtained in *Crump v My Travel Plc.*[85] In this case the consumers took a package holiday in Cancun, Mexico which was severely disrupted by hurricane Emily. They sued the tour operator on the basis that they should never have been flown into Cancun in the first place. This aspect of the claim was rejected. More importantly for present purposes, they also complained that the alternative arrangements made for their accommodation during and after the hurricane struck (government provided shelters) were woefully inadequate and not suitable alternative arrangements. The limb of the claim as also rejected. The judge accepted the tour operator's contention that Emily put them in an impossible position regarding alternative arrangements. My Travel had 3,000 customers in the area & the Claimant's hotel was not fit for habitation afterwards. They looked after their clients as best they could in an extreme situation in officially sanctioned and managed shelters. What is reasonable or suitable had to be judged in context – and in this instance everyone was kept safe and returned home expeditiously. The tour operator had complied with its regulation 14 obligations and it was *not appropriate* to compensate the consumers for the curtailment of their holiday once regulation 14 was engaged due to severe adverse weather conditions. Every contractual relationship imposes benefits, burdens and risks on each party to the contract. Holiday contracts are no different, and whilst regulations step in to give consumers added protection they would not get at common law, this does not mean that a consumer's holiday contract is *risk free*. Insurance for holiday curtailment is available.

The consumer could, of course, sue for loss of enjoyment damages under regulation 15 in tandem with a claim under regulation 14(2), but it is possible that under regulation 15 the other party to the contract would be able to rely on one of the statutory *force majeure* defences. No such defence is available to the organiser under regulation 14.[86] It is submitted that damages under regulation 14 are not intended to cover loss of enjoyment. Indeed this is why, it is submitted, regulation 14 is not qualified by statutory defences. The objective of the regulations is compensate for diminished value under regulation 14 where post departure alterations have to be made, thus ensuring that any claim for loss of enjoyment is brought under regulation 15 in the context of which the organiser *can* where appropriate deploy the statutory defences if the circumstances are right. The fact that regulation 14 is not qualified by statutory defences, therefore, does not matter.

---

[85] 30 November 2006 Bow County Court – Unreported.
[86] But see *Hibbs* (above).

Return to place of departure

The organiser's obligation to return the consumer by equivalent means of transport to the place of departure arises under regulation 14(3) only where it is *impossible* to make suitable alternative arrangements, or where the arrangements are not accepted by the consumer for good reason. Even then the obligation bites only where it is "appropriate". Transport back to the place of departure by equivalent means indicates that the type and class of travel should be the same as that enjoyed by the consumer on the outward journey.

Impossibility

The organiser is relieved from the mandatory requirement to make available suitable alternative arrangements only when it is *impossible* to do so. The burden of proving this impossibility, it is suggested, must rest on the organiser. Where it proves impossible to make suitable alternative arrangements, the organiser must return the consumer to his place of departure. But how often will it be *impossible* to make suitable alternative arrangements? It may be difficult; it may be expensive; but seldom impossible — at least in the context of the majority of standard package trips. Upgrading accommodation, restaurant, sports or transport facilities may well involve the organiser in significant expenditure, but regulation 14 makes no allowance for this. However, where the organiser has the choice of upgrading the package services, or downgrading them and paying the difference in value as compensation, there is nothing in regulation 14 which suggests that the organiser must *first* try to upgrade.

Alternative not accepted

Regulation 14(3) assumes that there may be occasions when the consumer can justifiably refuse to accept the alternative arrangements even though they might objectively be considered "suitable". This is probably intended to draw a distinction between objective suitability when considered in the context of the original package contract, and subjective suitability in the context of the consumers themselves[87]. For example, an organiser may be able to arrange for a group of package tourists perfectly appropriate alternative accommodation in a hotel of equal standard and with equivalent facilities. However, the alternative hotel may involve a long climb up steep hillside steps, or may not have a lift, or there may be a busy road between

---

[87] Although not apparently a decision on regulation 14 *Forsdyke v Panorama Holiday Group Limited* [2002] CLY 2321 illustrates how a particular consumer may find alternatives reasonably unacceptable – e.g. a disabled consumer refusing an alternative hotel that was built on a hillside with difficult access.

the hotel and the beach where the original was built on the beach. Whilst, objectively speaking, there may be no material difference between the two hotels and the majority of the consumers taking the package may be entirely satisfied with the compromise, there may be an elderly or infirm couple, or a family with very young children who subjectively find the alternative far from attractive. In such circumstances it is possible to imagine accommodation that is a "suitable" alternative but which for "good reasons" is rejected by a minority of the visitors. Where "appropriate" the organiser should arrange to return the elderly infirm or young families home.

Another example of circumstances where a consumer may have "good reasons" for refusing an offer of suitable alternative arrangements is where the consumer has been given good reason to lose all confidence in the ability of the organiser to make reasonable arrangements. For example, where a number of manifestly unsuitable alternative hotels or apartments have already been tendered but rejected, or where the organiser has repeatedly tried to "fob-off" the consumer with excuses for inaction in the face of persistent or continuing accommodation or transportation difficulties.[88]

When is it appropriate?

It might not be considered "appropriate" to return the minority of consumers home, if the alternative accommodation was only needed for one or two nights whilst the original hotel was made available again, or where the return home could not be arranged due to flight schedules until a day or two before the intended date of return in the original contract. It is submitted that in practice what is "appropriate" will be measured against what is reasonable in all the circumstances, and this is likely to include consideration of the financial implications of the return journey for the organiser. If the cost of a return home is out of all proportion to the inconvenience suffered by the consumer (good reasons for disputing the suitability of the alternative arrangements notwithstanding).

Compensation under regulation 14(3)

Where the consumer is returned to the place of departure under regulation 14(3) there is an additional entitlement to compensation. Unlike regulation 14(2) the compensation is not limited or defined to any "difference" in value. It would, therefore, seem appropriate under regulation 14(3) to claim not only damages representing the value of that proportion of the package that had been curtailed by the return home, but also damages representing loss of enjoyment, disappointment and distress. The logic underlying this distinction

---

[88] See e.g. *Rhodes v Sunspot Tours Limited* [1983] CLY 984 – before the PTR 1992.

is that those consumers who have been provided with "suitable" (though cheaper) arrangements under regulation 14(2) are not likely to suffer more than minimal loss of enjoyment; whereas those for whom such alternatives have proved impossible to arrange, have lost the benefit of an enjoyable trip.

Comparing Regulations 12, 13 and 14

All of these regulations imply terms into the package contract. However, a discrepancy between them is worthy of note. The terms implied by regulation 12 apply where the organiser is constrained to make changes *before the departure*. Regulation 13 invokes remedies for the consumer where the organiser cancels the package or the consumer withdraws from the package before the date when it is due to start. Regulation 14 applies to changes *after departure*. Accordingly, whilst there is a measure of compatibility between regulations 12 and 14 which are both based on the actual departure of the consumer, regulation 13 *prima facie* only applies to cancellations or withdrawals *before the date when the package is due to start*. Regulation 13 appears, therefore, to exclude those cases where the departure is delayed and there is then a cancellation. In cases where the due date of departure or contractual date of departure has passed before the organiser cancels (*e.g.* the consumers delayed and herded together at the airport awaiting news of what is to become of their holiday at a destination affected by significant civil disturbance) the consumer it seems must resort directly to regulation 15 remedies or the common law for an appropriate remedy.[89] The pre-*actual* departure but post *contractual date* of departure cancellation is still likely to give rise to a failure in the performance of the package contract on the part of the organiser or other party to the contract under regulation 15(2) which (subject to the statutory defences) will give rise to a claim in damages. Alternatively, and at the very least, the consumer may have recourse to restitutionary remedies for the price of the holiday at common law on the basis that the consideration moving from the other party to the contract has wholly failed.

---

[89] For a more detailed discussion about some possible intricacies in these circumstances see: Kilbey (1998) ITLJ 110; Saggerson (1999) ITLJ 6.

Contrasting Regulations 12, 13 and 14

Chapter 4

LIABILITY FOR NON-PERFORMANCE

Regulations 15(1) & (2)

Introduction

This chapter is concerned with the liability of "the other party to the contract" to the consumer under regulation 15 of the PTR 1992. The liability is in respect of the proper performance of the obligations under the contract. The relevant contract is plainly the package holiday contract.[1] Regulations 15(1) and (2) are arguably responsible for the most radical shift in the consumer's favour (at least in holiday cases) in recent years (or so it has been perceived and often received in practice). In the first edition of *Travel Law and Litigation* (1996) the liability arising under regulation 15 was described as a "qualified strict liability" by which was meant that the "other party to the contract" would be liable for incidents arising in the course of the provision of package holiday services unless one of the statutory defences could be established by the defendant under regulation 15(2)(a), (b) or (c). This is how the operation of regulation 15 was commonly understood it the early days of the PTR 1992. However, this interpretation of the PTR 1992 overstates the level of consumer protection offered by the PTR 1992, as more recent case law has illustrated. It is a mistake to regard the PTR 1992 as imposing any form of strict liability across the board (at least so far as regulation 15 is concerned) and careful consideration has to be given to the nature and extent of "the obligations under the contract" in order to determine whether there has been any failure to perform or improper performance of those obligations. After all, it is impossible to determine whether there has been a "breach" of contract until one knows the nature and extent of the contractual term in issue. The regulation 15 liability is imposed on "the other party to the contract" wherever there has been a failure to perform the package contract or an improper performance of the package contract irrespective of whether such obligations are to be performed by that other party or by other suppliers of services.

A number or preliminary matters are worth emphasising.

---

[1] In regulation 2 "contract" is defined as the agreement linking the consumer to the organiser or to the retailer or both, as the case may be.

- liability under regulation 15 as we have seen is imposed on "the other party to the contract";[2]

- liability is imposed by the PTR 1992 in favour of the consumer — and the expression consumer includes "the principal contractor" as well as "other beneficiaries" and transferees;[3]

- the liability is in respect of the failure to perform or improper performance of the obligations *under the contract*. That is to say not everything that goes wrong during the course of a package holiday is to be laid at the door of the "other party to the contract";

- the regulatory liability created by regulation 15 applies irrespective of whether "the other party to the contract" itself or other suppliers of contract services actually provides or carries out the service or facility about which complaint is made.

- liability is for damage caused by either a failure to perform any part of the package holiday contract or an improper performance of any part of the contract.[4]

- such damage will often be injuries, loss of bargain and loss of enjoyment of the holiday together with any incidental or consequential loss and expense incurred as a result of the failure in the proper performance of the contract..

In short, the other party to the contract (usually a tour operator) is liable for the damage caused by the failures or improper performance not only of its own staff but of the likes of carriers and hoteliers as well as other package service providers.[5] This liability does not necessarily involve proving that the tour operator is itself at *fault* for what has gone wrong. Provided that the failure or improper performance is in respect of an obligation under the contract, the tour operator is the primary target for the consumer's recovery of damages. The intention of the regulators was clearly to provide the consumer with the most accessible target for complaints. Once the validity of the complaint is established and the operation of the statutory defences excluded, it is then up to the tour operator to seek an indemnity from the other service provider.[6] Usually the other service provider will based abroad.

It has been noted above that the attempt to describe the impact of regulation 15 as imposing a regime of qualified strict liability has been proved to have

---

[2] Regulation 15(1).
[3] Regulation 2(2).
[4] Regulation 15(2).
[5] Such as transfer coach companies or the providers of pre-arranged inclusive excursions.
[6] As expressly provided for (out of an abundance of caution) in regulation 15(1).

been misconceived. All regulation 15 appears to do is to extend the liabilities of the other party to the contract to cover the shortcomings of its agents (suppliers and subcontractors) for whom it may not have been liable under ordinary principles of the English law of contract. It might be said, therefore, that regulation 15 in respect of regulated package holidays imposes a framework of extended "vicarious" liability. In other words the other party to the contract is liable for damage caused by the failures of a wider class of persons than its employees.

Regulation 15 is so important that it is worth setting out in full. It provides as follows:

> 15.-(1) The other party to the contract is liable to the consumer for the proper performance of the obligations under the contract, irrespective of whether such obligations are to be performed by that other party or by other suppliers of services but this shall not affect any remedy or right of action which that other party may have against those other suppliers of services.

> (2) The other party to the contract is liable to the consumer for any damage caused to him by the failure to perform the contract or the improper performance of the contract unless the failure or the improper performance is due neither to any fault of that other party nor to that of another supplier of services, because —

> (a) the failures which occur in the performance of the contract are attributable to the consumer;

> (b) such failures are attributable to a third party unconnected with the provision of the services contracted for, and are unforeseeable or unavoidable; or

> (c) such failures are due to —

> (i) unusual and unforeseeable circumstances beyond the control of the party by whom this exception is pleaded, the consequences of which could not have been avoided even if all due care had been exercised; or

> (ii) an event which the other party to the contract or the supplier of services, even with all due care, could not foresee or forestall.

Framework

Determining the liability of the *other party to the contract* involves passing through several linked stages each of which is discussed in more detail below. However, the stages can be summarised in this way.

1. Was the *other party to the contract* under *any* contractual duty to the consumer?[7]

2. What was the *scope* of the duty; that is, what services, facilities or activities did the duty cover?[8] Allied to this issue is whether the party responsible for the provision of the service, facility or activity is an agent, supplier or subcontractor for whom the other party to the contract is deemed to be liable.[9]

3. What was the *content* of the duty; that is, in respect of matters within the scope of the duty what was required to be done?[10]

4. By what standard do the actions of the *other party to the contract* fall to be judged?[11]

5. Given scope, content and applicable standard has there been a breach of the duty?

6. If a *prima facie* breach of duty is identified, do the statutory defences exonerate the *other party to the contract*?

7. If not, has the breach caused any recoverable loss?

Obligations under the contract

The other party to the contract's liability is wide, but it is restricted to liability for the obligations under the contract. The contract referred to in regulation 15 of the PTR 1992 can only be the package holiday contract.[12] This important qualification is often overlooked. Claims brought under regulation 15 of the PTR 1992 are first, and only, claims *in contract* – not in tort and not for breach of statutory duty.[13] Regulation 15 does not (save in one very minor respect) create free-standing, actionable statutory duties where breach would give rise to a cause of action in damages. The one very minor respect is this. Theoretically it might be possible to characterise the statutory imposition of liability for the proper performance of the obligations under the contract as a statutory duty to accept liability for that proper

---

[7] The answer will invariably be "yes" if there is a holiday contract of any sort, but this is only the starting point.

[8] The scope of the duty is limited to matters within the holiday contract – not e.g. locally booked excursions or extras.

[9] Pursuant to PTR 1992 regulation 15(1).

[10] E.g. Is the other party required to take positive steps or only required to warn?

[11] The locally applicable standard of reasonableness or the standard imposed by uniform international regulations.

[12] See the discussion on "Excursions" in Chapter 5.

[13] *Watson v First Choice Holidays and Flights & Others* [2000] QB/APP/0031B (Unreported) James Goudie QC.

performance whatever the contract itself actually said and whoever is at fault for causing the damage. Even if this is a correct analysis, the statutory duty is only to accept liability for the performance of the obligations under the contract as a result of which one is immediately thrown back into a consideration of what those contractual obligations are. As with any conventional contractual framework it is first necessary to identify the contractual terms (the obligations under the contract) in order to determine whether there has been a breach (a failure in performance or an improper performance). It is not necessarily everything that goes wrong in the course of a package holiday that can successfully the subject of a claim against the tour operator or whoever the "other party to the contract" may be. Liability under regulation 15 must be approached in at least three stages.

However, before deciding the nature and extent of the package contract obligations, it is necessary for the consumer to determine what *type of contract* that has been concluded with "the other party".

Providers and co-ordinators

Does the "other party" make a contract with the consumer to *provide* or ensure the provision of the package obligations; or does "the other party" only contract with the consumer to act as a co-ordinator, facilitator or go-between — an "arranger" of services to be provided by others? The difference between a contract to *provide* package services and a contract merely to arrange the package services has been a matter of some controversy at common law[14] However, as far as the 1992 Regulations are concerned it is submitted that the position is now more than tolerably clear. Anyone who organises packages (otherwise than occasionally) is a regulated organiser; any seller of regulated packages is a regulated retailer; and one or other of the retailer or organiser *must* be "the other party to the contract".[15] Regulation 15 imposes liability in appropriate circumstances on "the other party to the contract". It is submitted therefore that it is immaterial whether the contract purports to be a facilitating or co-ordinating contract or a contract promising the actual provision of the services. In either case the organiser or the retailer or both will be "the other party to the contract" and liable to the consumer pursuant to regulation 15.

Strict and fault-based obligations

For what exactly is the other party to the contract liable? Even though the "other party" may contract to provide the contract services (albeit through agents, suppliers and subcontractors in many instances) is this obligation a

---

[14] Discussed at greater length in Chapter 5.
[15] As set out in regulation 2.

strict one, or is it satisfied by the exercise of reasonable care? A holiday brochure may particularise the accommodation on offer as being air-conditioned. Thus[16] it is a term of the contract or an obligation under the contract[17] that the rooms will have air-conditioning. If it emerges that the rooms are not air-conditioned after all, there has been a failure in the performance of that contractual obligation for which the "other party to the contract" must surely be liable even if every practicable precaution was taken to ensure that the hotel complied with the brochure description. The *fault* may be that of the hotelier who failed to inform the tour operator that due to refurbishment of the system the air-conditioning would be removed just prior to the relevant season, but we already know from regulation 15(1) that liability attaches to the tour operator irrespective of whether the failure is his or that of one of his suppliers. It cannot avail the tour operator to say that every reasonable step was taken to make sure as far as was practicable that the hotel implemented the services advertised. The same would apply to all advertised and promoted services and facilities. Does it make any difference that the obligation under the contract in question is an implicit one? Assume for the purposes of this discussion[18] that a court would readily imply a term into a package contract to the effect that the food served in the package holiday hotel would be fit for human consumption. There is no reason why this implied term should not carry the same weight as the express term in respect of the air-conditioning, so that if the food turned out not to be fit for human consumption and caused food poisoning, the tour operator would be liable (even though not necessarily at fault) for a breach of this implied obligation. Provision of food not fit for human consumption would thus be characterised as a failure to perform an obligation under the contract or an improper performance of such an obligation for which the tour operator would have pay compensation in respect of the resulting damage.

In practice a contract for the provision of a package holiday contains a variety of terms. Some of these terms give rise to strict obligations, others only require that reasonable care should be exercised by whosoever delivers the service.[19] By way of summary the following examples are offered.

Where a package holiday contract includes promises that certain facilities will be available (e.g. air-conditioning, swimming pools and other leisure facilities and restaurants) or is based on specific descriptions (e.g. the hotel is 1.5 kilometres from the beach or 500 metres from the town centre) we encounter obligations that are strict in character. The obligation on the other party to the

---

[16] As provided for in regulation 6
[17] An implied warranty in the language of regulation 6.
[18] An this is not a ludicrous assumption.
[19] For an exposition of a contrary view see McDonald *Revisiting Organiser Liability Under The Package Travel Directive* [2003] ITLJ 131.

contract is to provide the services or facilities as described. The liability of the other party to the contract is comparable to a sale of goods liability if the wrong goods are supplied. No amount of protest to the effect that the tour operator did whatever was humanly possible to check its facts and correctly describe the facilities in the holiday particulars will give rise to a defence in an action for breach of contract if one of the advertised facilities is not available after all.[20] The closure of the swimming pool,[21] for example, means that there has been a failure to perform that term in the holiday contract that made provision for a swimming pool. The other party to the contract will be strictly liable for the damage[22] that results. The possible number of similar examples is legion. *Forsdyke v Panorama Holiday Group Ltd*[23] will serve as an illustration. F, booked a last minute one week package holiday at a hotel for himself and his wife, sought damages from P. At the time of booking, F had specifically requested a hotel with a heated swimming pool because his wife was about to have a hip operation and wished to exercise in warm water. In addition, F's wife was able to enjoy only a restricted range of holiday activities because of her arthritic hip. It was accepted by P that it was a term of the contract that the pool be heated. The pool in fact was cold. It was held, giving judgment for F that the principal purpose of the holiday was to swim in a heated pool and that was made clear to P at the time of booking. In the circumstances, F was entitled to damages for diminution in the value of the holiday assessed at £450.00 equivalent to approximately two thirds of the value of the holiday, and £75.00 for the distress suffered.

On the other hand there will be obligations under the holiday contract that demand no more than that the other party to the contract or its suppliers will exercise reasonable skill and care. A hotel will often have gardens and footpaths. Just as a Highway Authority is not expected to ensure that public pavements are as smooth as bowling greens[24] so a hotelier cannot be expected to warrant that every inch of footpath or terracing on the premises is similarly flat and blemish-free. In *Thompson v Thomson Holidays*[25] The Claimant fell into a sunken footbath adjacent to a garden path at her package holiday Hotel in Cyprus and claimed damages for her injuries (a fractured foot). This was a classic PTR 1992 Regulation 15 case. The footbath, she claimed, was at the side of a narrow pathway and was a hazardous obstruction. There should have been a warning about it in the form of a clearly delineated boundary, fencing. Better still the footbath should have been moved to a safe place out of the way of

---

[20] But one of the statutory defences under regulation 15 might still be invoked.
[21] Unless it be in the ordinary course of maintenance and cleaning for short periods.
[22] Loss of bargain and loss of enjoyment and the cost of going elsewhere for a poll of similar standard.
[23] 13 November 2001 (Kingston CC) Unreported.
[24] *Littler v Liverpool Corporation* [1968] 2 All ER 343.
[25] 17 January 2005 (Stoke on Trent CC) Unreported.

pedestrians walking round the hotel gardens. The Claimant relied on the fact that the footbath was subsequently moved and also on the fact that at the time of the incident it was very sunny to the extent that the footbath and adjacent pavement appeared to be the same colour and one was not distinguishable from another. The Claimant's case was supported by expert evidence from a Cypriot lawyer to the effect that the standard of care for hoteliers in Cyprus was the same as under the Occupier's Liability Act 1957 in England.

The Defendant contended that the sunken footbath had been in situ for many years without incident and the fact that the footbath had been moved as a result of the Claimant's accident such 20-20 hindsight did not render the hotel or the tour operator in breach of any duty to the Claimant. The Defendant relied on the dicta in *Staples v West Dorset District Council*[26] to the effect that a responsible occupier is not to be criticised for taking action after an accident to avoid a recurrence. The Defendant also relied on expert evidence from an engineer. The Engineer concluded that by Cypriot regulation the Hotel was obliged to have a footbath and that the one in question is consistent with others he had observed in Cyprus and that Cypriot Regulations in respect of such facilities did not impose any requirements on occupiers as to size, depth, configuration, colour or design of such a footbath or its positioning. The judge concluded that the accident occurred because the Claimant was not looking where she was going - this had been an isolated incident. Furthermore, although it was correct to look at the general Occupiers' Liability standard of care that standard had to be approached in the context of what was both required and conventional in Cyprus by the regulations. As the regulations demanded that there be a footbath and the evidence was that this footbath was in keeping with local customs, neither the positioning nor construction constituted any breach of duty on the part of the Defendant or the Hotel. Finally, there was no obligation on the Hotel or the Defendant to issue warnings about such incidental property features that form part and parcel of many holiday resort hotels. Judgment was given for the Defendant.

The holiday contract obligation, it is submitted, is an obligation to the effect that reasonable care will be exercised by those in charge of the operation of the hotel in the maintenance and repair of the paths and terraces. The exercise of reasonable care would usually involve the implementation of a reasonable system of repair and maintenance which standard is unlikely to demand that every blemish is eradicated. What reasonable care demands in all the circumstances will depend largely on whether the defect amounts to a dangerous hazard, and this in turn may depend in part on whereabouts in the hotel grounds the problem arises, for what period it has existed and whether it has been reported or ought to have been identified by the hotel's routine

---

[26] (1995) PIQR at P445.

inspection system. It is worth pointing out that the burden of proving a failure on the part of the hotelier to exercise reason skill and care[27] would be on the claimant. Accordingly, to succeed against a tour operator for a failure to exercise reasonable care in the maintenance of the grounds on the part of a hotelier (which would constitute an improper performance of the package holiday contract) one would be deploying familiar principles[28] derived from routine highways and occupiers' liability cases. The difference is that the foundation of the allegation of improper performance cannot arise out of the Highways Act 1980 or the Occupiers' Liability Act 1957. To a limited extent, therefore, one could paraphrase the liability arising under regulation 15 as the liability of the other party to the contract for the "negligence" of its suppliers and subcontractors even though one must remember that the liability of the "other party" is a liability in contract for the "negligence" of another, the tour operator's liability is not itself a liability in tort. All that is likely to be required of the occupier of an hotel would be that reasonable care was exercised in maintaining and repairing the fabric of the buildings and grounds or maintaining and cleaning facilities such as swimming pools. Without proof of "fault" against the service provider there is no improper performance of the holiday contract and, therefore, no liability of the tour operator either.

It is not always obvious, however, whether an obligation to provide a holiday service or facility falls to be considered as a "strict" obligation or a "reasonable care" obligation. Returning to the food hygiene example given above[29], the implied obligation under the package contract was described as being an obligation to provide food that is fit for human consumption. Is this the position? The obligation may be one that only requires that reasonable and appropriate steps will be taken by the relevant service provider to maintain the food storage and preparation systems in a reasonable and hygienic condition. Few, if any, catering systems (however impressive) are capable of guaranteeing freedom from food poisoning. Indeed the fact that consumers get food poisoning as a result of eating at their resort may not even presumptively demonstrate that there is a flaw in the food preparation systems employed at the resort. All that can be required of any catering establishment is that a proper hygiene protocol is devised and implemented. Thus it would not be the mere

---

[27] For which the other party to the contract would be liable under regulation 15(2).

[28] *James v Preseli Pembrokeshire District Council* [1992] PIQR 114.

[29] See *Pelling* [2000] ITLJ 7 where a case is made for considering the supply of food as part of a package holiday contract as the *transfer of goods* within the meaning of section 4 of the Supply of Goods and Services Act 1982 thus rendering the hotelier and tour operator liable where the food turns out to be not of satisfactory quality irrespective of any fault. See also *Lockett v Charles* [1938] 4 All ER 170 for a domestic application of this principle and *Martin v Thomson Tour Operations Ltd.* [1999] CLY 3831 for a travel related cryptosporidium infection case allegedly caused by food or water- where the duty in respect of the supply of refreshments was qualified as being one of reasonable care.

fact that a consumer had contracted food poisoning that gave rise to a tour operator's liability,[30] but that the hotel had failed to devise and implement a reasonable food hygiene protocol. Where a specific pathogen is implicated in the cause of the consumer's illness and that pathogen can be eradicated by reasonable food hygiene (such as the killing of salmonella in chicken by appropriately thorough cooking) it is likely that the consumer will have at least a prima facie claim to the extent that an evidential burden will fall on the Defendant to demonstrate that reasonable care in and about the food preparation was exercised. This is not likely to be easy where the guilty pathogen survives in undercooked food. On the other hand where even impeccable food hygiene does not necessarily kill the guilty pathogen[31] the consumer may encounter some difficulty in demonstrating that it is poor food hygiene that has caused the illness. Nonetheless, if the facts demonstrate that a particular service provider has been responsible for poor hygiene the service provider's argument that even good hygiene may not have eradicated the pathogen is likely to be treated with some judicial scepticism. The basic principle remains, however. It is submitted that in food poisoning and other illness-related claims[32] it is necessary for the Claimant to prove that there has been a failure to exercise reasonable care on the part of the service provider and/or the tour operator.[33] It may well be that the content of the duty to exercise reasonable care is such that in the provision of food and other hygiene-related services demands a greater degree of reasonable care (on the basis that the more perilous the activity, the more care is required in the implementation of reasonable hygiene systems) – but nonetheless, the liability of the provider and the tour operator are not "strict".

The same could be said of other maintenance and safety procedures. Providers or suppliers such as coach companies must take reasonable steps to ensure that their vehicles are properly maintained and serviced to minimise the risk of accidents, breakdowns and delays. No coach company can guarantee that its vehicles will never break down; no hotelier could possibly warrant that its lifts would never go out of commission due to unforeseen technical breakdown.

The importance of the distinction between contractual obligations of the "strict" and "reasonable care" sort has been recognised by the courts. *Hone v Going Places Leisure Travel Limited*[34] is an example.

---

[30] *Martin* (above).
[31] As may occur with *staphylococcus aureus*.
[32] Cryptosporidium outbreaks in hotel pools and Legionnaires' disease being two common examples.
[33] See Prager: *The Standard of Care in Food Poisoning Cases* [2008] ITLJ 26 and *Kempson v First Choice Holidays & Flights Ltd*. Birmingham CC Unreported 26 May 2006.
[34] [2001] EWCA CIV 947.

The claimant booked a package holiday to Turkey using the defendant's Teletext service for himself and his family. All went well until the return journey. However, a short time into the return flight from coastal Turkey to Manchester the aircraft was diverted to Istanbul due to a bomb scare on board the aircraft. Passengers were told to prepare for an emergency landing. The aircraft landed at Istanbul far form any terminal buildings and passengers were required to disembark via inflated chutes. The Claimant left the aircraft via the chute on the port side and as he descended he noticed that a "huge" lady weighing about 25 stones was stuck at the bottom. He collided with her and his wife coming down the chute behind him struck Mr. Hone in the back as a result of which he sustained serious spinal injuries. He sued the defendant (the "other party to the contract")[35] and alleged that there was inadequate supervision of the evacuation and no proper instructions given as to the use of the chute. It was contended in addition on his behalf that regulation 15 of the PTR 1992 imposed an "absolute" liability on the other party to the contract rendering the defendant liable for the injuries sustained. Therefore, Mr. Hone's case was put on the basis that either as a result of the fault of those managing the aircraft or because liability under the PTR 1992 was "absolute", he should be entitled to recover damages.

Douglas Brown J. at first instance[36] dismissed the claim. He said this as regards strict liability:

> In both the House of Commons and the House of Lords, government ministers used the same language: 'Regulation 15 is important and makes the organiser or possibly in certain circumstances the retailer, strictly liable for the performance of the contract'. If that was the objective of the regulations in their draughtsmanship the object has not been achieved. Much clearer words would be required to impose strict liability in all circumstances on organisers and retailers.

Mr. Hone could not succeed without proof of a failure to perform or improper performance of the obligations under the holiday contract and the relevant obligation was that reasonable care would be exercised. In other words Mr. Hone had to prove that someone was at fault for whom the defendant was, in law, responsible. The judge said: "... the claimant has wholly failed to establish that this accident was anyone's fault. Before criticising employees of an airline in respect of failure arising in an emergency crash I would need to know much more than I am told in the evidence in this case." The essence of the problem for Mr. Hone was that there was no expert evidence from the claimant to the effect that the evacuation procedure fell short of that to be reasonably expected on board an aircraft of the relevant type. The judge concluded: "It is not sufficient...to look at this on the basis of common sense. Common sense is all very well, but in dealing with safety precautions and manning in aircraft, there must be some standard set either by the employer, or by authority or both and the claimant has wholly failed to satisfy the burden which is on him, or proving his case in this regard."

In the course of his judgment Douglas Brown J. drew an intriguing and workable distinction between "improper performance" under regulation 15(2) which would relate to the "reasonable care" terms of the contract and a "failure" to perform the contract which would relate to the "strict" liability terms of the holiday contract. One improperly performs the contract where there is a failure to exercise reasonable skill and care whereas one fails to perform an obligation under the contract where a promised facility or service is simply not delivered.

The case reached the Court of Appeal on the issue of whether the PTR 1992 imposed strict liability as contended at first instance. The appeal was dismissed. Longmore LJ said:[37]

> In the absence of any contrary intention, the normal implication will be that the service contracted for will be rendered with reasonable skill and care. Of course, absolute obligations may be assumed. If the brochure or advertisement ... promises a swimming pool, it will be a term of the contract that a swimming pool will be provided. But in the absence of express wording, there would not be an absolute obligation, for example, to ensure that the holiday-maker catches no infection while swimming in the swimming pool. The obligation assumed will be that reasonable skill and care will be taken to ensure that the pool is free from infection. A similar term will be implied in relation to transportation in the absence of any express wording viz. that reasonable skill and care will be exercised.

So consideration of the tour operator's liability proceeds as follows on the basis of *Hone*.[38] Where food poisoning occurs, or an infection or injury is sustained in a swimming pool as a result of, say, broken tiles, or there is tripping or slipping on hotel premises or a transfer coach beaks down causing an accident or delay, the tour operator (the "other party to the contract") will only be liable where a failure to exercise reasonable care is proved against the supplier of the service responsible. Once the fault of the supplier is proved, the other party to the contract is irredeemably liable for that fault unless one of the statutory defences can be invoked. No liability

---

[37] Judgment paragraph 12.
[38] See also *Codd v Thomson Tour Operations Limited* [2000] CA B2/1999/1321 paragraph 24 where Swinton Thomas LJ noted in the context of an allegedly defective hotel lift: *"This is not a case in which ... it is appropriate to say that the hotel or the tour operator is liable for this accident without proof of negligence."*

attaches to the tour operator or the other party to the package contract unless fault is first proved against the supplier or subcontractor which fault leads to some failure of the holiday contract or constitutes an improper performance of it.

The counter-argument against this mixed regime of fault-based and strict liability suggests that the *only* exonerating circumstances available to the other party to the contract are those specified in the statutory defences set out in regulations 15(2) (a) to (c). The argument is to the effect that if the tour operator cannot show that the failure in contractual performance was *because* of an event canvassed in the statutory defences then strict liability for the failure in the performance inexorably followed irrespective of fault on anybody's part.

Whatever might have been the conventional wisdom when the PTR 1992 were first introduced, it is submitted that this counter-argument is now unsustainable. The opening words of regulation 15(1) are sufficient to put paid to any such reasoning. *"The other party to the contract is liable to the consumer for the proper performance of the obligations under the contract."* Without identifying the content of the obligations under the contract, it is impossible to know whether there has been a proper performance of them. When one considers that some of the obligations demand strict compliance and others merely the exercise of reasonable care, and given that the PTR 1992 says nothing at all in this context about the content of the package holiday contract, it becomes obvious that in many instances the consumer must prove some fault on the part of the service provider in order to render the other party to the contract liable for an improper performance. This reinforces the proposition referred to above. Namely that package holiday cases (whether involving damages for injuries or otherwise) are first and only claims in *contract*. In some, fault must be proved as in a conventional action based in "negligence", in others, no fault is necessary.

Before turning to consider the *standards* applicable in determining whether fault has been proved, and before turning to consider what, if any, role is left to the statutory defences under regulation 15(2) it is worth considering some of the different types of contractual obligation that arise in package holidays cases. In anticipation of this brief look at different sorts of contractual obligations the most important of all is worthy of emphasis. This is the "Acceptance of Liability Clause".

It is very common indeed to find in the small print of any holiday brochure a provision along the following lines (although there are many variants).

> We accept liability for the proper performance of our contract with you and in the event that the services we have promised to supply fall below a reasonable standard we will pay you compensation. In the event that you or any member of your party suffers death, injury or illness as a result of the

negligence of ourselves, our employees or any of our suppliers, subcontractors or agents we will pay you compensation in accordance with English law.

Another variant is:

We expect all our suppliers to carry out their functions and supply their services properly. If they do not and their fault results in any damage to you we will accept responsibility and pay you compensation.

What "properly" means involves consideration of two linked factors. First, the nature of the duty itself (does the obligation demand strict performance for it to be done "properly" as with the supply of the advertised accommodation, or does it merely require the exercise or reasonable care to ensure the accommodation is reasonably safe?). Secondly, by what *standard* is the obligation to be judged.[39]

Such brochure clauses are always worth close consideration. First, because where they apply to a holiday contract one may wonder whether it is worth relying on the PTR 1992 at all.[40] Secondly, when printed in a brochure the clause is will apply to *all* holidays supplied to which the brochure conditions apply whether or not the arrangements are regulated package holidays. In other words the blanket application of the clause extends to non-regulated holidays[41] as well - which is a real bonus for the consumer. Thirdly, it is not unknown for such clauses to be drafted in a way that goes further than would liability under regulation 15 of the PTR 1992. Examples that include wording such as "If you are injured *whilst on holiday* we agree to pay you compensation[42]....". Being injured *whilst* on holiday is not *at all* the same as being injured as a result of some improper performance of the obligations under the package holiday contract. Fourthly, depending on the drafting of the brochure clause the tour operator may (wittingly or otherwise) accept liability for ancillary service providers (such as organisers of excursions) which services would not ordinarily be obligations under the package holiday contract within the meaning of the PTR 1992.

Different types of obligation

It will be remembered that a regulated "package" is the pre-arranged combination of qualifying services sold or offered for sale at an inclusive

---

[39] As to which see further below.
[40] If a clause states baldly that the other party to the contract accepts liability for the negligence of hoteliers and negligence can be proved the claim would be simply couched as claim for damages under the contract itself regardless of the PTR 1992.
[41] For example, accommodation only holidays.
[42] This is an example from a real brochure disseminated by an independent tour operator.

price.[43] Therefore, any service or facility that falls outside the scope of this definition cannot form part of the obligations under the package contract and any failure in respect of such collateral or extra services cannot be brought within the regulatory framework created by regulation 15.[44]

Package contract obligations are likely to fall into the following categories.

1. Express liability terms

These are the booking condition terms referred to above whereby the tour operator accepts liability for the negligence, fault or some other behaviour causing damage on the part of holiday service providers, whether limited to package holiday service providers or not. Strictly speaking the tour operator's liability under such clauses is purely contractual and not dependant on regulation 15 of the PTR 1992. The obligation undertaken by the other party to the contract is to accept liability to pay compensation in any of the circumstances envisaged by the contractual clause. The question is, therefore, has an event occurred on the proper construction of the liability clause, which triggers the tour operator's contractual acceptance of liability? A claim brought under such a clause is not technically even a claim for breach of contract[45] but a claim for compensation *pursuant* to the contract. These "acceptance of liability" clauses can themselves give rise to subsidiary problems. If the tour operator accepts liability to pay compensation when the negligence of hotel staff causes injury, and the holiday contract is subject to English law,[46] is the triggering event to be assessed under common law principles of negligence and English standards of care applied, or by some other standard, such as the standard applicable in the place where the harmful event takes place? Usually, the tour operator will have made express provision for this also by stating in its brochure conditions that the applicable standard is the standard of the place where the triggering event has occurred.

2. Express supervisory terms

These include the terms by which the other party to the contract promises that it will closely monitor the performance of its agents, suppliers and subcontractors. This category could also include the common promise made by tour operators to the effect that all its service

---

[43] Regulation 2.
[44] The classic example of such a collateral service would be an excursion booked and paid for after the consumer arrives in resort.
[45] Save to the extent that the tour operator refused to pay.
[46] As will invariably be the case by express choice or otherwise.

providers are reputable and efficient businesses and/or licensed or accredited by all relevant local authorities. It is submitted that such clauses are something of a hostage to fortune for tour operators. What amounts to "closely monitoring" is inevitably a matter of fact and degree, but plainly such terms create much leverage for findings of fact that adequate monitoring would have forestalled the event about which the consumer subsequently complains. It should be noted once again that clauses of this type give rise to *direct* claims for breach of contract against the other party and the liability of the other party in respect of breaches of such clauses does not necessarily have to be based on regulation 15 of the PTR 1992. Another direct contractual obligation frequently assumed by tour operators is reflected in the promise that great care has been taken in the *selection* of the accommodation or other services and facilities forming part of the package holiday. This is another hostage to fortune, even if "great" care is construed as being no more than such reasonable care as was required in all the circumstances. Tour operators make a further rod for their own backs when adding to their small print a promise to the effect that great care has been taken to select "the best" available facilities whether generally or in a given price range. In practice one rarely finds breach of these "supervisory" promises relied on by claimants. This is almost certainly the result of a number of factors. First, it is surprisingly still rare for package holiday claims to be based on the contents of the contractual promises found in the holiday brochure. Secondly, where breach of such a clause is likely to be made out there will usually also be a claim based improper performance by an agent, supplier or subcontractor under regulation 15 for which the tour operator will be liable in any event.

3. Express descriptive terms

The *express descriptive* terms of the package contract are usually to be found in the package holiday brochure, promotional material, the confirmation invoice and any fair trading charter ("small print") disseminated by the tour operator.

For example, the brochure particulars might describe a hotel as being 30 minutes', transfer from the airport; having air-conditioned bedrooms, with sea view balconies and an Olympic-sized swimming pool. The fair trading charter promises that all local safety standards have been complied with in the provision of package facilities. In fact, the rooms assigned to the consumers are at the rear of the hotel, they are not air-conditioned, the balconies do not have a sea view and the swimming pool is a kidney-shaped splash pool that breaches local rules on depth markings. Transfer from the airport takes two hours on reasonably clear roads. In each of these respects there has been a failure to perform the obligations under the package contract for which the other party to the contract will be liable regardless of the amount of care taken in the preparation of the brochure, and irrespective of the extent to which (*if at all*) the other party to the contract was let down by the hotel proprietor in the assignment of rooms to its guests.

4. Hybrid terms

These are particularly virulent in holiday contracts. For example, accommodation (or indeed any other service or facility) may be described as being of a luxury standard. But what *is* the standard of luxury accommodation? One might confidently speculate at the extreme end of the scale that a luxury villa would be rat-free.[47] The promise that the accommodation would be "luxury" is an express term of the holiday contract, but the extent to which the promise is alleged to be unfulfilled will often mean implying from the context[48] what was reasonably to be expected. The provision of a villa that is rat infested would be a breach of the express term of the holiday contract to provide luxury accommodation but the boundaries of what luxury connotes is implicit.[49] Does a luxury coach necessarily offer more leg room than an ordinary coach? How appetising does "gourmet" food have to be? How badly does one have to interfere with a "spectacular" view before breaching the contract?

5. Implied descriptive terms

Terms or promises to be *implied*[50] from photographs or other information printed in a brochure or other sales or advertising material which can reasonably be attributed to the specific package in question, or can reasonably be attributed to a class of packages offered by the tour operator, or to all of their packages advertised.

The part of a brochure promoting holiday villas in, say, France may be prefaced with a large photograph of rolling countryside in which picturesque villas are depicted nestling on the tranquil hillsides. On arrival the consumer discovers that whilst the standard of the villa is otherwise than described in the brochure, it is part of a small town housing estate nowhere near the hillside shown in the picture. In this example the picture may be sufficiently proximate to the particulars of

---

[47] *Buhus-Orwin v Costa Smeralda Holidays Ltd.* [2001] CLY 4279.
[48] Including price, location, type of holiday or activity.
[49] It would be unusual to find a contractual term explicitly promising rat-free accommodation
[50] The courts are quite ready to imply terms into holiday contracts notwithstanding regulation 9(1)(b) of the PTR 1992 which states that all the terms of the contract should be set out in writing.

the villas in the brochure to give rise to the conclusion that it formed part of the promotional material from which the reasonable consumer could properly assume that the picture was intended to be associated with the villas advertised. If the court was satisfied that the picture was indeed so associated with the villa descriptions as to amount to "particulars" of the villas in the brochure, the provision of the housing estate villa would be an improper performance of the package contract for which the other party to the contract would be liable regardless of how much care and attention went into the preparation of the brochure. In other words, the tour operator could not escape liability on the grounds that the photograph was misplaced by the publisher of the brochure and that the tour operator was without fault in the creation of the impression that the photograph was closely associated with the accommodation offered.

6. Terms implied by the 1992 Regulations.

Regulation 14 provides a good example. It implies[51] a term into every package contract to the effect (amongst other things) that where, after departure, a significant proportion of the services contracted for is not provided, the organiser *will* make suitable alternative arrangements. So, if the beach and water sports facilities of a resort hotel are closed for refurbishment during the course of a package and the tour operator does nothing about it (such as making available the facilities at the neighbouring hotel), there will be a failure in the performance of the package contract for which the tour operator is liable, regardless of whether the tour operator knew about the planned refurbishment. The absence of fault on the part of the tour operator plays no part in assessing whether there has been a failure in the performance of the contract.

The PTR 1992 also makes provision for other implied terms. Regulation 10 implies into every contract a term permitting the consumer to transfer the booking to another in certain circumstances. Regulations 12 and 13 imply terms relating to significant alterations to contract terms and withdrawal from the contract in certain circumstances and the consumer's options where a withdrawal takes place. The "particulars" in a brochure are deemed to be implied warranties by virtue of regulation 6

7. Terms to be implied by law irrespective of the Regulations

These are terms requiring the exercise by service providers and suppliers of reasonable care in the adoption of good practice in terms of, for

---

[51] This also appears to pay little heed to regulation 9(1)(b).

example, hygiene or safety.[52] Put another way, there is an implied term of the holiday contract that reasonable care *will be exercised* by whoever provides the service.[53] This category of implied term given the effect of regulation 15 of the PTR 1992 is analogous to a non-delegable duty imposed on the other party to the contract.

It is not difficult to imagine a court implying a term into many package contracts to the effect that restaurant and kitchen facilities would be operated and maintained to a standard commensurate with the standard of accommodation promoted by the tour operator in its brochure, and that the premises of the accommodation would be kept and maintained to such a standard as to keep consumers reasonably free from obvious risk of personal injury. The mere fact that a consumer contracts food poisoning as a result of eating in the hotel restaurant, or slips and falls on a marble surface staircase, does not necessarily mean that there has been failure in the performance of the contract or an improper performance of the package contract. If the consumer is poisoned because the hotelier fails to maintain hygiene standards commensurate with the standard of the accommodation (fails, for example, to keep a reasonably hygienic kitchen), or if the hotelier adopts an unreasonable cleaning or maintenance programme which renders the marble surface wet and slippery, then the fault of the hotelier (or other relevant service provider, supplier or subcontractor) will be attributed to the tour operator or other party to the contract. The tour operator's ordinary vicarious liability for the faults of its employees is *extended* to its independent subcontractors — but the liability is still based on a finding of fault on the supplier's part. If it could not be shown that there was anything wrong with the standard of hygiene in the hotel kitchens or the cleaning and maintenance system adopted by the hotelier, the tour operator should not be held accountable for the illness or accident in the absence of fault on anyone's part. This limitation on the scope of the tour operator's liability is not the result of the statutory defences (of which more in due course). The limit on the tour operator's liability arises because there has been no failure in the performance or improper performance of the package contract in the first place. The contractual obligation was to the effect that reasonable care would be taken to observe good practice in food hygiene or property maintenance. Where it is not shown that there has been a lapse of good practice or a failure in the exercise of reasonable care on the part of the supplier, then there is

---

[52] Context is everything – see *Williams v First Choice Holidays & Flights Ltd.* [2001] CLY 4282 where at a Greek "plate smashing event" reasonable care did not require the organiser to provide paper or plastic plates.
[53] *Wong Mee Wan v Kwan Kin Travel Services Ltd.* [1996] 1 WLR 38.

no breach of the package contract, and nothing for which the tour operator ought to be held liable. Many consumers would no doubt like to think that the transport provided for them would be safe. However, it is submitted that this is not quite the term that a court is likely to imply into the package contract. The implied term may well be that the driver of any transport would exercise reasonable skill and care in driving the transfer coach. If an accident occurred between the airport and the hotel due to the fault of a negligent third party driver and through no fault of the transfer coach driver, it is unlikely that there has been any improper performance of the package contract. The transfer driver has exercised all reasonable skill and care. The accident was not his fault. There is, therefore, no fault to be attributed by regulation 15 to the tour operator.[54]

8. Terms implied by law to the effect that the other party to the contract itself will exercise reasonable care

The implied terms considered above to the effect that reasonable skill and care *will be exercised* irrespective of who delivers the service, are different from implied terms demanding that the tour operator *itself* exercises reasonable skill and care. A breach of this implied term gives rise to a direct liability on the part of the tour operator not merely a liability under the PTR 1992 for some improper performance of the holiday contract on the part of some third party supplier. This species of implied term would include the duty to warn[55] of known dangers the consumer was likely to encounter at or in the vicinity of any package facility delivered. It may extend[56] as far as an implied duty to provide information about appropriate medical services, or even a list of "dos and don'ts" in certain destinations. Such a direct implied duty almost certainly extends to checking that excursions sold by the tour operator's representative in resort are going to be supplied by reasonable operators and to a reasonable and safe standard. An implied duty to monitor the place of contractual performance would also be readily implied.[57] For example, consumers may be sold package tours to a Mediterranean hotel which looks pretty from the outside and even at a first glance inside, but where it emerges as the season progresses that the sanitation is increasingly dangerous and foul smelling due to complacency on the part

---

[54] See *Hone v Going Places Leisure Travel Ltd.* – above.
[55] *Spencer v Cosmos* [1994] CA - Unreported - no duty to warn of risks of "mugging" in the Algarve. A duty to warn only arises where there is a particular danger of a "marked character" to *tourists* over and above that to the general population.
[56] The limits of these direct implied contractual duties have yet to be tested in this jurisdiction.
[57] In so far as there was no express promise to this effect in the brochure conditions.

of the hotel management, high staff turnover, or the sale of the property into new ownership. In this example there may well be a variety of breaches of both express and implied terms within the package contract, but the example also illustrates an additional contractual term which the courts are likely to be willing to imply in order to give effect to the presumed common intention of the parties, namely, that the other party to the contract will exercise such care as is reasonable in all the circumstances to ensure that the accommodation it allocates to its customers remains as described to them, and reasonably fit for human habitation. If the tour operator fails to notice through its local representatives or through a failure to respond to consumer complaints, that the hotel has seriously deteriorated since the beginning of the season, a breach of this implied term is likely to be made out. That is, it is not enough for the other party to the contract (particularly when that other party is a commercial tour operator) simply to assume that in the middle or the end of the season all will be as it was at the beginning. This obligation too only demands the taking of reasonable steps (this time on the part of the tour operator directly) and the institution of a reasonable system of inspection and monitoring of the accommodation allocated to consumers on the part of the tour operator. This obligation is one that is often over-stated in cases brought by consumers. Wherever an accident befalls a consumer as a result of some operational problem at a hotel – such as a trip hazard - one often finds it alleged that the tour operator should have inspected and monitored the accommodation so to spot the fault and either prevented it from happening or ordered its correction before the accident occurred. Where this general supervisory duty has a more realistic application is perhaps where there have been previous accidents or illnesses in respect of which the tour operator or its local representatives have failed to take any action to ensure there is no repetition or recurrence.

Summary

The other party to the contract is liable under the PTR 1992 for *proper performance*. The proper performance in question is the performance of the *obligations under the contract*. The nature of the obligations under the contract are many and various. Some obligations are strict, but other obligations are fault based. Some absolutely require the provision of some service or facility, others require only that due care is exercised and reasonable skill is brought to bear in the provision of a service or facility. It remains of vital importance in deciding whether regulation 15 attaches liability to the tour operator, to consider what precisely it is that the other party to the contract has agreed to supply either itself or through the agency of other suppliers or subcontractors.

Latent Defect

It probably goes without saying that where an alleged improper performance or failure to exercise reasonable care is said to have caused an accident (or some other failure in the holiday contract) liability will not be established if it emerges that the cause of the problem was a latent defect that reasonable care could not have identified. It might be considered that liability in respect of latent defects would be excused under the statutory defences[58] but in fact, where the contractual obligation is to the effect that reasonable care will be exercised in the provision of facilities and services the scheme of regulation 15 liability means that in cases of latent defect there is simply no improper performance of the holiday contract in the first place. Consider the case of *Barlow v Thomson Holidays Ltd.*[59] The Claimant claimed damages from the Defendant tour operator as a result of suffering injuries caused by an apparently malfunctioning automatic sliding door at her package holiday hotel (Hotel Venus in Benidorm) in 2002. As she walked through the door which had opened for her, it suddenly closed on her knocking her to the ground. She fractured her right wrist and suffered various other associated injuries. It was alleged that the tour operator and the hotel had failed to maintain or service the door properly and that these failings constituted negligence and an improper performance of the holiday contract. The judge ruled in the tour operator's favour essentially on the following grounds. There had been no pre-existing problem with these doors. Clearly they went wrong, but automatic equipment does from time to time without there being any fault on the part of a hotelier or tour operator. The problem was not known about and there was no reason to think that a problem would develop. Expert engineering evidence had concluded:

> Faults in these types of systems tend to occur without prior warning or manifestation of the condition. Where there is an intermittent fault, these are difficult to detect due to the lack of regular repeatability ...

In *Moncrieff v Cosmos*[60] a married couple were on an extended winter holiday in Cyprus. On day 26 whilst in the restaurant of their hotel a section of the ceiling collapsed some tiles hitting Mr. Moncrieff and the consequences allegedly causing Mrs. Moncrieff post traumatic stress disorder. The claim proceeded against the tour operator on the basis that there was a form of strict liability in that the premises were not safe and also on a res ipsa loquitur basis that this sort of incident does not occur without there being a rebuttable presumption actionable negligence. However, in

---

[58] As to which see further below.
[59] 1 & 2 October 2005 (Liverpool CC) Unreported.
[60] 6 October 2006 (Swansea CC) Unreported.

giving judgment for the tour operator the judge concluded that the flaw in the ceiling that had given rise to what had been a very limited and non-structural collapse had been a problem probably caused originally in 1998 by local earthquakes and had been latent since then to the extent that no amount of inspections would have identified the problem.

A latent defect in the mast of an excursion yacht was the subject matter of unsuccessful action brought by Mrs. Jay against TUI UK Ltd when it broke and fell on her head.[61] The issues in this action were complex and arose out of express contractual terms between the tour operator and the injured claimant. However, the judge concluded on the facts that no reasonable yacht surveyor could have been expected to identify the latent defect in the mast that caused it to fall and injure Mrs. Jay. Accordingly there was no liability on the tour operator even if one assumed that the contractual liability clause in the holiday contract was one imposing strict liability subject to exoneration of the tour operator proved that all reasonable precautions had been taken to avoid the problem.

Scope of the Package Holiday Contract

It has already been noted that however one characterises the nature of the other party to the contract's liability under regulation 15 of the PTR 1992, such liability can only relate to improper performance or failure to perform obligations under the package holiday contract. Not everything that the consumer does or buys whilst on holiday is done or bought within the framework of the obligations under the package holiday contract. The most obvious example of additional or extraneous services arises in the context of excursions booked and paid for once the consumer arrives at the holiday destination. Excursions are dealt with separately in Chapter 5. An excursion is not usually part of the package holiday and it is not usually provided under the package holiday contract.

Excursions aside it is not always self-evident where the package holiday services and facilities begin and end. It is likely that any service or facility included on the tour operator's confirmation invoice will be regarded as falling within the ambit of the package holiday. Even so, precisely where those named services and facilities begin and end can be the subject of some debate. It is submitted that if the consumer is supplied with hotel accommodation as part of a package holiday, the hotel itself is clearly something for which the tour operator is likely to responsible under PTR 1992 regulation 15. But what facilities and services make up the hotel?[62]

[61] 26 October 2007 QBD Bristol reported on *lawtel*.
[62] See also Chapter 1 on the definitions of the regulated package contract components.

Jones v Sunworld[3] is a useful example of marginal facilities. In 1998, the claimant ('J') and her husband had decided to spend their honeymoon on a holiday resort of Fun Island in the Maldives run by Sunworld Ltd ('S Ltd'). J brought an action for damages for nervous shock and post traumatic stress disorder arising out of the accidental death of her husband. She contended that her husband had drowned in a lagoon while wading in shallow water when he experienced a ten foot drop. S Ltd denied that the drop had been that big. J had claimed that the pool was a hazard and that S Ltd had been under an implied contractual duty to use reasonable care and skill to warn her and her husband about it. The hotel was advertised in the holiday brochure as being one that had the advantage of the lagoon and that the lagoon gave relatively straightforward access on foot to a neighbouring, uninhabited island. She argued that if an appropriate warning had been given her husband would not have been surprised upon encountering deep water. Contractual services provided by the tour operator should have extended to taking steps to ensure that the accommodation and facilities (including the lagoon) at Fun Island had been such that guests could stay there and use the facilities in reasonable safety. In the event that the failure to warn was a failure on the part of the resort rather than S Ltd, the claimant relied on regulation 15 of the PTR 1992.

However, Field J. held that S Ltd was not liable for the death of J's husband. The pool in which J's husband had drowned was between six and eight feet deep. The deceased had found himself unexpectedly in water up to his chin which caused him to panic and drown. The Judge concluded that a beach or lagoon *could* be within a holiday package depending on the wording of the holiday brochure and the package's terms and conditions, and so within the compass of the tour operator's and the resort's duty to warn. *Although the lagoon was a natural phenomenon it was an integral part of the resort over which the resort owners had legal control.* It would have been artificial on the facts of this case to draw a line in the sand along the water's edge and say that the landward area was within the resort and hence within the package but the lagoon marked off as it was from the open sea by the house reef, was not part of the resort and was therefore outside the package. However, it did not follow that S Ltd had been obliged to assess the safety of the lagoon in the same manner as it had assessed the safety of the buildings and paved areas on the island which could relatively easily be inspected for such things as fire safety and other risks to physical harm. Given the nature and size of the lagoon, S Ltd was not under any obligation to survey it to discover features that might have a bearing on its safety. S Ltd was obliged to undertake a visual inspection of the lagoon although there was no evidence

---

[63] [2003] EWHC 591 (QB) - Field J.

that S Ltd had carried this out. However, even if an inspection had been undertaken, the physical characteristics of the lagoon and the pools within it had *not* been such that S Ltd should have warned J and her husband about them. S Ltd had not given the impression that guests could wade anywhere in the lagoon. Adult holiday makers had to be taken to know that the seabed was not even.

Jones emphasizes two important points. The first is that the package services may not end at the hotel door, or at the beach front. The second is that in each case where a service or facility is held to be within the package services or facilities, it is necessary to consider the nature and extent of the duty owed by either the tour operator or the local service provider in order that there be proper performance of the package holiday contract. In *Jones* (on the assumption that the lagoon was part of the "package") the nature of the duty on the hotel was limited. There was certainly no duty to eradicate unevenness on the seabed (and such was never contended) and no duty to undertake a survey of the seabed in places likely to be used by visitors to the hotel. In so far as there was a duty at all it was alleged that the duty was a duty to *warn* visitors about possible dangers. On the facts, however, the Judge concluded that even in the context of such a limited duty the sort of hole that caused the deceased's drowning was not such that any warning should have been issued by the hotel given that the hotel had not created the impression that consumers were free to roam at will across the lagoon and given that adults should be alert to such unevenness in any event.[64]

In *Martens v Thomson Tour Operations Limited*[65] a consumer, in the dead of night, fell down an unguarded well right outside the gate of his holiday campsite. The well itself had nothing to do with the campsite and was not managed or controlled by the campsite operators (agents of the tour operator). Nonetheless, the court held that it constituted a known hazard of a serious nature in hours of darkness that was likely to be encountered by tourists staying at the campsite and in respect of which a warning should have been issued. This claimant succeeded, but on the basis that he had consumed at least 21 Bacardis and Coke at the time of the accident (as illustrated on his bar bill for the evening) his award was subject to a 60% deduction for contributory negligence. The decision was not based on any finding that the well formed part of the package services or facilities but rather on the fact that as the well was so dangerous and so close to the entrance as to be likely to be a significant hazard to visitors, that proper

---

[64] See also *Djengiz v Thomson Holidays Ltd.* [2000] CLY 4038 where the tour operator was liable for the failure of the hotel to ensure that a beach volleyball court used by the hotel for organised games on a public beach was in a reasonable condition.
[65] Unreported – Mayor's & City of London County Court May 2000.

performance of the holiday contract demanded the issue of a warning. The obligations under the package holiday contract might, in similar cases, therefore, include an obligation to issue warnings in respect of significant and dangerous hazards off holiday premises that the consumer is likely to encounter.

It is submitted that the need for such warnings as part of the proper performance of the holiday contract is likely to be limited to circumstances where the hazard is serious and the risk of significant injury is manifest to the hotelier or tour operator[66] but may not be obvious to the visitor. Based on the facts in *Jones* and *Martens* it is doubtful that the courts would regard as realistic any contention that a hotelier should warn consumers about routine pavement trip hazards on the public road outside the hotel.[67]

What is clear, however, is that however widely the package contract facilities and services are drawn in respect of the other party to the contract's regulatory liability for proper performance it is *only* contractual obligations for which the tour operator is liable. This may seem obvious but it is surprisingly easy to overlook the fact that certain services provided even by the tour operator *whilst the consumer is on holiday* are not part of the pre-arranged combination of components sold or offered for sale at an inclusive price in the United Kingdom.[68] Two skiing holiday case illustrate the point. They are *Gallagher v Airtours Plc*[69] and *Rochead v Airtours Holidays Ltd.*[70]

Both cases[71] involved package holidays regulated by the PTR 1992. In each case the defendant sold to the consumer international air transport, coach transfers to and from the resort airport and accommodation. All this was clearly evidenced by their respective confirmation invoices. In each case, whilst on the transfer bus from airport to resort the consumers were sold ski-packs. That is, they chose from a list of items offered by the tour operator, the things they needed or wanted in order to go skiing whilst on their skiing holiday. In *Gallagher* the claimant's pack included skiing lessons, the *Rochead* pack included the provision of skis. Both claimants paid for their ski-packs whilst on board the transfer coach. It follows from this arrangement that in neither case did the ski-pack form part of the package holiday contract. Neither pack was part of the pre-arranged combination of components sold at an inclusive price in the United Kingdom. Accordingly,

---

[66] The analogous issue of dangerous destinations is discussed in Chapter 5.
[67] See also *Beales v Airtours Plc* [1996] ITLJ 167 – and PTR regulation 15(2)(b).
[68] Regulation 2.
[69] [2000] CLY 4280.
[70] Unreported – Central London County Court June 2000.
[71] For a more detailed discussion of excursions and more case examples see Chapter 5.

when Mrs. Gallagher was seriously injured as a result of skiing off a precipice and (she alleged) the negligence if her ski instructor[72] she could not make out a claim under the PTR 1992. Certainly she was *on* a package holiday supplied by the defendant at the time of the accident but her accident was not caused due to any improper performance of *that* package holiday contract. Ms. Rochead was negligently fitted with skis she had rented as part of her ski-pack which caused her to break her ankle when she fell on the piste. Again, the accident undoubtedly occurred whilst she was *on* her package holiday but it was not caused by anything that formed part of it so the tour operator was absolved from any responsibility for the negligence of the ski fitter.[73]

Local standards

Of equal importance in judging whether there has been a failure to perform or an improper performance of the package contract where "reasonable care" is in issue concerns the standards by which reasonable care falls to be judged. Standards of reasonable care are not universal.

The following type of clause (with many variants) is commonplace in tour operators' brochures.

> Standards of hygiene and safety vary dramatically throughout the destinations included in this brochure and should not be compared with the standards applicable in the United Kingdom. Tourism is new to many destinations in this brochure and whilst we use our best endeavours to ensure that the standards of transport, accommodation, food and hygiene offered to consumers comply with local laws, regulations and standards, these standards will often be lower than you would expect to find at home. We will monitor the standards of the services offered by our suppliers even though we have no direct control over them, but their standards must be judged in accordance with the standards and customs in the country where they are based and the services are to be provided.

In those instances where the obligation under the package contract is to the effect that reasonable care will be exercised by the supplier or service provider, by what standards apply? It is very common in practice to find consumers relying on current British standards and producing evidence from British quality or safety experts about the "kite mark" or general standard of

---

[72] An allegation that was not made out because she led no evidence of what standard was to be expected locally.

[73] See also *Costelloe v Thomson Tour Operations Ltd* [2000] CLY 4046 where the claimant sued over a ski-lift accident but failed because his ski-lift pass had been sold to him separately from his package holiday so the PTR 1992 did not apply to impose any liability on the tour operator. There was no breach of the package holiday contract.

equipment of facilities that would apply in the United Kingdom. Here are a few common examples:

- glass patio doors should have toughened glass and/or warning stickers;

- lifts must have an interior emergency bell or telephone;

- glasses and bottles should not be served or allowed in the vicinity of swimming pools; swimming pools must have specific depth markings and warning notices;

- stones steps or stairs should have non-slip treads or nosings; passenger-carrying vehicles should have seat belts;

- tents and caravans should have a certain level of fire resistance;

- cold and raw meats should be stored and displayed in separate cooler units.

- balcony walls or rails must be of a certain critical height.

Failure in respect of any of the above safety or hygiene features would usually, in this country, be conclusive of liability either by operation of specific statutory regulations or by the operation of general laws such as the Occupiers' Liability Act 1957. However, standards in other places differ. In Western Europe different standards (which are not necessarily inferior) apply. In some parts of the world standards may be distinctly inferior — but does the tour operator owe a duty to its customers to offer higher standards than those of the local norm?

In *Wilson v Best Travel*[74] the consumer went on a package holiday organised by Best Travel. In the course of his holiday he fell through a glass balcony door. The glass in the door was not toughened in the way that would have been expected in the United Kingdom, but there was nothing wrong with it when judged by the local, Greek standard. It was pleaded on behalf of the claimant that there was an implied term in the holiday contract[75] to the effect that the accommodation would be reasonably safe. Phillips J. rejected this contention and instead held that the tour operator's duty was to exercise reasonable care in the selection of accommodation for its clientele and that this duty was discharged if the accommodation complied with the local standards.

He said:

> Save where uniform international regulations apply, there are bound to be differences in the safety standards applied in respect of many hazards of

---

[74] [1993] 1 All ER 353.
[75] Which predated the PTR 1992.

modern life between one country and another. All civilised countries attempt to cater for those hazards by imposing mandatory regulations. The duty of care of the tour operator is likely to extend to checking that local safety regulations are complied with. Provided that they are, I do not consider that the tour operator owes a duty to boycott a hotel because of the absence of some safety feature which would be found in an English hotel unless the absence of such a feature might lead a reasonable holidaymaker to decline to take a holiday at the hotel in question.

He went on to say in effect that had this particular hotel been removed from the tour operator's portfolio because of the lack of strengthened glass in the balcony doors, then much of the holiday accommodation available in Greece would also have had to be withdrawn. *Wilson v Best Travel* still represents the law today, even though the 1992 Regulations have since come into force. There is nothing in the 1992 Regulations which addresses the *standard* of care required of "the other party to the contract" where the obligations under the contract are obligations that require the exercise of reasonable care. The standard of care is, of course, "reasonable" care as a matter of English law[76], but the crucial question in most cases will be: *what does reasonableness demand* in all the circumstances of a particular package contract; or alternatively, what does the other party have to do in order to exercise reasonable care? The answer to this question will, in most cases, be that the duty to exercise reasonable care is discharged where local standards are complied with. It follows that where local standards or regulations have been complied with, there will have been no failure to perform the obligations under the package contract, no improper performance of those obligations and, thus, no liability to the consumer.

Wilson was a case to which the law prior to the implementation of the PTR 1992 applied. A number of cases have confirmed that the position remains the same post-PTR 1992. In *Codd v Thomson Tour Operations Limited*[77] the Court of Appeal affirmed the general principle. The Claimant damaged his hand in the door of a lift in a Spanish hotel which stuck and then slammed shut without warning. There had been no previous incidents and there were no subsequent problems with the lift or the doors. The lift would not have complied with appropriate regulatory standards in the United Kingdom (or so it was assumed) but it was properly designed had been properly maintained and serviced in accordance with prevailing Spanish standards at that time. Swinton Thomas LJ said:[78]

> [The claimant] then submits that the judge was in error in not applying the British standards to this particular lift ... with the result that there was a

---

[76] The law applicable to any case brought under the PTR 1992 will be English law
[77] [2000] CA B2/1999/1321
[78] At paragraph 22 et seq.

breach of duty according to English law. That is not the correct approach to a case such as this where an accident occurred in a foreign country. The law of this country is applied to the case as to the establishing of negligence, but there is no requirement that a hotel, for example, in Majorca is obliged to comply with British safety standards.

The decision in *Wilson* was cited with approval. Both *Wilson* and *Codd* have been followed in many first instance decisions. In *Logue v Flying Colours Limited*[79] the claimant claimed damages for injuries to his arm and shoulder as a result of his falling through a glass balcony door at his Spanish holiday hotel. He complained that the glass should have been toughened and that it should have had warning stickers on it. Spanish building and hotel regulations demanded neither. Here it was contended on behalf of the claimant that regulation 15 of the PTR 1992 extended the tour operator's liability beyond its ordinary contractual liabilities and that the regulation itself established a regime under which the court was equipped to assess whether the standard of the facilities provided was proper and appropriate. The Judge[80] rejected any such notion. The submission of the claimant simply ignored the wording of regulation 15, namely, that the *"other party to the contract is liable for the proper performance of the obligations under the contract"*. The contractual obligation was that reasonable care would be exercised for the Claimant's safety and on the basis of *Wilson* the duty was discharged by selecting properties that complied with local safety standards.

A further example is to be found in *Johnson v First Choice Holidays and Flights Ltd.*[81] The Claimant and his wife embarked on a 14 night package holiday at the RIU Ventura-Maxorata Hotel, Fuerteventura, Spain in September 2001. The accident happened on 11 September 2001 when the Claimant slipped and fell while leaving the Hotel swimming pool. The Claimant slipped at a location close to the edge of the swimming pool. The Claimant commenced an action against the Defendant by reference to the PTR 1992. The key allegations of negligence centred on four discrete matters. First, that the area adjacent to the swimming pool where the Claimant slipped was wet. Second, that there was no warning notice to the effect that the area adjacent to the swimming pool was wet. Third, that there was no hand rail. Fourth, the absence of non-slip material in the construction of the swimming pool surround. The Defendant relied on evidence from an employee of the relevant Hotel group (a specialist in matters of health and safety and the assessment of risks). It was her evidence that the relevant area was safe, constructed of a non-slip substance and complied with such local standards of health and safety as were relevant. The Claimant had no expert or other

---

[79] Unreported – Central London County Court 7 March 2001.
[80] HHJ Zucker QC.
[81] Unreported – Northampton County Court 22 August 2003.

evidence as to the relevant local safety framework, nor as to the Hotelier's alleged failure to comply with the same. The claim was dismissed. The standard of care and, therefore, breach of duty was to be assessed by reference to local, Spanish, rather than British safety standards. Furthermore, the claimant had failed to discharge the burden on him to prove that the Defendant had failed to comply with the relevant local standard insofar as any of the matters about which he complained were concerned and warning notice would not have told the Claimant anything that he did not know already.[82]

Johnson draws some of the threads of this chapter together. The nature of the duty, the standard of care required and proof of breach of duty in accordance with the relevant applicable standard are all interlinked. It is a common feature of several cases[83] that the claimant has failed to produce any evidence of what the applicable safety standard or standard of reasonableness is and has equally failed to produce any evidence of in what respects the facility or service fell short of the applicable standard. Despite efforts in several of these cases to suggest that it is for the defendant (the other party to the contract) to show what the standard is and that it has been complied with, or simply to rely on the application of judicial common sense, the authorities[84] show that the burden of proving compliance does not shift to the defendant and "common sense" is not enough. There is no substitute for evidence.

Entrenchment of Local Standards

In recent years the principles derived from the decisions in *Wilson; Codd* and *Johnson* have become entrenched in a sequence of cases decided at first instance. This entrenchment can be traced to a High Court appellate decision in the cases of *Holden v First Choice & Flights Ltd.*[85] In 2002 the Claimant was involved in an accident whilst on a package holiday booked with the Defendant. She fell from the third step of a flight of stairs leading from the hotel ground floor down to the lower ground floor restaurant in the El Ksar hotel, Sousse, Tunisia, sustaining fractures to her left thumb and right wrist. In her Particulars of Claim she asserted that the accident was caused by breach of contract, negligence, and breach of the Workplace (Health, Safety and Welfare) Regulations 1992 (SI 1992/3004) and the Occupiers' Liability Act 1957 on the part of the Defendant. Essentially, she alleged that the steps were wet and slippery, and that she ought to have been informed that the

---

[82] *Staples v West Dorset District Council* [1995] PIQR P439 (CA).
[83] *Wilson, Hone, Codd, Logue and Johnson* all cited above.
[84] Particularly the passages cited from *Hone* and *Codd* above.
[85] 10th. May 2006 QBD Reported on *lawtel*.

hotel lifts provided access to the lower ground floor of the hotel, in which the restaurant was situated. The Defendant denied that English standards applied to the provision of the services under the holiday contract, and that either the Workplace Regulations or the Occupiers' Liability Act applied in Tunisia. However, it accepted that the PTR 1992 applied to the contract. At trial First Choice adduced evidence to the effect that the hotel had an appropriate cleaning system in place at the time of the accident, and that spillages were swiftly dealt with. In addition, the restaurant manager stood at the doorway of the restaurant preventing people from taking drinks into and out of the restaurant, although this was not for health and safety reasons but because drinks were more expensive in the restaurant than elsewhere in the hotel. A Recorder tried the case at first instance and found that the Defendant was in breach of its tortious duty to the Claimant. He found that Mrs. H had slipped as a result of the presence on the stairs of a colourless, odourless liquid, that the hotel was alert to the perils of people moving about with drinks, and that it ought to have instructed some-one in the restaurant to check the stairs whenever a person came into the restaurant with a drink in an open container (it was common ground that the hotel did not do so). First Choice appealed to the High Court. Goldring J. allowed the appeal. Whilst it was open to the judge to find that the Claimant had slipped on a colourless, odourless liquid, it was for the Claimant to prove that in failing to operate the system proposed by the judge (of instructing some-one in the restaurant to check the stairs whenever a person came into the restaurant with a drink in an open container), the hotel was in breach of local safety standards. Even if he had been applying English standards of reasonableness, it would not have been reasonable to require the hotel to operate the system proposed by the judge; furthermore, any distinction between cases involving allegations of failures in equipment and cases involving allegations of failure in systems was irrelevant to the issues the judge had to decide. The judge went further and stated that the applicable local safety standards could not be inferred from the standards aspired to at a given hotel; the mere fact that an establishment tried to provide safety standards that were arguably higher than the local standards[86] is not evidence of what the applicable local standard of safety actually is. The Claimant had not adduced any evidence of the applicable local standards. It was not for the Defendant to prove

---

[86] E.g. If there was evidence that yellow warning cones were often put out in the wet at a particular hotel, but not on the occasion of the accident in question, this would not prove that the local standard demanded yellow cones, and so the absence of cones on the occasion of the accident would not be actionable just because the hotel did not follow its own usual practice. Although the binding nature of the decision in *Holden* is still overlooked form time to time – see e.g. *Wilkes v TUI UK Ltd* 3 March 2007 (Birmingham CC) Unreported where the tour operator's request for yellow cones was (wrongly it is submitted) regarded as setting the applicable standard.

anything and the appropriate legal standard could not be inferred from what the hotel did or did not do in practice.

The Claimant's failure to adduce any relevant evidence of what reasonable care requires in the country or region where an accident has occurred is a common theme in the cases following *Holden*. There have been many. The judge in *Gallagher*[87] put it succinctly:

> I have no expert evidence to advise or help me as to whether or not the activities of [the skiing instructor] ... on that day did, in the eyes of a properly qualified professional, fall below the standard of care to be exercised by a reasonably prudent ski instructor of the variety of which he was. The burden of proof lies on the party who brings the action. It is plain from what I am going to be referring to in my judgment that there is no such expert evidence. It is a complete mistake to think that the court possesses any expertise in this field whatsoever. I am a judge. It is a basic principle that a claimant bears the burden of proof in a civil action. The standard of proof is the balance of probabilities. It is unfortunate if a claimant comes to court without the requisite evidence. ... [Counsel for the Claimant] has sought to persuade me that the matter was so obvious that the case was proved. But, with respect to him, I beg to differ.

These remarks and the result in *Gallagher* illustrate how dangerous it can be to assume that a court will conclude that there has been a breach of the applicable standard of care simply on the basis of a submission that "it is obvious".

- In *Murphy v First Choice Holidays*[88] the Claimant alleged she had fallen and hurt herself on a step in an amphitheatre used for hotel entertainment in Egypt. The claim was based on allegations that the amphitheatre was not adequately lit and she had not been issued with any warnings. The claim was dismissed because she had failed to adduce any evidence as to what the applicable standard of lighting was for a hotel in Egypt using this kind of facility.
- *Greenwood v My Travel UK Limited*[89] involved a teenager on holiday with his elder brother. Returning early to their shared room one evening the Claimant fell out of the bedroom window, he alleged because there was insufficient room to maneouvre between the furniture in the room. His claim was dismissed because he had adduced no evidence of the standards required space-wise in a hotel in Benidorm.

---

[87] See above.
[88] 22 February 2007 (Birmingham CC) Unreported.
[89] [2007] 20 November, (Altrincham CC) Unreported

- In *O'Grady v Cresta Holidays Ltd*[90] there was evidence from a single joint expert to the effect that in Spain the terrace of a pool should incline away from the pool's edge, so when the Claimant slipped on the slope and alleged the terrace was unsafe, the claim was bound to fail.
- Mrs. Fellows[91] stepped off a high kerb in her hotel's grounds in the Dominican Republic and caught her foot in a deep storm drain. Her claim failed in the absence of any evidence that there was anything wrong with the height of the kerb or the nature of the storm drain when assessed by standards in the Dominican Republic. On this occasion the tour operator had taken the precaution of supplying photographs from all over the island showing that such kerbs and drains were almost *de rigour* in the Dominican Republic.
- In *Prynn v Romano Travel*[92] the Claimant was unable to show that material local regulations relating to interior staircases in Spanish holiday villas were in force at the time of his accident, and furthermore, the judge was prepared to conclude that the staircase, although steep and in some ways treacherous, was similar to that encountered in many holiday villas. Accordingly, there was no improper performance of the holiday contract in failing to issue warnings or provide a suitable handrail.
- *Potter v TUI UK Ltd.*[93] the Claimant's case failed where he had adduced no evidence to prove that a private villa tennis court in Spain had to be maintained to such a high standard as to eradicate all moss and damp patches on which he had slipped breaking his leg.
- *O'Brien v TUI UK Ltd*[94] is another example. The Claimant in this case alleged that she had slipped over in the shower in the bathroom at her Majorcan Hotel as a result of a loose shower head which had become detached while she was showering and struck her on the chin. She also alleged that the water pressure had increased and it was suggested that this might have caused the shower head to detach. The trial Judge rejected the Claimant's account of the accident (which bore little resemblance to the post-accident reports which she had signed), but also held that the Claimant had failed to prove negligence by reference to the applicable Spanish standard of care.
- In *Grimshaw v Airtours Holidays Ltd*[95] the Claimant tripped over a boarded step at the entrance of a Hindu temple in Singapore. The temple had been erected in the 1830s, and the board had been there

---

[90] 18 October 2007 (Liverpool CC) Unreported.
[91] *Fellows v TUI UK Ltd* 28 October 2007 (Bristol CC) Unreported.
[92] March 2006 (Guildford CC) Unreported.
[93] 26 March 2006 (Mayor's Court) Unreported.
[94] 17 January 2006 (Bury CC) Unreported.
[95] 25 October 2005 (Mayor's Court) Unreported.

continuously ever since. The Claimant failed to adduce any evidence that it was regarded as dangerous or inappropriate by the standards applicable in Singapore and she lost her claim.

Regulations and General Standards

Regulations
How does one measure and prove the local standard? Where regulations exist or where there are guidelines issued by a local trade or professional organisation such will be a good measure of what the local standard is in respect of a particular facility or service. There are many possible examples of which the following represent only a random few.

Cyprus - The Public Swimming Pools Regulations 1996 direct[96] that

> Regulation 47(2): Trained supervisors ... shall be on duty during the entire time of the operation of the swimming pool ... at least one safety supervisor is required for small pools.

> Regulation 48(9): No bather is allowed to enter the swimming pool area without the presence of a supervisor or any other competent employee.

> Regulation 49(1): Signs ... with the rules for the proper use of the swimming pool shall be posted up at points which are clearly visible and are located near each swimming pool.

Spain – recommendations differ from region to region but Spanish architectural and design practice usually demands that annealed (that is ordinary unlaminated glass[97]) of 4-5mm thickness is in place in hotels and other public buildings. More often than not the thickness required is greater for wind resistance purposes at high levels and not for safety purposes for visitors to the premises.

Spain – by Ministerial Order dated 31 May 1960 (as amended by Decree 53/1995) applicable in the Balearic Islands hotels are under an obligation to provide swimming pool attendants during opening hours.[98]

---

[96] *Singh v Libra Holidays Ltd.* [5 February 2003] QBD Unreported.
[97] See e.g. *Hayden v Airtours* – [1999] ITLJ 94.
[98] *Roberts v Iberotravel* [2001] QBD 26 March – Gibbs J- in which the absence of a compulsory pool attendant and rescue equipment was crucial as a causative factor in the catastrophic asphyxia injuries suffered by an unsupervised child using a hotel swimming pool.

Barbados – building regulations require that hotel balcony walls or rails are at least 1.3m high. In Mexico, however, local regulations demand that balcony railings are at least 36 cm high.

Italy – fire safety is governed by detailed technical requirements for buildings and rules relating to building fire safety certification, staff training and public notices all of which are to be found in the *Decreto Ministeriale* of 9 April 1994.

Portugal – regulates health and safety in holiday accommodation of various descriptions by *Decree Law No: 328* of 29 September 1986 and the *Decreto Regulamente 8/89* as a result of which specific health and safety requirements must be met.

Greece – has a system of regulations issued by the Ministry of Transportation and local *nomarchia* (prefectures) that cover the provision of excursion coaches including a requirement that no vehicle over 18 years old is used, and making provision for the Greek equivalent of MOT testing (and other technical requirements) as well as regulating the (small) proportion of seating that shall be designated as "no smoking".

As already indicated and as will be abundantly obvious, the above list is only intended to provide some examples of the type of activities, services or facilities that can be subject to specific regulation. There are many others. A common type of regulation to be found in many jurisdictions relates to the provision of trained or accredited staff for the provision of certain services (such as diving or other sports or activity instruction). There is, regrettably, no substitute for checking in individual cases whether and to what extent a government of public authority has issued regulations that are relevant to a consumer complaint – particularly in injury cases.

The point is this. Where it can be shown that local regulations apply, and that those regulations have been breached, it is highly likely that a court in any jurisdiction would be satisfied that the breach of the local regulations constituted an improper performance of the holiday contract on the part of the service provider for which the other party to the contract will be liable pursuant to regulation 15 of the PTR 1992. Conversely, where a defendant can show that local regulations apply and that they have been complied with it is less likely that an improper performance of the holiday contract will be proved.[99] If breach and improper performance are established (by this means or any other) it remains necessary for the claimant to prove that the

---

[99] Which is what happened in *Codd v Thomson Tour Operations Limited* – above.

improper performance caused the loss and damage complained of. Indeed a breach of local regulations gives rise to two different species of complaint by the consumer. The first is that the breach of the local regulations itself constitutes an improper performance of the holiday contract for which the other party to the contract is liable by statute in this country; the second approach is that the other party to the contract is itself *directly* in breach of contract either because it expressly promised that the holiday facilities would comply with local rules or because it failed to check that there was such compliance.[100]

The case of *Singh v Libra Holidays Ltd*[101] illustrates how this works, although the Claimant lost his claim for damages because he failed to establish a causal link between the local regulatory non-compliance that was proved and his swimming pool accident. The claimant sustained compete tetraplaegia as a result of diving from the shallow end of a swimming pool at his package holiday hotel in Ayia Napa, Cyprus. The hotel catered for a young and boisterous clientele interested in sampling the "clubbing" atmosphere of Ayia Napa, as a result of which they would often be intoxicated. The Hotel itself catered for its guests and others on their return from the local nightlife often as late as 3.00 or 4.00 in the morning by maintaining an all-night bar which was adjacent to the hotel's swimming pool and at its shallow end. So it was that after a night on the town the claimant and a group of his friends returned to the hotel and sat around the bar drinking vodka and beer. The guests using the bar overnight routinely used the pool to swim and soak in without apparent let or hindrance. So it was that at about 8.30am the following morning the intoxicated claimant dived into the shallow end of the pool [1 metre deep] - something he had done countless times before during his week's holiday without untoward consequences. On this occasion his hands slipped apart on the bottom of the pool he hit his head with catastrophic results.

In its standard booking conditions the Defendant accepted liability for the negligence of its suppliers and for "deficiencies" in the facilities it was contractually bound to provide. The Claimant sued for damages for breach of these express contractual terms and pursuant to regulation 15 of the PTR 1992, which for all practical purposes in this case, imposed liability on the Defendant to similar effect. It was common ground between the parties that in assessing whether the hotel had been "negligent" or the facilities

---

[100] In breach of an implied term of the holiday contract that reasonable steps would be taken to ensure compliance with local regulations.
[101] [2003] EWHC 276 (QB) Holland J.

"deficient", the hotel had to be judged by the standards of swimming pool management prevailing in Cyprus in 1998.

The Claimant's case was as follows.

(1) Cypriot local standards in the form of *The Public Swimming Pools Regulations 1996* demanded in mandatory form that:

(a) There be a supervisor on continuous duty at the pool during all of its hours of operation.
(b) Signs (e.g. "No Diving" signs) for the safety of pool users should be posted up at points which were clearly visible near the pool.

(2) In breach of these regulations there was neither constant supervision whilst the pool was in operation (it being in operation more or less continuously) nor was there adequate or adequately positioned "No Diving" signage.

(3) The breaches of duty complained of caused the accident because:

(a) Constant supervision throughout the Claimant's stay at the hotel and generally would have prevented the development of a culture of high-jinx and horseplay around the pool which routinely led to guests diving into the pool at the shallow end. Had the high-jinx been stopped or guests warned after foolish behaviour in the pool it is likely that further such behaviour would have been eradicated.

(b) Supervision would have moderated the Claimant and his group's behaviour through the night and on the morning of the accident.

(c) Clear and conspicuous signs would have alerted or reminded intoxicated guests of the risk they faced when diving into shallow water.

(4) The Claimant also relied on the fact that the tour operator had done nothing to see that local regulations were enforced – the tour operator did not know the local regulations existed until the case was pleaded against them. Pool safety recommendations of the Federation of Tour Operators had also been ignored.

(5) Given that both hotel and tour operator admitted that they were aware of the fact that hotel guests dived into shallow water oblivious to the risks and that such risks carried the prospect of catastrophic injury the standard of care tourists were entitled to expect was a high one.

The Defendant denied liability on the following grounds.

(1) Whilst the Cypriot pool regulations applied to this hotel, the pool itself was not in operation at the time of the accident. There was clear signage stating that the pool was not be used after 10.00pm. Supervision was not, therefore, required.

(2) The general level of supervision during the hours of operation comprising patrols by the hotel manager and the bar and other staff was reasonable given that any misbehaviour (including diving into the pool at the shallow end) was met with a reprimand when witnessed.

(3) To the extent that it was shown by the Claimant that there were technical breaches of the Cypriot pool regulations, this did not matter because the hotel had been regularly inspected by the tour operator, the Cyprus Tourism Organisation and the local department of health, none of whom had ever raised any concern about supervision or signage. Thus, the real local standard was that enforced by the local regulatory authorities and as they were not concerned about the hotel's compliance there could not be said to have been a breach of local standards.

(4) The "No Diving" signs (of which there were 3) were clear and reasonably placed and the fact that there had been subsequent improvements did not alter that fact.

(5) In any event, any breaches of duty by the hotel were not causative of the accident because the Claimant was drunk, he knew (as was admitted) that the water was shallow and the hotel staff on duty on the morning of the accident had tried but failed to persuade him and his friends to go to their rooms. He would have taken no notice of any supervisory presence or better signs.

Holland J. gave judgment for the Defendant. In the course of his judgment he observed as follows:

(1) The potential for serious spinal injuries to the Claimant was "notorious" and the injuries were typical even though the risk of an accident happening the first place was modest to low.

(2) With that assessment of the magnitude of the risk in mind[102] the "No Diving" signs were inadequate. Two were in the eaves of the roof of the poolside bar and could not easily be seen by users at the shallow end. The third was large, but distant from the pool adjacent to a an accommodation block door the claimant never used. The claimant was unaware of any of the signs. The hotel was in breach of its duty under the Cypriot regulations in respect of the sufficiency and location of its warning signs.

(3) The fact that local regulatory enforcers had not done anything about such deficiencies in signage was irrelevant and did not absolve the hotel or the defendant. It was for the trial judge to assess whether regulations had been properly implemented and the fact that local regulators ignored them could not excuse the hotel. The pool regulations spoke in mandatory language and should be obeyed.

(4) The swimming pool *was* in operation at the time of the accident. Whilst it was supposedly closed after 10.00pm, and there were notices to this effect, there were no, or no obvious, signs telling guests when it opened and guests could be excused for thinking that it would be open at 8.30am on a summer morning so as to give rise to the appropriate duty on the part of the hotel.

(5) Unfortunately for the claimant, having always admitted that he knew perfectly well that the water was shallow, having used the pool on many previous occasions, and having admitted in cross-examination that he did not need anyone to tell him not to dive into shallow water, the absence of proper signs did not cause his accident.

(6) As to supervision, there was no basis in the event to condemn it as substandard albeit low key and benign, but in addition and ironically, the presence of at least 2 members of staff at the pool bar (more supervision than normal) attempting to soothe boisterous behaviour by the claimant and his party had failed to moderate their behaviour and thus it appeared that the claimant would have taken his dive come what may.

The case, naturally, turns on its own facts, but there are a number of points of interest over and above the particular factual matrix. First, the Defendant attempted to dilute the applicable local standard as laid down in the Cypriot

---

[102] Derived from *Morris v West Hartlepool Steam Navigation C. Ltd.* [1956] AC 552 per Lord Reid at 574.

regulations by the submission that an English judge should *not* merely read, construe and apply those regulations, but take into account whether or not, and the extent to which, the local regulators actually enforced them in Cyprus. The argument is that if the locals don't enforce their own regulations, then the local standard does not require compliance with them. This was an interesting, but it is submitted, doomed approach to local standards. The fact that a complacent hygiene inspector in London fails to enforce the Food Safety Act against a restaurant does not mean that the restaurant is not responsible for a subsequent food poisoning outbreak, neither does an overlooked building regulation necessarily prevent an occupier being liable under the Occupiers' Liability Act 1957 to a visitor when a wall collapses and causes injury.

Secondly, it is a matter of some continuing concern that some tour operators seem oblivious to whether local regulations actually exist *at all.* Libra Holidays did not know the Cypriot regulations existed, and they (wrongly) assumed that the local regulators would enforce them if they *did* exist. This was a mistake. *Singh* is a classic case where the tour operator could potentially have been liable for breaches of regulations that the local tourist and health authorities did not properly enforce. There is an element of unfairness in this as tour operators must strive to enforce local regulations about which the locals seem to care very little, but there it is. In the present case the tour operator served (but in the end did not use) evidence from its own managerial staff stating in terms that they did not attempt to comply with myriad local regulations because they always applied UK standards which were higher. No explanation of the alleged UK standards was given, and one is forced to wonder (as did the trial judge in passing) in what possible respects *anyone's* standards could be higher than the stringent requirements demanded by the Cypriot regulations.

Finally, there is no escaping the dynamics of the *evidence* as it emerges in the court room. Causation will always be a problem in cases of this character when the Claimant candidly admits that he did not need anyone to tell him not to dive into 1 metre of water. Of course this admission was qualified by the observation that he had done it without reprimand repeatedly over the course of a week, as had many others, and accordingly, he considered it to be alright to do so. Many honest Claimants will make such admissions in the course of their evidence, but the point surely is this. Where the risk of catastrophic injury is manifest (as in these cases) the duty on the occupier of premises should be a high one, *not* because the danger is not obvious to any sober and reasonable adult thinking logically with the benefit of 20-20 hindsight, but because in any leisure context (not just holidays) those at risk are not likely to be sober or thinking logically about their own health and safety and many, whilst appreciating the risk of some injury, do not appreciate the risk that the injury will be so serious.[103]

There is a further possible twist in the application of the local health and safety standard in assessing whether there has been an improper performance of the holiday contract. Occasionally local regulations or legislation impose on the overseas service provider a strict or even absolute obligation. For example, imagine that local health regulations in an overseas jurisdiction specify that hotel floors shall be maintained in such a dry condition as to ensure that visitors do not slip. In imposing such an obligation on the foreign service provider the local regulators may be taken to have imposed on the local hotels an obligation akin to the statutory obligation in England and Wales relating to the safety of workplace floors.[104] In other words the obligation imposed on the operator of the Hotel is very nearly the obligation of an insurer. If the Hotel fails to ensure that the floor is slip-free and is in breach of its local regulations, does this mean that the *tour operator* is liable for this as an improper performance of the contract between itself and the consumer? This is a vexed question in a minority of cases and as yet it has not received a conclusive answer in the courts. At the crudest level one could say that as the tour operator[105] is in effect "vicariously" liable for the Hotel's shortcomings, then the tour operator must be liable to the consumer for any ensuing injury subject always to the tour operator's right to pass on that liability down the supplier chain to the hotelier. However, things are unlikely to be quite as simple as that. It must be remembered that the tour operator's liability to the consumer is for the proper performance of *the contract*; the contract can only be the holiday contract between the tour operator and the consumer. The law is[106] that unless by contract the tour operator assumes a greater liability,[107] the default position is that the tour operator is liable only for a *negligent* failure in the provision of holiday services and facilities because the contractual duty is merely that reasonable care will be exercised. So, where an accident occurs despite the exercise of reasonable care by the hotelier, it can be argued that the tour operator is not responsible for an improper performance of the holiday contract because there has been no negligence even though the hotelier if sued directly might be liable for breach

---

[103] Nonetheless, *Singh* must now be listed with *Ratcliffe v McConnell* [1999] 1 WLR 670; *Darby v National Trust* [2001] PIQR P372; *Bartrum v Hepworth Minerals* [1999] 29 October QBD Unreported, and *Donoghue v Folkstone Properties* [2003] 2 WLR 1138 CA – as another example of the courts dismissing claims by those injured by using shallow water for leisure (whether open water or swimming pools) on the grounds that adults should know better. See also *Tomlinson v Congleton Borough Council* [2003] HL.
[104] See Workplace (Health, Safety and Welfare) Regulations 1992 reg. 12.
[105] The *other party to the contract*.
[106] *Hone v Going Places Leisure Travel* CA (see above).
[107] Such as occurs where the existence of certain facilities is promised as part of the contract.

of some absolute regulatory liability in the courts of its own jurisdiction. The tour operator's position would be that all it had agreed to do was have services and facilities provided with reasonable skill and care, and given the absence of negligence it should not be held responsible because in another jurisdiction a different defendant[108] would liable for breach of a different[109] type of obligation. This conclusion has a certain symmetry in English law and is likely to be considered an attractive solution by some – not least of all the tour operators. It is tentatively submitted, however, that it is not correct for 4 reasons – even though the dictum of Longmore LJ in *Hone*[110] would need some fine-tuning.

First, it would lead to the position where English Claimants would fail against the tour operator, but local Claimants would succeed against the hotel. *Secondly*, this outcome would surely not be consistent with the underlying objective of the PTR 1992 which are designed to allow consumers access to a remedy in the courts of their own domicile through the tour operator. *Thirdly*, and perhaps most important of all, such a get-out for tour operators pays insufficient heed to the PTR 1992 liability imposed on them. The PTR 1992 liability is in respect of the proper performance of the holiday contract. It is not stretching a point to say that the holiday contract implies a term not only that reasonable care is exercised in the provision of facilities, but that such facilities are provided to the standard required[111] in the place where they are offered, such that proper performance in the provision of hotel facilities means "proper" as demanded by those regulating the hotels. Finally, it is not irrelevant that many tour operators already *expressly* accept liability where a service or facility fails to match the standard required in the place where it is provided, so the apparent additional liability being discussed here is not in reality adding anything to the liabilities already accepted by many tour operators in their small print.

To the extent that there has been any legal authority on the topic it supports the proposition that an improper performance of a holiday contract can arise where a hotel has failed to comply with some unattainable but absolute health and safety standard imposed on it by its local regulators.

First Choice Holidays v Hotetur Club[112] is the case in point, although the issue arose in third party proceedings, and as a result the decision is unlikely to be taken as the final judicial word on the matter. First Choice

---

[108] The hotelier.
[109] Absolute.
[110] See above.
[111] Even if that is an absolute standard.
[112] 30 January 2006 (Birmingham CC) *Lawtel.*

compromised a large number of illness claims related to summer holidays at the Lagomonte Hotel in Majorca over the course of the summer of 2000. The illnesses were all triggered by cryptosporidium (a water-borne pathogen that thrives in swimming pools following faecal "accidents"). Having settled the Claimants' claims, First Choice pursued the Spanish hotel owner (Hotetur Club) in Part 20 proceedings. The basis of the tour operator's Part 20 claim was its contractual indemnity with Hotetur Club whereby the owners had warranted in effect that visitors to the Lagomonte Hotel would be safe, and *the facilities would comply with locally applicable standards.* The problem facing the hotel proprietor in this instance was that the local (Majorcan) swimming pool regulations came with a water purity specification. That specification was that the pool water should be "pathogen free". Despite expert evidence claiming that cryptosporidium was not known as a pathogen in Spanish swimming pools in 2000, and worse, once in the pool it was virtually impossible to get rid of it (it is not killed by chlorine other than in "nuclear" doses that would also harm human users) – the Hotel was unable to overcome the problem that the Majorcan water specification was a severe one. The outcome was that the Hotel had to indemnify First Choice in respect of all the Claimants' claims and costs, and were ordered to pay costs to First Choice on the indemnity basis (as the indemnity contract provided). The trial judge was satisfied that the "pathogen free" specification prevailed and the effect of this was to throw all the risk of illness occurring onto the Hotel in order to protect public visitors and the local tourist industry. There was no reason for giving the water specification anything but its apparently clear, literal meaning. Such "absolute" technical specifications or standards are likely to be few and far between – and must be proved in each case they are relied on but this case illustrates the value of a solid indemnity contract with the overseas hotelier.

General Standards

It is incumbent on the claimant to establish breach of duty and so it is incumbent on the claimant to prove what local standards apply and the extent to which they have been broken.[113] Does this mean that unless the claimant can establish the existence and breach of some local regulatory standard the claim will fail? The answer to this question is an emphatic "no". There are two main reasons. First, it should be borne in mind that the express terms of the holiday contract (as printed, for example, in a brochure) may impose on the other party to the contract and its suppliers a different standard. Secondly, and more importantly in this context, the standards applicable to a service or facility in a foreign jurisdiction may be governed not only by specific regulations or guidelines, but also by the local general law.

---

[113] A proposition derived from Longmore LJ in *Hone* (above).

If a visitor to a hotel in England tripped over the wire of a vacuum cleaner trailing across the foyer floor and sustained injury it is unlikely that in prosecuting a civil claim a claimant would waste much energy researching the existence or otherwise of the "Wires Across Floors (Prohibition) Regulations 2009". The claimant's adviser would have a shrewd idea that such regulations did not exist and in any event would project the claim under the common duty of care pursuant to the Occupiers' Liability Act 1957 and possibly in common law "negligence". In this instance English general law imposes the standard on the occupier of the hotel in respect of hazards affecting visitors. The occupier can be in breach of duty (and in breach of the standard to be expected of a reasonable hotelier in England) without there being in existence any specific regulations or industry guidelines. If a European package tourist was the victim of this imaginary accident and sued his domestic tour operator under the Package Travel Directive, there is no logical reason why such a tourist could not succeed on the basis that the English hotel had failed to satisfy its local standard by being in breach of the common duty of care. Such a breach would be an improper performance of the holiday contract on the part of the hotel for which the foreign tour operator would be liable under its equivalent of regulation 15 of the PTR 1992.

The same surely applies when considering foreign standards and English tourists abroad. This is not the application of foreign law as the applicable law of the dispute because the holiday contract will invariably be governed by English law. English law (for example) may imply a term to the effect that reasonable care will be exercised by the supplier of holiday services and facilities, what reasonable care requires in the context of a given incident is governed by the locally applicable standard. In some cases that standard is measured by reference to regulations or guidelines. In other cases the standard required of the local supplier is governed the local general legal standard – if you like by the local equivalent of the Occupiers' Liability Act 1957.

It is not unreasonable to start with the proposition that in most jurisdictions the occupiers of buildings and providers of transport (amongst others) owe a duty to exercise reasonable skill and care to persons using their premises or services (amongst others). This duty comes about in different ways in different jurisdictions. In Germany owners and occupiers of buildings open to the public owe a duty to take adequate measures to protect third parties if in the view of a diligent person a risk of injury has been created.[114] Article 1.902 of the Spanish Civil Code provides that *"He who by an act or omission causes damage to another, there being blame or negligence, is obliged to remedy the*

---

[114] *Bundesarbeitsgericht:* VersR 1975, p 812.

damage caused"[115] In France[116] *"Every act whatever of man that causes damage to another, obliges him by whose fault it happened, to repair it."* In common law jurisdictions the general legal standard is more accessible. For example in Australia *"a person must take reasonable steps to ensure that his actions do not cause damage to that person's neighbour"* a statement English lawyers will find familiar.[117] The Turkish Civil Code includes provisions that are very similar to those found in our own Occupiers' Liability Act 1957. These few examples are only intended to illustrate that almost everywhere one might visit there is some general law duty on the part of service providers to exercise reasonable care (or some local variant of this concept) in the provision of the service they are providing.

It is unlikely that a claim against, say, a Swedish hotelier in Sweden would fail simply because no specific regulation or guideline had been broken. If a claim succeeded in Sweden because the hotelier had failed to exercise the degree of care required by Swedish law, then surely that hotelier has fallen below the required "local standard" in the delivery of the service or facility? There is no reason why the same logic should not apply when considering whether the local standard has been met in the context of a package travel case litigated in England. Despite the absence of regulations, the local supplier of a package holiday service may have delivered substandard facilities when judged by the general rules applicable in his own jurisdiction. This is as much a breach of local standards as, say, a failure to comply with statutory swimming pool regulations.

In essence, if the foreign service provider has broken local laws relating to the locally applicable duty and standard of care there has been an improper performance of one of the obligations under the English package holiday contract, namely that reasonable care would be exercised in the provision of holiday components when judged by local standards. A short-cut to the right answer in most cases would be to pose the question: would a claimant win an action against the service provider in the provider's own jurisdiction? This is a useful question, but it must be emphasised that it is a short-cut. It is for the judge seised of the action (an English judge in an English court) to apply the local, foreign rules relating to duties and standards of care and decide whether that there has been a failure constituting an improper performance of the holiday contract. Therefore, expert evidence[118] should be confined to the nature of the duty and standard of care applicable in the place where the harmful event occurred, and a cogent explanation of how the duty and

---

[115] *International Personal Injury Compensation Sourcebook* [Campbell] Sweet & Maxwell 1996.
[116] Article 1382 of the Civil Code.
[117] IPIC Sourcebook (above) page 2.
[118] And there must surely be expert evidence if this approach is adopted.

standard are applied in that jurisdiction. It is going too far for such evidence to conclude that this or that claim would or would not succeed in the foreign court. However, there is no reason why foreign illustrative case law cannot be provided as part of the evidence to substantiate the opinion as to how the duty and standard of care work in practice in the place where the relevant incident happened.

We have already seen in the context of local regulations[119] that the fact that local enforcement officers fail to enforce local regulations is irrelevant in determining whether the local standard demands compliance with such regulations. Where a claim is based on a standard imposed by the general law the position is likely to be different. This is due to the fact that what reasonable care requires of a service provider will differ from jurisdiction to jurisdiction. An example may help.

It is all too common for British tourists to fall victim to injuries resulting from shattering, non-laminated glass doors[120] whether as a result of walking into them or otherwise. As a result it has become common in some places to place warning stickers on glass patio and balcony doors in holiday accommodation. In some jurisdictions such stickers are placed at suitable heights for both adults and children. Let us suppose that the standard of care demanded at a holiday destination by the local general law is that the hotelier should exercise reasonable care to minimise the risk of foreseeable personal injury. An English judge *might* conclude in the light of the common nature of these accidents that the failure to place stickers on glass balcony doors was a breach of this local duty and that the hotelier had fallen below the relevant standard of reasonable care in failing to put stickers in place. An improper performance of an obligation under the package holiday contract would thus be proved. Judges in the local jurisdiction might take an entirely different view. They might conclude that *reasonable* care in their locality did not require hoteliers to go to such lengths to protect visitors from their own stupidity and that, far from being reasonable, an insistence on warning stickers was tantamount to unnecessary "nannying" of a relatively few imbecile tourists. There would, therefore, be no duty – and obviously no substandard facility. The reverse is also possible. An English judge might conclude that *"... the risks to competent swimmers of bathing in the pond were obvious, and that there was, therefore, no duty to warn against swimming"*[121] Elsewhere judges might be inclined to consider that the risk of serious injury or death arising out of an adult beguiled into bathing at an

---

[119] *Singh v Libra Holidays Ltd* (above).
[120] *Wilson v Best Travel; Logue v Flying Colours Holidays Ltd* and *Hayden v Airtours Holidays Ltd* [above].
[121] *Darby v National Trust* [2001] PIQR P27 (CA).

attractive open water facility would not be at the forefront of a visitor's mind and therefore it was a risk requiring a conspicuous warning. In other words the foreign assessment of what reasonableness required would, perish the thought, be higher abroad than at home.

It is submitted that it is the local application of the relevant general standard that should prevail. The short-cut approach as already noted is that a claimant would lose an action against the service provider in the place where the incident occurred which is at least strongly indicative of proper performance of an obligation in accordance with prevailing local standards. It is not that local enforcers (the *courts* in examples where the general law is in play) ignore their own national regulations but that the local general law does not recognise a duty or in so far as it does would not recognise any breach of duty on the basis of the relevant consumer's complaint. If the local courts do not accept that there is a duty on local hoteliers to stick warnings on glass doors it is difficult to see how a failure to do so could properly be characterised as an improper performance of the holiday contract any more than the hotelier in *Codd v Thomson Tour Operations Ltd.*[122] was guilty of improper performance for failing to put an emergency telephone it the lifts as would have been required in England. Conversely, if the local application of the duty to exercise reasonable care would require the hotelier to provide conspicuous warning notices to the effect: "*Do Not Bathe In The Crocodile Tank*" a visiting tourist tempted to do just that might have good grounds on which to succeed given that the absence of a warning in breach of the local standard would surely be an improper performance of the holiday contract.

In practice expert evidence about the applicable duty and standard of care and the approach of the local courts to the application of such general local standards will not always be necessary. In some of the older cases, claimants were able to succeed by deploying alternative means to prove that the facilities giving rise to an accident were actionably substandard.

Wren v Unijet Holidays Ltd.[123] was a good example, but it must now be seen in the light of *Holden*[124] and the many cases decided since *Holden* which allow no scope for the sort of evidential own goal that proved Mrs. Wren's case for her. The essence of the claim was that the foyer of the claimant's holiday hotel included a disguised step in the marble surface which was a hazard. As the claimant walked across the foyer on the first day of her package holiday, partially blinded by sunlight she had thought that the floor

[122] See above.
[123] Guildford County Court 17 December 2002 (Unreported).
[124] See above.

was flat. It was not – and she fell down the step sustaining injuries. This, it was alleged, constituted a failure on the part of the hotel to exercise reasonable care for which the tour operator was liable. The step was in fact a menace and had caused other accidents. The tour operator in its terms and conditions accepted liability for accidents caused by the provision of "deficient" services and, of course, regulation 15 of the PTR 1992 applied.

In its Defence the tour operator maintained:

1. that there was, in fact, a white stripe across the step to mark it out clearly from the rest of the dark floor;
2. as the Claimant had failed to adduce any expert evidence to the effect that the hotel failed to comply with local standards, the claim was bound to fail.

Neither line of argument prevailed and the claim succeeded. It turned out that the white line had been placed across the top of the step *after* the Claimant's fall (as contemporaneous photographs clearly showed). Secondly, the judge accepted that the contractual obligation on hotel and tour operator was to supply facilities of a reasonable standard that were not deficient. Given previous accidents and the dark colouring of the floor, this aspect of the hotel's facilities were not reasonable irrespective of any local standards. Furthermore, as the hotel had put down a white line after the event this was good evidence that even by local standards it was considered reasonable to warn visitors that the step was there.

The success of the claimant's case in *Wren* was largely the result of the fact that the defendant's contention that there already existed a white line before the accident was not accepted. Furthermore, the defendant was badly placed to argue that local reasonableness had not been shown to require such a line when they themselves contended that there already was one and it was common ground that one was in place immediately *after* the accident. This example might be extended to cover a whole range of possibilities. A repair or alteration to defective premises immediately after an incident may be a good indication that the condition of premises was, at the time of the incident, substandard. Placing warning stickers on glass doors or erecting notices about slippery floors immediately after an accident may be a good indication that something of the sort was both necessary and reasonably required beforehand. However, one needs to bear in mind the observation of Kennedy LJ in *Staples v West Dorset District Council*[125] "*The fact that* [the occupier] *took ... action after the accident does not enable me to draw the*

---

[125] [1995] PIQR P439 (CA) at page P445.

inference that, in order to discharge the common duty of care ... they should have done so before the accident occurred."Whether remedial action enables an inference to be drawn that something was amiss *before* an accident will depend on the facts of each individual case. In *Staples* Kennedy LJ felt unable to draw any such inference because although the occupier owed no duty to warn visitors about the slipperiness of the Cobb at Lyme Regis before the index accident, the occupiers of the Cobb acted responsibly after the accident in appreciating that they should do everything possible to avoid a recurrence. It appears to follow from this that even *after* the accident caused by the slipperiness of the Cobb the occupier was not under a duty to warn adult visitors of such obvious dangers but had chosen to do so out of an abundance of caution.[126]

Uniform international regulations

Phillips J. in *Wilson v Best Travel*[127] indicated that the applicable standard of care might alternatively be governed by uniform international regulations relevant to a particular facility or service, but he did not develop this possibility in any greater detail. An attempt was made to develop this possibility in *Evans v Kosmar Villa Holidays Plc.*[128] In August 2002, three weeks short of his eighteenth birthday, James Evans was on holiday with a group of friends at the Marina Beach Apartments in Kavos, Corfu. The holiday had been booked with a tour operator, Kosmar Villa Holidays plc ("Kosmar"). The apartment complex was under independent Greek ownership and management but was contracted exclusively to Kosmar and was featured in Kosmar's brochure. It included a small swimming pool. Towards the end of his stay, in the early hours of the morning, Mr Evans dived into the shallow end of the pool and hit his head on the bottom, sustaining serious injuries which resulted in incomplete tetraplegia. He brought a claim for personal injuries against Kosmar. His Honour Judge Thorn QC, sitting as a judge of the High Court, found Kosmar liable for the accident, subject to a finding of 50 per cent contributory negligence. The judge found that Kosmar's lay witnesses had "*variously committed themselves to an early and false joint account to save their backs*" and on several issues was driven to the conclusion that "*not only have they lied, but that they also put their heads together, probably at several stages, and conspired together to deceive*". The deception the judge concluded was all about the nature and quality of warning signs posted about the swimming pool at the time of the accident. The judge also found that the signage failed to comply with the guidance issued by the Federation of Tour Operators

---

[126] *Johnson v First Choice Holidays and Flights Ltd* [above].
[127] See above.
[128] [2007] EWCA Civ 1003.

("FTO"). The FTO's Health and Safety Handbook contains a section headed "Suggestions for Swimming Pool Safety", which also appears to be available as a separate leaflet to be given to hoteliers and others. The judge referred in particular to the following paragraphs:

> 4. Depth markings should be placed at regular intervals. Minimum 2m apart on small pools, 3m apart on large pools ....
> 5. Gradual changes in depths should be indicated at these regular intervals as indicated.
> 6. Sudden changes in depths should be clearly marked ....
> ...
> 8. No Diving signs should be displayed in a prominent position, especially in areas with depths of less than 1.5m.
> 9. Opening hours and emergency procedures should be clearly visible.

Suffice it to say that the trial judge found that there were material breaches in respect of these paragraphs of the FTO's guidance and whilst he said nothing about the status of the Guidance these "breaches" were sufficient to secure judgment for the Claimant. The decision was overturned on appeal. One of the reasons for this was that the FTO Guidance was simply that; Guidance. It was not a substitute for or analogous to *uniform international regulations* even though the tour operator used the Guidance as part of its safety training for local representatives and compliance with the Guidance was expected on the part of tour operator's Greek hotels. Neither was the legal analysis affected by the fact that the tour operators had lied in pretending that the compliance had been handsomely complied with at the relevant hotel on the night of the accident. Richards LJ[129] giving the judgment of the court of Appeal said:[130]

> In the present case, there was no evidence to support the pleaded claim of non-compliance with local safety regulations, and that way of putting the case was not pursued at trial. In my view, however, it was still open to the claimant to pursue the claim on the other bases pleaded in the amended particulars of claim. What was said in Wilson v Best Travel Ltd did not purport to be an exhaustive statement of the duty of care, and it does not seem to me that compliance with local safety regulations is necessarily sufficient to fulfil that duty. That was evidently also the view taken in Codd, where the court found there to be compliance with local safety regulations but nevertheless went on to consider other possible breaches of the duty of care. I can deal briefly with the pleaded failure to comply with minimum standards laid down by the FTO. I have already described the FTO's Health and Safety Handbook and the "Suggestions for Swimming Pool Safety" contained within it. In my view the handbook is referred to correctly as

---

[129] With whom Arden and Hooper LLJ agreed
[130] From paragraph 24 onwards

guidance. It is advisory in character and has no legal force. It does not lay down standards with which Kosmar is required to comply. As I understood [the respondent's] submissions to us, he did not contend otherwise but relied on the handbook simply as "informing" the standard of care and as casting light on whether Kosmar had exercised reasonable care in this case.

There are 2 intriguing elements to be drawn from this passage.

(1) Safety *guidance*, even if followed or recommended internationally does not have sufficient (or any) legal status to form the basis (whether directly or indirectly) of the appropriate standard of care in overseas accident cases.

(2) Compliance with local safety standards is *not* necessarily *sufficient* to fulfil the service provider's duty of care and Phillips J's judgment in *Wilson* was not to be taken as an exhaustive statement of the tour operator's duty of care.

Richards LJ did not go on to say in what circumstances a tour operator might be found liable where local safety standards had been complied with. It is submitted that from the context of this part of the judgment it is plain that all Richards LJ was intending was that the two exceptions to the "local standards" test set out by Philips J. in *Wilson* could still form the basis of an allegation of breach of duty without recourse to proof of breach of local standards. When Richards LJ states that *Wilson* was not intended to be exhaustive, he surely meant that the local standards test was not exhaustive and that breach uniform international regulations could still be the basis of an allegation of breach of duty. The second exception to the local standards principle was also set out by Philips J. in *Wilson.* It might be summarised in this way. If the standard of safety is so low, or the absence of a safety feature is such that a fully informed and reasonable holidaymaker might reasonably decline to stay in the accommodation or use a facility, then the tour operator could owe a contractual duty to the consumer. To Philips J's exception a refinement can be added. Where a tour operator knows that a certain feature of the premises or facility is potentially dangerous (perhaps as a result of previous accidents or near-misses) then the tour operator is likely to be regarded as owing a contractual duty to the consumer[131] and if the other party to the contract has direct control over the premises or venue, then there may be a duty to exert that control by enforcing safety improvements.

But a contractual duty *to do what?* It is submitted that the duty in the circumstances canvassed by Phillips J. would be a duty to warn and provide reasonable information about the standards in respect of the facility the consumer could expect to meet. It is likely that the lower the local standard

---

[131] *Brannan v Airtours Plc* [1999] CA The Times 1 February.

of facilities and services the greater the need for such a warning and the clearer the warning would have to be in order for the other party to the contract to discharge the duty placed upon it. However, this duty only arises in circumstances where the local standard is already so low that a fully informed consumer might reasonably refuse the accommodation. Phillips J. held that such was not the case where the local standard demanded no more than ordinary, annealed glass in its balcony windows.

A duty to do what?

In cases falling within the two exceptions originally canvassed by Philips J. in *Wilson*, what is the nature and extent of the tour operator's duty? The nature and extent of the tour operator's duty will almost certainly depend on the nature of the hazard and the level of danger and likely risk of injury that hazard creates. The duty is likely to involve one of three things: either the removal of the facility from the tour operator's books in the worst imaginable instances, or at least the provision of a warning to consumers that the hazard exists and that they beware accordingly. It is submitted that any obligation to remove the facility from the tour operator's books will arise only in rare cases of deplorably low health and safety standards because this obligation on the tour operator *only* arises where the reasonable consumer would refuse to use the facility if properly informed. The time at which the consumer reaction should be judged is the time when the package contract is made. Examples are bound to reflect extreme circumstances, but such examples might include the removal of a hotel from the portfolio where the restaurant facility was adjacent to a open sewer or where the complex's ponds and streams were inhabited by alligators. It is easy enough after the event for a consumer to say that had it been known that a certain safety feature was not available, then the package would not have been purchased and it is tempting for courts to conclude after an accident that the missing safety feature was so important as to demand at least a clear warning. If the accident had never happened would there have been the same level of concern about the relevant missing safety feature? The duty to warn (as opposed to the duty to remove property from the market) is likely to arise more frequently, but even then probably only if the hazard has previously given rise to problems.

If the accident in *Wilson v Best Travel* had been to a child, would the result have been different? In *Wilson* Philips J makes a point of emphasising that it was not alleged on behalf of the claimant that a warning should have been given; neither was it suggested that a warning would have helped to prevent the accident. Mr Wilson fell through the glass door in circumstances which remain obscure, but in circumstances in which one infers that a prior warning would not have done any good. However, if the facts are changed only slightly, the position could well have been different. Might a reasonable parent refuse to stay in accommodation without safety glass in the balcony doors, or where the standard of balcony rail levels was lower than might be expected in the United Kingdom? If the lower standard was common place throughout a given destination the parent would probably not refuse to take the package. But would a warning help? In some circumstances it would. The parent who is warned of the absence of toughened glass, and advised that British tourists due to unfamiliarity with frequently used glass balcony or patio doors is likely to be more watchful particularly on first arriving at the resort until the family becomes accustomed to their change of surroundings. The parent herself could profit from the warning as many similar accidents occur when adults fail to see that the doors are closed and proceed simply to walk into them. In these instances it may well be that the consumer should be warned that if an accident occurs the safety margin is narrower due to the lack of a safety feature, and they may, therefore, be induced to take greater care themselves to minimise the risk of an accident happening.

Another example illustrates the difference between removing facilities from the market and issuing warnings. At some continental destinations it is common to find swimming pools which are at their deepest in the centre and are shallow around their entire circumference. These pools comply with local standards in some parts of Spain and France for example. However, the depth configuration of such pools can be a dangerous distraction for the uninitiated. A warning would do nothing to prevent or minimise head injuries sustained if a visitor were to be pushed or accidentally slips into the pool. However, such a warning may well minimise the risk of new arrivals or forgetful, established guests diving around the edge of the pool and to that extent may act as an alert to consumers that they need to take additional care. The difficulty for tour operators in the context of a duty to warn is to identify where this duty ends in practice. The difference in standards across a wide variety of destinations and in respect of a massive array of services, facilities, accommodation, transport and equipment deployed in the provision of a package tour could impose an unattainable obligation on the tour operator to warn of every discrepancy between local and UK safety standards. The inclusion in the "small print" of a general warning to the effect that local standards may not be what the consumer is accustomed to at home will probably not be enough to discharge the duty to warn. On the other hand, it is unreasonable to expect every feature of a package to be the subject of a specific warning. The tour operator's duty, it is submitted is, therefore, limited in a number of related ways. First, the duty will only arise where the other party to the contract has or ought to have some knowledge of the hazard and the risks arising from the hazard in question. Secondly, whether a specific warning is required will depend on the nature of the hazard and the seriousness of the consequences likely to occur if the hazard is encountered by the consumer. In other words, the greater the risk to consumers of different categories and the greater the consequences of encountering the hazard (judged on the basis of the experience and knowledge of the tour operator) the greater the need for specific and clear warnings. The hazard may be a temporary one. Many tour operators recognise the need to warn their consumers and do so not only by means of the general clauses in Fair Trading Charters, but by the provision of advice sheets to consumers before they depart, and immediately upon their arrival.

A duty to warn?

It is not every hazard (indeed it may be that it is not many hazards) that give rise to a legal duty on the part of the tour operator to warn its customers. It is worth revisiting *Evans v Kosmar Villa Holidays Plc.*[132] Richards LJ said this in the context of the submission that the Claimant should have had the benefit of warnings against diving into the shallow pool:

> If there was a duty to exercise reasonable care to guard against what the claimant did in this case, then in my view the judge was entitled to find a breach of duty. It was open to him to accept the evidence of the claimant's expert ... as to the deficiencies of the signage, and to find non-compliance with the FTO guidance; and his conclusion that there was a failure to exercise reasonable care, in particular as to the prominence of the "no diving" signage around the pool, is not one with which there is any reason to interfere. But did the duty of care extend that far? The essence of Kosmar's case is that there is no duty to guard against an obvious risk of the kind that existed here, namely that diving into shallow water (or into water of unknown depth) may cause injury. That risk was obvious to an ordinary able-bodied adult such as the claimant. The evidence shows that he knew of the risk and was able to assess it for himself. He took a deliberate decision to dive in. Kosmar was under no duty to warn him against such a course or to take other measures to prevent it. The fact that he dived in, as the judge found, in a brief state of inadvertence does not affect the position: that could be said of almost all accidents, and again there is no duty to guard against it. Nor is the position affected by the fact that a lot of people were taking the same obvious risk by diving in.

This part of the judgment in *Evans* is based on the observations of Lord Hoffman in *Tomlinson v Congleton Borough Council:*[133]

> 45. I think it will be extremely rare for an occupier of land to be under a duty to prevent people from taking risks which are inherent in the activities they freely choose to undertake upon the land. If people want to climb mountains, go hang-gliding or swim or dive in ponds or lakes, that is their affair ....
> 46. My Lords, as will be clear from what I have just said, I think that there is an important question of freedom at stake. It is unjust that the harmless

---

[132] See above – at paragraph 27.
[133] [2004] 1 AC 46 – a case where a young man was injured in the shallow water of a natural mere.

recreation of responsible parents and children with buckets and spades on the beaches should be prohibited in order to comply with what is thought to be a legal duty to safeguard irresponsible visitors against dangers which are perfectly obvious. The fact that such people take no notice of warnings cannot create a duty to take other steps to protect them. I find it difficult to express with appropriate moderation my disagreement with the proposition of Sedley LJ ... that it is 'only where the risk is so obvious that the occupier can safely assume that nobody will take it that there will be no liability'. A duty to protect against obvious risks or self-inflicted harm exists only in cases in which there is no genuine and informed choice, as in the case of employees whose work requires them to take the risk, or some lack of capacity, such as the inability of children to recognise danger ... or the despair of prisoners which may lead them to inflict injury on themselves ....

So a duty to warn in respect of perfectly obvious dangers or in the context of risky activities freely undertaken simply does not arise. There was no reason in principle to distinguish holiday accident cases from domestic occupiers' liability cases.[134] Richards LJ concluded:[135]

[It was] argued that, on the particular facts as found by the judge, the claimant was not aware of any risk. At the moment when he dived, he assessed it as safe for him to dive, as others were doing. As the judge said, any prior and useful knowledge left him and he acted in a brief state of inadvertence. [It was submitted] that this case should be about the need for prominent signage to reduce the risk of people in the claimant's position reaching a wrong conclusion as the claimant did. The point, in effect, was that it is not a matter of guarding against an obvious risk but of guarding against the possibility of a mistaken assessment of the risk. That is a clever way of seeking to meet the argument based on Tomlinson, but I would reject it. The risk in this case remained an obvious one of which the claimant himself was previously aware and should have been aware at the moment he dived. The fact that at that moment he acted thoughtlessly, in a brief state of inadvertence, is not a good reason for holding Kosmar to have been under a duty that it would not otherwise have owed him. Accordingly I take the view that there was no duty to give the claimant any warning about the risk of diving into the pool, let alone to have better placed or more prominent signs than those actually displayed, or to take any other step to prevent or deter him from using the pool or from diving into it. His dive and its terrible consequences are matters for which he must take full personal responsibility.

---

[134] See e.g. *Ratcliffe v McConnell* [1999] 1 WLR 670; *Donoghue v Folkstone Properties Ltd* [2003] EWCA 231.
[135] Paragraph 42

A further observation needs to made about compliance with local standards, where those standards are so low that the reasonable consumer might refuse to use the facility. How would the *reasonable* consumer react to the absence of a safety feature? Whether there has been a breach of the duty to remove a package facility from the market, depends on the destination of the package, the type of package involved and the way in which it is promoted to the consumer. For example, it is possible to envisage many third world destinations where adventurous packages are offered, and where there are no, or virtually no local safety standards affecting the maintenance of accommodation or transport facilities. In these instances the reasonable consumer would not usually expect to find local safety standards remotely approaching those to be found in western Europe. For instance, the reasonable consumer who purchased a Thai trekking holiday in the Golden Triangle would not expect to find that the raised tribal huts which constituted the accommodation were provided with safe balcony rails or even sturdy floors and would certainly not expect to find that any system of structural inspection was adopted. The destination and "adventure" style of the package in this example reduce the extent to which any reasonable consumer could refuse to use the facilities offered as part of the package. The reasonable expectations of a consumer travelling in the developed world or to a destination promoted as part of or equivalent to the developed world would be much higher.

Examples
Two cases illustrate the correlation between local standards and a tour operator's duty where local standards fall below expected UK standards. The first is the unreported county court case of *Codd v Thomson Tour Operations Limited*. This was a case where a child was using a lift in a hotel in Majorca. Access to the lift was through a self-closing swing door controlled by a hydraulic hinge, after which automatic doors closed within the lift itself. On the occasion of the accident, the swing door got stuck a few centimetres from the frame as a result of which the inner doors failed to operate and the lift would not work. The child attempted to close the swing door by grabbing the edge of the door with his hand whereupon the door snapped shut injuring his fingers. He sued the tour operator on the grounds that the hotel had failed to carry out its duties "properly" in accordance with the Fair Trading Charter for which the company contractually accepted responsibility. No claim was made under the 1992 Regulations, but the case might equally have been brought under regulation 15(2). The facts of the accident were not materially in dispute, but the tour operator relied on the fact that the evidence from the hotel was that these lifts were of a type standard in Spain and Majorca, and also on the fact that a systematic inspection regime existed to check periodically the lifts once a month, which inspection system was in accordance with Spanish regulations. Accordingly,

the tour operator's case was that there had been no failure on the part of the hotel to act "properly"; the hotel was not in any way at fault when judged by local standards and as a result there was no fault for which the tour operator should be held responsible either under the express terms of the contract or under the 1992 Regulations. There had been no previous incidents (and there were no subsequent incidents) involving the hotel lifts and the child and his family had themselves used the lifts without incident for nine days before the accident occurred. The claimant based his case on the fact that there was no emergency alarm or telephone to call for assistance (making it necessary for the child to try and close the door himself) and on the grounds that there was no handle on the inside of the outer swing door by which means the child might safely have pulled the swing door shut. The precise reason why the door became stuck on this one occasion was never identified. Judgment was given for the defendant tour operator. *Assuming* that additional safety features might have been incorporated into the equipment — such as an emergency bell or telephone, or an interior handle, and assuming that the inspection check list might have been more rigorous in other jurisdictions, it was inappropriate to go behind the prevailing local standard. Given that the hotel had installed standard equipment and inspected it in accordance with local requirements, it was not appropriate to criticise the hotel for failing to do more to prevent the accident and in the absence of fault on the part of the hotel, there was no fault capable of being attributed to the tour operator under the package contract (or the 1992 Regulations it might have been added). As in *Wilson v Best Travel* the court refused to import (assumed) British standards into a foreign jurisdiction.

Brannan v Airtours plc is an example of one of the exceptions to the general rule. In that case an intoxicated Mr Brannan stepped on a table in a crowded night club in Tunisia in order to get out of his seat to go to the toilet. As he did so he walked into an overhead fan which caused him facial injuries. There was no evidence at all about what local standards demanded in Tunisia, and so no basis for any conclusion that the facility had failed in any way to comply with appropriate local rules. However, the court at first instance held that because the tour operator had effective control over the night club and that a previous accident had occurred involving injury caused by an overhead fan, the tour operator owed to Mr Brannan a duty to ensure that tables were not placed directly under the low fans. Because the tour operator had effective control of the premises (where consumers might be expected to have more to drink than was good for them) this would have been very easy to accomplish. This part of the decision at first instance was not challenged by the tour operator on the claimant's appeal — the appeal being concerned entirely with the degree to which Mr Brannan was contributorily negligent.

Questions concerning compliance with foreign standards and comparative UK standards are intricately connected with the evidence that is available to a court in a given case. A good recent example of the interplay between principles and evidence is *Foster v Olympic Holidays* where a tourist fell from his holiday balcony which would not have complied with British standards. The case was settled at the door of the court on the basis that the tour operator was 75% to blame for the shortcomings of the balcony balustrade, there being no evidence that the local destination standards were any different from those in the United Kingdom.

In this case the claimant fell from a balcony at his holiday hotel and sustained grievous injuries as a result. There was evidence that the height of the balcony balustrade would have breached UK safety standards, and had the height accorded with the British standard the accident may have been averted. The case was settled at the door of the court on the basis of the tour operator accepting 75% liability. One cannot but suspect that this settlement was forced on the tour operator by reason of the fact that there was no available evidence as to what local standard required of balcony rails. Had the balcony complied with local building regulations it is difficult to see why the tour operator should have been held liable.

Local standards — foreign culture

Notwithstanding *Wilson v Best Travel* there is a discernible reluctance amongst judges at first instance to accept that foreign standards can be different without necessarily being worse than UK standards. There is also something of a cultural assumption that the British standard is likely to be better (*e.g.* "that would not be good enough in this country") even in the absence of any evidence as to what current practice and regulation requires in the United Kingdom. For example, the assumption in *Codd v Thomson Tour Operations Limited* that lifts of the exact type at issue in that case would not have been allowed in this country would have been seriously undermined by a visit to at least one of the major resort hotels in Torquay where the case was contested and where the court would have found exactly the same type of lifts installed in an apparently top class hotel.

The attitudes of hoteliers and other service providers in some parts of Europe are also at odds with what might be described as the Anglo-American culture of litigation or blame. For example, in Spain and Greece profound and genuine puzzlement is expressed over any requirement to install warning stickers on glass patio doors (they can be regarded as a needless eyesore amongst people who are used to constant access to patios and balconies in sunny climates and who need no reminding not to walk into them when they are shut); and the courts of southern Spain are beginning to tire of tripping claims brought by British tourists against local and district authorities arising out of uneven public pavements (cases which would have every prospect of success in Britain). The Greek hotel proprietor can look on in honest bewilderment as the recently arrived visitor from northern Europe dives head first into the shallow end of the swimming pool and then blames the hotelier for not putting in place regimented depth markings; or who walks into an open manhole cover whilst maintenance is being carried out to the pool drainage system.

Local standards of reasonableness, and local law

There may be situations where no local specific regulations apply. The standard form of tripping or slipping case may provide a good example. If a consumer is injured as a result of tripping over an uneven flagstone or on an icy path on the main entrance to the hotel, but no local regulations are in force which apply to the circumstances of the accident, how is the English court to measure whether the hotel has performed the package contract improperly, thus rendering the tour operator liable for damages under regulation 15(2)?

It cannot be right for the English court simply to apply British standards of care and reasonableness in order to adjudicate. The standard must be the standard to be expected of the service provider in the local jurisdiction. Potentially this gives rise to a confusion between the application of foreign *standards* and foreign *law*. Many jurisdictions have a system of occupiers' liability which approximate to the principles applicable under the Occupiers' Liability Act 1957. So, even where there has been no local breach of a specific local regulation it may be possible for the tourist to state that when judged by the general standards of care applicable in the place where the accident took place, the service provider has failed to exercise reasonable care, and that this failure amounts to a failure in the performance of the package contract for which the other party to the package contract must accept responsibility. This is not at all the same as applying foreign law to the package contract (governed by English law) but it is another, less specific, example of the *local standard* of care being properly applied to the facts of an accident. In the absence of specific regulation, the general standard at the destination where the accident occurred requires the occupier or manager of the premises to take certain steps to protect consumers. It may well be that this standard demands that reasonable care or a colourable imitation of reasonable care is exercised, or the local general law might demand that care of a different standard is taken. Whatever the standard required locally, it is submitted that this is the standard that the English courts should apply. In order to do this, it is necessary for the English court to have evidence of what test a local court would apply to the circumstances of the accident. Would it require the exercise of reasonable care, or the standard that all practicable precautions should be taken. Would a local court regard an uneven flagstone of five centimetres actionable, or would the application of local standards lead to a metaphorical shrug of the shoulders and a dismissal of the claim?

The point is this. If a specific local safety regulation applies and is complied with, the other party to the contract should not be held liable if the service provider has complied with that local standard. Equally, if there is no local regulation, it is difficult to see why the hotelier should be liable for a "dodgy" paving stone in the hotel grounds if by local standards the unevenness would be regarded as acceptable — or at least not actionable. Of course, if no evidence is placed before the court as to what local general standards would required it would not be surprising if the English court proceeded on the assumption that reasonable care was required, and then proceed to judge what is reasonable care demanded by the standards usually adopted in the United Kingdom. Again, the real question is *what does reasonableness require* given the circumstances and the location of this accident? If by Italian standards the Alpine hotelier is not under any obligation to keep his paths ice free (on the basis that visitors should know perfectly well that paths get icy and slippery in the ski season), there is no logical reason why any higher or different standard should be imported into the package contract on which the injured consumer sues when he takes a tumble on the uncleared path. The presentation of Italian evidence to this effect will be essential of course, to overcome the assumption in the Anglo-American culture that *any* reasonable hotelier would "keep and maintain the paths of the hotel ice free, and reasonably free from foreseeable risks of causing injury to guests".

Tour operators and raising standards

In the interests of consumer protection it could be argued that tour operators should be responsible for exercising their economic power over their service providers in order to drive up safety standards. That is, no one is better placed to *insist* that health and safety measures are enforced at foreign destinations in order to protect the hapless tourist as much as possible. This argument assumes of course that the tour operator controls sufficient economic muscle to impose its will in respect of health and safety measures and rather ignores the fact that the tour operator is not only constantly battling to keep its prices low, but is competing for package tour space with hundreds or even thousands of other tour operators and organisers from other developed jurisdictions. Whilst a degree of co-operation amongst local service providers can be expected (*e.g.* stickers on glass patio doors, or warning cones to be placed on recently sluiced marble floors) an attempt by tour operators to import too many outside [e.g. British] standards could well result in the service-provider simply selling his services to other competing organisations and cutting out the "fussy" safety-minded operator. Furthermore, it is submitted that it is not in the public interest to demand the importation of British standards in foreign travel arrangements that would either reduce the available market for the travelling public, or increase the price of travel for consumers. After all, it would come as a surprise to British hoteliers and other service providers if foreign courts started imposing pan—European standards of safety on facilities in this country.

Causation

It is stating the obvious to say that whatever breaches of the relevant standard may be proved in the delivery of a travel service or the provision of a facility, such breaches must have some *causative potency* as regards the alleged loss or damage claimed. *Singh*[136] is a classic illustration of this. Despite breaches of relevant Cypriot swimming pool management regulations the Claimant was unsuccessful in his action for personal injury damages because he had candidly accepted that whatever additional safety precautions had been taken to stop him from diving into shallow water, he would have ignored them. Another such example in a similar context is *Healy v Cosmosair Plc & Others*[137]. Mr. Healy (a family man in his mid-thirties) went on holiday to the Colina Da Lapa apartments in Carvoeiro in Portugal. At about 8pm one evening after a day out in the town with his children (part of which was spent watching Ireland play World Cup football) he returned to the apartments where he was persuaded to join his son Jack in the pool. As he went to jump in he lost his footing and fell, twisting in the air as he did so, and landing at about 90 degrees with his head hitting the bottom of the pool. He broke his neck as a result. The basis of the Claimant's claim against the tour operator was pursuant to the express terms of the package holiday contract and regulation 15 of the Package Travel (Etc.) Regulations 1992. It was alleged that:

(a) The pool terrace tiles caused Mr. Healy to slip;
(b) The tiles were deficient and not of a reasonable (non-slip) standard;
(c) The tiles did not comply with Portuguese regulations that required a 2 metre non-slip ring around the edge of the pool (there being only 410mm of non-slip material);
(d) These failing constituted a breach of contract and an improper performance of the obligations under the holiday contract that had caused the accident entitling Mr. Healy to damages.

The Defendant raised a number of issues:

---

[136] See above.
[137] 28 July 2005 QBD Eady J. (EWHC 1657).

(i)   On the facts it was alleged with the help of a number of eye witnesses that the Claimant had deliberately dived into the (shallow) pool;
(ii) The Claimant's judgment was impaired by alcohol;
(iii) In any event the terrace tiles on which the slip was alleged *did* comply with Portuguese non-slip regulations for 3 reasons. First because they were sold and supplied under the description of non-slip. Secondly, because they were indeed non-slip when dry and thirdly the Portuguese architect and local authority regulator had certified the complex as compliant with local regulations at the time the recently built resort had been completed.
(iv) The Claimant could not prove he had slipped on a deficient tile.

Save that he was sure that he would not have dived into the pool, Mr. Healy did not know what caused him to lose his footing. Endless evidence was forthcoming from various eye witnesses. Those in the pool (all relatives of Mr. Healy) describing an accidental loss of control, and those standing by (all independent) describing a dive – but importantly all describing a sort of shallow or racing dive of the sort one might expect to form an entry into shallow water.

There was also evidence from the Defendant's local representative to the effect that one member of the family had more or less admitted to seeing the whole thing in the immediate aftermath of the incident and that it was a dive. The judge thought this evidence unconvincing. The clincher for the Claimant on this vital issue of fact was probably the medical evidence which described the nature of his neck fracture and concluded that the type of injury sustained was only consistent with a (more or less) 90 degree impact with the floor of the pool – head first in other words. This flatly contradicted the independent eye witnesses various descriptions of a shallow or racing dive. Accordingly, the judge was able to conclude on the balance of probabilities that the entry into the pool came about other than by means of a voluntary dive and that the probabilities pointed to an "uncontrolled fall". So far so good from the Claimant's point of view, but was this uncontrolled fall triggered by a slip on tiles that were wet, slippery and failed to comply with Portuguese non-slip requirements? There was a volume of anecdotal evidence from various family and independent sources (including the Defendant's own local representative) to the effect that the terrace tiles surrounding the pool were slippery when wet and a number of previous slipping incidents were revealed. The expert health and safety evidence was agreed that when wet the tiles were as slippery as smooth glazed tiles even though they were to some extent "textured". Again, one senses from the judgment that the expert evidence was more compelling than the anecdotal evidence which was repeatedly described as being "impressionistic". When dry, the non-slip effect was as good as the 410mm dedicated non-slip surface that was there (which the Claimant alleged should have been 2 metres wide to accord with Portuguese standards).

The judge said, no doubt risking a statement of the obvious:

> I came to the decision, as a matter of construction, that the local stipulation for a two-metre (non-slip) strip is not met by the provision of a strip of 410mm.
>
> ...I should have been inclined to hold that the Defendant was to that extent liable for improper performance.

The Defendant's contention that the court could not go behind the certificates provided by the architect and the local authorities (each by implication accepting that the textured terrace tiles constituted non-slip tiles for the purpose of measuring the required 2 metre strip) was rejected – not least of all because the stipulation that there should be a non-slip "strip" (as indeed there was if only of 410mm) was inapt to describe the whole of the pool terrace covered by the terrace tiles. For the second time in the space of 12 months (see *Clough v First Choice Holidays and Flights Limited*[138]), despite the judge's findings of fact indicating that the Claimant and his witnesses were truthful the Claimant's case fell apart on causation. The Claimant had two hurdles to surmount on causation. First, that his uncontrolled fall was caused by a slip (as opposed to a dive), and secondly, that he slipped on a wet terrace tile. The judge reminded himself by quoting from Clough that people do slip from time to time whether or not the surface is non-slip or wet. He was also concerned about expert biomechanical evidence suggesting that a fall (from the general area where the Claimant recalled being) straight into the pool without touching the ground was not a physical possibility, whilst accepting that the Claimant's understandably "patchy" recollection of events meant it was possible he had touched the ground on his way into the pool but simply did not recollect so doing. Of even more concern was the fact that originally (and for some time as the proceedings progressed) the Claimant's contention had been that the terrace tiles were wet because they were in an area shaded by the pool bar and would not have dried in the period since most guests had finished using the pool at the end of the afternoon. At trial, the Claimant's attention had re-focused on the suggestion that the tiles were wet because his son had hopped out of the pool to get a soft drink from the bar dripping water on the tiles in the process. The "shaded area" theory was not supported by the health and safety experts who concluded in broad terms that the area would not have been shaded for long enough for this to be an issue. The problem with the evidence about the son was that it was a very late addition to the factual

---

[138] Discussed further below.

matrix (the evidence was served only a few months before the trial) with the almost inevitable consequences that the judge was hesitant about its reliability. In the event, the trial judge did not decide even on the balance of probabilities what had triggered the Claimant's "uncontrolled fall" and he concluded that the Claimant had failed to prove (the burden being on him) that he had been on a wet terrace tile at the time the uncontrolled fall was triggered.

> It is of course possible that the Claimant slipped on a wet tile less than 2 metres from the edge of the pool; it is also possible that the area had become wet by reason of Jack getting out of the pool. Nevertheless in these circumstances it is difficult conscientiously to draw the conclusion that the Claimant has proved on the balance of probabilities that he actually slipped on a wet area of tiling within the relevant margin.

The outcome on the main action was a resounding "not proven" and in this the result shares some startling similarities with that of Clough.

Clough v First Choice Holidays and Flights Ltd[139] is another example on similar lines. The claim followed a catastrophic accident on 13th November 1999 when the appellant, a young man then 26 years old, slipped from a wall and broke his neck in a swimming pool accident at a holiday complex in Lanzarote. The judge[140] made specific findings of fact. He concluded:

> (a) The horizontal surface of the pool wall was not coated in a proprietary brand of non-slip paint.
> (b) The paint with which it was coated was less effective in minimising the risk of slipping than a proprietary brand of non-slip paint: effective brands for use around swimming pools were available in Spain.
> (c) The horizontal surface of the wall was such that someone walking upon it with wet feet would be exposed to an increased risk of slipping compared with a surface coated with a proprietary brand of non-slip paint.
> (d) The wall was an attractive feature of the complex, regularly used by holiday makers, and indeed "a dive allurement".
> (e) The failure to use non-slip paint constituted a negligent breach of duty by the respondents for the purposes of the contractual arrangements between them and the appellant, and a breach of contract. It was "incumbent" on the owners of Las Lomas to have used good quality non-slip paint. Their failure to do so constituted a breach of the local regulations, and a failure to exercise reasonable skill and care in the provision of facilities at the complex, and the respondents were responsible in law for this negligence.

---

[139] [2006] EWCA Civ 15.
[140] Mr. David Foskett QC [Foskett J.]

(f) A physical barrier should have been provided around the wall, for the protection, not of adults, but children.

On the judge's findings, the appellant slipped on a surface which should have been but was not painted with non-slip paint. His feet were wet, and he had consumed a great deal of alcohol, but by walking where he did and being where he was when he slipped, he was not doing anything abnormal or prohibited by the rules of the complex. He did not dive into the shallow pool, nor miss his footing because he was walking too close to the edge, nor topple from it in a drunken stupor. The claim failed on causation: hence the appeal. In summary, the judge concluded that the negligence and breach of duty established against the respondents lacked "*causative potency*". The judge highlighted a number, but not all, of the features of the evidence relevant to this conclusion. Other users of the fountain pool, and in particular the wall from which the appellant slipped, had used it safely on previous occasions: so had the appellant himself on the day of his fall for part of his journey on foot. The judge commented that Mr Morgan, an expert called on behalf of the appellant, was able to walk safely on the wall when examining it some eighteen months after the accident, when the surface would have become even more slippery than it had been at the time of the accident. The judge thought that it was virtually "*inevitable*" that, given the mixture of water and suntan oil, even the best quality of non-slip paint would not have been sufficient to make the surface of the wall completely non-slip. He was not prepared to conclude that there was any individual "*particularly slippery area*" from which the appellant fell. The judge reflected further on the issue of the alcohol consumed by the appellant. Notwithstanding his conclusion that the appellant was "*not behaving in a reckless fashion*" when he was on the surface of the wall, the judge found it difficult to resist the inference that if the appellant had not taken alcohol, he would probably not have gone on to the wall, but even if he had done so, and slipped, he would probably have been able to avoid the consequent fall. The claim was dismissed as too subsequently was the Claimant's appeal.

Stockman v First Choice Flights and Holidays Limited[141] is perhaps a more obvious case in point on causation. Ms Stockman, a seasoned holidaymaker at 73 years of age, booked a package travel holiday to Tenerife in June 2004. When she arrived at Tenerife Airport she was met by the Defendant's local representative, who in turn introduced her to a 'taxi driver', who would be transferring her to the hotel. Ms Stockman claimed that she was 'marched' across the airport all the way to the Coach Station, whereupon a 25-seater 'coach' (a "micro bus") was waiting for her. In spite of her protestations that

---

[141] 28th April 2006 (Eastbourne CC) Unreported.

she was too old and too frail to climb up onto the step at the back of this vehicle, Ms Stockman attempted to do so and lacerated her leg. The Standard Terms and Condition of booking stated that "*the basic holiday cost as shown in the price panels includes: transfer to and from the resort airport, which will usually be by private taxi or shared mini-bus*". The judge concluded that the transportation provided to Ms Stockman was *not* a mini-bus, since the Defendant itself did not label it as such. This was, according to the judge, a breach of contract. However, the fact that the step on the micro-bus was *lower* than the mini-bus would have been meant that Ms Stockman had failed to establish that the provision of alternative transportation would have made any causative difference to her accident.

Putting lessons together

Priddle v TUI UK Limited[142] combines lessons about local standards, causation and contribution. The Claimant and her husband went on a Package Holiday to Spain that had been supplied by the Defendant. On the 8th day of the holiday she descended a marble-effect staircase that led from the terrace of an external swimming pool to an internal corridor and children's club activity room. Moments earlier an entertainment officer from the hotel had led a group of dripping wet holidaymakers out of the swimming pool and down the staircase. There was also evidence that the staircase was frequently used by children running up and down from the pool, without making any effort to dry off. The Claimant successfully negotiated the first flight of steps, followed closely behind by her husband. She reached a small landing, upon which there was a very large plastic yellow warning sign in the shape of a small man, upon which had been stuck a piece of A4 paper with the words 'Wet Floor' and a warning about the staircase become very slippery. The paper was partially torn but was perfectly legible. As she began to descend the second flight of steps, the Claimant noticed that the staircase was wet and, the Defendant alleges, *turned around* to warn her husband to this effect. At the same time she reached out for a handrail on her right, lost her footing and fell to the bottom of the steps, injuring her elbow. The Claimant brought an action pursuant to Regulation 15 of the PTR 1992 claiming a breach of the implied contractual term to exercise reasonable skill and care for her safety.
There were five specific allegations:

1) Failure to provide sufficiently clear or adequately positioned warning signs;
2) Failure to provide some form of non-slip treads on the staircase;
3) Failure to provide a handrail along the full length of the steps;

---

[142] 19th November 2004 (Taunton CC) Unreported

4) Failure to undertake an adequate risk assessment;
5) Failure to ensure that the holidaymakers, led by the entertainment officer, dried off before descending the steps.

The Defendant contended that the staircase was typical of the hundreds of marble-effect staircases found in resorts throughout Spain, that there was nothing inherently wrong with its construction or design and that it was, bluntly, difficult to imagine a larger or more prominent warning sign than the one already in place. It also pointed to the numerous other signs around the hotel that warned holidaymakers not to walk about in bare feet. The Claimant, the Defendant alleged, was wearing trainers with thick soles at the time of the accident such that step treads would not, causally, have made any difference. Ultimately, it was argued, this was a simple case in which a holidaymaker, through a momentary lapse of concentration, had suffered an unfortunate accident but one for which it could not reasonably said the Defendant should bear responsibility.

The trial judge concluded that of the five alleged breaches of contract, only the suggestion that there should have been step treads in place (for which a risk assessment would have to be carried out) was sustainable. On this point, however, he rejected the Claimant's submissions that the relevant standard of skill and care to be exercised by the hotel was that which would have applied had the accident occurred in England. The correct approach, he said, was that put forward by Phillips J in *Wilson* and confirmed by the Court of Appeal in *Codd* that whether or not reasonable skill and care has been exercised is to be judged by the standards and practices prevailing in the specific locality at the relevant time. On this basis, the Claimant had failed to establish that the staircase was unsafe: not only had it had passed monthly safety audits carried out by the Defendant, but the hotel been granted an operating licence by the relevant Spanish Authority for the use of the staircase which continued to have effect.

The judge also concluded that even if he was wrong on the question of breach of contract, the Claimant could not succeed on causation. The hazard created by water on the steps was well signed. The Claimant knew of the sign, having used the staircase up to four times a day, every day, prior to the accident, and had, by her own admission, perceived the danger before proceeding down the steps in any event. It was also possible, and indeed likely, that the water on the steps had been produced by children using the staircase rather than by the guests who had been led down the steps by the entertainment officer. Failing that, the judge said, he would have found that the Claimant had contributed substantially to her own injuries, not only in the manner set out above, but by failing to use an alternative route available to her through the hotel reception, even though the entertainment officer had led the other guests down the staircase.

This case provides a useful illustration of what many proprietors of foreign hotels would consider to be self-evident: that the mere existence of water on stone or other surfaces cannot, *in the absence of some other specific evidence*, give rise to a finding of liability. It is also a salutary reminder of the fact that *local standards apply* and further it is not enough for Claimants simply to allege breach of Local Standards: Claimants must be able positively to prove such a breach on the balance of possibilities.

Other Suppliers of Services

For whom exactly is the *other party to the contract* liable apart from itself and its own employees? Regulation 15(1) gives the general answer. The other party is liable for the proper performance of the contract irrespective of whether such obligations are to be performed by that other party *or by other suppliers of services.*[143] Other suppliers of *what* services? Plainly this must mean other parties supplying services that form part of the package holiday contract. This would invariably include the hotel operator and the provider of the transfer transport, for example, to and from the airport. To the extent that *other suppliers* are providing specifically identified components of the package holiday the expression should give rise to no particular difficulties. Nonetheless, the boundaries of the tour operator's liability for the defective services provided by others are not always easy to identify. For example, is the tour operator responsible where an accident is caused by the fault of an airport authority through whose airport the consumer must walk from aeroplane to transfer coach in order to enjoy the holiday; or where due to municipal shortcomings a trip hazard exists on a pavement outside a hotel on which the consumer is likely to need to walk to get access to the holiday accommodation? There have been some decisions that assist.

Langton v TUI UK Limited[144] is a reasonable example that touches on this issue, suggesting that a hotel or a tour operator is not to be held responsible where the electricity supply to a hotel fails. The Claimant took a package holiday in Corfu supplied by the Defendant. Unfortunately, during the course of his holiday, and on an occasion when he was in the shower at his hotel, there was a power cut. He reached out of the shower cubicle stretching for the door and had an accident. The Claimant blamed the Defendant tour operator and claimed compensation. The basis of the claim was either that the Hotel was responsible for the power cut because it had embarked on a

---

[143] Tour Operator standard conditions often unnecessarily extend this to agents and subcontractors – should they be different from "other suppliers".
[144] 27 January 2005 (Warrington CC) Unreported.

deliberate campaign of cutting of the electricity in order to save overloading its system due to "overuse" of air-conditioning in guests' rooms. Alternatively, at trial the Claimant sought permission to amend the claim to assert that the Greek Electricity Board was *a supplier of package holiday services* pursuant to regulation 15(1) of the PTR for whose failure (the failure to warn of the impending power cut) the tour operator was responsible.[145] On the claim based in "negligence" against the Hotel the judge concluded that the hearsay evidence available from Corfu demonstrated that:

- The Hotel was concerned about misuse of air-conditioning units although more from an economic stand-point than anything else but their concern was not shown to be related to the power cut.
- Electrical failures were not so commonplace as to suggest the Hotel should have warned its guests about them.
- The electricity supply was checked regularly by maintenance staff and records were available to show this.
- What evidence there was suggested that the power failure was the result of an emergency arising in the village for which neither the Hotel nor the tour operator could be held responsible.

This had been an unlucky accident for which liability could not be attached to the Defendant.

James v Travelshere Limited[146] also touches on this issue, albeit in passing. The Claimant took a package holiday to Sri Lanka in the course of the holiday on 14 February 2001 she visited the Pinnawela Elephant Sanctuary to watch the elephants bathe. She was escorted with the rest of her group to the water's edge where along with many others she stood on an apron of rocks to take photographs. She turned her back to return to the pathway just as the elephants left their bathing in the river to make their way back to the sanctuary; a person shouted "the elephants are coming"; the Claimant was taken by surprise and fell, breaking her ankle. The Claimant blamed the Defendant tour operator and claimed compensation. Essentially the Claimant's allegations boiled down to this and that accordingly there had been "negligence" on the part of the guide responsible for the visit.

- She was allowed to stand where it was unsafe; and
- She was not warned that the elephants were leaving the river.

---

[145] This allegation was regarded as being so feeble that permission to amend in the event was not granted.
[146] 2 February 2005 (Cardiff CC) Unreported.

It also emerged that usually a handheld klaxon was sounded when the elephants were on the march to alert people to the need to get of the way – but that such a klaxon had not been used on the day in question – in breach of the sanctuary's usual system. *In the original claim the Claimant had alleged that the sanctuary was a "supplier" of services within the meaning of regulation 15(1) of the PTR 1992*, but this basis for the claim was abandoned at trial and the Claimant accepted that the Defendant was not liable for any shortcomings on the part of those who operated the sanctuary. The judge concluded that indeed the sanctuary and its personnel had fallen short of their usual standards on the day of the accident and that had the klaxon been sounded the Claimant would have been alerted to the approaching elephants and the accident would have been avoided[147]. However, as it was, at trial *not alleged that the tour operator was liable* for the negligence of this provider of a public facility the Defendant was not liable to the Claimant on this basis.[148] Neither was the tour operator in breach of any duty through its own guide. The rocky apron was reasonably safe; many people used it for photographs; there had been no history of accidents and any warning to the effect that "elephants can move quickly" would not have made any difference to the outcome anyway because she had her back turned at the point when the elephants started to move.

One might provisionally conclude from these decisions that those responsible for the provision of public facilities or utilities are not *other suppliers of services* within the meaning of regulation 15(1) – at least not to the extent that their services and facilities are not designated specifically as components of the regulated package holiday contract.

The Statutory Defences

Where there is proved a failure in the performance of the package contract, or an improper performance of it irrespective of whether such is the fault of the other party to the contract or one of the suppliers, the other party to the contract will still be excused if one of the defences set out in regulation 15(2) applies. However, these defences are of narrow scope.

Regulation 15(2) provides that the other party is liable to the consumer for damage caused by the failure to perform or improper performance of the package contract *unless the failure or improper performance is due neither to*

---

[147] Unless of course she had fallen over as a result of being shocked by the blaring klaxon.
[148] Curiously it was not alleged as it might have been that entry to the public elephant sanctuary was an included element within the touring package holiday, thus rendering the tour operator potentially liable due to the routine application of PTR 15(1) for the improper performance of inclusive components of the package holiday.

any fault of that other party nor to that of another supplier of services, because ... and the statutory defences are then set out. It will be noted that these statutory defences only apply in the absence of *any* fault on the part of the other party or a supplier. So where the supplier or the other party is partly at fault — even to an extremely modest degree — the statutory defences have no application.

A preliminary point of emphasis is important. Before one gets to consideration of whether one of the statutory defences applies, it is first necessary for the Claimant to establish that there has been a failure to perform the contract or on improper performance of the contract. In other words, there must first be a *breach* of contract. It is only in the event of a breach that the Defendant should have need of the statutory defences because, in the absence of breach, recourse to a defence is unnecessary. This may appear to be an obvious point but it highlights the nature of liability under regulation 15 as a whole: liability for the proper performance of the obligations under the contract. So it appears as with all other contract cases, there is only a liability when there is a breach. In order to determine whether there has been a breach one must first ask what the *terms* of the contract are, or what the *obligations* under the contract are. If the obligations under the contract are roughly divided into two categories: those requiring that reasonable care is exercised in the delivery of a service or facility; and those demanding strict compliance, it will be understood that the statutory defences have no role to play in the first category, and in the second category foreshadow defences that might not otherwise have been available to the tour operator at common law.

Reasonable Care Terms

If it is proved by a Claimant that the other party to the contract or one of its agents, suppliers or subcontractors has failed to exercise reasonable care, it is difficult to see how the other party could discharge a burden under regulation 15(2)(c)(ii) for example, by showing that the improper performance was due to an event that could not have been foreseen or forestalled even with the exercise of all due care. The proof of a "breach" of contract (lack of reasonable care) by the Claimant against the other party (or its suppliers) necessarily implies that the improper performance could have been foreseen or forestalled had the relevant degree of care been exercised[149]. Does it make any difference that the expression used in regulations 15(2)(c)(i) and (ii) is *all due care* rather than reasonable care?

---

[149] Longmore LJ in *Hone v Going Places Leisure Travel Ltd.* (above) discusses this without reaching any firm conclusion.

This raises the possibility[150] that even where the Claimant proves a failure to exercise reasonable care it remains open to the "negligent" Defendant to try and prove that even with *all due care* the consequences of the breach of contract or the event giving rise to it could not have been foreseen or forestalled. This looks more like an argument on causation than breach of duty and it is submitted that the preferable approach is to begin with the proposition that the care that is *due* under the holiday contract is *reasonable care* in which case a failure to exercise *all due care* is the same as a failure to exercise reasonable care. In any event it would a rare case where the consumer proved lack of reasonable care where the other party to the contract could excuse itself on the grounds that no amount of care would have avoided the consequences of or the event leading up to the improper performance.

The same issue often arises in the context of a tour operator's express contract terms. *Jay v TUI UK Ltd*[51] illustrates this. It will be remembered that Mrs. Jay was injured on a yacht (called *Tiami*) in the Caribbean whilst on a holiday excursion. The trial judge concluded that the defect in mast that broke and fell on Mrs. Jay was a latent defect. The judge also concluded that the tour operator had not by either contract or by regulation accepted any form of strict liability to the Claimant for her accident, but went on to deal with the contractual defence of *force majeure* (the contract mirrored the statutory provisions in regulation 15(2)(c)(ii) that *even if* the *prima facie* liability under the contract had been strict, the tour operator would have made out the contractual defence. He said this:[152]

> The clear inference is that Tiami had been operating without problem ever since its date of construction and there is no suggestion of any relevant defect (or symptom) at any time. I repeat the fact that there has never been any allegation on behalf of Mrs. Jay of any want of maintenance. Moreover, [the expert witness] said that "a skilled yacht surveyor might possibly be able to detect a fault in the mast by careful inspection and tap sounding ...". And indeed the same paragraph goes on heavily to qualify even that possibility. The alleged defects are latent defects" (emphasis added). This provides no basis whatever for the contention that even a skilled yacht surveyor would probably have detected these defects, even if engaged to undertake a major survey of Tiami. Nor, applying a degree of common-sense when looking at the various photographs of the broken mast can I conceive of any contrary evidence. In all the circumstances, I rule that there is no proper basis to allow this issue to be re-opened for further evidence. For all the above reasons, I consider that the answer is inevitable, namely that Mrs. Jay's injury was caused by an event which the relevant party could

---

[150] As yet untested in the courts
[151] [2006] EWHC B1 (QB) (23 November 2006)
[152] Digested from paragraph 94 of the Judgment onwards

not have predicted or avoided even if it had taken all necessary and due care. In those circumstances, there is no liability of Thomson under clause 7, even on the assumption that the word "duties" in that clause does include strict contractual duties. If that assumption is removed, it is clear from all the above that was no want of care by any relevant party; accordingly, a much shorter route would lead to the same conclusion.

Strict Liability Terms

Where the contractual obligation to provide a facility is a strict obligation (the camp site has a swimming pool) and there non-performance is proved (the camp site does *not* in any meaningful sense have a swimming pool) there remains a role for the statutory defences. If the absence of the swimming pool is the result of debris from neighbouring building work collapsing into the pool rendering it unusable, the other party to the contract may have recourse to Regulation 15(2)(b) or (c)(ii). The problem may be attributable to unforeseeable behaviour by an unconnected third party or an event that the other party could have forestalled even with the exercise of all due care. In such situations the other party to the contract may be given a statutory defence to breach of contractual term of apparent strict liability. So, at least in the context of the so-called strict liability terms of the contract, that strict liability does appear to be qualified by the statutory defences.[153] To this extent the regime under regulation 15 of the PTR 1992 may be *less* demanding of tour operators than would the common law.[154]

How the Statutory Defences Work

It is submitted that the language of regulation 15 (2) suggests that the burden of proving the application of one of the statutory defences in the case of a contractual term of apparent strict liability is on *the other party to the contract.* Assuming a breach of contract (non-performance) is proved, first, the other party to the contract must show that no fault attaches to itself or a supplier for one of the reasons set out in the remainder of the subparagraph. Secondly, the list of excusing events set out in subparagraphs (2)(a) to (c) is exhaustive. If the other party cannot bring itself within one of the specified exceptions, the statutory defences cannot apply. The threshold imposed by these defences is a high one and it is rare to find a successful defence based on any one of them. They are often pleaded by way of defence, but seldom successful. It is perhaps for this reason that much discussion and effort has been concentrated on the extent of the package contract obligations themselves of which there must be a *breach* before any question of the

---

[153] At common law the other party would have to rely on doctrines such as Frustration.
[154] Or at least it removes the need for the other party to the contract to rely on the law of Frustration.

application of the statutory defences arises. Assuming a breach is proved, the other party to the contract must cross two thresholds. First, to prove the absence of any fault on its own part or that of a supplier of package services; secondly, to demonstrate that the absence of fault was *because* of one of the reasons set out in the statutory defences.

Failures that occur in the performance of the contract are attributable to the consumer

In short, if the damage is *entirely* the consumer's own fault the statutory defence excuses the other party to the contract from any liability. It should be emphasised that this is not the equivalent of a contributory negligence provision. The other party to the contract is excused only if the failure in the performance of the contract is not due to *any fault* on its own part or that of a supplier. Plainly there is no contributory negligence without primary liability, so where contributory negligence is the issue, the statutory defence under regulation 15(2)(a) is not the instrument to be deployed. Failures that are wholly attributable to the consumer might include:

- a fall at the hotel pool as a result of intoxication;

- a missed flight due to the misreading of a clear itinerary;

- larking about on a transfer tender leading to a fall overboard;

- over-reacting to administrative problems and booking into an alternative hotel.

Had regulation 15(2)(a) been intended as a contributory fault mechanism, it would have been very easy for the regulators to have said so. However, the absence of a contributory fault mechanism in the 1992 Regulations does not mean that contributory negligence cannot be validly and successfully raised by the other party to the contract. In order to rely on the partial defence of contribution, recourse must be made to the general law.[155]

A good example of the sort of situation envisaged by regulation 15(2)(a) is *Hartley v Intasun*[156] - although it pre-dates the implementation of the PTR 1992. In this case the Claimant misread his ticket and arrived at his departure airport 24 hours late. The tour operator nonetheless got him to his holiday destination where he found that his accommodation had been reallocated. An alternative of inferior standard was provided instead. His own late arrival at the airport did not stop the Claimant from claiming damages against Intasun. He lost. His late arrival at the airport was the only relevant breach of contract, and he had been lucky that the tour operator

---

[155] Law Reform (Contributory Negligence) Act 1945.
[156] [1987] CLY 1149.

had been able to provide any sort of alternative arrangements. Consider also the case of *Mauro Tarantini di Maggio v Lunn Poly*[157] which describes facts that in a package travel context would almost certainly trigger the defence under regulation 15(2)(a). Mr. di Maggio was also late for his flight, and missed it. In his case he blamed the travel agent for providing a poor photocopy of directions to the car park at Heathrow Airport as a result of which he and his navigating girlfriend got hopelessly lost. They had to purchase alternative flights to Cairo and sued the travel agent for the price. The judge treated the case as one in negligence[158] and dismissed the claim. The fault was nobody's but Mr. di Maggio's.[159]

The Court of Appeal has decided[160] that contributory negligence is available as a partial defence to a claim brought in contract[161] only where the liability in contract is coextensive with liability in negligence. It follows that where the breach of contract alleged is a breach of a duty of strict liability, the 1945 Act has no part to play in the apportionment of liability between the parties. So, the apportionment of loss permitted by the 1945 Act is of limited scope in contract claims and arises for present purposes only where the contractual duty is the same as the duty to exercise reasonable skill and care and will bite in cases to which the PTR 1992 applies only where a breach of a "reasonable care" contractual term is at issue. Where a claim is based on an alleged breach of statutory duty it has been clear since before the passing of the 1945 Act that at common law the defence[162] of contributory negligence was available to the alleged wrongdoer.[163] However, claims under regulation 15 of the PTR 1992 are not claims for damages fro breach of statutory duty. This gives rise to potential problems for tour operators that have as yet not been the subject of litigation in the higher courts.

In summary:

- Contribution is not available as a partial defence to the other party to the package contract under regulation 15(2) or the PTR 1992 because the other party must prove that non-performance occurred without *any* fault on its own part of that of its suppliers.

---

[157] Unreported – 2 May 2003 – Woolwich County Court
[158] No argument was based on the PTR 1992 because the chosen defendant was the travel agent and the contract was for flights only.
[159] See also on the related topic of "*parental negligence*" cases such as *Roberts v Iberotravel* [QBD 1996-08118] Gibbs J. and *Murphy v JMC Holidays Limited* [2003] ITLJ 16 in both of which cases the judges took the view that parents were 50% responsible for aspects of their respective offspring's injuries for not keeping the children under proper supervision. In such cases of course it is necessary to join parents as Part 20 Defendants.
[160] *Forsikringsvesta v Butcher* [1989] AC 852
[161] Claims under the PTR 1992 are claims in contract
[162] Then a complete defence
[163] *Caswell v Powell Duffryn Associated Collieries Ltd* [1940] AC 152

- An action under the PTR 1992 is an action for breach of contract. An action brought under the 1992 Regulations is *not* an action for breach of statutory duty, neither are the regulatory duties necessarily co-extensive with the tour operator's duties in negligence (on the contrary some of the duties imposed on the tour operator are duties of strict liability).

- It would appear, therefore, that as a matter of general law, the partial defence of contributory negligence is only available to the other party to the package contract where the alleged breach of duty is a breach involving the failure on the part of the tour operator or a supplier to exercise reasonable care.

The apparent limits of the usefulness of the partial defence of contributory negligence, could pose a serious restriction on the tour operator's ability to defend itself in some cases. Suppose a consumer is promised the allocation of a villa with swimming pool but on arrival discovers that there is no pool at the villa in question. This is a failure to perform the package contract which imposes strict liability on the tour operator. It avails the tour operator nothing to say that it took all reasonable care to check that the owner was telling the truth when he described the villa as having a pool. The tour operator cannot even partially defend itself by saying that if only the consumer had mentioned his dissatisfaction a neighbouring villa of comparable quality with a pool was empty and available for the consumer's occupation. The consumer's disappointment and the diminished value of his holiday without a pool was, therefore, partly or even largely his own fault. Such a partial defence (based on contributory negligence) will not work because the tour operator cannot maintain that the failure in the performance of the package contract occurred without *any* fault on the part of itself or a supplier, neither can it maintain that the continuing problem was (entirely) the fault of the consumer pursuant to regulation 15(2)(a). It may well be that the drafters of the PTR 1992 considered that regulation 15(2)(a) *should* have been that which permitted the court to apportion responsibility between a defaulting tour operator and the unreasonable consumer[164] but if this was the intention it has not been achieved. The answer in these instances for the other party to the contract must look elsewhere for a mechanism to limit the Claimant's claim. The other party to the contract is liable only for damage *caused* by the failure to perform the holiday contract and the assessment of such damage is subject to the usual principles of mitigation.[165]

The position will be different where the tour operator or supplier is in breach of a contractual requirement to exercise reasonable care. If the service

---

[164] Perhaps by deploying PTR 1992 regulation 15(9).
[165] See Chapter 7 – Damages and Other Remedies.

provider fails to take reasonable care in the implementation of a sensible maintenance system, or the transfer coach driver drives negligently, the tour operator may be able to avail itself of the general law of contributory negligence where the injuries sustained by the consumer are partly the result of his own fault — for example, in being too intoxicated to notice that the wall was not safe to jump over; or for failing to wear the seat belt provided. In these instances the contractual duty under the package is likely to be co-extensive with the other party to the contract's duty to the consumer in negligence, and the partial defence of contribution could be successfully raised under the 1945 Act.

Therefore, whether the consumer's damages fall to be reduced by reason of his own fault, much will turn on the type of contractual obligation that has been improperly performed. This issue has yet to be the subject of any reported litigation.

Failures attributable to a third party

Regulation 15(2)(b) excuses the other party to the contract where the failures in the performance of the contract are attributable to a third party *unconnected with the provision o f the services contracted for, and are unforeseeable or unavoidable.*

The scope of this defence remains obscure which may explain why it is little used by defendants. When is a third party "unconnected"? Does this expression mean that the third party should not be a supplier or an employee of a supplier of package contract services[166] or is it wider than this? The employee of a package airline or hotel is almost certainly "connected" with the provision of contractual services in a very real sense. But what of other collateral service providers? Are airport or municipal authorities, or air traffic controllers "unconnected" with the provision of contractual services? Are the utility providers which supply services to the package accommodation "unconnected" so that when there is an electricity workers' strike, the tour operator is excused under regulation 15(2)(b)? Are baggage handlers, airport maintenance staff, railway porters, customs officials "unconnected" with the provision of services contracted for? There is, as yet, no authoritative decision which answers any of these questions.

In many respects it is absurd to say that the persons identified above are "unconnected" with the services contracted for, because collateral though they may be, proper performance of their functions is essential to the successful performance of many a package tour. When baggage handlers are on strike, or fail to deliver the baggage as directed, a package trip is likely to be

---

[166] I.e. those services itemised on the confirmation invoice.

compromised. If the municipal authority has failed to maintain and repair the necessary highway at the airport or outside the hotel and an accident occurs as a result, is the other party to the contract liable to the consumer for the damage? Unfortunately, it remains to be seen whether these, or some of these, collateral persons will be regarded as "unconnected" or not. The pro-consumer view would be that they are certainly connected persons whose performance is essential to the smooth running of package arrangements. The opposite view takes a narrower approach to the meaning of "package services". On this side of the argument it would be said that the unconnected person only had to be unconnected *literally* with the services contracted for. Whilst air traffic controllers, railway signallers and baggage handlers may be collaterally essential to a successful package tour, they are not persons in any way connected with the service which appears *in the contract*. The transport arrangements — flights or rail journeys — may well form an integral part of the package contract, but the incidental services which keep the transport operation moving (however essential) are not services which figure in the contract itself. However, where these essential but collateral services fail the failure is likely to trigger a failure in the performance of the package holiday[167] contract and such a failure would be attributable to a third party who is connected with the transport of accommodation service that is mentioned in the contract. It is tentatively submitted that a pro-consumer view of regulation 15(2)(b) is likely to prevail. It is likely that to be unconnected, the third party should in all senses be an "outsider" to the services contracted for. The collateral but essential service providers (baggage handlers or air traffic controllers) may not be mentioned in the contract under the heading "transport services" but their services are intimately connected with transport services which will be set out in the package contract and without them the contractual services could not be properly performed.

Accordingly, a "connection" with the travel services contracted for, may cover much more than those who are directly contractually linked with the consumer and the other party to the contract — whether as principals, agents or employees. Had it been the intention of the regulators to provide for a wide category of "unconnected" parties it is not likely that they would have chosen to adopt the term "unconnected" third party in the context of regulation 15 (2) (b). Had the regulators intended the other party to the contract to have a generous escape route through regulation 15 (2) (b) it would have been relatively easy for them to provide that the tour operator should not be liable where a failure in the performance of the package contract was due to the fault of a person who was not a *contractual* service

---

[167] A strike at the airport is likely to lead to a failure to deliver passengers' luggage at their destination, for example, which will have a knock-on effect on the performance of the package contract itself.

supplier, or such a supplier's servant or agent. The fact that the regulators did not do this suggests that they intended the scope of the regulation 15 liability to apply to the tour operator even though the fault lay with an incidental provider of a collateral service the provision of which was *implicit* in the express agreement made between the consumer and the tour operator.

The classic operation of regulation 15 (2)(b) is intervening criminal activity,[168] or local government action as in *Griffith v Flying Colours Holidays Ltd*[169] where the tour operator was absolved from liability for inconvenience caused by replacement sewerage works in the vicinity of a holiday hotel. It is likely that the connected and "unconnected" third party cases will continue to be decided on a fact sensitive basis adopting the favourite approach of the English courts, namely considering all the circumstances of the case.

Unforeseeable or unavoidable — regulation 15 (2)(b)

Establishing that the failure in the performance of the contract is due to the fault of an unconnected third party is only the *first* hurdle for the other party to surmount if regulation 15 (2)(b) is to form the basis of a successful defence. Once it is established that the third party is "unconnected" with the services contracted for it must further be shown that the failure in the performance of the contract attributable to the third party was unforeseeable *or* unavoidable.

Let us suppose that a consumer is injured whilst sitting on a hotel veranda by a bottle thrown by a passing football hooligan. This particular third party would almost certainly be unconnected with the services contracted for. Whether the action was unforeseeable or unavoidable depends on the circumstances. The consumer on holiday during the "Portugal 2004" football competition at a resort near to where English, Dutch or German football teams were playing may argue with some force that the intrusion of football thugs was entirely foreseeable, and the incident entirely avoidable if adequate security measures were taken; or a warning issued; or fencing erected. Some resorts in the Caribbean are plagued with armed intruders who paddle small boats ashore onto private beaches. Injury caused by these "unconnected" intruders is eminently foreseeable and resorts often take elaborate measures to avoid the consequences by mounting armed guards of their own. There is almost no foreseeable event which is not also avoidable,

---

[168] *Beales v Airtours* [1996] ITLJ 167 – where consumers sued the tour operator having been attacked by street robbers in their Algarve resort. The Court of Appeal refused leave to appeal against the dismissal of the action at first instance. It was held that a tour operator might only owe a duty to consumers to warn against criminal activity where tourists were specifically targeted by criminals.
[169] [1999] CLY 5473.

and there are likely to be many unforeseeable events which may be avoidable with proper security and safety systems. Criminal activity is a good example. A visit to certain parts of the United States may involve the provision of open and insecure accommodation on the grounds that crime is unheard of, for example, accommodation in an Amish village or some islands off the coast of Virginia where the crime rate is literally zero. Package accommodation may, as a result of prevailing local conditions have no security. However, a failure in the performance of the package contract may arise as a result of a serious one-man crime wave which might be described as unforeseeable in the circumstances — but surely avoidable if modest security precautions had been put in place at the package accommodation.

Furthermore, by *whom* should the incident be avoidable. Presumably the regulators mean avoidable by a person or party connected with the services contracted for, rather than avoidable by the unconnected third party to whose fault the failure in the performance of the package is attributable. Imagine that the airport transfer coach is involved in an accident on the way to a city centre hotel. The accident is entirely the fault of a driver other than the coach driver. Such accidents are only too foreseeable. Would it be unavoidable? The entirely innocent coach driver would plausibly maintain that the accident was utterly unavoidable. However, the accident was certainly avoidable if the unconnected third party had exercised reasonable care in his driving. One assumes that unavoidability relates to the conduct of the parties delivering the contract services, although the PTR 1992 do not make this unambiguously clear.

How literally are we to take the expression "unavoidable"? Is it to be taken literally, irrespective of the expense or effort involved or the extent of the risk that exists? Again in the absence of authority one can only surmise that in English courts the gloss of reasonableness and proportionality will be imposed on this part of regulation 15 (2)(b). Would it be reasonable or proportional to invest in accommodation security measures at a destination with no or virtually no crime at all? The answer would probably be that some security would be reasonable, but the extent of that security would not be expected to match measures put in place in New York or Los Angeles. Would it be reasonable or proportional to invest in high security fencing to ward off passing football hooligans? It is likely that the expression "unavoidable" will be taken to mean in this jurisdiction *unavoidable in all the circumstances, taking into account the nature and consequences of the risk to the consumer and the extent and cost of the measures reasonably required to avoid that risk.*

Force majeure

Force majeure is a convenient short-hand for the circumstances envisaged by regulation 15 (2)(c). This particular part of the statutory defences applies regardless of whether the failure in the performance of the contract was due to the fault of a person connected or unconnected with the package services. Regulation 15 (2)(c) applies as much to problems originating from the "other party" as it does to difficulties arising from the actions of unconnected third parties. It also applies more commonly to circumstances where it is envisaged no person or party is to blame at all — but the failures in the performance of the contract arise due to outside influences over which the other party to the contract has little or no control. It is worth noting in passing that throughout the statutory defences under regulation 15(2) the other party to the contract appears to be excused for *"failures"* which occur in the performance of the contract. There is no reference to *"improper performance"*. This is probably of no consequence. Whilst regulation 15(2) draws a distinction between "the failure to perform the contract" and "improper performance of the contract", the *"failures"* referred to in regulation 15(2)(a) to (c) are almost certainly failures of all types – including improper performance. However, it is possible that the regulators had well in mind the difference between a "failure" to perform a term of strict liability and the "improper performance" of a term requiring the exercise of reasonable skill and care[170] and recognised that there was little if any role for the statutory defences in cases where a breach of a "reasonable care" obligation arises.

Unusual and unforeseeable circumstances — regulation 15 (2)(c)(i)

In order to take advantage of this defence the other party to the contract must be able to show that the failures in the package contract performance were due to:

* unusual circumstances;

* unforeseeable circumstances;

* beyond the control of the party pleading reliance on the defence;

* the consequences of which could not have been avoided;

* even if all due care had been exercised.

The other party to the contract must show that *all* of the above factors apply before the defence is made out. Small wonder that in the light of such a tough threshold this defence is seldom made out in practice.

The circumstances must be *both* unusual and unforeseeable. Where something is unforeseeable it is almost bound to be unusual one would have thought, but the reverse is not necessarily true. Some things may be very

---

[170] The distinction identified by Douglas Brown J. in *Hone v Going Places Leisure Travel PLC* (above).

unusual, but *foreseeable*. An earthquake in Japan or San Francisco may be unusual, but it is surely foreseeable. Foreseeability, or *reasonable* foreseeability, does not necessarily require the degree of clairvoyance needed to predict with certainty the happening of a given event at a given time with a given ferocity. All that is required is that the circumstances should, with reasonable knowledge of the destination, be of a type that could have been reasonably anticipated. Earthquakes, tropical storms and other freak weather conditions will, in some parts of the world, be statistically unusual, but foreseeable; and the same probably applies to riots, coups, civil disturbances, epidemics and other health emergencies. It might be *unusual* for tourists to be attacked by terrorists in central Africa, but any knowledge of the current political turmoil in that part of the world could render such attacks reasonably foreseeable. One of the conundrums faced by tour operators in particular when faced with the high demands of regulation 15 (2)(c) (i) is that the more warnings issued and precautions taken, the more it looks as though the circumstances that might give rise to the failure in the performance of the package contract were foreseeable. Another conundrum is that tour operators often rely on information supplied by other agencies, such as the Foreign Office, national and local governments and tourist boards in order to inform themselves of any likely trouble spots. The draw-back here is simply this. Lack of information about potentially damaging circumstances does not render an event unforeseeable — merely unforeseen.

The tour operator must also be able to show that even where circumstances were unforeseeable and unusual the consequences (*i.e.* all the consequences) of the circumstances could not have been avoided even if all due care had been exercised. If the there are unusual and unforeseeable circumstances beyond the control of the tour operator, it is the *consequences* of the circumstances that should be addressed in the context of deciding whether all due care could have made a difference. The tour operator must devise and where necessary implement a system designed to eradicate or at least minimise the consequences of the circumstances for the consumer. It may be virtually impossible for a tour operator to avoid the physical impact and effect of a hurricane, but the tour operator *can* avoid all, or at least some, of the consequences of the failure in the performance of the package contract that results from the hurricane by devising adequate strategies to cope with such emergencies when they foreseeably arise. The tour operator cannot "shore-up" the crumbling resort in the midst of a tropical storm, but it can and should have a reasonable protocol in place to avoid the consequences or some of the consequences of the storm as they affect the performance of the contract. These steps might include evacuation measures, alternative accommodation or even an early and cautious implementation of the options permitted by regulations 12–14 of the PTR 1992.

Devastating hurricanes hit Grand Cayman only about once every 25 years — or less. However, there is a near miss about once every five years and a very near miss once in ten. Tempting though it must be, it is not enough, it is submitted, for a tour operator metaphorically to shrug and tell consumers that their ruined package holidays were the result of a piece of chronological bad luck which was unforeseeable, the consequences of which could not have been avoided even with the exercise of all due care. Bad luck it may be, but it was reasonably foreseeable bad luck, and the *consequences for the package trip* or some of them could have been avoided with the exercise of due care — by evacuation perhaps to resorts in Jamaica or Cuba. One consequence — the unavailability of the package accommodation on Grand Cayman may indeed have been unavoidable; but others, such as a washed-out and utterly compromised holiday, ruined belongings and several days of terror amidst the storms *could* have been avoided if care had been taken to implement alternative strategies for the consumers affected. In this sense, the defence set out in regulation 15 (2)(c)(i) is a close ally of regulations 14 and 15(7). In this way, it can be seen that the tour operator (or other party to the contract) is excused liability for only those consequences which could not have been avoided but will remain liable for those consequences which could have been avoided *if all due care had been exercised.*

Another alternative for tour operators facing this sort of problem would be to take a radical approach to the packages they agree to supply. The supply of a package promoted as being to a hurricane zone could well raise the issue as to whether the striking of a hurricane caused any failure in the performance of the package contract in the first place.

It will be noted that this defence requires that *all due care* is exercised. This probably means no more than *reasonable* care, though the matter is not free of ambiguity. The regulators could easily have said *reasonable care* if that is what they had intended, and there is a respectable argument to the effect that *all* due care implies a greater degree of care than mere reasonable care — the taking of all *practicable* precautions. Nonetheless, it is submitted that the care that is "due" under regulation 15(2)(c)(i) is reasonable care.

First instance decisions where regulation 15(2)(c)(i) has been discussed have yielded patchy results from which it is difficult to discern any consistent principles. In *Bedeschi v Travel Promotions Limited*[171] the tour operator avoided liability for gastrointestinal illness aboard a Nile cruise vessel on the basis that expert evidence was adduced to show that such illness was commonplace in these circumstances and the risk of contracting it could not

---

[171] Unreported.

be eradicated due to the prevailing local standards of hygiene.[172] On the other hand in *Jordan v Thomson Holidays Limited*[173] the tour operator was held liable for the fact that a burst water pipe caused a flood in the Claimants' accommodation which led to the consumers being moved to alternative accommodation for which they claimed compensation. According to the judge, burst pipes are neither unusual nor unforeseeable nor are they beyond the control of the occupier[174] and as Thomson had not discharged the burden of proving that the consequences of the burst could not have been avoided even if all due care hade been exercised, it was liable to its customers for the resulting inconvenience. The curtailment of a skiing holiday as a result of extreme weather conditions was held in *Charlson v Mark Warner Limited*[175] not to be the responsibility of the tour operator as a result of the operation of the statutory defence and the tour operator was similarly absolved in *Hibbs v Thomas Cook*[176] because a ferry suffered a mechanical breakdown.[177]

Glover v Airtours Holidays Limited[178] is a strange case where the statutory defences were not apparently raised, but given the facts, may well have had some prospect of success. Mr. and Mrs. Glover noticed that a peep hole had been drilled in the wall of their hotel room, and worse that some of their clothes were contaminated with unmentionable stains. The hotel identified a scapegoat employee and dismissed him. The Glovers refused alternative hotel accommodation because they wanted to stay close to their friends at the offending hotel but successfully sued for damages on their return home. The focus of the hearing seems to have concentrated on whether the employee was in the scope of his employment in doing what he did, and to the surprise of some it was held that he was. Thus it was that the hotel and the tour operator were held liable for his misdemeanours in that the resulting invasion of privacy was an improper performance of the holiday contract. Even so, it is submitted that this is the sort of bizarre situation that might attract the application of regulation 15(2)(c)(ii). Surely the circumstances were both unusual and unforeseeable, and as such it is unlikely that the tour operator could have been expected to exert any control over them. Would due care on the part of the hotel or the tour operator have avoided the

---

[172] Another approach would be to consider whether in fact there had been any improper performance of the holiday contract.

[173] [1999] CLY.

[174] Neither was a burst pipe an "event" that could not be foreseen or forestalled within the meaning of regulation 15(2)(c)(ii).

[175] [2000] ITLJ 196.

[176] [1999] CLY 3829 – and see Chapter 3.

[177] Also *Grahame v JMC Holidays Limited* [2002] CLY 2324 – where the tour operator was absolved for a flight delay caused by technical problems experienced mid-flight. The claimant failed to prove that the mechanical failure was due to the defendant's systematic failure to maintain its aircraft adequately.

[178] Unreported.

consequences of such behaviour? Unless either had some basis in fact for anticipating that the relevant employee might act in such a fashion it is difficult to see what care would have been required by the hotel or the tour operator.

An event which the other party could not forestall — regulation 15 (2)(c)(ii)

The final statutory defence is set out in regulation 15 (2)(c)(ii). This applies where there is:

- an event;

- which the other party or supplier even with all care;

- could not foresee; *or*

- could not forestall.

This is more promising for the other party to the contract. Foreseeing or forestalling in regulation 15(2)(c)(ii) are probably *alternatives*. So even where an event might be foreseeable and foreseen, if even with the exercise of all due care the event could not be *forestalled*, the tour operator is excused liability. If foreseeing and forestalling *are* alternatives this is potentially a wide-ranging defence for the other party to the contract. In this instance it is the *event itself* that is the object of the statutory defence, not the *consequences* of the circumstances which lead to the failure in the performance of the contract as appears in regulation 15 (2)(c)(i). So, whereas in regulation 15 (2)(c)(i) it is the *consequences* that the other party to the contract has to try and avoid by the exercise of all due care, in the context of regulation 15 (2)(c)(ii) it is the event that one has to look to see if it could have been either foreseen or forestalled.

To return to the example of the hurricane on Grand Cayman[179] (though the same applies to an infinite number of other disaster scenarios), the storm may have been foreseeable and some of the consequences of the resulting failure in the package contract performance may well have been avoidable with the exercise of all due care. *However*, the event (the hurricane) could not have been forestalled by the exercise of any amount of care on the part of the tour operator or a supplier. This interpretation of the last of the statutory defences under regulation 15 potentially opens up a wide-ranging escape clause for tour operators in many different circumstances.

- the onus of proving that the defence applies remains on the tour operator;

---

[179] For a detailed discussion of hurricanes and their impact on travellers see *Kilbey, "Of Holidays and Hurricanes"* [1999] ITLJ 46.

• the liability of the other party for himself and other suppliers of package services remains firmly in place.

However, subject to these important matters, Regulation 15 (2)(c)(ii) gives a tour operator more latitude than may have previously been considered. Some of the cases decided under regulation 15(2)(c)(i) might be decided differently on an application of regulation 15(2)(c)(ii).

Examples

• The air traffic control or baggage handlers' strike or other industrial action may well have been eminently foreseeable, but the event could surely not have been *forestalled* with the exercise of any amount of care on the part of the other party to the contract.

• Freak weather conditions or geological incidents may be foreseeable, but as *events* it is unlikely that even the most optimistic consumer would consider it likely that the tour operator could *forestall* them however much due care was exercised. *Hayes v Airtours*[180] is a case in point.

• Mechanical breakdown to aircraft or other transport facilities and things like electricity or computer failures at airports are foreseeable potential irritants, but as *events* it may well be that a tour operator could successfully maintain, they could not have been forestalled — breakdowns occur in the best managed establishments without any failure to exercise all due care in the maintenance of systems and equipment.

• Illness as a result of questionable food hygiene combined with changed environment is commonplace in parts of the underdeveloped world — Egypt and India being two destinations where holiday illness is very common. Illness at these (and some other) destinations is clearly foreseeable. Nonetheless, as an *event* the illness cannot usually be forestalled given the prevailing, ordinary standards applicable at such destinations.

This statutory defence is of such potentially wide import and effect that it appears to restore a semblance of fault-based liability where a partially no-fault regime has been constructed. The true limits and scope of this defence have not yet been fully explored in the small number of decided cases. One such case is *Bensusan v Airtours Holidays Limited.*[181] The Claimants had booked two back-to-back Caribbean cruises, the first departing Montego Bay through the Panama Canal, the second from Montego Bay around the

---

[180] [2001] CLY 4283.
[181] First instance at [2001] CLY 4277 – unreported on appeal.

Gulf of Mexico. They were to be transported to Jamaica by air departing Gatwick airport. However, due to a catalogue of circumstances they ultimately arrived in Jamaica after the cruise vessel had already left on the Panama Canal tour. They stayed at a Hotel at Montego Bay until they were able to join the second cruise around the Gulf of Mexico. They sued Airtours for improper performance of the holiday contract on the, not unreasonable, grounds that they had a legitimate expectation that they would be transported to Jamaica in time to catch the cruise vessel before it departed. However, Airtours' defence was that regulation 15(2)(c)(ii) applied and absolved the tour operator from any liability. It was argued that a confluence of factors had conspired against the tour operator getting the tourists to their destination on time. Those circumstances included the fact that the in-bound aircraft had been delayed; a pot-hole in the runway at Gatwick had further delayed their departure; when the aircraft took off it was confronted by unusually strong head-winds, the crew had to put down in the United States because their permitted flying hours had been exceeded and finally, the cruise vessel had to depart before the flight arrived in Jamaica because otherwise it would have missed its slot at the Panama Canal. This confluence of circumstances it was argued or any one of the individual factors was an "event" that they could not have foreseen or forestalled even with all due care. The Claimants succeeded on appeal. However, the judge on appeal was satisfied that the word "event" in regulation 15(2)(c)(ii) was *capable* of comprising a chain of events or a series of separate events as well as individual events themselves. Even if each individual event was foreseeable (as the Claimants had argued) a combination of foreseeable or forestallable events might itself be unforeseeable or unforetsallable. Nonetheless, the judge was not satisfied that the defendant had discharged the burden of proving that all due care had been exercised and the appeal succeeded on the facts. The construction put on "event", it is submitted, is a curious one. First because the expression used in regulation 15(2)(c)(ii) is "*an* event", but secondly because if each link in the chain or series is itself foreseeable and or forestallable with all due care, such due care should be exercised to prevent a failure in the performance of the holiday contract as each link in the chain emerges. If this were to be done at each stage there would be no such failure in performance, or alternatively, if the due care had been exercised in respect of the first link in the chain the others would not have occurred. *Bensusan* is a case in point. The first problem identified was that the in-bound aircraft was late.[182] This can be both foreseen and forestalled. Had the in-bound aircraft not been late the passengers for Jamaica would not have had their journey further delayed by the runway problems, the headwinds would not have presented such difficulties and the crew would not have run out of

---

[182] As if this had nothing to do with the tour operator whose aircraft it was.

flight time. Despite the dictum in *Bensusan* the preferable approach is to identify *an* event (whether it forms part of a chain or not) and ask whether the defendant can prove that such an event could not be foreseen or forestalled even with all due care in the circumstances and conditions prevailing that give rise to that event *and* that it was *that* event which caused the failure in the performance of the contract. So, if the runway pot-hole and the headwinds were unforeseeable and could not be forestalled with all due care, did either event cause[183] the passengers to miss their cruise?

Other Regulation 15 Provisions

Regulation 15(3)

In the case of damage arising from the non-performance or improper performance of the services involved in the package, the contract *may provide for compensation to be limited in accordance with the international conventions which govern such services.* It is assumed that this means that the categories of compensation as well as the amounts can be limited in line with the limitations permitted by the international convention that applies to the carriage in question. Chapter 10 deals with some the international conventions in more detail. However, debates that have raged for some years as to whether regulation 15(3) is merely a "quantum capping"[184] provision or permits the other party to the contract to limit its liability *as if* it were the carrier subject to the relevant convention; and whether international conventions prevail over the domestic PTR 1992, and the European Package Travel Directive from which the PTR are derived have largely been resolved recently.

First of all, four things are of particular importance in the consideration of regulation 15(3). The first is that it concerns *services involved in the package* — which is not quite the same thing as services in the package contract. It is likely, therefore, that regulation 15(3) can be invoked in respect of failures in the performance of a package even though the services in respect of which the failure arises are not expressly set out in the package contract,[185] provided those services are *involved* in the package supplied to the consumer. The second point is that the other party to the contract is entitled to limit the amount of *compensation* payable as a result of any failure in the package performance arising from one of these "involved" services. In other words, the other party to the contract can *limit* its liability to pay damages in line with the applicable international convention, but cannot *exclude* its liability

---

[183] In the sense of materially contributing to.
[184] Apparently it is – see *Norfolk v MyTravel Plc* – below.
[185] Disembarkation procedures at an airport may keep a passenger within the rules of the Warsaw Convention but the airport services may not be specifically mentioned in the package holiday contract.

or *restrict* its liability to those situations in which liability would be recognised by any of the conventions.[186] A non-performance of the package is a non-performance whether it arises on board an aircraft, in the course of one of the operations of embarking or disembarking or anywhere else. So whilst under Article 17 of the Warsaw Convention, the airline may escape from liability altogether due to the location of the accident giving rise to the non-performance of the package, the tour operator has no such good fortune. The third factor of importance is that the other party to the package[187] contract must make provision for limiting its liability to pay compensation in the package contract. Tour operators conventionally do this simply by rehearsing the contents of regulation 15 (3) at some point in their "small print". Last but by no means least, there are a number of different international conventions, protocols and agreements in force, particularly with regard to international air travel. The tour operator, however, cannot limit its liability to pay compensation in respect of international carriage by air in those cases where the non-performance or improper performance of the package contract arises out of an incident involving an airline which is not governed by any of the conventions. There are circumstances, therefore, where a tour operator could be exposed to pay damages for injuries *in full* because the airline at the centre of the non-performance of the package is not subject to any of the conventions currently in force. This would be to the advantage of the consumer of course. However, where the airline was subject to the unamended Warsaw Convention, *both* airline and tour operator would be able to take advantage of the extremely low compensation rates originally set.[188] Thus, the other party to the contract may limit payable compensation to the extent that the carrier can, according to the provisions of such of the many conventions (if any) that might apply to that carrier.

In *Norfolk v MyTravel Plc*[189] the Claimant took a package holiday aboard the Cruise vessel "Carousel" on which she had an accident. She issued proceedings outside the 2 year limitation period sanctioned by the Athens Convention. The main issue was whether the Claimant's action was time-barred by virtue of article 16 the Convention or whether she had a claim under the PTR 1992 which would allow her a 3 year limitation period. Article 14 of the Convention provides that "*no action for damages for ... personal injury to a passenger ...shall be brought against the carrier otherwise than in accordance with this Convention*".

---

[186] See *Akehurst v Thomson Holidays Limited* – below.
[187] Assuming that the other party to the contract is not also the carrier.
[188] As to which see Chapter 10.
[189] 21 August 2003 [unreported] decision of HHJ Overend.

The Claimant argued that the Defendant had not incorporated the provisions of the Athens Convention into the package holiday contract and as a result could not rely on the Convention and the shorter 2 year limitation period. Regulation 15(3) of the PTR 1992 provides that the holiday contract "*...may provide for compensation to be limited in accordance with the international conventions which govern such services.*" In other words, without incorporation into the package holiday contract, the Defendant could not rely on the provisions of the Athens Convention. The Defendant's case was that the Convention applied automatically as a matter of law.

The judge concluded that the claim arose out of a contract for international carriage. Like the Warsaw Convention governing carriage by air, the Athens Convention was intended to provide a uniform code applicable to international carriage by sea. The Convention was not either expressly or implicitly compromised by the PTR 1992. Judge Overend said:

> If the effect (of the Convention) was to have been qualified, indeed partially repealed so as to make the Convention applicable only in circumstances where there had been an express reference in the contract involving the carrier, rather than the Convention applying a as a matter of law, then in my judgment the draughtsman would and should have said so in clear terms.

> ...the limitation (in regulation 15(3) of the Package Travel [Etc.] Regulations) can be interpreted as being a reference to the damage-capping provisions of articles 7 and 8 rather than to the time-bar provisions of article 16. Accordingly, I hold that there is no conflict between the (Regulations and the Convention) on the issue of the time-bar. The Regulations do not contain any provisions relating to a specific time-bar and the Athens Convention applies without the need fro any express reference.

Therefore, where a package holiday includes international carriage by sea *and the Defendant is the performing or contracting carrier*, the Athens Convention "prevails" over the PTR 1992 at least in respect of those parts of the holiday concerned with the sea carriage. There is no reason to suppose that the same would not be the case under a convention such as the Warsaw Convention concerning international travel by air.

In *Akehurst & Others v Thomson Holidays Limited and Britannia Airways Limited*,[190] the Claimants' package holiday flight crash-landed at Gerona Airport. The Claimants suffered physical and psychological injuries. Britannia admitted that they were liable in respect of the physical injuries

---

[190] Cardiff County Court – HHJ Graeme Jones [Unreported].

pursuant to article 17 of the Warsaw Convention (but not, of course, for any psychological elements)[191]. The tour operator argued that it too was entitled to rely on the limiting provisions of the Warsaw Convention (both in respect of the amounts of compensation payable and the bar to claims for psychological injury) *because their Fair Trading Charter purported to incorporate Britannia's conditions of carriage which referred to the Warsaw Convention* in purported compliance with PTR 1992 regulation 15(3).

A number of preliminary issues were tried. The important ones for present purposes were these:

1.   Were Britannia's conditions of carriage incorporated into the holiday contracts via the Thomson Fair Trading Charter?

2.   Were the holiday contracts subject to article 17 of the Warsaw Convention which restricts compensation for accident resulting in "bodily injury"?

In this action Thomson conceded that it was not the "carrier" for the purposes of the Warsaw Convention (compare with MyTravel in the *Norfolk* case above where it was conceded that the tour operator was the contracting carrier). Accordingly, it was conceded that the Warsaw Convention did not apply directly or automatically to the holidays as against Thomson, but would only do so *if expressly incorporated into the holiday contracts by the tour operator.*

The Judge concluded as follows.

1.   The tour operator's terms and conditions expressly stated that all holiday components (including international transport) would be supplied to a reasonable standard and the tour operator accepted liability for injuries (not limited to bodily injuries) caused by any failure to provide the holiday services properly or by the fault of a service provider (such as an airline).

2.   The small print also included the following: "The Conditions of Your Ticket": *Conditions of Carriage will apply to your journey. You can ask your travel agent booking your holiday to get you a copy of any conditions that apply to your journey …*

3.   The attempt by Thomson to incorporate the carrier's ticket conditions was an attempt to qualify the otherwise clear fault-based acceptance of liability in the body of the small print.

---

[191] See further Chapter 10.

4. An objective observer would not realise that *despite* the liability provisions in the small print, Thomson was trying to exclude liability for psychological injury. The reference to "The Conditions of Your Ticket" was at best ambiguous and would be taken not to be limiting the tour operator's liability but as a reference to the liabilities arising between the consumer and the *carrier - airline.*

5. The provisions attempting to incorporate Britannia's ticket conditions and thus the Warsaw Convention were at best ambiguous and had to be construed against Thomson. Any ambiguity being resolved in favour of the Claimant led to the only sensibly available conclusion that the ticket conditions applied only to the relationship between consumer and *carrier* and did not water-down Thomson's otherwise clearly expressed and accepted liability for injury sustained in the delivery of any of the package holiday services.

6. Furthermore, the attempt at excluding Thomson's liability for psychological injury had not been brought properly to the attention of the Claimants, and what's more this failure offended against regulation 9(1)(b) and (2) of the PTR 1992 which demands that written copies of the terms and conditions applicable to the holiday contract are supplied to the consumer. In seeking to rely on exclusionary provisions in the Warsaw Convention not properly communicated to the consumer under regulation 9 Thomson was attempting to take advantage of its own wrong and should not be permitted in law to do so.

As a result the judge concluded that the Warsaw Convention had *not* been incorporated into the package holiday contract by reference to the Britannia ticket conditions or otherwise. Accordingly, the tour operator was bound by its own contract terms to the effect that in injury cases (including psychological injury) it accepted liability for the proper performance of contract services *and* delivery of the services to a reasonable standard. So, there is no inconsistency between *Akehurst* (no direct application of Warsaw Convention) and *Norfolk* (direct application of Athens Convention) not least of all because the exclusivity of the remedies permitted under the respective international conventions affects only the performing and contracting *carriers.* In *Norfolk* (as with many cruise holidays) the tour operator was at least the *contracting* carrier. In *Akehurst* the tour operator conceded that it was not any species of carrier.

Two things emerge from these cases when considered together. The first is that regulation 15(3) is a compensation "capping" provision and does not allow organisers to limit their liabilities to "bodily injury" under the Warsaw Convention; neither does it allow organisers to take advantage of the shorter convention limitation periods. Secondly, where the organiser or the other party to the contract is also a contracting or performing *carrier* the conventions will apply as a matter of law *irrespective* of whether any incorporation into the package contract has been attempted by the tour operator.

Where an international convention applies directly or is incorporated into the package contract, the other party to the package contract may limit the compensation payable to the consumer for personal injury and death to the extent permitted by the relevant convention, as well as for other non-injury-based losses arising out of non-performance of the package[192].

Regulation 15(4)

With the exception of personal injury and fatal accidents cases the other party to the package contract may limit the *amount* of compensation which will be paid to the consumer provided that the limitation is *not unreasonable*. Regulation 15 (4), therefore, applies to "quality" complaints about regulated packages which will be the vast majority of claims. The burden of establishing that the amount is *not unreasonable* will be on the other party to the contract. The unreasonableness or otherwise of the limitation imposed on the amount of compensation payable in non-injury cases falls to be judged at the time the package contract is made, and not surprisingly, where reasonableness is at the heart of the regulation, the PTR 1992 offers no guidance as to what is and what is not to be considered unreasonable under regulation 15(4).

It is very common for commercial organisers to set out a limit on their non-personal injury exposure to pay compensation. This is sometimes a combined figure for loss of bargain and loss of enjoyment, sometimes discreet figures are given for the latter. Figures of twice or three times the invoice price are within the customary range.[193] Sometimes one sees compensation limits expressed in terms of specific sums per consumer per day (*e.g.* £100.00), coupled with a statement to the effect that the maximum imposed by the limitation is intended for those cases where no identifiable benefit was obtained from the package contract at all after which *all other claims of lesser severity should be judged in proportion to the stated maximum*. In the worst imaginable cases of non-performance or improper performance, therefore, the tour operator should be able to point to the limitation clause in the contract and say that this is the measure of loss agreed (and presumably regarded as not unreasonable) between the parties when the contract was

---

[192] Such damages for loss of or delay to baggage.
[193] *Grant & Mason* "Holiday law" (2003) point out (perhaps optimistically) that "quality" complaint damages seldom exceed twice the cost of the holiday so the utility of such limiting provisions is questionable.

made for the worst imaginable case of improper performance by which all other shortcomings in the performance of the package should be proportionally measured.

One possible draw-back for tour operators who specify scales of compensation applicable to consumers in quality complaint cases, is that the presence of a scale of loss may encourage some consumers to claim more by way of compensation than they otherwise might have considered viable. Sometimes a sum stated as a *maximum* in the contract becomes an irreducible *minimum* in the mind of the consumer. Perhaps the solution is for tour operators to specify as low a compensation limit as *they* consider reasonable in all the circumstances given that the worst that can happen is that a judge will disregard it if a contrary view is taken. This is precisely what happened in *Lathrope v Kuoni Travel Limited*[194] where the trial judge appears to have ruled that the provision of *any* blanket compensation figure[195] (in that case £50 per day) was unreasonable and that in any event given the consumers' 26 hour delay at the start of their holiday, £50 was manifestly inadequate – and thus unreasonable – he held.

Regulation 15(5)

Other than as expressly permitted by the PTR 1992[196] the other party to the contract's liability for the proper performance of the package contract cannot be excluded by any contractual term. Naturally, liability presupposes some breach of contract; failure to perform or improper performance of the contract in the first place so that in defining the contractual obligations one is not excluding a liability.

Are *procedural bars* to be construed as contractual terms excluding liability for the proper performance of package contracts? The classic example is the requirement that any complaint arising out of alleged failures to perform or improper performances of the package contract should be reported to the organiser's registered office within 28 days of the consumers return home, failing which the claim will not be considered. It is submitted that such clauses *do* offend against regulation 15(5).[197] There will have been an improper performance of the holiday contract for which the organiser is liable in contract law; the fact that the complaint does not arrive at the organiser's registered office until more than 28 days have elapsed since the consumer's return home does not affect the organiser's technical legal

---

[194] [1999] CLY 1382.
[195] This is judicial hyperbole as it must surely depend entirely on what figure was stipulated.
[196] Such as "quantum capping" under regulations 15(3) or 15(4).
[197] And probably against other general consumer protection regulations as well, such as UTCCR 1999 [SI 1999/2083].

liability as such, but the organiser is attempting to exclude the liability to pay compensation for the breaches of contract by imposing a procedural bar. The procedural bar is an attempt to exclude a liability to *pay* even if it is not excluding the technical legal liability for the breach.

Regulations 15(6) to (8)

Regulation 15(6) implies into every package contract the terms set out in regulations 15(7) and (8). These terms concern assistance that the other party to the contract must offer to the consumer in the event of difficulties encountered in the course of the package.

Regulation 15(7)

Regulation 15(7) applies only where the other party to the contract would be able to avail itself of a statutory defence under regulation 15 (2)(b) or (c) (but not where the failure in the performance of the contract is not due to any fault of the other party or a supplier because it is the consumer's own fault). It states:

> In circumstances described in paragraph 2(b) and (c) of this regulation, the other party to the contract will give prompt assistance to a consumer in difficulty.

So even where a *force majeure* statutory defence applies, the other party to the contract is still obliged "*to give prompt assistance to a consumer in difficulty*". The PTR 1992 do not suggest of what this prompt assistance might comprise, neither is it clear whether it is intended to stop short of the expenditure of money, or whether if money is spent in rendering the assistance the cost can be passed on to the consumer.[198] It appears to be little more than an exhortation to exercise good practice to help out where the package is compromised as a result of unforeseeable or uncontrollable events. It is submitted that this regulation is of limited scope. The other party to the contract is not on the surface obliged to spend money returning the injured or distraught consumer home, neither is the other party *obliged* to settle hospital bills or pay for other resources necessary to comfort the consumer — such as alternative hotels or resorts. What is envisaged is that, where available, the tour operator should deploy its staff both locally and in the United Kingdom to provide translation and communications services, to liaise with family at home and insurers, and to offer comfort and support. A failure to supply these modest services will itself be a failure in the performance of the package contract which should sound in damages —

---

[198] There is a story (perhaps an urban myth) that one tour operator recently paid a "gratuity" to local police in North Africa to secure the release without charge of a tourist who had been taken into custody for allegedly having a sexual relationship with a woman guest under the age of 21 (but over 18) – the complainant being the woman's father.

although the damages are likely to be modest unless the consumer can show that the other party to the contract had resources reasonably available to it which it failed to deploy to the consumer's assistance, and which caused the consumer some additional loss or damage. Such cases as have arisen under regulation 15(7) tend to support the contention that it is not very demanding.

Perry v TUI (UK) Limited[199] is an example. Mr. and Mrs. Perry experienced a terrible holiday. They claimed damages for an extra, unplanned week in Malta which they said they had to endure because of the tour operator's failure to provide them with adequate assistance pursuant to Regulation 15(7) of the PTR 1992. The holiday went wonderfully right up to the moment that Mr. Perry tried to board his flight home, whereupon the pilot refused to let him on-board. In an instant, the holiday had become a "nightmare". The reason for this refusal, (described by the Claimant as a breach of an express term of the holiday contract insofar as Mr. and Mrs. Perry had already paid for their flight home) was because it had come to the pilot's attention that Mr. Perry had spent some of his time on Malta in one of its hospitals. Therefore, the pilot demanded to see a 'Fitness to Fly' certificate. He said that given that Mr. Perry's illness had been breathing related, a doctor needed to pronounce him as fit to fly. In fact, it was the tour operator's representative who had spoken to Mr. and Mrs. Perry on the coach to the airport and had learnt about Mr. Perry's hospitalisation. She subsequently informed the airline (also owned by the tour operator). Whilst in hospital, one of the tour operator's reps had visited the Perrys and told them that Mr. Perry should get a Fitness to Fly certificate from the doctor before they left the hospital. The discharge day came. According to Mr. and Mrs. Perry, the discharge doctor categorically refused to issue a Fitness to Fly certificate when asked: he said that it was for the tour operator to obtain said certificate. Mr. Perry also mentioned that he had spoken to the Chief Executive of the hospital, who had allegedly reprimanded the discharge doctor for not issuing a Fitness to Fly certificate when asked. Suddenly it appeared as though there was some blame that could be laid at the hospital's door since the discharge doctor did not follow the putative standard procedure.

Could the tour operator be liable in some way? After his discharge, Mr. Perry was never visited by any rep. Further, when the Perry's were visited in hospital, the rep who visited them told them that a new rep would be taking over and would "be fully informed about their case." That new rep never spoke to them and he himself only lasted a day before he was replaced. Therefore, there were three of four reps within a seven-day period. The learned judge levied some criticism on the tour operator in this regard by

---

[199] 13 April 2005 Bromley CC Unreported.

finding that the number of reps must have caused a "breakdown in communication". However, as to whether the tour operator should have done more than what it did and by such omission caused the loss claimed the judge found that it had not. One feature of this case in particular went against the claimant, namely that once Mr. Perry had left the hospital, he never informed the tour operator about how he had failed to obtain the Fitness to Fly certificate which he had been advised to seek from the hospital. The judge found that the tour operator had advised the claimant adequately. Although the rep never spelt out that Mr. Perry would not be able to fly home without a Fitness to Fly certificate, the purpose and import of such a certificate was obvious. Crucially, the tour operator was found to have offered the requisite "prompt assistance" pursuant to Regulation 15(7) of the 1992 Regulations. Any reasonable claimant would have let the tour operator know that no Fitness to Fly certificate had been obtained. There was nothing to suggest that the tour operator was anything other than always contactable. Moreover, the tour operator had offered prompt assistance to the claimant at the start of their extra week but this assistance had been declined. This little visited and seldom reported subsection of regulation 15 requires the tour operator to give prompt assistance to a consumer in difficulty. As usual the court has concentrated on the facts and come up with its decision (unfavourable to the consumer on this occasion). Even so, once again the court appears to have overlooked that the requirement to give prompt assistance to a consumer in difficulty only arises where that difficulty is itself caused by some improper performance of the holiday contract albeit that the improper performance is "excused" due to some "force majeure" event under regulation 15(2)(b) or (c). The first question must always be: in what way is the tour operator in breach of contract. The second is: should the tour operator be excused due to circumstances under 15(2)(b) or (c); only then does the question arise: has the tour operator rendered the prompt assistance required by regulation 15(7). This subsection does not impose on tour operators a free-standing contractual obligation to render prompt, or indeed any, assistance and it is difficult to identify on these facts what it was that was the foundation "improper performance" excused by force majeure that triggered the application of regulation 15(7) in the first place.

Regulation 15(8)

Regulation 15(8) is intended to demand of the tour operator immediate action to try and resolve any complaints the consumer may have in respect of the package contract services:

> If the consumer complains about a defect in the performance of the contract, the other party to the contract, or his local representative, if there is one, will make prompt efforts to find appropriate solutions.

It must be assumed that the complaint made by the consumer about "*the defect in the performance of the contract*" is justified — although the regulation does not say so. One must also assume that once an appropriate solution is found, it should be implemented. Again this may be regarded as an exhortation to good practice although this time it applies to defects in performance of the contract — which must mean defects caused by the other party to the contract or its suppliers. What is the point of regulation 15(8) given that the defect in the performance of the package contract will sound in damages pursuant to regulation 15(1) and (2) in any event? There seem to be two possible points. The first is that solutions to problems should be sought at the earliest opportunity and whilst the consumer is still in the course of "enjoying" the package. The second may be that if the other party to the contract does not make prompt efforts to find (and implement) appropriate solutions, the consumer may be entitled to greater sums by way of damages. That is to say, the failure of the other party to act in accordance with regulation 15(8) is itself a further breach of contract leading to additional damages if the consumer can show that the other party's failure to respond promptly and appropriately has *aggravated* the loss and damages sustained as a result of the original failure in the performance of the package contract. For example, the consumer who is allocated by mistake the wrong hotel may be faced with a local representative who does a "disappearing act". The vexation of the consumer may well be aggravated when it is found as soon as the representative surfaces three or four days later, that an immediate move to the proper accommodation can be organised — and could have been organised as soon as the problem had been identified if someone had been there to help.

Regulation 15(9)

This regulation has the effect of turning the tables on the consumer. It is designed to ensure that consumers take reasonable steps to mitigate any loss they might otherwise suffer as a result of any non-performance of the package contract.

> The contract must clearly and explicitly oblige the consumer to communicate at the earliest opportunity, in writing or any other appropriate form, to the supplier of the services concerned and to the other party to the contract any failure which he perceives at the place where the services concerned are supplied.

The inference to be drawn from this provision is that where the contract includes the appropriate clause and the consumer fails to communicate his complaint in an "appropriate" form to the supplier and the other party to the contract the consumer will be badly placed to recover any damages, *provided* of course that the supplier or the other party to the contract can show that had a complaint been received they would have been able to react satisfactorily to it. In other words, the consumer is under a contractual obligation to complain on pain of being found not to have reasonably mitigated such loss as is subsequently alleged.

A second reason for reinforcing to consumers that complaints should be made so far as is practicable at the time the complaint arises, is so that the supplier and the other party to the contract are able to check the facts. A complaint that surfaces for the first time towards the end of a limitation period, or less dramatically several weeks after the consumer returns home, does create difficulties for the tour operator and service provider in verifying, explaining, excusing or even accepting the reasons underlying the complaint.

Chapter 5

NON-REGULATED CONTRACTS

Introduction

Placing detailed discussion of the PTR 1992 and *regulated* packages before any discussion of general common law principles of contract and tort could be open to criticism as an example of putting the cart before the horse. Be that as it may, the PTR 1992 have had such a dominating influence on the package travel market, and the business to which they apply constitutes such a large (albeit declining) proportion of the business conducted by the travel industry, that the regulations deserve their pride of place. Important as they are, the PTR 1992 do not supplant, rather they supplement general common law principles. There are many occasions when the PTR 1992 either do not apply at all or where they add nothing to the rights and remedies recognised by the general law and there are occasions where common law principles are significant alongside considerations of a package that is regulated.

Regulated packages and common law principles

Common law principles are significant even where the arrangements in question qualify as a regulated package under the PTR 1992. There are at least four major areas in which general principles should remain at the forefront of the consideration of regulated packages. These are:

1. The *formation* of the contract.

2. The *contents* of the contract (or associated non-contractual duties) — particularly the inclusion or otherwise of implied terms — *i.e.* what services under the contract are subject to regulation and the regulatory liability regime.

3. Duties and liabilities arising in respect of additional services supplied alongside (but outside) the regulated package services — *excursions* being the most obvious and frequent example.

4.	The assessment of damages and related principles of causation[1] and remoteness.

The PTR 1992 say nothing about *how* a package contract is made, so, for example, the ordinary rules of offer and acceptance apply. Common law rules relating to the assessment of damages, agency, conflict of laws and frustration are still very much at the forefront of travel cases even where the regulations undoubtedly apply. Where the package is regulated, the consumer may still have a cause of action against the other party to the contract even when the incident complained of arises out of a service or facility that forms no part of the regulated package services. For example, an incident arising out of a badly organised excursion or event, booked locally, and paid for separately may still be actionable against a tour operator even though because the incident or event does not involve the improper performance of a component that formed part of the pre-arranged combination of arrangements sold at an inclusive price, the PTR 1992 cannot be deployed against the organiser.[2] If the tour operator is found liable in respect of a *direct* contractual duty to the consumer for failing to select, monitor or supervise a non-regulated excursion, the consumer may still have a viable remedy against the tour operator notwithstanding that the PTR 1992 apply only to the components of the package *not* the excursion because it is outside the scope of the package. This duty may arise out of a separate excursion contract made locally, or it may be the result of a direct duty imposed by law[3] to the effect that the tour operator should exercise reasonable care in the selection and monitoring of excursions, services or facilities offered to consumers once they have arrived at their destination.[4] Where a consumer books a local excursion at the destination and pays for it separately, an "excursion contract" is made. It will often be the case that this excursion contract is made with the same tour operator who supplies the regulated package even though the excursion is not part of the package itself and even though the tour operator does not actually provide the excursion service itself but subcontracts this to a local excursion provider. Issues often arise as to whether the sale of the excursion is made through the tour operator's local representative as an agent for the tour operator or as an agent for the excursion provider. Only in the former situation is the tour

---

[1] *Stockman v First Choice Holidays* (28th April 2006 – Eastbourne CC Unreported) is a case in point on causation. Mrs. Stockman was promised a transfer from the airport by mini-bus. In the event she proved that what was provided was a *micro-bus* on the step of which she had fallen ulcerating her leg. Technically a breach of contract, the provision of the wrong sort of bus was not causative of any damage as it was shown that the step on a mini-bus was higher than that on the micro-bus provided.
[2] See e.g. *Brannan v Airtours* [1999] The Times 9 February.
[3] This duty may be a package contract duty or a duty in tort.
[4] See further the section on Excursions below.

operator likely to be liable for any breach of the excursion contract. On issues of this character the PTR 1992 provide no help at all.

Another example illustrates how common law principles still maintain a vital role in regulated package travel arrangements. As has been discussed in the context of the PTR 1992, the *contents* of the package contract may include a number of implied terms. Terms as to the standard of health and safety in place at a resort or in respect of food and hygiene are often the subject of implication.[5] Whether a term can properly be implied or not is a matter for the implementation of general legal principles; the regulations themselves do not help. On the existence or otherwise of an implied term may depend a finding of whether there has been any failure in the performance of the contract or improper performance of it. After all, there can be no failure to perform the contract if the obligation on which the alleged failure depends is not either an express or implied term[6] of the regulated package contract.

In addition there will be cases where a consumer chooses a common law route instead of claiming under the PTR 1992. This will occur, for example, in an action based on fraudulent or negligent misrepresentation where the consumer suffered *consequential* but not *foreseeable* losses as a result of a failure to perform the package contract.

Formation of the Contract

Offer and acceptance

Detailed consideration of matters such as offer and acceptance and the incorporation of terms is not part of the scope of this book. However, in respect of both the formation of the contract, and the incorporation of terms, there are some special situations that arise in the context of travel contracts which are worth discussing briefly here.

* Brochures and other material of a promotional nature are likely to be treated as invitations to treat, not offers to sell packages or other travel arrangements. This would be entirely consistent with other retailing

---

[5] As to which see Chapter 4.
[6] The cases have as yet not got to grips with the fact that PTR regulation 9(1)(b) requires the other party to the contract to ensure that the terms of the contract are set out in writing or in some other form as is comprehensible and accessible and are communicated to the consumer before the contract is made. Regulation 9(1)(c) requires a written copy of the contract terms to be supplied to the consumer. Regulation 9 certainly has not prevented the continued wholesale implication of terms as to quality and fitness in regulated package contracts.

arrangements.[7] It is the consumer who offers to buy the product promoted by the organiser in a brochure.[8]

- When the consumer has considered the brochure or other promotional material, she may contact the tour operator or organiser direct; in many cases, however, a look at the brochure will result in a visit to a travel agent. Alternatively, some consumers may go straight to the travel agent and make use through the desk clerk of the travel agent's direct computer links with various commercial organisers. The common law principles still apply in their full vigour at this stage of the purchasing process. The problem here is *how* those principles apply. The consumer who makes use of the travel agent's clerk as a quasi-consultant to review a number of options available as displayed on the computer screen is in a similar position to the consumer who scans a brochure or a number of brochures in order to find a destination or a hotel, or a package that suits them. The main difference between this consumer and the consumer who has previously considered a brochure is that the computer is likely to be able to show the current state of availability which a brochure cannot. It is submitted that in this situation the organiser is still only inviting the consumer to treat, and not making an offer to sell the arrangements on display. The position should not, pragmatically or logically be any different for the consumer who *has* previously considered brochures and is now fine-tuning a request for information by means of the travel agent's computer. The invitation to treat of the tour operator may be considered to be at a more advanced stage than the invitation to treat in the brochure if only because the computer data will be able to say more about availability, perhaps more about the number of people already booked on a specific package and perhaps more details will be available as to price. Nonetheless, this type of computer display remains an invitation to treat. It would be unreasonable to bind the organiser or tour operator to a contract simply by the consumer sitting at a travel agent's desk stating "I accept the offer now on the screen" particularly when the organiser has regulatory obligations to ensure that certain information is conveyed to the consumer before the contract is made.[9]

---

[7] *Fisher v Bell* [1961] 1 QB 394 and *Partridge v Crittenden* [1968] 1 WLR 1204.
[8] Although on the facts of any particular case one must be careful to distinguish an offer to buy from a mere enquiry (e.g. as to price). *Harvey v Facey* [1893] AC 552.
[9] *Gow v TUI UK Ltd [Trading as Crystal Holidays]* 27th. April 2006 (Unreported) Watford County Court – where Mr Gow argued that the contract between himself and Crystal was concluded at the end of the telephone conversation with the organiser, and so: (a) Crystal's standard terms and conditions were not incorporated as no mention had been made of them at the time of the contract: Crystal's invoice was irrelevant as it was a post contractual document; but the judge disagreed, he found it was standard practise for such contracts not to be formed when the travel agent provisionally accepts the holiday maker's offer on the tour operator's

- Computer screen displays and brochures often now inform consumers that no contract will come into effect until such time as the consumer receives or the organiser despatches written confirmation of the booking made — whether the booking was made directly or through a travel agent. Whilst the peremptory refusal of the tour operator to recognise the existence of a contract before the confirmation is despatched would not *necessarily* prevent an objective application of the rules of offer and acceptance leading to the conclusion that there was indeed a contract in place at an earlier stage of the negotiations, if such a warning is issued in clear and unambiguous terms, the tour operator's warning must be a factor that helps to feed the assumption made here that computerised communications (through a travel agent or directly via the Internet, for example) are likely in most cases to be firmly placed at the negotiations stage of the formation of the travel contract especially as the existence of such a notice or warning would be good evidence that the parties to the negotiations had at least implicitly agreed as to the mechanism by which any contract should come into existence. There are many ways of looking at this kind of issue. It may be described in terms of offer and acceptance, as above. In addition to this, pre-conditions may be attached to the making of any offer. The organiser may validly state that no approaches from consumers will be considered unless they are accompanied by the consumer's signature to a written form accepting the standard terms and conditions.[10] Alternatively, for those who insist that the consumer is accepting the tour operator's offer to sell in these situations, it may be that the requirement of written notice of acceptance is the agreed manner in which acceptance of the consumer's offer *has* to be communicated before a contract comes into existence; or even that until a certain stage of the negotiating process the organiser has no intention to create a legal relationship between itself and the consumer. Whichever way these problems are configured the likely result is that in most cases it is the tour operator who accepts the consumer's offer to purchase by one means or another. Or at least, that no contract comes into being until any pre-conditions clearly promoted by the organiser have been complied with.

A good example of the importance of treating every situation on its own facts arose in *Bowerman v Wallace*[11] - a unusual case of a unilateral contract.[12] In this case the consumers had purchased a skiing holiday from a company that went into insolvent liquidation and sought a refund of the

---

behalf. The practise is for travel agents to state the booking as being subject to the tour operator's standard terms and conditions and their written confirmation.

[10] See *Gow* (above).

[11] [1996] New Law Publishing (daily transcripts).

[12] See also *Carlill v Carbolic Smoke Ball Co* [1893] 1 QB 256.

holiday price under an ABTA refund scheme. ABTA obliged with the refund, but deducted the insurance premium paid by the consumers. The consumers complained on the grounds that notices displayed by ABTA member travel agents had promised a full refund in the circumstances in which the consumers found themselves. The consumers argued that a full refund must include the insurance premium which ABTA had withheld. The Court of Appeal agreed. The consumers had made travel contracts with ABTA members partly on the strength of the promise contained in the Notice promising a full refund. The Notice was designed to attract consumers and did attract them to ABTA secured holidays. The language of the Notice was in part colloquial, but consumers would take it to mean precisely what it said. In these circumstances the Notice was itself a *contractual document* offering the full refund in circumstances that applied to the consumers in question. That offer was held out to the whole world in respect of which it was only necessary for the consumer to buy an ABTA bonded holiday in order to accept the offer. In other words, the ABTA promise was a unilateral contract and the consumers were entitled to enforce the ABTA promise to a full refund which included the disputed insurance premium.

Scope of Express Terms

Apart from the terms implied by virtue of the PTR 1992 or otherwise as a matter of law,[13] there will invariably be express terms on which the parties wish to rely. Often it will be the organiser who seeks to rely on some express provision as to the limitation of damages or procedural precondition as to liability, but there are circumstances in which it is distinctly to the consumer's advantage to have, for example, a tour operator's standard terms or brochure conditions incorporated into the contract. Those tour operators who are ABTA members are obliged to include in their contract terms a provision to the effect that the tour operator will accept responsibility in personal injury cases, for the negligent acts or omissions of their servants, agents, suppliers and subcontractors.[14] There are at least two important situations where the express terms of the contract may give the consumer the benefit of protection that goes further than the PTR 1992.

The two situations that extend the other party to the contract's liability further than the PTR 1992 are as follows. The first arises because in almost all cases, the tour operator will adopt a liability clause in its brochure conditions irrespective of whether the arrangements supplied to the consumer qualify as a regulated package. That is, the brochure "small print"

---

[13] See e.g. regulation 6 of the PTR 1992 and section 13 of the Supply of Goods and Services Act 1982.
[14] Clause 2(8)(ii) of ABTA's Code of Conduct for Tour Operators.

will apply to *all* travel arrangements booked by the consumer with the tour operator not just to regulated packages. If this happens, by the express terms of the contract, the tour operator accepts a wide-ranging liability for improper performance including personal injury, *as if* all the arrangements in the brochure were regulated packages. Accordingly, if a consumer books accommodation only and the booking is subject to terms and conditions accepting liability for improper performance of the contract, the other party to the contract will be liable as if the accommodation only arrangements constituted a regulated package. The second and equally common situation is where by means of its brochure terms and conditions the tour operator or the other party to the contract expressly accepts liability in respect of the proper performance of *excursions* or other services that would otherwise be outside the scope of the package contract.

Jay v TUI UK Ltd[15] is worth considering, being a case where a tour operator's conditions were subjected to judicial scrutiny as to their scope and content. In December 2000, the claimant Zoe Jay booked a "Late Deal" holiday with Thomson for herself, her husband and others, to go to Barbados for one week, departing on 28 January 2001. It was common ground that this booking gave rise to a package holiday contract. The party duly flew to Barbados where they attended an introductory meeting, presented by a number of Thomson representatives. As a result of what they were told (and saw on a video), they booked a day's sailing excursion on the catamaran "Tiami II". This booking constituted a local excursion bought through a uniformed Thomson holiday representative, within the meaning of clause 6 of the Contractual Terms. A voucher was issued to the party headed "St James Travel and Tours Ltd" ("St James Travel") and acknowledging receipt of the relevant deposit. St James Travel was the duly appointed agent of Thomson for the purpose of organising and contracting local excursions for Thomson holidaymakers. On arrival at the quayside at the start of the excursion, Mrs. Jay's party paid the balance of the excursion price and received in return the receipt. This receipt was headed in the name of Cruise Management Ltd ("CML"). The outward leg of the journey occupied the morning and was uneventful. But on the return leg Tiami was hit by a sudden gust or squall of wind. Within seconds the mast broke and fell to the deck. As it did so, it struck Mrs Jay, first on the head and then on the back. As a result, she suffered serious injury. It was common ground between the parties at trial that a cause of the accident was the manufacturing defect in the mast of the vessel.

---

[15] [2006] EWHC B1 (QB) – HHJ Adrian Palmer QC.

Mrs. Jay claimed against Thomson on the basis that Thomson is liable in respect of the accident, pursuant to clauses 6 and 7 of the Contractual Terms. Clause 6 and the relevant parts of clause 7 were as follows so far as relevant (emphasis added):

> *6. Our responsibility for your holiday*
> ...if you buy a local excursion or tour through a uniformed Thomson Holiday Rep, *we will pay you reasonable compensation if it is not as advertised* on the Thomson Noticeboard or in the Visitors Book or Thomson Resort Guide. We have taken all reasonable care to make sure that all the services which make up the holidays advertised are provided by efficient, safe and reputable businesses, and that they follow the local and national laws and regulations of the country where they are provided.

> *7. Personal Injury 1*
> This section covers injury, illness or death while you are using the services that we have arranged for you. We have no direct control over the way our suppliers provide their services. But everyone employed or contracted by us or by our suppliers is expected to carry out their duties properly. If they do not carry out their duties properly or at all and that fault results in your injury, illness or death, we may make a payment to you. We will not make any payment if your injury, illness or death was caused by an event or circumstances which that person could not have predicted or avoided even if they had taken all necessary and due care. We will not make any payment if your illness, injury or death was your own fault. *If we do make a payment it will be similar to one you would receive under English law in an English court.*

Mrs. Jay claimed under clause 6. Her claim was simplicity itself: by reason of the accident, the excursion was not "*as advertised*" in the Thomson guide. Thus Mrs. Jay sought to construe clause 6 so as to create strict liability of Thomson for any accident (causing injury) or other mishap, however occurring. The sole requirement for liability being that the excursion was not "as advertised". If correct that construction would create a very wide range of strict liability on the part of Thomson and it would render clause 7 of the booking conditions entirely superfluous. The judge concluded that a different construction prevailed when clauses 6 and 7 were considered together.

Clause 7 stipulated that Thomson would make a payment in certain circumstances, which will be "*similar to one (the consumer) would receive under English law in an English court*". That is to say, Thomson would pay damages for personal injuries suffered, but only in certain circumstances. The judge concluded:

> It seems to me that there is then a clear distinction between clause 7, which deals with personal injury, and clause 6, which does not deal with personal

injury. Under clause 6, Thomson will pay "reasonable compensation" for spoiled excursions (akin to the spoiled holiday), falling short of personal injury.

Mrs. Jay's claim based on clause 6 of the contract terms failed. The reasoning appears to have been on the following lines. Whilst it might be possible to maintain that where a mast breaks and injures a passenger on an excursion, that excursion cannot have been *as advertised* by the tour operator, clause 6 only entitled passengers to damages so far as damages related to the spoilt or curtailed excursion. If personal injury resulted, then recourse had to be made to clause 7 which expressly provided that the tour operator would only pay damages if certain conditions were satisfied, and the most important condition was that the payment would only be made in circumstances where it was *"similar to one you would receive under English law in an English court."* As an English court would only award damages where failure to exercise reasonable care was proved,[16] the liability of the tour operator for personal injury was thus subject to proof of *fault* even though on the proper construction of clause 6 in the present case liability for loss of bargain and enjoyment might be a strict form of liability. The judge said[17] as follows:

> Basically, a holidaymaker can expect proper performance of those services, by the use of reasonable care. This is reinforced by (a) Hone v Going Places Leisure Travel Limited, to the effect that a contract of this type will not create an absolute liability unless there is a (clear) intention to do so; and (b) the use of the word "fault"... ... if this is the proper interpretation, the apparent extension to any contractor to a supplier turns out to be self-limiting, because it applies only to those contractors who bore duties of proper performance of the immediate services that constituted the excursion. By this circuitous route, we would in effect be back to the old-fashioned situation ... – having simply added recognition of the fact that the provision of services is often "outsourced" to contractors, rather than mere servants or agents.

One cannot but suspect that the drafters of clause 7 of the booking conditions had nothing of the sort in mind, and that the limiting words of clause 7 were intended to cover the *amounts* of damages payable, but if nothing else the case illustrates the common dislike of any form of strict liability in the English courts in the absence of the clearest possible acceptance of such a liability. In the event the judge concluded that the problem causing the mast to break was a latent defect and the

---

[16] See generally Chapter 4.
[17] Judgment paragraph 67.

manufacturer's fault, for which the tour operator could not be contractually or by statute held responsible.

There is no substitute for looking at and construing the express written terms of the travel contract even in those cases that *are* plainly regulated packages. A further, if extreme, example serves to illustrate why. A small, independent tour operator had its "small print" drafted to include this provision. *"We accept responsibility in the event that you suffer personal injury whilst you are on holiday"*. This may well have been an attempt to convey in writing what was perceived to be the effect of PTR 1992 regulation 15, but one can see immediately that it is far more wide-ranging than that.

Incorporation of terms

The most sophisticated set of terms and conditions covering every imaginable eventuality will be of no effect unless the conditions are incorporated into the contract and obviously this must happen *before* the contract is made. All the best laid plans of a contracting party can be laid waste if booking staff and agents fail to understand that contracts can come into existence merely in the course of a conversation by oral agreement. Particularly where a consumer has not or *may not* have seen the organiser's brochure or its standard terms and conditions. Strictly monitored procedures are essential to ensure so far as possible (whether with travel agents or with direct booking staff) that consumers are warned that no travel or package contract is to be concluded until certain pre-conditions are satisfied or until a written confirmation is despatched by the organiser.

The PTR 1992 deals indirectly with the incorporation of contractual terms in regulation 6. This is the provision that provides the *"particulars"* in a brochure are to constitute implied warranties in the contract. There is no apparent reason why *"particulars"* should not extend to the terms and conditions and other general information at the front and back of most tour operators' brochures.[18] Had the regulators wished to restrict the meaning of "particulars" to particulars in respect of the holidays, services or facilities promoted in the brochure there is no reason why they should not have said so. If this broad interpretation of "particulars" is acceptable, then the contractual terms (printed at the back of the brochure) become by regulation 6(1) implied warranties in the travel contract. At a stroke, therefore, the PTR 1992 themselves may be thought to incorporate the contents of the brochure including the terms and conditions as implied warranties in the contract. This leads to the undoubted curiosity that terms *expressed* in a Fair Trading

---

[18] With the exception of particulars about security of money in the event of insolvency which are expressly excluded as implied warranties by regulation 6(2)(a).

Charter would be described as *implied* warranties. An alternative construction of regulation 6 to the effect that "particulars" means only the particulars of the arrangements, services and facilities described in the brochure (to the exclusion of the small print) is, however, equally plausible and one that it would certainly be open to the courts to adopt. In practice it may not matter in most cases because tour operators invariably require the consumer's signature signifying that the booking conditions have been provided and are accepted on behalf of the consumer and all those travelling with the consumer pursuant to the travel arrangements that are the subject of the contract.

Nonetheless, whether by regulation 6(1) or by obtaining the consumer's signature the terms contained in a brochure Fair Trading Charter (which usually includes all the cancellation charges, scales of compensation applicable to non-injury cases and procedural or time bars applicable to any claim made against the supplier) plainly have to be incorporated into the travel contract before the terms can be relied on by either party. Where or if regulation 6 is not appropriate for the purposes of deeming the terms to be incorporated into the contract, the normal rules of incorporation apply. Essentially, *notice* must be given to the consumer that terms are intended to be incorporated into the contract, and the notice that must be given needs to be looked at in the context of three distinct requirements.

- *The time when notice is given.* Notice of terms and conditions intended to be incorporated into a contract must be brought to the attention of the consumer before the contract is made. Giving notice after the contract is concluded is too late. In *Olley v Marlborough Court Hotel*[19] property was stolen from a hotel guest due to the hotel's negligence. The hotel attempted to avoid liability by reason of a notice on the wall of the claimant's bedroom excluding their liability in such circumstances. The Court of Appeal held that the notice could not have the intended exclusionary effect because the accommodation contract had been made by the consumer at the time of checking-in at the reception desk. By the time the claimant got to her room the contract had been made and it was too late to introduce additional terms by reference to notices on bedroom walls. The notice was of no effect.

- *Sufficiency of notice given.* Even if given at the right time the Notice or the circumstances in which Notice is given must be sufficient to draw the contractual term to the attention of the consumer. In *Richardson, Spence & Co v Rowntree*[20] the House of Lords concluded that sufficient notice had not been given to a steam ship passenger where the passenger had

---

[19] [1949] 1 KB 532.
[20] [1894] AC 217.

been handed a folded ticket where no writing on the inside of the ticket was visible to her. The conditions printed on the inside of the folded ticket purported to exclude liability for damages for personal injury[21] but the clause was held to be ineffective due to the failure of the defendants to draw the passenger's attention to the existence of conditions before the contract was made.[22]

- *The type of contract made.* There are situations where the consumer is expected to appreciate that the type of contract made is one that is likely to be subject to special terms and conditions.[23] Where travel tickets are issued by railway, ferry or airline companies the consumer is likely to be taken to have known that the ticket would be subject to conditions. The same principle applies, it is submitted, to consumers who book travel arrangements with a tour operator. Tour operators' brochures are commonplace in the modern consumer world and few consumers could honestly maintain that they were ignorant of the fact that many special terms and conditions would be printed in the back of a brochure. Whilst there are circumstances in which the consumer may not be expected to appreciate that a ticket was a contractual document, or more than merely a receipt for payment,[24] travel and transport tickets on which reference is usually made to other conditions[25] are usually within the class of examples where the reasonable consumer would be expected to know that conditions of carriage would be imposed. Reference to any general book on the principles of contract law will confirm that adequate *reference* to terms and conditions is enough. It is not necessary that the consumer should have *read* them.

Incorporation and construction

Akehurst & Others v Thomson Holidays Limited & Others[26] illustrates the problems that may arise where contractual terms are not adequately incorporated or are loosely drafted. The claimants sued the tour operator

---

[21] Long before this was regarded as unacceptable.
[22] See also *Hollingworth v Southern Ferries* [1977] 2 All ER 70 an example of a pre-regulation case in which an exclusion clause printed in the supplier's brochure had not been sufficiently brought to the attention of the passenger.
[23] Many of the "railways" cases where incorporation of contractual terms was by a reference printed on the reverse of a ticket can only be explained on the basis that the passenger must have been taken to know that conditions were likely to apply because at the time the ticket is handed to the passenger the contract would already have been concluded – see for example *Thompson v London, Midland & Scottish Railway Company* [1930] 1 KB 41.
[24] *Chapleton v Barry UDC* [1940] 1 KB 532 (a deck chair receipt) and *Thornton v Shoe Lane Parking* [1971] 2 QB 163 – in which the consumer was not expected to know that terms and conditions referred to on the back of the ticket excluded liability beyond loss and damage to the car.
[25] Whether in the form of posters or printed leaflets.
[26] Unreported – Cardiff County Court 6 May 2003.

and the airline following a crash landing at Gerona airport at the beginning of a regulated package holiday. A significant proportion of the passengers suffered psychological injuries and as a result were unable to pursue that element of their claims against the airline.[27] Instead the claimants pursued the tour operator for psychological injury damages. By way of defence the tour operator maintained that it too was able to limit its compensation to such bodily injuries as could be proved. The standard terms and conditions provided as follows: *"The Conditions of your ticket. When you travel by air or on water the transport company's 'Conditions of Carriage' will apply to your journey. You can ask the travel agent booking your holiday to get you a copy of any conditions that apply to your journey ... "*. It was argued by the tour operator that the conditions of carriage of the airline had thus been incorporated into the package holiday contracts, and the conditions of the airline *in turn* incorporated the provisions of the Warsaw Convention limiting claims to those in respect of bodily injury.

Although the judgment in the claimants' favour largely proceeded on the basis that as properly *construed* the clause quoted above was inapt to bring about the exclusion the tour operator was seeking but because of inappropriate, ambiguous drafting the airline's terms and conditions had not been incorporated into the package holiday contracts and without the incorporation of the airline's terms and conditions there was no incorporation of the Warsaw Convention. It followed that the tour operator was liable for psychological injury in circumstances where the carrier was not.

Similar problems with the incorporation of terms arose in *Lee & Lee v Airtours Holidays Limited*[28] in which the Defendant tour operator failed to secure the benefit of Athens Convention limitations on damages because it failed to incorporate the Convention into its package holiday contracts. No contract terms were produced for the consumer's consideration until they appeared on the reverse of the confirmation invoice[29] and even then the terms limiting damages were not drawn to the consumer's attention.[30]

Another example where the drafting of a tour operator's terms and conditions caused a problem was *Horan v Neilsen Holidays Limited*.[31] The claimant complained about the leg room in his economy class seat on the return flights to and from Canada for a skiing holiday supplied by the

---

[27] Due to article 17 of the Warsaw Convention that permits recovery only in respect of bodily injury against the carrier.
[28] Central London County Court – October 2002 – Unreported – but see *Saggerson* [2002] ITLJ 198 at 200.
[29] By which time a contract already existed.
[30] See also Chapters 4 & 10 for discussion about the questionable basis of this decision on other grounds.
[31] Unreported – Chester County Court April 2002.

defendant.[32] At first instance the trial judge found that the conditions on board for the claimant were very cramped and that he had been unable to walk up and down on the plane, which findings could not be challenged on appeal. On appeal the circuit judge concluded that the contractual promise in the defendant's brochure that package holiday facilities would be provided to a *reasonable standard* was one that justified the trial's judge's conclusion that there had been a breach of contract in the provision of cramped seating notwithstanding that the seating complied with Civil Aviation Authority recommendations.

A third example of inept drafting appeared in *Spencer v Cosmos Air Holidays Limited*[33] a case where tourists had been ejected from their hotel due to allegedly rowdy behaviour. Alas, as son often happens, when the tour operator was sued for failing to provide the contractually promised accommodation it was unable to furnish evidence of the rowdiness that led to the eviction. Furthermore, Cosmos attempted to rely on a contractual clause in its booking conditions that excluded liability for the negligence of its suppliers causing injury, death, loss or damage. The Court of Appeal ruled that the clause as drafted was simply inadequate to cover the claimants' eviction because it had nothing to do with situations where holidaymakers were evicted or where the promised holiday accommodation was not provided or made available for them (for whatever reason).

Contractual Purpose

In *Chapleton v Barry UDC*[34] the Court of Appeal held that a consumer could not have anticipated that a deck-chair ticket was anything more than a receipt for the price paid. The document did not have necessary contractual force to incorporate the terms and conditions referred to on the back of the ticket. Similarly, it is not every conversation between consumer, travel agent or organiser which will be regarded as having contractual effect. In *Kemp v Intasun Holidays*[35] the consumer visited a travel agent at the beginning of the year with her daughter to choose a summer holiday for the family. In the course of a conversation with the travel agent she mentioned that her husband was presently ill suffering from asthma and a bronchial attack to which he was prone. Due to his ill-health she said, extra insurance would be required. She chose a holiday in Mallorca and in due course completed a booking form which was accepted by Intasun. The family went on holiday in

---

[32] The claimant alleged initially that he suffered a deep vein thrombosis but he suffered nothing of the sort.
[33] [1989] – Lexis.
[34] See above.
[35] [1987] 2 FTLR 234.

August, and all too predictably were put in substandard accommodation which induced an asthma attack for Mr. Kemp which in turn caused considerable alarm and distress. The trial judge found in favour of the claimants both in respect of the substandard nature of the accommodation and the asthma attack suffered by Mr Kemp. However, the second part of the judgment was overturned on appeal. Kerr LJ said:

> *One can put the matter in many different ways, but there is none whereby this casual conversation can possibly have any contractual consequences for these defendants.*

The case is also an important one with regard to the status of travel agents[36] and also has implications in respect of foreseeability and remoteness of damage. However, for present purposes, suffice it to say that mere passing reference between consumer and travel agent (and one might add tour operator or organiser) will not necessarily have any contractual implications between the parties to the travel contract.

A linked issue arises in cases of "Special Requests". Tour operators routinely include a clause in the terms and conditions to the effect that whilst they will use their best endeavours to provide any special requests[37] made by the consumer, such cannot be guaranteed and the requests do not form part of the package contract. This is usually taken up on the confirmation invoice which will set out any special request and reaffirm that their provision is not guaranteed. These are examples of non-contractual communications between the parties save to the extent that there might be implied or expressed an obligation on the other party to the contract to exert some effort in an attempt to bring the special request into effect.[38]

Effectiveness of Incorporation

It is all very well incorporating contractual terms, but when incorporated will they be effective? Once again this is a matter for the general law whether one is dealing with a regulated package contract or not. In the context of, for example, exclusion of liability clauses, limitation of damages clauses, liquidated damages or penalty clauses; procedural bars, definitions clauses — travel contracts (including regulated package contracts) are no different from any other form of contract and will be governed by ordinary principles of

---

[36] See further Chapter 8.
[37] Special requests are usually concerned with things like "quiet" or adjoining rooms, or rooms with a view, or additional leg room on aircraft seats.
[38] In *Thompson v Airtours Holidays Limited (No.2)* [2002] CLY 2323 the trial judge concluded that to accept a request for the allocation of a quiet room and then do nothing about bringing the request into effect was misleading, but the effect of this conclusion is unclear from the case report.

contract law either pursuant to statute or the common law. Each of the above types of clause will be looked at briefly in a travel contract context.

Exclusion and limitation clauses

The Unfair Contract Terms Act 1977 (UCTA) is almost always going to apply to a travel contract, either because one party is acting in the course of a business and the other is a consumer, or because one party is contracting on another's standard terms of business.

Section 2(1) of UCTA is of general application and prohibits the exclusion or limitation of liability for death or personal injury resulting from negligence by reference to any contract term or any form of notice[39]. Section 2(2) applies to other forms of loss and damage resulting from another's negligence, in respect of which exclusion or limitation of liability by notice or contract term is effective only in so far as the exclusion or limitation satisfies the test of reasonableness.[40] "Negligence" includes any contractual duty to take reasonable care; common law duties to take reasonable care and the common duty of care under the Occupiers' Liability Acts.[41]

Section 3 of UCTA applies to *all* breaches of contract whether covered by section 2 or not. It includes cases where liability under the contract is a *strict* liability (not just a liability to exercise reasonable care). The party in breach cannot by reference to any contract term exclude or restrict any liability for the breach, or claim to be entitled to render a performance substantially different to that which was reasonably expected of him, except and in so far as the term on which he relies satisfies the requirement of reasonableness.

There have been examples where the courts have held that the common nature of some types of exclusion clause in the travel industry was evidence of their reasonableness[42] (particularly where such terms have the approval of a trade organisation such as ABTA). However, the fact that the industry (whether abetted by a trade organisation or not) chooses to adopt universal types of exclusion and limitation clauses for non-injury cases seriously *restricts* the consumers' choice which may be a factor which points to the *unreasonableness* of the terms on which reliance is placed. The consumer has little if any negotiating power to change the conditions he is offered, and little choice if he decides to look elsewhere.

[39] Except that by section 29 the provisions of international transport conventions permitting personal injury limitations prevail – as to which see Chapter 10.
[40] UCTA section 11 and schedule 2.
[41] Although the Occupiers' Liability Act 1957 as such has no extra-territorial effect.
[42] *Usher v Intasun Holidays Limited* [1987] CLY 418 and *Markham-David v Bluebird Holidays Limited* [5 November 1998 – Salisbury County Court] unreported.

Procedural bars

UCTA applies to procedural bars as well as the more conventional type of exclusion or limitation clause. Section 13 provides:

> To the extent that this part of this Act prevents the exclusion or restriction of any liability it also prevents:
>
> (a) making liability or its enforcement subject to restrictive or onerous conditions;
>
> (b) excluding or restricting any right or remedy in respect of the liability, or subjecting a person to any prejudice in consequence of his pursuing any such right or remedy;
>
> (c) excluding or restricting rules of evidence or procedure.

Therefore, to the extent to which a contractual clause purports to impose procedural bars in the context of claims for negligently caused personal injury, the clause will be of no effect. In other circumstances, such a clause would be subject to the test of reasonableness — the burden of proving which would be on the party relying on the clause.

A contractual provision which requires a consumer to complain in writing within a certain period of time is a clause which could potentially fall within the prohibition imposed by section 13(1)(a). Whether the condition or the procedural bar was a "restrictive or onerous" condition would fall to be judged at the time the contract was made. Similarly, a clause providing that the absence of a written complaint by the consumer in a given form by a given time would be conclusive evidence that the consumer was entirely satisfied with the travel services provided would potentially fall foul of section 13(1)(b).[43] Procedural bars are, however, commonly encountered in the standard conditions of many commercial organisers and there is nothing necessarily offensive about them in non-personal injury cases[44] provided that they are not restrictive, onerous or unreasonable. Very often in cases of quality complaints a period of 28 days or a calendar month is imposed within which the consumer should complain in writing to the tour operator's head office or principle place of business in the United Kingdom.

Some sort of procedural bar may well be both justifiable and reasonable for the organiser of the travel arrangements — whether a regulated package or otherwise — on the grounds that the other party to the contract or the service-provider may have to investigate the complaint in circumstances

---

[43] Such as by threatening to put consumers on a "black-list" or refusing them privileges such as future discounts or offers available to others.

[44] But see *Sargant v CIT* [1994] CLY 566 where a 28 day complaints clause was upheld in a personal injury case on grounds which are hard to discern or justify on the basis of the cryptic case report.

where there may be a high turn-over of local staff; almost certainly a high turn-over of other visitors and potential witnesses; and where changes to itineraries, premises and working practices can take place very quickly. In these circumstances any failure of reasonable notification of a complaint can be extremely prejudicial to the organiser.[45] Whilst the reasonableness or otherwise of the procedural bar must be judged at the time the contract is made, it by no means follows that the requirement's reasonableness will be judged in the same way in every case. *At the time the contract is made* it may be perfectly reasonable to expect consumers to make quality complaints about their food or the opening hours of the bar within 28 days of their return home. However, the same consumers *at the time the contract is made* might legitimately regard the same period as wholly unreasonable where their arrangements are wrecked by a major weather incident from which they take several weeks to recover after their return home. Accordingly, in the example given here, where the procedural bar clause demands written complaint within 28 days of a return home, that clause could comfortably be regarded by the same court as reasonable in the context of some types of complaint, but not reasonable in respect of others.

Another type of procedural restriction is encountered in those clauses which purport to limit the *scope* of the consumer's complaints, for example, to those complaints already foreshadowed on an official claims notification form. A provision to the effect that the organiser will not entertain or meet claims not included in an official claims notification or holiday report form are difficult to justify if the consumer has in some other appropriate manner brought the complaint to the attention of the service-provider or the organiser. In those increasingly rare circumstances where such clauses arise, their intended effect is almost certainly to dissuade unrepresented consumers from bothering to pursue their complaint rather than a serious attempt reasonably to confine the scope of the consumer's potential recovery.

Definitions clauses

Apart from attempting to exclude or limit liability in certain circumstances or attempting to erect procedural bars, one contracting party can endeavour to restrict its liability to another by closely defining the scope of its contractual obligations. Before it becomes necessary to restrict liability for breach, there must first *be a breach of contract*.[46] If the obligations of the organiser of the travel arrangements are carefully defined in the first instance, the consumer may be faced with a situation in which there has been

---

[45] See in particular regulation 15(9) of the PTR 1992 which requires the other party to the contract in a regulated package case to include a term in the contract requiring the consumer to complain about defective performance at the earliest opportunity.

[46] See e.g. *Cooper v Princess Cruises Limited* discussed in Chapter 1.

no failure on the part of the other party to the contract to perform properly the obligations under the contract and so no need to invoke an exclusion or limitation clause.

Anglo-Continental Holidays Limited v Typaldos Lines (London) Limited[47] is a good example of a "definitions" clause in action; although one that was ultimately unsuccessful. A party of tourists booked a cruise to Israel. A short time before departure the cruise company substituted an inferior cruise ship to the one chosen by the customers and made significant changes to the itinerary. The travel agent who booked the cruise for the tourists, refunded their money and in turn sued the cruise company. The cruise company relied on a clause in its contract with the travel agent which provided that its cruise steamers, sailing dates, rates and itineraries were subject to change without notice. However, the cruise company had gone too far. The Court of Appeal would have none of it. Even at common law a party to a contract was not permitted to alter the substance of the agreed transaction. It was not open to the cruise company to say *"We will change you from this fine modern ship to an old tramp"*[48] neither could it unilaterally and without notice put the sailing dates back a week. As a matter of construction of the contract, the Court of Appeal would not allow the cruise company to define out of existence the substance of what had reasonably been expected by way of performance. This sort of situation today would often be covered by section 3(2)(b)(i) of UCTA which prohibits one party by reference to a contract term from claiming to be entitled to *"render a contractual performance substantially different from that which was reasonably expected of him"* or (ii) to *"render no performance at all"*.

Another example of a definitions clause in action can be seen in *Williams v Travel Promotions Limited (Trading as "Voyages Jules Verne")*.[49] This again was failed attempt by a tour operator to define away its liability to a consumer, although it is submitted somewhat less cynically than in *Anglo-Continental*. Mr Williams booked a holiday at Victoria Falls on the Zimbabwe side. Days before his departure he was informed that for the last night before his return home, he would be transferred to a luxury hotel on the Zambian side of the falls to avoid border crossing delays. Mr Williams claimed damages for this change in accommodation for his last night in the sum of £148.20. At arbitration the district judge ruled against him stating:

> I have heard some horror stories about holidays, but this is not one of them. I am looking at a booking form signed by the Plaintiff. It states: 'I accept the

[47] [1967] 2 Lloyd's LR 61.
[48] Per Lord Denning MR.
[49] [1998] *The Times* – 9 March.

Booking Conditions as set out in the Conditions of Passage'. Mr Williams told me very frankly that he read the Booking Conditions in detail.

The Conditions of Passage were lengthy and included the following under the heading "minor changes":

> The arrangements featured in this brochure are by their very nature complex with services from many different airlines, hotels and ground transportation companies ... it is not always possible to guarantee particular domestic flights, the aircraft type and/or the hotels featured on a particular departure date, or the precise itinerary. We therefore have to reserve the right to change any flight or hotel listed and, if necessary, even to modify the itinerary itself without prior notice ... No compensation is payable in such circumstances.

The circuit judge agreed with the district judge, so the matter came before the Court of Appeal in February 1998. The Court dealt mainly with the construction of the contract and the Conditions of Passage.[50] The company's downfall was the use of the word "*necessary*" in the passage quoted above and the link made on the proper construction of the clause between "*necessary*" accommodation changes and "*overbooking*". The court was not satisfied that the company had demonstrated that the change in Mr Williams' accommodation for his last night on holiday was *necessary*[51] neither was it satisfied that any necessity that might have existed was the result of overbooking. So as a matter of *construction* of this particular clause the tour operator again failed by means of a definitions clause to limit the scope of potential breaches, and limit by this route any exposure to pay compensation. However, *in principle*, the notion that a properly drafted definitions clause could successfully restrict the organiser's liability received some measure of support from the Court. Sir Brian Neill said:

> It might have been very sensible for the respondents to have included in their brochure some different form of words which made it clear to the reader that they had a wider discretion which would entitle them to make such changes as were reasonably required for the better performance of the contract. But they have chosen ... to use the word "necessary".

Schiemann LJ said that (as had been argued in the course of the respondent's submissions):

> ... there were all sorts of circumstances in which it would be sensible to allow [tour operators] to change pre-existing arrangements, and I can see that there might well be. But this court ... had to distinguish between what would be a sensible clause and what this particular clause provides ... There is no difficulty in saying 'reasonably required' if that is what is meant."

---

[50] Sir Brain Neill deciding that it was unnecessary to go on and consider the PTR 1992 or UCTA.
[51] As opposed to convenient or expedient.

Accordingly, it should be possible to devise properly drafted clauses which restrict the scope of the organiser's contractual obligations without offending the provisions of UCTA and where the consumer is not being offered something substantially different from what was reasonably expected, but on the contrary, is being provided with *exactly* the kind of arrangements contemplated by the parties at the time the contract was made. The successful definitions clause allows the organiser a reasonable degree of latitude to change the details of the product without being in breach of contract, or offending against UCTA, provided the real substance of the contract is not undermined.

Non-Regulated Arrangements

General principles must be invoked where the package or travel arrangements are not a regulated package, or where there remains scope for reasonable doubt as to whether the arrangements in question constitute a regulated package. Plainly, if the arrangements do not constitute a regulated package the PTR 1992 do not apply. With the increasing availability on the market of so-called "dynamically packaged" arrangements it is likely that there will remain a considerable grey area in which the application of the PTR 1992 is debatable. Where there remains some doubt as to whether a set of arrangements constitutes a regulated package it is often wise to present a case both under the regulations and at common law. In the context of those arrangements which *are* unquestionably regulated packages there will arise disputes as to the actual content of the regulated package i.e. what formed part of the pre-arranged combination of services offered at an inclusive price, the answer to which will make a difference to whether the other party to the package contract is liable in the vent that something goes wrong.

What is it that the other party to the contract has agreed to provide to the consumer? What is the contract *for.* These questions are important for at least three reasons. First, in order to determine whether the contract is regulated or not; secondly, even if it *is,* whether the service or facility giving rise to the problem is part of the content of the regulated package and thirdly to establish in what *capacity* the other party has adopted[52] in the making of the contract in question. Two excursion cases show how the answer to these questions can determine whether or not a tour operator is liable to a consumer for injuries.

These excursion cases invariably include an issue as to whether the tour operator is contracting with the consumer as principal – being thus liable on the excursion contract, or as agent, and so not liable on the excursion contract.

---

[52] That is, Principal or Agent.

The answer lies always in the facts and the documents. In *Moran v First Choice Holidays and Flights Ltd*.[53] the claimant and her husband were on a holiday provided by the defendant in the Dominican Republic in 2001. On arrival at their hotel a welcome pack was provided giving information regarding excursions available through the defendant. At a welcome meeting the following day a tour representative employed by the defendant, gave more information about excursions. The claimant and her husband booked and paid for the jeep safari excursion. The excursion took place. Later in the holiday they booked an excursion called 'Crazy Quads' through Rachel. It was paid for by travellers' cheques. The claimant states that they received a white piece of paper, presumably a booking confirmation or receipt. She recalls that the paper was torn out of a book and there was a carbon copy which the rep retained. The claimant and her husband were collected from their hotel and taken to the compound where the quad bikes were stored. Some instructions were given, crash helmets were provided and bikes were allocated. A convoy of bikes set off. Ahead of the claimant at the front of the convoy was a bike driven by an employee of the quad bike company. About thirty minutes into the journey the bike was approaching a clump of grass in the middle of the track. Mr Moran turned the handlebars to the left to go round the grass, he then turned the handlebars to the right but the wheels did not turn. He grabbed hold of the clutch and pulled it in, he took his thumb off the throttle but it remained in position and the machine kept revving. The bike went off the edge of the track, down a ledge and dropped some thirteen to fourteen feet. Mr and Mrs Moran were thrown from the bike and sustained injury. The evidence of the claimant and her husband was that they at all times believed the contract was made with First Choice; they relied upon three matters:

1. documentation provided by the defendant;
2. the manner in which the earlier safari excursion was dealt with and performed;
3. the fact that they could have bought a cheaper quad bike excursion but did not do so because of the defendant's guarantee of insurance and the safety checks.

The relevant documentation included:

a) Welcome Pack
b) Booking Form (used for the safari expedition).

The Welcome Pack had two logos at the head of this document: 'First Choice' and 'Unijet'. It began with the words: '*On behalf of First Choice and Unijet, it is a pleasure to welcome you to the Dominican Republic*'. A further

---

[53] [2005] EWHC 2478 (QB).

paragraph stated: '*Tours and Trips - First Choice and Unijet offer an exciting selection of trips to suit everybody from relaxing aboard a catamaran to discovering the wild countryside on a jeep safari. All our excursions are fully insured and regularly checked to ensure that they meet our safety standards. First Choice cannot be held responsible for any excursion not supplied by First Choice as they probably will not meet our stringent insurance and safety requirements, at First Choice your safety and enjoyment are our first priority.*' There was no reference within this document to the fact that excursions which are 'supplied' by First Choice are operated or provided by another company.

The Booking Form also had logos: *First Choice, Barcelo Viajes* and *Outback Jungle Safari*. Also on the front of the form were the following statements: "*There are several 'Pirate' companies operating excursions in the Dominican Republic, these companies are not used by British tour operators because they do not reach the quality, safety and hygiene standards that we as your tour operator demand. We cannot accept any responsibility for illness, injury or death caused as a result of participating in a pirate excursion.*'

It was unsurprising that provided with this documentation the claimant and her husband believed that First Choice was supplying the excursion and with it the relevant safety checks and insurance and equally unsurprising that the judge was unimpressed with the tour operator's attempts to distance itself from the provision of this excursion. The result was otherwise in *Mason v Titan Travel Ltd* (as to which see further below).[54]

The judge in *Moran* concluded thus:[55]

> I am satisfied that the cause of the accident was a defect in the quad bike which Mr. Moran was driving as part of a tour excursion. As to the excursion contract the defendant was at all times the undisclosed agent for the local principal Dominican Tour Bike Adventure who provide the quad bike and as such is liable for its undisclosed principal. The defendant has produced no satisfactory evidence to demonstrate that the defective bike had been regularly and competently maintained prior to the accident and was thus free from defect. It has also failed to provide any post accident inspection evidence to negative the allegation of a defect. The claimant succeeds in her claim based upon the failure of the defendant to exercise reasonable skill and care in the provision and performance of the excursion. The claim is made out both in terms of breach of the contract and breach of the duty of care."

---

[54] Grimsby County Court June 2005 HHJ Moore (Unreported)
[55] Nicola Davis QC from judgment paragraph 27.

In *Mason* the tour operator supplied to the Claimant a package holiday to Canada in May 2001. Whilst on the package tour the Claimant purchased an excursion (for an extra $45) called the Canoe Float Trip at Jasper. Whilst on the excursion on the river the canoe collided with an overhanging branch and capsized. The Claimant sustained injuries. The Claimant sued Titan for damages pursuant to the PTR 1992 regulation 15 – having expressly abandoned other causes of action. The facts were not controversial and for the purposes of the preliminary issue tried it was assumed that the Claimant had made out a case in "negligence" against the canoe operators and excursion providers. A preliminary issue was ordered to be heard: *whether or not the canoe float trip was a component of the package holiday.* If the excursion *was* a component of the package holiday then Titan was liable for any improper performance in the provision of the excursion. If the excursion was *not* part of the package holiday the trip falls outside the scope of the PTR 1992 which accordingly would not apply to this accident. The Claimant contended that because the excursion was advertised in the Defendant's holiday brochure and was *available* to be purchased pre-departure (although it was not so purchased on this occasion) it was being supplied by the Defendant as a principal. The Defendant countered by pointing out that the holiday brochure not only advertised the excursion as a voluntary add-on at a separate price but had expressly stated in clear, distinctive lettering in its brochure that the excursion was not part of the package holiday; that it would be supplied and provided by an independent local company in Canada and no liability for its provision would be accepted on the part of the Defendant.

The judge concluded that it was clear beyond any room for doubt that the excursion had not been part of the regulated package holiday[56] and in addition that the sale of the excursion in Canada by a representative of the Defendant tour operator had clearly been in the latter's capacity as an agent for the local excursion supplier. Commenting on the nature of the information the Defendant had supplied to the Claimant about the supply of the excursion one of the judge's comments, namely: "*you can't say fairer than that*" probably sums up the factual complexities that bedevil the issue of who is liable on an excursion contract. If the tour operator makes it clear in conspicuous language and plain documentation that the excursions are being supplied by someone else; names that other party and states in terms that they are not tour operator managed excursions then the greater the likelihood that the tour operator will not be regarded as the principal to the excursion contract. If, on the other hand, the tour operator cannot resist the

---

[56] So much was surely obvious given that a separate price was paid after departure in Canada in Canadian dollars.

temptation to cover adverts, receipts and vouchers with its own logos and its own eulogistic commendations of the excursions on offer, it should not come as a surprise that is regarded as either a principal to the contract (for an undisclosed agent or otherwise) or liable on the contract as a contracting agent.

Common Law – Provider or Facilitator?

Does an organiser whose arrangements fall outside the scope of the 1992 Regulations agree to provide the facilities and services described in the brochure or the contract making himself liable if those services or facilities are not provided, or not provided adequately? Alternatively, does the organiser merely agree to act as a co-ordinator or facilitator of the arrangements, thus absolving himself from liability for the quality of the services that he has co-ordinated and which are actually provided by others?[57]

Is the common law organiser (usually the tour operator) the provider of the services and facilities under the travel contract or merely the facilitator of the consumer's arrangements. If the former, the tour operator will have a contractual liability for both the *existence* and *quality* of the services and facilities that the organiser agrees to provide as part of the travel contract[58]. A number of cases appear to justify the conclusion that at common law the tour operator agreed to *provide* the travel services — albeit through service-provider agents — but nonetheless remained liable on the contract for what it had agreed would form part of the holiday.

In *Jarvis v Swan Tours*[59] Edmund Davies LJ said: "*If ... Travel agents*[60] *fail to provide a holiday of the contract quality, they are liable in damages*". In *Adock v Blue Sky Holidays*[61] Cumming-Bruce LJ said:

> The Jarvis case establishes that where the subject matter is a contract for the provision of facilities for a holiday, the parties to that contract foresee that upon the payment of the financial consideration to the tour operator company, the tour operator company is under an obligation to provide those facilities ... ".

Mustill LJ in *Spencer v Cosmos*[62] said:

---

[57] See Grant: *The Last Resort* [1991] NLJ 134 where various common law options in respect of an organiser's liability are discussed.
[58] This looks a very similar liability to that which arises under regulation 15 of the PTR 1992.
[59] [1973] QB 233.
[60] By which he surely meant tour operators.
[61] [1980] reported on Lexis.
[62] [1981] Lexis.

> A reading of the brochure leaves no room for doubt that the defendant [tour operator] personally undertook to secure, subject to specified exceptions, that accommodation in the stated hotel and for the stated period of time together with transportation, was provided for the plaintiff.

In *Glover v Kuoni Travel*[63] the tour operator was also held liable for the low standards of its subcontractors which compromised the package holiday supplied to the consumer, namely, the poor quality of water sports' instruction and facilities available at a resort which had been described as a "haven for water sports". Unfortunately, the report of the case is silent as to the precise basis of this liability. Each of the above examples underlines the pithy statement of the contractual liability approach provided by Lord Goddard in *Cooke v Spanish Holiday Tours:*[64] *"It isn't much good booking a room if you can't have a room"*.

These examples illustrate a respectable thread of authority for the proposition that even without the intervention of the PTR 1992, tour operators made contracts (subject to the construction of the individual arrangements) for the *provision* of the travel services albeit through intermediaries and the tour operator was responsible for the provision and the *quality* of the services that were to be provided[65]. In each case it was of no help to the tour operator to be able to say that all due or reasonable care had been exercised in the making of the arrangements for the consumer, and therefore, any failure in supply or quality was down to the local service provider. It was not in these cases a question of the tour operator acting reasonably as a co-ordinator or facilitator in booking facilities for the consumer. If the rooms were not available due to double-booking or some other reason, it was the tour operator who was in breach of contract. This common law contractual liability approach is based on the proposition that the tour operator or other organiser agrees that the travel services *will be* provided and services *will be* carried out reasonably. This basis of liability is analogous to liability for the sale and supply of goods and services — the goods being the travel arrangements made by the tour operator.[66] However, before the implementation of the PTR 1992 the approach of the courts was not uniform.

Other decisions imply that the pre-regulation role of the tour operator was that of a facilitator or co-ordinator of travel services not responsible for their

---

[63] [1987] CLY 1157.

[64] [1960] *The Times* 6 February.

[65] An interesting overview of the non-statutory liability of tour operators as mere co-ordinators or facilitators not responsible for the quality or safety of the services sold can be seen in *Survey of United States Travel Law: Karp* [2001] ITLJ 87.

[66] *Wilson v Best Travel* [1993] 1 All ER 353 was a pre-regulation case brought pursuant to the Supply of Goods and Services Act 1982.

actual provision or the quality of such provision. The organiser's pre-regulation duties were as identified in these cases, essentially three-fold. The first duty was that the organiser was under a duty to exercise reasonable skill and care in acting as a booking agent (with hoteliers and transportation services), co-ordinator or facilitator. That is, the organiser would be under a duty to select reasonable and competent subcontractors or service providers, and itself under a duty to *take reasonable care* in its co-ordinating role. The second duty was that the tour operator or organiser was to act reasonably to ensure that care was exercised by service-providers and local suppliers. The third, (subtly different form the second) and a more popular option was that the tour operator or organiser was under a contractual duty to the effect that *reasonable care* would be exercised not just by his own personnel but by the service providers.

It has to be said that the reports of many cases, particularly holiday cases, are incomplete; as a result it is sometimes difficult to discern the precise basis on which the court found for the consumer or absolved the tour operator. One such decision was regarded as important before the implementation of the PTR 1992.

Wall v Silver Wing Surface Arrangements[67] probably represents the high-point of the restricted theory of tour operator liability for travel arrangements at common law. In this case a family group booked accommodation in Tenerife. A fire broke out, and they attempted to use the fire escape from their third floor accommodation only to find that the gate at the bottom of the fire escape had been locked. Returning to their rooms they made their escape by way of knotted sheets out of the window, and in the course of descending in this way sustained very serious injuries. It was alleged (pre-regulation) that the tour operator owed the family a duty to the effect that they would be reasonably safe in using the hotel accommodation, it being common ground that the tour operator itself was not at fault for the locking of the fire escape gate. Hodgson J. refused to imply any such term into the contract and dismissed the action on the grounds that the tour operator had not been at *fault*. He said:

> ... the tour operator neither owns, occupies nor controls the hotels which are included in the brochure ... It is also ... clear ... that if an officious bystander had suggested either to the tour operator or, I think, to most customers that the tour operator would be liable for any default on the part of any of these people, both would, to put it mildly, have been astonished. I would find it wholly unreasonable to saddle a tour operator with an obligation to ensure the safety of all components in a package over none of which he had any control...

---

[67] An unreported decision of Hodgson J. QBD 1981.

The fact that the tour operator through its local representative had earlier inspected the hotel including this very fire escape and found all to be in working order, it is submitted, is immaterial to the decision of the court. As the facts of the case itself illustrate, even if there had been no inspection of the hotel before the fire broke out, it would have been difficult, if not impossible, for the consumers to prove that an earlier inspection would have prevented the accident from occurring.

Fortunately, for consumers in non-regulated cases more recent decisions have consigned *Wall* to the museum of cases "not followed" on one pretext or another.

Far from being "astonished" to find that the tour operator was liable for the failure to provide safe accommodation facilities, it is submitted that most consumers would be aghast if they were told that there was no implied term in their travel contract to the effect that the accommodation allocated to them would be put and kept in a reasonably safe condition.[68]

Wong Mee Wan v Kwan Kin Travel Services

More recently the Privy Council[69] has brought the obligations of the organiser at common law much closer to those imposed by regulation 15 of the PTR 1992.

The claimant was the representative of the estate of her deceased daughter who had been killed in a holiday accident in the Peoples Republic of China in the course of a package supplied to her by Hong Kong tour operators.[70] The package services were to be performed by the tour operator's subcontractors. One of the advertised package services was a trip across a lake in China by ferry. The party missed the ferry and so the subcontractors arranged for alternative transport across the lake by speedboat. Whilst being carried across the lake the speedboat was in collision with a junk due to the negligence of the driver and as a result of the collision the deceased was killed. In their Lordship's view[71] "*it was an implied term of the contract that those services would be carried out with reasonable skill and care*". So, by 1996, the common law- recognised a duty on the part of the package contract organiser to the effect that reasonable care would be exercised by those charged with performing the contract and supplying the services to the consumer, and for any lapse in the exercise of such due care the organiser would be liable regardless of whether the organiser itself was at fault. This is

---

[68] Hodgson J.'s judgment is rightly applauded elsewhere for the clarity of its exposition on how terms come to be implied into contracts – see: Grant & Mason *Holiday Law* (2nd. Edition at 103).
[69] [1996] 1 WLR 38.
[70] The PTR 1992 do not apply in Hong Kong.
[71] The advice was given by Lord Slynn with whom the others agreed.

a form of extended vicarious liability very similar (if not identical) to that imposed by regulation 15 of the PTR 1992. Indeed in the course of his advice, Lord Slynn referred in passing to the PTR 1992 as part justification for the conclusion that such a duty was not too onerous for tour operators to bear. However, there is an important qualification to this general interpretation of the Privy Council's decision, namely, that great weight was put on the construction of the particular package contract in issue and the wording of the particular brochure in which the package had been promoted. The tour operator had stated repeatedly in the brochure that in the course of the package "*we will do ...*" (this, that and the other). In characteristically overstated fashion the organiser had aggressively created the impression that it was itself participating in and providing the arrangements that would be undertaken. According to Lord Slynn:

> The issue is thus whether in this particular contract the [tour operator] undertook no more than it would arrange for services to be provided by others as its agent ... or whether it itself undertook to supply the services when ... there would be implied into the contract a term that it would as supplier carry out the services with reasonable care and skill ... Taking the contract as a whole their Lordships consider that the [tour operator] here undertook to provide and not merely to arrange all the services included in the programme, even if some activities were to be carried out by others. The [tour operator's] obligation under the contract that the service would be provided with reasonable skill and care remains even if some of the services were to be rendered by others...

The duty recognised in *Wong Mee Wan* is not tantamount to a warranty that a consumer *will* be safe, any more than the tour operator's liability under regulation 15 of the PTR 1992 is based on a guarantee of safety or freedom from the risk of injury or ill-health (provided that reasonable care is exercised). How far is the *Wong Mee Wan* duty limited to those situations where eulogistic promises are made integrating the tour operator with the services to be provided? If the tour operator in *Wong Mee Wan* had refrained from the constant use of the first person plural, and instead substituted expressions such as: *You* will go ... or *you* will be taken by our *agents* ... Or *customers* will be shown by local guides ... would the tour operator still have faced liability for the negligent driving of the speedboat driver?

On the facts of *Wong Mee Wan* the answer may well have been "yes". In the course of his advice Lord Slynn also observed: *"no steps were taken to see that the driver of the speedboat was of reasonable competence and experience ... "* which might have formed a different basis altogether for the decision in favour of the deceased's estate. It is submitted that the extreme language adopted in the *Wong Mee Wan* brochure by which the provision of the package services was expressly personalised by the tour operator, was only one factor which confirmed the court's basic reasoning, and made it unnecessary to overrule *Wall v Silver Wing Surface Arrangements Limited.*[72]

Their Lordships also concluded that:

> if the tour operator agrees that services will be supplied, whether by him or by others on his behalf, to imply a term that those services will be carried out with reasonable skill and care is not imposing ... a burden which is 'intolerable'[73] ... nor is it wholly unreasonable ... "[74]

This passage indicates that *as a general rule* the tour operator can expect to be the subject of the *Wong Mee Wan* duty at common law. That is a duty to the effect that the package services *will be* provided with reasonable skill and care irrespective of who is responsible for their performance or provision. Where the tour operator *may* escape the imposition of such an implied duty is where the tour operator makes it explicitly clear that the obligation it undertakes is the obligation only to exercise reasonable care in the organisation of the services, their co-ordination, their facilitation and the selection of reasonable subcontractors and accepts no responsibility for the actual supply of those package services.[75] By *defining* the scope of what it is the tour operator agrees to do in this way avoidance of the *Wong Mee Wan* implied (non-delegable) duty may be possible. Otherwise, it is suggested the consumer will reasonably assume that a package is being bought from the tour operator the components of which will themselves be supplied to reasonable standards. In *Wong Mee Wan* the tour operator did not expressly or in so many words accept liability for the negligent performance of its subcontractors or third parties, the language of the brochure simply made it easier for such an obligation to be implied.

Wilson v Best Travel[76] has already been considered in the context of applicable standards of safety,[77] and although the consumer was unsuccessful in his claim, it represents another example of the courts accepting that tour operators do owe contractual obligations that could give rise to a liability for the shortcomings of subcontractors outside the PTR 1992. It was a case arising out of a holiday contract performed before the introduction of the regulations, but the decision is unaffected by the regulations. It will be remembered that in this case the consumer fell through a glass patio door and sued the tour operator on the basis that there was an implied term in the contract to the effect that the hotel would be reasonably safe. Philips J.

[72] See above.
[73] As the Hong Kong Court of Appeal had decided.
[74] As Hodgson J. had decided in *Wall v Silver Wing Surface Arrangements* (above).
[75] But tour operator members of ABTA would not be able to so confine their obligations by express contract terms.
[76] [1993] 1 All ER 353.
[77] See Chapter 4.

declined to imply any such term. However, he *did* accept that the tour operator would owe a two-fold duty to its consumers to:

- check that all local safety standards and regulations had been complied with;

- warn consumers (or remove property from its books) where the lack of a safety feature was such that a reasonable consumer might refuse to stay in the accommodation (or, it may be assumed, use another facility) if they had known of the absence of the safety feature.

In both of these respects the tour operator or any other party to the package contract is going to be liable for failures on the part of its subcontractors and third parties to comply with local regulations and standards, or any failure to provide an obvious safety feature without which the reasonable consumer might refuse to use the facility offered.

The introduction of the PTR 1992 has reduced the number of situations in which the common law contractual duties form the basis of the cause of action against organisers, but after *Wong Mee Wan* and given the influence of ABTA which imposes voluntary obligations on members in respect of things that go wrong in the course of package travel arrangements[78] which obligations are invariably set out in the tour operator's terms and conditions there now appears to be little to choose between the obligations imposed on organisers for the faults of their subcontractors by the PTR 1992[79] and the obligations imposed at common law for such faults.

Nonetheless, the common law duties (whether implied by contract or imposed as direct duties in tort) are still likely to figure in those situations identified at the head of this chapter in respect of services that fall outside the scope of the regulated package contract, or those situations where the arrangements supplied do not or might not constitute a regulated package. The most common recurring example of a situation where such issues will arise are excursions.

Excursions and Extras

Excursions frequently cause accidents, illness, injury and quality complaints in the same way as package arrangements themselves do. Road accidents, activity-related injuries, food poisoning, incidents arising out of badly maintained facilities or equipment are as likely to occur in the course of an excursion as they are to arise in the course of the provision of the original package services. There are five commonly encountered types of excursion.

---

[78] The ABTA Code of Conduct is available through their website.
[79] Especially regulation 15.

1. Inclusive excursions

An "*inclusive package excursion*" is an excursion which forms part of the original all-inclusive arrangements booked with the principal services as part of the contract with the organiser before departure usually at the time the package contract itself is made. That is, the excursion forms an integral part of the package services. These excursions are often found in the organiser's brochure — and often, but not always, relate to orientation tours or visits to primary sites at the travel destination. In these instances, no particular problem arises as the terms of the package contract and the PTR 1992 in their full vigour apply to the excursion as much as to any other part of the package contract. It is merely a matter of identifying precisely which services are included as part of the pre-arranged combination of qualifying components within the meaning of regulation 2 of the PTR 1992. If an excursion forms part of the pre-arranged combination of qualifying services sold at an inclusive price in the United Kingdom that excursion is just as much part of the package as the hotel accommodation or transport.

2. Pre-bookable excursions

Sometimes the consumer encounters *pre-bookable* excursions in a tour operator's brochure for which a separate price is quoted. The excursion and the price are often to be found in a panel in the brochure promoting the destination chosen by the consumer. For example, holidays in Cyprus will sometimes advertise a trip to Egypt which will be an "add-on" to the original or basic package. The same thing happens on occasions with outings such as destination "City Tours". Often consumers are invited to purchase these add-ons before departure rather than locally on the grounds that it is cheaper to do so, or on the grounds that space is limited and early booking will avoid disappointment. The fact that these excursions are priced as *optional* extras in the brochure, and may appear as separate items on the confirmation invoice indicates that they are not intended to be part of the pre-arranged combination of qualifying components of the package holiday. The fact that they are offered on an optional basis and charged for separately suggests that such excursions are neither part of a pre-arranged combination[80] nor offered for sale at an inclusive price. It is worth being reminded of an example given by Chadwick LJ in *ABTA v CAA:*[81]

> Now suppose that the agent has informed the customer that the cost of flights will be £X, the cost of accommodation will be £Y and the cost of

---

[80] See generally Chapter 1 for a discussion of pre-arranged combinations and inclusive prices.
[81] [2006] EWCA Civ 1356.

transfers[82] will be £Z; and has explained to the customer that he can purchase any one or more of those services, as he chooses, without any need to purchase the others. He has explained, in effect, that the customer can choose to purchase the other services elsewhere; or to make other arrangements. In that case – as it seems to me – there would be little doubt that the services are not offered for sale as a pre-arranged combination and at an inclusive price.

In these situations the excursions, albeit booked before departure with the package organiser and notwithstanding the fact that they are itemised on the confirmation invoice appear to fall outside the scope of, or is not part of the content of the regulated package contract. The other party to the package contract is only liable under the regulations for the proper performance of the *package* contract so these types of excursion will not be covered by the PTR 1992 as part of the original package. Such difficulties as there may be with whether pre-bookable excursions are or are not something for which the organiser is responsible under the PTR 1992 should not obscure the fact that whether or not the tour operator is liable for their proper performance can often turn on two other factors. First, even if pre-bookable excursions are not regarded as part of the original package they will be the object of separate *excursion contracts*[83] which may render the tour operator liable. Secondly, the terms and conditions of the tour operator may accept or be taken to accept liability for the proper performance of such an excursion. Whether the booking conditions render the tour operator liable is a matter of construction but, for example, a tour operator whose booking conditions provide that *"we accept liability for the proper performance of the arrangements we make for you that form part of your holiday"* is badly placed to argue that the pre-booked excursion is not one of those arrangements. Furthermore, the tour operator who states *"we accept liability for the negligence of our suppliers and subcontractors"* without the qualification that such suppliers and subcontractors must be of the package holiday services (to the exclusion of excursions) is likely to be at the wrong end of a finding that the excursion provider *is* such a supplier or subcontractor of the tour operator albeit in the context of the excursion rather than the original package.

3. *Local Excursions & Extras*

Still by far the most common excursion booking is made *after arrival* at the destination. Excursions are promoted or offered by local representatives of the tour operator and purchased by the consumer on

---

[82] We might substitute the example of a pre-booked excursion.
[83] As to which see section 3 below.

the spot, frequently at "welcome" meetings. Because these are paid for separately long after the package contract has been made and of necessity after the consumer has arrived at the holiday resort such local excursion cannot be regarded as falling within the scope of the liabilities covered by the PTR 1992.[84]They are not pre-arranged; sold or offered for sale at an inclusive price and are not sold in the United Kingdom.[85] Nonetheless the tour operator may still be liable for the proper performance of these excursions. The cases of *Moran* and *Mason* have already been discussed earlier in this chapter. A further illustration is warranted here, and concerns the provision of *extras* rather than an excursion – but the principals are just the same. In *Derbyshire v First Choice Holidays and Flights Ltd*[86] The Claimant booked a package holiday to Canada with the Defendant tour operator in 2000. The price paid for the package holiday included the following elements: accommodation; return flights from London Gatwick to Calgary; transfer from airport to Hotel; the services of a local representative. C could have pre-booked and paid in advance for his skiing equipment and lessons through First Choice. However, he neither pre-booked nor paid in advance for the hire of ski equipment or ski lessons (the combination of these two elements was referred to as a "*ski pack*"). He arrived at Calgary airport and was met by the transfer coach and the local representative. On arrival at the Hotel he and his partner hired ski equipment and booked skiing lessons which were provided by Altitude Sports: an independent local business. The Claimant made a payment to the tour operator's local representative for the hire of the ski equipment and the lessons and the representative issued a "*Ski Pack Ticket*" with Altitude Sports written at the top which was presented to Altitude Sports for the provision of the equipment and the lessons. The ticket also featured First Choice's logo. The evidence was that Altitude Sports supplied ski equipment to all of the tour operator's guests. The Claimant was provided with ski boots and skis which he wore for his first lesson and first day's skiing without incident, but the next day he was attempting a snowplough turn and as he pressed down on his left ski, his ski stopped suddenly while his body continued to rotate in a clockwise direction and he fell to the ground. His right ski detached from his foot, but his left ski was still attached. The reason for this was that the assistant in the Altitude Sports shop had (as the Judge found at trial)

---

[84] The same principles apply as in *Gallagher v Airtours Holidays Limited* and *Roochead v Airtours Holidays Limited* discussed in Chapter 4.
[85] See Chapters 1 and 4 – PTR 1992 regulations 2 and 15.
[86] Central London County Court 18 October 2004 HHJ Kennett (Unreported).

negligently supplied the wrong sized boot for the Claimant's left ski and bindings. The Claimant sued for damages under the PTR 1992 regulation 15 for an improper performance of the package holiday contract and he also argued, in the alternative, that he had a separate contract, parallel to the package contract, for the fitting and hire of his ski equipment which he had entered into in Canada with the tour operator through its local representative. In dismissing the claim the judge concluded:

(1) the purchase of the ski pack was not regulated in accordance with the PTR 1992 because it was neither pre-arranged nor inclusively priced and was sold separately outside the United Kingdom;
(2) on a true construction of the contract made for the fitting and provision of skiing equipment the contract was with Altitude Sports and the tour operator's local representative had simply acted as their agent (the local representative had disclosed the existence and identity of Altitude Sports and the tour operator's promotional literature for ski packs made it clear that it only "*recommended*" suppliers of ski packs, rather than supplying the same itself);
(3) this status as agent was not affected by the fact that the local representative had taken the money for the ski pack;
(4) there was no evidence that the tour operator had been negligent in failing to select an appropriate local supplier for the fitting and hiring out of ski equipment and, therefore, no liability arose on this basis (the accident was the result of an isolated lapse).

Phillips v First Choice Holidays and Flights Ltd[7] is another recent example of the excursion factors at work. The Defendant provided the Claimant, and 3 others, with a package holiday to the island of Margarita, in Venezuala in 2005. During the course of the holiday the Claimant booked, and paid for, a 'Canaima Camp' excursion. The excursion involved a trek through rainforest and, 'weather permitting', a flight in to the Angel Falls Gorge. The Claimant alleged that the flight had not flown into the gorge, in breach of the package holiday contract. He claimed that the air hostess on board had stated that the plane was 'too big' to fly into the gorge. He claimed that another excursion group had flown in to the gorge earlier the same day and accordingly that the failure of his plane to fly in to the gorge could not be attributed to the weather. The Defendant relied upon the 'excursion planner' brochure which it alleged the Claimant had been provided with, in resort. The brochure terms and conditions specifically stated that First Choice were

---

[87] Medway County Court 7 February 2007 DDJ Beech (Unreported).

acting only as agents for the excursion provider, Iberoservice, whose logo was clearly displayed on the front of the brochure and on the ticket issued. Alternatively, the Defendant claimed that the plane upon which the Claimant had travelled was the same model that had been used for the excursion for many years and that the weather conditions in the gorge were extremely volatile, thereby explaining why a different group had been able to fly in on the same day. In evidence, the Claimant denied ever having received the excursion planner. He produced a further single-page photocopy document which he claimed he had been provided by the representatives in resort. This document did not contain any terms and conditions, nor did it refer to Iberoservice. Nonetheless, the judge concluded that the Defendant had been acting as an agent for the local supplier when it sold the excursion to the Claimant. The Claimant's excursion contract made locally was with Iberoservice not the Defendant and the Defendant was no liable on it.

If the tour operator is in such circumstances regarded as liable on the excursion contract how does one determine the nature and extent of the liabilities and seek a remedy against the tour operator. So far as remedies are concerned the courts of England and Wales will have and exercise jurisdiction against a company registered in this jurisdiction and this is likely to cover most tour operators serving the domestic market.[88] What system of law applies to locally booked excursions? The fact that the English court has jurisdiction does not necessarily mean that English law will be applied to the issues.[89] However, because both principals are based in England and Wales;[90] the principals make the excursion contract during the currency of a package holiday governed by English law[91] and the language of the documents is likely to be English, it is not difficult to reach the conclusion that the parties had chosen English law to apply to the *excursion contract* which choice is demonstrable with reasonable certainty from all the circumstances of the case.[92] Even if an express choice of law cannot be demonstrated from the surrounding circumstances[93] the law applicable to the excursion contract will usually be the law of the country where the tour operator has its central

---

[88] Section 42 Civil Jurisdiction & Judgments Act 1982.
[89] Section 11 and 12 Private International Law (Miscellaneous Provisions) Act 1995. See further Chapter 6.
[90] The consumer by residence and the tour company by its seat.
[91] In the overwhelming majority of cases.
[92] Article 3 of the Rome Convention – Contracts (Applicable Law) Act 1990.
[93] The express choice is not likely to one articulated in the contract (whether in writing or orally).

administration[94]. This is also highly likely to lead to the conclusion that English law applies. Even if an express choice of law cannot be discerned and a presumed choice is inappropriate, unless and until one party asserts[95] that foreign law applies and proves by expert evidence what that law provides, an English court will assume that the foreign law is similar to English law. Finally, even if the tour operator asserts the application of a foreign law there is a high probability that any such foreign law will impose on the principal to the excursion contract the same or similar obligations[96] as would be implied into an excursion contract by English law[97].

4. Independent excursions

There are excursions booked locally by consumers that have nothing to do with the original package organiser where as supplier of the original package or as provider or promoter of the excursion itself — such as those bought from a local supplier through the concierge of a resort hotel, or directly from a local supplier, who may or may not have a desk or shop front at the resort hotel accommodating the consumer. These are wholly independent of the tour operator and it is most unlikely that the tour operator would have any responsibility for the proper performance of such an excursion.

5. Package within a package

Finally there is the "*package within a package*", that is, excursions that are themselves regulated packages within the meaning of the PTR 1992. This may happen in many instances where pre-arranged transport and other tourist services are provided as part of an inclusive excursion deal. The excursion itself may satisfy all the necessary qualifying elements of a regulated package. The example given above of the trip to Egypt as part of an original package to Cyprus may offer both transport and accommodation as part of an all-inclusive excursion. If the excursion is booked with the organiser in the United Kingdom the regulations will undoubtedly apply to these "packages within packages" or "secondary packages". If the package within a package is booked locally after the consumer arrives in resort, then the same principles apply as discussed in section 3 above.

---

[94] Article 4 and in particular the presumptions set out in articles 4(2)-(4) of the Rome Convention.
[95] In a Statement of Case.
[96] For example, to exercise reasonable skill and acre and provide safe equipment to appropriate local safety standards.
[97] See further Chapman: *Excursions: Tour Operators and the Negligence of Local Suppliers* [2002] ITLJ 123.

Given that in many excursion cases English law will be applied, whether as a result of express choice or statutory presumption, the common law principles clarified in *Wilson v Best Travel* and *Wong Mee Wan v Kwin Kin Travel* will also apply to contracts for the provision of excursions (whether or not they form secondary packages). In summary, therefore, where an excursion contract is made with an organiser and is subject to English law, the following implied terms or duties are likely to apply.

- The tour operator should exercise reasonable care in the selection and monitoring of its subcontractors and suppliers.

- The tour operator should ensure that all relevant local safety standards and regulations are complied with.

- The tour operator should advise and warn consumers in respect of any safety features not provided by the service provider which might induce a reasonable consumer to refuse to take the excursion.

- The tour operator should (absent a clear health warning) refuse to promote, advertise or sell excursions where the absence of a safety feature was such that a reasonable fully informed consumer would refuse to undertake the excursion.

- Reasonable skill and care in and about the provision of the excursion services and facilities *will be exercised* by those actually performing the excursion. That is, the organiser of the excursion will be liable for the proper performance of the excursion irrespective of whether the excursion services are carried out directly by the organiser or by a subcontractor or third party; the organiser will be subject to a non-delegable duty to the effect that due care *will be exercised* in the provision of the excursion services on the basis of the same principles as were applied in *Wong Mee Wan*.[98]

Tour operators should be alert to the fact that many consumers taking part in package and especially excursion events will be undertaking activities of a type, and requiring a degree of fitness (albeit a modest degree) which the consumer is not accustomed to deploying at home. There is nothing like a foreign holiday excursion to induce the consumer to attempt an undertaking that would never have been considered other than as part of a holiday. The consumer who would not usually contemplate mounting a horse at home, happily gallops off on a camel in the desert; the holidaymaker who has driven nothing more exciting than a Ford KA at home, thinks nothing of participating in water sports and jet-skiing whilst on holiday in the Mediterranean. The reluctant swimmer at home, enthusiastically dives head-

---

[98] See above.

first into unknown waters abroad. Organisers would be wise to take into account this factor when devising their promotional literature in respect of activity excursions, and in respect of any decision they make as to who should be the proper or target audience for such excursions.

Some tour operators expressly accept contractual liability for the proper provision of excursions of all types so excursion complaints are amongst those where careful consideration of the tour operator's brochure conditions is required. In some instances the drafting of the tour operator's booking conditions is ambiguous in that the contract provides that the tour operator accepts liability for damage *"save where the damage arises out of something not connected with the package holiday or an excursion provided by us..."*. The implication here is that even if the tour operator does not expressly accept liability for excursions the wording of the exception in the contract *implies* that liability for both package arrangements and excursions *is* intended to be covered by the tour operator's liability promise. Any ambiguity in drafting will be resolved against the tour operator in the consumer's favour.

General Contractual and Non-Contractual Duties

The incidence of accidents and illness whilst in the course of foreign travel is probably no less than the incidence of accidents in every day life. There is no known research about the incidence of accidents and illness abroad which would indicate that consumers are more vulnerable abroad than they are at home although it sometimes *appears* that they are. Are there circumstances in which the organiser, or other party to the contract will owe a contractual or tortious duty to a consumer regarding services, facilities or equipment which has, on any view, nothing to do with the services provided pursuant to the package contract or any excursion linked (however indirectly) with the organiser of the original package arrangements?

Regulation 15(7) of the PTR 1992

This little visited and seldom reported subsection of regulation 15 requires the tour operator to give prompt assistance to a consumer in difficulty. The court in *Perry v TUI UK Ltd.*[99] appears to have overlooked that the requirement to give prompt assistance to a consumer in difficulty *only* arises where that difficulty is itself caused by some improper performance of the holiday contract albeit that the improper performance is "excused" due to some "force majeure" event under regulation 15(2)(b) or (c). The first question must always be: in what way is the tour operator in breach of

---

[99] See further below [13 April 2005 Bromley County Court Unreported].

contract or rendered *prima facie* liable for improper performance. The second is: should the tour operator be excused due to circumstances under 15(2)(b)or (c); *only then* does the question arise: has the tour operator rendered the prompt assistance required by regulation 15(7). This subsection does not impose on tour operators a free-standing contractual obligation to render prompt, or indeed any, assistance and it is difficult to identify on these facts what it was that was the foundation "improper performance" excused by force majeure that triggered the application of regulation 15(7) in the first place.

Mr. and Mrs. Perry experienced a terrible holiday. They were claiming damages for the extra, unplanned week in Malta which they said they had to endure because of the tour operator's failure to provide them with adequate assistance pursuant to Regulation 15(7) of the PTR 1992. The holiday went wonderfully right up to the moment that Mr. Perry tried to board his flight home, whereupon the pilot refused to let him on-board. In an instant, the holiday had become a "nightmare". The reason for this refusal, (described by the Claimant as a breach of an express term of the holiday contract insofar as Mr. and Mrs. Perry had already paid for their flight home) was because it had come to the pilot's attention that Mr. Perry had spent some of his time on Malta in one of its hospitals. Therefore, the pilot demanded to see a 'Fitness to Fly' certificate. He said that given that Mr. Perry's illness had been breathing related, a doctor needed to pronounce him as fit to fly. In fact, it was the tour operator's representative who had spoken to Mr. and Mrs. Perry on the coach to the airport and had learnt about Mr. Perry's hospitalisation. She subsequently informed the airline (also owned by the tour operator).

Could the tour operator be liable in some way for failing to advise Mr. Perry about the need for a Fitness to Fly Certificate? After his discharge, Mr. Perry was never visited by any rep. Further, when the Perry's were visited in hospital, the rep who visited them told them that a new rep would be taking over and would "be fully informed about their case." That new rep never spoke to them and he himself only lasted a day before he was replaced. Therefore, there were three of four reps within a seven-day period. The learned judge levied some criticism on the tour operator in this regard by finding that the number of reps must have caused a "breakdown in communication". However, as to whether the tour operator should have done more than what it did and by such omission caused the loss claimed the judge found that it had not. One feature of this case in particular went against the claimant, namely that once Mr. Perry had left the hospital, he never informed the tour operator about how he had failed to obtain the Fitness to Fly certificate which he had been advised to seek from the hospital.

The judge found that the tour operator had advised the claimant adequately. Although the rep never spelt out that Mr. Perry would not be able to fly home without a Fitness to Fly certificate, the purpose and import of such a certificate was obvious. Crucially, the tour operator was found to have offered the requisite "prompt assistance" pursuant to Regulation 15(7) of the 1992 Regulations. Any reasonable claimant would have let the tour operator know that no Fitness to Fly certificate had been obtained. There was nothing to suggest that the tour operator was anything other than always contactable. Moreover, the tour operator had offered prompt assistance to the claimant at the start of their extra week but this assistance had been declined.

ABTA Code of Conduct

All members of ABTA are exhorted by the Code of Conduct[100] at clause 4E to the effect that they should *"Where appropriate and subject to their reasonable discretion, provide prompt assistance to Clients in difficulty."* One would hope that where the difficulty has arisen due to an actionable improper performance of a regulated package holiday, most organisers would see that it was in their own interests to help out any consumer in difficulty given that such assistance would be likely to reduce the amount of damages recoverable. It may even be thought desirable for some proportionate assistance to be offered when the problem arises due to something entirely outside the control of the package holiday organiser. However *desirable* it may be the exhortation to help only where *"appropriate"* and *"subject to ... reasonable discretion"* might be regarded as more an expression of hope than contractual expectation, let alone contractual entitlement.

Implied Terms and Duties in Tort

When considering the general duties of the other party to any travel contract, it is important to recognise that such duties may arise in at least two distinct contexts. First, as part of the *contractual* duties implied by law, which duties would form part of the package contract with the consumer. Secondly, such duties may arise outside the scope of the contract, and be imposed as duties of care in tort.

Implied contractual terms

Terms will be implied into the travel contract[101] as they would in any other contract if:

---

[100] 2006 edition (effective 1 September 2006).
[101] Whether it is a regulated package or not.

- the implication is necessary in fact to give effect to the presumed common intention of the parties — sometimes described as the "officious bystander" test.[102]

- the implication is required as a matter of law in respect of certain types of contract.[103]

The sort of implied contractual duties that are commonly encountered – such as the contractual duty to exercise reasonable and care, or the non-delegable duty to the effect that reasonable skill and care will be exercised by service providers – are discussed earlier in this chapter[104] and in Chapter 4.

Duties in tort

Apart from implied contractual duties, will the tour operator or whoever is *the other party to the* [travel] *contract* be subject to concurrent or additional duties in tort?

> ... in addition to the foreseeability of damage, necessary ingredients in any situation giving rise to a duty of care are that there should exist between the party owing the duty and the party to whom it is owed a relationship ... of proximity ... and the situation should be one in which the court considers it fair, just and reasonable that the law should impose a duty of a given scope...[105]

The three requirements for the imposition of a duty of care at common law[106] are by now adequately entrenched to provide a general framework within which to consider the tour operator's or the organiser's general non-contractual duties towards the consumer. These duties may of course arise as implied terms of the travel contract, but could also be regarded as duties imposed by the common law in tort. In outline the three components are:

- foreseeability of damage;

- proximity of the relationship between the parties;

- fairness, justice and reasonableness.

---

[102] *Shirlaw v Southern Foundries Limited* [1939] 2 KB 206 and see also *Wall v Silver Wing Surface Arrangements Limited* (above).
[103] Implication by statute or statutory regulation is the most obvious situation - common examples including: The Sale of Goods Act 1979; The Supply of Goods and Services Act 1982 and the PTR 1992.
[104] See : *Hone v Going Places Leisure Travel Limited* [2001] The Times, 6 August, and *Wong Mee Wan v Kwan Kin Travel Services Limited* [1996] 1 WLR 38.
[105] *Caparo Industries Plc v Dickman* [1990] 2 WLR 605 per Lord Bridge at 617. See also Balcombe LJ in *Marc Rich & Co. v Bishop Rock Marine Co. Limited* [1994] 3 All ER 686 at 704.
[106] See generally works such as *Clerk v Lindsell* 2003 edition paragraph 7-13 – 7-23.

The issue for travellers and tour operators alike is just where the application of these three features will lead the courts in respect of the general duties owed by organisers to their customers. This issue is most likely to arise in circumstances where the consumer faces difficulties which are not the result of a failure or improper performance of the travel *contract*,[107] but where the tour operator should have been able to exert some influence on the circumstances in which the consumer suffers loss or damage. However, whether or not the duty arises as a contractual or tortious duty inevitably depends on the scope of the contract. The future in this context (both as to the scope of implied contractual terms, and the existence of non-contractual or tortious duties) is unclear. The following are a few of the many examples where duties might be imposed on organisers which may be characterised as implied contractual (package contract or non-package) duties, or duties imposed in addition to any contractual relationship.

- Does the tour operator owe a duty to the consumer to advise in respect of those medical practitioners (by recommended list or otherwise) who should be used in the event that local medical treatment is required?[108]

- Does the organiser owe a duty to the consumer in respect of providing warnings or advice as to which outside service providers are to be preferred?[109]

- Is there a duty to advise or warn consumers against the use of certain restaurants or clubs of bad repute which they may encounter in the course of their travel?

- Should the tour operator advise consumers with regard to "no go" areas in the vicinity of their accommodation, in their resort generally?[110]

- In the context of an example used before, would an organiser be under a duty to give security advice to consumers staying in a resort likely to be

---

[107] Simply because implied contractual duties will fulfil the same role whether or not the contract is a regulated package contract.

[108] It is not uncommon to encounter consumers who consider that their tour operator is liable for clinical accidents resulting from treatment offered by local doctors – but this overlooks the fact that the doctor is supplying independent professional services even if he is called out by the tour operator or the managers of the consumer's hotel. Such professionals services would not usually be offered by the doctor as the supplier or agent or subcontractor of the holiday organiser.

[109] For example, a duty to warn against the use of services offered by local beach touts (e.g. paragliding; jet-skiing; walking tours) on the grounds that such persons may not be insured or may use un-serviced equipment or vehicles.

[110] The obligation of the tour operator has been limited to some extent by authority in this regard: *Beales v Airtours Holidays Limited* [1996] CA Unreported but digested at [1996] ITLJ. 167 where the duty to warn the tourist was said to be limited to those destinations or places where tourists were particularly the *target* of local criminals.

concurrently inhabited by national supporters for teams in a sporting tournament?

• What obligations does the organiser have in respect of potentially dangerous destinations?[111]

The solution as to these wider duties, it is suggested, is most likely to be found in a *contractual* context. The fairness and reasonableness of imposing extra-contractual duties is likely to be closely scrutinised. Whilst a close proximate relationship exists between the organiser and the consumer in which it is entirely foreseeable that certain types of loss or damage may be sustained by the consumer in certain circumstances, it is tentatively suggested that the court is unlikely to discover the existence of a duty of care that extends the duties already imposed by contract and statutory regulation. Given that the proximate relationship is already governed by contract *and* by statutory regulation, the courts are usually likely to determine the scope of the organiser's duties to the consumer by reference to the contract — and the express and implied terms to be found in that contract. Where the contract, a system of regulation and the intervention of industry codes of practice apply it could be regarded as not in the public interest to impose additional, non-contractual burdens on the organiser for loss and damage sustained by the consumer in respect of matters that are not connected with the travel contract (whether it is a regulated package or not). This still begs the question: what contractual duties or concurrent duties in tort will be implied as a matter of fact in travel, and specifically package travel contracts?

Based on the decisions such as *Davey v Cosmos*[112] the *contractual* implied terms or duties in a travel contract are likely to include the following, and are likely to be largely supervisory or monitoring in their nature and scope:

• a duty to warn of a known or suspected hazard affecting the organiser's customers or tourists in general;

• a duty to ensure that excursions, trips or events likely to be offered and sold by unconnected third parties to the organiser's consumers are operated by reasonable service providers to a reasonable standard and at a reasonable level of exertion;[113]

---

[111] Bowers: *Dangerous Destinations* [1999] ITLJ 53 – which discusses the role of the Foreign and Commonwealth Office and the problems associated with some destinations recently affected by insurrection or terrorism – and see further below.

[112] [1989] CLY 2561 – a duty to warn tourists of the known risk of sewage on the sea.

[113] *Brannan v Airtours Holidays Limited* [1999] *The Times*, 1 February – where the tour operator was under a duty to warn consumers of low overhead fans that posed a danger to those visiting a nightclub for an "Airtours" cabaret – in circumstances where a visitor had previously

- a duty — where the organiser has administrative and managerial control of extra-contractual facilities or premises — to ensure that due care is exercised by the service provider in the provision of the extra-contractual services.

Some examples will help to illustrate these general implied contractual duties which probably apply in addition to those provided for in the PTR 1992 and in addition to the generally implied contractual term to the effect that reasonable skill and care will be exercised.[114] There may well be others.

- A tour operator may well be subject to a duty to warn its customers in respect of certain holiday activities provided by local operators known to have poor health and safety records, or where it is known that the service or facility providers do not insure their activities, maintain or licence their equipment, or train their staff. Such a duty may even be extended to situations where the tour operator has no actual knowledge of a potential problem, but could have obtained such knowledge on making reasonable enquiries or keeping itself reasonably informed.

- A similar duty may arise with regard to known trouble-spots at otherwise safe destinations even though their management and control is unconnected with the tour operator — particularly where tourists are targeted by a local criminal element.[115]

- It is not impossible to envisage developments in which tour operators would be regarded as duty bound to make *positive* recommendations as to safe and reputable local service providers (taxi companies, shopping centres, doctors) which consumers could trust particularly in the more dangerous or less well regulated parts of the world.

- Where recommendations *are* made, however, it is submitted that the party making the recommendation needs to ensure that the recommendation is made on reasonable grounds and following reasonable research. To advise nothing is almost always better than to advise badly.

---

damaged themselves on such a fan and the claimant suffered head injuries when he stood on a table and walked into one.

[114] See Chapter 4.

[115] A good example in this context from the 1990s may be the targeting of new arrivals at Miami airport who hired cars with easily identifiable hire car plates who were subsequently car-jacked by local criminals. The practice is now less of a problem as the hire companies have changed their registration system — but at its height it should have been a difficulty anticipated and known to tour operators operating fly-drive holidays out of Miami. In some parts of the Caribbean, resort hotels go to considerable lengths to advise guests not to leave their accommodation compounds unaccompanied due to targeting by local criminals. Cf. *Beales v Airtours* (above) where the tourist was mugged but the destination was no more dangerous than many other places and the tourist no more of a target than anyone else.

Such contractual (or possibly tortious) duties would be based on what might be described as the inequality of knowledge. The organiser of any travel arrangements — particularly package travel arrangements — might in many circumstances be reasonably expected to have access to local information that is not available to the majority of travellers. One should emphasise that such duties — if they are found to exist — are duties to warn, advise and recommend; it should be no part of the organiser's obligations to take steps to prohibit or prevent consumers acting as they see fit, provided they are possessed with reasonable information about their activities and their destination.

If such general contractual duties are properly described as implied terms of the travel contract, or the package contract in regulated cases, then breach of such a duty will itself be capable of amounting to a failure in the performance of an obligation under the package contract and subject to the liability framework imposed by regulation 15 of the 1992 Regulations.

Misrepresentation

In *Chesneau v Interholme Ltd*[116] a judge at first instance decided that the claimants' claim for damages for *misrepresentation* should be such as would put them in the position they would have been in if the representation had never been made. As a result he concluded that if the representation had never been made, the claimants would never have gone on the holiday in question, but booked alternative arrangements with another company, and they would certainly not have incurred over £200.00 in expenses looking for suitable alternative accommodation; neither would they have suffered any distress or disappointment. He awarded £30.00 in damages. This was a little hard on the claimants as they did not discover that the representations made by the tour operator were false until their arrival at their villa, and as a result they incurred the expenditure of obtaining reasonably appropriate alternative holiday accommodation. The Court of Appeal recognised the reality of their predicament and held that the £200.00 odd spent on the alternative accommodation represented a proper sum spent in attempting to mitigate the loss caused by the tour operator's misrepresentation.[117] One important feature of the case that is not clear from the report is why the claimants brought their claim in misrepresentation at all. Had the action been framed as a straightforward breach of contract, the loss sustained was perfectly foreseeable, so the claimants should have recovered their expenditure plus damages for loss of bargain and loss of enjoyment[118] without a visit to the

---

[116] [1983] *The Times* 9 June.
[117] Although this begs the question as to what loss it was that was being mitigated.
[118] In so far as this was not mitigated by their alternative arrangements.

Court of Appeal. The likely answer is that before the 1992 Regulations and the re-statement of the common law in cases like *Wong Mee Wan*[119] the uncertain scope of an organiser's contractual obligations at common law tempted many litigants to try their luck with a claim in misrepresentation. It seems that the *Chesneau* claimants did not take the precaution of suing for breach of contract in the alternative.

Given the advent of the PTR 1992, voluntary control in the form of codes of practice such as those produced and imposed by ABTA and *Wong Mee Wan*, is there now much call for claims based in misrepresentation? In most cases there may not be. However, there is one, as yet unexplored possibility open to the consumer. Damages for misrepresentation under section 2(1) of the Misrepresentation Act 1967 (so-called statutory negligent misrepresentation) are measured in the same way as damages for fraudulent misrepresentation.[120] The measure of damages is the same as that for the tort of deceit.[121] All *consequential* losses are recoverable whether foreseeable or not. In theory this is an uncovenanted bonus for the consumer who is restricted to foreseeable losses in actions for breach of contract.[122] Suppose in an extreme case that a consumer of vulnerable personality is so dismayed by the misrepresented accommodation or facilities that he tries to commit suicide by throwing himself off a high wall in a fit of uncontrollable self-destruction. In doing so he succeeds only in causing himself permanent damage of a type and to an extent entirely unforeseeable by the other party to the package contract. The injury flows directly from the effect of the misrepresentation on a vulnerable client. The fact that the damage may not have been reasonably foreseeable is neither here nor there in assessing damages on the statutory basis.

The point is that in situations where the loss sustained by the consumer goes beyond that which was reasonably foreseeable but which nonetheless flowed directly from the misrepresentation, the consumer would be entitled to recover under the 1967 Act but not in an action for breach of contract. A similar advantage in rare cases may accrue to the consumer who alleges fraud. The tour organiser will probably be able to avoid liability in fraud where a representation has been made to the effect that a luxury hotel is ready and available for immediate occupation. However, a hotelier or hotel management company may be more vulnerable to findings of fraud in respect of any misrepresentations made about the state of completeness of its accommodation or associated facilities. Where consequential but unforeseeable (or arguably

---

[119] See above.
[120] *Royscott Trust Limited v Rogerson* [1991] 2 QB 297.
[121] *Doyle v Olby (Ironmongers) Limited* [1969] 2 QB 158 and *Saunders v Edwards* [1987] 1 WLR 1116.
[122] See further Chapter 7.

unforeseeable) loss has resulted directly from the fraudulent misrepresentation, the consumer would be well advised to consider the hotel management company as at least one of the targets for the claim.

The effect of the PTR 1992 in respect of regulated packages, the ABTA code of conduct and recent developments in the common law which recognise the non-delegable contractual duties on the part of travel organisers (in some circumstances) to the effect that reasonable care will be exercised (irrespective of who actually performs the travel service), have combined to the effect that actions in misrepresentation[123] in travel and holiday cases should now be very much the exception rather than the rule. Nonetheless, they are still encountered but almost always, misrepresentation is a make-weight cause of action of little additional utility. In *Mawdsley v Cosmosair Plc*[124] where the claimant complained about a brochure that stated that a holiday hotel had "*lift in main building*" when in fact the lift in the main building did not visit the mezzanine restaurant level, action was brought for breach of contract, pursuant to regulation 4 of the PTR 1992 and in misrepresentation. Neither the judge at first instance nor the judge sin the Court of Appeal appeared to consider that the cause of action in misrepresentation added anything to the substance of the claim in contract of under the PTR 1992.

The Unfair Terms in Consumer Contracts Regulations 1999

Application

These Regulations[125] came into force on 1 October 1999. They apply to terms in contracts[126] between *consumers* and *sellers and suppliers* of goods or services which have not been individually negotiated and which are unfair[127]. Any term not satisfying the requirement of *fairness* is void under regulation 8(i)[128]. Schedule 2 of the 1999 Regulations gives examples of what *might* be

---

[123] Not including the statutory "misrepresentation" provisions in regulation 4 of the PTR 1992.
[124] [2002] EWCA Civ 587 discussed in Chapter 3.
[125] SI 1999 No: 2083.
[126] Not specifically package or travel contracts.
[127] That is, a term which is in breach of the requirement of good faith; causes significant imbalance in the parties' rights and obligations, and is to the detriment of the consumer – Regulation 5(i) and *Director General of Fair Trading v First National Bank Plc* [2001] 3 WLR 1297 in which the requirement of good faith under the 1994 regulations (predecessors to UTCCR was considered.
[128] The Director General of Fair Trading is given a general power in regulation 10 to apply to the court to restrain the use of unfair terms in consumer contracts — a power clearly designed to deal with industry-wide abuse of exorbitant commercial power where individual consumers

regarded as unfair, but the examples are not intended to be exhaustive. The application of the 1999 Regulations to package and travel contracts has an important qualification. Where a term in the contract is incorporated by reason of the PTR 1992 or accords with restrictions permitted by an international convention, the 1999 Regulations do not apply.[129] Therefore, what is permissible by one set of regulations or an international convention, is not rendered impermissible by the 1999 Regulations ("UTCCR"). UTCCR may be seen as an additional mechanism available to consumers only where the PTR 1992 or an international convention is silent in respect of the type of clause challenged.

UTCCR will have a modest impact even where the PTR 1992 apply.[130] UTCCR only protects consumers who are natural persons[131] and acting for purposes that are outside his business.[132]

Standard terms and subject matter

UTCCR apply only to terms which have *not* been individually negotiated, but cannot in any circumstances be deployed in respect of terms concerning the *price* of the service offered or which define the main *subject matter* of the contract. So a consumer is not permitted even to *argue* the unfairness of a standard term simply on the grounds that it was expensive or that no discount was given (*e.g.* where a direct booking is made with a tour operator, and the latter saves the commission otherwise payable to the travel agent). Neither can the consumer complain that a term is unfair simply because he did not like the destination and was at a disadvantage when buying his holiday due to the greater knowledge of the organiser or supplier.

Plain and intelligible

Terms must be written in plain and intelligible English. In the event of an ambiguity the uncertainty must be resolved in the consumer's favour.[133] What is plain and intelligible and what is not should be easier to spot than it is to describe. Increasingly, tour operators obtain "Plain English" accreditation for their booking conditions, but sometimes at the expense of *legal* clarity. It is all well and good having intelligible booking conditions, but such

---

might be disinclined to take action, or where the loss of a case or two against individual consumers would not deter the supplier from keeping the standard clause in its contracts.

[129] 1999 Regulations – 4(2).

[130] See e.g. Schedule 2, clauses 1(e) and (f) which describe imposing oppressive cancellation charges as potentially unfair.

[131] UTCCR Regulation 3(1) compared with the potentially broader meaning of "consumer" under the PTR 1992 – see Chapter 1.

[132] It remains open to question, therefore, whether the business traveller is covered by UTCCR.

[133] UTCCR Regulation 7 – but the position is much the same at common law.

conditions must still be capable of bringing about the intended contractual effect.

Sanctions

Simply because a term in the contract offends against UTCCR and is, therefore, not binding[134] on the consumer, the consumer is not guaranteed to succeed in any claim against the supplier neither does it mean that the rest of the contract does not remain binding on the parties. The consumer must also suffer a detriment — though this need not necessarily be a financial detriment. An example given in the UTCCR of an unfair term[135] concerns clauses which purport to deprive employees and agents of the power to make promises on behalf of the principal supplier, or, for example, to make such promises subject to confirmation in writing from a company director of the supplier. This is the sort of contractual term that one may well find in travel contracts where, for example, a tour operator wants to limit the extent to which it is bound by statements made by travel agents or telesales operators. However, the simple fact that such a contractual term may be regarded as unfair and rendered of no effect does not necessarily mean conversely that the supplier *will* automatically be bound by any promises made by employees and agents. Despite the removal of the offending clause the court still has to determine whether *in fact* the promisor (travel agent) had actual or apparent authority to bind the principal (tour operator), and the court will *still* have to be satisfied that the "promise" was made with contractual intention and force[136] *and* that the relevant promise was made in time and circumstances enabling it to be incorporated into the travel contract.

The most effective sanction devised by UTCCR arises out of the power given to the Director General of Fair Trading[137] to seek undertakings and if necessary an injunction[138] restraining the continued use of offending contractual terms. This may arise either where a particular company is using an unfair term or where a particular variety of contractual term is used generally in a particular industry. Such general measures are more likely to have an impact on the use or abuse of unfair terms in consumer contracts than individual cases brought by disgruntled consumers. In October 2002 the Director General of Fair Trading secured agreement[139] from most of the major UK tour operators and ABTA in respect of important industry-wide

---

[134] UTCCR regulation 8
[135] Schedule 2(1)(n).
[136] On facts such as *Kemp v Intasun* - see above.
[137] UTCCR regulations 10-12.
[138] And similar powers are given to local trading standards departments and the Consumers' Association to name but two other "qualifying bodies" listed in UTCCR Schedule 1.
[139] It is assumed under threat of action pursuant to the powers vested in him by UTCCR.

changes in tour operator's standard booking conditions. Some of the more important "unfair" terms that were subject to the agreement and which as a result of the agreement we can expect to see much less often than previously (particularly as new post 2003 season brochures are circulated) are as follows:

1. Conditions requiring consumers to make a complaint within 28 days of the end of their holiday failing which liability would be denied.[140]

2. Provisions that did not make clear the consumer's PTR 1992 Regulation 13(2) options in the event that the arrangements are cancelled pre-departure and requiring the consumer to pay a surcharge for a more expensive substitute holiday taken pursuant to PTR 1992 regulation 13(2)(a) .

3. Exclusive Jurisdiction and Choice of Law clauses relating to the English courts and English law which could prejudice consumers in other parts of the United Kingdom.

4. Terms stating that 21 days notice is deemed a reasonable period for a consumer to give under PTR 1992 regulation 10 in the event that the booking is to be transferred to an alternative consumer.

5. Clauses that specify what is to be regarded as a significant alteration to an essential term and limiting compensation to the happening of those specified events.[141]

The threat of proceedings from the Director General of Fair Trading[142] is, therefore, demonstrably more potent than the threat posed by individual consumers.[143]

---

[140] As in *Sargeant* – above.
[141] *Williams v Travel Promotions* – see above.
[142] Or local trading standards offices or the Consumers' Association.
[143] It is not thought that Travel Promotions altered their terms and conditions after their defeat in the Court of Appeal at the hands of Mr. Williams.

Chapter 6

ACCIDENTS: CHOICE OF LAW & JURISDICTION

Introduction

The chapters in which the PTR 1992 and the common law approach to the contractual duties of travel organisers are considered, proceeded on the assumption that the consumer is likely to be able to obtain remedies in the courts of England and Wales, and that the laws of England and Wales will apply.[1] Even where the English courts should apply foreign *standards*[2] these foreign standards are applicable as a matter of *English law*. That is to say, English law requires that in order to discharge its implied contractual duties (*e.g.* to take reasonable care or ensure that reasonable care is taken), the organiser or the other party to the contract need "only" ensure that local standards of health, safety and hygiene are met. The question for the court in these circumstances is, *what does reasonable care require of the organiser?* Where an English travel contract exists between consumer and organiser and the consumer's difficulties have been caused by a tour operator or a tour operator's subcontractors, the consumer simply sues the organiser for breach of the English contract, which was almost certainly concluded in England. There are many circumstances, however, where the traveller has an accident which is not attributable in any way to breach of contract or duty on the part of the travel organiser.

This chapter considers those accidents or incidents that may affect the traveller who has not made travel arrangements through a party based in England and Wales, or whose problems derive from an accident or incident completely unrelated to any package or travel contract made in the United Kingdom. In these examples the English traveller may be the aggrieved party, but equally, it may be important for the English traveller to appreciate those circumstances in which as a tortfeasor he may be subject to the jurisdiction

---

[1] Tour operators invariably state in their terms and conditions that the law of the constituent part of the UK from where the consumer is booking apply to a package contract and the courts of that part of the UK will have jurisdiction.
[2] *Wilson v Best Travel Limited* [1993] 1 All ER 353 and other cases discussed in Chapter 4.

of foreign courts. Such incidents would include the following obvious examples:

- road accidents between persons of different nationalities;

- skiing or other sports-related accidents between persons of different nationalities;

- food poisoning or other illnesses caused by facilities or services that are unrelated to any contractual arrangements made in the United Kingdom;

- quality complaints for those who have organised their travel arrangements independently.

The motorist travelling in France who has a collision with a Dutch driver is unlikely to have any contractual remedy against a package organiser based in England and Wales. The traveller injured in a private-hire jet-ski accident in the Mediterranean may have no recourse against his tour operator. Similarly, the family poisoned as a result of poor hygiene in a Greek restaurant in Rhodes may have no come-back against any party based in England. There are still many travellers — both for leisure and business purposes — who are not travelling as a result of contracts made through agents or organisers in this country and many more who are not travelling pursuant to regulated package contracts.

In any of the above examples the following two questions are of fundamental importance.

1. Does the English court have *jurisdiction* over the dispute in other words can proceedings be issued and the action tried in this country?

2. If the English court has jurisdiction, *which law* should be applied in resolving the dispute?

It is not only feasible but commonplace to encounter circumstances in which the English courts have jurisdiction over a dispute, but where the applicable law will be the law of another country.

JURISDICTION

Whether or not the courts of England and Wales or any other country have jurisdiction over a dispute depends on the law of that country. Accordingly, if a claimant wants to takes action in England, English rules of jurisdiction apply. If an English litigant is made the object of proceedings in Spain, it is the Spanish rules on jurisdiction which will dictate whether or not the English defendant is subject to the jurisdiction of the local court.

So when can proceedings be issued and an action tried in the courts of England and Wales[3]?

The answer to this question depends on the rules of four different jurisdictional regimes. They are:

1. The regime of the European Union[4] as set out in the Council Regulation (EC) 44/2001.[5]

2. The Brussels-Lugano Convention[6] regime which applies to the countries of the European Free Trade Association.[7]

3. The "modified" Brussels regime which applies to the constituent parts of the United Kingdom.[8]

4. The residual regime as it applies to the rest of the world.[9]

These regimes will be considered in turn.

Regulation 44/2001 and The Brussels Convention

It is more than a little regrettable that with the introduction of Regulation 44/2001 (with effect from 1 March 2002) and the continued application of the Brussels-Lugano Convention to EFTA countries, there has been a splintering of jurisdictional rules. Nonetheless, although Regulation 44/2001[10] and the Brussels Convention are now distinct regimes and contain subtle[11] differences it is convenient to deal with these 2 regimes together. Regulation 44/2001 is directly applicable in the United Kingdom as it is in the other Member States. The text of the Brussels Convention is to be found in Schedule 1 to the Civil Jurisdiction and Judgments Act 1982. Regulation 44/2001 applies[12] to all civil and commercial matters whatever the nature of the court or tribunal[13]. The presumptive rule is that defendants are entitled to be sued in the courts of the country where they habitually reside[14]. In outline,

---

[3] Regulation 44/2001 and the Brussels Convention are concerned with "Member States" and for our purposes the Member State is the *United Kingdom*. Jurisdiction within the United Kingdom is dealt with separately but for the purposes of clarity, "England and Wales" is used throughout this section.
[4] From 1 July 2007 Regulation 44/2001 applied to Denmark as well as all other members of the EU.
[5] Referred to hereafter as Regulation 44/2001.
[6] Referred to here as the Brussels Convention.
[7] Norway, Iceland, Switzerland & Liechtenstein .
[8] Referred to here as the "modified Convention".
[9] The common law regime.
[10] Effective in respect of proceedings instituted as from 1 March 2002.
[11] Or treacherous *Briggs: The Conflict of Laws* (Clarendon Press 2002).
[12] As does the Brussels Convention.
[13] Article 1.
[14] Regulation 44/2001 article 2.

for cases likely to be interest to those concerned with travel contracts, the courts of England and Wales will have jurisdiction[15] over a matter to which Regulation 44/2001[16] applies in six situations namely where:

1. The defendant submits to the jurisdiction of the English courts by entering an appearance for purposes other[17] than to contest jurisdiction.[18]

2. The defendant is domiciled in England and Wales.[19]

3. The harmful event occurred in England and Wales or a contract for the supply of services was to be performed in England and Wales.[20]

4. The defendant is one of a number of defendants[21] (including Part 20 defendants[22]), and one of the *other* defendants is domiciled in England and Wales.

5. In cases of consumer contracts[23] where the defendant pursues commercial activities in England and Wales where the consumer is domiciled.[24]

6. Where the consumer is domiciled in England and Wales and as insured, beneficiary or policyholder, is suing an insurer.[25]

---

[15] The outline of jurisdictional rules set out here in respect of the UK and England and Wales can be modified to provide a jurisdictional answer to any other Member State subject to Regulation 44/2001 or the Brussels Convention.

[16] Article references are to Regulation 44/2001 unless otherwise stated.

[17] By following the provisions of CPR Part 11.

[18] Article 24 – irrespective of prior jurisdiction agreement unless another court is given exclusive jurisdiction under Article 22.

[19] Irrespective of the nationality of the defendant; domicile is the key and English law applies to determine domicile [Article 59(1)]. For this purpose section 41 of the Civil Jurisdiction and Judgments Act 1982 applies for individuals [CJJ Order 2001, Schedule 1 paragraph 9].

[20] Article 5(1) for matters relating to a contract for the supply of services and 5(3) for matters relating to tort or delict. For present purposes the harmful event is the accident that causes the damage.

[21] Article 6(1) – but subject to an important restriction that it is necessary to join the additional defendants to avoid the risk of irreconcilable judgments. This has been restrictively interpreted – *Reunion Europeene SA v Spliethoff's Bevrachtingskantor BV* [1998] ECR I-6511 – Case C-51/97 to mean that joinder is only justified where the joined parties are sued in respect of the same cause of action. See also, *Watson v First Choice Holidays and Flights* [2001] CA Civ. 972 in which the Court of Appeal noted the difficulties this caused a claimant who sued a tour operator under the PTR 1992 and sought to join the occupier of Hotel premises in respect of serious injuries sustained on holiday. The case against the tour operator was in contract, that against the Hotel being in delict. The case was referred to the ECJ but compromised.

[22] Third Parties under article 6(2) – provided that the purpose of the *original action* was not simply to secure jurisdiction over third parties.

[23] Excluding transport contracts.

[24] Article 15 and 16.

[25] Article 9.

As far as the European Union and EFTA countries are concerned the same regime is deployed in determining whether an English domiciled defendant is subject to the jurisdiction of a foreign court.

Each of the above situations will be considered separately in outline.

Submission to the jurisdiction

Article 24 of Regulation 44/2001 provides:

> Apart from jurisdiction derived from other provisions of this Regulation, a court of a Member State before which a defendant enters an appearance shall have jurisdiction. This rule shall not apply where appearance was entered solely to contest the jurisdiction, or where another court has exclusive jurisdiction by virtue of article 22.

In other words, a defendant who submits (deliberately or otherwise) to the jurisdiction of the English courts by participating in the proceedings — without challenging the jurisdiction of the court at the first available opportunity will be bound by that submission. Participation in proceedings on the merits is not prejudicial to a defendant who challenges jurisdiction provided the jurisdictional challenge is entered before or simultaneously with a substantive defence. The Civil Procedure Rules ("CPR")[26] make provision for a defendant to challenge the jurisdiction of the court at a preliminary stage. In the light of the CPR it is unlikely that a defendant would be either required or able to participate substantively in the proceedings once a jurisdictional challenge has been entered. It will be remembered that procedural rules vary from place to place though and the defendant domiciled in England who finds himself the target of litigation elsewhere is subject to the procedural rules of the local forum.

> The challenge to jurisdiction may have the result attributed to it by [Article 24] only if the plaintiff and the court seised of the matter are able to ascertain from the time of the defendant's first defence that it is intended to contest the jurisdiction of the court.[27]

In England it is now unlikely that a defendant would get as far as filing a defence on the merits before mounting a jurisdictional challenge. CPR Part 11(1)-(5) provide as follows:

> (1) A defendant who wishes to —
>
> (a) dispute the court's jurisdiction to try a claim; or

---

[26] Part 11.
[27] *Elefanten Schuh v Jacqmain* [1981] ECR 1671.

(b) argue that the court should not exercise its jurisdiction, may apply to the court for an order declaring that it has no such jurisdiction or should not exercise any jurisdiction it may have.

(2) A defendant who wishes to make such an application must first file an acknowledgement of service in accordance with Part 10[28].

(3) A defendant who files an acknowledgement of service does not, by doing so, lose any right that he may have to dispute the court's jurisdiction.

(4) An application under this rule must —

(a) be made within the period for filing a defence; and

(b) be supported by evidence.

(5) If the defendant —

(a) files an acknowledgement of service; and

(b) does not make an application within the period for filing a defence, he is to be treated as having accepted that the court has jurisdiction to try the claim.

Nothing could be clearer.

Domicile

Article 2 of Regulation 44/2001 provides:

Subject to this Regulation, persons domiciled in a Member State shall, whatever their nationality, be sued in the courts of that Member State...

The domicile of individuals is still governed by section 41 of the Civil Jurisdiction and Judgments Act 1982[29] which provides that a person is domiciled in the United Kingdom or in one constituent part of the United Kingdom if that person is resident *and* has a substantial connection there by reason of the nature and circumstances of the residence. This specific definition of domicile for the purposes of the Brussels Convention might be reduced to the short-hand of "habitual residence".

This Article applies in two common situations relevant to travellers. The first is where the person responsible for causing the accident or incident which has caused the claimant damage, is himself habitually resident in England and Wales (whatever his nationality); for example, where an English traveller is injured in a road accident in Italy caused by an American driver who is normally resident in London.[30] The second type of incident where Article 2

---

[28] The Acknowledgement of Service standard form includes a specific "tick-box" for jurisdictional challenges.
[29] Civil Jurisdiction and Judgments Order 2001 – Schedule 1 Paragraph 9.
[30] Plainly the same applies if the tortfeasor is English and lives in England.

may have an important bearing is where the same accident is partly the responsibility of a Swedish driver. The Swedish driver will be subject to the jurisdiction of the English courts if sued as the second defendant[31] in an action properly instituted in England against the habitually resident American. In situations where there is alleged to be multiple responsibility for causing the accident or injury to the claimant, provided one of the proposed defendants is domiciled in England, the court has jurisdiction over the others (provided of course the others are domiciled in one of the other Member States). Where Article 2 can be deployed against one or more tortfeasors, the court has no discretion to decline jurisdiction on the grounds that the English court is not the most suitable or natural forum, or indeed on any grounds other than those set out elsewhere in Regulation 44/2001.

Article 2 is also of importance for English domiciled tortfeasors who *cause* accidents abroad. Unless they are one of a number of defendants properly joined in an action in another member State, the English tortfeasor *must* be sued in England unless Article 5(3)[32] applies.

Harmful event

Article 5.3 of Regulation 44/2001 provides:

> A person domiciled in a Member State may, in another member State be sued —
>
> In matters relating to tort, delict or quasi-delict, in the courts for the place where the harmful event occurred or may occur.

Article 5.3 essentially applies to all breaches of duty other than those in respect of obligations freely assumed by agreement.

The choice of jurisdiction is the claimant's. This poses no problem if the harmful event occurs in England or Wales. Where the harmful event is in another Member State, the English claimant may choose the place of the accident as the venue for court proceedings (especially if there are multiple defendants). Equally, the English defendant has no choice but to submit to the jurisdiction of the foreign court if the accident occurred within its jurisdictional boundaries. So, if an English driver injures a German pedestrian in Portugal, and the German claimant chooses to sue in Portugal, the English defendant (and the Portuguese court) has no grounds on which to object to the jurisdiction of the Portuguese court. If, however, the injured German pedestrian can properly allege that the accident was caused by the English driver and another driver — a Dutchman domiciled in Germany —

---

[31] Under article 6(1).
[32] In respect of the place where the harmful event occurred.

then proceedings can legitimately be instituted in Germany against the Dutch driver, with the English driver as a second defendant.[33]

If the courts of England and Wales do not have jurisdiction by virtue of either Article 2 or 5.3 of Regulation 44/2001 (and indeed even if they do) the claimant should exercise his choice of forum not only on grounds of familiarity and convenience, but by considering the differences that will exist between the level and types of damages that will be recoverable in different jurisdictions. Plainly, subject to counter-veiling inconvenience, inconsistency or unpredictability of decisions, or procedural factors such as the amount of time it takes to get an action to trial, the claimant will want to choose that jurisdiction which permits — and is likely to award — the greatest sum in damages for the injury sustained. On the other hand, for a defendant domiciled in England it is not necessarily disadvantageous to submit to the jurisdiction of another court, particularly where the types or level of damages recoverable may be more limited than in England and Wales.[34]

The *harmful event* itself will often be easy enough to identify. It will be the accident in which the claimant is first injured. However, the expression is wide enough to encompass both the place where damage is suffered *and* the place where the event giving rise to the damage took place. If the *event* and the *damage* occur in different jurisdictions the claimant will have a choice between the two appropriate legal systems. However, for the traveller who is involved in an accident it is the *event* that will govern the choice of jurisdiction under Article 5.3 of Regulation 44/2001. The injured English-based claimant will not succeed in an argument to the effect that because some aspects of the loss are *sustained* after a return home[35] the English court has an Article 5.3 jurisdiction in respect of a road accident in Denmark caused by the negligence of an Austrian driver in which the English-based defendant was injured. In *Marinari v Lloyds Bank PLC*[36] the court held that Article 5.3:[37]

> ...should not be construed so extensively as to encompass any place where the adverse consequences of an event that has already caused actual damage elsewhere can be felt.

As a general rule, therefore, once some actual damage has been suffered, the place where that damage (of whatever character) has arisen will be regarded as the place where the harmful event occurred for the purposes of Article 5.3

---

[33] Both claims being in tort or delict.
[34] Heads of loss are governed by the law applicable to the issues, but assessment of damages is a matter of English procedure and governed by English law – *Hulse v Chambers* [2001] 1 WLR 2386.
[35] E.g. deterioration in physical condition or continuing loss of earnings.
[36] [1996] 2 WLR 159 at 171.
[37] Of the Brussels Convention – but the result would be the same under Regulation 44/2001.

even though further consequences may develop later in another jurisdiction. The claimant who breaks his leg in France as the result of the negligence of a Belgian driver may well sustain *most* of his consequential loss in England where he is domiciled, however the physical injury arising in France is almost certainly conclusive of the French court's jurisdiction under Article 5.3.

Multiple defendants

Provided that an action is properly maintainable against a person domiciled in England (for incidents occurring in other Member Sates), any other joint or several tortfeasors may be brought into the English proceedings. Article 6.1 provides:

> *A person domiciled in a Member State may also be sued — Where he is one of a number of defendants, in the courts for the place where any one of them is domiciled provided the claims are so closely connected that it is expedient to hear and determine them together to avoid the risk of irreconcilable judgments resulting from separate proceedings.*

The claimant in *Watson v First Choice Holidays & Flights Limited & Others*[38] relied on this provision.[39] The claimant and a friend took a package holiday in Spain. Whilst they were there they were invited back to the accommodation of 2 girls they had met on a night out. The girls' accommodation was not in the same hotel as the claimant as his friend but, it was, they alleged, part of the same hotel complex sharing a number of common facilities. On reaching the girls' accommodation the lads' entry was barred by truncheon bearing security guards who proceeded to chase them through the unlit grounds. As the lads ran away, they spotted a gap in a fence and a low wall over which each hurdled only to find that the drop on the other side of the wall was about 20 metres onto a dual carriageway below. One of the lads sued in England and brought action in the first instance against the tour operator responsible for his own package holiday alleging that there had been an improper performance of the holiday contract in that the security guards had overreacted and there was insufficient lighting and inadequate fencing at the point of the low wall. As the guards and the wall were all services forming part of the same complex of hotels as their own, it was alleged that the tour operator was responsible for this pursuant to PTR 1992 regulation 15. The claimant then attempted to join the proprietors of the girl's hotel mindful of the fact that if the "complex" as a whole was not within the services forming part of the lads' package holiday contract, the claim under the PTR 1992 was likely to fail. The problem that arose for the claimant was that his claim against the tour operator was in

---

[38] [2001] CA EWCA Civ 972.
[39] As it then was under the Brussels Convention.

contract[40] but his claim against the Spanish hotelier proprietor was in delict under Spanish law. Case law from the European Court of Justice[41] had earlier ruled that where the cause of action against the additional defendant[42] was different to that against the defendant domiciled in the court seised of the original action, there was insufficient connection between the actions to justify joinder under Article 6.1. This was a judicial gloss on the actual words of Article 6.1[43] but it stood in the way of the claimant. It was argued on his behalf that because any liability on the part of the tour operator was *for the delict* of the hotel proprietor and that the *improper performance of the* [holiday] *contract* comprised the hotelier's delict, there was a sufficient connection in the interests of avoiding irreconcilable judgments to justify joining the Spanish hotel proprietor in the extant English proceedings. The hotel proprietor maintained that there was no such justification[44] because the claimant could have brought proceedings against both the tour operator and the hotel in Spain – the place where the harmful event took place. The issue was referred to the ECJ by the Court of Appeal but the action compromised before the reference was heard.[45]

Article 6.2 permits in certain circumstances the joinder of a *third party* (Part 20 Defendant) where the English (or any other court of a Member State) court is seised of the original action. As was pointed out above, the same applies where a tortfeasor domiciled in England and Wales (irrespective of nationality) falls to be sued for causing or partly causing an accident in another Member State. Again, the reverse is true. The defendant domiciled in England and Wales may find himself properly joined as an additional party in the courts of another Member State even though the courts of that state would not be the appropriate court under Article 2 or 5.3.

Kinnear v Falconfilms[46] is a good illustration of Article 6[47] in operation. In 1988 the actor Roy Kinnear was making a film near Toledo in Spain. In the course of filming he was thrown from a horse and suffered serious injuries. He was taken to hospital in Madrid where he died the following day. It was

---

[40] At first instance deputy judge Mr. J. Goudie QC made it clear that regulation 15 cases are actions in contract, not in tort and not for breach of statutory duty.

[41] *Reunion Europeene* (above).

[42] The Spanish hotelier defendant not domiciled in England and Wales in this instance.

[43] Even though additional words have been added to article 6(1) of Regulation 44/2001 this judicial gloss apparently remains.

[44] And the Hotel operator may well have been right. Article 6.4 as it now stands expressly allows for multiple causes of action as well as parties in cases where a claim is combined with rights *in rem* over immovable property. This express provision would suggest that the regulators only intended departure from a narrow construction of the Article 6 exceptional jurisdiction in these limited circumstances.

[45] [2001] EWCA Civ 972.

[46] [1996] 1 WLR 920.

[47] Of the Brussels Convention as then applied.

alleged that the accident was caused by the breach of contract and negligence of the defendant film company. This was denied; but it was further alleged that death was the result of clinical negligence at the hospital in Madrid. The defendant sought to join the Spanish doctor and hospital as third parties to an action commenced against them in this country on behalf of the deceased's estate. On appeal, Phillips J. held that Article 6.2 of the Brussels Convention (as it then was) applied.

> If one carries out the artificial exercise of comparing the issues that are raised by the plaintiffs' claim against the defendants and the defendants' claim against the third parties, it is apparent that the issues largely overlap. In the action between the plaintiffs and the defendants, the following issues arise. (1) Was Mr. Kinnear's accident caused by breach of duty on the part of the defendants? (2) Was Mr. Kinnear's death caused by medical malpractice on the part of the third parties? If so, (3) did that medical malpractice break the chain of causation? In the third party claim the first two issues arise again and, if the court finds that breach of duty on the part of both the defendants and the third parties contributed to Mr Kinnear's death, the court then has to decide how liability should be apportioned between them. This analysis further demonstrates that the facts of this case abundantly satisfy not merely the letter of article 6.2 but the considerations that have given rise to this head of special jurisdiction.

The jurisdiction conferred by Article 6 is an *exceptional* or special one[48] intended to be exercised where there is a close connecting factor or nexus between the issues in the main action and a Part 20 claim *"with a view to the efficacious conduct of the proceedings. The Convention thus enables the entire dispute to be heard by a single court.*[49] *"*

A nexus sufficient to justify an English court giving permission (where required) allowing a Part 20 claim to proceed[50] in respect of parties within the jurisdiction might be considered sufficient for the purposes of Article 6.1 of Regulation 44/2001 and the judgment of Phillips J. seems so to imply. However, a word of caution is justified. A sufficient nexus between the main action and third party proceedings might be sufficient to warrant the bringing of an Additional Claim under CPR Part 20 and permission to bring such a claim may well be correctly granted in circumstances where it is shown that there is an *insufficient nexus* for the purposes of Article 6.1 of Regulation 44/2001. In other words, what's good for CPR Part 20 may *not* always be quite good enough for the purposes of Article 6.

---

[48] Exceptional in the sense that article 2 jurisdiction base don domicile is the presumptive jurisdictional rule under Regulation 44/2001 and the Brussels Convention.
[49] *Kongress Agentur Hagen GmbH v Zeehaghe BV* [1990] ECR I 1864.
[50] CPR 20.9(1)(a) & (b).

Waterford Wedgewood PLC & another v David Nagli Ltd & Others[51] was such a case. Waterford Wedgewood PLC brought proceedings in respect of the sale or attempted sale by the Defendants of counterfeit Waterford crystals. It alleged both trade mark infringement and passing-off. Following the issue of proceedings Waterford Wedgewood PLC applied for summary judgment. The Defendants sought and were granted permission to issue and serve third party proceedings on a practising solicitor in the Republic of Ireland. Although permission for the issue and service of those proceedings was given the Master refused an application to adjourn the summons for summary judgment in the action between Waterford Crystal PLC and the Defendant. Judgment in the application for summary judgment was duly given. Then the Third Party sought orders setting aside the Third Party Notice. That application came before a Deputy Judge. The Deputy Judge made the following crucial findings of facts:-

> [Following their obtaining summary judgment] I am told that the plaintiff has since taken no further step in the action other than to enforce payment of their costs .... Realistically they will probably take no further steps in the proceedings other than for the purpose of enforcing their order for costs................In any case the Defendants are probably not worth pursuing............If this is right, it means that there are unlikely to be any further proceedings in the main action, by which it is or may be necessary to have the third-party bound.

The following principles apply to Article 6[52] as summarised by the Deputy Judge:

1. The purpose behind the special jurisdiction conferred by Article 6(2) is to secure the rational and efficient disposal of trials and in particular to avoid the risk of irreconcilable judgments which would follow if third party claims were tried separately.

2. Although in *Kinnear* Phillips J stated that the nexus between the Plaintiffs claim against the Defendant and the Defendants claim against the Third Party required to satisfy Order 16 1(1) RSC [for which read CPR Part 20] is likely to be sufficient to justify the special jurisdiction granted by Article 6(2), one should read this passage only as illustrating where it may be *expedient* for the claim and third party claim to be heard together. The Judge was not intending to derogate from the principle of the Convention that to override the basic right of the third party to be sued separately in the Court of his domicile it must be shown

---

[51] [1998] FSR 92.
[52] The Brussels Convention as it then was.

to be expedient in the interest of justice and good administration that the two actions or claims be heard by the same Court.

3. Absent this ingredient, domestic third party proceedings which merely happen to satisfy CPR Part 20 will not necessarily be regarded as "*any other third party proceedings*" within Article 6(2). Article 6(2) is intended to have the same meaning and effect in each Member State.

4. Where therefore the main proceedings are for whatever reasons no longer active, it will only be in exceptional circumstances that claims can be pursued by way of third party proceedings under Article 6(2), as where it is necessary the same tribunal which has already tried the issue in the main action should determine similar or related issues in the third party claim.

5. Save in exceptional circumstances "other third party proceedings" refer to the joinder of third parties into active proceedings so that both be heard together.

6. Even in the cases falling within Article 6(2) the Court *retains the discretion*. If otherwise the third party claims ought to be pursued abroad, the Court can in appropriate cases exercise its discretion and decline jurisdiction. Where it might do so it would equally refuse leave under domestic rules.

The Deputy Judge held that the third party proceedings before him were not "third party proceedings" *within Article 6(2)*. These principles were adopted in a tour operator group action brought by sick Claimants in which the tour operator attempted to join the overseas hotelier as a Third Party. Unfortunately it did not do so until the claims of the Claimants had been compromised in the main action. So, in *Barton & 12 others v Golden Sun Holidays Limited (in liquidation) and Avlida Hotel Limited*[53] the judge concluded:

> In my judgment there is no close connection between the sets two of claim in the instant case. In the claim brought by the claimants they relied exclusively on causes of action and remedies solely based in English law existing for the protection of English consumers. The claim brought by the defendants inevitably will require an investigation on what happened in Cyprus and, probably, the consequences for those parties in Cypriot law. Further there is no basis to conclude that the administration of justice will be achieved more efficiently if the Part 20 claim is determined by the Birmingham county court. ... The claim between the claimant and defendant is no longer active and is unlikely ever to be revived. There is no realistic possibility that the claim between the defendant and part 20

---

[53] 3 August 2007: Birmingham District Registry (Unreported) Wyn Williams J.

defendant will be tried with the claimants' claim. There is no risk of an irreconcilable judgments. There has never been and never will be any prospect of the part 20 defendant being a party in the determination of the proceedings brought by the claimants against the defendant.

Consumer contracts

In matters relating to consumer contracts the consumer has a choice and may bring proceedings in the courts of the place either where the consumer is himself domiciled or in the place where the other party to the consumer contract is domiciled.[54] The consumer's choice is plainly important. Someone is regarded as consumer where he contracts for a purposes that can be regarded as being outside his trade or profession *and* where the other party to the contract is someone who pursues commercial or professional activities in the Member State of the consumer's domicile or directs activities to that country *and* where the contract falls within the scope of those activities.[55] Transport only contracts are excluded from these provisions.[56]

Many foreign-based[57] holiday and travel service suppliers direct their commercial activities to all parts of the United Kingdom, particularly on the internet, and in doing so they are likely to find themselves subject to the jurisdiction of the English courts. The same will apply to a foreign service provider promoting accommodation and other tourist facilities through British newspapers and magazines. The consumer's choice is between the courts of his own country of domicile or that of the service provider – and no doubt the choice will usually be that of the consumer's domicile.[58] So, the Irish publican promoting on the internet stag-nights in Dublin; the Tuscan property company selling do-it-yourself holiday cottage rentals and the Corsican adventure company pedalling activity breaks by similar means may all find themselves as defendants in an English court in the event that things go wrong. It is submitted that in determining whether the contract falls within the scope of the activities of the commercial or professional supplier or promoter[59] the courts are likely to take a broad pro-consumer approach.

Where the Brussels Convention still applies[60] the consumer's choice is rather more constrained. There Articles 13 and 14 require that the consumer contract is made as a result if the conclusion of the contract was preceded by

---

[54] Article 16.
[55] Article 15.1(c).
[56] Article 15.3.
[57] Although the base must be a Member State for the purposes of Regulation 44/2001.
[58] Article 38 ff of Regulation 44/2001 deal with automatic mutual recognition of judgments obtained in member States.
[59] Article 15.1(c).
[60] EFTA.

a specific invitation addressed to the consumer or by general advertising and the consumer took in his own country all the steps necessary for the conclusion of the contract. Where this applies, the consumer may choose to sue the other party in the courts of the country where he is domiciled. The following example may illustrate the thrust of Articles 13 and 14.

A tour operator having its principle place of business and being domiciled in Luxembourg publishes a brochure offering French villas for holiday rental. The brochure is promoted and circulated throughout the European Union including England where the consumer is domiciled. The consumer is on a mailing list, as a result of which a copy of the brochure is dispatched to him. On receipt the consumer decides to hire one of the villas for a family holiday and contacts the tour operator by telephone. Subsequently as a result of exchanges of fax which include the tour operator's standard terms and conditions, the hire contract is concluded in Luxembourg and is made subject to Belgian law by agreement. In this example the *purpose* of the contract is outside the scope of the individual's trade or profession; it is a consumer contract for the supply of services (the provision of the French holiday villa) and the consumer has taken all necessary steps for the conclusion of the contract in England. If the performance of the contract goes wrong, the customer in this instance may sue the tour operator in England by virtue of Articles 13 and 14 of the Brussels Convention.

In the modern era of the Single Market, where travel related services or facilities may be offered from any part of Europe, cross-border advertising or the furnishing across borders of promotional material by virtue of mailing lists is likely to become increasingly common, even if it not already commonplace. Articles 15 and 16 of Regulation 44/2001 and articles 13 and 14 of the Brussels Convention will assist the consumer in these situations (at least as regards choice of forum) regardless of the domicile of the other party to the contract or the place of performance of the contract.

Insurance claims

Section 3 (Articles 8-13) of Regulation 44/2001 applies to jurisdiction in matters relating to insurance. The presumptive rule (Article 9) is that an insurer should be sued in the courts of the place where the *insurer* (or his co-insurer) is domiciled[61] or in another Member State if the Claimant is domiciled there *and* is the policyholder, the insured or a beneficiary of the insurance. Article 10 further permits actions against *liability insurers* in the courts of the place where the *harmful event* occurs.

---

[61] Although if the insurer is the Claimant (Article 12) proceedings must be brought in the place where the Defendant is domiciled.

Article 11 of Regulation 44/2001 provides:

> 1. In respect of liability insurance, the insurer may also, if the law of the court permits it, be joined in proceedings which the injured party has brought against the insured.
>
> 2. Articles 8, 9 and 10 shall apply to actions brought by the injured party directly against the insurer, where such direct actions are permitted.
>
> 3. If the law governing such direct actions provides that the policyholder all the insured may be joined as a party to the action, the same court shall have jurisdiction over them.

Although article 11.1 does not specifically say so, it was thought that this was intended to apply and should be construed as only applying to *third-party proceedings* brought by the insured person and it does not permit the insurer to be joined in as a Co-Defendant in the main action.[62] The primary basis of this conclusion is the history of the provision now contained in article 11. Section 3 of the Civil Judgments and Jurisdiction Act 1982 is headed "*Interpretation of the Conventions*" and, so far as relevant reads as follows:

> (1) Any question as to the meaning or effect of any provision of the Brussels Convention shall, if not referred to the European Court in accordance with the 1971 Protocol, be determined in accordance with the principles laid down by and any relevant decision of the European Court.
>
> (3) Without prejudice to the generality of subsection (1), the following reports (which are reproduced in the Official Journal of the Communities), namely-
>
> (a) the reports by Mr P . Jennard on the 1968 Convention and the 1971 Protocol"
>
> ... may be considered in ascertaining the meaning or effect of any provision in the conventions and shall be given such weight as is appropriate in the circumstances.

The report of M. Jenard, in so far as it relates to the relevant part of the Brussels Convention reads as follows:

> The provisions of this section may be summarised as follows: matters relating to insurance, actions against an insurer domiciled in a Contracting State may be brought in the following courts, i.e. either:

---

[62] This construction has been approved twice in the High Court: *Susan Pimblett Kevil v Clelland and Ethniki Insurance S.A.* [2005] QBD Unreported 10th. June following *Louise Patterson and Others v Richard Carden and others* [Morland J. 14th. September 2000 unreported].

(2) as a *third-party*, in the court seised of the action brought by the injured party against the insured if, under its own law, that Court has jurisdiction in the third-party proceedings. (Article 10)[63]

It was thought to be more than tolerably clear, therefore, that as far as English law is concerned the victim of a European traffic accident cannot directly sue the *insurer* of the guilty party in England as a second Defendant in proceedings brought against the tortfeasor even if the law of the insurer's domicile permits direct actions against insurers. The tortfeasor or guilty party could, however, join the insurer as a third party. The accident victim is *not*, it is submitted, a "beneficiary" of the liability insurance[64] of the defaulting driver within the meaning of Article 9 of regulation 44/2001. There are two obvious reasons for this. The first is that at the time the insurance policy is issued such a "beneficiary" is completely unidentifiable and the second is that such a "beneficiary's" right to recover is dependent on the insured party committing some tortious act that triggers the liability provisions of the policy.

Then there came *FBTO Schadeverzekeringen NV v Jack Odenbreit.*[65] This was a case in which a German resident (Mr. Odenbreit) was injured in a traffic accident in the Netherlands. He sued the (one presumes) Dutch insurer in the German courts. The ECJ in its judgment[66] set out the statutory background thus:

Legal context of the dispute:

> Regulation No 44/2001
>
> Recital 13 in the preamble to Regulation No 44/2001 states, '[i]n relation to insurance ... contracts ..., the weaker party should be protected by rules of jurisdiction more favourable to his interests than the general rules provide for.'

Article 9(1)(a) and (b) of Regulation No 44/2001 provides:

> 1. An insurer domiciled in a Member State may be sued:
>
> (a) in the courts of the Member State where he is domiciled, or
>
> (b) in another Member State, in the case of actions brought by the policyholder, the insured or a beneficiary, in the courts for the place where the plaintiff is domiciled...

---

[63] Bearing in mind the changes of Article numbers & subtle but important changes of wording between the Brussels Convention and Regulation 44/2001.

[64] But the Polish Government thought otherwise in its submissions to the ECJ in the *FBTO* case (see further below).

[65] ECJ 13 December 2007 [2007] EUECJ C-463/06.

[66] Delivered without obtaining any written Opinion from the Advocate General.

Article 11 of that regulation states:

> 1. In respect of liability insurance, the insurer may also, if the law of the court permits it, be joined in proceedings which the injured party has brought against the insured.
>
> 2. Articles 8, 9 and 10 shall apply to actions brought by the injured party directly against the insurer, where such direct actions are permitted.
>
> 3. If the law governing such direct actions provides that the policyholder or the insured may be joined as a party to the action, the same court shall have jurisdiction over them.

Directive 2000/26/EC of the European Parliament and of the Council of 16 May 2000 on the approximation of the laws of the Member States relating to insurance against civil liability in respect of the use of motor vehicles[67] and amending Council Directives 73/239/EEC and 88/357/EEC (OJ 2000 L 181, p. 65), as amended by Directive 2005/14/EC of the European Parliament and of the Council of 11 May 2005 (OJ 2005 L 149, p. 14) ('Directive 2000/26'), provides in Article 3, entitled 'Direct right of action':

> Each Member State shall ensure that injured parties referred to in Article 1 in accidents within the meaning of that provision enjoy a direct right of action against the insurance undertaking covering the responsible person against civil liability.

In addition, Recital 16a in the preamble to Directive 2000/26 states as follows:

> Under Article 11(2) read in conjunction with Article 9(1)(b) of... Regulation ... No 44/2001 ..., injured parties may bring legal proceedings against the civil liability insurance provider in the Member State in which they are domiciled.

The question asked of the ECJ by the German court was as follows:

> Is the reference to Article 9(1)(b) in Article 11(2) of ... Regulation ... No 44/2001 ... to be understood as meaning that the injured party may bring an action directly against the insurer in the courts for the place in a Member State where the injured party is domiciled, provided that such a direct action is permitted and the insurer is domiciled in a Member State?

All the Member States who submitted observations and the Commission of the EU considered that the short answer to this question was "yes" because such an interpretation would reflect the need to protect the economically weaker party (the injured person). The very aim of article 11(2) of Regulation 44/2001 was to extend to injured persons the right to sue in the courts of that person's domicile provided to plaintiffs by article 9(1)(b). The

---

[67] The Fourth Motor Directive.

ECJ did not accept that the injured party was to be regarded as a "beneficiary" but rather that such an injured party had in his own right a direct right of action on the courts of his own domicile by virtue of 11(2) when read in conjunction with 9(1)(b) and the answer given by the Court was as follows:

> In light of all the foregoing considerations the reply to the question referred for a preliminary ruling must be that the reference in Article 11(2) of Regulation No 44/2001 to Article 9(1)(b) of that regulation is to be interpreted as meaning that the injured party may bring an action directly against the insurer before the courts for the place in a Member State where that injured party is domiciled, provided that a direct action is permitted and the insurer is domiciled in a Member State.

The Court was conscious of applying a teleological interpretation of the provisions of Regulation 44/2001 but added:[68]

> To deny the injured party the right to bring an action before the courts for the place of his own domicile would deprive him of the same protection as that afforded by the regulation to other parties regarded as weak in disputes in matters relating to insurance and would thus be contrary to the spirit of the regulation. Moreover, as the Commission correctly observes, Regulation No 44/2001 strengthened such protection as compared with the protection resulting from application of the Brussels Convention.

The consequences of this decision have to be understood in conjunction with changes required by the Fourth Motor Directive, pursuant to which the law of England and Wales was changed to permit direct action against insurers in respect of traffic accidents occurring *in the UK*. The Motor Directives are considered in more detail immediately below, but a summary of the jurisdictional position might be helpful here.

- An injured party may sue a liability insurer in the courts of the injured party's domicile *where such direct actions are permitted.*

- English law now permits direct action against liability insurers for accidents in the UK.

- If the applicable national law of a member State relating to liability for an accident permits direct actions against liability insurers, then an action can be brought pursuant to that applicable law in the courts of the injured person's domicile.

- All Member States should now permit such direct actions against liability insurers as a result of the Fourth Motor Directive.

---

[68] Judgment: paragraph 28.

- Therefore, it should always be possible for an EU injured party to sue an EU liability insurer in the courts of the injured party's domicile.

Fourth & Fifth Motor Directives

The European Fourth Motor Insurance Directive[69] provides that *"...each Member State shall ensure that injured parties ... enjoy a direct right of action against the insurance undertaking covering the responsible person against civil liability ..."* in respect of accidents. This was given effect in English law by the European Communities (Rights Against Insurers) Regulations 2002[70]. The 2002 Regulations provide as follows by clause 3(1) and (2):

> (1) Paragraph (2)... applies where an entitled party has a cause of action against an insured person in tort or ... delict, and that cause of action arises out of an accident.[71]

> (2)... the entitled party may,[72] without prejudice to his right to issue proceedings against the insured person, issue proceedings against the insurer which issued the policy of insurance relating to the insured vehicle[73], and that insurer shall be directly liable to the entitled party to the extent that he is liable to the insured person."

The Directive also establishes a regime intended to provide injured parties with easier access to information about insurers covering vehicles of foreign drivers involved in accidents and all EU insurers are required to have a claims system in each Member State which system should include the power to negotiate claims made against them wherever the location of the accident. Reciprocal arrangements between the uninsured drivers' compensation schemes[74] are also implemented by the Directive.

Before the Fourth Directive, faced with an unfamiliar legal system in a foreign language, many claimants may have abandoned their claims. However, under the Directive UK claimants need only contact the UK information centre (the MIIC) to pursue a claim. The simplification of this process should encourage more UK victims to claim. The benefits of the Directive are backed by the Motor Insurers Bureau (MIB). If the insurer fails to appoint a claims representative; the responsible driver is uninsured; the vehicle cannot be identified; or if the insurer or the insurer's claims representative has not made a reasoned response to the claim within the

---

[69] 2000/26/EC of 16 May 2000 – effective from 19 January 2003.
[70] SI 2002 3061.
[71] An "accident" is an accident on a road or other public place in the UK caused by, or arising out of, the use of any insured vehicle – clause 2(1).
[72] A resident of a Member State.
[73] A vehicle is a motor vehicle *normally based in the United Kingdom*.
[74] Such as the Motor Insurers' Bureau in England.

compulsory timescale, the claimant will not suffer further delay. They will be compensated by the MIB, which will in turn recover the amount paid from the compensation body in the relevant European Member State. That compensation body may then turn to the insurer or driver responsible to recover its own expenses. This system should reduce delays in the claims process to the claimant significantly, leaving the procedural obstructions to the designated bodies. The Directive should also assist rapid access to damage repair and early assessment of the need for medical rehabilitation, allowing better claims handling, and hence cost control, by the insurer.

It is not this Directive that confers *jurisdiction* on the English courts in respect of foreign motor accidents. For jurisdictional provisions one must still have regard to Regulation 44/2001[75] as now construed in *FBTO*.[76] The court's of the claimant's domicile in liability insurance cases derives from the purposive construction of Regulation 44/2001 as now approved by the ECJ.

Paragraph 15 of the preamble of the Fourth Directive presupposes that any action of a claims representative appointed by an insurer under the Directive will be subject to the supervision of the national courts of the Member State where the representatives acting *but only if and "so far as this is compatible with the rules of private international law on the conferral of jurisdiction"*. Paragraph 16 of the recitals accompanying the Fourth Directive states: *The activities of claims representatives are not sufficient to confer jurisdiction on the courts in the injured party's Member State or residence if the rules of private international law on the conferral of jurisdiction do not so provide."* In combination it is submitted that the obvious intention of the regulators was that the Fourth Directive *itself* should *not* be construed as conferring jurisdiction on the Courts of a Member State where none previously existed. Thus the importance of the Information Centres set up under the auspices of the Directive is as potential sources of information and claims processing. This in turn might mean easier or more efficient claims settlement, but if legal action is required against an insurer the insurance jurisdiction provisions of Regulation 44/2001 still apply – but they apply as now interpreted by *FBTO*.[77]

Article 4d of the Fifth Directive simply provides: *"Member States shall ensure that injured parties to accidents caused by a vehicle covered by insurance ... enjoy a direct right of action against the insurance undertaking covering the person responsible against civil liability."* Arguably, this is already achieved by the 2002 Regulations. Article 5 of the Fifth Directive adds a new recital (16a) to the preamble of the Fourth Directive which now

---

[75] Or where appropriate the Brussels Convention.
[76] See above.
[77] See above.

reads, "*Under Article 11(2) read in conjunction with Article 9(1)(b) of Regulation 44/2001 on jurisdiction and the recognition and enforcement of judgments, injured parties may bring legal proceedings against the civil liability insurance provider in the Member State in which they are domiciled.*" This is quite correct as a matter of general principle – but only in the very limited circumstances already defined in articles 9 and 11 of the Judgments Regulation. What the Fifth Directive has *not* done is to alter the wording of the Judgments Regulation or to require further amendment to the wording of the 2002 Rights Against Insurers Regulations.

Unlike the 4th Directive, the 5th EU Directive on Motor Insurance[78] does not have a single aim; it covers a range of topics, some of which might have an impact within the UK, but most of which will not. The Directive was adopted on 11 May 2005 and came into force on 11 June 2005. Member States had 24 months (i.e. until 11 June 2007) in which to implement its provisions.

Compensation for victims where vehicles have false or no registration plates

In the event of an accident where a vehicle cannot be identified by its registration plate, MIIC[79] may not be able to identify a liable insurer. In such case the guarantee fund in the country of the accident will meet the claim – if the accident is in the UK, this will be the MIB.

Compensation for victims where the vehicle was not required to be conventionally insured

Some vehicles are exempt from the normal third party insurance requirement. Where the liability on these vehicles is accepted by a particular body, the UK Regulations require those vehicles to be traceable through MIIC. Where this is not possible the compensation body (MIB) must meet any claim. This is already the case in the UK.

Liability towards pedestrians and cyclists

This provision is intended to ensure that pedestrians and cyclists always have a right to seek compensation in the event of an accident, but does not guarantee it, if, for example they are wholly liable themselves.

---

[78] EC 2005/14.
[79] Motor Insurers' Information Centre.

Role of information centres

Information centres set up under the 4th Directive will be obliged to provide insurer information to domestic as well as foreign claimants. This is already the case in the UK, so the position of MIIC remains unaffected.

Parallel proceedings

Both Regulation 44/2001 and the Brussels Convention deplore parallel proceedings. The object is to ensure so far as is practicable, that connected or interrelated disputes are heard together by the same court, and that the potential for inconsistent findings of fact and decisions is minimised. Articles 27 and 28[80] apply in respect of parallel proceedings,[81] in the course of which it is important to draw a distinction between *staying* second or subsequent sets of proceedings and *declining* jurisdiction over such additional proceedings. Thus Article 27 provides:

> Where proceedings involving the same cause of action and between the same parties are brought in the courts of different Member States, any court other than the court first seised shall of its own motion stay its proceedings until such time as the jurisdiction of the court first seised is established. Where the jurisdiction of the court first seised is established, any court other than the court first seised shall decline jurisdiction in favour of that court.

This prevents changes of mind on jurisdiction on the part of a claimant — who may consider on reflection that he had a chance to recover greater damages in a jurisdiction other than that which he first chose. It also prevents a counterclaiming defendant from issuing fresh proceedings by way of a tactical weapon in the courts of a country other than the court chosen by the claimant. Whether a court is seised of a matter is a question judged by the rules of the national court. So, a French court deciding whether an English court was "seised" of a matter would apply English rules, and the English court would apply Spanish procedural rules in order to determine whether the Spanish court was seised first. If both Spanish and English courts have to determine chronologically which court was first seised of a matter the answer (whichever court it is) should be the same in both countries. In England and Wales the court will be seised of a matter when the Claim Form is *served* on the defendant. Once it is determined which court was first seised of the matter, any other court is obliged to *decline* jurisdiction. Some jurisdictions permit applications for negative declarations, or declarations of non-liability. This can be a source of procedural difficulty for claimants where a defendant applies for such a declaration in order to get its retaliation

---

[80] Of Regulation 44/2001.
[81] Article 21 and 22 of the Brussels Convention.

in first so to speak. The operation of Article 27 may in these circumstances stifle any intended proceedings in England and Wales.

Article 28 provides:

> Where related actions are brought in the courts of different Member States, any court other than the court first seised may while the actions are pending at first instance, stay its proceedings.

A court other than the court first seised may also, on the application of one of the parties, decline jurisdiction if the law of that court permits the consolidation of related actions and the court first seised has jurisdiction over both actions. For the purposes of this Article, actions are deemed to be related where they are so closely connected that it is expedient to hear and determine them together to avoid the risk of irreconcilable judgments resulting from separate proceedings.

Article 28 gives rise to the exercise of a judicial *discretion* where there are connected proceedings underway in the courts of another Member State. The main differences between Articles 27 and 28 are that Article 27 applies only in respect of action involving the *same parties* and the *same cause of action* where the court which is not first seised *must* decline jurisdiction. Article 28 applies where the parties or the causes of action may not be the same as in other proceedings in another Contracting State but where, nonetheless, there is an intimate connection between the two sets of proceedings. Secondly, the Article 28 power to decline jurisdiction has to be invoked by application of one of the parties, whereas Article 27 requires the court to exercise its powers of its own motion.

The Modified Convention

Schedule 4 of the Civil Jurisdiction and Judgments Act 1982 applies as between the three constituent parts of the United Kingdom — England and Wales, Scotland and Northern Ireland. Similar rules[82] are applied regarding the distribution of business between the three parts of the United Kingdom as apply between the different Member States[83] and Contracting States[84] within the European Union and EFTA.

The Modified Convention has two main implications. The first is that as between persons domiciled in the United Kingdom, the Modified Convention applies in order to determine whether an action be brought in England, Scotland or Northern Ireland. Secondly, foreign claimants need to have regard to the Modified Convention in order to determine which part of the

---

[82] See The Civil Jurisdiction and Judgments Order 2001: 2001 SI 3929.
[83] Regulation 44/2001.
[84] Brussels Convention.

United Kingdom should be seised of an action. That is, if a foreign claimant is obliged, or wishes, to commence proceedings against a UK resident, in which part of the United Kingdom should the proceedings be instituted? The special rules on domicile are broadly the same as between the different constituent parts of the United Kingdom as they are between the different Member and Contracting States in Europe.

Where Regulation 44/2001 or the Brussels Convention do not apply

There are many parts of the world and, therefore, many accidents or injuries, to which the Regulation 44/2001 and the Brussels Convention do not apply. There is no other unifying system of rules relating to jurisdiction. Therefore, outside the EU and EFTA a piecemeal approach has to be taken depending on where the accident or incident giving rise to the action occurred.

The courts of England and Wales have jurisdiction over defendants (where Regulation 44/2001 or the Brussels Convention do not apply) where:

- the defendant submits to the jurisdiction of the English court;[85]

- the defendant is validly served with the initiating process *within* the territorial jurisdiction of the English court, and the defendant does not apply for, or is refused a stay of proceedings on the grounds that England is not the most suitable forum;

- the court is satisfied that the case is a proper one in which to give permission for the service of proceedings out of the jurisdiction;[86]

- the claimant's claim is founded on tort and the damage was sustained in or resulted from an act committed in England;

- proceedings are *validly* served on one party either within or without the jurisdiction of England and Wales and the party who the claimant seeks to add as an additional defendant is a necessary or proper party to those existing proceedings.[87]

The English *defendant* is subject to the same kind of process in reverse where action is contemplated in a jurisdiction outside the EU or EFTA. The national law and rules of private international law of the country seised of the case[49] will be applied in determining whether the court in which it is proposed to sue the English defendant has jurisdiction. It is not possible to

---

[85] The principles applicable on determining submission being the same as those applicable to submission under Regulation 44/2001.

[86] CPR Part 6.20(1)(c) applies.

[87] The commentary at CPR 6.20 in the *White Book* remains one of the more accessible outlines of the circumstances in which permission will be granted for the service of proceedings out of the jurisdiction.

review even in outline the almost unlimited number of different sets of
national laws which might be applied where the English based defendant
finds himself the subject of litigation in the courts of the "rest of the world".

APPLICABLE LAW

Torts

For torts committed on or after 1 May 1996 Part III of the Private
International Law (Miscellaneous Provisions) Act 1995 applies. Section 11
provides:

> (1) The general rule is that the applicable law is the law of the country in
> which the events constituting the tort or delict in question occur.
>
> (2) Where elements of those events occur in different countries the
> applicable law under the general rule is to be taken as being:
>
>> (a) for a cause of action in respect of personal injury caused to an
>> individual or death resulting from personal injury, the law of the
>> country where the individual was when he sustained the injury …
>>
>> (b) …
>>
>> (c) in any other case, the law of the country in which the most
>> significant element or elements of those events occurred.

The applicable law is to be used for determining the issues that arise in a
claim *including the issue of whether an actionable wrong has been
committed at all*. This means that an event or incident can be actionable in
the English courts irrespective of whether the incident would be a tort in
England. Breach of a foreign statute or regulation which was actionable as a
delict by virtue of the applicable law will be justiciable in England even
though there may be no equivalent regulation here. Similarly, whether the
wrongdoer's liability is strict or fault-based and the existence of or limit and
extent of principles such as vicarious liability are matters for the applicable
law irrespective of the position in English law. The availability or otherwise
of defences[88] is an issue for the applicable law.

The general rule applies to matters of substance. Matters of procedure[89] are
governed by the procedural law of the country seised of the case.[90] The

---

[88] Such as contributory negligence or the voluntary assumption of risk.
[89] Identifying recoverable heads of damage is a matter of substance for the applicable law.
Assessing the level or amount of damages under each recoverable head is a procedural matter
governed by the procedural law of the forum – e.g. English law. See *Hulse v Chambers* [2001] 1
WLR 2386 where Greek law applied to determine whether damages for pain and suffering were
recoverable (they were) but English principles of quantification applied to the amount awarded.
[90] See *Dawson & Dawson v Broughton* discussed below.

application of the general rule means that even where the English court exercises jurisdiction over a dispute, the substantive law which it applies may not be English law. Accordingly, where two drivers both domiciled in England have a road accident in Finland and the claimant sues the other driver in England[91] it should be the Finnish rules of the road that are applied. Or to take a more convoluted example, where German, Dutch and English drivers find themselves as co-defendants in an action in England[92] brought by a French pedestrian arising out of an accident on the Costa del Sol, it should be the Spanish rules of the road that are applied to the dispute.[93]

Substance and Procedure

As indicated above the conventional view has been that the recoverable *heads of damage* fall to be identified in accordance with the applicable law but the *quantification* or *assessment* of the amount of damages under each recoverable head of loss is a matter of procedure and thus governed by the law of the court seised of the case – the *lex fori*. Section 14 of the 1995 Act preserved the traditional distinction between matters of substance (the applicable law) and matters of procedure (the law of the forum).

Section 14 as material provides:

> (2) Nothing in this Part affects any rules of law (including rules of private international law) except those abolished by section 10 above.

> (3) Without prejudice to the generality of subsection (2) above, nothing in this Part — ...

> (b) affects any rules of evidence, pleading or practice or authorises questions of procedure in any proceedings to be determined otherwise than in accordance with the law of the forum.

In Parliamentary debate on 27 March 1995 the Lord Chancellor, Lord Mackay of Clashfern, made a statement about the intended effects of the 1995 Act:

> With regard to damages, issues relating to the quantum or measure of damages are at present and will continue under Part III to be governed by the law of the forum; in other words, by the law of one of the three jurisdictions in the United Kingdom. Issues of this kind are regarded as procedural and, as such, are covered by Clause 14(3) (b).

---

[91] Pursuant to article 2 of Regulation 44/2001.

[92] By virtue of article 2 and 6 of Regulation 44/2001.

[93] A short review of some basic causes of action in a selection of foreign jurisdictions can be found in *International Personal Injury Compensation Sourcebook* (Campbell) Sweet & Maxwell 1996 – although there is no substitute for taking local legal advice as to what the applicable law demands.

It follows from this that the kind of awards to which the noble Lord referred of damages made in certain states, in particular in parts of the United States, will not become a feature of our legal system by virtue of Part III. Our courts will continue to apply our own rules on quantum of damages even in the context of a tort case where the court decides that the 'applicable law' should be some foreign system of law so far as concerns the merits of the claim. Some aspects of the law of damages are not regarded as procedural and, in accordance with the views of the Law Commissions in their report on the subject, Part III does not alter this. These aspects concern so-called 'heads of damages'—the basic matter which is being compensated for—such as special damage relating to direct financial loss. Whether a particular legal system permits such a head of damage is not regarded as procedural but substantive and therefore not automatically subject to the law of the forum. This seems right given the intimate connection between such a concept and the particular nature of the case in issue. But again, I foresee no significant increase in awards of damages because a particular head of damage permitted by some foreign system of law would continue, so far as the quantum allocated to it in any finding is concerned, to be regulated by our own domestic law of damages.

Harding v Wealands[94] concerned an accident that happened on 3 February 2002 on a dirt track near Huskisson in New South Wales, when Ms. Wealands lost control of the vehicle she was driving and it turned over. Negligence was admitted.[95] Mr. Harding, who was a passenger, was severely injured and rendered tetraplegic. He was English and Ms. Wealands Australian. They had formed a relationship when Mr. Harding visited Australia in March 2001 and in consequence Ms. Wealands had come to England in June 2001 to live with Mr. Harding. At the time of the accident they had gone together to Australia for a holiday and a visit to Ms Wealand's parents. The vehicle belonged to Ms. Wealands and she was insured with an Australian insurance company. After the accident, Mr. Harding and Ms. Wealands returned to England. The action was tried by Elias J, who applied English law to the *assessment* of damages for two reasons. First, because the assessment of damages was a matter of procedure governed by the *lex fori* and secondly, because even if it was a matter of substantive law, it was in this case "substantially more appropriate" to apply English law.[96] The Court of Appeal (Waller LJ. dissenting) overturned the judge, whose decision was subsequently restored by the House of Lords. The matter was one of considerable importance because the Claimant maintained that under the provisions of the Motor Accidents Compensation Act 1999 then applicable to claims brought under the law of New South Wales he would recover about 30% less than he would under English law.

---

[94] [2006] UKHL 32.
[95] The following commentary is taken largely from the speech of Lord Hoffman.
[96] See discussion about section 12 below.

Chapter 5 of the Motor Accidents Compensation Act 1999 ("MACA") which was in force at the time of the accident provided[97] that "*a court cannot award damages to a person in respect of a motor accident contrary to this Chapter.*" The provisions of Chapter 5 which would have been relevant to an award of damages by a court in New South Wales to the Claimant are:

> (a) The maximum recoverable for non-economic loss (pain and suffering, loss of amenities of life, loss of expectation of life, disfigurement) is A\$309,000 subject to indexation (section 134);
>
> (b) In assessing loss of earnings, an excess of net weekly earnings over A\$2500 must be disregarded (section 125);
>
> (c) There is no award for the loss of the first 5 days of earning capacity (section 124);
>
> (d) No award may be made for gratuitous care which does not exceed 6 hours a week and is for less than 6 months and the amount recoverable for care exceeding these minima is limited to sums specified in section 128;
>
> (e) The discount rate for calculating the present value of future economic loss is prescribed as 5% (section 127);
>
> (f) Credit must be given for payments made to the claimant by "an insurer" (section 130);
>
> (g) No interest is payable on damages for gratuitous care or non-economic loss and entitlement to interest on other damages is subject to conditions, principally relating to the timely provision of information by the claimant (section 137).

None of these provisions forms part of English law but if the court applied the law of New South Wales to matters of substance in issue in the action, and these restrictions on the recovery of damages were regarded as being substantive law then in quantifying the award the English court would have to apply the statutory damages restrictions to the Claimant's considerable disadvantage. The House of Lords concluded that the quantification of damages (which is what the NSW statute was in part about) remained one of procedure and so the limitations imposed had no application when damages came to be quantified in the English courts.

Lord Hoffmann said:[98]

> ...the courts have distinguished between the kind of damage which constitutes an actionable injury and the assessment of compensation (ie damages) for the injury which has been held to be actionable. The identification of actionable damage is an integral part of the rules which

---

[97] Section 123
[98] Paragraph 21

determine liability. As I have previously had occasion to say, it makes no sense simply to say that someone is liable in tort. He must be liable for something and the rules which determine what he is liable for are inseparable from the rules which determine the conduct which gives rise to liability. Thus the rules which exclude damage from the scope of liability on the grounds that it does not fall within the ambit of the liability rule or does not have the prescribed causal connection with the wrongful act, or which require that the damage should have been reasonably foreseeable, are all rules which determine whether there is liability for the damage in question. On the other hand, whether the claimant is awarded money damages (and if so, how much) or, for example, restitution in kind, is a question of remedy.

And continued:[99]

There is accordingly in my opinion no English authority to cast any doubt upon the conclusion of the Australian High Court in *Stevens v Head* (1993) 176 CLR 433 that, for the purposes of the traditional distinction between substance and procedure which treats remedy as a matter of procedure, all the provisions of MACA, including limitations on quantum, should be characterised as procedural.[100]

In *Roerig v Valiant Trawlers*[101] the Court of Appeal decided that section 4 of the fatal Accidents Act 1976 which provides that the receipt of benefits should be disregarded in the calculation of any loss of dependency claim was procedural, so that even if Dutch law applied to a fatal accident claim brought by a widow in the English courts[102] it was the procedural law of the court seised of the action that should apply in quantifying damages and so benefits should not be deducted form the compensation for loss of dependency.

Substantially more appropriate to apply law of another country

The general rule under section 11 of the 1995 Act is relatively straightforward. Unfortunately, it can be displaced by the application of section 12 which provides:

(1) If it appears, in all the circumstances, from a comparison of —

(a) the significance of the factors which connect a tort or delict with the country whose law would be the applicable law under the general rule; and

(b) the significance of any factors connecting the tort or delict with another country,

---

[99] Paragraph 43.
[100] This had also been the view of the Court of Appeal in *Roerig v Valiant Trawlers Ltd.* [2002] 1 WLR 2304.
[101] Discussed further below.
[102] Which as it happened it did not.

that it is substantially more appropriate for the applicable law for determining the issues arising in the case, or any of those issues, to be the law of the other country, the general rule is displaced and the applicable law for determining those issues or that issue (as the case may be) is the law of that other country. The factors that may be taken into account as connecting a tort or delict with a country for the purposes of this section include, in particular, factors relating to the parties, to any of the events which constitute the tort or delict in question or to any of the circumstances or consequences of those events."

With great respect to the legislators, section 12 seems to represent a loss of nerve. The general rule under section 11, it is submitted, did not need displacing and the potential for displacement created by section 12 in circumstances that are defined only in the broadest terms, creates unnecessary uncertainty. In *Roerig v Valiant Trawlers*[103] Waller LJ said:

At first sight Section 12 seems less than clear when the question is whether some other law should be applied in relation to an issue such as damages or a head of damage. It requires comparison of the significance of the factors which connect a tort (not the issue) with the country whose law would be the applicable law under the general law, and the significance of any factors connecting the tort (not the issue) with another country, and from that comparison to decide in all the circumstances whether it is substantially more appropriate for the law of that other country to be the law to determine the issue.

For the general applicable law rule to be displaced the court must be satisfied that it is *substantially* more appropriate for a law other than the law of the place where the tortious events occurred to be applied to any or all of the issues. The factors that *may* be taken into account have been included in section 12 — but they are couched in the most general fashion and the examples provided are not exhaustive.

In *Roerig* the Claimant was a Dutch lady who brought an action as a dependant of a Dutchman. She did so on her own behalf and on behalf of their Dutch children in the English courts under the Fatal Accidents Act 1976, the Dutchman having been tragically killed on a trawler registered in England and owned by the Defendants, an English registered company. There was no dispute about liability or about the Claimant's entitlement to bring the action under the 1976 Act. It was not in issue that under Section 4 of the Fatal Accidents Act it is provided that in relation to actions brought under that Act:

---

[103] [2002] EWCA 21.

Assessment of damages: disregard of benefits

In assessing damages in respect of a person's death in an action under this Act, benefits which have accrued or will or may accrue to any person from his estate or otherwise as a result of his death shall be disregarded."

The Defendant contended that under Dutch Law the position is different put in this way by Dutch expert evidence:

...under Dutch law the level of compensation is determined by the financial requirements of the claimant. All benefits received by the claimant - whether emanating from social security or from a collective labour agreement's provision - will be taken into account and deducted from compensation. The reasoning behind this is that society provides for its victims and their dependants to an acceptable and reasonably high minimum, which is usually elevated by provisions arranged by the industry they are working in.

The Defendant contended that when a comparison was made of the significant factors connecting the tort with England, and the significant factors connecting the tort with Holland, it was substantially more appropriate for the applicable law relating to the issue of damages to be the law of Holland and thus the deduction of benefits from an award of fatal accident damages should be undertaken.

Waller LJ carried out the section 12 balancing exercise at the Defendant's invitation:

The next task is to identify the factors that connect the tort with England and those that connect the tort with Holland. The factors that connect with England seem to me to be that the events occurred on a boat registered in England, and that the defendant is an English company. What then are the factors that connect with Holland? The deceased was a Dutchman, and his death would lead to damage being suffered by his dependants, who are Dutch, in Holland where they live. The incident occurred when the deceased was under the supervision of the Dutch Fishing Master albeit the skipper of the boat was English. In real terms the vessel was on a Dutch fishing expedition in that the boat set off from a Dutch port and would return with its catch to a Dutch port. The defendant was a subsidiary of a Dutch company, and the deceased was on board the trawler as an employee of a Dutch company also a member of the same Group.

What then is the significance of the Dutch factors when compared to the significance of the English factors which might make it substantially more appropriate for Dutch law to determine the loss of dependency issue? ...the deceased was Dutch, employed by a Dutch company paying Dutch taxes and making contributions to obtain Dutch security benefits, and the fact that the dependants will suffer their loss of dependency in Holland as Dutch citizens, which are the most significant factors.

...it seems to me that the logic of that argument leads almost inevitably to the consequence that where a claimant, injured in England, is a foreigner living and employed in that foreign country, any head of damage should be assessed in accordance with the law of his or her country. Indeed in one sense I suppose it could be said to be "appropriate" that that should be so since the injured party or the dependants thereof are likely to feel their loss only in that foreign country. But it seems to me that it was not intended that the general rule should be dislodged so easily. Where the defendant is English, and the tort took place in England, it cannot surely be said that it is substantially more appropriate for damages to be assessed by Dutch law simply because the claimant or the deceased is Dutch. One can entirely understand that if fortuitously two English persons are in a foreign country on holiday and one tortiously injures the other, the significant factors in favour of England being the place by reference to which the damages should be assessed may make it substantially more appropriate that damages should be assessed by English law. But say the position were that an English defendant under English principles relevant to assessment of damage would have to pay aggravated damages to a claimant, and would thus have to pay English plaintiffs such damages, why should a foreigner not be entitled to have such damages awarded in his or her favour simply because by the law of where they reside those damages would be unavailable?

In my view the word "substantially" is the key word. The general rule is not to be dislodged easily. I thus think the judge was right in the view he formed that the defendants had failed in their attempt to do so.

Thus, the Dutch widow was permitted to recover damages under the Fatal Accidents Act 1976 without the deduction of benefits that would have occurred had section 4 of the Fatal Accidents Act 1976 been substantive (and displaced by substantive Dutch law in the English courtroom).

Factors relating to the parties

No doubt this *includes* nationality, domicile and residence and factors such as language. If any of these factors are shared by the litigants (or possibly the majority of them) is it *substantially* more appropriate to apply a different law to that indicated by the general rule? It is not clear whether factors relating to one party alone (such as whether one party is a consumer;[104] or less probable whether one is a litigant in person or under some form of legal disability) are supposed to have any bearing on the decision as to which law is the applicable law of the tort.

Factors relating to the events

It was originally suggested by the Law Commission working party that the general rule would only be displaced where there was an *insignificant*

---

[104] But see *Prince v Prince* discussed further below.

connection between the place where the harmful event occurred and the parties. However, it may be possible to envisage some circumstances — such as cross-border incidents, or accidents involving vessels or vehicles, or in the course of day trips organised in the course of package holidays — where it is purely coincidental that the happening of the harmful event took place in one jurisdiction rather than another.

Factors relating to any of the circumstances or consequences of those events

This factor appears to underline the intention of the legislators that it is *all* the circumstances that a court should take into account in exercising its judgement under section 12, and these general features are probably wide enough to include factors such as the *interests of justice, the expectations of the parties*, as well as *administrative convenience.*[105]

It is submitted, that however broadly drawn the section 12 factors may be, their purpose is to help the court identify the most appropriate law applicable to the tort, *not* to allow the parties (even less one of the parties) to choose the "best" system of substantive law for their purposes. It remains to be seen how closely the courts scrutinise the section 12 factors when the general rule of applicable law[106] is displaced, and it will be interesting to see the extent to which courts find it easy to displace the general rule in favour of the section 12 exception where displacing the general rule leads to the application of the substantive law of the forum. A good example of section 12 in action is *Clive Dawson & Kimberley Dawson v Ian Broughton.*[107]

The claimants claimed damages for personal injury against the defendant and the first claimant alone claimed on behalf of the estate of his partner under the Law Reform (Miscellaneous Provisions) Act 1934 and the Fatal Accidents Act 1976. They had been passengers in a car driven by the defendant in France when it was involved in a collision with another vehicle. Primary liability was not in dispute but an issue arose as to contributory negligence in respect of the wearing of seat belts. A preliminary issue was tried as to whether English or French law was to be applied. It was a significant issue since in France, under the *Loi Badinter*, the failure to wear a seat belt did *not* result in any reduction in damages. Under the Private International Law (Miscellaneous Provisions) Act 1995 section 11(1), the general starting point was that French law applied. However, the effect of

---

[105] Such as how long a case is likely to take to reach trial, the recoverability of costs and funding.
[106] Where all the parties are English it seems the displacement of any presumptive rule that foreign law applies is relatively easy – see *Edmunds v Simmonds* [2001] 1 WLR1003 where both negligent driver and injured passenger were English.
[107] 31 July 2007 Manchester County Court :HHJ Holman (reported on *Lawtel*).

section 14(3)(b) of the Act was that matters of evidence and procedure were to be determined by English law. Therefore, 2 questions arose:

(a) whether the *Loi Badinter* was substantive or procedural law; if it was procedural, English law (including the law of contributory negligence) applied because English law governed all matters of procedure;

(b) even if the *Loi Badinter* was substantive should French law be displaced under section 12 and English law applied instead.

The Claimants submitted that (1) the *Loi Badinter* was substantive and therefore French law applied. They argued that contributory negligence was firmly rooted in issues of liability, causation and blameworthiness and was substantive, notwithstanding that it might result in a reduction in damages; (2) if the *Loi Badinter* was found to be substantive, the general rule should not be displaced under s.12 since the collision occurred in France, the other driver was French and they had moved to and settled in France.

The Judge concluded that contributory negligence was relevant to the scope of a defendant's liability for a victim's injuries and the identification of actionable damage. Therefore, contributory negligence was a *substantive* issue and it was incorrect to treat it simply as part of the assessment of damages. In the instant case, the issue of causation was inextricably linked with the issue of contributory negligence. It was wholly inappropriate to regard contributory negligence simply as a matter of quantification. On that basis, the general rule operated and French law applied. *Nonetheless*, under section 12 the court had to consider all the circumstances and be satisfied that it was substantially more appropriate that English law should apply. The general rule (French law) was not to be dislodged easily and the exercise of discretion required a balancing exercise. Using "substantially" in its ordinary meaning, it was not enough if the scales tipped only marginally in favour of one party. In the instant case, the factors connecting the parties to England were stronger than those connecting them to France. The fact that the accident happened in France did not assist the Claimants because the discretion could only *arise* if the accident occurred other than in England and Wales. The involvement of the French driver was irrelevant because he was not to blame. It was relevant but not determinative that the Claimants continued to live in France. It was also relevant that they had *chosen* to bring their action in England, and it was of note that wearing a seat belt was a matter of custom in England with criminal penalties for failing to do so. It was inherently inequitable for the Claimants to submit to the English jurisdiction, but then seek to avoid the disadvantage of the consequences of contributory negligence that might flow if it was established that the deceased had not been wearing a seat belt, particularly when that was closely intertwined with issues of causation of injury. That was plainly a relevant circumstance for the purposes of section 12. On balance, therefore, it was held to be substantially more appropriate to displace the general rule and apply English law instead of French law.

It seems obvious from this case that what struck the judge as unfair was the idea that a Claimant should chose the English courts in which to sue but nonetheless seek to take advantage of and apply French *law* (the presumptive law of the road traffic accident) which in the circumstances did not give any scope for a partial defence of contributory negligence. One suspects that the Claimants hoped for higher English damages without risking a deduction for contribution – the best of both worlds. So one can see why the judge thought and concluded as he did. Even so, there are a number of interesting points that arise out of this decision. The first is that a ruling under section 12 to displace the presumptive applicable law is not in any true sense the exercise of a judicial *discretion* rather it is the exercise of judgment on a permitted statutory basis. Secondly, it will be remembered that the Claimants were passengers in the negligent driver's car and he (the defendant) was domiciled in England. Thus the Claimants were not only perfectly *entitled* to sue him in England they were *supposed* to do so under Article 2 of Regulation 44/2001 on jurisdiction.[108] Thirdly, having reminded himself that French law should not be displaced easily merely on the tipping of the scales, yet his conclusion was that "on balance" it was substantially more appropriate to apply English law.

Prince v Prince[109] is another example. Married British nationals domiciled in England went to France in July 2003 on a touring holiday in the course of which they were in a road traffic accident that was the fault of a French driver. The injured Claimant however, sued her husband as being the driver of the car in which she was a passenger under the no-fault provisions of the French *Loi Badinter*. It was contended that, although the English court had jurisdiction it was French law that applied pursuant to the presumption contained in section 11 of the Private International Law (Miscellaneous Provisions) Act 1995. Under the French *Loi Badinter* the Claimant's husband would be liable to her in relation to the accident, because in road traffic cases a Claimant is entitled proceedings either against the negligent driver or against the driver of the car in which she was travelling at the time of the accident[110]. At a preliminary hearing the District Judge ordered that the law under which the claim would be heard would be French rather than English. The Defendant appealed the order on the grounds that the judge had failed to pay sufficient heed to the fact that both parties to proceedings were English nationals domiciled in England, and the consequences of the accident

---

[108] Although they could also have sued in the place where the harmful event occurred.
[109] 22nd June 2007 (Lincoln County Court) Unreported.
[110] It would then be a matter for him or his insurers to pass the liability down the chain of fault.

were largely felt in England; and had given too much weight to the fact that
the other driver, who was not a party to proceedings, was a French national.
Counsel for the insurer relied heavily on the following *dicta* of Waller LJ in
the Court of Appeal in *Harding v Wealands:*[111]

> ...I would fully understand, having regard to the settled relationship that
> Mr Harding and Ms Wealands were in, that if they had been on holiday in
> France when this accident occurred England might have been found to be
> substantially more appropriate and to have displaced French law...

The Defendant's appeal against the District Judge's conclusion failed. Apart
from the general balancing of factors required under section 12 the Judge
considered that he was entitled to have regard to the difficulties the Claimant
might face if English law displaced the presumption. If English law applied,
the claim as against the Claimant's husband was doomed to fail because he
simply was not at fault. The Claimant would be left in the position of having
to sue the French driver France,[112] which, in the context of a fast track claim,
might not be economical. Taking all of this into account, the presumption
was not displaced and the applicable law remained that of France and the
no-fault *Loi Badinter*.

The 1995 Act applies between the component parts of the United Kingdom
just as it applies to "foreign" incidents and actions.

Contracts

Consumers travelling abroad will frequently make contracts for the provision
of services on or after their arrival. Even those travelling by virtue of
regulated packages will often make local contracts — the most obvious
examples being those for the provision of excursions or entertainment by or
through the organiser of the package or some other local party linked with
the organiser. Excursions linked to package holidays have already been
discussed in Part 1.

The Contracts (Applicable Law) Act 1990 applies to contracts made on or
after 1 April 1991. The 1990 Act gives the force of law to the Rome
Convention and other contractual conventions which are reproduced as
Schedules to the Act, the objective being to apply uniform rules concerning
the law applicable to contractual obligations. The ambition is that all
Member States of the European Union would apply the same choice of law

---

[111] [2005] 1 All ER 415.
[112] Or (he might have added) her husband in France. Why this is regarded as such
insurmountable prejudice in 2007 is not an issue entertained by the Judge. Whilst people holiday
in France in their millions, the thought of having to *litigate* there still sends many into
paroxysms of vapours.

rules in respect of contractual obligations. The 1990 Act and the Rome Convention are, therefore, of general application.[113]

Express or inferred choice

Unlike the position in tort or delict, the applicable law in contract is, wherever possible, that chosen by the parties.[114] The choice must be express or demonstrated by the circumstances with reasonable certainty. If an express choice is not made, or a choice cannot be inferred from circumstances of reasonable certainty, then the law of the contract is the law of the country with which the contract is most closely connected.[115] With the exception of certain consumer contracts it is presumed that a contract is most closely connected with the country where the party who is to effect "*the performance which is characteristic of the contract*" has his habitual residence or in the case of a corporation the country where it has its central administration. However, where the other contracting party is a corporation and the contract is entered into in the course of that party's trade or profession, the law of the contract will be the law of the country where the corporation has any place of business through which the performance of the contract is to be effected.

However, before one needs to approach any of the presumptions applied by the Convention it should be remembered that the parties' *choice* can be implied or inferred from all the circumstances as well as expressly articulated. It may well be that for many consumers contracting abroad[116] with or through tour operators or other travel organisers, the circumstances may be such as to enable a clear inference to be drawn that the parties intended their contractual obligation to be governed by English law. Factors such as the residence and nationality of the parties, the language of the contract, the currency in which the price is paid, provisions in the primary travel contract[117] concerning guides and general standards applicable to the consumer's resort, may be such as to justify the conclusion that a choice has been made to apply English law to the excursion contract albeit a clear choice inferred from the all the surrounding circumstances.

---

[113] I.e. not limited to contracts affecting residents of Member States of the EU.
[114] Rome Convention article 3(1).
[115] Article 4.
[116] Such as in the case of excursions in the course of package holidays.
[117] E.g. choice of law clauses in the package holiday contract as reflected by the tour operator's brochure conditions.

Presumption in the absence of choice

In the absence of an express choice of law or one that can be inferred from the circumstances, Article 4 indicates that the law of the contract should be:

- the law of the country where the party who is to *effect performance* habitually resides (or in the case of corporations where they have their central administration[118]) — *not* the place of performance of the contract;

- *except* that where performance is effected through some *other place of business* it is the law of the country of that other place of business that should apply to the contract.

This gives rise to problems in the context of contracts for the provision of excursions and entertainment to holidaymakers and it is by no means self-evident which system of law should govern such contracts made during the currency of a holiday abroad. It is necessary in all such cases to analyse the contractual background carefully.

- Was the excursion contract made directly *with* the tour operator (with or without the intervention of a tour operator's representative)?[119]

- Was the contract made with some other party who can properly be characterised as a servant or agent of the tour operator such that the excursion contract is in effect with the tour operator?

- If either of the above applies, does the tour operator have or operate through a local office through which will be effected the characteristic performance of the contract?

- Was the contract made with or through parties entirely unrelated to the provision of the original travel services and if so, was this fact made transparently clear to the consumer?[120]

It is thought that in the case of most local travel contracts — such as for excursions, trips, entertainment and refreshment — the performance characteristic of the contract will be the delivery of the service promised at the local level. It follows that in the event (for example) that a tour operator[121] has a local place of business which administers contracts of this type, in the absence of any clause in the contract to the contrary, the law of the *place of performance* should be the law applicable to the contract *unless*

---

[118] If it is the tour operator who is to effect performance of an excursion English law becomes the most obvious contractual choice of law once again.

[119] A separate contract from the package holiday contract.

[120] And just as importantly from the tour operator's point of view, can the unconnected nature of the excursion supplier be demonstrated on the excursion vouchers or tickets?

[121] Always assuming that the tour operator is indeed the other party to the excursion contract.

the totality of the circumstances is such as to lead the court to conclude by inference that the parties chose English law even if they did not articulate their choice in writing. The customer may well be a consumer, but because the contractual services are being performed exclusively in a country other than that of the consumer's habitual residence[122] the consumer has no special protection in this sort of situation. It has yet to be decided whether, all other things being equal, an excursion contract between tour operator and consumer made after the consumer's arrival on holiday is automatically governed by their implied choice of English law, or whether because it is administered from the tour operator's local office the law of the place of performance is to be preferred.

EVIDENCE

Foreign law is a matter of fact. It should be pleaded and proved just like any other matter of fact. It has already been noted that where no point is taken the court will assume that English law applies.[123] Proof is by expert evidence which would usually set out the substance of the law to be applied, and deal if necessary with the manner in which the appropriate foreign court whose law is being applied would approach the exercise of any relevant discretion. Matters which need to be dealt with by expert evidence should include the following:

- What general principles of foreign law apply?

- What specific duties does the foreign law impose; on whom and what is the content of those duties?

- From where are those duties derived?[124]

- How are those rules applied in the foreign court?

- How would the foreign court adjudicate on alleged breaches of any of the identified duties?[125]

- Are there any special defences or bars to action, and if so do they go to liability, apportionment of liability or quantum?

- From what are the defences derived?

- Does a discretion arise and if so, what factors carry weight in the exercise of that discretion and is there a hierarchy of such factors?

---

[122] Article 5(4)(b).
[123] See generally *Dicey & Morris: The Conflict of Laws* – 13th edition 2000 – Chapter 9.
[124] E.g. Civil Code; Statute, Treaty or case law – or a combination of such sources.
[125] Is there a system of precedent?

Expert evidence should not give an opinion as to how the foreign court would rule on the case in hand. It is for the judge seised of the action to decide who should win albeit based on the principles of foreign law. For the foreign law expert to conclude that such-and-such a case would be won or lost in the local jurisdiction would be like a traffic reconstruction expert concluding that X was "negligent". This trespasses on the judge's function and should be avoided. The point of the expert evidence is to provide the foreign legal material that forms the basis of a judicial decision in this country.

Whilst it is not unthinkable that an English court would approach a matter of foreign law without expert evidence, it is only likely to do so where the issue of foreign law is a matter of simple construction of documents originally drafted in English. Courts do not as a general rule respond well if they have to approach issues of foreign law from original or translated sources without any expert assistance. Of course, foreign law can be admitted or agreed like any other issue of fact, and efforts to reach agreement or instruct joint foreign law experts will be encouraged at an early case management stage under the Civil Procedure Rules 1998.

LIMITATION PERIODS

Section 1 of the Foreign Limitation Periods Act 1984 provides:

> (1) Subject to the following provisions of this Act, where in an action or proceedings in a court in England and Wales the law of any other country ... falls to be taken into account in the determination of any matter —
>
>> (a) the law of that other country relating to limitation shall apply in respect of that matter for the purposes of the action or proceedings; and
>>
>> (b) except where that matter falls within subsection (2)[126] below, the law of England and Wales relating to limitation shall not so apply.

Actions brought in England and Wales over which the courts in this country have jurisdiction, where the contractual or tortious issues are governed by foreign law are subject to the limitation periods imposed by the foreign law which governs the substantive issue. Where the foreign limitation period involves the exercise of a judicial discretion, the court in England and Wales must exercise that discretion in the manner that would be adopted in the courts of the law to be applied.[127] Except in rare cases[128] the rule of thumb is that where foreign law applies to an issue it is the foreign limitation that will be applied to that issue.

---

[126] The common law double-actionability rule – now abolished.
[127] This is likely to call for expert evidence.
[128] Involving elements of public policy.

Chapter 7

DAMAGES AND OTHER REMEDIES

Introduction

This chapter is concerned with damages recoverable in travel cases and with other incidental remedies. The PTR 1992 create a number of remedies specifically relevant to regulated package travel, some of which are available to tour operators against consumers. Criminal sanctions are dealt with in Chapter 12. One should also be aware that pursuant to the provisions of both the PTR 1992 and the Unfair Contract Terms Act 1977, the supplier is entitled to rely on the limiting and exclusionary provisions of various international conventions. These conventions are dealt with in greater detail in Chapter 10.

Breach of Travel Contracts

General principles

In contract cases the claimant is generally entitled to recover such damages as will put him in the position he would been in had the contract been properly performed. In travel cases damages are usually divided into two broad categories.

1. General damages comprising that element of the claim where a loss is proved but cannot be quantified in a pecuniary sense. Essentially the court has to do the best it can to value in monetary terms that which has no apparent financial value. Damages for personal injuries and for loss of enjoyment are classic examples of non-pecuniary general damages.

2. Special damage representing such losses as can be arithmetically calculated caused by the breach of contract and usually reflect specific sums lost by a claimant or expenses incurred (including damages for loss of bargain). The expense incurred by a tourist in arranging for alternative hotel accommodation, or the costs of telephone calls home are examples of special damage that should be specifically pleaded.

Whether categorised as general or special damage, the claimant in an action for breach of contract is entitled to compensation reflecting:

(i) that loss which is:

> such as may fairly and reasonably be considered either as arising naturally, i.e. according to the usual course of things, from such breach of contract itself, or such as may reasonably be supposed to have been in the contemplation of both parties, at the time they made the contract, as the probable result of the breach of it.[1]

And

> (ii) that loss which arises out of special circumstances (outside the ordinary course of things) which was foreseeable by, or should have been in the contemplation of, the contract breaker by reason of his actual knowledge of the special circumstances pertaining to the contract at the time the contract was made.[2]

These general principles apply to both general and special damage. Special damage should be itemised and specifically pleaded in the body of the claim or in a schedule attached to the claim. General damages need not be specifically pleaded other by reference to the claimant's claim being for "Damages".

In this chapter a distinction will be drawn between:

- holiday cases;

- carriage cases;

- hybrid cases.

Holiday Cases

In holiday cases damages fall broadly into three categories based on the above general principles. The categories are as follows:

- damages for loss of bargain or the diminution in the value of the holiday contract as a result of the breach;

- damages for loss of enjoyment (which includes items such as distress, anxiety, and vexation),

- special (pecuniary) damage or loss and expense specifically arising as a result of the breach of the holiday contract.[3]

---

[1] *Hadley v Baxendale* [1854] 9 Exch 341 – Alderson B.
[2] *Victoria Laundry (Windsor) Limited v Newman Industries* [1949] 2 KB 528.
[3] For an example of the accumulation of all 3 heads of loss see *Doneck v First Choice Holidays and Flights Limited* [1999] CLY 3823 in which diminution in value damages were assessed as the equivalent of the cost of the original holiday; £500 was added for loss of enjoyment and the claimant recovered the additional cost paid for a change of hotel.

In respect of the first two categories in holiday cases — loss of bargain and loss of enjoyment — Bridge LJ noted:[4]

> ...in this kind of case it is even more difficult than in personal injuries cases to arrive at the appropriate figure with any degree of precision.

It is increasingly common to find holiday cases reported in much the same way as personal injuries cases have been reported by the legal profession for many years.[5] The growing volume of such voluntary reporting is bound to produce greater consistency not only in the level of awards but in the manner in which the awards are sub-divided. Furthermore, the framework of damages identified above is not yet universally applied in all courts. Finally, the great variation in the awards annotated illustrates the importance of judging each case on its own particular facts. The importance of paying particular regard to the *facts* of individual cases is especially significant when attempting to value claims for loss of enjoyment. Sticking too close to a formula can be dangerous when attempting to assess the value of a claim given that a court is likely to be concentrating on what figure when looked at in the round constitutes adequate compensation for the particular claimant or group of claimants. One still finds examples, however, where judges have assessed the loss suffered in undivided lump sums. *Stainsby v Balkan Holidays Ltd*[6] is a recent example. The claimant holidaymaker (S) sought damages from the defendant tour operator (B) arising from a spoilt holiday. S had booked a package holiday in Bulgaria for two weeks at a cost of £718. The holiday was S's honeymoon. On arrival at the two star hotel, which had no lift, S was allocated a room on the fourth floor, despite having requested, on the ground of her pregnancy, a room on the lower floors. The room allocated to her was dirty and damp. S was offered an upgrade to three star accommodation at an additional cost of £600. She declined the offer, as she was unable to afford the upgrade. She was eventually given a room on the lower floors. However, the room was incredibly noisy, and S and her husband were unable to sleep or relax. B offered S an alternative hotel at an additional cost of £422, which S accepted. However, construction works, which had not been mentioned to S, were being carried out at this alternative hotel; S found the works very noisy and disruptive. Further, the food was of a poor standard, causing S to incur extra expenses in eating out. Having regard to the matters complained of, the judge concluded that S would be awarded damages of £1,000 for combined loss of bargain and loss of enjoyment.

---

[4] *Adock v Blue Sky Holidays* [1980] CA Unreported.
[5] *Current Law* is a rich source of information.
[6] Middlesbrough CC September 29, 2005 (Unreported).

Loss of bargain or diminution in value

This is a familiar concept and the starting point for any claim for damages in holiday cases. It includes:

- the monetary difference between what was bought and what was supplied; and

- a sum representing any physical discomfort[7] and inconvenience suffered as a result of the breach of contract (this being the converse of the degree of comfort which the consumer should have enjoyed pursuant to the contract).

Although there will be many instances where diminution in value damages could be arithmetically calculated, loss of bargain is almost always approached as if it were an element of non-pecuniary loss. Quantification of damages for loss of bargain, therefore, often appears haphazard and unscientific, although the haphazard appearance of some reported awards may be as much a problem of the reporting as with the decision-making itself.

Some examples will illustrate how damages for loss of bargain may be approached.

Example 1

A consumer contracts for first class transport to a four-bedroomed villa with an Olympic-sized swimming pool and air-conditioning, for 14 nights. The cost is £2,500.00. In breach of contract the supplier provides standard class travel to a three-bedroomed cottage with no air-conditioning and a small kidney-shaped splash pool. The cost of this reduced package would have been £1,250.00.

On facts such as these it should be simple to approach loss of bargain in an arithmetical way. For example, it should be possible to discover what the cost of the package actually supplied would have been, either by reference to the supplier's own brochure or a similar one. In the example given, the measure of damages for loss of bargain should be £1,250.00.

Example 2

Using the same facts as in Example 1, but this time the supplier is able to provide the appropriate four-bedroomed villa for the second week of the holiday, and provides first class travel on the journey home.

---

[7] This is well recognised as part of the damages for loss of bargain and is distinct from damages fro loss of enjoyment: *Bailey v Bullock* [1950] 2 All ER 1167 – an accommodation overcrowding case arising from solicitor's negligence.

On these altered facts, the loss of bargain would be 25% of the price paid — that is, one half of the value of the first week.

It is easy to tinker with the examples given to produce an almost infinite number of similar situations. Where a five-star hotel is booked, and a three-star hotel is provided, the difference in the price of the two from the supplier's brochure or similar brochures should produce a relatively reliable figure by which the diminution in value can be assessed. Where economy class flights are provided in place of the agreed business class, the loss of bargain is the difference between the cost of the two or the cost of any upgrade paid by the passengers.

The same arithmetical approach can be adapted with a little ingenuity where, say, a resort advertised as being to five-star standards fails to meet the advertised standard. If it is possible by reference to specific facilities and services to say that the accommodation provided was in reality little more than of two-star standard, then the diminution in value ought to be the difference between the prices charged to the consumer and that which would have been charged for a two-star hotel in the same area. This approach might be described as the *price comparison* approach.

Unfortunately, assessment of damages, even for loss of bargain, is seldom as straightforward as this. It can be seen in the context of the comparison between the five-star resort and the two-star hotel referred to above, a degree of subjectivity affects the outcome. Whilst the price comparison approach gives the appearance of objectivity, fixing the price difference is itself dependent on the court's acceptance of the comparison the claimant or defendant attempts to make. Very often it will be clear that accommodation falls below the standard advertised, but more difficult to assess with any objectivity *the degree* to which the advertised standard is not achieved. Sometimes courts adopt an alternative price-based approach. This alternative method involves attempting to place a value (at least in percentage terms) on the facilities that should have been supplied but are not supplied pursuant to the contract. So, in Example 3 below, some courts might say that the sports facilities at this particular resort appear to represent about 15% of the cost of the accommodation, and award such a figure by way of the loss of these facilities. It will readily be appreciated that this method of assessment is subject to the same difficulties as that involving price comparisons between the notional standard of the accommodation provided and its advertised standard. The appearance of objectivity is more apparent than real. Another court in another place at another time might value the sports facilities in Example 3 at only 10% of the cost of the accommodation.[8] What percentage

---

[8] In *Forsdyke v Panorama Holiday Group Limited* [2002] CLY 2321 the judge valued diminution in value as two-thirds of the cost of the booked holiday where the tour operator

is chosen as a suitable measure of damages will sometimes depend on what special facilities were expressly required by the consumer and communicated to the tour operator at the time of the booking.[9]

Example 3

The contract is to provide four-star accommodation in a beach-side hotel with a range of dining and sports facilities. In reality the hotel is a mile from the beach, it has only one restaurant with a fixed menu and the sports facilities are closed. Otherwise, the accommodation is of four-star standard, clean, and modestly luxurious.

In this example it *may* be possible to compare the prices of other local hotels with limited facilities, but it will often happen that what the consumer has been provided with is a mixture of what was agreed and some sub-standard services which does not lend itself to easy comparison. Examples of this sort are commonplace. If prices for a comparative, lower standard hotel are not readily available, the court would usually take a general and inherently subjective view of the facilities supplied and assess loss of bargain damages in a non-pecuniary manner "in the round". This non-pecuniary approach in practice is frequently justified because the consumer has suffered more than merely the pecuniary loss of bargain. Quite apart from any loss of *enjoyment* (dealt with below) the consumer may well suffer physical discomfort and inconvenience in addition to the pecuniary loss described by a price difference. Such could arise in Example 1 above. The provision of accommodation without air-conditioning would certainly be reflected in the *price* and any price comparison made, but in addition to the price factor, the consumer will almost certainly have suffered *physical discomfort* which the contract had promised to avoid. This physical discomfort forms part of the award for loss of bargain. The same sort of consideration would apply in a case where the consumer found it particularly inconvenient or uncomfortable to reach a distant beach or other facilities that were advertised as being close-by. Accordingly, even when considering damages for loss of bargain alone, the consumer will often have sustained a loss that is difficult to measure in purely arithmetical terms by means of price comparison.

Example 4

The consumer purchases a package tour to China based in a succession of international joint venture luxury hotels. In fact, on tour, the consumer is provided with hotels of local character. In this example, a direct comparison

---

failed to provide a hotel with a heated swimming pool in circumstances where the need for a heated pool had been specifically drawn to the attention of the defendant before the holiday was booked.

[9] In accordance with the *Victoria Laundry* case (above).

is likely to be possible. A similar tour based on Chinese hotels should be relatively easy to find, and the loss of bargain will be the difference between the luxury and the local tours — and "twin" tours are often offered by the same company. It is frequently the case, however, that claimants do not produce any price comparison evidence to underpin, support or otherwise on which to base their claim for loss of bargain damages. Defendants seldom produce their own price comparison in an effort to reduce the level of a likely award for damages for loss of bargain. It may well be that it is the lack of such evidence which leads the courts to adopt so frequently a broad, "non-pecuniary" brush.

Loss of enjoyment

Damages for breach of contract are often based on pecuniary losses, but there is no reason in principle why certain types of non-pecuniary loss should not also be recoverable in some categories of contract cases. Damages for personal injuries arising out of a breach of contract is the most obvious example. Physical discomfort and inconvenience is also recognised as a head of recoverable loss for breach of contract, such loss often arising in the context of residential property disputes where a claimant has been put to physical discomfort and inconvenience by reason of a landlord or vendor's breach of contract. In *Bailey v Bullock*[10] for example, the claimant recovered damages for a breach of contract the consequence of which was that he was accommodated in overcrowded circumstances. These damages included a sum for his discomfort and inconvenience. However, the damages reflect the diminished value of the bargain of the claimant.

In most contract cases, however, damages for mental distress, anxiety, annoyance and disappointment have not been recoverable. The distinction between discomfort on the one hand and distress and annoyance on the other, is illustrated by cases like *Hobbs v London & South Western Railway Co.*[11] The plaintiff sued a railway company for breach of contract. He had purchased tickets for himself and his family to Hampton Court, but they had been deposited at Esher and forced to walk the remaining five miles to their intended destination in the middle of the night. The Court of Appeal approved the jury's award of £8.00 damages for the physical inconvenience but overturned the award of £20.00 designed to compensate for the fact that the plaintiff's wife caught a cold as a result of the walk home. Mellor J said:

> ...for the mere inconvenience, such as annoyance and loss of temper, or vexation, or for being disappointed in a particular thing which you have set your mind upon ... you cannot recover damages.

---

[10] See above.
[11] [1875] 10 LRQB 111.

A distinction was drawn between "mere" inconvenience on the one hand, and "physical" inconvenience on the other. The first was sentimental according to Mellor J and irrecoverable.

To this general principle there are a number of limited exceptions. Holiday cases (as a subspecies of travel cases) fall into one exceptional category. To this extent, as actions for breach of contract, holiday cases are distinctive. The recovery of general damages for mental anguish, distress and disappointment is justified where the object of the contract was to provide a measure of peace of mind or freedom from distress. Limiting disappointment damages to contracts of this type was regarded by the Court of Appeal in *Hayes v Dodd*[12] as a matter of policy.

The underlying purpose of all holiday contracts is to provide a degree of peace of mind and freedom from vexation — even where the holiday in question involves strenuous activity. Given that the primary objective of a holiday contract is to provide enjoyment it would be astonishing if damages for the loss of enjoyment or disappointment could not be recovered[13]. Freedom from disappointment as well as and distinct from freedom from discomfort are clearly matters such as may reasonably be supposed to have been in the contemplation of the parties at the time the holiday contract was made.

In *Jarvis v Swan Tours*[14] Lord Denning MR said in the context of Mellor J's observations in *Hobbs*:

> I think those limitations are out of date. In a proper case damages for mental distress can be recovered in contract just as damages for shock can be recovered in tort. One such case is a contract for a holiday, or any other contract to provide entertainment and enjoyment. If the contracting party breaks his contract, damages can be given for the disappointment, the distress, the upset and frustration caused by the breach.

The distress, upset and frustration referred to by Lord Denning is usually all encompassed in the expression *loss of enjoyment*. In *Jackson v Horizon Holidays*[15] Lord Denning MR noted:

---

[12] [1990] 2 All ER 815.

[13] For a different view see: *Mason: Damages For Distress and Disappointment – Why Us?* [2001] ITLJ 8. The ECJ in *Leitner v TUI Deutschland GmbH & Co KG* [2002] All ER (EC) 561 stated that it was implicit that the Package Travel Directive recognised "non-material damage" (i.e. damages for loss of enjoyment and disappointment) apart from personal injury damages, in case where it had been held by the national court that Austrian law did not recognise such a head of contractual loss.

[14] [1973] QB 233 at 237-8.

[15] [1975] 1 WLR 1468 at 1473.

People look forward to a holiday. They expect the promises to be fulfilled. When it fails, they are greatly disappointed and upset. It is difficult to assess in terms of money; but it is the task of the judges to do the best they can.[16]

Unrelated tortfeasors

A third case from the same era as *Jarvis* and *Jackson* is *Ichard v Frangoulis*[17] which is worth mentioning at this juncture. This was a case where the plaintiff's holiday was ruined by a pre-departure road accident unrelated to the provision of the subsequent holiday. The plaintiff's loss of enjoyment on that holiday was nonetheless reflected in the damages recovered from the tortfeasor:

> ...not as a separate head of damage but as one of the factors to be taken into account when assessing general damages, and as a factor which would lead me to give rather more by way of general damages than I otherwise would do. (Pain J).

The ruined holiday was one of the plaintiff's amenities compromised by the road accident which was reflected in the total award for general damages against the party responsible for the accident, even though the party responsible had nothing to do with the provision of the holiday. It is foreseeable that some amenities lost or compromised by such an accident will include leisure activities such as holidays. Where this happens, the loss of this amenity can be reflected in a non-specific manner in the totality of the award. Such a general approach was not followed in *Graham v Kelly & East Surrey NHS Trust (No.2)*.[18] The plaintiff was due to travel on holiday to Tenerife two days after a road traffic accident in which he was injured. Despite his injuries, the plaintiff took the holiday in order to minimise the disappointment to his family. Due to the injuries it was held that the family got no real benefit from the holiday and the plaintiff was awarded a sum reflecting both the cost of the holiday (loss of bargain) plus a *separate* figure for loss of enjoyment. However, judicial approaches to compensation are individual and there are still instances where an award does not distinguish between various different types of general damage (e.g. personal injury damages for loss of amenity and damages for loss of enjoyment). *Doree v First Choice Holidays & Flights Limited*[19] is just such a case. D, female, aged 53 at the time of the incident and 57 at trial, suffered an acute gastrointestinal infection 3 days from the end of a package holiday. The

---

[16] A view taken up by Clark LJ in the surveyor's negligence case of *Farley v Skinner (No.2)* – annotated at [2001] ITLJ 8.
[17] [1977] 1 WLR 556.
[18] [1997] CLY 1819.
[19] Redditch County Court (12 January 2005) Reported in Kemp & Kemp on the issue of damages for food poisoning.

acute phase of diarrhoea and stomach cramps lasted 3 days. Whilst visiting the bathroom she fainted and injured her face and knee. On her return to the UK she was off work for 6 weeks and was treated for worms in her stools as well as a campylobacter bacterium infection. She had existing depression which was worsened as a result of her symptoms. She recovered from her facial injury within 3 weeks and her knee within 2 months. Her condition developed into post infective irritable bowel syndrome which showed some improvement although at the date of trial she was suffering diarrhoea approximately every week, constipation every 2-3 weeks, swelling of the stomach every 2-4 weeks, and wind every 2-3 weeks. Once every 3 months she suffered acute symptoms of diarrhoea as well as severe stomach cramps. She was careful as to what she ate and her condition could be embarrassing in company, she was unable to pre-plan events as much as before and had to take medication. The prognosis was that she would have symptoms indefinitely but that they would improve with time. The judge awarded £15,000 by way of general damages for pain, suffering and loss of amenity *which included loss of enjoyment of the holiday.*

Assessment of loss of enjoyment damages

Each case must turn on its own facts, and because of this, the search for scientific formulae is probably a sterile exercise. Judges must take Lord Denning in *Jackson* at his word, and simply do the best they can in the circumstances. Such observations are not finely tuned to produce easily accessible guidelines for advisers to follow, and for the courts, previous cases can only be regarded as authoritative in the most general sense. Given the importance of the particular facts as they affect a particular consumer it is hardly surprising to find in multi-claimant actions, a wide variety of awards. Such variety is not necessarily symptomatic of inconsistency[20]. Equally, different members of the same party may be entitled to damages at different levels for loss of enjoyment (and indeed for loss of bargain) if the impact of any breach of contract has been significantly greater on some than others. For two couples travelling together as part of the same package to a resort, the couple with children may suffer more in both lost bargain and enjoyment than the couple without children where the breach is the closure of the children's clubs at the relevant resort.

Proportionality

There is no general principle articulated in the reported cases to the effect that damages for loss of enjoyment should be proportional to the cost of the

---

[20] Mummery LJ in *Farley* (above) thought otherwise.

holiday. In *Scott & Scott v Blue Sky Holidays*[21] the report states: "*damages are at large and are not to be determined by reference to the sum spent on the holiday.*" For example, there is no reason in principle why a modestly priced holiday taken by a family in relatively straightened circumstances should not be reflected in damages for loss of enjoyment amounting to several times the cost of the holiday.

> "There can be no doubt that there is an increasing tendency on the part of ... judges ... to award damages well in excess of the value of the holiday concerned. A notional ceiling on these damages based on the cost of the holiday can no longer necessarily be assumed ..."[22]

In fact awarding damages well in excess of the price of the holiday has been a feature of holiday cases since at least *Jarvis v Swan Tours*.[23] The trial judge awarded Mr Jarvis approximately 50% of the cost of the holiday. The Court of Appeal overturned this award and substituted a figure of approximately double the cost of the holiday taking into account damages for both loss of bargain and loss of enjoyment. A case that never ceases to excite the anger of the industry is *Clarke and Greenwood v Airtours Holidays Limited*[24] but the high level of damages awarded was not the subject of any appeal. A counterveiling view was expressed by the trial judge in *Davis v Thomson Holidays Limited*[25] but having expressed the view that in cases concerning damages for disappointment regard should be had to the cost of the holiday, the judge proceeded to award 30% of the holiday cost as damages for disappointment where the beaches of contract had been "modest". Certain factors can and should be taken into account when non-pecuniary damages for loss of enjoyment are awarded. It is interesting to note how infrequently such factors are explicitly addressed in the reports of cases. It is not known whether this is a problem with the reporting of such cases, or whether, like damages for loss of bargain, the reality is that little if any evidence relevant to loss of enjoyment is actually presented.

Evidence

The following factors ought to have a bearing on the amount of damages awarded in individual cases:

• the type of holiday — for example: special occasions, honeymoons, celebrations, birthdays and retirement;

---

[21] [1985] CLY 943.
[22] *Brown & Stratton* [1997] ITLJ 176.
[23] See above.
[24] [1995] CLY 1603 where the damages awarded in total amounted to 4 times the cost of the holiday for particularly bad examples of breach of contractually promised standards.
[25] [1999] CLY 3826.

- the number of holidays — those who travel infrequently, particularly where they have to save for holidays may reasonably be entitled to feel their disappointment more keenly than frequent travellers to whom expense is a secondary consideration;

- the nature of the breaches, and the particular effect they have on the consumer complainants. For example, the loss of sports facilities may be felt severely by some, but less so by others. The absence of promised choices of restaurant may be of less significance to a young family than to the retired couple. The lack of advertised baby-sitting facilities will have quite the reverse impact;

- proximity to certain outside facilities such as beaches, night clubs, activities for teenagers or shopping will be a factor of variable significance according to the particular inclination of the consumer in question.

The closure of the hotel diving school may well go unnoticed by many resort users, but in other cases the facility may have been at the centre of the consumer's decision to use that resort. In all these situations, and many others, there is no substitute for evidence of the real impact of the breach of contract on the consumers who have taken action. This may seem an abundantly self-evident point, but it cannot be over-stated. The production of evidence verifying a complainant's previous diving or other relevant experience will underline the importance of the facility for that consumer.

Answering the following questions may help in the preparation and presentation of evidence designed to identify the appropriate level of loss of enjoyment damages, even if the evidence has to be principally based on the statements of those affected themselves.

- *Why* was a particular holiday selected?

- *What* features of the holiday were regarded as primary features for the complainant's party, and what were the breaches? *Forsdyke v Panorama Holiday Group Ltd*[26] is a case in point. F, booked a last minute one week package holiday at a named hotel for himself and his wife, sought damages from a tour operator, P. At the time of booking, F had specifically requested a hotel with a heated swimming pool because his wife was about to have a hip operation and wished to exercise in warm water. In addition, F's wife was able to enjoy only a restricted range of holiday activities because of her arthritic hip. It was accepted by P that it was a term of the contract that the pool be heated, notwithstanding that

---

[26] Kingston upon Thames CC November 13, 2001 (Unreported).

P's brochure did not advertise the hotel as having a heated pool. The pool in fact was cold. F complained and was offered three alternatives, namely (1) move to another hotel A; (2) upgrade to hotel B at a cost of £150, or (3) use the pool at hotel B at no extra cost. F rejected the first offer because hotel A was built into the side of a hill and unsuitable for people with walking difficulties. He rejected hotel B because, on visiting, he found the pool temperature to be only 20 degrees celsius which he considered too cold to use. Giving judgment for F, the judge concluded that hotel A was clearly not a viable alternative and the pool at hotel B, whether heated or not, was too cold to swim in comfortably. The principal purpose of the holiday was to swim in a heated pool and that was made clear to P at the time of booking. In the circumstances, F was entitled to damages for diminution in the value of the holiday assessed at £450, equivalent to approximately two thirds of the value of the holiday, and £75 for distress suffered.

Another illustration involving a specific facility required by holidaymakers can be found in *Westerman v Travel Promotions Ltd.*[27] W brought an action for damages against a tour operator, T, after he and his wife returned from a package holiday in Switzerland, Italy and the Mediterranean. The holiday consisted of a sightseeing programme with transport between locations to be provided by rail, bus and boat. The cost of the holiday was £795 per person. The holiday brochure promised that part of the travel arrangements on days 3 and 10 of the holiday would be on a "unique" 1939 built train, "the Red Arrow". W's evidence was that himself and his wife were rail enthusiasts and would not have booked the holiday but for the attraction of the Red Arrow and the rail travel thereon. Days before the tour commenced W was informed by letter that the Red Arrow had been withdrawn from service. T provided an alternative itinerary which provided instead for first class travel on Swiss Rail and for a significantly longer period to be spent travelling by train than would have been provided on the Red Arrow as originally scheduled. T also made provision for a flight in place of a stretch of the journey that was scheduled to be covered by bus and the Red Arrow. W and his wife embarked on the holiday and upon their return, sought compensation for the failure to provide the Red Arrow train journeys. T provided a £50 per person refund and argued that, given only three hours in total would have been spent on the Red Arrow and that more than adequate alternative arrangements had been made, that satisfied their liability to compensate W under the PTR 1992. Judgment was given for the claimants: (1) the primary reason why W

---

[27] Stafford CC November 26, 1999 (Unreported).

and his wife had booked the package holiday was the Red Arrow element of the package; (2) the changes to the Red Arrow element of the package, which also formed a major part of T's brochure advertising for the holiday, constituted a significant alteration to the itinerary and/or a failure to provide a significant proportion of the package holiday services; (3) while T had made alternative arrangements and had paid £50 per person in compensation, that did not amount to adequate compensation in accordance with T's duty under the 1992 Regulations, and (4) in the circumstances, W and his wife would be awarded £100 each for the diminution of the value of their holiday and a further £100 each for their distress and disappointment.

Finally, perhaps a more traditional complaint arose in *Dickinson v Thomson Holidays Ltd.*[28] D brought an action against T seeking damages for the diminution in the value of her holiday and loss of enjoyment. D had booked a holiday with T to a hotel in La Pineda, Spain for herself, her husband and their 10-year-old son. They were attracted to the particular hotel by the fact that it was advertised in the brochure as being directly on the beach and particularly suitable for families. The brochure depicted a pool at the front of the hotel with the beach immediately across the road. D claimed that shortly before departure she received two telephone calls and two letters from T about building works in the resort. The first call and letter informed D that there were works going on behind the hotel which might cause a disturbance. The second call and letter informed D that the works would after consideration cause no disturbance as they were actually being carried out some distance from the hotel. However, on arrival at the hotel, D discovered that the beach opposite the hotel was like a building site as a consequence of ongoing sand works. D had not been informed of these works. The beach was unusable. The works caused a disturbance in terms of noise and dust, both during the day and during the night. D's view was obscured by lorries and machines on the beach, and she was unable to use the balcony to her hotel room, which was at the front of the hotel, or open the patio doors due to the noise and the dust. D was unable to use the pool, which was also situated at the front of the hotel, or use the hotel's eating facilities situated by the pool without being disturbed. D and her family avoided the disturbance by taking additional day trips and walking 15 minutes to a usable beach. It was held, giving judgment for D, that (1) for D's family, the holiday would have been a disappointment; (2) there had been a breach of contract and of the Regulations; (3) breach was foreseeable and

---

[28] Leeds CC October 20, 2003 (Unreported).

avoidable; (4) measures should have been in place to deal with such storms as did occur in holiday resorts, and (5) in the particular instance there was sufficient time before D departed to alert the family to the works and give them the opportunity to make alternative arrangements. Damages of £660 were awarded amounting to two thirds of the cost of the holiday and £750 for loss of enjoyment, representing £250 for each family member.

- *How* was the complainant's party able to overcome any breach of contract? *Thomson v RCI Europe.*[29] although not a package travel case, illustrates the self-help issue. T claimed accommodation costs and also sought to recover damages for disappointment, distress and inconvenience having paid a fee to RCI to exchange the use of an apartment which she owned in Portugal for an apartment in the US for the duration of a holiday for herself and members of her family. T alleged that the accommodation in the US was totally unacceptable, principally because the apartment could only be reached by climbing 87 open wooded steps. The steps were covered in leaves and, as such, were totally inappropriate for the party, which included a two year old child and T herself, aged 69. T immediately made it clear to RCI that the apartment was unsatisfactory and unsuitable and she was informed that no alternative accommodation was available. T initially found a motel for three nights and, thereafter, a house where the party stayed for the remainder of their holiday. RCI submitted that it merely offered an accommodation exchange service and that the case was not analogous to a package holiday claim. Giving judgment for the claimant, the judge concluded that the case *was* analogous to a package holiday claim. T was awarded £1,030 for the cost of the alternative accommodation and £1,000 by way of general damages for upset, distress and inconvenience.

- *When* had the complainant or his party last been able to enjoy such facilities or when are they likely to be able to take another, similar holiday?

- *Is* any evidence available to verify independently, the consumer's past experience or pre-contractual intention?

Total failure of consideration

This is closely linked with *proportionality*. Consumers often claim on the basis that they are entitled to a "refund" of the holiday price. Such an understandable approach is nonetheless flawed. The response from the supplier will be to point out all those things that the consumer actually got

---

[29] Manchester CC February 14, 2001 (Unreported).

for the price even if the holiday did not meet with expectations. In this way, the price of the holiday becomes a false ceiling above which the consumer's entitlement to damages cannot rise. The holiday company argues that the holiday was not *worthless*, that some value was given (albeit only for return flights and substandard accommodation) and in this way the supplier can chip away at the claim confined as it is within the glass ceiling of a "refund". The recovery of the price paid for the holiday on the basis that the consideration has wholly failed is a restitutionary remedy. In order to succeed the consumer must show that the price was paid to secure a performance by the supplier that has utterly failed, has not in any single respect been fulfilled, and where no part of the promised performance has been delivered.[30]

The cases where the consumer's action is soundly based on this restitutionary basis will be very rare.[31] *Buhus-Orwin v Costa Smeralda Holidays Ltd*[32] may be a rare case in point. B brought a claim against a tour operator, C, with whom he had booked a two week holiday in Sardinia promised by C in its brochure to be "opulent luxury in a dramatic landscape and a beautiful villa with private garden and swimming pool". On arrival, B and his family found that the villa was infested with rats. B complained to C, who eventually offered smaller alternative accommodation with only a communal pool and no private garden. No compensation was offered. B declined the alternative accommodation and returned home. B contended that C was in breach of (1) an implied contractual term to exercise reasonable care and skill in the provision of holiday services, and (2) the terms of the PTR 1992. C argued that the rodent infestation was mice rather than rats and was unavoidable in that area. Further, that B, by declining the alternative accommodation, had failed to mitigate his loss.

The judge found in the claimant's favour. C had failed to provide luxury, rat-free accommodation in breach of the implied warranties in the descriptive material in its brochure; had failed to comply with its regulatory duties and had failed to exercise reasonable care and skill in the provision of contractual services. B's refusal of the alternative accommodation had to be judged by reference to the luxury holiday that he had booked. In the circumstances, he

---

[30] In cases where a full refund is awarded in addition to damages for loss of enjoyment – such as *Doneck* (above) and *Currie v Magic Travel Group (Holidays) Limited* [2001] CLY 4278 one wonders *if no benefit at all* was obtained and no performance of any kind delivered pursuant to the holiday contract, bad though the experience may have been for the tourists in those cases.

[31] Although a prosecution under regulation 5 of the PTR 1992 for failing to provide a hotel with disabled access to a consumer known to be wheelchair bound rather than a damages case *Inspirations East v Dudley MBC* [1998] 162 JP 800 may be just such a case. *Buhus-Orwin v Costa Smerelda Holidays Limited* [2001] CLY 4279 another (see further under "Mitigation").

[32] August 2001 – see above.

had acted reasonably and mitigated his loss, particularly as C's offer had not included an offer of compensation. B was awarded a sum representing the *whole of the holiday cost* and consequential losses, together with the sum of £2,000 for loss of enjoyment.

The case of *Powell*[3] discussed in Chapter 9 (Hotels) provides another illustration of apparent total failure. Mrs Powell booked herself and her husband a half board Thomsons "Late Deal" in Majorca over the telephone from Tracy. Under the deal, the guests would take pot luck and be allocated accommodation of a minimum standard on arrival in Palma. Mrs Powell was adamant that she had been expressly told by the sales rep. "Sharon" the accommodation would be in "a hotel", a fact the Defendant denied. On arrival in Majorca the Powells were sent to the "Ivory Playa Apartments", a complex with a bar, restaurant, room service, chamber maids and other facilities one might expect of a hotel. The Powells' room had a bed, table and chairs, and a small kitchenette. The Powells were furious with their accommodation. They were convinced they had booked "a hotel" and that they were in an apartment. Mrs Powell telephoned Thomsons' 24 hour holiday line to complain. She was told that, if she wanted to move to a bona fide hotel she would have to pay the difference between her (very cheap) Late Deal and the brochure price for the hotel, and this was £700. The next morning the Powells booked themselves on the next flight home. In the afternoon they met the local tour representative and told him they were leaving. On their return to the UK the Powells claimed the full cost of their holidays, plus the cost of the flight home. The Defendant contended that no guarantees had been made about the accommodation, save that it would be of a minimum standard. The Defendant argued that, even had a hotel been guaranteed, the "Palm Beach Apartments" provided all the services of a hotel and to all intents and purposes was a hotel. The Defendant noted that there could have been no claim at all had the block called itself a "hotel" and had the Powells not had a kitchenette in their room. The Defendant argued that, had there been a breach of contract, damages should be calculated on a loss of amenity basis, and that any loss of amenity was very small indeed. Further, the Powells had behaved wholly unreasonably in booking a flight home before they had either given their accommodation a chance or even spoken to the tour representative. However, in the absence of any evidence from Sharon to the contrary, the Judge found that Sharon had indeed guaranteed the Powells would be accommodated in a hotel. The Judge then held that the "Palm Beach Apartments" was not a hotel. In DJ Wainwright's words, "hotels are different from a block of apartments – they have communal areas, a formal dining area, and a general air of hustle and bustle

---

[3] 28 April 2005 (Exeter CC) Unreported.

not evident in a block". Finally, the District Judge held that it was entirely reasonable for the Powells to curtail their holiday as they did, and that their only other option was to pay £700 to upgrade to a hotel. Damages were awarded *equivalent to the total cost of the holiday* plus the flight home.

Cases of total failure may well arise where the supplier fails to provide transport to the destination and leaves the consumer stranded, but in the overwhelming majority of examples the consumer will have been given something for his money — however lamentably short of the contractual ideal. Such was the decision in *Dale v Golden Sun Holidays Ltd.*[34] D sought damages for breach of contract from G under the Package Travel, Package Holidays and Package Tour Regulations 1992 Reg.15. D had booked a 14-day package holiday to Greece for himself and his family with G at a total cost of £1,300. The two studio apartments allocated to them were completely unsuitable. Both were below ground, dark, dirty and infested with ants and cockroaches. The door handle on the entrance door to one studio was broken, cooking facilities were inadequate and the only cooking utensils provided were rusty and unusable. The swimming pool and showers around the pool were dirty. Although G had provided alternative accommodation for D's wife and daughter that accommodation was just as dirty, and D and his son were not moved. D and his family came home early, leaving after only one week. The problems that D had experienced were sufficient to give rise to a breach of contract and it had been reasonable for D and his family to return home early. D could *not* recover the *full* cost of the holiday (as damages for loss of bargain) because the family had stayed in the accommodation for a week and would have had some enjoyment of the holiday – although in total the damages awarded exceeded the holiday cost. D was awarded £975 for the cost of the holiday, £310 for the cost of the return flights home and £750 for loss of enjoyment.

Richards v Goldtrail Travel Ltd[35] serves to illustrate the same point. R claimed damages from G for loss of enjoyment and the diminution in value of her holiday. R and her four travelling companions had booked a 14-night holiday with G to apartments in Turkey on an all inclusive basis for a total cost of £2,195. When the party arrived at the apartments they were informed that no room was available as the apartments were overbooked. They were taken to another hotel, 10 minutes from the apartments, for the first night of their holiday. The following day the party was taken back to the apartments and were given a small room that was used by staff and were told that there was no alternative room available. Although R had been told, when making

---

[34] Ipswich CC February 12, 2003 (Unreported).
[35] Bromley CC September 15, 2003 (Unreported).

the booking, that English food was provided at the apartments, the food was only suited to Turkish tastes and in addition R had concerns over food hygiene. There had been no hot water available during the evenings, the apartments experienced frequent power cuts and the telephone in R's room did not work. Giving judgment for R, it was held that total damages would be awarded of £4,917, being £1,317 in respect of diminution in value of the holiday, £3,400 loss of enjoyment and £200 for food expenses.

However, it is submitted that most cases should be pleaded and presented as claims for damages for breach of contract whatever scale of damages is sought. References to total failure of consideration and sums in the Claim Form specifying the right to recover liquidated amounts (such as refunds) should be avoided unless they are clearly associated with concurrent and alternative claims for damages. *Samuels v My Travel Tour Operations Ltd (t/a Cresta Holidays)*[36] may, however, be such a case. (S) sought damages for breach of contract against the defendant (M), a tour operator. S had booked a luxury holiday in Mauritius for two weeks for his honeymoon at a cost of £3,778. The hotel was rated as an all inclusive four star. Upon arrival at the hotel S found construction work taking place. S was woken early every morning because of the noise and found that the construction work continued all day, with the workmen working late into the evening, using floodlights once it became dark. Since S received no help from M's representatives he had spent many hours trying to rectify the situation. When M's representatives told him that no alternative accommodation could be found, S found some on his own and moved there at his own cost. S was be awarded damages of £3,778 representing the full cost of the holiday, £1,000 to compensate him for loss of enjoyment, and £135 to compensate him for unnecessary expenses including taxi fares and telephone calls.

Making out a case with reference to the recognised heads of damage has three advantages:

1. It represents more accurately the legal framework within which claims should be brought.

2. It avoids the creation of the glass ceiling represented by the holiday price (which allows defendants to erode the claim by reference to all the benefits conferred by even a substandard performance of the contract);

3. It helps claimants and defendants alike to focus on the fact that damages for loss of bargain reflects but one head of recoverable loss in holiday contract cases, and highlights the fact that when combined, damages for

---

[36] Barnet CC February 27, 2004 (Unreported).

loss of bargain, enjoyment and out of pocket expenses may well greatly exceed the price paid for the services.

Holiday cases — more illustrations

Some examples are given below. They represent only a small proportion of the cases reported in the *Current Law Yearbook*, but generally illustrate the assessment of damages in holiday cases.

Clarke & Greenwood v Airtours [1995] CLY 132

The Clarke and Greenwood families booked three-star hotel accommodation in Tenerife for two weeks. The hotel was to be allocated on arrival. The price was just over £2,000.00. On arrival the families were billeted in self-catering apartments infested with cockroaches; wild dogs roamed the apartment complex and the amenities were otherwise generally poor. Airtours failed to remedy any of the defects or deal with the consumers in a humane way. The consumers were told that if they wanted to return home they would have to pay for the return trip themselves.

The award was as follows:

- £500.00 to each of the two families for loss of bargain;
- £320.00 to each family for expenses incurred in eating outside the complex;
- £800.00 to each of the eight plaintiffs for distress and disappointment.

The total award exceeded £8,000.00. The award was met with angry noises from the defendant tour operator, but despite threats no appeal was launched. Damages far exceeded the notional cost per consumer (about £250.00) for the holiday and illustrates the extent to which the courts are increasingly inclined to break through the glass ceiling of the holiday price in assessing damages for inconvenience and loss of enjoyment.

Rebello v Leisure Villas [1995] CLY 320

Instead of a detached holiday villa, the plaintiff was allocated a studio apartment with very limited facilities. The cost for 14 nights exceeded £1,400.00. It was accepted that the holiday was not a complete disaster, but the disappointment was considerable because the trip was the plaintiff's principle holiday of the year.

The court awarded:

- 50% of the holiday price representing loss of bargain;
- £450.00 representing damages for distress and disappointment.

The total award of £1,100.00 was clearly significant even though the holiday gave the plaintiff some enjoyment and relaxation and was far from a complete wash-out. The award is very nearly the equivalent of a "money-back" claim even though the plaintiff was provided with many of features of a holiday that she had expected.

Lynes & Graham v Airtours [1997] CLY 1773

Two consumers paid a total of £592.00 for self-catering accommodation. The accommodation was not of the three-star quality demanded, it was filthy and broken down. It was acknowledged that the plaintiffs had obtained some value from their holiday.

They were awarded;

- £750.00 *each* in respect of loss of bargain and disappointment.

This award represents very nearly three times the cost of the holiday even though it was common ground that some benefit had been obtained.

Crump v Inspirations East Limited [1998] CLY 157

This was a two-week holiday for two in Goa costing just over £2,000.00 with first class travel supplements. The five-star hotel was not finished and 24 hour a day refurbishment works were being carried out. The consumers were moved to a neighbouring three-star hotel.

The plaintiffs were awarded £1,097.00 by way of damages for diminished value of the holiday, plus a further £625 each (£1,250.00) for disappointment.

Again it can be seen that the plaintiffs got something of value from their holiday even though it was far from what they had booked. The total in damages marginally exceeded the original holiday cost.

Cherry v Malta Bargain Ltd[37] is a more arithmetical approach to the same heads of loss. The claimant (C) brought an action against the defendant travel agent (M). C had booked a seven day holiday for her, her husband and their four children at a three star hotel in Malta for £1,848. She found the bedrooms and bathroom assigned to the family dirty, the bedding being stained. She was offered an upgrade to a four star hotel in return for £546. In making the move in the midday heat, she incurred taxi fares of £10 and paid £3 for drinks. The new hotel was clean but unsuitable for her family. On the third day of the holiday, she was allowed to move to another hotel, which proved satisfactory. C alleged that the first three days of the family's

---

[37] May 5, 2005 (Gravesend CC) Unreported.

holiday had been ruined. It was held that M was responsible for the standard of the hotel, where cleanliness was a basic requirement. M was accordingly liable to C. Damages were awarded in the sum of £1,207, which comprised: £546, being the sum paid to upgrade hotel; the sum of £13 incurred in moving hotel on the first occasion; £198 for the diminution in the value of the holiday, the accommodation, according to standard custom, being 25 per cent of the cost of the holiday; and £450 for loss of enjoyment, calculated at the rate of £25 per person per day.

Brown v Thomson Tour Operations Limited [1999] CLY 1412

This was a case where the claimant claimed damages for personal injury arising out of the defendant's breach of a package holiday contract. The claimant had been injured before his departure, but whilst away, and walking on crutches he slipped on a wet floor. As a result of the fall he sustained aggravating injuries including an infection (septic arthritis) which was triggered by the holiday fall. The tour operator argued that his damages should be limited to a small amount for the additional bruising to his knee because the infection was not foreseeable *at the time the contract was made* and was accordingly too remote. The court disagreed. Although damages for personal injury were claimed arising from a breach of contract, once personal injury was foreseen as a likely consequence of the breach *all that could he classed as personal injury* fell within the recoverable category of loss.

Brown should be compared and contrasted with three other cases. The first is *Ashcroft v Sunset Holidays plc.*[38] In this case a terminally ill and psychiatrically disturbed holidaymaker lost her claim for damages for a nervous breakdown following a poor holiday with Sunset. Such dramatic psychiatric consequences were simply not foreseeable and it was held, psychiatric illness of this magnitude was not in the contemplation of the parties at the time the contract was made. The reporting of the cases makes it difficult to know whether *Ashcroft* is irreconcilable with *Brown* or whether the grounds of reconciliation are just difficult to fathom from the known facts. It may well be that the reconciling element is that *psychiatric illness per se* (in the form of a nervous breakdown as opposed to distress and annoyance) is just not reasonably foreseeable at all as a result of a bad holiday in the absence of special knowledge whereas in *Brown* some physical injury and indeed injury to the knee would have been eminently foreseeable in the event that the customer encountered wet and slippery floors — the fact that the injury was of a more serious magnitude than might usually have been expected being irrelevant.

---

[38] *The eggshell personality and package holidays* [1997] ITLJ 173.

The second case of comparative interest to *Brown* is *Kemp v Intasun.*[39] In this case the tour operator was liable for the foreseeable upset, distress and anxiety caused by a filthy hotel room, but not for *personal injury* arising from a severe asthma attack which it was held was not the foreseeable consequence of being accommodated in a dirty room in the absence of the tour operator being in possession of special knowledge.

The third case is that of *Wiseman v Virgin Atlantic Airways.*[40] Dr. Raphael Wiseman purchased a return flight to Port Harcourt, Nigeria, with Virgin Atlantic Airways. The outbound flight was uneventful. When, however, he presented himself at the check-in desk to return to London, the Virgin Atlantic staff refused to allow him to board the plane. Eady J., who heard his claim, stating that Dr Wiseman's evidence indicated that he had been treated '*appallingly*'. By all accounts, he had certainly suffered an extraordinarily unfortunate series of events. To begin with, he was asked by the Virgin Atlantic Staff for a bribe. When he refused to comply, he was accused of carrying a fake passport, publicly ridiculed and accused of being a criminal. His humiliation was exacerbated by the fact that he was travelling with his "entourage" (a group of friends from his church), some of whom heard the accusations, causing him to "lose face". To add insult to injury during the time that he was forced to stay in Nigeria, he was assaulted by a gang of robbers. The final blow came when, after finally being allowed to return to London, his former fiancée ended their engagement and asked him to reimburse the expenses that she had incurred whilst he had been abroad. None of the facts was disputed by Virgin, who admitted that they were in breach of contract. The only issue before the court was the quantum. Dr. Wiseman was seeking to recover £19,999, most of which comprised a claim for general damages for the mental distress, anguish and humiliation that he had suffered.

The judge awarded Dr. Wiseman £2,147.42 special damage in respect of the expenses that he had incurred as a result of his forced stay in Nigeria. This included the cost of reasonable hotel accommodation, restaurant bills, taxi fares, and postage and telephone calls. His claim for the expenses incurred by his ex-fiancée was, however, dismissed. Returning to first principles, the judge concluded that the loss was suffered not by Dr Wiseman, but by his ex-fiancée herself, with whom Virgin had no contractual relationship. In respect of those expenses that Dr Wiseman had actually paid to her, these were simply to too remote in all the circumstances of the case. The Claim for upset and distress caused by the failure of his relationship was also unsuccessful.

---

[39] [1987] FTLR 234.
[40] [2006] EWHC 1566 (QB).

Not only had Dr Wiseman failed to establish causation, but the judge, citing *Watts v Morrow*,[41] held that damages for "loss of society" were not recoverable as a matter of law. The 'entourage' was equally unlucky. They had incurred expenses overnight because it was not safe for them to return home until the following day. These too were held to be too remote.

The judge then turned his attention to Dr. Wiseman's wider claim for 'mental distress and trauma'. He held that it was well established that, save for a number of exceptional circumstances, damages for injury to reputation or hurt feelings were not recoverable in a claim for breach of contact. This was not a situation in which Dr. Wiseman had contracted for a 'holiday' (which would fall into the exceptional group of contracts which are entered into for the purposes of providing "peace and enjoyment"), but was a straightforward contract of carriage. Furthermore, given that Dr Wiseman had stayed in comfortable hotel accommodation, albeit at his own expense, his distress could not be said to have resulted from '*physical*' inconvenience, another of the limited exceptions to the general rule. The Court concluded that there was no convincing evidence that Dr Wiseman had actually suffered a 'personal injury' in the form of psychological damage. If this had been established, then damages could have been recovered, as a matter of principle, but only if Dr Wiseman had been able to prove that they were in the reasonable contemplation of the parties, when the contract was formed, as a 'not unlikely consequence' of a breach of the contract. In a passage that will come as a great relief to many in the airline industry Eady J. said:

> In this context, I must conclude that it would not have been in the contemplation of the parties that the mere fact of not permitting a passenger to board the aircraft for his return flight would lead to a breakdown in health (although obviously it would cause inconvenience and, quite possibly, also frustration, temporary anxiety and distress).

Finally, the Court concluded that Virgin Atlantic could not be held liable for the fact that Dr Wiseman was assaulted by robbers during his stay in Nigeria. The robbery was a supervening event that could simply not be said to have been caused by the breach of contract. It was, according to Eady J., the '*causa sine qua non*' but not the '*causa causans*'.

Personal injury cases

Where a holiday is ruined or compromised by a personal injury accident for which the organiser is responsible, but the services are otherwise as promised

---

[41] [1991] 1 WLR 1421.

in the contract, how do the personal injury damages inter-relate with the damages awarded for loss of bargain and loss of enjoyment?

The personal injury damages for pain and suffering, it is submitted, should be assessed along conventional lines. However, does the loss of *amenity* element of the general damages award overlap with the loss of enjoyment damages otherwise recoverable for the compromised holiday? The answer to this is no. There are two distinct types of amenity under discussion here. The first is the loss of amenity that goes with the physical injury — for example, the inability to walk, or the lost agility that comes with a back injury. The second type of lost amenity, is the loss of that amenity (and the enjoyment of it) that should have come with the holiday — for example as a result of the loss of physical amenity (such as would have been experienced with the same injury at home), the consumer loses the ability to enjoy the normal activities associated with the holiday purchased (such as site seeing trips or seven sunbathing). Accordingly, loss of enjoyment damages should be awarded in addition to general damages for pain and suffering.[42]

But is there a loss of bargain or diminution in value as well, where all the contractual services are otherwise up to scratch? After all, with the exception of the event that caused the accident the consumer has available all the services and facilities that were promised by the contract and they are up to the appropriate standard it is assumed. Nonetheless, it seems as though there is a loss of bargain — although one that is very difficult to calculate in any arithmetical sense. Whilst the services and facilities promised by the contract are *available*, the injured consumer may not be able to take advantage of them by reason of the injury. Certainly this, in part, will be reflected in an award for loss of enjoyment. However, it should also result in an award for diminution in value because as a result of the injury the consumer has been deprived of the opportunity to use the contract services and facilities. For the injured consumer the facilities may as well have been closed or the services not available.

Special Damage

Out of pocket expenses and losses sustained that are materially attributable to the breach of the holiday contract are recoverable as consequential pecuniary damages. The number of possible examples is almost limitless. Before identifying some of the many possible examples it is worth bearing in mind that expenditure by a consumer whilst on holiday may have the effect of *reducing* the level of damages for loss of enjoyment if that expenditure is incurred in replacing a service that should have been available as part of the

---

[42] Which will be awarded as would be appropriate in a non-travel personal injury case.

original holiday cost. However, this does not present claimants with *carte blanche* to spend excessively in an effort to reduce their disappointment.[43] Special damage will include items such as the following:

- The cost of alternative accommodation (see further below)[44]

- The wasted cost of additional insurance[45]

- The cost of flights home[46]

- Additional car parking fees[47]

- Replacement clothing and toiletries[48]

- Payment for facilities[49] that should have been included to a reasonable standard in the holiday cost, such as sports equipment, ski-passes, access to swimming pools, beaches and restaurants[50] (and the cost of transport to such alternative facilities)[51]

- Telephone and other communications costs[52]

- Cost of hiring a car[53] or alternatively wasted costs of car hire[54]

- The notional cost of gratuitous care attributable to the personal and domestic assistance rendered by family members in the aftermath of an injury.[55]

---

[43] See below the commentary and cases cited on "mitigation".
[44] *Doneck* [1999] CLY 3823; *Duthie* [1988] CLY 1162; *Maciak* [1992] CLY 1536 and *Kelly* [1995] CLY 1605.
[45] *Coughlan v Thomson Holidays Limited* [2001] CLY 4276 and *Parr* [1996] CL Oct 131.
[46] *Currie* and *Buhus Orwin* (above).
[47] *Harris v Torchgrove* [1985] CLY 944.
[48] Common in food poisoning and illness cases – *Davey v Cosmos* [1989] CLY 2561.
[49] See also *Dickinson* discussed above.
[50] See *Bellinger v TUI UK Ltd* (Unreported CLCC 21 August 2006) where the judge held that "half board" meant one main meal comprising 3 courses – the Claimant would have been entitled to the cost of alternative meals or ta least the cost of the additional courses that were not supplied at the holiday hotel.
[51] *Coles* [1994] CLY 1477; *Gover* [1987] CLY 1151; *Harris* (above); *Scott* [1985] CLY 943 and *Skratowski* [1990] CLY 1543.
[52] *Tucker* [1986] CLY 383 and *Jacobs* [1986] CLY 976.
[53] *Suttill* 1994] CLY 1475.
[54] *Charles* [1994] CLY 1476.
[55] This particularly rich vein of additional compensation is recoverable in respect of any serious personal injury, and is particularly prevalent in the acute phase of food poisoning cases. See e.g. *Giambrone v JMC Holidays Limited* [2003] 4 All ER 1212 (first instance) and [2004] *The Times* 4 March (CA) in which Brooke LJ considered that a figure of no more than £50 per week might be appropriate in respect of the notional extra care given to children made seriously ill with gastroenteritis.

Thomson v RCI Europe[56] illustrates facts in which the cost of alternative accommodation may be recovered. T claimed accommodation costs and also sought to recover damages for disappointment, distress and inconvenience. T had paid a fee to RCI to exchange the use of an apartment which she owned in Portugal for an apartment in the US for the duration of a holiday for herself and members of her family. T alleged that the accommodation in the US was totally unacceptable, principally because the apartment could only be reached by climbing 87 open wooded steps. The steps were covered in leaves and, as such, were totally inappropriate for the party, which included a two year old child and T herself, aged 69. T immediately made it clear to RCI that the apartment was unsatisfactory and unsuitable and she was informed that no alternative accommodation was available. T initially found a motel for three nights and, thereafter, a house where the party stayed for the remainder of their holiday. RCI submitted, inter alia, that it merely offered an accommodation exchange service and that the case was not analogous to a package holiday claim. Judgment was given for the claimant: the case was analogous to a package holiday claim. T was awarded £1,030.00 for the cost of the alternative accommodation and £1,000.00 by way of general damages for upset, distress and inconvenience.

Carriage Cases

In *Lucas v Avro*[57] it was held that for breach of contract involving only the provision of seats on a charter flight, general damages for loss of enjoyment, disappointment and distress were not recoverable. A "flights only" contract was considered to be a contract of carriage, and not a contract designed to give peace of mind or enjoyment to the passenger. So whereas in holiday cases the provision of peace of mind and relaxation is inevitably within the contemplation of the parties at the time the contract is made, the same is not necessarily true of carriage contracts or contracts for the provision of transport where there is no association with other leisure services.

This does not mean that the passenger with a carriage contract cannot recover any damages at all[58]. In *Lucas*, for example, it was conceded that the carrier should pay compensation for certain out-of-pocket expenses.[59] We have already seen that damages for *discomfort* are recoverable as part of a claim for diminution in value and noted *Hobbs v London & South Western Railway Co.*[60] where the plaintiff recovered £8.00 for the physical

---

[56] Manchester CC February 14, 2001.
[57] [1994] CLY 1444.
[58] See also *Wiseman* (above).
[59] Which included some taxi fares and loss of earnings.
[60] See above.

inconvenience of walking five miles from Esher to Hampton Court — but recovered nothing for the vexation of it all. In *Horan v Neilson Holidays Limited*[61] a tall passenger recovered £500 for the discomfort of a transatlantic charter flight in conditions which the judge accepted were like a "veal crate".[62] Even though damages for out-of-pocket expenses are recoverable in carriage cases, the exposure of the defaulting carrier is not unlimited. For example, in *Le Blanche v LNWR*[63] the plaintiff failed to recover the cost of a special train commissioned to take him to his intended seaside destination for a dinner engagement.

In *Lucas* a small amount was awarded to compensate the plaintiff for consequential loss of earnings. Once again there are limits. In *Hamlin v Great Northern Railway*[64] a salesman who needed to be in Hull for a sales engagement was diverted to Grimsby for the night, but failed to recover compensation for his lost business. In the modern era the availability of mobile telephones, faxes and mini-cabs suggests that it will be only in extremely rare cases that a delayed or diverted passenger would not be able to alert his customers to a delay or diversion in order to avoid the worst consequences of missed appointments. It is also worth noting that where a carrier's standard terms and conditions have been successfully incorporated into a carriage contract the published timetable will almost never constitute a warranty that the advertised times will be met.[65] Consequential losses, therefore, will usually only be recoverable (even in part) in cases where the passenger has been diverted and not merely delayed (however badly).

As far as damages for *discomfort* and inconvenience are concerned the following factors should be taken into account in assessing the level of any award of general damages in carriage cases.

•   the availability of alternative means of transport;

•   the availability of accommodation where necessary;

•   the comfort and suitability of alternative transport or accommodation;

---

[61] Chester County Court – 16 April 2002 – Unreported.
[62] Notwithstanding that the seat pitch complied with the recommendations of the Civil Aviation Authority.
[63] [1876] 1 CPD 286.
[64] 1 H&N 408.
[65] The National Conditions of Carriage prepared on behalf of the train companies operating in the UK exclude compensation for all loss including consequential loss with the exception of delays in excess of one hour where discount vouchers for future travel are payable up to 10% of the value of ticket (or portion of the ticket) compromised by the delay or diversion.

- the time and place where the breach of the carriage contract has occurred (*e.g.* was it in the middle of a winter's night, and many miles from the intended destination?);

- any assistance rendered by the carrier in breach;

- the physical characteristics (age, infirmity or disability) of the passenger.

Reference should be made to Chapter 10 for cases in which the special rules derived from international transport conventions apply.

Hybrid Cases

These cases may not self-evidently involve holiday or leisure travel, but include examples where the contract is ostensibly one of carriage but where the carrier knows or ought to know that the underlying purpose of the carriage is for leisure or holiday purposes. A good example of this sort of hybrid case is *Konczak v Spacegolden*.[66] In this case a plaintiff's coach journey to Poland was badly interrupted by mishap and mismanagement. Although the contract was for carriage only the court awarded the plaintiff damages of £255.00 (against a price of £45.00) which damages included an element for "annoyance". The report is short and it is impossible to know from the report whether *Konczak* properly represents the hybrid cases being discussed here or whether it is actually a departure from cases such as *Lucas*. Nonetheless, this may be the sort of case where the carrier knew, or could reasonably infer that the passenger was travelling for leisure purposes, or to a holiday destination, and as a result of that special knowledge[67] the court is entitled to reflect the loss of enjoyment or annoyance and distress of the passenger in the general damages awarded. This may arise where:

- The leisure aspect of the carriage contract is manifest so that the loss of the leisure element is one of the natural and ordinary consequences flowing from the carrier's breach of contract. This category of hybrid cases is likely to include examples like extended railway journeys, sea or river voyages (particularly if the contract does not qualify as a regulated package); or cases where the carriage is provided by the same party as supplies separate leisure services as well (as where a timeshare co-ordinator sells transport facilities along with timeshare exchange services).

- The leisure element may have been specifically drawn to the carrier's attention in such a way that the carrier ought to have had it within its contemplation. This category (as well as the first above) may apply to

---

[66] [1994] CLY 1474; [1995] ITLJ 143.
[67] On *Victoria Laundry* principles.

those who are travelling for mixed business, educational, social and leisure purposes or where some members of a party or family are travelling for leisure and others for business reasons.

If there *is* a separate hybrid category of travel cases, the principles underlying the assessment of damages for loss of enjoyment will be the same as in holiday cases; and the calculation of damages for loss of bargain, out of pocket expenses and consequential losses will of course be the same as in both holiday and non-holiday cases.

Mitigation

The line between mitigation and causation is a fine one. Consider *Jewsbury v Thomson Tour Operations Ltd. & Britannia Airways,*[68] The Claimant and her husband booked return flights from Birmingham International airport to Las Palmas airport. The First Defendant was the tour operator and the Second Defendant was the carrier in respect of the flights. The couple requested wheelchair assistance so that Mrs. Jewsbury, who suffered from arthritis, could be transported from the arrivals gate to the baggage reclaim hall at the airport. On arrival at Las Palmas, a wheelchair was provided, but no escort, and it was therefore necessary for Mr. Jewsbury to push his wife through the airport from the arrivals gate, through passport control, and towards the baggage reclaim hall and customs. In order to access the hall they had to descend one floor. It was common ground that there were lifts and escalators obviously available, but the Jewsburys did not think that the lifts would be operational, because on previous trips an escort had unlocked them with a key. Mrs. Jewsbury chose to use the escalator, therefore. It was stationary as she approached it, but as she stepped onto it, she triggered a motion detector, and it began to move. As a result, she fell, sustaining injuries. The District Judge found 'wheelchair assistance' comprised a wheelchair and some assistance, namely the provision of an escort. The tour operator was therefore in breach of its contractual duty to Mrs. J in failing to provide an escort. However, her failure even to attempt to use the lift was so unreasonable that it negated any breach of contract. It could not have been reasonably foreseen that any failure to provide an escort would lead to an accident of this nature. The judge also concluded that as the passengers had already gone through passport control, the Warsaw Convention was no longer engaged and claims against both Defendants were dismissed.

The claimant in a travel case is subject to the normal rules of mitigation.[69] The onus is on the *defendant* to show that a claimant has failed to take

---

[68] May 13th 2005, DJ Mort (Unreported - Sheffield County Court).
[69] The commentary and case cited in the major works such as *McGregor:* paragraphs 295-318 are of general application.

reasonable steps to mitigate or reasonably minimise the loss alleged. The standard of judgement required of the consumer faced with difficult decisions as a result of the other party's breach of contract, is not a particularly high or exacting one. The courts are slow to criticise a claimant faced with problems caused by the other party's breach of contract. Even if not all such decisions arise in the "agony of the moment" the consumer is not always best placed to make fine judgements in foreign countries as to what his best course of action might be. One can confidently expect that the standard of mitigation expected of a holiday consumer would be lower than that expected of a commercial party — this is particularly likely to be the case where the consumer is expected to spend more money in order to reduce his loss elsewhere. Some consumers may not have much in the way of additional money at their disposal, which in turn may affect their ability to mitigate a loss.

There are three areas related to the mitigation of loss that can be summarised as follows:

- Where the loss complained of arises out of a breach of duty on the part of the defendant but could have been avoided by the claimant's taking reasonable steps, that loss will not be reflected in an award of damages.

- Where the claimant has in fact avoided the loss by his own efforts, even though such efforts might be more than reasonableness would have dictated, the claimant will not be compensated for the additional efforts that have been made. The claimant who does more than reasonableness requires mitigates his loss, but is not usually rewarded for having done so in the absence of additional expenditure save to the limited extent that such additional efforts might have caused some additional inconvenience or aggravation.

- Where a claimant incurs expenditure in taking reasonable steps in an attempt to minimise the loss, this expenditure is recoverable from a defendant irrespective of whether the additional expenditure actually succeeds in reducing the loss suffered by the claimant.

Reasonable steps

Whether or not steps are reasonable depends on the particular facts of individual cases and in particular the circumstances of the claimant concerned. What may be reasonable for one consumer may not be reasonable for another. For example, in *Tucker v OTA*[70] a consumer booked a package holiday with direct day-time flights. His outward flight was over-

---

[70] [1986] CLY 383.

booked and he refused the offer of alternative flights for himself and his four-year old daughter on the grounds that the alternative did not guarantee him his flight connections and his daughter was insecure and likely to be disturbed and troubled by night-time flights. The court held that the defendant had failed to prove that *this* consumer's decision was unreasonable. In *Robson v Thomson Holidays Limited*[71] the claimant was informed shortly before her skiing holiday in Colorado that the promised direct flights were in fact indirect and necessitated a change of aircraft at an intermediate US airport. The claimant treated the defendant's failure as a repudiatory breach of contract and booked her own club-class direct flights with an alternative airline.[72] She recovered the cost of these alternative flights even though the cost was double that of the original holiday.[73]

However, in *Markham-David v Bluebird Holidays*[74] the defendant successfully demonstrated that the claimant had acted unreasonably when following long airport delays caused by technical failure of the aircraft engine, the claimant returned home and booked alternative scheduled flights to South Africa. Had he exercised reasonable patience at the airport he would have learnt that an alternative aircraft was on its way, and would have got him to South Africa within a short time of the alternative he booked and paid for. His claim for the cost of the scheduled alternative flights was dismissed.[75]

Consumers are more likely to find themselves in difficulty with the mitigation of loss in circumstances where they act too hastily in rejecting alternative arrangements[76] offered by organisers, or when they do not give the organiser adequate opportunity to make alternative arrangements than in any other situations.

---

[71] 5 April 2002 – Luton County Court – Unreported – see Chapter 3 for a more detailed statement of the facts.

[72] In *Golby v Nelson's Theatre and Travel Agency* [1967] 111 Sol Jo 470, the consumer who terminated the travel contract in the mistaken belief that his direct flight had been changed to an indirect one was not entitled to compensation. The inference is that *had* his mistaken belief been true termination would have been justified. It seems, therefore, that changing a non-stop flight to one requiring a change is a 2significant alteration"" of an "essential term".

[73] But see generally *Ruxley Electronics v Forsyth* [1995] 3 WLR 118 (HL) in which the general principle was stated that the cost of reinstatement should not be disproportionate to the contract price.

[74] Salisbury County Court – 5 November 1998 – Unreported.

[75] His claim for damages for loss of enjoyment was also dismissed on the grounds that this was a contract of carriage only.

[76] *Czyzewski v Intsasun* [1990] CLY where the claimant rejected alternative accommodation and flew home cf: *Buhus-Orwin v Costa Smerelda Holidays Limited* (above) and *Toubi v Intsasun* [1988] CLY 1060.

Other examples where the consumer is likely to be shown to have acted unreasonably in failing to mitigate a loss would include the following:

- Where the consumer does not report faults or quality complaints to the local service provider or to his organiser until it is too late to do anything about them — *e.g.* the day of departure [despite the duty imposed on the consumer by PTR 1992 regulation 15(9)][77] provided that the service provider can show that there was at least a reasonable prospect of the complaints being addressed.

- Where reasonable alternative accommodation is offered but refused by the consumer — even if the alternative is not literally equivalent in all respects to that which was booked. An interesting variant on this theme is illustrated by *Travel Promotions Limited v "Weekend Watchdog".*[78] The consumers booked a package holiday at the Savoy Hotel in Madeira. On arrival they discovered that building works were being undertaken in part of the gardens about which they were dissatisfied. They complained, not through the courts, but to the BBC television programme "*Weekend Watchdog*". The company's complaint to the Broadcasting Standards Commission about the fairness of the programme's coverage of the consumers' complaints was upheld on a number of grounds. However, at the centre of the three-cornered dispute between the BBC, the consumers and the company was the fact that the consumers had been offered and had refused alternative accommodation in another five-star hotel a short taxi ride away. The alternative was built in modern style whereas the Savoy was a traditional villa-style hotel. The peremptory refusal of the consumers even to consider, let alone view, the alternative offered by the company illustrates two things. First, it shows that where reasonable (if not identical) alternatives are available but refused, consumers can be shown to have acted unreasonably. Secondly, it demonstrates how a refusal to consider solutions offered by the travel company can be used *evidentially* to demonstrate that the complaints made by the consumers must have been exaggerated (on the grounds that had the building work noise been as disturbing as was claimed by the consumers, serious consideration would have been given to the modern alternative hotel of equal standard). The evidential point was reinforced by the fact that the consumers refused even the offer of alternative rooms further away from the noise they claimed was so damaging to their enjoyment of the holiday.

---

[77] *Scott Blue Sky Holidays* [1985] CLY 943 is a case where the claimants failed to complain on the spot about the food at their hotel and as a result were denied compensation for the cost of alternative eating arrangements.

[78] BSC- Complaint BSCFP048.98.CM – 24 February 1999.

- On the same theme is *Martin v Travel Promotions Ltd.*[79] The consumers purchased first class airline tickets from Bombay to London at the conclusion of a package holiday in India because they missed the flight included in the package due to other transport delays, which in turn compromised a connection they intended to make to their home in Menorca. The tour operator had made arrangements for alternative return flights to London, but by the time these were communicated to the consumers they had already independently booked their own first class tickets. Whilst the consumers were entitled to a small sum by way of damages for the inconvenience of missing the original inclusive flight,[80] their action in buying independent first class tickets was hasty and disproportionate and their loss was thus not caused by the tour operator's breach of contract.

- A German case reported in *Neue Juristische Wochenschrift*[81] illustrates a failure to mitigate on the part of consumers which raises the sort of absurd facts one often only encounters in travel related litigation. The consumers were a married couple. They wanted accommodation in a room with a double bed. Instead they were offered accommodation in a twin room and claimed damages as a result. They were successful — but only to a very limited extent. The court decided that for the price of some string the consumers could have tied their twin beds together in a way that would have prevented them separating with very little effort. The price of the string was the limit and extent of their recovery. This modest effort would have eradicated altogether the fault about which they complained.

- In less startling circumstances, at the cost of some cleaning materials and a little effort, consumers may be able to render a badly prepared and cleaned apartment perfectly acceptable. They should be compensated for their time and effort as well as their additional expenditure — but not for inhabiting a dirty apartment for a fortnight.

Aggravation

There are circumstances in which the behaviour of a tour operator or supplier can make matters worse and aggravate the damage suffered. A good example is *Halpern v Somak Travel Ltd*[82] where two young ladies were virtually imprisoned in a dingy room in their three-star hotel and felt that staff were laughing and mocking their discomfort and predicament

---

[79] [1999] CLY 3819.
[80] £250.00 each seems more than adequate.
[81] I3-1995 – from a District Court in Bavaria.
[82] [1998] CLY 1428.

throughout their holiday. Their £1,000.00 awards for distress far exceeded the cost of the holiday.[83] A sympathetic and helpful response by service suppliers can save a tour operator a lot of money.

Additional expenditure

In the course of attempting to reduce the effects of a breach of contract the consumer may incur extra expenditure. The consumer may, for example, pay for alternative accommodation or make alternative transport arrangements at his own expense.[84] Provided that the cost is reasonable, it should be recovered. This is a positive form of mitigation that is likely to have a direct effect on other heads of damage claimed by the consumer. This type of expenditure is commonplace in travel claims,[85] for example, where due to unhygienic conditions or bad food the consumer elects to take meals outside an all-inclusive resort or outside the scope of the pre-arranged meal plan or where excursions are cancelled the consumer may choose to provide his own transport. The impact this expenditure and its recovery from the defaulting party has on other aspects of the claim is in the nature of a set-off against damages for loss of bargain and loss of enjoyment. Two different aspects of this sort of set-off need to be considered.

The first is simply where the consumer's loss of enjoyment and loss of bargain is reduced because of the additional expenditure. That is the consumer takes it into his own hands to minimise the loss of enjoyment or bargain he would otherwise have suffered. The second aspect is where the consumer purchases something *better* than that which should have been provided under the contract to the extent that he not only eradicates any loss of enjoyment but increases the level of enjoyment he might legitimately have expected under the contract.

Set-off

Coles v JSI Europe[86] illustrates the nature of the set-off. The claimants booked a family holiday in the United States and the Bahamas. They were flown to Orlando rather than Miami and incurred additional expense in hiring a car to get them to their intended destination. Subsequently, on arrival in the Bahamas they were charged for items which should have been included in the holiday price, they were not provided with free vouchers which they had been promised and they were surcharged by there Bahamas hotel. The family was awarded substantial general damages for loss of

---

[83] £730.00.
[84] *Trackman v New Vistas Limited* The Times 24 November 1959.
[85] See the footnotes in respect of special damage (above).
[86] [1994] CLY 1477.

enjoyment, but also recovered £830.00 to reflect the additional expenditure they had incurred in providing at extra cost items that should have been included as part of the contract. Had they not been able to fund these items, their general damages for loss of enjoyment were likely to have been considerably higher. However, they were able to mitigate the worst effects of the organiser's breaches of contract by purchasing the excluded items for themselves.

Betterment

To what extent will a consumer have to give credit for the fact that his position has been improved over what he could have legitimately expected under the travel contract, either by expenditure incurred himself, or as a result of accepting alternative arrangements made by the organiser?

It is submitted that credit for improved circumstances will seldom be necessary. If a consumer accepts (or pays for) accommodation in a four-star hotel for the second week of a fortnight's holiday where the hotel allocated for the first week has been below the contractual three-star standard, the consumer should not have to give any credit against his loss of bargain and loss of enjoyment in respect of that first week. It may well be that the shadow cast over the second week by the problems of the first will be minimal where he is provided with significantly higher standard accommodation and facilities, but this does not mitigate in any way the shortcomings of the first seven days. This situation is reflected in regulation 14 of the PTR 1992 which provides that suitable alternative arrangements should be made at no extra cost to the consumer.

Interest

Interest on general damages should be claimed at the rate of 2% from the date on which proceedings are issued. This applies to personal injury damages for pain, suffering and loss of amenity and also to damages for loss of enjoyment (and its allies, anxiety, distress and vexation). On special damage including damages for loss of bargain, the claim for interest can justifiably be put at 6%, except in those cases where a pecuniary loss is continuing over a prolonged period between the date of travel and the assessment or settlement. Where special damage consists of the diminished value of the holiday and incidental, consequential expenditure, 6% should be claimed from the date on which the price for the travel arrangements was paid; and on incidental expenditure from the date the consumer returns home. The addition or inclusion of interest in a claim can make a significant impact on its value. Interest should not be forgotten when formulating Part 36 Offers.

Limitation Clauses

In the case of damage other than personal injury resulting from the non-performance or the improper performance of the services involved in the package, the contract may include a term limiting the amount of compensation which will be paid to the consumer, provided that the limitation is not unreasonable.[87]

Although the language of regulation 15(4) is not identical to that employed by the Unfair Contract Terms Act 1977 (UCTA) the idea underlying the provision is the same. The limitation of damages payable to the consumer for quality complaints is permissible subject to its being *reasonable*. As a result, it is not uncommon to find commercial tour operators limiting the amount they will pay in the event of an improper performance of a regulated package by reference either to a maximum daily sum per person or to a scale set out in table form in the small print at the back of a brochure. Some commercial organisers make it clear that the daily sum they allow is intended to reflect the consumer's loss in cases of the worst type where there has been substantially no performance at all; and that other alleged failures should be measured in proportion to the maximum stated. Another perfectly legitimate device is for the organiser to limit exposure for "quality" damages to twice or occasionally three times the total invoice price of the holiday. The reasonableness or otherwise of the limitation agreed between the parties falls to be judged at the time the contract is made but the circumstances of the breach of contract cannot be ignored. The question will usually be formulated along the following lines: at the time the contract was made was it reasonable to limit the amount of damages payable to the consumer to cover the kind of breach that has arisen in the given case?

Limiting damages in non-injury case to twice the invoice price works in practice tolerably well for most commercial organisers. Not only will this limitation cater for all but the most horrendous examples of improper performance or non-performance, but in pragmatic terms, many consumers will be content to have their losses measured by reference to a table that is clearly set out in the relevant travel brochure without recourse to litigation or arbitration. Nonetheless, a distinction needs to be drawn between damages limitation clauses which attempt to restrict the sum payable where something has gone wrong in the course of a holiday (often clauses of the type described above), and those which seek to limit the amount payable to consumers where changes are imposed or cancellation occurs prior to the consumer's departure — which are dealt with below. Although both types of limitation clause are subject to the UCTA reasonableness test, it is suggested the clause which provides for the payment of *up to* twice or three times the

---

[87] PTR 1992 regulation 15(4).

holiday price in damages is inherently more likely to be found reasonable than the one which limits damages to, say, £50.00 where significant changes to the contract are made before departure and the consumer decides to withdraw.

Cancellation charges

Where the consumer cancels a contract otherwise than as a result of changes brought about by the organiser, the organiser will almost always have made provision in its standard booking conditions for the payment of a cancellation fee. The validity of cancellation charges imposed by tour operators has yet to be the subject of an authoritative decision in the courts. Cancellation fees usually appear in tabulated form in the tour operator's booking conditions and provide that in the event of cancellation by the consumer a certain proportion of the price remains payable or is not refundable if already paid. An example might be along the following lines:

Cancellation

> 42 days or more before departure — deposit forfeit.
>
> 41–29 days before departure — 30% of the price.
>
> 28–15 days before departure — 45% of the price.
>
> 14–28 days before departure — 60% of the price.
>
> 7–1 days before departure — 90% of the price.
>
> Departure date or after — 100% of the price.

This example errs on the side of generosity to the consumer and has been chosen at random from a large selection of tour operator cancellation clauses, some of which impose greater forfeits at earlier dates. Despite the apparent similarity between such cancellation charges and unenforceable penalties, it is by no means certain that such charges *are* penalties. Where a contract provides for performance in the form of alternative obligations the consumer's election to perform the contract by paying an agreed sum in lieu of continuing with the travel arrangements, is not self-evidently a penalty because the consumer's election does not amount to a breach of contract. On the contrary it is an alternative mechanism by which the contract is to be performed. The contract provides an option to cancel which when exercised carries with it a financial obligation on the part of the consumer.[88] Penalties and liquidated damages crystalise only where the consumer is in *breach* of contract.

---

[88] Careful drafting of the "small print" is necessary to ensure that the consumer is being given an option to cancel, so that such a cancellation is not a breach of contract giving rise to liquidated

An extreme example of cancellation charges in action is presented by *Weedon*.[89] In late 2006 the Claimant booked a ski-ing holiday for himself, 2 adults, 5 children and 1 infant. The holiday was booked via the internet and paid for using his American Express Card. Pursuant to the Defendant tour operator's standard terms and conditions (which it was accepted were incorporated into the contract) the Claimant was required to pay a deposit of £130 for each party except the infant. On 5th January 2007, 57 days before departure, the Claimant asked the Defendant to 'remove' 7 of the 9 parties from the booking. The reason for this, subsequently revealed at trial, was because the children's school had refused to allow them to take time out during an exam term. Clause 12 of the Defendant's standard terms and conditions stated as follows: "*If you want to cancel your booking or part of it, the lead name on your booking or your travel agent must advise us in writing at the address given in All You Need to Know. The letter must be signed by the person who made the booking. To cover the cost of processing your cancellation and to compensate us for the risk that we may not be able to resell your travel arrangements, we may make a cancellation charge on the scale shown below*" The scale indicated that where a booking was cancelled more than 56 days before departure, the consumer would lose his or her deposit, together with any insurance policy that had been taken out. Accordingly, the Defendant withheld 6 of the £130 deposits paid by the Claimant, as a 'cancellation charges'. The Claimant, outraged by the Defendant's conduct, alleged that since the booking confirmation number had not changed, there had been no 'cancellation', and that all he had done was to 'amend' the booking, thereby attracting an administrative 'amendment fee' of only £25 per person. He also alleged that the Defendant's standard terms and conditions were 'ambiguous'. In particular, he relied upon clause 11.5, which stated: "*Some types of accommodation (such as apartments, or hotel rooms with reductions for three adults) are priced according to the number of people staying there. If your booking changes because someone in your party cancels, we will recalculate your booking cost based on the new number of people going. If fewer people share the accommodation, then the cost for them may go up. This extra cost is not a cancellation charge, and is not covered by our recommended insurance*". The Claimant's argument was that this clause was so unclear that Clause 12, which he accepted he understood, should be 'struck out'. The district judge had little difficulty dismissing the claim. In particular, she found that Clause 12 could not be any clearer and was perfectly capable of being understood by a layperson (including the Claimant who was, for the record, both a 'musician' and a 'psychotherapist'). The clause expressly provided for the

---

damages, but an election to perform the contract in a different way. *Bridge v Campbell Discount Co. Ltd* [1962] 1 All ER 385.
[89] Cambridge CC 5 July 2007 DJ Pearl (Unreported).

possibility that a party would cancel 'part' of the booking, and it was precisely this situation that it was intended to cover. Clause 11.5 was also clear and provided for the fact that where a number of parties to a booking cancels, the consequent increase in the price of the holiday would be in addition to any cancellation fee and therefore would not be covered by insurance. Although it was not necessary to do so to determine the dispute between the parties, the judge also concluded that the scale of cancellation charges was not an unenforceable penalty, was but was a genuine pre-estimate of the Defendant's potential loss in the event that it was unable to re-sell the various components of the package holiday.

Liquidated damages

Even where tabulated cancellation fees cannot be characterised as an alternative method of performance (i.e. cancellation on payment of a price), and are construed as arising upon a breach of contract on the part of the consumer, it does not follow that the pre-set amounts payable to the organiser will be unenforceable penalties. Obviously, organisers will maintain that the fees represent no more than a genuine attempt to estimate the administrative losses likely to be suffered in the event of consumer cancellation. In order to avoid the cancellation charge if payable on breach, the *consumer* must show that the scaled fees charged do not represent a genuine pre-estimate of the organiser's loss and are extravagant and unconscionable in comparison to the greatest loss the organiser could suffer. This is a tall order for consumers who are not likely (in this context) to be part of larger action groups; where the amounts of money are relatively small and where a price equal to or greater than the cancellation charge is likely already to have been paid (as part of the price of the package) to the organiser[90]. Whilst nobody likes to pay a cancellation fee, there is no evidence from which one might conclude that the level of cancellation fees imposed by organisers is a burning consumer issue[91] at the moment.

Contributory Negligence

Contributory negligence technically goes to issues of liability rather than quantum but it may be useful here to review briefly some cases where contributory negligence has arisen. It will be remembered that contributory negligence is taken into account as a result of general law principles not by

---

[90] See *Milner*: "Liquidated Damages: An Empirical Study in the Travel Industry" [1979] MLR 508.
[91] Although the Office of Fair Trading has in the past challenged a scale of cancellation charges suggested by ABTA.

virtue of PTR 1992 regulation 15(2)(a).[92] Case references unless otherwise stated can be found in the Table of Cases.

- *Brannan v Airtours Holidays Limited* – 75% deduction due to claimant walking on a table top into an overhead fan about which he should have bee warned - reduced to 50% on appeal.

- *Martens v Thomson Tour Operations Limited* – 60% deduction due to intoxicated claimant walking into an unfenced well in the middle of the night about which he should have been warned.

- *Isle & Dean v Thomson Holidays Limited*[93]- 60% deduction for each of 2 intoxicated claimants who hopped over a terrace wall at night to relieve themselves only to find a cliff on the other side of the wall about which they should have been warned.

- *Logue v Flying Colours* – intoxicated claimant lost on primary liability but indication that had the result been otherwise there would have been a 75% deduction for contributory negligence.

- *Singh v Libra Holidays Limited* – intoxicated claimant who dived into a shallow swimming pool lost on primary liability (causation) but an indication was given that any award would in any event have been reduced by 75%. In *Evans v Kosmar Villa Holidays*[94] the deduction on similar facts would have been only 50% (had the Claimant succeeded on primary liability).

- *Roberts v Iberotravel Limited* and *Murphy v JMC Holidays Limited* – the related area of parental negligence contributing to injuries in each case to the extent of 50% for non-supervision of young children.

International Conventions

Regulation 15(3) of the PTR 1992 provides:

> In the case of damage arising from the non-performance or improper performance of the services involved in the package, the contract may provide for compensation to be limited in accordance with the international conventions which govern such services.

The most commonly encountered international conventions are dealt with in Chapter 10. However, such limitations as are permitted by regulation 15(3) will only apply in one of two situations. First, where *the other party to the*

---

[92] See further Chapter 4.
[93] Unreported – 2000 QBD Silber J.
[94] [2007] EWCA Civ 1003.

contract is itself a carrier within the meaning of the relevant convention[95] or secondly where the package contract expressly incorporates the convention limits.[96] It is only the "compensation capping" provisions limiting damages in international conventions that may be incorporated under regulation 15(3)[97].

Remedies under the PTR 1992

Regulations 12, 13 and 14

Regulations 12, 13 (pre-departure changes) and 14 (post-departure changes)[98] of the PTR 1992 are considered in more detail in Chapter 3. Where an organiser is constrained to alter significantly an essential term of the contract the consumer has the option to withdraw from that contract[99]. Organisers often attempt a definition in their standard terms of what constitutes an essential term, and what amounts to a significant alteration, in order to define or agree with consumers in advance the circumstances in which the consumer's option may be exercised.

Organisers often attempt to define in the contract what are "essential terms" and what will amount to a "significant alteration". Usually these are alterations such as changes of departure airport, changes in resort areas — but not often the resort itself — and delays in carriage of more than 12 hours as well as changes in accommodation to that which is substantially of lesser quality than that booked by the consumer. Having predefined what amount to "essential terms" and what is to be regarded as a significant alteration[100], the organiser usually then makes provision for compensation to be paid to the consumer in accordance with a table set out in the booking conditions. This compensation is usually payable irrespective of whether the consumer elects to withdraw from the contract under regulation 12, or proceed with the package contract notwithstanding the significant alterations as far as the contractual terms are concerned.

Two things are worthy of note. The first is that it does not necessarily follow that making "changes" (even if significant and of essential terms) will be a *breach* of contract – whether the changes are made before or after departure. The "changes" may not be changes at all if the contract itself permits the

---

[95] Assuming the convention to be a transport convention.
[96] *Akehurst v Thomson Holidays Limited & others* – 6 May 2003 – Cardiff County Court (unreported) discussed in Chapter 3 and further in Chapter 10.
[97] *Norfolk v My Travel Group PLC* – 21 August 2003 – Plymouth County Court (unreported).
[98] For a discussion of the niceties of regulations 12-14 see Kilbey: *Delayed departure, cancellation and the PTR* [1998] ITLJ 110 and a response: Saggerson: [1999] ITLJ 6.
[99] Regulation 12.
[100] Often by use of a distinction between "major" and "minor" changes.

organiser a degree of latitude in the performance of the contract. It will always be argued by organisers that where latitude is allowed in the contract for the making of changes, even "significant changes" (with or without compensation), then the making of such a change is not a *breach* of contract. A cruise holiday case – *Cooper v Princess Cruises Limited*[101] - illustrates the point.[102] This was a claim arising out of a luxury Caribbean cruise costing £7,460.00 1999. Regrettably the vessel was badly affected by a hurricane; according to expert evidence, the first in 113 years to take the unpredictable track this one did. The adverse weather conditions had a serious effect on the passengers including the claimants. They suffered badly with sea-sickness, they could not utilize all the restaurant and refreshment facilities aboard the vessel, their itinerary was curtailed and reworked and they were unable to enjoy some of the ancillary excursions and benefits such as bathing and snorkeling on stop-overs. Their socializing on board was limited as was their use of the Jacuzzi. The claimants sued for damages for breach of contract and pursuant to Regulation 14 of the PTR 1992. The contract had expressly reserved to the tour operator and the captain of the vessel the right to alter the itinerary [subject to the proviso that they acted reasonably] in order that the captain had ultimate control of the passenger's safety in relation to weather conditions. As the unpredictable hurricane followed the vessel around the Caribbean it was held that the captain's decision regarding changes in the itinerary were reasonable and, accordingly, there was no breach of contract – the captain was, in fact, performing the contract albeit in a different way to that envisaged by the itinerary. In the absence of any breach of contract there was no room for the application of Regulations 14 or 15 of the PTR 1992 in the context of the itinerary changes. The Judge went on to hold that the facilities on board that the Claimants were unable to use were, nonetheless, available and it was only the unusual weather conditions that prevented their use to the extent that passengers might have wanted. Sea-sickness was not attributable to the defendant or the operators of the vessel. In this context also there could not be said to have been a breach of contract. Furthermore, the Judge held that leaving aside the itinerary changes and the limited availability of the jacuzzi and pools and the failure to provide some entertainments, these did not when taken together comprise a "*significant proportion of the package*" within the meaning of Regulation 14. The judge applied the definition of "significant" in Chambers dictionary – "worthy of consideration" - and held that these items when taken in the context of the package as a whole were not such as to constitute a proportion of the package worthy of consideration to trigger the application of Regulation 14. The claimants abandoned the second week of

---

[101] Unreported – Chester County Court - 29 January 2002.
[102] See also *Williams v Travel Promotions Limited* [1998] The Times 9 March.

the cruise due to continuing sea-sickness, loss of confidence in the cruise and the fact that the itinerary included revisiting some of the places already visited during the first week. The judge concluded that this was not a case of the defendant offering alternatives under Regulation 14 (post-departure "changes"), but rather a case where the organiser was exercising its contractual right to alter the itinerary. The claim was dismissed and judgment entered for the defendant.

One may justifiably ask, why should such "changes" not be changes to which the PTR 1992 apply? The reason is a linguistic one. Where the contract itself permits changes to be made, and such changes occur, the contract is being performed as agreed. It is only where the "changes" are not foreshadowed in the contract, it is submitted, that the regulation rights arise. A similar situation occurs in many simple carriage contracts. If the carriage contract does not incorporate a promise to transport the consumer by a given route to a given destination at a given time, the consumer cannot complain where an alternative route is taken and some delay ensues.

The second point arising out of regulations 12-14 is that what constitutes and "essential term" or a "significant alteration" is, it is submitted, to be judged *objectively* in the context of the holiday contract as a whole. The mere fact that the tour operator or organiser designates something as "not significant" or "inessential" will not be the touchstone. The fact that the parties have agreed or have appeared to agree by means of the "small print" what is significant and what is an essential term may be of some evidential significance but is unlikely to be conclusive. Consumers should be able to deploy the Unfair Contract Terms Act 1977[103] to bring terms allocating a discretion to the organiser within the control of the statutory reasonableness test. The consumer's argument would be that an organiser cannot by the terms of the contract claim to be entitled to render a performance of the contract radically different to that originally booked save to the extent that it is reasonable to allow such radical departure.

There is no reason why organisers should not define what *they* mean by "essential terms" and "significant" alterations; neither is there any reason why the organiser should not seek the consumer's agreement to such definitions — however limited or non-existent the consumer's bargaining power might be. However, at least as far as the PTR 1992 are concerned, a court would not be *bound* (though it might be influenced) by the parties' apparent agreement as to what the essential terms were, or what has apparently been agreed would constitute a significant alteration of such a term.

---

[103] Section 3(2)(a).

It will be remembered from Chapter 3 that the purpose of regulations 12 and 13 of the PTR 1992 is to ensure that the consumer is offered options in the event that the contract as originally configured cannot be provided (pre-departure) and that of regulation 14 (after departure) is designed to ensure that suitable alternative arrangements are made to continue to package or bring the consumer back to their place of departure. In each case, "if appropriate" the consumer should be compensated in addition to the provision of the alternative arrangements required in regulations 12-14. All this assumes that the consumer is notified of his regulatory rights.

Regulatory mitigation

PTR 1992 regulation 15(9) provides:

> The contract must clearly and explicitly oblige the consumer to communicate at the earliest opportunity, in writing or any other appropriate form, to the supplier of the services concerned and to the other party to the contract any failure which he perceives at the place where the services concerned are supplied.

This imposes on the consumer a duty to report complaints to the service provider and to the other party to the contract, as it were, "on the spot". This consumer obligation only arises if the regulated package contract so provides. The purpose is no doubt to enable the service provider or the other party to the contract to resolve the complaint or improve the standard of service as soon as practicable, and thus be given an opportunity to reduce any exposure to pay compensation. This is a reflection of common sense but adds nothing to the consumer's common law obligations to mitigate loss where reasonably possible. If the contract does *not* "clearly and explicitly"[104] oblige the consumer to complain on the spot, and the other party to the contract can demonstrate that such complaint could have been successfully addressed, could the consumer successfully avoid a reduction in damages from failing to report the complaint because of the absence of a "mitigation clause" in the package contract? The answer to this must surely be an unambiguous "no". No doubt the function and purpose of regulation 15(9) is to impose on organisers a duty to remind consumers of their duty to mitigate by complaining on the spot when something goes wrong. A failure to remind consumers in the way envisaged in regulation 15(9) should not have any impact on the consumer's duty to mitigate, otherwise the consumer under a regulated package contract would be justified in acting in a way which would not have been regarded as reasonable under the general law. Regulation 15(9) also needs to be seen as part of the general scheme of regulation 15 as a whole — particularly regulations 15(7) and (8). The other party to the package contract can hardly

---

[104] The intended difference between clarity and explicitness is opaque.

be expected to offer appropriate solutions or prompt assistance if it has no knowledge of the consumer's difficulty.

Criminal offences

One option open to consumers is to report the commission of suspected criminal offences[105] to the appropriate enforcing authorities.

Regulations 5, 7, 8, 16 and 22 give rise to criminal penalties. The provision of misleading brochure information, failure to provide pre-contract information and failures to make provision for security in respect of purchase money can all be the subject of complaints to local weights and measures authorities which will usually be the local trading standards department[106]. It is incumbent on the prosecuting authority to give notice of intended prosecution to the Director General of Fair Trading.[107] The Director General's permission to prosecute is not required, but clearly it is envisaged that he will monitor and record prosecutions under the PTR 1992.

Criminal offences and statutory defences, both under the PTR 1992 and generally, are considered later in Chapters 12 and 13. Chapter 5 deals with some related issues that arise at common law and under the Unfair Terms in Consumer Contracts Regulations 1999.[108]

Trial by Media

One additional and increasingly popular "remedy" is worth mentioning. It is what might be described as trial by print and broadcast media, from which neither organiser nor consumer usually emerge with any credit — and indeed from which the consumer seldom emerges with a real remedy.[109] Nonetheless, the threat of a reference to the print or broadcast media is a weapon wielded with increasing frequency and diminishing discrimination by consumers at ever-earlier stages in their disputes with organisers.[110] There are two implications of this. The first is that organisers themselves are increasingly likely to have resort to complaints to the media's regulatory bodies, and secondly, those serious complaints of public importance that *do* arise from time to time are bound to be devalued in the scrum to complain in over-stated terms about the latest "holiday from hell".

---

[105] And such offences can be committed by the officers and managers of corporate organisers – section 25 PTR 1992.
[106] Schedule 3 PTR 1992.
[107] Schedule 3(2) PTR 1992.
[108] SI 1999 2083.
[109] That is, monetary compensation.
[110] In the case of BSCFP048.98.CM (above) the consumers alerted the BBC *Watchdog* team *before* they departed for their holiday.

Chapter 8

TRAVEL AGENTS

Introduction

It may be something of an exaggeration to say that travel law has been bedevilled by the uncertain status of the travel agent — but it is more than a little curious that a precise and complete definition of the travel agent's status in law has never been forthcoming. On the contrary, it seems as if judges do the best they can to duck the issue wherever possible. Where it becomes necessary to decide if the travel agent was acting as an agent, and if so whose agent, the courts usually adopt a piecemeal approach for the purposes and on the facts of a given case and in given circumstances. It is very easy to limit such authority as there is to the particular facts of the given case. In *Bowstead*[1] the leading common law text on agency — the travel agent gets barely a passing reference — and where it does it is in the context of "election" by the travel agent suing alternative defendants for the price of tickets.

The piecemeal common law approach to the status of the travel agent has its advantages — and as this chapter may demonstrate, the approach is probably justified. The fact of the matter is that the travel agent is to some extent all things to all men — at least some of the time. He is a commercial chameleon, changing his colours according to the context in which he is viewed. It is also important to distinguish between two different agency concepts. The first is where a party describes itself as a "travel agent" (the most obvious examples being High Street shops). Where this happens the travel agent may in fact be acting as an agent (and if so, for whom?) or as a principal, the title itself being inconclusive as to the role adopted. The second is simply where a supplier of services (internet sites often fall into this category) insists that it acts only as a booking agent – purporting to be neither a travel agent *as such* or a principal (but merely a booking

---

[1] *Bowstead & Reynolds* on *Agency* (2001).

facilitator). It is a question of fact whether the agent of this second type has successfully avoided any liability as a contracting party.

In what follows both categories will be discussed but the focus must be on the traditional High Street shop travel agency. A review of some of the different functions undertaken by travel agent is justified. Travel agents are variously:

- "agents" pursuant to written agreements with tour operators for the display and distribution of brochures and promotional literature;

- booking agents for the tour operators — particularly with regard to packages and holidays;

- stakeholders of money paid to them, which in turn must be transmitted to a service supplier, such as a tour operator, in due course;

- ticket agents — authorised to write tickets for bus companies, railways and ferries; travel consultants and advisers for the general public;

- booking clerks making reservations for the consumer, even if not authorised to issue tickets (and here internet sales sites need to be careful that they are not unwittingly acting as principal contractor with the consumer[2]).

Travel agents cannot be regarded as "commission" agents in any traditional sense, because whilst they clearly earn commissions from the likes of the tour operators, they will often have a large number of principals for whom they are acting at any one time. They are not usually tied to the products offered by a single supplier.

If one poses the question, "whose agent is the travel agent?" it is impossible to give a straight answer; and where a straight answer is impossible, the probability is that a poor question has been asked. The question "whose agent?" is not one that is susceptible to a single answer; and a single answer is neither necessary nor desirable. What is both necessary and desirable, is that the analyst looks at each transaction, and at each identifiable point within each transaction in the light of the *evidence* that is available, in order that a rather different sort of question might be answered. The *proper* and only question given the variable status of the ravel agent at common law is: "At a given point in any travel agency transaction, for whom was the travel agent acting"? The answer in some circumstances may well be that he was not acting as an "agent" at all — particularly when exercising his "consultancy" functions.

---

[2] See further below *International Life Leisure Ltd v Revenue & Customs Commissioners (vadt19649)* (2006).

Travel agents, security and regulated packages

The place of travel agents and retailers in the scheme of package travel sales has been the object of much recent indirect attention in the context of the ABTA v CAA litigation.[3] The CAA advised by a formal Guidance note that travel agents in an age of split contracting would be likely to need to provide consumer security by means of ATOL bonding.

The CAA was conceived (amongst other things) as the licensing authority concerned with the *financial* protection of consumers following a number of high-profile tour operator failures which left holidaymakers stranded abroad or abandoned at home without holidays for which they had paid.[4] Licensing provisions were introduced with regard to the provision of flight accommodation. By means of the ATOL Regulations 1995 introduced under the Civil Aviation Act 1982 as subsequently amended in 2003 the consumer was supposedly protected against tour operator business failures by means of the fact that any flight accommodation provided had to be directly traceable back to an ATOL holder, and the holding of an ATOL would itself be a badge of security protecting the consumer effectively guaranteeing repatriation and compensation in the event of insolvency. The relevant 2003 amendment to the ATOL Regulations provided that "*A person shall not make available flight accommodation which constitutes a component of a package in the capacity of an agent for a licence holder except where all the components of the package are made available under a single contract between the licence holder and the consumer.*"

The apparent objective of this amendment was to cure the perceived mischief of contract splitting - to put a stop to "unscrupulous" travel agents hiving off air transport from hotel services, and making each the subject of *separate* contracts so that only the air transport element was protected under the ATOL. The consumer, it was thought, was likely to believe that they were purchasing a package holiday (hotel and flights) whereas they were not, due to the separate contracts. The 2003 amendment to the ATOL Regulations simply provided that if the seller was acting as an agent for an ATOL holder, the flights sold to a consumer as part of a package had to be sold as part of a *single contract* between the ATOL holder and consumer encompassing all package elements. The amended regulations did *not* say that wherever split contracting was attempted by the travel agent the travel agent should be deemed to have entered into a package contract with the consumer. The ATOL Regulations as amended in 2003 adopted the same definition of a

---

[3] *The Association of British Travel Agents Ltd v Civil Aviation Authority* [2006] EWCA Civ 1356 - R. (*The Association of British Travel Agents Ltd*) *v Civil Aviation Authority and The Secretary of State for Trade and Industry (Interested Party)* [2006] EWHC 13 (Admin).
[4] Remember "Court Line" or as Professor Grant describes it at [2005] ITLJ 165, "the Court Line *disaster*".

"package" as the Package Travel (Etc.) Regulations 1992 - but it was not the 2003 amendment to the ATOL Regulations that was open to challenge but Guidance issued pursuant to it.

Guidance dated 4 March 2005 was issued under the rubric "*Sale of Air Package Arrangements: Advice on the need to provide consumer protection*" ("the Guidance") set out how the CAA intended to interpret and enforce (including by criminal sanction) applicable ATOL Regulations which incorporated the PTR 1992 definition of a regulated package. Who might need the protection of an ATOL and in what circumstances was at the heart of the Guidance which was couched in terms designed to encourage travel agents and retailers to err on the side of caution. Goldring J at first instance said this:[5]

> The Guidance has the clearest effect on travel agents. Most will obtain ATOLs on its basis. Doing so will incur substantial cost. That is not hypothetical. If the Guidance is not in accordance with the law, that cost will be unnecessarily incurred. Although [it is submitted] the travel agent may take his own advice and act accordingly, given the possible sanctions, it would be a brave travel agent who did so. In the final analysis he would leave himself open to the possibility of up to two years' imprisonment. It is not in the public interest for travel agents effectively to be pressurised into obtaining ATOLs if the law manifestly does not require them to.

The Guidance[6] itself had stated:

> As travel agents' sales of combinations of arrangements, including air transport, potentially become packages, there are circumstances in which travel agents will need an ATOL to provide the public with financial protection for this activity. The following sections describe the ways in which the sale by an agent of combinations of travel arrangements, including air transport, may become sales of a package with a consequent requirement of an ATOL; this guidance is based upon the regulatory requirements...

It was the *apparent* need for travel agents to be possessed of an ATOL for the sale of allegedly regulated packages including air transport that induced ABTA to issue judicial review proceedings challenging the interpretation placed on the PTR 1992 definition of a package by the CAA as part of its Guidance as to the application of the ATOL Regulations 2003. As it turned out both at first instance and on appeal, the courts concluded that the CAA had gone too far and ordered the withdrawal of the Guidance. Even so, the action and the judgments illustrate that in the contemporary travel contract market the role of the travel agent or retailer has more than ever before been under some considerable scrutiny.[7]

---

[5] At paragraph 81.
[6] At paragraph 3.4.
[7] Other features of the ABTA v CAA litigation – particularly in respect of the definitions of a regulated package are dealt with elsewhere in this book.

General Principles of Agency

> Agency is the relationship which exists between two persons, one of whom expressly or impliedly consents that the other should represent him or act on his behalf, and the other of whom similarly consents to represent the former or so to act.[8]

The person who agrees to be represented or to have another act for him, is the "principal".

Agents act under *express* or *implied* authority. Where the principal's consent to have the agent act for him is manifested directly to the agent — either expressly or implicitly — the agent's authority is *actual authority*. Where, on the on the hand, the principal's manifestation of consent is made to third parties (*e.g.* consumers), the authority of the agent is *apparent authority*. Actual authority and apparent authority can and do often overlap — but it is possible for an agent to have apparent authority by reason of the way in which he has been represented to third parties by the principal — without necessarily enjoying actual authority. Accordingly, an agent may still bind his principal even though he acts outside the scope of his actual authority in circumstances where the principal has represented to the world at large, by his words or conduct that the agent can so act.

Agency and Packages

It should be obvious that whether the PTR 1992 applies to a package holiday or not, holiday contracts are governed first and last by the ordinary principles of English law including the law of agency. Goldring J. has commented:[9]

> In my view, whether the agreement links the consumer to the organiser or retailer or both depends upon the application of the English law of contract, in particular the law of agency. So too do decisions as to whether the organiser or retailer or both are parties to the contract or whether under Regulation 15, the organiser or retailer or both are liable under it. If by application of the English law of contract the retailer is liable under the contract between him and the consumer, he cannot escape his liability by blaming the lack of proper performance of the obligations under it on someone else. For, additionally, he is responsible for the proper performance by others who may supply services under the contract. Equally under Regulation 16 the retailer must provide sufficient evidence of security. In short, that there may be such an additional obligation upon the

---

[8] *Bowstead* article 1.
[9] *R. (The Association of British Travel Agents Ltd) v Civil Aviation Authority and the Secretary of State for Trade and Industry (Interested Party) [2006] EWHC 13 (admin)* at paragraph 181.

retailer does not mean that the normal English law of contract has no
relevance. It means that in the case of the sale of a package, the retailer
cannot escape liability by pointing to someone else's failure: that he must
provide sufficient bonding to give that obligation value.

In the Court of Appeal Chadwick LJ[10] seems to have been less concerned about
laying down any overriding rules concerning the circumstances in which a
retailer might be acting only as the agent for the principal in the context of
regulated package contract. Rather, the issue of whether there was a regulated
package and if so *who the contracting parties were*, was first and foremost a
question of fact and degree depending on the circumstances. He said this:

> As I have explained, an offer to sell two or more separate travel services at
> the same time does not necessarily lead to the conclusion that the services
> are being sold of offered for sale as components in a pre-arranged
> combination at an inclusive price; but, on the facts of a particular case, it
> may be so.

Before one can determine whether a particular party is responsible for the
provision of ATOL security protection or is liable as a contracting party with
a consumer it is essential to determine whether the party identified is
contracting as a *principal* or its on account or as an *agent* on someone else's
account. Unhelpful though it may, the answer is inevitably one of fact,
degree and evidence. The fact that a party labels itself as only an "agent" is
far from conclusive. The extent to which the factual background is important
and the parties' stated intention can be unimportant is nowhere better
illustrated than in *International Life Leisure Ltd v Revenue & Customs
Commissioners (vadt19649)* (2006). The appellant company (L) appealed
against a refusal by the VAT commissioners to authorise its repayment
claims for VAT. L's business was to market and effect bookings of properties
and accommodation in hotels. In addition, L entered into agreements to
market properties for agents who in turn acted for a number of property
owners. L neither maintained the properties with which it dealt nor did it
furnish or clean them. L produced two annual brochures that detailed the
properties and accommodation it had agreed to market, which were supplied
direct to the public and also to travel agents. The brochures contained
booking conditions and other information relevant to bookings. If L
successfully marketed a property or accommodation it received commission
for its efforts. The amount paid by holidaymakers to L was in turn paid net
of commission to the holiday provider. The appeal concerned three types of
contract.

a. The first contract took a standard form where L agreed with private
    individuals to let their properties. Under the terms L had to pay any

---

[10] With whom the other judges agreed.

cancellation charges that might become due to the accommodation provider and it was authorised to set the rental rates for the accommodation to be paid by holidaymakers.

b. The second contract offered accommodation through a large number of hotels. L was allocated a set number of rooms but neither acted as sole agent nor guaranteed any payments before bookings were secured. Again L was responsible for cancellations and was under no obligation to inform the accommodation owner of the amount it charged for the rooms.

c. The third contract L again made its profit by charging more for the "residential units" than it was itself charged for the products but was restricted to charging the tariffs specified in the contract.

L argued that, as the accommodation supplies were made as agent, there was no requirement to include such supplies within the tour operators margin scheme as prescribed by the VAT (Tour Operators) Order 1987. But it was held to be plain that there was a contract between the customer and L and under that contract L undertook obligations to the customer. In return the customer undertook to pay L the package price. It was fatal to L's case that the customer did not undertake any obligation vis-a-vis any hotel or accommodation provider; the latter could not go to the customer and demand the package price. The booking conditions contained terms that were inconsistent with L acting as agent for a named principal. L could arrange and change the holiday destination and undertook contractual liability to the customer to ensure that the accommodation was provided to the requisite standard. The documentation failed to identify L's supposed principal by name; although the confirmation invoice issued to the customer "typically" specified the name of the owner, there was no indication of his status or position and certainly no indication that he was a party to the contract. As the hotel or accommodation provider did not know what its selling price to the customer was, it could not account for the VAT that, on L's argument, the provider was liable for. Accordingly for these reasons the documentation was clearly in error in stating that L acted as agent; therefore L was acting as principal under the Booking Conditions or at the very least acting in its own name. L was therefore liable to account for VAT on the relevant supplies under the tour operators' margin scheme.

Whose agent is the travel agent?

Where a travel agent is dealing with "packages" — whether regulated packages or otherwise — the probability, it is suggested, in most cases is that the agent will be the agent of the tour operator from the time the tour operator expressly authorises the agent to accept the booking. Before that, the travel agent will not, in most cases, be the agent of the tour operator — but he need not necessarily be the agent of the consumer either. When the

Travel agent and consumer

Does the fact that the travel agent is the operator's agent from the time a contract is concluded mean that before then, the travel agent must be the agent of the consumer?

The answer to this question is "probably not" — for at least two reasons. First, the travel agent may not be an "agent" at all — but acting as a consultant or travel adviser, owing the consumer rather different duties as we shall see later. Secondly, even if the travel agent is acting as an agent for someone, it does not necessarily follow from the above that before a contract is concluded his agency must be with the consumer.

If the written agreement between agent and operator provides that the agent shall not purport to *accept* bookings (and thus conclude contracts) for the operator until the operator gives the "all clear" — that is, gives express authorisation for the booking to be accepted; it is surely either *implicit* in this arrangement (or at the very least the operator must implicitly represent to the consumer), that the agent has authority to take bookings and thus conclude a contract at the shop counter before seeking the tour operator's confirmation. So even if, at a stage before a contract is concluded, the travel agent's authority may not be *implied actual authority*, it could be *apparent authority*. The consumer may very well think so.

By way of enlarging on the example given above in respect of a requirement for accommodation in a double room: if a consumer makes his choice of package holiday and informs the travel agent, and the travel agent accepts the booking for transmission to the tour operator, that consumer may well reasonably regard the agent as having *apparent authority* to bind the operator in respect of any special demands he makes at the time the choice is conveyed to the agent. The consumer may convey his choice to the agent with a special request to the effect that his two rooms are adjacent with connecting doors. The agent may make an error, and fail to transmit the special request to the operator, who in turn authorises the agent to conclude a contract on the basis of two rooms on different floors. This error could go unnoticed by the consumer — particularly if the booking was made at the last minute. If at all stages before the contract was concluded, the agent was an agent for the *consumer*, the consumer would have no redress against the tour operator for the improper performance of the package contract — because the package contract agreed between consumer and operator made provision for exactly what the consumer got, namely, two rooms on different floors. The *consumer's agent* with the *consumer's apparent authority* made a contract (albeit in error) on his behalf without provision for adjacent rooms. Accordingly, there would be no improper performance of the package contract on which the consumer could sue the operator.

If, on the other hand, the agent was agent for the tour operator at the time the booking was *transmitted* and by reason of his *apparent* authority had concluded a contract by accepting the booking from the consumer, then the tour operator would be liable for the error of his agent. The consumer's package contract would have already been made with the travel agent acting *for* the tour operator before any "green light" to accept the booking had been given. Whether this last scenario is feasible depends entirely on whether it can reasonably be said that the tour operator *represents* to consumers at large (either by words or conduct) that the agent has *apparent authority* to conclude contracts before a booking is transmitted to the operator.

On balance, it is thought unlikely that a court would conclude that the tour operator impliedly held out the travel agent as having apparent authority to *accept* rather than merely *transmit* bookings to the operator — to conclude them on the operator's behalf. There are a number of reasons for this.

1. The consumer will often be warned at the time he places his booking with the travel agent that no contract is concluded before the tour operator expressly authorises that the booking be accepted.

2. The tour operator's brochure will often state explicitly that the travel agent is *only the operator's agent once a booking has been "confirmed"* — meaning when the package contract is concluded.

3. If the travel agent was the agent for the tour operator when the booking was *received* from the consumer, a contract would be concluded at that point quite regardless of whether the tour operator had any *availability*. If the package the consumer had chosen was sold out at the time the consumer gave his choice to the travel agent — who by accepting the choice concluded the tour operator's contract as his agent — the consumer would have an action against the tour operator for failing to supply him (the consumer) with the package he had contracted for. Even in these highly computerised days, where bookings and confirmations might only take a few moments, this would appear to place an unreasonable burden on the tour operator.

4. If the travel agent becomes the agent of the tour operator at the time the package contract is made, the legal reality is consistent with the usual standard terms agreed between the operator and agent; it is consistent with ATOL provisions for "air-based" packages; and is consistent with the absence of any countervailing express agreement between the consumer and the travel agent. There is no apparent reason why an express agreement between two of the parties to the transaction should be set aside by the implication of another between two different parties to the transaction.

5. In practical terms, a line has to be drawn somewhere. If the agency line
    between operator and agent is not drawn at the point where the operator
    authorises the agent to accept the booking, and thus conclude a contract,
    it would have to be drawn at some earlier point in the transaction
    involving the agent and consumer. Whilst not impossible, it is very
    difficult to see precisely where in any given transaction this line should
    be drawn. Would it be at the point where the consumer communicates
    his choice to the travel agent? Or perhaps even earlier than that, when
    the consumer enters the travel agent's shop? Not only would it be
    difficult to draw a precise line, it would be quite unnecessary, due to the
    fact that before a package contract is concluded the agent owes other
    duties to the consumer — for example at common law in negligence.

There is no direct authority for the proposition that in package contract
cases the travel agent becomes the agent of the tour operator when the latter
expressly authorises the former to accept a consumer's booking on his
behalf, and a contract is made — but it is offered as a "rule of thumb" by
Grant & Mason;[13] and the proposition derives some comfort from the
judgment of Kerr LJ in *Kemp* v *Intasun Holidays.*[14]

In *Kemp* the consumer visited a travel agent at the beginning of the year with
her daughter to choose a summer holiday for the family. In the course of a
conversation with the travel agent she mentioned that her husband was ill
and that he was suffering from asthma and a bronchial attack, which he
sometimes did. She also said that due to her husband's ill-health some extra
insurance would be required. Mrs Kemp chose a holiday in Mallorca at the
"America I" hotel, and in due course a booking form was completed, sent to
Intasun and Intasun accepted the booking. All too predictably, when August
arrived and the family went on their holiday, they were allocated a different
and substandard hotel. As a result of the filth in the new hotel, Mr Kemp
suffered an attack of asthma, and considerable alarm and distress as a result.
The trial judge found in favour of the plaintiffs both in respect of the
substandard accommodation, and the asthma attack and its consequences.
Istasun appealed.

In the course of his judgment, Kerr LJ said this:

> One can put the matter in many different ways, but there is none whereby
> this casual conversation can possibly have any contractual consequences for
> these defendants. At the time of that conversation, Thomas Cook were not
> the agents of the defendants, let alone for the purpose of receiving or passing
> on the contents of that conversation/ Whether they became their agent at a
> later stage, and if so, for what purpose, it is unnecessary to decide.

---

[13] *Holiday Law* 4th. edition 2007.
[14] [1988] 6 TR.L. 161

Kerr LJ went on to say that in some circumstances it might well be possible to rely on the travel agent's knowledge of a consumer's physical condition (*e.g.* where the consumer enters the shop in a wheelchair), but reinforced his earlier observation by noting that even if such knowledge could be relied upon by the consumer it was a matter between consumer and travel agent — not the tour operator. This seems no more than a passing reflection on the fact that the consumer may be able to sue the travel agent in such circumstances for breach of duty, but even so, the travel agent would not be regarded as the agent of the tour operator *simply by reason of the quality of type of information that the consumer passed to the agent.* It might not, therefore, seem very likely that the courts would accede to the argument that the travel agent might become the operator's agent at an earlier stage than the conclusion of a contract due to the *nature of the information* they possessed. However, if and when the travel agent becomes the agent of the tour operator (thus often making the tour operator liable for promises made by the travel agent) is bedevilled by *facts.* In *Holland v First Choice Holidays and Flights Limited*[15] the trail judge rejected the "rule of thumb" in its entirety. Such a rejection was not surprising on the evidence presented to be the judge. The consumers had asked for a certain type of accommodation and the travel agent promised it would be provided even though such accommodation was not included in the booking made with the tour operator. The required accommodation was not provided and the consumers sued the tour operator for improper performance of the holiday contract pursuant to regulation 15 of the PTR 1992. They succeeded on the grounds that the travel agent had been the agent of the tour operator from the moment that the consumers had communicated their intention to buy a holiday to the travel agent. On the facts this was understandable because:

1. The agent – "Travel Choice" – was linked with the tour operator "First Choice" and part of the same corporate group.

2. The sales representative at the travel agent wore a uniform with the "First Choice" livery on it.

3. In evidence the sales representative *said in terms* that "Travel Choice" was an agent[16] for "First Choice" and had a quota of First Choice holidays that it had to sell to the public.

The opposite result was obtained in *Keppel Palmer v Exsus Travel Limited & Royal Westmorland Villas*[17] where the English based sales agent for Royal Westmoreland was absolved from liability because it had stated in clear

---

[15] Reigate County Court – Unreported 8 October 2003.
[16] It is unlikely that the representative knew of the legal consequences of agency and her view of the matter should not have carried much weight.
[17] [2003] All ER (D) 183 (June).

terms on documents supplied to the consumer that it acted only as a sales agent for the Barbados based defendant who actually rented the holiday villa to Mrs. Keppel Palmer.[18]

It may well be that the travel agent owes to the wheelchair-bound consumer a duty to advise that the chosen hotel is at the top of a hill. However, if such advice is not given, and the hilltop hotel is selected, the selection transmitted by the agent to the tour operator, and the contract then authorised by the operator — it is difficult to see why the tour operator should be any more liable in respect of this error on the part of the travel agent than was the agent in *Kemp*. The nature of the information in the wheel chair example was more obvious — it amounted to more than a passing conversation — but the offer the consumer makes to the tour operator through the travel agent is an offer to purchase the services of the hilltop hotel. That will be exactly the offer the operator accepts and precisely what the tour operator should provide — steps and all. Nonetheless, wise tour operators mark their packages in such a way as to identify those that are suitable for disabled consumers. Where they do offer such indications, however, they had better be right.

Post-contract communications

In package contract cases, it would seem to follow from the above, that where the consumer communicates some special request to the travel agent (after the contract has been made), and the travel agent (unwisely) states that the special request can or will be met as part of the package, the tour operator *will be bound*. The operator, in effect, will have constructive knowledge of the special request through his agent, the travel agent. Most travel agents are careful to ensure that all consumers are aware that changes to the intended package, or special requests made after the contract is concluded, either, cannot be confirmed other than with the express authorisation of the tour operator, and/or that the meeting of such requests cannot be guaranteed in any event.

Nonetheless the possibility of a court at some future date ruling that for the purposes of communicating such post-contract requests the travel agent remained the agent of *the consumer* cannot be ruled out. The courts have a habit of dealing with such cases on an individual basis in accordance with the evidence available in the context of a particular dispute.

Non-Package Cases

The travel agent sometimes issues of "writes" tickets for transport service providers. On these occasions the travel agent is probably the agent for the

---

[18] The Barbados based defendant was found liable for defects in the villa – see Chapter 4.

transport provider throughout the course of the transaction. The bus company, railway, airline or ferry operator authorises the travel agent to sell ticket on its behalf. This authorisation may go beyond that given to travel agents selling packages, in that the package vendor (the tour operator) only authorises the agent to transmit bookings for acceptance by the operator. Where the agent is actually "writing" the ticket, it is more probable than not, that he is expressly authorised to sell the transport space — even though it would be sensible for the agent to check availability before the ticket is written. The very writing of the ticket, and the authorisation to do so creates at the very least an "apparent" authority in the travel agent to sell the space on the transport provider's behalf. In allowing the agent to "write" the ticket, the transport provider holds out the agent as being authorised to sell the seat or space in question. Accordingly, if a travel agent writes a ticket as agent for the transport provider, the provider is bound by the contract that is made between the agent on his behalf and the consumer. So when the consumer arrives to take his place, and finds he has been allocated standard-class accommodation instead of first class, or has been allocated a couchette instead of a berth, the consumer will have an action for breach of contract against the transport provider. The ticket — an important contractual document — written by the travel agent with the authority of the transport provider-specifies the accommodation the consumer is entitled to expect under the contract. If he is not provided with it, it is the transport provider who must compensate him — though no doubt such a provider would look to the travel agent for an indemnity, either on the grounds that the agent did not follow the correct procedures in checking availability, or alternatively on the grounds that the agent exceeded his *actual* authority.

Hotels and overnight accommodation

Where, on the other hand, the travel agent is invited to book hotel or other accommodation for a consumer, it is most unlikely that he will have "ticket writing" authority for the hotel. In such situations it is more probable than not that the travel agent will be acting as the agent of the consumer (if he is anybody's agent at all). The travel agent's relationship with the accommodation provider is likely to be much closer to — if not precisely the same as — the relationship between travel agent and tour operator. This is because in all probability the agent will have had no regular prior dealings with a given hotel, and there will be no actual or apparent authority to create the relationship of principal and agent between the agent and the provider. In these situations the travel agent is acting as no more than a line of communication for the consumer with the hotel. Accordingly, if the agent transmits an *offer* to the hotel to the effect that the consumer requires two adjoining twin rooms, and the hotel accepts that offer by communicating assent to the travel agent, that accommodation is what the consumer will be taken to have contacted for — even though the consumer may have intended the agent to convey an offer for two double rooms.

In all these situations — packages, issuing tickets and booking independent facilities — the crucial questions are; when is the contract concluded; and who makes the contract?

Whose Agent?

Whilst there is clearly not a single, all-embracing answer to this question, its importance in individual cases arises in the context of a number of recurring issues in the travel industry.

- What are the *terms* of the particular travel contract? What the terms are, will depend on who makes, or who is authorised to conclude the contract.

- To whom should the consumer turn for redress in the event that he is not supplied with what he requested? This too depends on who concluded the contract, and when in the course of dealings with the consumer the contract was concluded, it also depends on what breach of contract is alleged by the consumer.

- To whom should the consumer turn in the event that the service provider becomes insolvent? He can only turn to the travel agent (in the absence of an express guarantee) if the travel agent was acting as the consumer's agent at *all* material times. Money handed to an agent as the consumer's agent may become money held on behalf of a tour operator if a travel contract is concluded between the money's deposit by the consumer and the insolvency of the service provider.

- Whether, and for what purpose, the travel agent is the agent of a tour operator or other "supplier" can be crucial in determining the vexed question of the liability of credit card companies for contractual failures under section 75 of the Consumer Credit Act 1974 (see p 534).

Retailers & the PTR 1992

The most important of the 1992 regulations from the travel agent's point of view must be regulation 4. It will be remembered[19] that this provides, *inter alia*, that

> No ... retailer shall supply to a consumer any descriptive matter concerning a package, the price of a package or any other conditions applying to the contract which contains any misleading information.

---

[19] Chapter 3.

The penalty for so doing is liability to compensate the consumer for any loss he suffers in consequence of the misleading information.

This provision is positively breathtaking in its scope as far as travel agents are concerned. There is no provision for the application of a statutory defence or limitation of liability under regulation 4. So where a tour operator misdescribes a package resort in a brochure, and that brochure is supplied to the consumer from the shelves of the travel agent, the travel agent (as a supplier) is as liable as the tour operator for the consequences of the misdescription. Fault doesn't come into it. In cases of misdescription therefore, the travel agent is made jointly and severally liable with the tour operator to compensate the consumer for the loss arising out of the misdescription. This loss will include loss of bargain, special damages and loss of enjoyment. The consumer may find this provision useful in a number of instances.

1. Where an operator has become insolvent, it may be easier for the consumer to claim directly against the travel agent rather than going through the rigmarole of claiming under a bonding scheme.

2. The tour operator or organiser may not have secured the consumer's money in the way required, there may be no bond, insurance or trust fund against which the consumer can claim.

3. The claim against any bond will almost certainly not include a claim for damages for loss of enjoyment, anxiety, distress and inconvenience; so any fund may not be sufficient to meet such claims in full.

4. The travel agent is almost certainly going to be a "softer" target than a credit card company under section 75 of the Consumer Credit Act 1974.

5. Joining the travel agent in an action with the tour operator may be tactically advantageous, just as a mechanism for applying additional indirect pressure from the travel agent on the tour operator.

6. Regulation 4 foreshadows an action in which the tour operator may escape by proving "no fault", the travel agent cannot have the opportunity to do likewise. (Fortunately, regulation 4 applies as much to tour operators as it does to travel agents so both are likely to be pursued under the same regulation.)

As discussed in Chapter 3 and seen in cases such as *Minhas v Imperial Travel Limited*[20] regulation 4 is used with increasing frequency against travel agents in respect of actions for the failure of a service provider to deliver what the consumer reasonably considered part of the holiday contract.

[20] [2003] CL February 263.

Regulation 5(2) of the 1992 Regulations is also of particular importance to a travel agent, who will be guilty of a *criminal offence*[21] if he *"makes available to a possible consumer a brochure which he knows or has reasonable cause to believe does not comply with the requirements of ... "* regulation 5(1), that is, one that is not *"legible, comprehensible an accurate".*[22]

Travel Agents as The Other Party to the Contract

The trial judge in *Minhas*[23] also concluded that as a retailer the travel agent was liable under regulation 15 of the PTR 1992 for improper performance of the holiday contract, although this was on the improbable basis that the travel agent had received the money for the holiday from the consumers. The receipt of the money for the holiday begs the question as to the *capacity* in which the money was received by the travel agent.[24] If received *as an agent of the tour operator* it is difficult to see how receipt of the money makes the travel agent the other party to the contract for the purposes of regulation 15. Reference should be made to the decision in *Hone v Going Places Leisure Travel Limited*[5] at first instance where Douglas Brown J considered that a travel agent would only be liable as *"the other party to the contract"* under regulation 15 where the agent made the holiday contract as agent for an *undisclosed principal* or where the agent had itself acted as an organiser of the package.

Travel Agents' Duties of Care

Where the travel agent is exercising a "consultancy" or advisory function, he owes duties of care at common law to his customers.

> it should be regarded as settled that if someone possessed of special skill undertakes, quite irrespective of contract, to apply that skill for the assistance of another person who relies on that skill, a duty of care will arise ... Furthermore, if ... a person takes it upon himself to give information or advice to ... another person, who, as he knows or should know, will place reliance upon it, then a duty of care will arise".[26]

There can be little room for doubt that a duty of care is imposed on travel agents in accordance with these principles[27]. There is certainly no policy

---

[21] Punishable by unlimited fine in the Crown Court and a fine of up to £5,000 in the Magistrates' Court.
[22] An offence subject to certain statutory defences discussed in Chapters 12 and 13.
[23] Above.
[24] See also R. (The Association of British Travel Agents Ltd) v Civil Aviation Authority and The Secretary of State for Trade and Industry (Interested Party) [2006] EWHC 13 (admin) discussed above with regard to the principles of ordinary agency law being applicable in a package travel context.
[25] [2001] ITLJ 153 – discussed in Chapter 4
[26] Lord Morris of Borth-y-Gest in *Hedley Byrne Co. Limited v Heller & Partners Limited* [1964] AC 465.
[27] Alternatively, a similar duty might be thought to arise in contract in most cases in that the travel agent acts as consultant or offers advice *in consideration* of the consumer booking travel

reason why the courts should refuse to recognise the actionability of any breach of such duties of care in respect of travel agents. Where the travel agent is exercising an advisory function in respect of a customer there is undoubtedly a "proximate" relationship between agent and customer justifying the recognition of the duty.

The scope of the duty

The statement of general principle recognising the existence of the travel agent's duty of care to the customer tells up nothing about the scope of that duty. At one extreme, travel agents could legitimately fear the imposition of such wide obligations as to make them the nannies of the travelling consumer. There is little authority to assist the travel agent in deciding just where the scope of his common law duty begins and ends. The following guidance is suggested in the absence of authority.

The travel agent is under a duty of care to exercise towards the customer such reasonable skill and care in the course of carrying out his advisory functions as is necessary for the proper performance of his professional role. His advisory functions are those functions in respect of which the reasonable consumer would ordinarily contemplate advice or assistance.

Accordingly, the travel agent cannot be expected to fulfil an officious role, proffering advice for which he is not asked on matters that he could reasonably expect to be common knowledge; neither can he be expected to offer detailed advice in respect of matters with which the overwhelming majority of customers would have no concern or interest, or about which the reasonably well-informed would know in any event.

Choice

Where a customer makes an unaided choice, be it of a holiday, conference facilities, accommodation or transport arrangements, the travel agent cannot be expected to launch into a gratuitous review of the "pros and cons" in respect of the choice that has been made. His advice has not been sought, and could not reasonably be expected. However, where the travel agent is aware or ought to be aware due to his professed expertise, of *special circumstances* he will be under a duty to offer advice on which the customer may reflect in order to review the choice that has been made.

Special circumstances

The wheelchair-bound customer and the hilltop hotel was an example of special circumstances discussed earlier. The duty on the travel agent may extend no further than asking the customer whether they have given due consideration to wheelchair access, particularly, but not only, in the context of destinations

---

arrangements using the agent. See e.g. Woolmuth: The Liability of Travel Agents [1966] *Temple Law Quarterly* 29.

where facilities for the disabled may be even less available than they are in some parts of western Europe or the United States. Another example of special circumstance may arise in the context of a case like *Kemp* — where the travel agent was casually alerted to the health problems of the proposed touring party. In cases such as this, however, the existence of facts giving rise to a duty of care may largely depend on the *quality* and *importance* of the information given, and the circumstances in which it was given. There will be cases (like *Kemp*) where the court finds it difficult to accept that a casual conversation or "off the cuff" remark on the part of the consumer was intended to, or could be expected to have any legal effect. The line between a customer *asking* for advice or assistance in respect of personal special circumstances, and *informing* the agent of such special circumstances as should have alerted the reasonable travel agent to the need to offer advice and assistance (or tell the customer to obtain advice elsewhere), may be a very narrow one indeed.

There will be a second class of "special circumstances". These will arise where the travel agent knows or should know about some factor relating not to the consumer but to the *destination* chosen by the customer, the type of accommodation or transport chosen or some other feature of the choice, about which the reasonably will-informed customer could not be expected to know. Such special circumstances should arise where civil unrest has recently occurred; where health problems have recently been experienced; where severe weather has disrupted the supply of services in a given location; or where a particular hotel, airline, ferry company or other service provider has had particular problems, perhaps relating to unfinished accommodation or the rerouting of transport services. This duty does not, it is submitted, extend to commenting on the obvious, such as "it can be cold cruising in Alaska", or "Majorca can be very busy in August".

The travel agent's task in the context of package holidays is often made easier by reason of the fact that tour operators usually go to some lengths to point out those packages that are offered that may not be suitable for the unhealthy or the elderly, or which may involve some minor risk to health, or where the social norms at a given destination are radically different from that which the customer might expect to encounter at home.

Transmission and ticketing

The travel agent will certainly be under a duty of care to transmit accurately the customer's offer to purchase the tour operator's package or the service provider's services. If the customer's choice is for the five-star hotel with hot and cold running flunkies, it is incumbent on the travel agent to transmit this accurately to the tour operator, because as we have already seen, if something else has been transmitted as an offer to purchase on behalf of the consumer, it will almost certainly be that "something else" that the tour operator agrees to provide in the package contract so that when the consumer is given "something else" on arrival at the destination there is no improper performance of the holiday contract. Closely allied with this duty is the obligation on the travel agent to *check* the details of what has been chosen by the customer before transmitting them to the operator, and checking the tour operator's acceptance of the offer in the terms in which it was made, on the grounds that the best time to correct errors is immediately after they have been made.

Where the travel agent is "writing" a ticket, even if he is the agent of the transport provider in so doing, he will probably be liable to the customer independently, in the event that he makes an error in the dates, the times or other particulars relevant to the ticket that he issues.

Where the travel agent, even where he is acting as an agent for a tour operator, neglects to transmit tickets or information about the package, such as changes in times and dates, or the facilities that are available in the course of the package, it is likely that despite the tour operator's liability under the 1992 Regulations, the travel agent would also be directly liable to the customer for failing to furnish the customer with documents or information intended for the customer by the tour operator.

Prices

In package contract cases, it is probably not the travel agent's duty, and the travel agent probably could not reasonably be expected, to be a talking encyclopaedia with all the prices, facts and figures at his fingertips. The customer will have made his choice from a selection of brochures, or have chosen not to look at the selection generally available. The customer can, therefore, be expected to exercise an informed choice as to price. However, if asked if a cheaper alternative is available, the agent's duty would extend to making reasonable enquiries, but he would seldom be taken to have warranted that a cheaper alternative was not available.

Where a customer is using the travel agent as a booking agent for airline, bus, rail or ferry tickets, it *is* probably incumbent on the travel agent to advise the customer in respect of the range of price possibilities available, usually the result of travelling at certain times, or booking a certain period in advance of the proposed travel. It lies particularly within the travel agent's expertise to know Apex, Super-Apex and other "bargain" fare rates for example. This is an onerous duty when one considers that a 1996 *Which?* Survey discovered that 90% of rail travellers surveyed were not given accurate price information about the cheapest rail fare available to them by railway booking staff.

Passports, visas, vaccinations

This is the sort of general information that falls or should fall within the expertise of the travel agent, and on which the customer may legitimately expect some accurate advice. Once again in the context of regulated packages, the travel agent's task is made simpler by reason of the fact that the brochure should include general information of this nature[28] and by reason of regulation 7 this information has to be given to the customer before the package contract is concluded. Even in package cases, however, there remains an implicit obligation[29] for the travel agent to have in place a system for checking that the information given in the brochures he displays or supplies is correct.

In non-package cases the travel agent must either decline to advise at all (perhaps the best policy), or *get it right*. Many travel agents supply general brochures of documentary and health requirements covering various parts of the world. Some offer advice desks or telephone lines at which customers' queries may be answered. Often the advice that is tendered is subject to a warning that the customer should double-check the requirements with the relevant embassy or high commission[30]. Where qualified advice of this nature is given it is absolutely vital that the customer is warned in the clearest imaginable terms (preferably in writing) that he must satisfy himself about the such requirements from a source related to his intended destination, or from a recognised travel centre (such as those run by the major international airlines) rather than rely on the information in the booklet (which may be out of date, or have been recently or temporarily overtaken by events).

When given advice, or referring the customer to some other source for advice, it is of vital importance for the travel agent to bear in mind that not all his customers will be holders of British passports, and different visa and health requirements can be imposed by countries in respect of different nationalities. If undertaking an advisory role regarding passports, visas and health requirements the *first* question the travel agent should ask is whether the customer and *all* members of his party are holders of British passports. If this question is not asked, the wrong advice may be given for which it is highly likely that the travel agent would be held accountable to the customer.

Contributory negligence

With the possible exception of "late bookings" where the consumer collects his tickets and itinerary at the airport or other place of departure, the consumer has an opportunity to check the terms of the contract to which he is committed and the particulars of the documents and tickets the travel agent has provided. The sensible consumer will always double-check their provisions. Most travel agents will expressly request that the consumer check all his travel documents.

---

[28] See PTR 1992 regulation 5 and Schedule 1 of the PTR 1992 clause 5.

[29] PTR 1992 regulations 4 and 5.

[30] It is common for travel agents to supply a leaflet from the US Embassy with regard to visa requirements for those travelling to the USA. The current accuracy of such information may be put to the test from October 2004 when the USA radically revises its visa waiver system for those travelling from the UK.

But is the consumer under a duty to do so? As a matter of common sense it is submitted that in those cases where the consumer has reasonable predeparture opportunity to check the accuracy of his contract and travel documents, he is under a duty to check for himself; on pain of being held contributorily negligent and the partial author of this own misfortune in the event that the documents do not accurately reflect the travel contract. Inevitably, questions of contributory negligence can only be considered on a case-by-case basis, and the consumer will be blameless where he has checked, but the documents are so ambiguous as to defy reasonable interpretation by the layman. It is doubtful whether this would occur very frequently.

Travel Agents and Employees

Vicarious liability
The common law duty on the travel agent naturally extends to all the travel agent's employees. It will be no defence to a claim in negligence for the travel agent to maintain that the advice was given by a junior member of staff, or someone working on the desk as part of a work experience programme. This is a plain and obvious application of the principle of vicarious liability.

Operational systems
Given the number of transactions that cross the travel agent's shop counter on a daily basis, it is hardly surprising that when a problem with a customer arises the travel agent or his employee is likely to have little, if any, personal recollection of the circumstances in which a booking was made, or what was said at the time a booking was made. This gives the customer almost *carte blanche* to "recollect" the events leading up to a particular transaction. The customer's recollection is more probably than not the one that will be accepted by a court in the absence of a contemporaneous note contradicting such recollection. After all, a judge has to accept someone's version of events, and the customer's recollection is not cluttered with one hundred and one identical booking incidents. The importance of noting "special requests" or concerns of the customer at the time they are made to the travel agent is vitally important. Not only will this help to avoid error in the issuing of tickets and the transmission of offers to the tour operators, it will assist the agent's recollection of one isolated transaction amongst many, when the inevitable dispute arises. Travel agents and their employees should be persuaded to treat every transaction as a potential legal dispute, and should take no persuading that every customer is potentially an "awkward customer". The care to be taken in the keeping of contemporaneous records extends to noting "no special requests" where appropriate.

In the sphere of the criminal law, it is of equal importance that operational systems should be properly devised, implemented and *recorded*. There is no point in devising a sophisticated due diligence system, be it for use under the Trade Descriptions Act, the Consumer Protection Act or regulation 5 of the PTR 1992, unless when the crisis comes, the travel agent can *prove* that the system was implemented. So, where as under regulation 5, it is incumbent on the travel agent to inform himself as to the accuracy, comprehensibility and legibility of the brochures he is displaying and supplying to the consumer, it is not only essential for him to devise and implement a system of random checks on the brochure information (in proportion to the number of packages he is offering); it is also essential for him to be able to *demonstrate* to trading standards officers and courts alike that the system has been implemented. An inability to show that a checking system is in place, and has worked, usually leads to the conclusion that the system cannot be a good or effective one. Indeed, it is often more important to *show* that a system of checking or due diligence exists, than it is to actually implement one. The necessity for well-documented operational systems is particularly acute for travel agents where the tour operator may issue corrections to a brochure, or bring out a second or subsequent edition. Plainly it is important for the travel agent to ensure that the corrections are passed on to all consumers who refer, or may wish to refer, to the brochure that has been corrected, or that all traces of the first edition of the altered brochure are eradicated so far as it lies within the control of the agent to do so. This not only involves using errata stickers on the brochure themselves, both on the pages where the corrections apply, and/or on the shelf-edge marking those brochures to refer the consumer for counter assistance and further details; it also involves recording in writing the *fact* that steps have been taken to implement the correction, the date and time, and the personnel responsible for undertaking the task of making the relevant corrections, and exactly what steps were taken. Where customers are referred for further information to members of staff, those members of staff should record the dates and times at which the "correcting" advice was given (they should, naturally know exactly where to look for it), exactly what advice was given and in what form, and wherever possible the consumer should be asked to sign to the effect that the "correcting" information has been passed on. The point being that even where all the proper and necessary steps have been taken to alert the consumer to errors or changes in brochures or other promotional literature, without a properly documented system the travel agent *may never prove it*. The major and leading travel agents (particularly the multiples) have written operational manuals showing what system had in individual agencies; and how the operation of the system is to be recorded for the purposes of proof. For small outlets and independents, there is no doubting the scale of the administrative burden, but it would be very risky to assume that the threshold of "due diligence" or any other form of statutory defence would be lowered out of sympathy to the small or independent travel agent.

Chapter 9

HOTELS AND TIMESHARES

Introduction

The original form of "timeshare" arrangement might be said to be an hotel - but this is never what is meant when people talk of timeshare property or ownership. Nonetheless, this chapter considers each of these two areas: first, the liabilities of Hotels in England and Wales, secondly, consideration of the provisions of the Timeshare Act 1992 as amended[1] and the liabilities and offences created by this legislation. Consideration is also given to the impact of other legislation such as the PTR 1992 on timeshare operations and consumers, and the chapter concludes with a short note on holiday rentals. The expression "Timeshare" is here used to denote not only those arrangements that fall directly within the scope of the Timeshare Act itself but also the increasingly bewildering array of exchange and points systems by which consumers buy-up their holidays years in advance in exchange for a capital payment.

Hotels[2]

Liability for loss and damage to property

Introduction

Within recent living memory a tour operator (who shall, as they say, be nameless) supplied a package holiday tour to South Africa to a small group of English tourists. The brochure had announced that whilst in Cape Town

---

[1] Timeshare Regulations 1997 SI 1081.
[2] For a comprehensive monograph on Hotel Law: *Grant, Douglas & Sharpley* - Northumbria Law Press 2007 (derived from a series of articles in the ITLJ 2005-7). The monograph provides references to a large number of additional illustrative cases and contains detailed historical discussion of the evolution of modern hoteliers' liabilities and as such has been an invaluable reference in the production of the summary that follows in this Chapter.

the tourists would be accommodated at a famously luxurious and historic 5-star hotel – "*or similar*" (as the brochure had it in a small footnote). History does not reveal what administrative problems the tour operator had but at all events on arrival in Cape Town the group was taken to a different (and obviously lower grade) establishment in the suburbs 30 minutes drive or more from the intended luxury hotel. Many of the guests (already disappointed at their accommodation's lack of sophistication) were surprised on waking the next day to see ranks of senior citizens exercising gently on a large tarmac courtyard. The guests had, in fact, been put-up in an *old peoples' home*. The tourists' many complaints resulted in a criminal prosecution under the Trade Descriptions Act 1968 – one of the charges being centred on the allegation that when promised an hotel the visitors had not been provided with an hotel. This allegation proved more problematical for the prosecuting authority than might at first appear. The dictionary[3] has it that an hotel is: "*an establishment providing accommodation and meals for payment*". The place where the tourists were taken *was* an establishment; it provided accommodation and it provided meals all for which the tourists paid. In addition it had communal lounges, television and radio (though not in the rooms) a swimming pool, and gardens as well as some basic and gentle sports and leisure facilities. In what sense, the tour operator asked rhetorically, was this old peoples' home not an hotel? The resulting acquittal on this charge could hardly be described as triumphant, but one suspects it was inevitable in the circumstances. The tourists had not been allocated to the hotel they had good reason to think they would be sent to and they, no doubt, had good claims for breach of contract. None of this altered the fact that it was not self-evident[4] that their establishment fell outside that wide definition of an hotel.

On the other hand consider *Powell v Thomson Holidays Ltd.*[5] Mrs Powell booked herself and her husband a half board Thomsons "Late Deal" in Majorca over the telephone from Tracy. Under the deal, the guests would take pot luck and be allocated accommodation of a minimum standard on arrival in Palma. Mrs Powell was adamant that she had been expressly told by the sales rep. "Sharon" the accommodation would be in "an hotel", a fact the Defendant denied. On arrival in Majorca the Powells were sent to the "Ivory Playa Apartments", a complex with a bar, restaurant, room service, chamber maids and other facilities one might expect of an hotel. The Powells' room had a bed, table and chairs, and a small kitchenette. The Powells were furious with their accommodation. They were convinced they

---

[3] The Concise Oxford Dictionary.
[4] Bearing in mind the criminal standard of proof.
[5] 28 April 2005 (Exeter CC) Unreported.

had booked "a hotel" and that they were in an apartment. Mrs Powell telephoned Thomsons' 24 hour holiday line to complain. She was told that, if she wanted to move to a bona fide hotel she would have to pay the difference between her (very cheap) Late Deal and the brochure price for the hotel, and this was £700. The next morning the Powells booked themselves on the next flight home. In the afternoon they met the local tour representative and told him they were leaving. On their return to the UK the Powells claimed the full cost of their holidays, plus the cost of the flight home. The Defendant contended that no guarantees had been made about the accommodation, save that it would be of a minimum standard. The Defendant argued that, even had a hotel been guaranteed, the "Palm Beach Apartments" provided all the services of a hotel and to all intents and purposes was a hotel. The Defendant noted that there could have been no claim at all had the block called itself a "hotel" and had the Powells not had a kitchenette in their room. The Defendant argued that, had there been a breach of contract, damages should be calculated on a loss of amenity basis, and that any loss of amenity was very small indeed. Further, the Powells had behaved wholly unreasonably in booking a flight home before they had either given their accommodation a chance or even spoken to the tour representative. However, in the absence of any evidence from Sharon to the contrary, the Judge found that Sharon had indeed guaranteed the Powells would be accommodated in a hotel. The Judge then held that the "Palm Beach Apartments" was not a hotel. In DJ Wainwright's words, "*hotels are different from a block of apartments – they have communal areas, a formal dining area, and a general air of hustle and bustle not evident in a block*".

The starting point for the consideration of the liability of hotels and hoteliers has to be the basic, dual common law principle that an Hotelier:[6]

(i)   Is duty bound to receive all persons who present themselves subject to their being capable of paying reasonable compensation for the sustenance and accommodation provided to them; and

(ii) Is liable as an insurer for guests' property that is lost or stolen whilst on the Hotel premises.

Historically it was thought that travellers were subject to the special risk of being subjected to collusive dishonesty and criminal conspiracies between thieves and innkeepers as regards their property, (hence the innkeeper's liability as an insurer for lost and stolen goods) and that the risks and dangers associated with travelling abroad[7] were such that innkeepers should

---

[6] The liabilities of Innkeepers by common custom of the realm – see *Shacklock v Ethorpe Ltd* [1939] 3 All ER 372.
[7] In the general sense as opposed to the "overseas" sense.

be obliged to accommodate all-comers[8] for their greater comfort and protection. These basic principles are now of more historic than practical importance, save to the extent that in the development of the law in recent years, changes have been based on and adapted to these common law principles, which is to say that legislation has built on the common law foundations rather then substituted a code of legal liabilities. This is nowhere more apparent than in the Hotel Proprietors Act 1956.

Definition

Section 1(3) of the Hotel Proprietors' Act 1956 (the "HPA") provides as follows:

> In this Act, the expression "hotel" means an establishment held out by the proprietor as offering food, drink and, if so required, sleeping accommodation, without special contract, to any traveller presenting himself who appears able and willing to pay a reasonable sum for the services and facilities provided and who is in a fit state to be received.

The above subsection may be thought to beg as many questions as it answers. It is worth setting out section 1(1) which it is thought is better understood when considered *after* section 1(3):

> An hotel within the meaning of this Act shall, and any other establishment shall not, be deemed to be an inn; and the duties, liabilities and rights which immediately before the commencement of this Act by law attached to an innkeeper as such shall, subject to the provisions of this Act, attach to the proprietor of such an hotel and shall not attach to any other person.

One derives from the HPA the proposition that what is now termed an hotel is the same thing as an *inn*, and by a process of deduction, an hotelier is the same thing as an innkeeper. Inns and innkeepers were, as summarised above, historically things of special status at common law, but the combination of subsections (1) and (3) of the HPA means that we may now legitimately talk the plainer language of "Hotels" rather than that of the quainter "Inns". The key to the definition of an hotel it is submitted is the expression *"without special contract"* which effectively means *without advance booking or agreeing individual terms*[9]. Accordingly, where a proprietor holds out his establishment as offering food, drink and (if required) accommodation on

---

[8] Subject to certain exceptions discussed below. Thus a proprietor who specifically excludes children, or workmen or coach tours is likely by such truculence to excuse himself from the liabilities imposed by the customs of the realm and the HPA.

[9] Although the booking need not be very far advanced for a special contract to arise.

generally applicable terms to persons seeking such services[10] *without the precondition of prior booking* then he is running an hotel.[11]

Holding Out

Whether someone holds themselves out as offering the services and facilities of an hotel is a matter of fact and degree. A publicly displayed sign is likely to be *sufficient* evidence of a holding out, but not a *necessary* precondition.[12] One might call an establishment anything, but its legal character must be assessed by reference to what business is actually carried on there. According to section 1(3) of the HPA the proprietor must offer food, drink[13] and sleeping accommodation *to any traveller* in order that the business carried on at the premises can be characterised as an hotel. Nothing less will do, but if a proprietor is offering all the qualifying elements it matters not that he describes his establishment as a Lodge, Retreat or Resort – it will be an inn and thus an hotel.

Hodkinson v Humphrey-Jones (valuation officer): re: 2 Great Ormes Road, Llandudno[14] illustrates in practice (although this example refers to a boarding house rather than an hotel) how the issue of "holding out" must and can only be resolved by reference to all the particular facts and pointers of a given case. This was an appeal by the ratepayer from the decisions of the Gwynedd Valuation Tribunal relating to premises known as Cranleigh formerly 2 Great Ormes Road, Llandudno. The appeal was as to whether the property was properly entered in the Non-Domestic Rating List as "Boarding House". Under s.66(2A) *Standard Community Charge and Non- Domestic Rating (Definition of Domestic Property) Order 1990/162* the property was still to be regarded as a domestic property if during a year of assessment the property was available for the provision of short-stay accommodation for periods totalling less than 100 days and the persons intending to provide such accommodation also intended to reside there throughout any period during which accommodation was intended to be provided. It was accepted that the burden of proof that the premises lay within these exemptions during the relevant periods was with the proprietor. The property was advertised as a hotel in 1990 and as a desirable place to stay for a holiday in 1991. There was nothing in any of the advertisements to indicate a limitation

---

[10] Provided they fall within the definition of a "traveller".
[11] As opposed to a Motel, a Guest House; a Boarding House, "Private Hotel" or Bed-and-Breakfast Pubs offering drinking only facilities are not Hotels (and, therefore, not Inns) and neither are restaurants. However, an Hotel may and invariably will include bars and/or restaurants.
[12] *Parker v Flint* [1699] 12 Mod Rep 254.
[13] Not necessarily alcoholic drink – *Cunningham v Philp* [1896] 12 TLR 352 per Cave J (a temperance hotel).
[14] Rating Valuation Tribunal July 1995 – reported on *Lawtel.*

on the availability of the accommodation. The premises were laid out and equipped for the purposes of providing board and lodgings and were also licensed premises. The 'booking book' produced showed numerous examples of days when the accommodation offered was unoccupied but there was nothing to indicate that the accommodation was not available on offer on those days. The valuation tribunal had found that "there was an intention to offer accommodation for more than 100 days in the year". Other evidence of external signs and low fuel consumption did not lead to any contrary conclusion. The proprietor failed to establish entitlement to exemption from non-domestic rating. Whatever the reality, the proprietor had held himself out as offering accommodation that was *available* for paying guests for more than 100 days per year.

Without Special Contract

The "holding out" must be to everybody[15] "without special contract" which means the holding out must include a holding out to any casual travellers who happen to present themselves.

> A traveller who turns up unannounced at an hotel, without prior agreement or notice has a right to be accommodated by the hotel. This is the essence of an hotel – that it will receive travellers who simply arrive on the doorstep needing refreshment or a bed for the night. They cannot be turned away into the night, prey to robbers and bandits.[16]

The fact that most establishments properly described as hotels these days accept and encourage advance bookings, and many will accept longer term guests on specifically agreed terms does not of itself deprive that establishment of the characteristics (and liabilities) of an hotel. However, those whose visits are the subject of special contracts will not be afforded the benefit of the establishment's (or its proprietor's) liabilities *as an hotel* or *hotelier*. So one can see that the imposition of the common law liabilities as entrenched by the HPA depends on two essentials: *first* the proper characterisation of the establishment and *secondly* the nature of the visitor. This has the inevitable effect that different types of visitor to an hotel will be subject to different degrees of legal protection.

Travellers

Neither the common law nor the HPA provides any definition of whom or what a traveller is. One is supposed to recognise a traveller when one is encountered. The exclusionary attempts made by some judges are not

---

[15] So if a hotelier legally limits access – e.g. "No Children"; "No Dogs" the holding out is not likely to be a holding out as a common law innkeeper.
[16] *Grant et al – Hotel Law* page 13.

terribly helpful. The private guests of the innkeeper and those coming to the inn to undertake routine maintenance are unsurprisingly not travellers and not entitled to the protection of the customs of the realm in respect of a hotelier's common law liability. More usefully (albeit impressionistically) a distinction has to be drawn between travellers on the one hand and "boarders" on the other. The long-term guest it appears loses the characteristics of a traveller.[17] Given the importance of the status of travellers in the context of common law (and now statutory) hoteliers' liability it is perhaps surprising[18] that no firm definition of who a traveller is has been forthcoming. The following is tentatively offered by way of illustrating those factors that may incline against a finding that a guest is in fact a traveller and entitled to the protection of the customs of the realm and the HPA. None of the factors is, however, conclusive one way or the other.

- A traveller will not have made any advance booking.[19]

- A traveller will stay at an establishment for 7 nights or less[20] but will at least have engaged sleeping accommodation.[21]

- A traveller will pay the advertised day-rate chargeable by the establishment for his accommodation.

- A traveller will have a point of departure and destination other than at the establishment where he is accommodated.

- A person who is received as a traveller may forfeit that status by outstaying his welcome as such.

Granted that none of these factors is determinative one way or the other, it is still readily apparent that in the modern age the number of persons accommodated at hotels in England and Wales who enjoy the protection of the customs of the realm and the HPA as *travellers* staying at hotels is going to be rather limited. Many present –day guests at hotels will not be qualifying travellers.

---

[17] Just how long one has to stay to lose the status of a traveller is less than clear. It is now surely doubtful that the presumption of a 3 day stay (applied as the presumed result of the old cases in *Williams v Linnitt* – 1951 1 KB 565) is valid.

[18] Although the common law's case-by-case approach to all such factual issues is a common phenomenon.

[19] But see *R v Higgins* [1948] 1 KB 165.

[20] See: *Lammond v Richard & The Gordons Hotel Ltd.* [1897]1 QB 541 in which it was said that the length of stay was an important factor distinguishing lodgers or boarders from travellers – although in the instance case the length of stay was one of several months. See also e.g. *Pinkerton v Woodward* (1867) discussed by *Grant et al* at page 53.

[21] If the guest is to have enjoy the benefits of the hoteliers obligations as an insurer of property - HPA section 2(1)(a).

Exceptions

It will be remembered[22] that if any[23] *traveller* presents at an *hotel* that person is entitled to be *received* by the hotel, and once received the hotel is *liable* as an insurer for his property. To this general proposition there are some important exceptions.

(i) To be received the traveller must appear to be able and willing pay a reasonable price for the hotel services and facilities.

(ii) To be received the traveller must be in a fit state[24] to be received.[25]

(iii) To be received, sleeping accommodation must be available – that is, the hotel need not receive the traveller if it is fully booked or its accommodation fully occupied.[26]

(iv) Liability *as an insurer* does not extent to motor vehicles (or property left inside motor vehicles) or any horse or other live animal.[27]

(v) Liability as an insurer does not apply where the hotelier can prove that the relevant loss was the result of the guest's own negligence in that the loss would not have occurred if the guest had exercised that degree of care to be expected of the ordinary prudent guest.[28]

(vi) Provided the hotel conspicuously displays[29] the statutory notice under the HPA at or near reception where it could be conveniently read by guests, liability as an insurer is limited to the sum of £50 per article and £100 per guest.[30] If properly displayed and in clear writing the limits imposed by the display of the statutory notice illustrate the significant limitations

---

[22] Section 1(3) HPA – reversing the result in *Bennett v Mellor* discussed by *Grant et al* at page 36.

[23] See *Constantine v Imperial Hotels Ltd.* [1944] 1 KB 693 in which Birkett J. deplored an attempt by an hotel to exclude a black West Indian cricketer – any traveller has the right to be received by an hotel.

[24] This again will often be a matter of fact and degree, but drunks, rowdies and prostitutes are 3 obvious examples where an hotelier would be entitled to exercise an exclusionary discretion. Signs of contagious disease might be another. In *Rymer* [1877] 2 QBD 136 it was considered that a hotelier was within his rights to decline to receive a traveller with large and objectionable dogs that were likely to a disturbance to other guests.

[25] Each of these exceptions is accommodated in section 1(3) of the HPA itself.

[26] *Browne v Brandt* [1902] 1 KB 696.

[27] HPA section 2(2).

[28] *Shacklock v Ethorpe* (above) where the guest was found not to have been negligent on the facts where she left jewellery in a locked case in an unlocked room.

[29] Again a matter of fact and degree.

[30] Section 2(3) HPA – unless the goods are offered & accepted or ought to have been accepted by hotelier for safe keeping or unless the goods are lost due to the hotelier's (or his employee's) default, neglect or wilful act).

imposed on the hotelier's liability as an insurer. £100 will not stretch far in respect of the property of most modern travellers.[31]

Section 2 of the HPA is reproduced in full here for ease of reference.

Modifications of liabilities and rights of innkeepers as such

2.—(1) Without prejudice to any other liability incurred by him with respect to any property brought to the hotel, the proprietor of an hotel shall not be liable as an innkeeper to make good to any traveller any loss of or damage to such property except where —

(a) at the time of the loss or damage sleeping accommodation at the hotel had been engaged for the traveller; and

(b) the loss or damage occurred during the period commencing with the midnight immediately preceding, and ending with the midnight immediately following, a period for which the traveller was a guest at the hotel and entitled to use the accommodation so engaged.

(2) Without prejudice to any other liability or right of his with respect thereto, the proprietor of an hotel shall not as an innkeeper be liable to make good to any guest of his any loss of or damage to, or have any lien on, any vehicle or any property left therein, or any horse or other live animal or its harness or other equipment.

(3) Where the proprietor of an hotel is liable as an innkeeper to make good the loss of or any damage to property brought to the hotel, his liability to any one guest shall not exceed fifty pounds in respect of any one article, or one hundred pounds in the aggregate, except where

(a) the property was stolen, lost or damaged through the default, neglect or wilful act of the proprietor or some servant of his; or

(b) the property was deposited by or on behalf of the guest expressly for safe custody with the proprietor or some servant of his authorised, or appearing to be authorised, for the purpose, and, if so required by the proprietor of that servant, in a container fastened or sealed by the depositor; or

(c) at a time after the guest had arrived at the hotel, either the property in question was offered for deposit as aforesaid and the proprietor or his servant refused to receive it, or the guest or some other guest acting on his behalf wished so to offer the property in question but, through the default of the proprietor of a servant of his, was unable to do so;

Provided that the proprietor shall not be entitled to the protection of this subsection unless, at the time when the property of this subsection unless, at

---

[31] The aggregate limit first imposed by the Innkeepers Act 1863 was £30 which probably demonstrates that the value of money has slumped more in the last 50 years than the previous 100 years.

the time when the property in question was brought to the hotel, a copy of the notice set out in the Schedule to this Act printed in plain type was conspicuously displayed in a place where it could conveniently be read by his guests at or near the reception office or desk or, where there is no reception office or desk, at or near the main entrance to the hotel.

The display of a statutory notice[32] is not to be taken as an admission that the establishment is a hotel within the meaning of the HPA or that the person making a claim is a traveller entitled to rely on the common law rights preserved by the HPA. The statutory notice reads (and must be reproduced literally[33] to be effective):

Under the Hotel Proprietors Act 1956 a hotel proprietor may in certain circumstances be liable to make good any loss or damage to a guest's property even though it was not due to any fault of the proprietor or the staff of the hotel.

This liability however –

(a) extends only to the property of guests who have engaged sleeping accommodation at the hotel;

(b) is limited to £50 for any one article and a total of £100 in the case of any one guest, except in the case of property which has been deposited, or offered for deposit, for safe custody;

(c) does not cover motor-cars or other vehicles of any kind or any property left in them, or horse or other live animals.

This notice does not constitute an admission either that the Act applies to this Hotel or that liability thereunder attaches to the proprietor of this hotel in any particular case.

Hotel premises

Where a hotelier is liable as an innkeeper or insurer he is only liable where the loss or damage to property occurs in those parts of the premises that are legally subject to his insurer's responsibilities. This is somewhat circular, but can be summarised by the old common law expression that the hotelier is only strictly liable for a guest's property that is *infra hospitium*. This is not mentioned in terms in the HPA but as the Act is predicated on the common law liability of innkeepers which liability was limited to property *infra hospitium* there is no doubt that this territorial limit still applies. What is the *hospitium*? The answer in marginal cases will raise many issues of fact and degree. However, the *hospitium* it would appear is that part of the premises reasonably suitable for the reception of guests' property and intended by the

---

[32] As stated in terms in the statutory notice itself reproduced as the Schedule to the HPA.
[33] *Hodgson v Ford* [1892] 8 TLR 722.

hotelier to be used for the reception or acceptance of guests' property. In *Williams v Linnitt*[34] the *hospitium* of the hotel was held usually to include garages and in this instance (in the absence of garages) extended to the hotel car park. The case concerned a stolen car form the hotel car park which is a claim that would not arise in the same form after the HPA vehicles (and the contents of vehicles) being excluded from the hotelier's liability as an insurer under that Act.[35] In *Williams* Lord Tucker discusses some of the ancient common law authorities and concludes that originally the *hospitium* of an inn extended only to the inn itself and its stables (which would include any inner courtyard that the inn might have) and hence in the 1950s[36] to its garages too. The narrow confines of this *hospitium* he said could be extended by the innkeeper himself if he voluntarily accepted guests' property for keeping in some other area.

Lien

The common law *quid pro quo* for the hotelier's liability as an insurer of guests' property was that the hotelier could exercise a lien (detain) the guests' property as security in respect of unpaid bills for accommodation, food and drink. The lien can only be exercised over a guest's property[37] which is part of the luggage or baggage brought to the hotel as such, and can only be exercised in respect of the debts incurred by the guest to the hotel in respect of those services the delivery of which would render the hotel liable as an insurer. The hotel cannot exercise a general lien in respect of other alleged debts or liabilities of the guest, such as damage to hotel property. The *quid pro quo* might be best illustrated by reference to the hotelier's now abolished liability as insurer for the motor vehicles of guests parked in hotel car parks. If the hotelier was liable as an insurer for the car (and had to look after it accordingly), it was only fair that in the event of unpaid bills that he should be able to exercise a lien over the car. When the liability of the hotelier as a motor insurer was abolished in 1956, so was the right of the hotelier to exercise a lien over motor vehicles.[38]

---

[34] [1951] 1 KB 565.
[35] Section 2 (2).
[36] But not now due to the HPA.
[37] Not other people's property that the guest has had delivered to the hotel and *known* by the Hotel to belong to a third party – see e.g. *Broadwood v Granara* [1875] LR QB 210 (a piano lent to a hotel guest was not his luggage or baggage) but cf. *Threlfall v Borwick* (1854) 10 Ex 417 where the innkeeper did not know of the ownership of a piano brought to the inn as part of the guest's baggage and in respect of which the innkeeper had liabilities as insurer. See also *Robins v Gray* [1895] 2 QB 501 where sewing machines sent by the guest's (a salesman) employer were part of his baggage.
[38] HPA section 2(2).

The old cases have an air of unreality about them in the modern world. The loan of pianos to musicians staying at hotels will nowadays seem even more eccentric than it would have appeared in the 1870s and it is unlikely that many hotels would now accept a ring as a security deposit against the payment of the bill.[39] More to the point the problem of assessing an ability to pay[40] and that of extracting payment are invariably dealt with at the same time by the taking of a credit or charge card imprint pre-authorising expenditure at the hotel up to an anticipated total amount.

Liability for personal injury

In the first part of this chapter we have considered the hotelier's limited liability as an innkeeper that is to say as an *insurer* in respect of a guest's property. Where for any reason the liability as an insurer does not apply, a guest will have to resort to general law principles of liability for the loss of or damage to his goods – such as the law of negligence or bailment. Recourse to the general law is always necessary where a claim arises in respect of personal injury. The hotelier is under no distinct obligations as an innkeeper or as an insurer where safety is concerned and does not warrant[41] that guests will be safe whilst at hotel premises. In such cases it is always necessary for the injured party to prove negligence or breach of the common duty of care under the Occupiers' Liability Acts 1957 ("the OLA") or 1984, or to prove that goods have been supplied that contravene the general safety requirement in section 10 of the Consumer Protection Act 1987.

It is neither appropriate nor possible to review here the law relating to an occupier's statutory and common law liabilities for injuries sustained as a result of the state of premises controlled by an hotelier. For properties outside this jurisdiction reference should be made in particular to Chapters 4 and 5. In respect of properties within the jurisdiction the established texts on Tort[42] are the best option. Only the briefest summary is attempted here.

An occupier owes the *common duty of care* to all his visitors[43] and that duty is *to take such care as in all the circumstances of the case is reasonable to see that the visitor will be reasonably safe in using the premises for the purposes for which he is invited or permitted by the occupier to be there.*[44] In determining whether there has been a breach of the common duty of care regard must be had to all the circumstances including the degree of care the

---

[39] *March v Commissioner of Police* [1944] 2 All ER 392 – where the ring turned out to be stolen – but in respect of which the hotelier was still entitled to exercise his lien.
[40] Section 1 HPA.
[41] In the absence of an express contractual warranty.
[42] E.g. *Charlesworth & Percy* on Negligence: 11th. edition 2006.
[43] OLA 1957 section 2(1).
[44] OLA section 2(2).

visitor might be expected to take in respect of their own safety, bearing in mind the fact that children might be expected to be less careful than adults. Account can also be taken of any warnings[45] issued by the occupier in respect of an alleged material hazard.[46]

It should come as no surprise that premises used for leisure purposes, such as restaurants, hotels, bars, clubs and sports facilities have provided a rich source of case law under the OLA 1957. A few examples may be used as illustration. In *Perry v Butlins Holiday World*[47] liability was established when a 3 year old fell against a brick wall capped with a sharp engineering brick and in *Stone v Taffe*[48] where a visitor fell down a steep unlit staircase in a pub – after hours. *Davies v Tenby Corporation*[49] is a case where a local authority provided a swimming pool but placed the diving board over shallow water, and liability was established. Cruise operators have also been found liable where a passenger fell off an unstable chair in heavy seas[50] and where another slipped on shiny, sloping linoleum.[51] On the other hand, there is *no duty* owed by an occupier in respect of dangerous hazards or risks about which the visitor should be well aware[52] - such as the risk associated with diving into water the depth of which is not known and has not been ascertained[53]. In other instances it has been found that there was no breach of the common duty of care such as where a customer tripped over a sleeping dog in the bar of an hotel[54] and where a customer slipped on a icy forecourt where nothing could have been done in the prevailing weather conditions.[55] In *Sawyer v H & G Simmonds Ltd.*[56] a visitor to a pub failed in a claim for injuries arising out his falling on broken glass dropped by another customer.[57]

---

[45] Verbal or in writing.
[46] OLA section 2(3) and 2(4). Liability is subject to the conventional complete or partial defences of contributory negligence and *volenti non fit injuria*.
[47] [1998] Ed. CR 39.
[48] [1974] 1 WLR 1575.
[49] [1974] 2 Lloyds LR 469
[50] *Appleton v Cunard* [1969] 1 Lloyds LR 150.
[51] Charlesworth – Negligence – paragraph 7-40.
[52] *Tomlinson v Congleton BC* [2003] HL 47 and the many cases cited therein.
[53] See also *Evans v Kosmar Villa Holidays PLc* [2007] CA (discussed in Chapter 4).
[54] *Carroll v Garford* [1968] 112 SJ 948.
[55] *Wood v Morland* [1971] 115 SJ 569.
[56] [1968] 112 SJ 353.
[57] The occupier has to know about a problem before he can reasonably be expected to do anything about it – but such an occupier certainly has a duty reasonably to monitor and maintain his premises in a reasonable condition. Avoiding liability in cases like this will invariably depend on the occupier proving that some effective system of inspection and monitoring was in place.

In the case of children, the *dicta* of Devlin J. in *Phipps v Rochester Corporation*[58] and Lord Steyn in *Jolley v Sutton London Borough Council*[9] remain irresistible:

> **Devlin J.** ...the responsibility for the safety of little children must rest primarily with their parents; it is their duty to see that such children are not allowed to wander about by themselves or at least to satisfy themselves that the places to which they do allow their children to go unaccompanied are safe for them to go. It would not be socially desirable is parents, as a matter of course, able to shift the burden of looking their children from their own shoulders to those persons who happen to have accessible bits of land.

> **Lord Steyn:** In this corner of the law the results of decided cases are inevitably very fact- sensitive. Both counsel nevertheless at times invited Your Lordships to compare the facts of the present case with the facts of other decided cases. That is a sterile exercise. Precedent is a valuable stabilising influence in our legal system. But, comparing the facts of and outcome of cases in this branch of the law is the misuse of the only proper use of precedent, viz, to identify the relevant rule to apply to the facts as found.

Equality

In the provision of goods, services or facilities almost all forms of discrimination on grounds of sex,[60] race,[61] religion, belief or sexual orientation[62] (whether direct or indirect) are prima facie unlawful. The Equality and Human Rights Commission unsurprisingly lists hotels as one of its specific examples of "service provider" to which the discrimination legislation applies. The legislation applies as much to the ancillary services offered at or by hotels as it does to the provision of hotel accommodation itself. In outline the law prohibits any service provider from:

- refusing or deliberately omitting to provide any goods, services or facilities;

- refusing or deliberately omitting to provide such things of like quality, in the like manner and on like terms as are normal in relation to other members of the public;

- on the basis that the person seeking the goods, services or facilities belongs to one of the groups covered by the equality legislation.

---

[58] [1955] 1 QB 450.
[59] [2000] 1 WLR 1082 at 1089.
[60] Sex Discrimination Act 1975 sections 1 & 29.
[61] Race Relations Act 1976 sections 1 & 20.
[62] Equality Act 2006 sections 45,46 & 81.

One would have hoped that by now all service providers would at least have appreciated that it could not possibly be in their economic interests to refuse to provide a service or treat certain groups differently from others on the grounds of sex, race, religion or sexual orientation, even if by so doing a bigoted minority were put off or subjectively disturbed. Cases like *Constantine v Imperial Hotels*[63] where a West Indian cricketer was refused pre-booked accommodation at a London hotel on the grounds of his race and colour should not recur,[64] neither should there be any repetition of the facts of the *El Vino*[65] case, in which women rightly claimed to have been discriminated against because they were not permitted to stand at the bar of a famous Fleet Street establishment but rather had to sit in the room at the back of the premises.

The legislation referred to so far is essentially negative in the sense that it prohibits and penalises discrimination. Of particular interest and importance to the travel industry, however, is *disability discrimination* law which demands of service providers in certain circumstances positive action to ensure that premises, services and facilities are as available as practicable to those under some form of disability as they are to anyone else.

Disability Discrimination[66]

Legislation and Guidance

The Disability Discrimination Act 1995 ("the Act") has 70 sections, 8 Parts and 8 Schedules. This has been amended by the Disability Discrimination Act 1995 (Amendment) Regulations 2003, the Disability Discrimination Act 2005 and Equality Act 2006.[67] An extensive body of regulations have been made under the Act which cover a wide variety of areas which will be referred to where relevant. Guidance has also been issued by the Secretary of State under the Act. The Act requires Courts and Tribunals to take any guidance which appears to be relevant into account.[68]

---

[63] [1944] 2 All ER 171.
[64] But see *Hallam v Cheltenham BC* [2001] IRLR 312.
[65] [1983] QB 425.
[66] "Too fat to work" was the headline in the *Times* on 19th November 2007. Incapacity benefit is available to anyone under state pension age who cannot work because of illness or disability. The headline continued: "Almost two thousand people who are too fat to work have been paid a total of £4.4 million in benefit, it emerged last night. Other payments went to fifty sufferers of acne..."
[67] See also Chapter 10 for the impact of the DDA on air travel.
[68] See also a number of very useful and practical publications on the Equality and Human Rights Commission Website (http://www.equalityhumanrights.com).

Key concepts

The Act defines a disability as:

> a physical or mental impairment which has a substantial and long-term adverse effect on his ability to carry out normal day-to-day activities.[69]

The Act gives some further definitions[70] but provides for guidance to be given as to the meaning of these phrases.

Physical or mental impairment

The following points emerge from the legislation,[71] the regulations[72] and guidance:

- A mental impairment must be or result from a mental illness that is clinically well-recognised[73]
- Addiction to alcohol, nicotine or any other substance is not to be treated as an impairment for the purposes of the DDA[74]
- The following are also not impairments: a tendency to set fires, a tendency to steal, a tendency to physical or sexual abuse of other persons, exhibitionism, and voyeurism.[75]
- Hayfever sufferers are also excluded.[76]
- However where these conditions are the cause of an impairment rather than an impairment themselves, the applicant may be considered disabled. For example, someone who is depressed as a result of alcoholism may be disabled[77]

Substantial and long term adverse effect

The Guidance issued by the Secretary of State indicates that a 'disability' is a limitation going beyond the normal differences in ability which may exist among people. A 'substantial' effect is more than would be produced by the sort of physical or mental conditions experienced by many people which

---

[69] DDA s.1(1).
[70] DDA Schedule 1.
[71] DDA.
[72] Disability Discrimination (Meaning of Disability) Regulations 1996 ("DDMD Regs") SI 1455.
[73] DDA Schedule 1 Paragraph 1.
[74] DDMD Regs Regulation 3.
[75] DDMD Regs Regulation 4.
[76] DDMD Regs Regulation 4(2).
[77] *Power v Panasonic UK Ltd* [2003] IRLR 151 EAT.

have only minor effects. A 'substantial' effect is one which is more than 'minor' or 'trivial'.

If someone has a progressive condition (such as cancer or multiple sclerosis) which does not result in "substantial" effects, they are to be treated as disabled if the condition will lead to such an effect in the future.[78]

'Long term' means that the impairment has lasted at least 12 months; or the period for which it lasts is likely to be at least 12 months; or it is likely to last for the rest of the life of the person affected.[79]

Effect on normal day-to-day activities

An impairment is to be taken to affect the ability of the person concerned to carry out normal day-to-day activities only if it affects one of the following: mobility; manual dexterity; physical co-ordination; continence; ability to lift, carry or otherwise move everyday objects; speech, hearing or eyesight; memory or ability to concentrate, learn or understand; or perception of the risk of physical danger.[80]

Discrimination

There are two kinds of discrimination: that which involves one person being treated less favourably than another on account of a disability and that which involves a failure to comply with duties which require adjustments to be made for disabled people.

Less favourable treatment

The Act states that disabled person is discriminated against if for a reason which relates to his disability, he is treated less favourably than others to whom that reason does not or would not apply.[81]

What does this mean? The following examples may help:

1. A blind person with a guide dog might be denied access to a café because no dogs are allowed in the café. One argument is that the café has not treated him less favourably because other customers would not be allowed into the café with dogs. This interpretation has been held by the courts to be wrong[82]; the reason (relating to his disability) the blind man

---

[78] DDA Schedule 1 paragraph 8.
[79] DDA Schedule 1 Paragraph 2.
[80] DDA Schedule 1 Paragraph 3.
[81] DDA s.20(1).
[82] *Manchester CC v Romano* [2004] EWCA Civ 834.

is denied access is his dog. Accordingly the correct way of approaching the problem is to compare the blind man with other people going into the café without dogs. On this analysis, he has been treated unfavourably.

2. The second example was given in the Code of Practice on rights of access issued by the Secretary of State. In this example a waiter asks a disabled customer to leave the restaurant because she has difficulty eating as a result of her disability. He serves other customers who have no difficulty eating. The waiter has therefore treated her less favourably than other customers. The treatment was for a reason related to her disability her difficulty when eating. And the reason for her less favourable treatment did not apply to other customers.

In each case, there would have been discrimination unless it could be shown that the treatment of the disabled person was justified.[83] In order to show that the treatment was justified the provider of the services has to be of the opinion [subjective test] (reasonably held[84] [objective test]) that a number of conditions are satisfied:[85]

*   The treatment is necessary in order not to endanger the health or safety of any person including the disabled person. The example given in the Code of Practice is:

    > An amusement park operator refuses to allow a person with muscular dystrophy onto a physically demanding, high-speed ride. Because of her disability, the disabled person uses walking sticks and cannot stand unaided. The ride requires users to brace themselves using their legs. The refusal is based on genuine concerns for the health or safety of the disabled person and other users of the ride. This is likely to be justified.

    If however the ground of health and safety is relied upon the service provider must consider whether a reasonable adjustment can be made to allow the disabled person access to the service without concerns for health and safety

*   The disabled person is incapable of entering into an enforceable agreement or giving an informed consent and therefore the treatment was reasonable.

---

[83] DDA s.20(1)(b).
[84] DDA s.20(3)(b).
[85] DDA s.20(4).

• The treatment is necessary because the provider of services would otherwise be unable to provide the service to members of the public[86] (bungee jumping may not be suitable for a quadriplegic and it may not be possible to adapt it to make it suitable).

• The treatment is necessary in order for the provider of services to be able to provide the service to the disabled person or other members of the public[87] (an example may be of disabled access; the main entrance of a posh hotel may be at the top of a lengthy flight of steps but the only place a disabled access could be provided might be via a less attractive part of the hotel).

• In relation to discrimination in the terms on which a service is provided to a disabled person,[88] these may be justified where there is a greater cost to the provider of services in providing the service to the disabled person. (Providing the same service to the disabled person on the same terms as to other members of the public might be very expensive and therefore the terms on which the service is provided may be varied so that the service provider's costs are reduced). However the increased cost of providing a service may not be passed on to the disabled person and is expressly excluded from this justification for unfavourable treatment.[89] The following examples are given in the Code of Practice:

 (1) A guest house has installed an audio-visual fire alarm in one of its guest bedrooms in order to accommodate visitors with a sensory impairment. In order to recover the costs of this installation, the landlady charges disabled guests a higher daily charge for that room, although it is otherwise identical to other bedrooms. This increased charge is unlikely to be within the law.

 (2) A golf club charges higher fees to individuals with mobility impairments to cover the extra costs of purchasing a new electronic golf buggy which enables mobility-impaired members to access the course. This increase in fees is unlikely to be within the law.

What if the service provider does not know that a person is disabled? This does not seem to matter as it is a question of fact whether or not

---

[86] This only applies to a case falling within DDA 19(1)(a), refusal to provide to a disabled person any service which is provided to members of the public.
[87] This only applies to cases falling within DDA 19(1)(c) or (d) discrimination in the standard of service offered or the manner in which it is provided or discrimination in the terms on which the service is provided.
[88] This only applies to a case falling within DDA 19(1)(d).
[89] DDA s.20(5).

there was discrimination. The following guidance is given in the Code of Practice:

A pub employee orders a customer who is lying prone on a bench seat to leave the premises because he assumes she has had too much to drink. However, the customer is lying down as a result of a disability rather than alcoholic consumption. The refusal of further service is for 'a reason which relates to the disabled person's disability'. This will be unlawful unless the service provider is able to show that the treatment in question is justified, as defined by the Act.

Failure to carry out reasonable adjustments

The second type of discrimination is where a service provider fails to comply with a duty to make reasonable adjustments for disabled people in circumstances where such a failure cannot be justified (see below).

Specific Effects of the Disability Discrimination Act

Goods, facilities and services

Of particular relevance to the travel and tourism industry are the requirements relating to the provision of services.

"Provision of services" includes the provision of goods or facilities.[90] A 'provider of services' is someone concerned with the provision, in the UK of services to the public or a section of the public[91]. A number of examples of service providers are given in the Code of Practice and they include: hotels, restaurants, pubs, railway stations, airports, national parks, sports stadia, leisure centres, advice agencies, theatres and cinemas.

It is irrelevant whether or not the service is free.[92] Other than this, 'services' are not defined in the DDA. The following examples are however given:[93]

- Access to an use of any place which members of the public are permitted to enter
- Access to and use of means of communication
- Access to and use of information services
- Accommodation in a hotel, boarding house or other similar establishment

---

[90] DDA s.19(2)(a).
[91] DDA s.19(2)(b).
[92] DDA s.19(2)(c).
[93] DDA s. 19(3).

- Facilities by way of banking or insurance or for grants, loans, credit or finance
- Facilities for entertainment, recreation or refreshment
- The services of any profession or trade, or any local or other public authority.

Unlawful discrimination

The DDA makes it unlawful for a provider of services to discriminate against a disabled person on the following grounds:[94]

- By refusing to provide, or deliberately not providing, to the disabled person any service which he provides, or is prepared to provide, to members of the public.
- In the standard of service which he provides to the disabled person or the manner in which he provides it to him.
- In the terms on which he provides a service to the disabled person. An example of this might be as follows:[95] a person who has Usher's syndrome (and who, as a consequence, is deaf-blind) is booking a holiday. The travel agent asks her for a larger deposit than required from other customers. The travel agent believes, without good reason, that because of her disability she is more likely to cancel her holiday. This is likely to be unlawful.
- In failing to comply with a duty to make adjustments for disabled people under s.21 of the DDA in circumstances in which the effect of that failure is to make it impossible or unreasonably difficult for the disabled person to make use of any such service.

Duties to make reasonable adjustments

The DDA imposes duties on providers of services to make reasonable adjustments for disabled people. As mentioned, the service provider will have discriminated unlawfully against a disabled person if a failure to make an adjustment makes it impossible or unreasonably difficult for the disabled person to make use of any service. The Code of Practice suggests that when considering whether services are unreasonably difficult for disabled people to use, providers of services to the public should take into account whether the time, inconvenience, effort, discomfort, anxiety or loss of dignity entailed in using the service would be considered unreasonable by other people if they

---

[94] DDA s.19(1).
[95] Code of Practice p.154.

had to endure similar difficulties.[96] The duties to make adjustments are as follows:

- Reasonable steps should be taken to change any practice, policy or procedure employed by a service provider which makes it impossible or unreasonably difficult for disabled persons to make use of the service provided to other members of the public.[97] A good example of such a change might be the alteration of a blanket no-dogs policy which might be altered to allow guide dogs. Another example relevant to the travel industry is as follows:

    > A hotel refurbishes a number of rooms on each floor making them fully accessible to disabled guests. However, the hotel's reservations system allocates rooms on a first-come, first-served basis as guests arrive and register. The effect is that on some occasions the specially refurbished rooms are allocated to non-disabled guests, and late-arriving disabled guests cannot be accommodated in those rooms. The hotel decides to change its reservation policy so that the accessible rooms are either reserved for disabled guests in advance or are allocated last of all. This is likely to be a reasonable step for the hotel to have to take.[98]

- Where a physical feature (e.g. one arising from the design or construction of a building or the approach or access to premises) makes it impossible or unreasonably difficult for disabled persons to make use of such a service, the service provider is under a duty to take reasonable steps to:

    - Remove the feature
    - Alter it so that it no longer has that effect
    - Provide a reasonable means of avoiding the feature
    - Provide a reasonable alternative method of making the service in question available to disabled persons[99]

The Code of Practice states that "physical features include steps, stairways, kerbs, exterior surfaces and paving, parking areas, building entrances and exits (including emergency escape routes), internal and external doors, gates, toilet and washing facilities, public facilities (such as telephones, counters or service desks), lighting and ventilation, lifts and escalators, floor coverings, signs, furniture, and temporary or movable items (such as equipment and

---

[96] Code of Practice p.155 §10.26.
[97] DDA s.21(1).
[98] Code of Practice p.158.
[99] DDA s.21(2).

display racks). Physical features also include the sheer scale of premises (for example, the size of an airport)." An example

- Service providers are under a duty to take reasonable steps to provide auxiliary aids or services (such as the provision of information on audio tape or of a sign language interpreter or braille) which would enable disabled persons to make use of services provided or facilitate their use.[100]

What is reasonable? It depends on the circumstance and the Code of Practice states that it will vary according to:

- the type of service being provided;
- the nature of the service provider and its size and resources; and
- the effect of the disability on the individual disabled person.

The Code also suggests some of the factors which might be taken into account when considering what is reasonable:

- whether taking any particular steps would be effective in overcoming the difficulty that disabled people face in accessing the services in question;
- the extent to which it is practicable for the service provider to take the steps;
- the financial and other costs of making the adjustment;
- the extent of any disruption which taking the steps would cause;
- the extent of the service provider's financial and other resources;
- the amount of any resources already spent on making adjustments; and
- the availability of financial or other assistance.

A service provider is not required to take a step which would fundamentally alter the nature of the service he or she is providing or the nature of his trade, profession or business.[101] A restaurant may not be required to provide bright lighting for those with partial blindness as this would ruin the ambience. However, the restaurant would have to consider whether a reasonable adjustment should be made such as have one area which is well lit.

A service provider is also not required to take a step which would cause him to incur expenditure exceeding the prescribed maximum.

---

[100] DDA s.21(4).
[101] DDA s.21(6).

Transport

The provisions of the DDA 1995 in respect of discrimination in relation to goods, facilities and services did not apply to any service in so for as it consisted of the use of any means of transport.[102] The position has been altered by the DDA 2005 and by the Disability Discrimination (Transport Services) Regulations 2005 which came into force on 4 December 2006. Essentially, providers of transport services in respect of the provision or use of a vehicle covered by the 2005 Regulations, are now providers of services and must comply with the duties under the DDA 1995. The 2005 Regulations cover the following types of vehicle: buses and coaches (scheduled and leisure), private hire vehicles, taxis, trains, trams, light rail, vehicles used on modes of guided transport, rental vehicles and breakdown recovery services. The effect of the DDA 2005 and the 2005 Regulations is to impose similar duties as apply to other service providers on those providing a service in respect of the provision or use of a vehicle in the United Kingdom to the public, or to a section of the public. It is therefore unlawful to discriminate against a disabled person:

- refusing to provide (or deliberately not providing) any service which it offers or provides to members of the public

- in the standard of service which it provides to the disabled person or the manner in which it provides it; or

- in the terms on which it provides a service to the disabled person.

- by failing to comply with the duty to make reasonable adjustments in circumstances in which the effect of that failure is to make it impossible or unreasonably difficult for the disabled person to make use of any such service.

The reasonable adjustments required are the same as for those required for service providers except the duty to overcome a physical feature (see above) does not arise in relation to the provision or use of a vehicle. There are two exceptions to this: in the case of rental vehicles, the full duty to overcome physical features applies; and in the case of breakdown recovery vehicles, the duty applies only in part.

[102] DDA 1995 s.19(5)(b).

Other relevant provisions of the DDA

Certain contract terms void

The DDA stipulates[103] that any term in an agreement is void (that is, unenforceable) if its effect is to:

- require someone to do something which would be unlawful under Part 3 of the Act
- exclude or limit the operation of Part 3; or
- prevent someone making a claim under Part 3

Legal Responsibility for employees

Service providers are considered legally responsible for the discriminatory actions of their employees.[104] However in legal proceedings brought against an employer it is a defence that the service provider took such steps as were reasonably practicable to prevent the employee's action. There is a list in the Code of Practice of steps which might be taken to prevent discrimination by employees and compliance with which would undoubtedly assist in establishing an employer establishing a defence to his or her employee's discriminatory act.

Court proceedings

Proceedings may be brought in the County Court in England and Wales for discrimination.[105] Damages may be awarded not only for losses but also for injured feelings.[106] Proceedings must be brought within 6 months of the act which is being complained of[107] except where they are referred for conciliation; in the latter circumstances the limitation period is extended by 2 months.[108] The period of 6 months may be extended where the court considers that it is just and equitable to do so.[109]

---

[103] DDA s.26(1).
[104] DDA s. 58.
[105] DDA s.25(1).
[106] DDA s.25(2).
[107] DDA Schedule 3, Part II, paragraph 6.
[108] DDA Schedule 3, Part II, paragraph 6(2).
[109] DDA Schedule 3, Part II, paragraph 6(3).

Timeshares

> The essence of timeshare is that it is the division of the benefits of
> ownership of property amongst a number of people, none of whom
> therefore buys a particular property".[110]

Timesharing, as is now commonly understood, involves the right to occupy
property for a certain specified period of the year – or in the extended sense
of the term used here the right to use one's pre-purchased points to buy a
holiday from an exchange brochure. Timeshare property as such is usually
owned and managed by a corporation or trust[111] which holds the property on
behalf of individual members who in turn have rights to occupy the
individual units of accommodation and to use the common facilities.
Timeshare business has been booming since at least the early 1960s to the
extent that there are now in excess of 4,000 timeshare resorts throughout the
world[112]. Buying the right to occupy timeshare property for a specified period
of the year enables consumers to reserve accommodation in a resort of their
choice at the time of year of their choice (either permanently or for an
extended period of years) by making a capital payment in advance. The
capital payment is a hedge against future inflation[113]. An added facility
offered to many timeshare owners is the opportunity to "exchange" and
upgrade their accommodation to an alternative property, resort or period of
the year through one of the many exchange operators that have entered the
market. The fact that timeshare owners employ the services of exchange
operators to seek out new resorts, different periods of the year and higher
standards of accommodation gives rise to the intriguing question as to why
the original accommodation was purchased in the first place. To some there
seems little point in buying a permanent slot in the place of your choice only
afterwards to engage in exchange contracts when the time comes for booking
the annual holiday. However, 3.5 million people can't be wrong. This
introduction deals with English law. Many countries of the European Union
have now implemented regulations designed for the protection of consumers
within their own territories, but each is different in detail if not in ambition.
Where a timeshare agreement is subject to the law of another Member State
it is essential to have regard not only to the provisions of the Directive but to
the provisions of the regulations of the relevant Member State.

---

[110] *Clearer Drafting and the Timeshare Act:* Euan Sutherland (Parliamentary Counsel) 1993
Statutory Law Review 163.
[111] Ownership and management are often in the hands of different legal entities.
[112] Or such was the position in 1998 – *Bourne: Is Timeshare Coming of Age* [1998] ITLJ 67
where it was noted that in 1995 annual consumer expenditure on purchases amounted to US$5
billion. The increased level of participation of some of the larger international hotel groups is
also noted.
[113] Subject to the inevitable, recurring management charges and administration fees.

Leases

In *Smallwood v Sheppards*[114] the plaintiff orally agreed to let some waste ground to the defendant for three successive bank holidays on which occasions the defendant was to have exclusive possession for the purposes of erecting and running a small fairground. After the first bank holiday the defendant refused to honour the agreement and was successfully sued for the balance of the rent. The court held that there had been a single letting even though the occupation of the defendant was not continuous. This is timesharing by another name.

Where a holiday home in this country is let to a consumer for a specified period of time over successive years, such an agreement is capable of being a lease. The length of the lease will be the total period of the discontinuous occupation of the consumer.[115]

Timeshare sales

The activities of a few rogue traders involved in the sale of timeshare interests in the 1980s gave rise to growing concern. The concern was born out of high-pressure sales procedures which ranged from annoying harassment to downright dishonesty.[116] Consumers were commonly subjected to inordinate sales pressure in resorts where they were already enjoying a package holiday and beguiled with gifts and promises into signing purchase agreements on the strength of assurances that were not always honoured when the final deal was sealed. Timeshare "presentations" could be equally pressurising for consumers invited to attend meetings in this country. This concern was recognised in the form of legislation both in the United Kingdom and later in Europe.

The Timeshare Act 1992

The Timeshare Act 1992[117] as amended by the Timeshare Regulations 1997[118] implement European Directive 94/47/EC.[119] The TSA creates both civil and criminal liabilities. The principle purpose of the TSA is to regulate the conduct of timeshare sales and to protect consumers from the effects of high-pressure sales techniques for which by the 1980s a minority of timeshare companies

---

[114] [1895] 2 QB 627 Wright J.
[115] *Cottage Holiday Associates v Customs & Excise Commissioners* [1983] 2 WLR 861 – Woolf J.
[116] See *Briggs: Timeshare – what's in a word?* [1999] ITLJ 63 where the author reviews some popular "scams".
[117] Referred to throughout as "TSA".
[118] See above.
[119] OJ 1994 L280/83.

and sales representatives had become notorious.[120] In order to furnish this protection the TSA concentrates on the provision of *information* to consumers, the control of *advertising*[121] and the creation of a right to *cancel*[122] a timeshare agreement within certain time constraints.[123] The TSA does not regulate the management of timeshare properties or companies and provides no remedy for dissatisfaction arising out of administrative disputes which may emerge once the consumer has agreed to an enforceable timeshare contract. So whilst the TSA is unashamedly designed to maximise consumer protection, the protection of the TSA only extends to matters relating to the making of a timeshare contract and the information supplied in the pre-contract period. For remedies against errant timeshare managers in respect of the condition or management of property, the availability of exchanges, or indeed any other matter promised in the pre-contract negotiations, or in the timeshare contract itself the consumer must look to the general law.[124] To this broad statement an important qualification can be added. Where a complaint in respect of the management or quality of timeshare property can be conscientiously linked to any form of *misdescription* of matters which must be included in the timeshare agreement, then that misdescription is itself actionable.[125] Such actionable misdescriptions will be discussed further below.

Application of the TSA

The TSA applies to those who agree to become timeshare users and those involved in offering the use of timeshare accommodation to such persons in the form of timeshare agreements in the course of a business.[126]

A timeshare agreement[127] is:

> ...an agreement under which timeshare rights are conferred or purport to be conferred on any person and in this Act, in relation to a timeshare agreement.

---

[120] Estimates before the implementation of the TSA were that 10,000 consumers a year complained to local trading standards departments - *Bourne: Cooling Off on Timeshares* [1992] NLJ 418.

[121] Sections 1B and 1C.

[122] Section 2.

[123] There is also elaborate provision made for statutory Notices of consumer rights – see *The Timeshare (Cancellation Notices) Order 1992* SI 1942 and the *Timeshare (Repayment of Credit on Cancellation) Order 1992* SI 1943.

[124] This is a matter of some considerable importance to timeshare owners because disputes concerning management or operation of timeshare property is likely to arise in respect of real property in respect of which the courts of the place where the property is situated will invariably have exclusive jurisdiction.

[125] Sections 1C and 10 A(2) TSA.

[126] Private sales of timeshare interests are not covered.

[127] TSA section 1(4).

Timeshare rights means:[128]

> ...rights by virtue of which a person becomes or will become a timeshare user, being rights exercisable during a period of not less than three years.

Time share users belong to the class of persons who may use timeshare accommodation which itself is defined as:

> ... any living accommodation in the United Kingdom or elsewhere, used or intended to be used, wholly or partly, for leisure purposes ... all of whom have rights to use, or participate in arrangements under which they may use, that accommodation, or accommodation within a pool of accommodation to which that accommodation belongs for a specified or ascertainable period of the year.

"Accommodation" means[129]

> ...accommodation in a building or in a caravan...

The TSA covers not only those arrangements which might be described as conventional timeshare arrangements where the consumer buys a specified week or weeks in a given resort over a period of time, but those "floating" arrangements where the consumer buys the right to select accommodation from a pool of resorts made available by the developer or operator. The consumer who buys a conventional period in a chosen resort may of course participate in exchange facilities offered by an exchange company, but the TSA extends its remit well beyond these. It covers situations where the consumer does not take any occupational rights in respect of a given apartment or resort but rather purchases in the abstract a specified period of time within which accommodation may be selected from the range on offer by the organiser, provided the range of accommodation forms part of a class of accommodation at the time the timeshare agreement is made. These last arrangements (described here as "abstract" because they are not tied to any individual property) will usually entitle the consumer to take a pre-specified period in one of a number of properties in the organiser's brochure or list. The rights must be exercisable over a period of not less than three years. This is not only intended to exclude from the operation of the TSA those few arrangements where consumers might pre-book a couple of annual retreats to the same holiday home in succeeding years, but also the need for consumer protection in respect of agreements of relatively short duration is plainly less compelling. An agreement which is of indefinite[130] duration, it is submitted, is one that confers rights exercisable during a period of not less than three years to which the TSA would, therefore, apply. The TSA applies

---

[128] TSA section 1(b).
[129] TSA section 2(2)(a).
[130] Where no duration is specified or the duration is terminable on the happening of a future event.

to consumers' rights as the owner of shares and securities and rights under collective investment schemes.[131] Accordingly, a timeshare operator cannot now avoid the application of the TSA simply by selling shares in a company which shares confer rights of occupation on shareholders. The fact that section 1(1) covers those who have rights to *participate in arrangements under which they may use [time-share] accommodation* is a further anti-avoidance mechanism. In such a lucrative industry the avoidance possibilities are almost limitless. In the past this has been attempted by the implementation of convoluted share purchase, club membership and trust arrangements designed to put as great a distance as possible between the consumer and the right to occupy the property in question. For example, the purchase of shares might confer on the consumer the right to *apply* for membership of a club; if membership is granted a consumer is allowed (subject to availability) to *apply* for holiday accommodation which can be bought with points assigned in proportion to the number of shares purchased from a pool of accommodation managed by an organisation from whom the company or the club (or even a third organisation in which the club is interested) leases space in the resorts offered to consumers.

There have been many variants of such convoluted schemes whose principle objective appears to have been the avoidance of the protection afforded to consumers by virtue of the TSA. Until the amendments brought about by the Timeshare Regulations 1997 such schemes were probably effective because rights conferred on consumers as shareholders were excluded from the provision of the TSA in its original form. Since the 1997 amendments, however, it is thought much less likely that such avoidance schemes will work. If the consumer is allowed to *participate in arrangements* which have as their ultimate goal the occupation of leisure accommodation over an indefinite period of time or a period of not less than three years, then the agreement that confers the right to participate in those arrangements is likely to be regarded as a timeshare agreement and subject to the provisions of the TSA (as amended). As soon as the consumer purchases shares, that consumer has the right at least to *participate* in arrangements under which they *may* use accommodation within a pool of accommodation.[132] In these sorts of circumstances it is likely that the share purchase agreement is the "timeshare agreement" governed by the provisions of the TSA.

---

[131] As defined in the Financial Services Act 1986.
[132] If the consumer does not have at least the right to participate in arrangements (even if that participation is unsuccessful because club membership is refused, or accommodation is unavailable) it is difficult to see what possible benefit the consumer achieves from the purchase of the shares (given the presumed underlying objective of the purchase is to take holidays not to make a capital financial investment).

Jurisdiction

The TSA assumes an exhorbitant jurisdiction. It applies to:

- any timeshare agreement to any extent governed by the law of the United Kingdom or part of the United Kingdom;[133]

- any such agreement where one or both of the parties are in the United Kingdom when the agreement is entered into;[134]

- any agreement if the relevant accommodation[135] which is the subject of the agreement is situated in the United Kingdom;

- agreements at the time when they are made the offeree[136] is ordinarily resident in the United Kingdom and the property is situated in a country of the European Economic Area.

It is the last of these jurisdictional provisions which may excite the most interest. If the consumer is ordinarily resident in the United Kingdom (whatever their nationality) and the property is situated in an EEA country, the TSA applies, even though the mechanics of the sale, the negotiations leading up to it and the property itself, its management company and even its owner are conducted and located in another country. It is unclear how this provision is intended to operate alongside the provisions of Regulation 44/2001 where the presumption is that the courts of the *defendant's* domicile should have jurisdiction over disputes.[137] Furthermore, article 22 of Regulation 44/2001 provides that exclusive jurisdiction over rights *in rem*[138] in immovable property rests with the courts of the country where the property is situated and even exceptionally, where the object of the action is a tenancy of up to six months, then it is the courts of the country where the *defendant* is domiciled (if different) which also have jurisdiction. Consumer contracts for the supply of goods and services are usually subject to the special jurisdiction of articles 15 and 16. The outcome of the apparent inconsistency between Regulation 44/2001 and section 1(7)(A)(b) of the TSA is not easy to predict. It may well be, however, that the resolution of this apparent conflict will be achieved by limiting the scope of section 1(7)(A)(b)

---

[133] TSA section 1(7).
[134] This will cover all sales made at presentations in this country irrespective of the nationality of the timeshare company or the location of the property.
[135] This will include accommodation in the available pool of accommodation – such as where a Scottish castle and an English country club appear as properties alongside a preponderance of foreign beach resorts in the available pool.
[136] The purchaser or the consumer.
[137] See Chapter 6.
[138] Most timeshare disputes will not give rise to problems in respect of rights in rem but will be personal disputes.

of the TSA to those consumer situations canvassed by articles 15 and 16 of
the Regulation.

Right to cancel

> A person must not in the course of a business enter into a timeshare
> agreement ... unless the offeree has received, together with a document
> setting out the terms of the agreement or the substance of those terms,
> notice of his right to cancel the agreement.[139]

This is the very heart of the TSA. Consumers must be given notice of their right
to cancel any timeshare agreement to which the TSA applies. The notice must
allow a 14-day period in which the consumer is allowed to cancel without
penalty[140]. The calculation of the 14-day period starts with the day after the
timeshare agreement is entered into (day 1) and ends on the 14th day. The
trigger date is the date of the timeshare agreement (plus one). No timeshare
agreement must be entered into without the consumer being given both:

- a copy of the agreement or the substance of its terms; *and*

- a copy of the notice of the right to cancel.

Contravention is a criminal offence.[141] Furthermore the form of notice of
right to cancel must be in the prescribed form.[142] The timeshare agreement
cannot be enforced against the consumer during the "cooling off " period of
14 days where notice of the right to cancel has been given. If a notice of the
right to cancel is not given the timeshare agreement may not be enforced at
all unless the consumer affirms the agreement.[143] Affirmation of the
agreement by the consumer renders the agreement enforceable whether or
not the offeror gave notice of the right to cancel and affirmation by the
consumer prevents the consumer cancelling the agreement subsequently.
Where the consumer gives notice of cancellation to the offeror the agreement
is unenforceable, it cancels the timeshare agreement and the consumer is
entitled to recover from the offeror any money paid under or in anticipation
of the agreement to the offeror or an agent. The timeshare offeror is not
entitled to recover any sum from the consumer.

---

[139] TSA section 2(1).
[140] The Directive of 1994 required a minimum of 10 days but the UK has retained the longer period.
[141] Punishable on summary conviction to a fine of up to £5,000.00 or on indictment to an
unlimited fine – TSA section 2(3).
[142] TSA section 4.
[143] TSA section 5.

Affirmation

If the timeshare agreement is affirmed, notwithstanding the failure on the part of the offeror to give notice of the right to cancel, the consumer loses the opportunity to cancel the agreement. Whether or not there has been an affirmation is judged on general contractual principles. Affirmation may be express or it may be implied by the conduct of the consumer and all the circumstances surrounding the transaction. Mere inactivity is unlikely in itself to amount to affirmation because TSA section 5(2) provides that in the absence of proper notice the consumer may cancel "at any time". However, a failure on the part of the consumer to do anything at all may be regarded as part of the circumstances from which an implied affirmation may be inferred. The use of any timeshare property, facility or service is likely to be regarded as affirmation. Voluntary payment of money due without protest under the agreement is also likely to be taken as affirmation.

Additional rights to cancel

Section 5A of the TSA provides for a further cancellation period in those circumstances where the timeshare agreement does not include specified terms set out in Schedule 1 of the Timeshare Regulations 1997. For example, the timeshare agreement must include (amongst other things) accurate information about the location of the property, its state of completion or expected date of completion, whether the agreement is tied in with membership of an exchange programme and the date from which the consumer may start to exercise his timeshare rights and the period over which such rights extend. Note that failure to supply some the requirements of Schedule 1 does not give rise to an additional right to cancel.[144] Where there is a failure to provide the specified information in the timeshare agreement that agreement may not be enforced against the consumer[145] for a period of three months and 10 days after the date on which the agreement entered into. The consumer may give notice of cancellation at any time during this period. If the information is forthcoming from the offeror after the date of the agreement but within three months of that date, then the supply of that information shortens the additional cancellation period of the consumer. In this situation the consumer has just 10 days within which to cancel the timeshare agreement. Accordingly:

- if the timeshare organisation fails to supply prescribed information within Schedule 1 at all, the consumer has three months and 10 days to

---

[144] For example, information about refuse collection and utility services. The additional right to cancel only arises for a failure to provide information set out in Schedule 1 (a), (b), (d)(i), (d)(ii), (h) and (m) – see Appendices.
[145] TSA section 5(A)(1).

reflect and cancel if required during which period the agreement may not be enforced against the consumer;

- once that additional cancellation period of three months and 10 days has expired and the consumer has not exercised the right to cancel the timeshare agreement is enforceable against the consumer;

- alternatively, if the timeshare organisation fails to include the prescribed information as part of the contract, but provides it a week later, this later provision of the prescribed information immediately triggers the shorter additional cancellation period for the consumer — being 10 days.

The purpose underlying the additional cancellation period is no doubt first of all to allow timeshare operators or sellers to correct any administrative error or oversight and to provide the prescribed material. The second objective is plainly not to stand in the way of consumers who are not interested in receiving the information set out in Schedule 1 (or who are deemed not to be interested by reason of the passage of three months from the date of the agreement).

Advance payments

Advance payments or deposits are prohibited during any cancellation period specified in either section 5 or 5A of the TSA. Advance payments must not be requested or accepted, either directly or through an intermediary until the relevant cancellation period has expired.[146] Contravention is a criminal offence. Section 5(8) provides a civil remedy for the recovery by the consumer of any money paid in respect of an unenforceable deposit. Whether the sums were paid to the offeror or to an intermediary the consumer may recover the money from the offeror.

Information and advertising

The person[147] who in the course of a business proposes to enter into a timeshare agreement as offeror must provide any person who asks for information about the accommodation a document which gives:

- a general description of the proposed accommodation;

- the matters set out in Schedule 1 of the Timeshare Regulations 1997 [paragraphs (a) to (g), (i) and (l)] which information includes the identities and domicile of the offeror and the offeror's legal status and information about completion dates, utilities and common facilities

---

[146] TSA section 5(B).
[147] Including Companies and Trusts.

available at the accommodation as well as information on the right to cancel;

• information about how to obtain further information.

Any information included in the document is deemed to be a term of the timeshare agreement. Any timeshare advertising must indicate the possibility of obtaining the document referred to above. The timeshare agreement and any information document supplied must be in English where the consumer is resident in the United Kingdom.[148]

Remedies and penalties

The TSA in its original form created criminal offences enforceable by local weights and measures authorities on giving notice to the Director General of Fair Trading. In addition to the right to cancel, the consumer was also given a statutory right to recover from the offeror any advance payment made before or during the cooling off period. The framework of criminal enforcement and penalties in addition to the (now enlarged) cancellation rights remain in place following the 1997 amendments. On summary conviction a defendant is liable to be fined up to the statutory maximum.[149] On indictment the potential fine is unlimited. A statutory defence of due diligence is available to a defendant[150]. By TSA section 10A the obligations created by sections 1A (information document), 1C (obligatory terms in timeshare agreements), 1D (language) and 1E (translations) are deemed to be duties owed directly to consumers and any contravention is actionable by the consumer in the civil courts against the offeror.

Misdescriptions

In addition to the general law of misrepresentation[151] consumers now have a direct statutory cause of action against a timeshare operator guilty of misdescription. TSA section 10A provides that a contravention of section 1A shall be actionable. The obligation under section 1A to provide information of the type set out in Schedule 1 must include an obligation to provide reasonably accurate information — and much of that information is deemed to be incorporated as terms in the timeshare agreement. The supply of inaccurate information is likely, therefore, to be a breach of the timeshare agreement as well as being directly actionable by virtue of section 10A. It also seems likely by virtue of TSA section 10A that where a consumer intending to enter into a timeshare agreement on the strength of misleading information within

---

[148] See generally TSA sections 1A – 1D.
[149] Currently £5,000.00.
[150] TSA section 8(1).
[151] The Property Misdescriptions Act 1991 does not create civil remedies.

Schedule 1 incurs expenditure or suffers some other form of foreseeable loss, such expenditure or loss will be recoverable as the remedies created extend to all those to whom the information document is given.

Timeshare and Regulated Packages

It will be clear from the above that the TSA is mainly concerned with consumer protection at the stage where a timeshare sale is being negotiated. The TSA does not concern itself with liability for the quality of the services and facilities delivered by the timeshare providers once the timeshare contract has been lawfully completed. To whom then does one turn when complaints arise about management standards and often more seriously, in the event that accidents occur at a timeshare (or exchange) resort? Holidays taken at timeshare or exchange resorts often have the appearance of package holidays to the consumers concerned; few appreciate that it is far from self-evident that these holidays are regulated by the PTR 1992. Furthermore, given the complicated structure of many timeshare and exchange programmes it is not always evident to whom the consumer can turn for a remedy from amongst the ownership, management and trust organisations that assume responsibility for the sale, operation, management, care and exchange of timeshare developments or units of accommodation within them. Often recourse will have to be made to the domestic law of the place where the complaint arises or accident occurs.[152]

Reference should be made to Part 1 of this book for a detailed discussion of the PTR 1992. In the standard timeshare arrangement it is unlikely that the PTR 1992 would apply. Once accommodation has been purchased for a period of time pursuant to the timeshare agreement consumers will usually make their own transport and other tourist arrangements depriving the annual holiday of the necessary attributes of pre-arrangement and inclusiveness of price so that neither the timeshare operator nor the transport or other providers are likely to be caught by the PTR 1992 even if it transpires that transport or other tourist services are supplied by the same organiser as originally arranged the timeshare accommodation or exchange.

The express terms of a timeshare, management or exchange agreement may, however, be such that liability is accepted by the organiser for the safety and quality of accommodation where a holiday is to take place irrespective of whether the holiday is a regulated package[153]. In the absence of such express terms consumers will find it more difficult to obtain redress in their home

---

[152] For example, to take but one example, in Spain, the Community of Owners (that is the managing committee of the property itself is a legal entity capable of being sued as such).
[153] In much the same way as organisers of non-regulated holidays may be caught by express terms and conditions intended for regulated package holidays – see Chapter 5.

courts for accidents or quality complaints that arise in the course of a timeshare or exchange holiday.

The decision in *Rechberger and Others v Republic of Austria*[154] may have important implications for timeshare and exchange service providers especially where the consumer is offered by the same service provider a holiday component that is "free" and one for which payment must be made. Perhaps the classic example of this is where free accommodation is made available on a promotional basis provided the consumer purchases flights from the timeshare or exchange programme operator. After *Rechberger* it would seem that the provision of a "free" holiday component is immaterial. If there is a pre-arranged combination of qualifying components sold at the price of *one* such component (the others being "free") then there is an *inclusive price* within the meaning of the PTR 1992; the "free" element being offered inclusively with the other component for which the price is paid. Thus in two-for-the-price-of-one arrangements, there is an inclusive price and likely to be the necessary degree of pre-arrangement for the PTR 1992 to apply. So, where a promoter offers "free" accommodation provided flights are booked with the promoter, there is a regulated package holiday. This is not one component being sold and one given away free; it is two sold at the inclusive price attributable to one. *Rechberger* was a case where single newspaper prize winners only had to pay nominal sums[155] in order to get their accommodation and flights "free". The fact that the price for the holiday did not reflect its value was neither here nor there. The nominal fee paid was the necessary *inclusive price* to bring the arrangement within the ambit of the Package Travel Directive. Similarly disturbing for those engaged in package-avoidance tactics is the decision in *Club-Tour*[156] in which the European Court of Justice considered that the fact that the arrangements had been put together at the request of the consumer did not prevent those arrangements from being a regulated package.

The result seems to be that where a consumer purchases one component of a holiday from a supplier which supplier is also providing other components without extra charge, whether because the accommodation component is provided pursuant to an exchange programme or because the organiser is offering promotional accommodation[157] the promoter or organiser is likely to be considered to offering regulated package holidays and all the liabilities attendant upon being a regulated package holiday organiser will apply.[158] Where the consumer uses accumulated accommodation points to "buy"

---

[154] ECJ : C-140/97.
[155] Airport taxes.
[156] See Chapter 1 – "tailor-made" arrangements.
[157] In the hope, for example, that a timeshare will be purchased by the consumer.
[158] See Chapter 4 and in particular regulation 15 of the PTR 1992.

holiday accommodation and from the same exchange programme purchases flights this too takes on the appearance of a regulated package in the light of the European authorities. Unfortunately, the likely effect of all this will be that timeshare and exchange programme promoters will erect increasingly contorted corporate structures in an effort to ensure that each component of the travel arrangements whether sold or offered free is provided by a separate legal entity.[159]

It remains entirely unclear whether timeshare or exchange programme tourists will be able to take advantage of the PTR 1992. For the time being the individual arrangements made and the terms of the individual contracts need to be closely considered in order to discern whether action pursuant to the PTR 1992 is viable for timeshares and exchange programmes. If it is not, or the position is open to doubt, consumers must have recourse to the management and maintenance companies of their resorts[160] or in some jurisdictions the community of unit owners.

Holiday Lets

Renting holiday accommodation through an agency remains a popular choice for many tourists, but who is liable when the property turns out not to be as described or promised, or is positively hazardous?

- Where the property is rented directly from the proprietor there is no room for doubt that the proprietor must take responsibility both for the descriptions used to promote the accommodation, any hazards on the property or any failure to meet the quality promised or implied in the letting contract.

- If the rented property is in the United Kingdom the consumer is unlikely to be discouraged from pursuing a remedy against either the property owner or the organisation (if any) responsible for co-ordinating the advertising of the property and administering the letting arrangements — the letting "agent". In these situations the fact that the letting agent is careful to ensure that the promotional literature and the standard terms of any booking form and contract clearly state that the contract is made for and on behalf of the proprietor of the property, is likely to be of little procedural inconvenience to the consumer who can sue either proprietor or agent within the jurisdiction without difficulty.

---

[159] Thus the effect would be the same as those engaged in split-contracting or off-package sales – see further Chapter 4.
[160] Often incorporated in a non-EU jurisdiction.

- Where the property is abroad or there are concerns as to the ability of the proprietor to satisfy a judgment, the consumer may wish to direct any complaint against the letting agent — and this is the potential source of problems.

The letting agent is almost certainly not an organiser of regulated packages. The only component supplied is the accommodation. Consumers conventionally make their own transportation and other tourist service arrangements. In addition, letting agents are usually careful to claim that their status is no more than that of an agent and that complaints should be directed to the proprietor of the holiday property. The consumer saddled with misdescribed property in France or building works in Greece is then left with what to the consumer is regarded as the unenviable task of seeking a remedy in the courts of the place where the property is situated or where the proprietor is domiciled and he will be lucky if that happens to be England and Wales. The provisions of Regulation 44/2001[161] will apply.

Even where the letting agent insists that it is no more than a go-between, however, the contractual arrangements are always worth close scrutiny. The brochure containing the description of the property or other promotional material may contain an express term to this effect:

> We do not own any of the properties advertised in this brochure neither do we manage any of these properties. The descriptions are those supplied to us by the owners and we have no means of ensuring that all descriptions are accurate in every respect. Your letting agreement is with the owner of the property and your agreement is subject to the terms and conditions of the owner. We act only as agents and complaints should be addressed to the owner.

When faced with this sort of common express term the consumer may still have a remedy against the letting agent. A number of matters should be addressed. It is all very well having such clear terms in brochures, but the agent will be hard pressed to argue that the consumer is bound by such a term unless it is adequately brought to the consumer's attention.

- How prominent is the term describing the contractual status of the owner and the agent?

- How does this prominence compare with other matters advertised in the brochure — that is, would a reasonable consumer have had a reasonable opportunity to identify and consider such a term before entering into an agreement to let a holiday property?

---

[161] See Chapter 6 – but in particular article 22 which gives exclusive jurisdiction in respect of tenancies over property to the courts of the place where the property is situated or in short lest the courts of the defendant's domicile.

- Is the term repeated or drawn to the consumer's attention in the booking form or in some other clear manner before the letting agreement is finalised?

- Do other forms of words or descriptions in the brochure or the contractual documentation imply (strongly or at all) that it is the letting agent who is acting as principal?[162] How do these implications compare with the manner in which the "agency" term has been reproduced or included in the agent's promotional material?

It has been pointed out elsewhere that there may be occasions on which such agency terms (if inadequately publicised or brought to the attention of the consumer) could be avoided by virtue of the Unfair Terms in Consumer Contracts Regulations[163] as representing a form of "hidden" or "unexpected" term.

However, first and foremost, it should be remembered that simply because the letting agent insists that he is nothing more than an *agent* it does not necessarily follow that this is what he *is*. In determining whether a party contracts as principal or agent a court will look at the entire factual matrix and it is not a foregone conclusion that the "agent's" description of himself as enjoying that status will be conclusive. It is submitted that a letting agent will usually have to make his agency position abundantly plain and unambiguous to the consumer in language brooking no room for doubt; not only in brochures but also in forms of agreement and other formal documentation (such as letterheads), to avoid the otherwise understandable conclusion that *despite* the description of his status in the small print, what the "agent" is actually doing is offering to supply the holiday homes described to consumers in circumstances where the "agent" is far better placed to monitor and control the standards of service and safety. This understandable conclusion is only underlined where promotional literature is peppered with references to what "we" (the agent) are offering, supplying or promising. In these circumstances the "agent" is actually a principal and can be sued as such. In addition, consumers may take advantage of the general principles[164] which allow agents to be sued as *agents* in certain limited circumstances. It is not thought likely that the courts would today follow the traditional rule that an agent for a foreign principal could be sued as principal on any contract made in that capacity.

---

[162] Similar to the position of the tour operator in non-regulated package cases such as *Wong Mee Wan v Kwan Kin Travel Services Limited* [1996] 1 WLR 38.

[163] Not because the wording is necessarily ambiguous but because such an agency term may contradict a reasonable consumer's assumption as to his relationship with the agent as a result of other written terms or other things said or done by the agent in promoting the accommodation. See *e.g.* para 1(q) of Sched 2 to the 1999 Regulations, which now apply.

[164] As to which reference must be made to works such as *Bowstead & Reynolds*.

Chapter 10

INTERNATIONAL CONVENTIONS: CARRIAGE OF PASSENGERS AND BAGGAGE

Introduction

This chapter deals with some of the main provisions of the more important international transport conventions in so far as they concern the carriage of passengers and baggage. The carriage of domestic passengers and luggage is also considered in outline. International conventions governing the carriage of passengers and luggage — whether by air, sea or rail — impose similar (but by no means identical) international and independent regimes.

The Montreal Convention

History

An international summit held in Warsaw in 1929 produced a Convention for the unification of certain rules relating to International Carriage by Air. This was amended at a conference at The Hague in 1955 and the revised Convention came into force in 1963. The Warsaw Convention and the Hague Protocol are to be read together and as a whole are referred to as the *Warsaw Convention as amended at The Hague 1955*. The detailed picture is further complicated by the fact that not all parties to the original Convention were parties to the Convention as amended at The Hague. These complications compromised the original intention underlying the original Warsaw Convention which was to provide a uniform set of international rules. The resultant splintering of the liability system generated much confusion. In more recent years international agreements between airlines and rules imposed by the European Union further undermined the value of the Warsaw Convention as a uniform code of rules for international carriage by air. Increasingly, those whose travel took them to or from the USA or the EU, or where the carriage involved stopping in the USA or the EU, found themselves governed by systems of rules grafted onto the principles of the Warsaw Convention. Invariably, these other semi-detached systems of rules were more advantageous to the *passenger* compared with their position under the original and modified Warsaw Convention[1].

Modernisation

An attempt to modernise the Warsaw-Hague Convention was commenced as long ago as 1995. The attempt culminated in the *Montreal Convention* in 1999[2]. The Convention came into force on 4 November 2003, 60 days after ratification by the thirtieth State Party – this being the USA. The State Department said this on ratification:

> The Montreal Convention is the culmination of over four decades of efforts by the United States to eliminate the unconscionably low limits of liability provided under the 1929 Warsaw Convention when passengers are killed or injured in international air carrier accidents.
>
> The significant new benefits of the Montreal Convention include:
>
> • Completely eliminating liability limits for death or injury of passengers.
>
> • Allowing lawsuits in cases of passenger death or injury to be brought in the courts of the passenger's "principal and permanent residence" where the carrier has a commercial presence in that state, which will in almost all cases ensure that U.S. citizens and permanent residents can bring an action in U.S. courts

The Department for Transport was similarly eulogistic about the Convention albeit with a somewhat different emphasis:

> The Montreal Convention introduces a comprehensive and up-to-date set of rules defining and governing the liability of air carriers in relation to passengers, baggage and cargo. Provisions equivalent to some of the provisions of the Convention are already in force by virtue of Council Regulation 2027/97 and earlier amendments to the 1961 Carriage by Air Act.
>
> The main additional benefits implementation of the Convention will bring are as follows:

---

[1] For an introduction to the Warsaw-Hague regime and some of its complexities see the Third Edition of this book.
[2] It is the Montreal Convention 1999 that is referred to in the balance of this section of Chapter 10 as "the Convention".

a. The possibility of an electronic document of carriage (Article 3.2);

b. A liability limit in relation to damage caused by delay to passengers of 4150 SDRs (Article 22.1);

c. A liability limit in relation to the destruction, loss, damage or delay of baggage of 1000 SDRs (Article 22.2);

d. A mechanism for the periodic review of liability limits (Article 24);

e. A new jurisdiction (Article 33);

f. A State Party may require carriers from other States Parties to furnish evidence of adequate insurance (Article 50)."[3]

English law

The Convention has effect in English law by virtue of The Carriage by Air Acts (Implementation of the Montreal Convention 1999) Order 2002 and came into force in the UK and the rest of the European Union on 28 June 2004.[4] The Convention re-establishes a degree of urgently needed uniformity and predictability of rules relating to the international carriage of passengers and baggage, whilst maintaining the core provisions which successfully served the international air transport community for several decades under the Warsaw-Hague regime. The new Convention achieves a degree of modernisation in a number of key areas and protects passengers by introducing a modern two-tier liability system[5] and by facilitating the swift recovery of damages with the intention of avoiding litigation. Schedule 1 of The Carriage by Air Act 1961[6] extends the application of the Convention to the Channel Islands and the Isle of Man.

A New Regime

The Montreal Convention is a new treaty. It is not just a serious of amendments to the old Warsaw-Hague regime. Nonetheless, it is likely that the many domestic and international authorities on the construction of the Warsaw-Hague Convention will be deployed in construing the Montreal Convention where the words deployed in each are comparable.[7]

---

[3] Extracts taken from the US State Department and Department for Transport websites in 2003.
[4] European Union countries jointly ratified the Convention on 29 April 2004.
[5] See further below.
[6] Which still applies for these purposes.
[7] The meaning of "accident" in Article 17 being one of the most important – as to which see further below.

Applicability of the Convention
Article 1

1. This Convention applies to all international carriage of persons, baggage or cargo performed by aircraft for reward. It applies equally to gratuitous carriage by aircraft performed by an air transport undertaking.

2. For the purposes of this Convention, the expression "international carriage" means any carriage in which, according to the agreement between the parties, the place of departure and the place of destination, whether or not there be a break in the carriage or a transhipment, are situated either within the territories of two States Parties, or within the territory of a single State Party if there is an agreed stopping place within the territory of another State, even if that State is not a State Party. Carriage between two points within the territory of a single State Party without an agreed stopping place within the territory of another State is not international carriage for the purposes of this Convention.

3. Carriage to be performed by several successive carriers is deemed, for the purposes of this Convention, to be one undivided carriage if it has been regarded by the parties as a single operation, whether it had been agreed upon under the form of a single contract or of a series of contracts, and it does not lose its international character merely because one contract or a series of contracts is to be performed entirely within the territory of the same State.

International Carriage

It is the agreement for carriage that matters.[8] The agreement will be evidenced by the passenger ticket or tickets and it is the *entire* agreement[9] that counts for the purposes of determining whether the carriage is international. One agreement may involve several tickets and many flights or journeys. One must take the agreed carriage as a whole, rather than merely that limb of the journey during which a mishap has occurred in order to determine whether the incident is governed by the Convention. Some examples of international carriage may illustrate the implications of article 1(2) (where Outer Mongolia is not a High Contracting Party).

1. London—New York;

2. Belfast—London—Paris;

3. Glasgow—Brussels—London;

4. London—Outer Mongolia—London;

---

[8] Article 1(2).
[9] Particularly for return trips.

5. Brussels—Paris—Corsica.

Some illustrations may assist with the effect of article 1 in respect of *"international carriage"*.

(a) In the second example given above, where a passenger suffers an actionable accident on the limb of her journey from Belfast to London causing her to disembark in London, the Convention applies. The carriage was international because according to the *agreement between the parties* the places of departure and destination were situated in the territories of two High Contracting Parties (UK and France).

(b) If, in the third example, the flight is prevented from landing in Brussels and instead is diverted straight to London, the carriage remains international within the meaning of Article 1 because an *agreed* stopping place was within the territory of another High Contracting Party (Belgium) even though the stop-over failed to materialise.

(c) In the fourth example, the Convention applies even though Outer Mongolia is not a High Contracting Party because the place of departure and destination are within the territory of one High Contracting Party with an agreed stop-over in the territory of another country. This fourth example might be referred to for convenience as the *return ticket* principle. It is immaterial that the stop-over may be for the purposes of a fortnight's holiday. However, it should be noted that the return ticket principle does not operate the other way round. Someone working in a territory that is not a High Contracting Party who purchases a return ticket from there to visit family in the United Kingdom will not benefit from the Convention.

(d) The fifth example can be used as a good illustration of how it is the *agreement* between the parties that matters rather than the actual carriage undertaken by the carrier. If a passenger misses the flight in Brussels but takes a train to Paris to pick up the flight to Corsica, the agreement is for international carriage between Brussels and Corsica (two countries) even though the flight undertaken by the passenger involves departure and destination in the same country, so the Convention applies[10].

Some further examples illustrate occasions on which the Convention does not apply.

---

[10] Although it should be noted that current practice amongst most international airlines is that *all* flight coupons must be used. If they are not, the entire journey-ticket is cancelled. In this example, if the passenger is allowed to embark in Paris it would almost certainly in practice be the result of the airline cancelling the original arrangement due to a "no show" in Brussels and agreeing to issue a fresh ticket in Paris.

(a) A flight from Manchester to the Channel Islands (or the Isle of Man, or Gibralter) is not within the meaning of Article 1 because both departure and destination are within the territory of a single High Contracting Party. Although, for example, the Channel Islands are not part of the United Kingdom, the Convention has been applied by Order in Council to Jersey and Guernsey (as well as some other sovereign territories) by which the latter are deemed to be part of *the same* High Contracting Party as the United Kingdom.

(b) A leisure round-trip on Concorde[11] over the Bay of Biscay. Such a day-trip would only be governed by the Convention if, for example, it involved an agreed stop-over for lunch in Bordeaux. However, such an agreed stopping place need not (and probably would not in this example) be specified on the ticket. Many direct (as opposed to non-stop) international flights involve agreed stopping places which do not appear on the ticket.

(d) If the leisure trip on Concorde puts down in Bordeaux due to a technical fault or for some other emergency or unscheduled reason the Convention does not apply. The stopping place was not an *agreed* stopping place. The same principle would apply to an agreement for a flight from Belfast to London which is unexpectedly diverted to Dublin. Where the *agreement* is outside the scope of article 1, the carriage does not become international carriage governed by the Convention simply due to extraneous circumstances which create an international dimension that was not part of the original agreement.

Because it is the character of the *agreement* that matters and not the actual carriage undertaken it is entirely possible that in respect of the same flight some passengers will be covered by the Convention and others will not. In the case of two passengers travelling from Belfast to Brussels via London, one may purchase in Belfast a ticket for the provision of the entire journey. The other may travel to London intending to purchase an onward stand-by ticket to Brussels on arrival in London. The former has agreed for the provision of international carriage within the Convention which covers the complete arrangement, the latter has not and will only be subject to the Convention for the second limb of the journey. Furthermore, it is worth noting that because it is the agreement that matters, it is irrelevant that the carriage may involve one or more changes of aircraft.[12]

---

[11] Now a historical example.
[12] See e.g. *Collins v British Airways Board.*

State Parties

A country becomes a State Party to the Convention when the Convention is ratified by that state. It is possible for a State Party to pull out of the Convention by giving notice of denunciation. The identity of the High Contracting Parties from time to time is certified by Order in Council in the United Kingdom. There is, however, no reason why a carrier cannot incorporate the provisions of the Convention by reference into its contracts of carriage even where the Convention has not been ratified by the carrier's national government. Equally, there is no reason why a carrier should not incorporate the provisions of the Convention into its contracts of carriage[13] where the journey planned by a particular passenger would otherwise fall outside the scope of the Convention – covering for example the passenger travelling from Belfast to Brussels via London (above) who purchases a stand-by ticket in London.

Carriers

There will often be more than one carrier in respect of a passenger's trip, for example, where a passenger changes aircraft at a stop-over. Where this happens each *successive* carrier is:

- liable in respect of that part of the carriage for which it was responsible; or

- liable for those parts of the carriage for which it is *by contract* taken to have assumed responsibility[14] which will occur where the entire carriage is construed as being a *single operation* irrespective of the number of carriers involved.

This may render a carrier liable to a passenger under the Convention in less than obvious circumstances. For example, two carriers each may take responsibility for separate limbs of a journey from Belfast to New York via London. If the carriage is considered to be a *single operation*, then the first carrier will be liable for actionable damage on the Belfast to London limb under the Convention even though on its own this limb of the operation would not be considered international carriage. Whether it *is* a single operation depends on the intention of the parties to the contract. Such arrangements are likely to be considered a single operation in the increasingly common circumstances where two or more airlines have informal partnerships, share facilities[15] or where the two limbs of the journey appear on the same coupon.

---

[13] And many will do so by default simply because the same terms and conditions of carriage would apply across the board to all passengers.
[14] Article 1(3).
[15] Code sharing.

The passenger need not be the person who made the carriage contract with the carrier. There will be many circumstances in which the passenger is carried as a result of arrangements made by others. The rules of agency will often mean that this factor is of little importance, for example, where a tourist is carried on tickets provided by a travel agent or tour operator. However, passengers who travel as a result of contracts made for their benefit between a carrier and, for example, their employer are still being carried as *persons* within the meaning of the Convention.

Persons & Passengers

The Convention[16] applies to *all international carriage of persons (and) baggage.* However, it is important to look at each of the liability provisions in the Convention[17] to determine whether each individual provision applies to "persons" or only to "passengers" – and there is a big difference between the two. One might safely conclude that all passengers are persons, but the reverse is not invariably true. Flight crew will be persons, but not passengers. Thus, persons who are employees of the carrier who are performing duties as part of the crew on board the aircraft are not *passengers.* It remains unclear whether employees of the carrier who are not on board for the purpose of carrying out duties as part of the crew at the time of an incident are *passengers.* In the USA it has been held that such persons are *not* passengers (if they are being paid to fly in order to take up duties later in the flight) for the purposes of the Convention because they are on board as a requirement of their employment.[18] However, employees of third parties who are on board even to undertake employment duties *are* passengers within the meaning of the Convention[19] there being no relationship between them and the carrier[20] other than one of carrier-passenger. There is no apparent reason why carriage for military purposes should not be governed by the Convention but the provision of tickets which would permit the carrier to rely on the compensation limits in article 22 seems unlikely in the case of military flights.

---

[16] Article 1(1).

[17] Article 17 - liability for death or injury being a good example.

[18] *Re Air Crash Off Long Island, 1996* 26 Avi 16.174 – but see the commentary in *Shawcross & Beaumont* VII-663 where the validity of this conclusion is questioned.

[19] *Herd v Clyde Helicopters Limited* [1997] 1 All ER 775 (HL) a case concerning a policeman on surveillance duties in a helicopter.

[20] For example, a relationship of employer-employee or instructor and student.

Aircraft

The term *aircraft* is not defined in the Convention. It will include aeroplanes, gyroplanes, gliders, free and captive balloons, airships and helicopters.[21] The Carriage by Air Act 1961 also applies to carriage by hovercraft by reason of the Hovercraft Act 1968.[22] A paraglider is not an aircraft. In *Disley v Levine*[23] the Court of Appeal concluded that parliament could not reasonably have contemplated applying the Convention to a tandem paragliding training flight where the pilot was under the instruction of a paraglider school and accordingly on a purposive construction of the Convention paragliders were not aircraft not least of all because they are exempt from many of the regulations affecting air transport aircraft.

Reward

Reward is likely to be construed broadly. Usually it will mean a payment in money. It is also likely to include carriage where the only cost to the passenger is some contribution towards expenses and is likely to include cases where the contribution is in "kind" rather than in money.[24]

Gratuitous Carriage

Article 1 includes within its reach *gratuitous carriage by aircraft* performed by an air transport undertaking. An "air transport undertaking" is not defined in the Convention. It is, however, defined in the Air Navigation Order 2002.[25] It means an undertaking whose business includes the undertaking of flights for the purposes of *public* transport of (inter alia) passengers.[26] It would seem that the Convention, therefore, includes within its scope the carriage of all persons whether for reward or gratuitously (e.g. employees) where the carrier is an air transport undertaking so the distinction between fare paying passengers, passengers travelling free and employees (query working crew) has lost its importance under the Montreal Convention.

Documentation

Article 3 - Passengers and baggage

---

[21] All specified in the General Classification of aircraft in Schedule 2 of the Air Navigation Order 2000 SI 1562.
[22] Hovercraft (Civil Liability) Order 1986 – SI 305.
[23] [2001] EWCA Civ 1087.
[24] *Corner v Clayton* [1976] 1 WLR 800.
[25] SI 2000/1562 – 129(1).
[26] See further *Shawcross and Beaumont VII/279.*

1. In respect of carriage of passengers, an individual or collective document of carriage shall be delivered containing:
(a) an indication of the places of departure and destination;
(b) if the places of departure and destination are within the territory of a single State Party, one or more agreed stopping places being within the territory of another State, an indication of at least one such stopping place.

2. Any other means which preserves the information indicated in paragraph 1 may be substituted for the delivery of the document referred to in that paragraph. If any such other means is used, the carrier shall offer to deliver to the passenger a written statement of the information so preserved.

3. The carrier shall deliver to the passenger a baggage identification tag for each piece of checked baggage.

4. The passenger shall be given written notice to the effect that where this Convention is applicable it governs and may limit the liability of carriers in respect of death or injury and for destruction or loss of, or damage to, baggage, and for delay.

5. Non-compliance with the provisions of the foregoing paragraphs shall not affect the existence or the validity of the contract of carriage, which shall, nonetheless, be subject to the rules of this Convention including those relating to limitation of liability.

There are two things worth noting about the new provision relating to travel documentation. The first in that by Article 3(5) non-compliance on the part of the carrier does not invalidate the contract of carriage neither does it deprive the carrier of the right to rely on the rules that limit liability. Although the Convention uses the expression "*rules … relating to limitation of liability*" the purpose of the regulators is also to preserve the limits imposed on the recovery of damages when ticketing errors or omissions occur. The term "*limitation of liability*" will be construed broadly to include the rule son limitation and the rule relating to quantum under the Convention. This represents a change from the Warsaw-Hague regime, no doubt introduced because the limits on both liability and quantum in the Montreal Convention have been liberalised in the passenger's favour.

The second thing worthy of note is that Article 3 permits the use of what has become know as "e-ticketing" [Article 3(2)] even thought that term is not used in the Convention. A significant proportion of "tickets" are now issued on-line.

Jurisdiction

Article 33   (emphasis added)

1. An action for damages must be brought, at the option of the plaintiff, in the territory of one of the States Parties, either before the court of the domicile of the carrier or of its principal place of business, or where it has a place of business through which the contract has been made or before the court at the place of destination.

2. In respect of damage resulting from the *death or injury* of a passenger, an action may be brought before one of the courts mentioned in paragraph 1 of this Article, *or in the territory of a State Party in which at the time of the accident the passenger has his or her principal and permanent residence and to or from which the carrier operates services for the carriage of passengers by air*, either on its own aircraft or on another carrier's aircraft pursuant to a commercial agreement, and in which that carrier conducts its business of carriage of passengers by air from premises leased or owned by the carrier itself or by another carrier with which it has a commercial agreement.

3. For the purposes of paragraph 2,

> (a) "commercial agreement" means an agreement, other than an agency agreement, made between carriers and relating to the provision of their joint services for carriage of passengers by air;
> (b) "principal and permanent residence" means the one fixed and permanent abode of the passenger at the time of the accident. The nationality of the passenger shall not be the determining factor in this regard.

4. Questions of procedure shall be governed by the law of the court seized of the case.

The jurisdictional options provided by Article 33 of the Convention are exhaustive. The claimant[27] has a choice and may commence proceedings:

1. Where the carrier is ordinarily resident.

2. Where the carrier has its principal place of business.

3. Where the carrier has an establishment by which the contract is made.

4. The place of destination as disclosed by the contract.

5. The place of the passenger's permanent residence *provided* the carrier operates air carriage services from *and* has premises in that jurisdiction.

Option 5 (above) is a new option for Plaintiffs and it has all the hallmarks of compromise. It is not enough that the Plaintiff has his permanent and only residence in the jurisdiction of a State Party, it is also necessary that the carrier operates as an airline from that jurisdiction based at premises owned

---

[27] Plaintiff in the language of the Convention.

or leased by the carrier or by another airline with whom the carrier is in partnership.

There had been some debate under Warsaw-Hague as to whether, notwithstanding the choice of jurisdiction provisions,[28] a Plaintiff's choice might nonetheless be subject to arguments of *forum non conveniens*. In *Milar SrL v British Airways*[29] it was argued that where a claimant brought an action pursuant to a choice made within what was then Article 28, it was still open to the court to stay proceedings on the grounds that an alternative jurisdiction had a closer connection and was more suitable than the claimant's choice. It was argued that proceedings that were "brought" within the provisions of Article 28 did not have to be resolved or determined or even *heard* in that forum. The Court of Appeal did not succumb to this submission. Uniformity was best achieved without recourse to *forum conveniens* arguments. Accordingly, the Plaintiff's choice was regarded as unassailable. This firm conclusion was arrived at notwithstanding that as a result of a single major airline disaster a carrier may be subject to litigation in a number of different countries. Such is the price of certainty. There appears to be no obvious reason, however, why parties should not come to a jurisdictional agreement about where an action should be heard provided this is done after the damage complained of has occurred[30]. There is every reason to think that the same result would be achieved under the new jurisdictional provisions of Article 33.

Liability under the Convention

Three forms of liability will be considered.

1. Liability for death or injury.

2. Liability for damage or loss of baggage.

3. Liability occasioned by delay to passengers or baggage.

Death or bodily injury

Article 17 (1)

> The carrier is liable for damage sustained in case of death or bodily injury of a passenger upon condition only that the accident which caused the death or injury took place on board the aircraft or in the course of any of the operations of embarking or disembarking.

---

[28] Under Article 28 of Warsaw-Hague, now article 33.
[29] [1996] QB 702.
[30] *Rothmans of Pall Mall (Overseas) Limited v Saudi Arabian Airlines Corporation* [1980] 1 All ER 359.

Accident

The Convention (as did the Warsaw-Hague Convention) imposes *"a form of strict liability on carriers in respect of accidents causing death, [wounding] or bodily injury to passengers in return for the limitations of liability...."*[31]

The first essential is for the claimant to establish that there has been an *accident*. It is the cause of injury that must be the accident. "Accident" is a term of art under the Convention and it is almost certain that the same approach to the construction of the word "accident" will be taken under Montreal as under the Warsaw-Hague regime. Just because a passenger may suffer an accident in the sense understood colloquially in English does not necessarily mean that the accident is a qualifying accident that falls within Article 17. That the "accident" must cause death or bodily injury demonstrates that the "accident" cannot be the injury itself. One must distinguish cause and effect. So one must distinguish between the *event* which causes an injury and the injury as such.[32] There will be many injuries sustained by passengers which do not result from events which can be properly characterised as accidents within the meaning of Article 17. To be a qualifying accident under Article 17 there must be *an unexpected unusual event or happening that is external to the passenger*.[33] This definition is broad enough to encompass terrorist acts and torts committed by others on board the aircraft[34] including torts involving deliberate misconduct by one passenger on another. *Morris v KLM Royal Dutch Airlines*[35] concerned a male passenger who indecently assaulted a young girl in a neighbouring seat. The Court of Appeal was satisfied that such an incident was an "accident" within the meaning of Article 17[36] and further observed that there was no reason within the Convention to limit compensation to accidents that might be said to have some relationship to the operation of the aircraft. Lord Phillips MR[37] said:

> We have no doubt that the accident that befell the claimant exemplified a special risk inherent in air travel and that, whatever the precise test might be, it constituted an "accident" within the meaning of that word in article 17.

---

[31] Lord Steyn *Morris v KLM Royal Dutch Airlines* [2002] 2 WLR 578.
[32] *"...it is the cause of the injury that must satisfy that definition ["accident"] rather than the occurrence of the injury alone"*. Lord Hope in *Morris v KLM* (above)).
[33] *Saks v Air France* [1985] 470 US 392 a definition that was approved by Lord Phillips MR and subsequently the House of Lords in *Morris v KLM Royal Dutch Airlines* [2002] 2 WLR 578.
[34] *The Deep Vein Thrombosis and Air Travel Group Litigation* – 20 December 2002 – Nelson J. at paragraph 73 and the American cases cited therein and paragraph 226 – [2003] 1 All ER 935 affirmed in the Court of Appeal.
[35] [2001] 3 WLR 351 at 355 to 359.
[36] Of the Warsaw Convention.
[37] At page 359 paragraph 31.

The risk that was exemplified was the risks facing a 15 year old girl travelling in cramped conditions in close proximity to a stranger. It is submitted that another risk exemplified by air travel would include the need to remain in a confined space with other passengers some of whom may be agitated, angry or intoxicated. If this is right there is no reason why "air rage" incidents should not also be classified as *accidents* within the meaning of article 17.

Where the injury arises as the result of a passenger's own internal reaction to the "*usual, normal and expected*" operation of the aircraft, there has not been an accident within the meaning of the Convention. In *Chaudhari v British Airways Plc*[38] the claimant suffered from a left-sided paralysis rendering him partly disabled. In the course a flight to Los Angeles he attempted to leave his seat and being unable to stand up properly he fell injuring his hip. His claim failed in the Court of Appeal. This was not an "*accident*" covered by the Convention. It was an event occasioned by the claimant's own infirmity[39] when combined with the ordinary operation of the aircraft.[40]

Examples of "accidents" include the following:

- an air crash;[41]
- a collision on the runway;
- a collapsing seat-back;
- spilling of hot food or drink;
- food poisoning by airline food;
- falling items from overhead compartments.

The following would not normally be regarded as accidents within the meaning of the Convention:

- deep vein thrombosis caused by in-flight immobility;
- perforated eardrum resulting from normal decompression;

---

[38] [1997] *The Times* 7 May.
[39] Self-inflicted drunkenness leading to injury is not normally regarded as an "accident".
[40] As is likely to be the case in the event of heart attack or stroke and (would have thought) deep vein thrombosis. But see e.g. *Fulop v Malev Hungarian Airlines* 175 F.Supp2(d) 651 (SDNY)(2001) where a refusal to *divert* the aircraft in order to treat a passenger's heart attack was considered an "accident".
[41] *Akehurst v Britannia Airways Limited* [2003] Cardiff County Court 22 May *The Gerona Air Crash* [Unreported].

- seat belt injury sustained as a result of the ordinary process of deceleration on landing;

  - Back injury or swollen legs from prolonged sitting in confined space;

  - Allergic reaction to insecticide spray.[42]

The courts' attempts to draw a clear line between "*an unexpected or unusual event or happening that is external to the passenger*" (a qualifying accident if injury results) and a passenger's own internal reaction to the "*usual, normal and expected*" operation of the aircraft (not a qualifying accident), have led to some arguably curious decisions. Perhaps at this juncture it is vital to bear in mind that neither of the expressions quoted above appears in the language of Article 17 (in either the Montreal or Warsaw versions of the Convention). These words reflect the judicial gloss of the US Supreme Court.[43] It may well be that the introduction of the Montreal Convention justifies a fresh look at the meaning of "accident" and a re-visiting of some of the existing first instance authorities.

Justice O'Connor delivered the Opinion of the Court in *Saks*. It is important to bear in mind that the injury in *Saks* was permanent deafness caused by decompression as the aircraft landed at Los Angeles Airport. There was no hazard and there was no "happening" other than the landing of the aeroplane in the ordinary course of its flight. Justice O'Connor noted that "*An injury is the product of a chain of causes, and we require only that an injured passenger is to prove that some link in the chain of causes was an unusual or unexpected event external to the passenger.*" As a result of the almost statutory force given to the judgment in *Saks*, what Justice O'Connor (it is submitted) thought of as a principle mitigating the restrictive interpretation of constituted a qualifying accident has instead become something of a straight-jacket. Judges commonly look at each link in the chain of causation and ask themselves whether in respect of each whether the link constituted *an unexpected or unusual event.* Thus it has been held at first instance that a passenger who slips on something shiny on the cabin floor, falls and bangs her knee had *not* suffered a qualifying accident.[44] Similarly a lady who broke her leg after slipping on a wet floor in the vicinity of a cabin toilet had no Article 17 "accident" claim.[45] Neither did an elderly gentleman who fell as a result of stepping in a gulley at the edge of an air

---

[42] Examples taken from Nelson J. in *Deep Vein Thrombosis and Air Travel Group Litigation* (above) paragraphs 77 and 78.
[43] *Saks v Air France* (above).
[44] *Williams v Air UK Leisure Ltd.* (Unreported) Liverpool CC 28 April 1997.
[45] *Kedgley v Britannia Airlines* (Unreported) Wandsworth CC 1 September 2004.

bridge whilst in the course of one of the operations of embarking[46] or a lady who slipped on a marble ramp at Cardiff airport made treacherous by rain.[47] The decision in each of these 3 cases offends the ordinary usage of the English language given that it is impossible to describe what happened to each claimant without recourse to the word "accident". The problem facing the courts, however, glued as they are to the words of Justice O'Connor in *Saks,* is the search for an *event* or *happening external to the passenger* that causes the injury which is not the result of the *usual, normal and expected operation of the aircraft.* So, it is said, there is nothing unusual or unexpected about litter on the floor of a cabin, a wet toilet floor;[48] gullies on an air bridge or rain on an access slope at an airport.

But why is it not the case that the "event" external to the passenger in these cases is simply the fall itself?[49] The fall (event) causes the injury (it is plainly not the injury itself). A slip, trip or fall is invariably and by nature unexpected and such things are unusual, forming no part of the normal operations of the aircraft. If the fall is triggered by a hazard the occurrence is not something that could reasonably be described as being the passenger's "internal" reaction to anything. Baroness Hale said[50] "*If I fall over during a flight to New York and break an arm I suspect we would all agree that my broken arm was caused by the accident of my fall – we should not be agonizing too much over whether my fall was an event external to me …*". The primary consideration is the natural meaning of the language used in the Convention "*This definition*[51] *should be flexibly applied after assessment of all the circumstances surrounding a passenger's injuries*".[52] It would appear to be a very simple matter to conclude given the ordinary, plain language of the Convention, that Baroness Hale's broken arm has indeed been the result of a *qualifying* accident.

What appears to have stood in the way of such a simple and logical construction of Article 17 is that Courts have striven to ask in respect of each link in the chain of events whether that link is "unusual". It seems that littering or wet toilet floors are not unusual; these "normal" (albeit unedifying) occurrences create hazards of a type that should then be regarded as typical of the ordinary operation of the aircraft, and when a passenger encounters the hazard and falls, the fall is that passengers internal reaction to

---

[46] *Duffy v Britannia Airlines* (Unreported) Lancaster CC 19 September 2005 – a decision under the Montreal Convention.

[47] *Cannon v My Travel Airways Ltd* (Unreported) Manchester CC 8 July 2005.

[48] But see *Barclay v BA Plc* (below).

[49] Other than the undeniable fact that judges have hitherto been inclined to think otherwise. The search for the "event" has always taken place earlier in the chain of causation.

[50] *Deep Vein Thrombosis& Air Travel Group Litigation* [2005] UKHL 72 para 49.

[51] That is, the definition in *Saks.*

[52] Lord Mance at paragraph 59 *DVT litigation (above).*

the normal situation he was presented with because not everyone fell. This is tortuous indeed but may stem in part from English law's suspicion of strict liability. However, the first instance cases have not been unanimous. A Mrs. McKie[53] slipped on wet steps whilst disembarking at Newcastle airport and sustained bodily injury. Not following the line of authorities (none being binding) already referred to, the judge concluded that the provision of wet steps was the "unexpected event" because the reasonable passenger would legitimately expect an airline to make provision for the predictable contingency of rain at Newcastle, and the resulting incident (the fall leading to injury) was external to the passenger. One might tentatively conclude that *McKie* reflects the better view and is more consistent with the language of the Convention; is not *inconsistent* with the gloss imposed by *Saks* and happily accords with common sense.

It is possible that these problems will shortly be revisited by the Court of Appeal as a result of permission granted by the trial judge in *Barclay v British Airways Plc.*[54] In this case a lady slipped on a floor strip in the cabin of a BA aircraft whilst boarding a flight to London Heathrow and suffered bodily injury. The judge[55] introduced the issue thus:

> The nub of the dispute is that Mrs Barclay says that what she had was obviously an accident, and that there is no binding authority to displace the natural meaning of the word. BA say that she must show that there was something external to her which caused the fall, and that that "something" must be unusual or unexpected. A "mere" fall, with no (unusual) external cause, will not do. At the heart of that is that a fall, simpliciter, is not an event external to the Claimant, thus there needs to be proven a cause for the fall which is external, unusual or unexpected. At first blush, BA's proposition involves adding words to the Convention which are not present.

It is worth quoting the Recorder's decision at some length, not only for its impact on the particular facts as found in that case but because of some observations made in which the judge could be taken to have observed that some of the first instance decisions on which the airline industry customarily rely may be perceived to have excluded from the ambit of article 17 incidents that should more properly be regarded as qualifying "accidents".

> 72. The first question is: was the admitted slipping an event external to the Claimant? On the evidence and the law, I have come to the conclusion that the Claimant has failed to prove that it was. This is, in effect, a case of "mere fall", and I hold on the basis of *Chaudhari* (which in my judgment requires me to come to this conclusion) and the preponderance of opinion in

---

[53] *McKie v Thomas Cook Airlines UK Ltd.* (Unreported) Manchester CC 16 April 2007.
[54] 27 February 2008 Oxford County Court *Lawtel.*
[55] Mr. Recorder West-Knights QC.

the foreign case law, that a mere fall is not an event external to the Claimant for the purposes of determining whether there was an accident within the relevant meaning of the word. I regard the statement of Lord Steyn set out at paragraph 69 above as persuasive in the same direction: he refers to the *cause of the accident*, not merely the event comprising the accident, having to be external. In this case, all that can be said is that a slipping occurred on the plastic strip.

73. That is where it happened, but I cannot find that that is why it happened. It cannot be established that the slipping occurred *by reason of something to do with the strip* (except its passive and "usual" presence). The evidence, such as it is, tends to suggest that the initiation of what led to the slipping had no cause to do with the plastic strip, and indeed no cause outside the Claimant at all. It may have been no more external than the failure of Mr Chaudhari properly to stand up. All that is proved is that the Claimant fell over, albeit that part of the mechanics, place and timing involved the plastic strip - a point at which there was less friction than that afforded by the carpet. Put another way - what was the external event here? None is identified, and none is proved beyond the fall itself, which does not count.

74. And, even if the strip actually caused the slipping, somehow, and was thus a cause external to the Claimant, there was nothing unusual or meaningfully unexpected about that cause.

75. I am satisfied that these conclusions not only accord with the wording of the *Saks* test, but also that there is no warrant for limiting the ambit of the references in *Saks* to "external" to those situations where internal aetiology such as ear-drum or vein damage are being considered. The line has to be drawn somewhere, subject to the sensible application of flexibility to the test, and the one drawn in Saks is of general application - including the concept of externality.

76. On the basis of the US/Australian cases referred to above, and consistent with the "chain of events" statement in *Saks*, and with the underlying ratio of *Chaudhari* in mind, in this case I then look backwards, in terms of causation, for an unusual or unexpected cause for the slipping/loss of balance, to see if there was any *prior* (pre-fall) event passing the Saks test. In this case there is none. Moving about behind, and the fact of, reclined seats and putting a foot on/the presence of a standard and non-defective plastic strip, are the bare components of this "accident" and they do not include, I find, anything which is unusual or sensibly to be described as unexpected.

77. The Claimant's claim therefore fails on the ground that there was no relevant accident. This is a conclusion which remains, to my mind, mildly counter-intuitive, but intuition is not the only or the best guide in this field,

and I remind myself that "accident" in the Convention is, to a degree, a term of art.

78. The analysis has not been assisted by the artificiality engendered by the absence of cogent evidence as to the circumstances of the slipping, a situation caused in part by the preparedness of BA to admit the Claimant's case while not having fully understood it, but in the end that has probably not affected the outcome.

Application of this decision

79. In light of the potentially wide publication of this decision, of which I was reminded by BA after the parties had seen it in draft, I should add two things:

i) decisions of the County Court in England do not bind any court, including the same or any other County Court

ii) if this case, in the absence of clear English authority, is cited, particularly abroad, for the purposes of persuasion it should be recognised that this is a decision on its peculiar facts. In particular, this case is not about tripping over a bag in the aisle or on the wet floor of a lavatory or by reason of other external causes which, in my view, **are** causes which are unexpected from the point of view of the passenger and which **do** pass the *Saks* test. In common with the court in *Singhal v BA, supra,* I consider that the cases deciding to the contrary have, with respect, arguably strayed too far from the ordinary meaning of the word "accident" and may have resulted in a regime which is not "no fault liability" but, in practice in falling-over cases, something closer to "no fault liability".

Death or bodily injury

The meaning to be given to the expression "*bodily injury*" has been a matter of considerable controversy.

In *Morris v KLM Royal Dutch Airlines*[56] the House of Lords concluded that somebody who suffered no physical injuries but suffered mental injury or illness has no claim under article 17. Lord Steyn[57] said:

> "...in two respects mental injury and illness may be relevant. First, there is no reason in principle to exclude from consideration pain and suffering caused by physical injury ... Secondly, I would hold that if a relevant accident causes mental injury or illness which in turn causes adverse physical

---

[56] [2002] 2 WLR 578.
[57] At page 589 paragraph 20.

symptoms, such as strokes, miscarriages or peptic ulcers,[58] the threshold requirement of bodily injury under the Convention is also satisfied."

Lord Hobhouse said:[59]

> ...bodily injury simply and unambiguously means a change in some part or parts of the body of the passenger which is sufficiently serious to be described as an injury. It does not include mere emotional upset such as fear, distress, grief or mental anguish. A psychiatric illness may often be evidence of a bodily injury or the description of a condition which includes bodily injury. But the passenger must be prepared to prove this, not just prove a psychiatric illness without evidence of its significance for the existence of a bodily injury.

Thus it might be thought that the prospects for any claimant pursuing damages for psychiatric illness under article 17 would be bleak. *Bodily injury* means *physical* injury.[60] Things are not yet that clear-cut. In an American case[61] a passenger suffered from post traumatic stress disorder as a result of an emergency landing and made a claim under article 17. Whilst the court recognised that there could be no claim for "fright" it concluded that because there was medical evidence to the effect that the post traumatic stress disorder had caused brain injury, the claimant had indeed sustained a *bodily injury* to her brain. The judge concluded that the issue of whether there was *bodily injury* or not was essentially a medical not a legal issue and the medical issue in the instant case had to be resolved in the claimant's favour.

Lord Steyn in *Morris*[62] thought that this conclusion should not be followed, however, in the extract from the speech of Lord Hobhouse (above) there may be thought to be a hint of support for the American judge's approach, which is to some extent mirrored in observations made in short speeches by Lords Nicholls and Mackay[63]. Perhaps proof of *bodily injury* to the brain that manifests itself in psychiatric symptoms is only a matter of medical evidence after all.

The location of the accident

The location of the accident causing the damage is also of great importance. To be actionable under the Convention the accident must occur:

- on board the aircraft; or

---

[58] As was the case in the concurrent appeal of *King v Bristow Helicopters Limited* [2002] 2 WLR 578.
[59] At page 623 paragraph 143.
[60] Article 17.1 of the Montreal Convention 1999 (not yet in force) drops references to "wounding" but retains the expression "bodily injury".
[61] *Weaver v Delta Airlines Inc.* 56 F Supp 2d 1190.
[62] See above.
[63] pages 581 and 582.

- in the course of any of the operations of embarking or disembarking.

In 1929 the scope of the Convention may have been tolerably clear to the regulators. Even today, leaving aside bizarre incidents, it should be reasonably plain where an accident has occurred "*on board*" the aircraft. The operations of embarking and disembarking are more problematical and have led to an immense volume of case law — particularly in the USA. In 1929 when aircraft and airports were tiny by modern standards, and the passengers embarked and disembarked via stairways that were little more than sturdy stepladders, the process of embarking or disembarking may have been relatively easy to identify. Even in 1929, the drafters of the Convention must have had in mind some notional line at which point embarking commences and disembarking stops. If they did they left it out of the Convention. In the modern era the matter has become more opaque. Different jurisdictions have come up with different answers to the question: where does embarking begin and disembarking end? Accordingly, it is quite feasible that a passenger may be regarded as embarking in one jurisdiction but not in another. Some jurisdictions regard the *control* exercised by a carrier at a given point in the airport procedures as a compelling factor in deciding where the process of embarkation begins. Other jurisdictions have devised multi-faceted tests taking into account not only the control exercised by the carrier, but the location of the incident together with the functions being undertaken by carrier and passenger at the time the incident occurs. However, physical location is usually paramount.

The Court of Appeal has taken a pragmatic view of the difficulties presented by the concepts of embarkation and disembarkation at modern airports. In *Adatia v Air Canada*[64] the claimant and her infirm mother arrived at Heathrow. The airline's ground agent made provision for a wheelchair for the claimant's mother, but as the airline's representative pushed the wheelchair along a moving walkway in the terminal building, the wheels became stuck in the jaws at the point where the walkway joined the ordinary floor. The claimant herself, propelled by the movement of the walkway became trapped between the wheelchair and the edge of the walkway and sustained injury. Was the claimant in the course of one of the operations of disembarking at the time of the accident? The Court of Appeal thought not, but refused to succumb to the temptation to lay down an all-encompassing test as to when the disembarkation ended. Reference was made to the tests developed in other jurisdictions, but these tests were not adopted. In this instance the Court concluded that the claimant had reached a point of safety in the terminal building and could not be regarded as being in the course of one of the operations of disembarking.

---

[64] [1992] 2 S&BAvi VII/63.

Whether a passenger is in the course of one of the operations of embarking or disembarking is essentially a matter of fact and degree depending on the circumstances of passengers, procedures and airport geography in individual cases. In all the circumstances can it be said that the passenger is at the time of the accident engaged in an operation of embarking or disembarking?

The issue of embarkation was dealt with equally pragmatically by Morison J. in *Philips v Air New Zealand Limited.*[65] This was a case where Dr. Phillips ("P") claimed damages against the defendant airline for personal injuries said to have been sustained as a result of an accident in March 1997 at Fiji international airport. P had asked for assistance from the airline in advance of her arrival at the airport, since she could not carry heavy baggage. A wheelchair and helper, "T", were provided. T was employed by Air Terminal Services (Fiji) Ltd ("ATS") with which the airline had a ground handling agreement. After check-in T pushed the wheelchair in which P was sitting onto a moving escalator in order to take P to the departure area on the first floor. The chair fell back and P sustained an injury. The proceedings were commenced after expiry of the two-year period for bringing a claim under the Convention. Just like Mrs. Adatia, Dr. Phillips needed to demonstrate that the Convention did not apply otherwise her claim would be time-barred. Morison J's. conclusions can be summarised as follows:

(1) Before a person could be said to be in the course of any of the processes of embarkation there must be a *particular identified* aircraft and flight.

(2) There may be a number of 'operations' of embarkation. The word 'operations' is plural. Article 17 cannot be confined in its application to the process of actually climbing over the threshold of the aircraft at the point of embarkation or walking up the steps to the aircraft if the aircraft is loaded from the ground.

(3) The question of article 17's application is best answered by reference to three criteria: *where*, geographically, did the accident occur; *what* was the passenger doing at the relevant time; *was* the passenger under the carrier's control? If the accident happened in the terminal building or otherwise on the airport premises, was the location of the accident a place where the injured party was obliged to be in the process of embarkation?

He concluded:

> "In this case, the accident happened at a time when a specific flight had

---

[65] [2002] EWHC 800.

been called and during a necessary process towards embarkation. Dr Phillips was going upstairs because the airline had called passengers to go to the embarkation point, namely the departure gates. Standing back, it seems to me that going to the embarkation gate after the flight has been called is one of the several processes which passengers must perform in order to embark on their flight. The processes of embarkation will, I think, include the checking-in; the passage through security and passport control and the 'departure routine'; that is, going to the gate to be cleared for embarkation and proceeding thereafter to embark. In the most general sense, these activities are required by the airline of its passengers. In a perfect world, one would arrive at an airport or aerodrome, as it was when the Convention was agreed, and go straight on board. The fact that air travel is bedevilled by security checks and waiting time does not alter the gist of what I think the draftsmen of the Convention intended to be covered by article 17. If a passenger is required to take a particular step or go to a particular place for boarding then he or she is engaged in a process of embarkation. That means, I think, that during the many minutes a passenger spends in the public or private lounges or goes shopping or eats or drinks in restaurants or cafés, then he or she could not be said to be in the process of embarkation. At this stage the passenger is waiting, more or less reluctantly. But he or she may have already been through a process of embarkation [e.g. security, boarding card check and passport control] and will inevitably have to go through other such processes, such as going to the gate and getting on the aircraft. The process of embarkation does not have to be a continuous one. In my judgment this makes good sense of the realities of modern air travel. For some of the time a passenger is able to do what he or she wants; for some of the time he or she has to comply with directions and requirements imposed by the carrier. Accordingly, I am satisfied that Dr Phillips was injured in an accident which occurred in the course of one of the processes of embarkation."

Death or Injury Damages

Article 21

1. For damages arising under paragraph 1 of Article 17 not exceeding 100,000 Special Drawing Rights for each passenger, the carrier shall not be able to exclude or limit its liability.

2. The carrier shall not be liable for damages arising under paragraph 1 of Article 17 to the extent that they exceed for each passenger 100,000 Special Drawing Rights if the carrier proves that:

(a) such damage was not due to the negligence or other wrongful act or omission of the carrier or its servants or agents; or

(b) such damage was solely due to the negligence or other wrongful act or omission of a third party.

The damages limitations imposed by Article 21 are a model of clarity. The two-tier system is manifest. *Up to* 100,000 SDRs the carrier is not entitled to limit its liability at all. Once the pre-conditions of Article 17(1) are satisfied liability up to the stated figure follows automatically. Over and above that figure a fault regime is imposed, but with the burden of proving the *absence of fault* lying on the carrier. Damages within these limits for death and injury will be calculated in accordance with the law of the place where the action is being heard. Where a claim is made and is valued at more than 100,000 SDRs but the carrier demonstrates that there was no fault or the incident was caused by the negligence of a third party, the claimant will be able to recover the "no fault" damages of 100,000 SDRs even though the balance of the claim over and above that figure would have to be abandoned or dismissed.

The Special Drawing Right ["SDR"] is a notional unit based on a basket of international currencies and its value in relation to national currencies fluctuates daily.[66] The value of the SDR is usually about £0.80p. The Carriage by Air (Sterling Equivalents) Order 1999[67] makes provision for the automatic valuation of damages limits measured by SDRs but does so by reference to a unit called the Poincaré Franc (worth approximately one fifteenth of an SDR).

It was the miserably low level of damages the airlines exchanged for their strict liabilities that so angered American Governments over many decades and was responsible more than anything else for the splintering of the old Warsaw regime by special treaty arrangements involving the USA and ultimately the European Union. To some extent, therefore, the damages provisions in Article 21 might be regarded as the trigger to reunification bringing many countries back within a unified Convention regime – which after all has been the stated purpose of the international air carriage conventions since 1929.

Loss of or damage to baggage

Article 17 (2) & (3)

> 2. The carrier is liable for damage sustained in case of destruction or loss of, or of damage to, checked baggage upon condition only that the event which caused the destruction, loss or damage took place on board the aircraft or during any period within which the checked baggage was in the charge of the carrier. However, the carrier is not liable if and to the extent that the damage resulted from the inherent defect, quality or vice of the baggage. In

---

[66] Reference to the UK section of the web site of the International Monetary Fund gives the daily rates.
[67] SI 2881.

the case of unchecked baggage, including personal items, the carrier is liable if the damage resulted from its fault or that of its servants or agents.

3. If the carrier admits the loss of the checked baggage, or if the checked baggage has not arrived at the expiration of twenty-one days after the date on which it ought to have arrived, the passenger is entitled to enforce against the carrier the rights which flow from the contract of carriage.

Provided the damage caused to checked baggage is not the result of some inherent defect in the baggage itself, the carrier is liable for any damage caused to the baggage whilst it is in the carrier's "charge". The responsibility of the carrier for checked baggage is similar to the responsibilities of a bailee. It is for the passenger to prove that there has been some loss or damage and that such loss or damage occurred whilst the baggage was in the carrier's charge. The position is different for hand baggage and personal items taken into the cabin. Damaged *hand* baggage and personal items are only the responsibility of the carrier if the damage is caused by the *fault* of the carrier or its servants or agents acting in the course of their employment. In the case of hand baggage, therefore, it is for the Claimant to prove fault. This means negligence. The difference between checked baggage and hand baggage is because the latter remains largely in the keeping and control of the passenger and the passenger can be expected to look after it.

As can be seen below there are upper limits on the amount of damages that can be recovered in the case of either total loss or damage to baggage unless the passenger makes a special declaration of value and pays a premium in respect of the extra value claimed. The carrier's right to rely on the compensation limits set out below does not apply if it is proved by the passenger that the loss or damage was caused deliberately or recklessly (*and* with knowledge that damage would probably result) by the carrier of a servant or agent acting in the scope of their employment. Article 22(6) permits the recovery of costs, expenses of litigation (if different from costs) and interest *in addition* to the compensation specified if the law of the place where the action is taken permits such recovery. English law plainly so permits and one would expect the English courts to adopt the normal rules of costs recovery applicable to other forms of litigation under the Civil Procedure Rules 1998 subject to an exception as set out below.

The costs provisions of Article 22(6) are qualified by provisions that at first take on the appearance similar to the English procedural rules under CPR Part 36. The Claimant should not recover costs if the amount awarded does not exceed the sum which the carrier has offered in writing to the Claimant within a period of six months from the date of the occurrence causing the damage, or (6 months) before the commencement of the action, if that is later. The similarity with CPR Part 36 is deceptive. There is no express provision in the Convention allowing for the recovery of costs from the *Claimant* by the carrier in the event that the Claimant fails to do better than the written offer.

Damages Limits

Article 22 (2), (5) & (6)

> 2. In the carriage of baggage, the liability of the carrier in the case of destruction, loss, damage or delay is limited to 1,000 Special Drawing Rights for each passenger unless the passenger has made, at the time when the checked baggage was handed over to the carrier, a special declaration of interest in delivery at destination and has paid a supplementary sum if the case so requires. In that case the carrier will be liable to pay a sum not exceeding the declared sum, unless it proves that the sum is greater than the passenger's actual interest in delivery at destination.

> 5. The foregoing provisions of paragraphs 1[68] and 2 of this Article shall not apply if it is proved that the damage resulted from an act or omission of the carrier, its servants or agents, done with intent to cause damage or recklessly and with knowledge that damage would probably result; provided that, in the case of such act or omission of a servant or agent, it is also proved that such servant or agent was acting within the scope of its employment.

> 6. The limits prescribed in Article 21 and in this Article shall not prevent the court from awarding, in accordance with its own law, in addition, the whole or part of the court costs and of the other expenses of the litigation incurred by the plaintiff, including interest. The foregoing provision shall not apply if the amount of the damages awarded, excluding court costs and other expenses of the litigation, does not exceed the sum which the carrier has offered in writing to the plaintiff within a period of six months from the date of the occurrence causing the damage, or before the commencement of the action, if that is later.

Stipulation on limits

Article 25

> A carrier may stipulate that the contract of carriage shall be subject to higher limits of liability than those provided for in this Convention or to no limits of liability whatsoever.

---

[68] Delay – see below.

It is not immediately apparent why a carrier would want to make use of this permissive Article.

Delay to passengers or baggage

Article 19

> The carrier is liable for damage occasioned by delay in the carriage by air of passengers, baggage or cargo. Nevertheless, the carrier shall not be liable for damage occasioned by delay if it proves that it and its servants and agents took all measures that could reasonably be required to avoid the damage or that it was impossible for it or them to take such measures.

Limits of liability in relation to delay [and] baggage
Article 22 (1)

> In the case of damage caused by delay as specified in Article 19 in the carriage of persons, the liability of the carrier for each passenger is limited to 4,150 Special Drawing Rights.

The implementation of Article 19 is not as straightforward as its apparently clear wording suggests and this remains as true under the Montreal Convention as it was under the Warsaw-Hague regime. Although article 19 is not so expressly limited, it is highly unlikely that damage caused to a business due to the delayed arrival of an executive passenger, or his indisposition caused by diverted luggage, or any damage to a third party unconnected with the provision of carriage by air, would be recoverable. If it was recoverable in principle, the financial limitations of recovery would rarely make such a commercial claim worth the candle.

Article 19 is silent as to what constitutes a delay. *De minimis* delays are unlikely to be included, but subject to the *de minimis* principle, all delays appear to be covered. However, many relatively short and even medium term delays (be they to passengers or their baggage) are unlikely to occasion any or much loss or damage. Misdirected luggage, however, could result in a valid claim under the Convention subject to the financial restrictions on recovery, but the sums involved are only likely to involve enough to "tide over" the passenger until such time as the luggage is retrieved. It is probably the financial restrictions on recovery which have acted as a practical bar to extensive litigation under article 19 in this country as far as passengers and baggage are concerned.

The central issue under article 19 remains largely unresolved. *What is a delay and how is it to be measured?* Once that question is answered, how are damages to be calculated or the delay valued?

At first glance it might be thought that any departure from the published timetable or the arrival time written on the ticket could constitute a "delay". However, this logical conclusion assumes that the carrier has a contractual responsibility to stick to the timetable, which will not be the case unless time is of the essence of the carriage contract. Time, however, is *not* of the essence — at least not in so far as the carrier is able to convey the passenger and baggage to the agreed destination within a reasonable time taking into account all the circumstances. This test injects a degree of fluidity into the carriage contract that appals many passengers with connecting flights or other dependent obligations. Carriers are usually careful to include in their standard conditions (which often have the approval of IATA) an express provision to the effect that the timetable is not guaranteed and can be changed without notice. Standard ticketing conditions also invariably contain an express provision that responsibility for connecting flights (the commonest form of consequential loss) is not accepted. These parts of the standard conditions are invariably reproduced on the ticket coupons. The contractual obligation that is assumed by carriers is usually only to carry the passenger and baggage with *reasonable dispatch* to the agreed destination. Not even the route is guaranteed. To the extent that the carrier has behaved *reasonably* in terms of attempting to meet its timetable and in any dealings with intervening emergencies and factors such as weather conditions or other *force majeure* events, it is submitted that the carrier will not have offended against the provisions of article 19. However, not every flight that is *late* has been *delayed* within the meaning of article 19.[69] Hence the test in English law: has the carrier complied with its contractual obligation to carry with reasonable dispatch, taking into account all the circumstances? If the carrier has acted reasonably in all the circumstances, the flight may well be late — even very late — but carriage will not have been "delayed". Where a delay has occurred an attempt by the carrier to rely on the "*all necessary measures*" defence will almost certainly involve proof by the carrier that it has good engineering facilities; reasonable emergency procedures for substituting aircraft or even providing an alternative carrier; re-routing flights; offering alternative transport services; accommodation and meals.

One final problem presented by article 19 is this. Does the delay have to arise whilst the passenger or the baggage is airborne? Article 19 only covers *damage occasioned by delay in the carriage by air* not other types of delay. In the absence of compelling authority one way or the other, it is tentatively suggested that this provision should be construed purposively, as if article 19 read "damage occasioned by delay in *the performance of the contract for* the

---

[69] Delay depends on what the carrier has contractually agreed to do – see the discussion on Definitions Clauses in contracts in Chapter 5.

carriage by air".[70] If a narrower interpretation were to be employed, all delays occasioned other than whilst the passenger was airborne (or in the course of embarkation or disembarkation) would be excluded. The broader interpretation suggested here allows a passenger to deploy article 19 in respect of delays that arise as a result of events whilst still at the airport, for example, delay due to late in-coming aircraft, overbooking, technical breakdown, denied boarding or security alerts and this broader, purposive construction still leaves plenty of scope for the carrier to rely on the statutory defence that all necessary measures have been taken to avoid resulting damage; and ample room for the carrier to argue that the lateness is not a *delay* because in all the circumstances they have acted properly in getting the passenger to the agreed destination with reasonable dispatch.

Limitation of Actions[71]

Article 35

> 1. The right to damages shall be extinguished if an action is not brought within a period of two years, reckoned from the date of arrival at the destination, or from the date on which the aircraft ought to have arrived, or from the date on which the carriage stopped.
>
> 2. The method of calculating that period shall be determined by the law of the court seized of the case.

The limitation period for any claim (including a claim for death or injury) is 2 years. Any claim is extinguished after the expiry of 2 years from the date the flight arrived or should have arrived at its destination[72]. The period is absolute. There is no latitude given for minors or persons suffering under any disability, neither is there any opportunity to invite a court to disapply the limitation period under, for example, section 33 of the Limitation Act 1980 or due (one assumes) to fraud or concealment.[73] The method of calculating the period of limitation is determined in England by English law. Thus, time

---

[70] Some measure of support for this may be sought from the judgment of Morison J. in *Phillips v Air New Zealand International Limited* (above) in which it was made clear that the contract of carriage begins and the Convention applies from the point where the passenger checks-in. But what if the carrier prevents passengers checking-in due to a back-log in the timetable?

[71] See also Article 31 – time bars for making written complaints in the event of loss, damage or delay to baggage.

[72] Given the meaning of international carriage discussed at the beginning of this chapter the destination could be taken as the final destination on the ticketing arrangements i.e. the destination of the return journey or final journey on the ticket coupons issued. It would be safest where possible, however, to calculate the 2 year period from the date the flight was supposed to land at the destination intended at the conclusion of that limb of journey during which the incident giving rise to the claim occurs.

[73] *Joanne Elizabeth Higham v Stena Sealink Ltd* (1996) – unreported – lawtel – applying the Athens Convention on carriage by sea.

expires at midnight on the day that is the second anniversary of the incident giving rise to the claim.[74] If that day is a day on which the court offices are closed the period is extended until midnight on the next day on which the court offices are open.[75]

So it is that it will often be the carrier who is endeavouring to establish that a claim is one to which the Convention applies. Even though the application of the Convention might result in the carrier being strictly liable to the passenger or may result in the reversal of the burden of proof to the carrier's disadvantage, the Convention's application also brings with it the tighter limitation period, which if missed by the Claimant, puts an end to any claim once and for all.

The cases of *Adatia* and *Phillips*[76] are good examples illustrating the point. In each case the carrier wanted to demonstrate that the accident in question occurred during the course of one of the operations of embarking or disembarking. It was the airline in *Adatia* that sought to establish that the claimant was disembarking at the time of her accident on a travelator in the airport terminal. Similarly in *Phillips* it was the airline that sought to establish that the Convention applied in order that the claim would be time-barred in circumstances where the Claimant had been injured as a result of clumsy handling in her wheelchair by a ground handling assistant on an escalator in the terminal building.

Exclusivity of Convention

Article 29 - Basis of claims

> In the carriage of passengers, baggage and cargo, any action for damages, however founded, whether under this Convention or in contract or in tort or otherwise, can only be brought subject to the conditions and such limits of liability as are set out in this Convention without prejudice to the question as to who are the persons who have the right to bring suit and what are their respective rights. In any such action, punitive, exemplary or any other non-compensatory damages shall not be recoverable.

Article 26 - Invalidity of contractual provisions

> Any provision tending to relieve the carrier of liability or to fix a lower limit than that which is laid down in this Convention shall be null and void, but

---

[74] *Marren v Dawson Bentley & Co.* [1961] 2 QB 135 – by analogy with the 3 year personal injury limitation period under section 11 of the Limitation Act 1980.
[75] *Pritam Kaur v Russell* [1973] QB 336.
[76] See the section earlier in this chapter on *Location of the accident*

the nullity of any such provision does not involve the nullity of the whole contract, which shall remain subject to the provisions of this Convention.

The wording of the exclusivity provision in the Convention is different from that found under the Warsaw-Hague regime. Article 29 is relaxed about the possibility of a Claimant bringing a claim that is technically founded in contract or tort as distinct from relying on the *Convention* as creating the cause of action. However, where a contractual or tortious cause of action is adopted Article 29 ensures that the framework, procedures and limitations imposed by the Convention should be superimposed onto whatever that cause of action might be.

The exclusivity of the present Convention is still best illustrated by reference to *Sidhu v British Airways*[77] where exclusivity was determined conclusively by the House of Lords in the context of the Warsaw-Hague regime. Members of the Sidhu family were en route from Heathrow to Kuala Lumpur via Kuwait at the beginning of August 1990. The aircraft landed in Kuwait after the Iraqi invasion had commenced, and whilst passengers were waiting in a transit lounge the Iraqi army took over the airport. It was common ground that:

- there had not been an "*accident*" within the meaning of Article 17 of the Convention;

- the passengers were not on board the aircraft or in the course of one of the operations of embarking or disembarking;

- the psychological injuries suffered by members of the Sidhu family "probably" did not qualify as bodily injuries within the meaning of Article 17 (although other physical injuries were alleged);

- however, the passengers by dint of the fact that they were still en route to their ultimate destination in the transit lounge *were* in the course of "international carriage".

It was also conceded in *Sidhu* that if the claims *had* fallen within the provisions of article 17, no residual remedy at common law would have arisen. Therefore, the issue was whether such a residual common law remedy existed where the circumstances giving rise to the damage arose in the course of international carriage, but were *not* covered by the remedies in the Convention; because there had been no "accident" or the injuries did not qualify as "bodily injury". The claimants brought their action entirely at common law alleging negligence against the airline for allowing the aircraft to land in Kuwait at a time of expected conflict and danger, and the action was commenced after the two-year period allowed by the Warsaw Convention. The claimants' argument was

---

[77] [1997] AC 430.

based on the fundamental common law principle that where there is a wrong, there should be a remedy, and that as the claim was not covered by the provisions of then Convention, the residual remedies of the common law could be deployed to assist.

Lord Hope, speaking for the House of Lords, disagreed. He said of the Warsaw Convention:[78]

> It was not designed to provide remedies against the carrier to enable all losses to be compensated. It was designed instead to define those situations in which compensation was to be available. So it set out the limits of liability and the conditions under which claims to establish that liability, if disputed, were to be made. A balance was struck in the interests of certainty and uniformity.
>
> The conclusion must be therefore that any remedy which is excluded by the Convention, as the set of uniform rules does not provide for it. The domestic courts are not free to provide a remedy according to their own law, because to do this would be to undermine the Convention. It would lead to the setting alongside the Convention of an entirely different set of rules which would distort the operation of the whole scheme.
>
> I see no escape from the conclusion that, where the Convention has not provided a remedy, no remedy is available.

This will remain the position under the provisions of the Montreal Convention.

Carriers' defences

The defences available to any claim brought by a passenger offered to a carrier under the Montreal Convention have been reconfigured. It is no longer possible for a carrier to be exonerated from liability if it is able to prove that it took *all necessary measures*[79] or the *impossibility*[80] of taking such measures to avoid the damage.[81] Instead, the two-tier liability regime

---

[78] At page 453G.

[79] In *Chisholm v British European Airway* [1963] 1 LlLR 626 it was held that all *necessary* measures meant in effect all *reasonable* measures. Thus, where a passenger had ignored illuminated set-belt signs, public address announcements and warnings by the cabin crew, to leave her seat and walk around the cabin, it was held that all reasonable measures had been taken and the airline was exonerated.

[80] When was it *impossible* to take measures that would otherwise be regarded as necessary in the eyes of a reasonable man? One example might be *Barboni v Cie Air France* [1982] 1 S&B Av R VII/89 in which a passenger was injured using an escape chute in the course of an emergency evacuation. The airline was absolved on the grounds that it was impossible to take measures that would have avoided the injury.

[81] Such was the position under the original Warsaw Convention, but the usefulness of the defence was eroded by the proliferation of special contracts and treaties by which carriers in various jurisdictions were constrained not to rely on it.

in respect of liability for death or bodily injury contains the basis of a carrier's partial defence. Where a claim is for more than or is likely to exceed 100,000 SDRs, the carrier can escape liability if it proves[82] (the burden being on the carrier) that the damage *(a) was not due to the negligence or other wrongful act or omission of the carrier or its servants or agents; or (b) was solely due to the negligence or other wrongful act or omission of a third party.* So it is that the defence forms part of the definition of and limits applicable to the carrier's liability.

A second line of defence (causation and contributory negligence) is provided by Article 20. It will be noted that the concept of 100% contributory negligence is honoured in this provision.

A third line of defence is based on the provisions requiring the passengers to make timely complaints in the vent of loss, damage or delay to baggage.

Article 20 - Exoneration

> If the carrier proves that the damage was caused or contributed to by the negligence or other wrongful act or omission of the person claiming compensation, or the person from whom he or she derives his or her rights, the carrier shall be wholly or partly exonerated from its liability to the claimant to the extent that such negligence or wrongful act or omission caused or contributed to the damage. When by reason of death or injury of a passenger compensation is claimed by a person other than the passenger, the carrier shall likewise be wholly or partly exonerated from its liability to the extent that it proves that the damage was caused or contributed to by the negligence or other wrongful act or omission of that passenger. This Article applies to all the liability provisions in this Convention, including paragraph 1 of Article 21.

Even though Article 21 states that a carrier is not permitted to exclude or limit its liability up to 100,000 SDRs for death or bodily injury, Article 20 makes it clear that this prohibition does *not* apply to issues of contributory negligence. The Law Reform (Contributory Negligence) Act 1945 will be imported by English courts into the allocation of fault under Article 20 when such allocation is required. An English court will apply the same principles of fault allocation to accidents in the air as it would have done in respect of accidents on the roads. From what sum would the contributory negligence deduction to be applied? If a passenger is *prima facie* entitled to the maximum "no fault" sum allowable (100,000 SDRs) under Article 21, will the contributory deduction apply to that sum? Alternatively, would the deduction be applied to the total notional value of damage sustained by the

---

[82] Article 21.

passenger (let's say 200,000 SDRs), following which deduction the passenger would be entitled to recover up to the Convention maximum? That is, if after the deduction from the total notional value of the claim the passenger is still notionally left with the maximum (or more) allowed under the Convention, would the passenger still get 100,000 SDRs even though found, say, 50% contributorily negligent? Because the language of the Convention is "exoneration" in respect of liability for damages, it is submitted that the calculation of damages occurs before any deduction for contributory negligence. That is to say if the total notional liability exceeds the Convention maximum, the deduction for contribution is undertaken from the notional total that would have been awarded but for the Convention maximum. Once the deduction for contribution has taken place one then has to see if the Convention maximum is exceeded. If it is then the maximum obviously caps the payment due to the passenger. Theoretically, therefore, it may well be the case that in some cases, the passenger recovers the Convention maximum even though the passenger has been held to be 50% liable due to his own contributory negligence.[83]

Article 31 - Timely notice of complaints

> 1. Receipt by the person entitled to delivery of checked baggage or cargo without complaint is prima facie evidence that the same has been delivered in good condition and in accordance with the document of carriage or with the record preserved by the other means referred to in paragraph 2 of Article 3 and paragraph 2 of Article 4.
>
> 2. In the case of damage, the person entitled to delivery must complain to the carrier forthwith after the discovery of the damage, and, at the latest, within seven days from the date of receipt in the case of checked baggage... . In the case of delay, the complaint must be made at the latest within twenty-one days from the date on which the baggage or cargo have been placed at his or her disposal.
>
> 3. Every complaint must be made in writing and given or dispatched within the times aforesaid.
>
> 4. If no complaint is made within the times aforesaid, no action shall lie against the carrier, save in the case of fraud on its part.

Receipt of baggage without a complaint being made *forthwith* (and in any event within 7 days of receipt) is good evidence that there was nothing wrong with it – but only *prima facie evidence*. The presumption is plainly rebuttable on receipt provided a written complaint is lodged with the carrier within 7 days of receipt. Failure to lodge a complaint within 7 days is a bar to recovery of damages for any loss or damage to baggage. In the case of delay, the bar is put at 21 days. Time is measured from when the complaint

---

[83] It is understood that a similar logic applies in the determination of the amount payable in respect of compensation for Unfair Dismissal.

is dispatched. The time bars are absolute unless fraud is proved against the carrier and burden of proving fraud rests with the passenger.

Recklessness

Where the claim for damages arises out of a claim for loss or damage to baggage or delay, the carrier loses the right to rely on the fiscal limitations imposed by the Convention:

> if it is proved that the damage resulted from an act or omission of the carrier, its servants or agents, done with intent to cause damage or recklessly and with knowledge that damage would probably result; provided that, in the case of such act or omission of a servant or agent, it is also proved that such servant or agent was acting within the scope of its employment. **[Article 22(5)]**

Recklessness under Article 22[84] appears to *exclude* "thoughtless" recklessness, of the type where a person gives no thought to the consequences of an act presenting a real risk of harm which a reasonable person would have recognised and paid heed to.

The Warsaw test was applied by the Court of Appeal in *Goldman v Thai Airways.*[85] A passenger was injured as a result of being thrown in his seat by clear air turbulence. The pilot had not turned on the seat-belt signs despite the fact that turbulence was forecast. The Court of Appeal considered there to be inadequate evidence to justify the trial judge's conclusion that the pilot had been reckless and that there was *no* evidence that the pilot had knowledge that damage would probably result from the failure to light the seat-belt signs. The pilot was entitled to exercise his discretion as to the use of warning lights; he had not encountered any pre-turbulent air disturbances and had no indication of the likely severity of the turbulence which affected the aircraft and about which he probably did know. The passenger's damages were thus limited to the amount then allowed under Article 22 of the Convention and the limitation was not lifted.

In *Gurtner v Beaton*[86] the Court of Appeal upheld the trial judge's finding that it was necessary in the context of Warsaw Article 25 for the passenger to prove that the party criticised had a "*subjective awareness*" that damage would probably result — however unreasonable the *lack* of awareness might be. The importance of the subjective element was confirmed by the Court of Appeal in *Nugent v Michael Goss Aviation Limited*[87] a case of a fatal

---

[84] As was the case under the Warsaw-Hague regime.
[85] [1983] 1 WLR 1186.
[86] [1993] Lloyd's LR 369.
[87] [2000] Lloyds LR 222.

helicopter crash recognising that the threshold for a claimant to cross in an effort to prove recklessness was a high one.

Some illustrations of cases where reckless conduct under the Warsaw Convention has been found are as follows (there being no obvious reason why the findings would not be the same under the Montreal Convention):

- a helicopter pilot landing on a car park without detailed prior inspection;

- a light aircraft pilot at low altitude and speed waving to on-lookers;

- failure of flight attendants to secure a refreshment trolley;

- leaving baggage of delayed passengers unattended.

Denied Boarding Compensation

Regulation (EC) No 261/2004 (the '*Denied Boarding Regulations*' - hereafter "the Regulations") provides a system of compensation and assistance for airline passengers in the event that that their flight is cancelled, subject to delay, or they are 'denied boarding'. From the 17th February 2005 it has been 'directly applicable' in all EU Member States including the UK. In other words, if a relevant carrier fails to act in accordance with the Regulations, a claim can be brought in the County Court to enforce the passenger's rights (and possibly claim additional compensation). The Regulations apply only to 'motorised fixed wing aircraft', i.e. aeroplanes. The Regulations came into effect on 17th February 2005. They apply to all flights which have taken place after that date, whether or not the flights were booked (and the contract formed) before that date.

The Basic Scheme

Who is liable under the Regulations? The key question here, and one that is likely to arise in practice, is whether in the context of a Package Travel Holiday the correct defendant to a claim under the denied boarding Regulations is the tour operator, or the air carrier? The answer is that the obligations and duties relating to compensation and so forth only attach to the air carrier (and only if the flight criteria, below, are met.) Who or what is the 'air carrier' will be a matter of fact in all the circumstances of case. A tour operator will be liable under the Regulations *only* if it also acts as the air carrier. A further point to note is that in order to bring themselves within the scheme of the Montreal Convention, Tour Operators will often include a term in the contract to the effect that they are acting as the 'air carrier'. Finally, one should not fall into the trap of thinking that the Regulations do not apply in the case of flights that form part of Package Holidays. They do (with some exceptions): the only question is *who is the correct defendant?* Claims should be made against *carriers* and any residual and related holiday claim should account for the fact that the consumer has a claim against the carrier pursuant to these Regulations.

Which flights are covered?

The Regulations apply to the following flights, provided always that the passenger has confirmed reservation and has presented himself at check-in (unless the flight has been cancelled):

- All flights departing from an airport located in the EU and arriving anywhere in the world, whether or not the air carrier is an EU air carrier (i.e has a operating licence granted by an EU member state).

- All flights departing from an airport outside the EU and arriving in the EU provided that 1) the air carrier is a EU air carrier and 2) the passenger has not already received benefits or compensation in the non-EU country from which they have just departed. This means that the Regulations do not apply to non-EU air carriers flying into the EU from outside the EU.

What about passengers who are travelling under a special price-saving scheme?

- Passengers on frequent-flyer schemes are covered.
- Passengers travelling for free, or on deals which are not available to the general public (e.g. crew; employee discounts & families; the Prime Minister; the Queen's Flight) are not covered.
- Flights which form part of a Package Holiday are covered unless the Package Tour is cancelled for reasons other than cancellation of the flight (for example, the 'accommodation' is destroyed).

Categories of Flights

Irrespective of whether the flight is cancelled, delayed, or the passenger is denied boarding, the extent of compensation and assistance that the air carrier is obliged to offer depends upon the 'category' that the flight falls into.

- Category (a): all flights of 1,500km or less.
- Category (b): all flights inside the EU of more than 1,500km, and all other flights between 1500km and 3000km.
- Category (c) all flights that do not fall into categories (a) or (b) above.

The Triggering Events

There are three triggering events:

(a) Denied Boarding
(b) Delay
(c) Cancellation

(a) Denied Boarding

Denied boarding is defined[88] as '*a refusal to carry passengers on a flight, although they have presented themselves for boarding under the conditions laid down in Article 3(2), except where there are reasonable grounds to deny them boarding, such as reasons of health, safety or security, or inadequate travel documentation*'. If a carrier can demonstrate that the passenger has been denied boarding for 'reasonable grounds; (i.e. they are carrying a prohibited object) then whilst they have been 'denied boarding' as a matter of fact, they will not have any rights under the Regulations. A good example arises out of *Limbert v My Travel Group Plc.*[89] The Limberts' flight from Palma to Manchester was delayed by over 6 hours. Finally it was announced that the aircraft to be used would be smaller than intended because the original aircraft had been damaged in a runway incident by part of the airport structure. The Claimants were unlucky in that they were not able to board due to the smaller number of seats available, and instead they were out on an alternative flight to Cardiff whence they made their way to Manchester by coach. They sued for denied boarding compensation, but the judge concluded that they had not been denied boarding at all within the meaning of the Regulations because the airline had proved that it had to substitute a smaller aircraft for safety reasons because of the damage sustained to the original aircraft. Accordingly, one of the exceptions within Article 2(j) applied and the question of denied boarding compensation did not arise at all.

Where a carrier reasonably expects to deny boarding on a flight, it *first* has to ask for 'volunteers' who are willing to surrender their reservations in exchange for 'benefits':[90]

• These benefits are not defined and are to be agreed between the passenger and the air carrier.

---

[88] DB Article 2(j).
[89] 7 June 2006 Pontefract CC (Unreported).
[90] DB Article 2(k).

- Whatever is agreed is additional to the passenger's right to re-routing or reimbursement under the scheme. However, by becoming volunteers passengers do lose their right to compensation and care/assistance under the Regulations.

- The agreement for the additional benefits is not enforceable under the Regulations themselves. It is a straightforward matter of private contract law between the 'volunteer' and the air carrier.

Right to Compensation

In the event that insufficient 'volunteers' come forwards, and the carrier denies boarding, the effected passengers are entitled to the following compensation.[91] This must be paid in cash, by electronic bank transfer, bank order, bank cheque or, with the signed agreement of the passenger, in travel vouchers or 'other services':

- Category (a): 250 euros
- Category (b): 400 euros
- Category (c): 600 euros

If, however, the carrier is able to reroute the effected passenger to their final destination within the following time-scales, the compensation that they receive will be reduced by 50%.

- Category (a): no later than two hours after the scheduled arrival time;
- Category (b): no later than three hours after the scheduled arrival time;
- Category (c): no later than four hours after the scheduled arrival time.

Right to reimbursement or re-routing

Passengers who are denied boarding (including volunteers) must also be offered the choice between:[92]

(i) Reimbursement (within 7 days) of the full cost of their ticket for any part of their journey not made. This means that if the passenger takes it upon themselves to complete their journey with, for example, a different carrier, they are not entitled to reimbursement.

(ii) For parts of the journey which have already been made but where the flight is no longer serving any purpose. For example, if a passenger is

---

[91] DB Articles 4 & 7.
[92] DB Article 8.

flying from the UK to Australia, via Holland, and the flight is cancelled after they arrive at Holland, the passenger is entitled to reimbursement for the UK to Holland stretch, even though they have made that part of their journey.

(iii) Where relevant, a flight to their starting point at the earliest opportunity or alternatively, re-routing to the passenger's final destination at the earliest opportunity or at a later date to the passenger's convenience, subject to availability of seats.

The right to reimbursement will apply to flights which form part of a package[93] unless that right also arises under the Package Travel Directive (90/314/EEC).

Right to care

Passengers who are involuntarily denied boarding (i.e. excluding volunteers) are entitled to the following forms of care[94] and assistance, for free:

- Meals and refreshments in reasonable relation to their waiting time;
- Two telephone calls, telex or fax messages or emails;
- Hotel accommodation in cases where a stay of one or more nights becomes necessary or where a stay additional to that intended by the passenger becomes necessary;
- Transport between the airport and place of accommodation, as required.

(b) Delay

Where a flight is delayed, the passenger's rights are more limited.[95] There is *no* right to compensation. If an air carrier reasonably expects the scheduled time of departure to be delayed by the following periods of time, passengers are entitled to reasonable meals and refreshment and telephone calls/faxes etc as set out above:

- Category (a): delay of 2 hours or more
- Category (b): delay of 3 hours or more
- Category (c): delay of 4 hours or more.

Where a carrier reasonably expects the scheduled time of departure to be delayed by 5 hours, the passenger is entitled to reimbursement. Where a

---

[93] DB Article 8(2) – and see further below about the relationship between Denied Boarding Compensation and Package Holidays.
[94] DB Article 9.
[95] DB Article 6.

carrier reasonably expects the scheduled time of departure to be delayed by *at least* a day, the passenger is entitled to hotel accommodation and transport under the same conditions as apply to passengers who are denied boarding (as to which see above).

(c) Cancellation

Cancellation is defined as: *'the non-operation of a flight which was previously planned and on which at least one place was reserved'*. In the event that a flight is cancelled, the Regulations provide passengers with the following rights: the same right to reimbursement and re-routing as applies to passengers who are denied boarding (see above); meals and refreshments and the right to telephone calls and faxes; and where the cancelled flight is rerouted and the departure time of the new flight is at least a day after the intended departure time of the cancelled flight), passengers are entitled to hotel accommodation and transportation under the same conditions as apply to passengers who are denied boarding.

Passengers whose flights are cancelled are also entitled to compensation in the same amounts as set out at above unless:

*   they are informed of the cancellation between 2 weeks and 7 days before the scheduled time of departure and are offered re-routing which would allow them to depart no more than 2 hours before the scheduled time of departure and arrive at their final destination less than 4 hours after the scheduled time of arrival; or

*   they are informed of the cancellation less than 7 days before the scheduled time of departure and are offered re-routing which would allow them to depart no more than 1 hour before the scheduled time of departure and arrive at their final destination less than 2 hours after the scheduled time of arrival.

*   The 'extraordinary circumstances' provisions (below) apply.

Extraordinary circumstances

It is crucially important to note that when a flight is cancelled the right to compensation will not apply where the cancellation is caused by *'extraordinary circumstances which could not have been avoided even if all reasonable measures had been taken'*:[96]

---

[96] *Eivind F Kramme v SAS Scandinavian Airlines Danmark A/S* – ECJ Case: C 396/06. In the AG's opinion technical problems with an aircraft can qualify as extraordinary circumstances provided the technical problem itself is *atypical* and provided that there are also unusual reasons

Whilst extraordinary circumstances[97] are not defined within the Regulations themselves, the *preamble* states that they may occur in the following situations: political instability; meteorological conditions incompatible with the operation of the flight concerned, security risks, unexpected flight safety shortcomings and strikes that effect the operation of an air carrier. The 2005 catering strike affecting British Airways would clearly have been covered, provided that they could not have been avoided by exercising all reasonable measures. The preamble also states that extraordinary circumstances should be deemed to exist where the impact of an air traffic management decision in relation to a particular aircraft on an particular day gives rise to a long delay, an overnight delay, or the cancellation of one or more flights, even though all reasonable measures had been taken by the air carrier to avoid these occurrences. The "extraordinary circumstances exemption *only* applies to the right to *compensation* in the event of *cancellation.* It has no application to either denied boarding, or to delay neither does it have any application to the other remedies available to inconvenienced passengers.

Carriers and tour operators who are likely to be affected by claims under these Regulations should bear in mind that the burden of proving the existence of *extraordinary circumstances* lies on the carrier or other likely defendant to proceedings. In practice it is probable that courts will require something more than the mere assertion that a flight was adversely affected by the weather or industrial action

The Regulations do not affect a passenger's right to claim compensation in respect of the same events, under a different legislative scheme[98] (e.g. the Package Travel Regulations 1992). However, any further compensation that is received may be deducted from the compensation that is awarded under the Denied Boarding Regulations.

Upgrading and downgrading

If, as a result of delay, denied boarding or cancellation, the air carrier decides to place the passenger in, for example, business class rather than economy class (for which the ticket was purchased), it may not request any additional payment from the passenger. If, by contrast, the air carrier places the passenger in a lower class, it shall, within 7 days, reimburse a fixed percentage of the price of ticket, depending upon the category of flight:[99]

---

why the carrier has been unable to provide a substitute aircraft. If the ECJ follows the opinion of the AG (and it usually does) technical breakdowns are going to provide acrriers an easy get-out to their Denied Boarding obligations. See also: *Butler* Regulation 261/2004 [2008] ITLJ 7.

[97] It must be noted that this statutory defence applies only to the *cancellation* of flights. It is not a general defence applicable across the whole range of rights and remedies under these Regulations.

[98] DB Articles 3(6), 8(2) & 13.

[99] DB Article 10.

- Category (a): 30% of the price of the ticket.
- Category (b): 50% of the price of the ticket.
- Category (c): 75% of the price of the ticket.

Notices and warnings

The carrier is obliged to ensure that a clearly legible notice is displayed at check-in, containing these exact words: '*If you are denied boarding or your flight is cancelled or delayed for at least two hours, ask at the check-in counter or boarding gate for the text stating your rights particularly with regard to compensation and assistance*'. The carrier must also provide each passenger who is denied boarding, or whose flight is cancelled or delayed by at least 2 hours, with a written notice setting out their rights. The notice should also contain the contact details of the national body responsible for ensuring that the passenger's rights are not infringed. In the UK, this is the Air Transport Users Council or the Civil Aviation Authority. Some Member States have not yet designated authorities to deal with complaints. If that is the case, the Commission will use all means, including infringement procedures, to compel them to apply the relevant provisions.

The carrier is specifically prohibited from limiting or waiving any of the rights.[100] In the event that a carrier purports to apply such an exclusion, the passenger can claim additional compensation through the Courts.

Vulnerable passengers

The carrier is required to give priority to persons with reduced mobility or special needs. In particular, these passengers, along with persons accompanying them, shall be provided with meals and refreshments (the so called 'right to care') 'as soon as possible'. This obligation extends to the means of notifying passengers of their rights. For example blind passengers would be entitled to expect a notice in Braille.

The right to redress

Article 13 provides that nothing in the regulations will affect the right of the tour operator or the air carrier to seek compensation from each other, if necessary. This may arise, for example, where passengers are stranded abroad as a result of flight cancellation, and the air carrier has sought to rely upon the 'extraordinary circumstances' provisions. In these circumstances the Tour Operator may be liable to provide assistance in any event under the Package Travel Regulations, and may seek to recover the cost of doing so

---

[100] DB Article 15.

from the air carrier, pursuant to Article 13, if it considers that the carrier did
not reasonably rely upon the 'extraordinary circumstances' exclusion.

In July 2004 two sets of judicial review proceedings were brought against the
Department of Transport, the purpose of which was to mount a prospective
challenge to the validity of the Regulations that have now come into force.
The matter was referred to the European Court of Justice for their
consideration. On 8th September 2005 Advocate General Geelhoed handed
down his opinion upholding the validity of the Regulations[101] and predictably
the Regulations were subsequently upheld by the Court.[102]

Relationship with Montreal Convention

The European Court of Justice decided that there was no conflict between
the Montreal Convention and the Denied Boarding Regulations. The former
deals with individual passenger's rights to bring an action before a court, as a
matter of private international law, to claim damages for loss caused to him
by delay. By contrast, the Regulations create (with some exceptions) a strict
liability scheme for air carriers whereby passengers are afforded care and
assistance during the delay, whether or not there is any fault. The Advocate
General noted that whilst a claim can be brought for breach of the
Regulations in national courts (as a matter of public law), the purpose of any
such action is to force air carriers to comply with their rights, and not to
compensate the passenger for loss.

The Regulations are not disproportionate, nor are they invalid for lack of
legal certainty or reasoning. The preamble (although not legally binding)
clearly states the intended purposes of the regulations, and this is reflected in
the substantive rules themselves. He concluded that the Community
Legislature, in drafting the Regulations, struck a balance between the air
carriers and passengers, and paid particular attention to the fact that
passengers are heavily dependant on the 'efficiency and good will' of the
airline when things go wrong. Finally, the Regulations are not discriminatory
simply because other forms of transport (i.e. by land or sea) were not subject
to similar rules, or because they were likely to have a greater, and more
damaging, impact on budget airlines. He said that there is a fundamental
difference between air travel and other kinds of travel, and that the idea that
economic differences which are the direct result of market behaviour and
strategies would mean that airlines are subject to less onerous rules would

---

[101] Which had been challenged by a conglomerate of budget airlines.
[102] *R (on the application of (1) the International Air Transport Association; (2) the European
Low Fairs Airline Association) v Department for Transport* [2004] EWHC 1721 (Admin).

stand the system 'on its head' and ignore the fact that consumer protection legislation must be of general application if it is to exist at all.

Relationship with the Package Travel Regulations 1992

There is no doubt that the Denied Boarding Regulations apply to flights that form part of regulated package holidays and it is not surprising that many consumers approach their package holiday tour operator fro compensation when something goes wrong with their flight arrangements within the meaning of the Denied Boarding Regulations. It is doubtful that the tour operator will be the right party from whom to seek compensation under the Denied Boarding Regulations.[103] The party responsible for compensation for denied boarding[104] is the *operating carrier.* The *operating carrier* means an air carrier that performs or intends to perform the flight under a contract with the passenger (or someone else contracting as agent for the passenger).[105] So:

- To the operating carrier (liable for the regulatory remedies) the carrier must be an *air carrier.*

- An *air carrier* is an *air transport undertaking* with a valid operating licence.[106]

Neither of these preconditions will usually apply to a tour operator even if the tour operator purports to accept liability as a *contracting carrier* in its standard terms and conditions. It is the *airline* that is responsible for the remedies under the Denied Boarding Regulations and consumers should be pointed in their direction when a claim is made. Indeed the consumer should have received written information about their rights as against the *operating carrier* by the operating carrier at the time the facts giving rise to the consumer's right to claim arises.

Where a flight is part of a regulated package holiday any delay, cancellation or denied boarding[107] is likely to be consider an *improper performance* of that part of the package holiday.[108] Such a conclusion is almost unavoidable[109]. The tour operator would conventionally be liable for such an improper performance because the operating carrier would an agent or supplier of the tour operator within the meaning of the PTR 1992. So unless

---

[103] Although the corporate integration of tour operators and some airlines makes it uneconomic or unnecessary for the tour operator to take a stand on this point.
[104] DB Article 4 – and the same applies to the remedies for delay and cancellation under DB Articles 5 & 6.
[105] DB Article 2.
[106] DB Article 2(a).
[107] That is any circumstances giving rise to remedies under the Denied Boarding Regulations.
[108] Regulation 15 PTR 1992.
[109] Subject to the statutory defences in regulation 15(2) PTR 1992.

the operating carrier can deploy the limited defence of exceptional circumstances, the tour operator is likely to be *prima facie* liable for damages for the improper performance of the flight element of the package holiday due to the operating carrier's default. What constitutes *exceptional circumstances* is likely to be regarded an event that could not have been forestalled even with the exercise of all due care under PTR 1992 regulation 15(2)(c). So:

- Any claim under the Denied Boarding scheme should be targeted at the operating carrier of the aircraft. This will not usually be the same company as the tour operator supplying the package holiday even if the carrier is part of the same group of companies as the tour operator.

- If such a claim is not directed against the operating carrier, the damages that the passenger would be entitled to, or the money in lieu the carrier's failure to provide some other remedy under the Denied Boarding Regulations could technically (subject to what follows) be regarded as recoverable from the tour operator as damages for improper performance of the holiday contract (and any claim should be so pleaded).

- Any defence that the operating carrier has in respect of a Denied Boarding scheme claim is available to the tour operator including the defence of *exceptional circumstances* in the limited situations where that defence applies. Either because of the operating carrier's defence there has been no improper performance of the holiday contract, or due to that defence the tour operator has a *force majeure* defence under regulation 15(2) (c) of the PTR 1992.

- But if a claim is not or has not yet been made against the *operating carrier*, of the aircraft or flight the amount the consumer is entitled to as Denied Boarding Regulation compensation should not be awarded under the PTR 1992 or should be deducted from any recovery of damages for *improper performance of the holiday contract* under the PTR 1992. Such damages would not be awarded against the tour operator unless claimed as damages under the PTR 1992, and if they were so claimed should be deducted form the final award to the consumer on the grounds that the passenger has not reasonably mitigated any package travel losses by making a claim against the operating carrier. The failure reasonably to mitigate should be pleaded by the tour operator as part of its defence in any package travel claim and it will be remembered that the burden of proving a failure to mitigate is on the tour operator.

- The only surviving claim against the tour operator for *improper performance* of the holiday contract is likely to be:

(a) a claim for damages for *loss of enjoyment* relating to that part of the holiday that the operating carrier has compromised by offending against the Denied Boarding Compensation rights of the passenger (e.g. loss of enjoyment of the flight element of the holiday);

(b) a claim for damages for *loss of enjoyment* for the knock-on effect on the package holiday of the Denied Boarding scheme problem (see example given below);

(c) a small element of damages for loss of bargain – *not* relating to the air carriage part of the holiday contract because that is covered by the Denied Boarding scheme remedies – but for any impact on the value of the package holiday to the consumer flowing directly from the Denied Boarding scheme problem. For example, due to the Denied Boarding scheme default of the operating carrier, the passenger arrives 2 days late in resort and loses the value (in addition to the enjoyment) of the first 2 days of the package holiday.

In *Harbord v Thomas Cook Airlines & anor*[110] a flight that was due to leave from Stansted airport but was altered so that it departed from Manchester 24 hours later was held to amount to a cancelled flight rather than a delayed flight, therefore a passenger was entitled to claim compensation where no exceptional circumstances existed for the cancellation. The claimant claimed compensation from the defendant in relation to an alteration to an air flight. He had booked a flight from Stansted to Vancouver, however that flight did not happen and he was told that a flight was available 24 hours later from Manchester to Vancouver. The court had to determine whether the flight from Stansted was cancelled or was delayed. The court also had to determine whether, if the flight had been cancelled, it was cancelled due to extraordinary circumstances. The judge concluded: (1) The flight from Manchester to Vancouver was not the same thing as a flight from Stansted to Vancouver. The fact that the carrier might have provided other passengers booked on the original flight from Stansted with transport from Stansted to Manchester did not go to the issue of whether the original flight was cancelled or delayed. The carrier was merely mitigating its liability to compensate the frustrated passengers. The common sense of the situation was that a time differential of 24 hours was indicative more of cancellation than delay. The movement of the point of embarkation from Stansted to Manchester was also suggestive of an entirely alternative flight rather than merely the delay of a flight. The fact that the flight had the same flight number had no bearing on the issue. Accordingly, the flight was cancelled.

---

[110] CC (Oxford) (District Judge Jenkins) 30 January 2006 (reported on Lawtel).

(2) The aircraft defect on which the carrier had relied as amounting to a flight safety shortcoming affected one of the aircraft in its fleet. It was not a defect that affected the particular aircraft on which the claimant was due to travel. It was not sufficient for the carrier to escape liability by simply being able to point to some technical defect affecting flight safety somewhere or other in its fleet of aircraft even if it was asserted this had a knock-on effect on its fleet. For the carrier to have had the benefit of an exemption from liability it had to be able to point to some flight safety shortcoming affecting the aircraft on which the passenger was due to travel. Accordingly, the claimant was entitled to recover the compensation sought.

No Additional Denied Boarding Rights of Action

In *Helen Parker v TUI UK Limited (T/A AusTravel)*[111] it was argued on behalf of the airline that the Denied Boarding Regulations did not create any cause of action capable of being the subject matter of proceedings in the English (or any) courts.

In July 2005 the Claimant booked a return flight from London Heathrow to Sydney, through AusTravel. The flight itself was provided by the Defendant, trading as ThomsonFly. The Claimant alleged that she had been informed, when she spoke to an AusTravel representative on the telephone, that she had booked a scheduled flight with Quantas. When she discovered that the flight was a charter flight with ThomsonFly she asked to be upgraded to a premium economy sear and duly paid an additional £325. The outbound flight departed from London on 26th December 2005. On the date of the return flight, the Claimant arrived at Sydney Airport to be told that her flight had been delayed by at least 24 hours. The cause of the delay was a mechanical fault, as a result of which a 'part' had to be flown from London to Australia. In accordance with its obligations under Article 9,[112] the Defendant, through its local operating agents, offered all passengers overnight accommodation (including free transport to and from the airport), free meals and free telephone calls. The Claimant refused the offer and stated that she would prefer to stay at a friend's house in Sydney. The flight was in fact delayed by 49 hours. After approximately 24 hours, and having tried to contact AusTravel without success, the Claimant decided to pay for an alternative flight home to Gatwick, with Quantas.

The Defendant reimbursed the Claimant the cost of the delayed flight from Sydney to London flight, pursuant to Article 8(a) of the Denied Boarding Regulations. The Claimant's claim was for the cost of £325 upgrade, the cost

---

[111] Central London County Court 30th October 2006.
[112] EC Regulation 261/2004 (the 'Denied Boarding Regulations').

of taxis to and from the friend's house in Sydney, the cost of a taxi from Gatwick to Heathrow, the cost of a mobile phone voucher, and £500 damages for 'loss of enjoyment'. The Particulars of Claim pleaded reliance upon the Denied Boarding Regulations and s.13 of the Supply of Goods and Services Act 1984.

The judge accepted that the level of service provided to the Claimant had been abysmal, and that the whole experience had been very upsetting and disappointing for her. However, he was constrained to conclude that The Denied Boarding Regulations did not create a free-standing, private law cause of action. Instead, they provided for a public-law remedy to enforce the obligations set out therein. If passengers had complaints about breaches of the Regulations, these could be referred to the Civil Aviation Authority who could take up matters if they wished. The Claimant's rights were exclusively encompassed within the Regulations. Article 8 of the Denied Boarding Regulations provided passengers with a choice between rerouting, or reimbursement of the part or parts of their flights not made together with a return flight to the first point of departure, where relevant. On the facts of this case, the Claimant had received a reimbursement of the part of her journey not made, including half of the cost of the £325 upgrade. She was not entitled to a 'flight to the first point of departure' because it was not relevant. The Claimant had also been provided with care and assistance under Article 9 of the Regulations. The Court was precluded from ordering the Defendant to pay the cost of Claimant's taxis to and from her friend's house because Article 9 only referred to transport between the hotel and airport, which was provided. Similarly, the claim for the mobile phone voucher, and the taxi from Gatwick to Heathrow, were not costs to which the Claimant was entitled under the Regulations.

As to the claim for loss of enjoyment, the Defendant had no reason to know that the Claimant had come to Australia on holiday. She could have come on business or for a number of other reasons. This was a contract for carriage only, not a contract for a holiday.[113] Furthermore, contracts for carriage by air are governed by the Montreal Convention 1999.[114] Therefore *even if* the Claimant was claiming for some other breach of contract (other than her claim for loss of enjoyment) she could not succeed.[115]

---

[113] *Lucas v Acro* (1994) CLY 1444 was authority for the proposition that general damages for loss of enjoyment are not recoverable for breach of a contract for carriage only.

[114] In *Sidhu v British Airways* (1997) 1 AC 430, the House of Lords held that where the Convention applies, no alternative remedy was available at common law or otherwise.

[115] Defendant referred to other cases – *Patel v India Air* (1999) CLY 4904, *Nanuwa v Lufthansa* (1999) CLY 4885 and *Brunton v Cosmosair* (2002) CLY 232 - which lay down guidance for the

Air Travel & Disability Discrimination

Introduction

The principal piece of legislation governing the rights of disabled persons, and the responsibilities of individuals and other entities towards them, is the Disability Discrimination Act 1995, as amended.[116] The 1995 Act provides a comprehensive framework of provisions covering a range of situations, from the obligation on employers to make physical adjustments to the workplace, through to generalized duties on the providers of services not to discriminate against disabled persons. As ever, the position relating to air travel (and transport generally) is complicated by a series of exemptions and ambiguous definitions within the legislation.

The basic position is as follows.

a.   A claimant only has a cause of action if they are 1) 'disabled'[117] and 2) have been unjustifiably 'discriminated' against ('treated less favourably') for reasons related to their disability.

b.   Pursuant to Section 19 of the Act, it is unlawful for a 'provider of services' to discriminate against a disabled person:

 i.   In refusing to provide, or deliberately not providing, any service.

 ii.   In failing to comply with any duty imposed on him by section 21 (the duty to make 'reasonable adjustments') in circumstances in which the effect of that failure is to make it impossible or unreasonably difficult for the disabled person to make use of any such service.

 iii.   In the standard of service which he provides to the disabled person or the manner in which he provides it to him.

 iv.   In the terms on which he provides a service to the disabled person.

c.   A person is "a provider of services" for the purposes of the Act if he is concerned with the provision, **in the United Kingdom,** of services to the public or to a section of the public (my emphasis).

---

proposition that even if the Claim had been made under the Montreal Convention 1999, damages for loss of enjoyment would not be recoverable.
[116] By the Disability Discrimination Act 2005.
[117] A physical or mental impairment which has a substantial and long-term adverse effect on his ability to carry out normal day-to-day activities.

d.   When the 1995 Act first came into force the obligations set out above did not apply to services which involved the use of *any means of transport*. In December 2006 *the Disability Discrimination (Transport Vehicles) Regulations 2005* removed this exemption in so far as it related to trains, taxis, coaches and other land-based public service vehicles. It did not, however, extend to air transport.

The effect of these provisions is that the 1995 Act does not apply to air transport itself, nor to facilities which are provided on board the aircraft. Air transport continues to occupy a legal 'no-mans land' somewhere outside the ambit of the statute. It should be noted, however, that the 1995 Act does apply to the services and facilities which form part of the airport infrastructure, and to the administrative process of booking flights and holidays. Thus, for example, it is potentially unlawful to discriminate against disabled persons in relation to:

- Booking facilities (including websites, telephone reservations and brochures advertising flights);
- The airport building and services therein (for example lifts, car parks, escalators etc);
- Check-in services.

The Act does not however apply to any of these 'infrastructure' services if they are provided outside the United Kingdom. A disabled passenger who experiences discrimination at a foreign airport terminal before his or her return journey currently has no cause of action whatsoever under the 1995 Act.

The Code of Practice

The airline industry did not escape completely. In March 2003 the DFT introduced a code of practice in relation to the access to air travel by disabled persons. The code is not statutory and does not have the force of law. It states that airlines are 'expected' to meet the minimum standards set out within it, but it also acknowledges that the basic position under the 1995 Act remains the same. Therefore a failure to comply with the code does not, by itself, give a disabled passenger a cause of action. It might be argued that there would be an implied term in the holiday contract or carriage contract that the airline will comply with the code, but a Court should be reluctant to reach this conclusion since it would entirely emasculate the current exemption in section 19 of the 1995 Act.

The Guidance sets out in exhaustive detail the facilities and services that airlines are expected to have in place. Everything from pre-booking seats to the design and accessibility of websites is covered. In 2006 the Department for Transport published a report setting out the findings of a committee which had monitored compliance with the code of guidance since its implementation in 2003. Perhaps not surprisingly, given the breadth of the guidance and its uncertain legal status, the report was not effusive in its praise of the industry. It found 'work in progress' but concluded that there had been little substantive change in a number of key areas since 2004. In particular, the report noted that many airlines were awaiting the outcome of EC proposals for a regulation governing the rights of disabled people on air transport. That regulation has now arrived, and the legal landscape is set to change for good.

European Dimension

EC Regulation 1107/2006 ('the Regulation') takes effect in two stages. Articles 3 and 4 came into force on 26th July 2007, and the remainder of the Regulation takes effect one year later on 26th July 2008.

The enabling legislation in England and Wales is the *Civil Aviation (Access to Air Travel to Disabled Persons and Persons with Reduced Mobility) Regulations 2007* ('the 2007 Regulations'). In so far as these Regulations relate to Articles 3 and 4 of the EC Regulation, or deal with designation of enforcement and complaints bodies, they came into force on 26th July 2007. The remainder of the Regulations come into force on 26th July 2008, in accordance with European Legislation.

Regulation 8 of the 2007 Regulations amends Section 19 of the Disability Discrimination Act 1995 to provide that where there is any conflict between section 19 and the rights and obligations under the EC Regulations, the latter will prevail. In a single step, this provides a tidy and workable solution to the current exemption of air transport services from national disability legislation (which, strictly speaking, continues to apply).To Whom does the 2007 Regulation Apply?

Pursuant to Article 1, the Regulation applies to:

> any persons whose mobility is reduced due to any physical disability (sensory or locomotory, permanent or temporary) intellectual disability or impairment, or any other cause of disability, or age, and whose situation needs appropriate attention and the adaptation to his or her particular needs of the service made available to all passengers.

Immediately the open-ended nature of this definition is strikingly apparent. Potentially, the obligations under the regulation extend to persons who are *not* presently covered by the 1995 Act, for example those with a temporary injury such a broken leg or twisted ankle as a result of an over-enthusiastic football tackle. It should be noted, however, that despite the width of the definition of disability, the focus of the Regulations is on a person's *mobility* rather than any other aspect of disability. In this respect, the scope of the regulations is significantly narrower that the 1995 Act. They do not apply, for example, to persons with a broken arm, impaired speech or deafness, save insofar as such problems prevented those persons from moving around the airport and on the aeroplane. For present purposes, the term 'disabled persons' is used to describe any person who falls within the definition set out above.

Which Flights and Transport are Covered?

The Regulation as a whole

The rights and obligations created by the Regulation apply to all disabled persons who are:

a. Using or intending to use;
b. Commercial passenger air services;
c. On departure from, on transit through, or arrival at;
d. An airport situated in the territory of a member state.

A commercial passenger service is defined as "*a passenger air transport service operated by an air carrier through a scheduled or non-scheduled flight offered to the general public for valuable consideration, whether on its own or part of a package*". The following points should be noted:

*   Both scheduled and charter flights are included.
*   Flights which are not available to the general public, or which are free (the queen, Air Force One, staff discounts) are not included.
*   It is immaterial that the flight is a component of a package holiday. It is still covered by the Regulation.
*   This definition is more limited than the one used in EC Regulation 261/2004 (Denied Boarding[118]), which applies to 'air carriers' generally, unqualified by the 'commercial' criterion. Articles 3, 4 and 10

Articles 3, 4 and 10 (which concern the general prohibition on refusal of carriage, and the assistance to be provided by air carriers) are of even wider application. They additionally apply to all flights departing from an airport outside the EU but flying into an airport within the EU, provided that the

---

[118] See above.

operating carrier is a Community Air Carrier (i.e. has a valid operating licence). There is no need for the flight to be a commercial passenger service. This definition is effectively the same as that used in the Denied Boarding Regulations.

Article 3 – Refusal to Carry

Article 3 prohibits an air carrier, its agent, or a tour operator, from refusing on grounds of disability or reduced mobility, to:

- Accept a reservation for a flight departing from or arriving at an EU airport; or
- Embark a disabled person at an EU airport, provided that that person has a valid ticket and reservation.

Perhaps the most notable aspect of this provision, and many others in the Regulation, it that it extends to the *tour operator* as well as the air carrier. In this respect the Regulation is markedly wider in scope than the Denied Boarding Regulations - EC Regulation 261/2004. 'Tour operator' is defined as an 'organiser' or 'retailer' within the meaning of Article 2(2) of the Package Travel Regulations 1992. Since Article 2(2) itself refers to a 'package' within the meaning of the Regulations, it would seem that if a tour operator manages successfully to 'split contract' or 'dynamically package' a holiday, it will not be covered by the Discrimination Regulation, irrespective of whether it has sold the relevant flight to the disabled person. If the air-transport 'wing' of the tour operating company has also provided the flight, however (e.g. Thomson Fly or First Choice Airlines), it will not be quite so easy to escape the grip of the 2007 Regulation.

Article 4 – Exceptions and Derogations

An air carrier, its agent, or a tour operator may refuse to accept a reservation or embark a disabled person for two reasons:

- In order to meet applicable safety requirements established by international, Community or national law or safety requirements established by the authority that issued the carrier's AOC[119]; or
- If the size of the aircraft or its doors makes embarkation or carriage of the disabled person physically impossible.

It will be noted that the second of these two exceptions creates a high hurdle. It is not enough that the size of aircraft makes embarkation difficult or even

---

[119] Air Operator's Certificate.

reasonable impracticable. It must be physically *impossible.* Article 4(1) also provides that any passenger who is refused embarkation or reservation for a reason set out above must be offered the right to reimbursement or rerouting pursuant to Article 8 of the EC Regulation 261/2004 (Denied Boarding). This raises several issues.

a. 'Denied Boarding' under EC Regulation 261/2004 is defined as " *a refusal to carry passengers on a flight...except where there are reasonable grounds to deny them boarding, such as reasons of health, safety or security*". Thus if a passenger is denied boarding for a reasonable ground, Article 8 is simply not triggered. This exception seems to be preserved by article 4, in so far as it relates to rerouting and a return flight[120], but not in relation to reimbursement. There is a clear tension between the two Regulations in this regard, which will need to be resolved.

b. Article 4 seemingly also requires the *tour operator* to offer reimbursement etc. This also sits uncomfortably with EC Regulation 261/2004, which applies only to air carriers, not tour operators.

c. If an air carrier, agent or tour operator is relying upon an Article 4 exception: must also:

   i.   Immediately inform the disabled person of its reasons for refusing carriage, which must be communicated to the disabled person in writing within 5 working days of a request by the passenger for a written notice.
   ii. Make reasonable efforts to propose an 'acceptable alternative' to the disabled person.
   iii. May require the disabled person to be accompanied by another person who is capable of providing assistance required by that person.

Assistance

Information about safety rules and restrictions

An air carrier or its agent is required to make publicly available in an accessible format in at least the same languages as the information made available to other passengers:

---

[120] Article 4 states "the right to the option of a return flight or re-routing shall be conditional upon all safety requirements being met".

(i)   The safety rules that it applies to the carriage of disabled passengers; and
(ii) Restrictions on the carriage of disabled passengers or their mobility equipment due to the size of the aircraft.

A *tour operator* must make such safety rules and restrictions available for flights included within packages.

Information at the point of sale

- The air carrier, their agents and tour operators must take all necessary measures to ensure sufficient mechanisms are in place at the point of sale in the EU to enable disabled persons to notify the carrier etc of their need for assistance, and to determine whether there is a reason for refusal of carriage for safety reasons.
- In practical terms, this means for example that a tour operator's website must have free-text boxes into which passengers can enter and explain the full extent of their disability, or at least a telephone number which can be used to communicate this information. It will no longer be appropriate to take a passive stance and wait for the disabled person to inform the operator of its 'special request'.

Transmission of information to airports

When an air carrier, agent or tour operator is provided with information by a disabled passenger at least 48 hours prior to departure of the need for assistance, the carrier etc must transmit the information at least 36 hours prior to departure to the managing bodies of the airports of departure, transit and arrival (even if not in the EU); and to the operating carrier (if different from ticketing carrier) unless the identity of the carrier is not known at the time of notification of the information, in which case transmission must taken place as soon as practicable.

As soon as possible after departure, the operating carrier must also inform the managing body of the destination airport (if in an EU state) of the number of disabled passengers aboard the aircraft requiring assistance from the airport and the nature of that assistance.

Assistance on board the aircraft

The air carrier (but *not* the tour operator) must provide the assistance specified in Annex II of the 2007 Regulation to the disabled person *without additional charge*. That assistance includes:

- Carriage of recognised assistance dogs in the cabin, subject to national regulations;

- In addition to medical equipment, carriage of up to two pieces of mobility equipment per disabled passenger, including electric wheelchairs (subject to: advanced warning of 48 hours; possible limitations of space aboard the aircraft; and the application of regulations concerning carriage of dangerous goods);

- Communication of essential information concerning the flight in accessible formats;

- Making all reasonable efforts to arrange seating to meet the needs of disabled passengers on request and subject to safety requirements and availability;

- Assistance in moving to toilet facilities, if required;

- All reasonable efforts to seat any accompanying carer next to the disabled passenger.

The obligation is conditional, however, upon:

- The carrier/agent/tour operator receiving notification from the disabled passenger at least 48 hours prior to departure (subject to the obligation on the carrier to have proper mechanisms in place for receipt and transmission of such information). The 'notification' will cover the return flight provided that it is purchased through the same carrier as the outward flight.

- Any notification in relation to the carriage of assistance dogs being made pursuant to applicable national law.

- The disabled person presenting him or herself for check-in or at the designated disabled arrival point, at the time stipulated in advance, or if not stipulated, at least 1 hour before departure at check in and at least 2 hours before departure at the arrival point.

Article 7 – Airport Assistance

The Managing body of the airport is responsible for ensuring the provision of assistance specified in Annex I of the Regulation, also *without additional charge.*

The assistance includes:

- Designating in co-operation with airport users (normally through the Airport Users Committee), sufficient points of arrival and departure within the airport at which disabled persons can announce their arrival and request assistance;

- Providing clear signage to those designated points of arrival and departure and providing basic information about the airport in accessible formats;

- Providing assistance and arrangements necessary to enable disabled persons to move through the airport, including moving through check-in and security/emigration, embarkation onto and dis-embarkation from the aircraft, moving from aircraft door to seat on embarkation and from seat to aircraft door on disembarkation, assistance with storing and retrieving hand baggage on the aircraft at embarkation and disembarkation and assistance in transiting through the airport.

- Providing wheelchairs, lifts and other necessary equipment for embarkation/disembarkation;

- Handling necessary mobility equipment and providing temporary replacements for lost or damaged mobility equipment;

- Handling recognised assistance dogs;

- Communicating information in accessible formats needed for disabled passengers to take flights.

These obligations are however subject to the disabled passenger notifying the air carrier/agent/tour operator, and presenting themselves for check-in, in the same manner as set out above.

Division of Responsibility

One of the problems with the residual set of obligations imposed by the DDA 1995 in relation to services and facilities within the airport infrastructure was that it was not at all clear who, as between the air carrier and airport authority, was responsible for providing the respective services. For example, if a disabled traveller was denied a wheelchair to allow him or her to access the plane from the departure lounge, was it managing body of the airport, or the airline, who was responsible? This problem came a head in *Ross v (1) Ryanair (2) Stansted Airport Limited*[121] in which Ryanair and Stansted Airport each denied that they should reimburse the Claimant for the cost that he incurred in having to hire a wheelchair to allow him to board the flight. In that case the evidence demonstrated a relatively clear contractual matrix pursuant to which Ryanair had agreed to be responsible for certain services within the airport, including the provision of such wheelchairs, and they were accordingly held liable.

As is clear from the discussion above, the relative responsibilities of the air carriers and the managing body are now clearly demarcated by Articles 8 and 10 of the Regulation. However, pursuant to Article 8(3), the managing body of the airport may pass on its costs/charges of compliance with Article 8 to the air carriers using the airport. Any charge must be reasonable, cost-related, transparent and established in co-operation with airport users.

The Regulation also permits a carrier to agree with the managing body of the airport that the latter will provide a higher standard of assistance to that carrier's passengers than is strictly required, in which case the airport can levy an additional charge against the carrier.

Training

Air carriers and managing bodies must provide adequate training to ensure that:

a. All their personnel (including employees of sub-contractors) who provide direct assistance to disabled persons have knowledge of how to meet the needs of passengers.
b. All their personnel working at airports who deal with the travelling public have disability equality and awareness training.
c. On recruitment, all new employees attend disability-training courses and all current employees receive refresher training where appropriate.

Compensation and Enforcement

As with all EC Regulations, Regulation 1107/2006 is directly applicable in England and Wales and its terms and provisions, with the exception of those relating to penalties for infringement,[122] are enforceable in the civil courts.

---

[121] (2006) Lawtel.
[122] Member states are required to introduce effective, proportionate and dissuasive rules on penalties applicable to infringement of the Regulation. These penalties, which take the form of criminal convictions and fines payable on the standard scale for breach of obligations under the EC Regulations, are now governed by Regulations 3 and 4 of the 2007 Regulations. It is a

Liability under the Regulation cannot be excluded or waived. Each member state is required to designate an enforcement body. In England, Wales and Scotland this will be the Civil Aviation Authority, which is already occupying an equivalent role enforcing the provisions of EC Regulation 261/2004.[123] The Department for Transport has also indicated that the Disability Rights Commission (which, from 30th September 2007, will be subsumed into the Commission for Equality and Human Rights) will be the designated complaints handling authority. It is notable that this is different to the Complaints authority under Regulation 261/2004, which is currently the Air Transport Users' Council.

The Regulation provides no explicit right to compensation for disabled passengers for infringement of its provisions, save in respect of loss of or damage to mobility equipment. Furthermore, the recital to the Regulation suggests that where a disabled passenger has a right to reimbursement or rerouting under Regulation 261/2004, the Package Travel Regulations 1992, or under the present regulation, he or she will only be entitled to exercise that right once, to avoid double recovery.

The question is whether a passenger has a right to compensation generally if he or she is unlawfully refused carriage etc in breach of the regulation. Does the absence of any specific provision dealing with this issue imply that the European Commission did not intend the Articles to create free-standing, actionable duties giving rise to compensation claims in the national courts? A similar dispute is already raging in County Courts up and down the country in relation to the Denied Boarding Regulations. Airlines continue to argue that there is no right to compensation over and above that already provided in Article 7 of that Regulation. By and large, anecdotal evidence suggests that they appear to have been successful in this respect.

It appears, however, that the legislative draftsmen are alive to the possibility of a similar argument being employed in the present context, and have already put appropriate mechanisms in place to prevent it from succeeding. Regulation 9 of the *Civil Aviation (Access to Air Travel for Disabled Persons and Persons with Reduced Mobility) Regulations 2007*,[124] provides as follows:

---

defence for the air carrier, managing body of the airport or tour operator (as the case may be) to prove that they took all reasonable steps to avoid committing an offence (Regulation 5). Where members and officers of corporate bodies have contributed to the bodies failure to comply with an obligation under the EC Regulation, they are also liable to prosecution (Regulation 6).
[123] Denied Boarding.
[124] Available on the DFT website.

Compensation claims by disabled persons etc.

(1) A claim by a disabled person or a person with reduced mobility for an infringement of any of his rights under the EC Regulation may be made the subject of civil proceedings in the same way as any other claim in tort or (in Scotland) in reparation for breach of statutory duty.

(2) For the avoidance of doubt, any damages awarded in respect of any infringement of the EC Regulation may include compensation for injury to feelings whether or not they include compensation under any other head.

(3) Proceedings in England, Wales or Northern Ireland may be brought only in a county court.

(4) Proceedings in Scotland may be brought only in a sheriff court.

(5) The remedies available in such proceedings are those which are available in the High Court or (as the case may be) the Court of Session.

(6) A county court or a sheriff court is not to consider a claim under this regulation unless proceedings in respect of it are instituted before the end of the period of six months beginning when the infringement complained of occurred.

(7) Where, in relation to proceedings or prospective proceedings under this regulation, the dispute concerned is referred to conciliation before the end of the period of six months mentioned in paragraph (6), the period allowed by that paragraph is to be extended by three months.

(8) A court may consider any claim under this regulation which is out of time if, in all the circumstances of the case, it considers that it is just and equitable to do so.

The position under the Regulation could not therefore be any clearer: if a disabled passenger's rights are infringed, there is a prima facie right to damages for any loss caused. Regulation 9 is also likely to breathe new life into the airlines' argument that a breach of Regulation 261/2004 does not create a similar free standing right to damages. After all, if it did, parliament would presumably have said so in the Civil Aviation (Denied Boarding, Compensation and Assistance) Regulations 2005, the equivalent statutory instrument dealing with enforcement and prosecution of air carriers for breach of those regulations.

Finally, any claim under Regulation 9 must, however, be brought within 6 months of the infringement complained of, unless:

a.	The dispute is referred to conciliation before the end of the six month period, in which case the limitation period is extended by a further three months. (Regulation 10 of the 2007 provides that the Commission for Equality and Human Rights may make arrangements for provision of conciliation services).
b.	The court exercises its discretion to hear a claim out of time if it considers it 'just and equitable' to do so (the same test that is applied under 1995 Act).

The Athens Convention

The Carriage of Passengers and Luggage by Sea

The 1974 Athens Convention is given effect in the United Kingdom by section 183 of the Merchant Shipping Act 1995 which came into force on 1 January 1996. The Athens Convention is reproduced in Schedule 6 of the 1995 Act It follows a pattern and imposes a regime which shares similarities with the Montreal Convention but it is by no means identical.

Application

The Athens Convention covers a carrier's liability to passengers for death and personal injury, and for loss and damage to luggage. Loss and damage to luggage includes pecuniary loss arising out of the non-delivery of luggage to the passenger within a reasonable time of arrival at the destination unless the delay is the result of a labour dispute. The Athens Convention does not cover liabilities in respect of quality complaints that might arise in respect of a spoilt cruise holiday, or sub-standard berth accommodation. In this regard the Athens Convention respects the distinction between contracts of carriage and contracts which have as a primary purpose the provision of enjoyment and comfort — *e.g.* holiday contracts.

Exclusive

Like its air travel counterpart the Athens Convention applies to the exclusion of other remedies where a *carrier* is liable in respect of losses covered by the Convention.

Article 14
Basis for claims
No action for damages for the death of or personal injury to a passenger, or for the loss of or damage to luggage, shall be brought against a carrier or performing carrier otherwise than in accordance with this Convention.

Jurisdiction

Article 17
1. An action arising under this Convention shall, at the option of the claimant, be brought before one of the courts listed below:
(a) the court of the place of permanent residence or principal place of business of the defendant, or
(b) the court of the place of departure or that of the destination according to the contract of carriage, or
(c) a court of the State of the domicile or permanent residence of the claimant; if the defendant has a place of business and is subject to jurisdiction in that State, or
(d) a court of the State where the contract of carriage was made, if the defendant has a place of business and is subject to jurisdiction in that State.

Thus any action under the Athens Convention can be brought by at the election of the claimant in:

- the court of the place where the carrier has its principal place of business or permanent residence;

- the court of the place of departure or destination as set out in the contract;

- the court of the permanent residence of the claimant;

- the court of the country where the contract of carriage was made provided the defendant has a place of business in that State and is subject to its jurisdiction.

International carriage

The Athens Convention applies to any international carriage by sea[125] if:

- the ship is flying the flag of a State Party to the Convention;[126]

- the contract has been made in a State Party to the Convention;

---

[125] Article 2.
[126] There are only 34 signatories to the Athens Convention even though it has been in force since April 1987. An up to date list of State Parties can be found on the International Maritime Organization website.

- the place of departure or destination according to the contract is in the territory of a State Party.

International carriage is carriage which according to the contract has a place of departure and destination, or a scheduled intermediate port of call, in different states.

The following examples illustrate the scope of the Athens Convention.

- a journey by cross-Channel ferry;

- a ferry scheduled to cross from Wales to Ireland which is diverted to England due to bad weather;

- a round trip cruise starting and finishing in Southampton with various Mediterranean ports of call.

Carrier, ships, passengers and luggage

- A carrier may be either the party on whose behalf the contract of carriage has been made or a "performing carrier", being the party who actually performs the carriage contract. The carrier with whom the contract is made remains liable under the provisions of the Athens Convention even if the actual carriage is entrusted to another carrier (the "performing carrier") However, the performing carrier is liable jointly and severally with the actual carrier for such parts of the contract as are performed by him.

- A ship is a sea-going vessel excluding air-cushion vehicles such as hovercraft.[127]

- A passenger[128] is any person who is carried in a ship under the contract of carriage, or who with the consent of the carrier is accompanying a vehicle or live animals which are covered by a contract for the carriage of goods. Employees are not passengers within the meaning of the Athens Convention.

- Luggage[129] is any article or vehicle carried by the carrier under a contract of carriage, but excludes articles and vehicles carried under a charterparty, bill of lading or other contract primarily concerned with the carriage of goods.

---

[127] To which the Warsaw Convention applies.
[128] Article 1.4.
[129] Article 1.5.

Relationship to PTR 1992

The Convention applies by operation of law to any *carrier* even if the carrier is also a tour operator within the meaning of the PTR 1992.[130] The Convention is not qualified by or limited in its effect by virtue of anything in the PTR 1992 and prevails over the PTR 1992 where the carrier happens also to be a tour operator.[131]

> "If the effect of section 183 of the Merchant Shipping Act 1995, and indeed the earlier statute which was codified therein, was to have been qualified, indeed effectively partially repealed so as to make the Convention applicable only in circumstances where there had been an express reference in the [package holiday] contract involving the carrier, rather than the Convention applying as a matter of law, then ... the draftsman would and should have said so in clear terms."[132]

So it was in *Norfolk*[133] that the Claimant, who brought her claim within the 3 year personal injury limitation period in English law but outside the 2 year period permitted against carriers under the Athens Convention, was time barred. The judge noted that there was no inconsistency between the PTR 1992 and the Athens Convention in this regard because the PTR 1992 did not specify any limitation period at all and, implicitly, therefore, there was no reason why for accidents on board vessels to which the Convention applied the limitation period should not be that specified in the Athens Convention. In any event the Convention, having the force of law, applied as against (or as in this case *in favour* of) performing and contracting carriers irrespective of the PTR 1992.

Liability

Article 3 provides:

> "1. The carrier shall be liable for the damage suffered as a result of the death or personal injury to a passenger and the loss or damage to luggage if the incident which caused the damage so suffered occurred in the course of the carriage and was due to the fault or neglect of the carrier or his servants or agents ...

---

[130] *Norfolk v Mytravel Tour Operations Limited* [2003] 8 August Plymouth County Court HHJ Overend – unreported.
[131] Which may often be the case in the case of cruise holidays. There is no reason in principle why this should not be the same under the Warsaw Convention where the tour operator is also the *carrier*.
[132] *Norfolk v Mytravel* (above). But for a different (and it is submitted mistaken) view to the effect that the PTR 1992 provide a parallel remedy see *Lee & Lee v Airtours Holidays Limited* [2002] ITLJ 198.
[133] Fn 109.

2. The burden of proving that the incident which caused the loss or damage occurred in the course of the carriage, and the extent of the loss or damage, shall lie with the claimant.

3. Fault or neglect of the carrier ... shall be presumed, unless the contrary is proved, if the death or personal injury to the passenger or the loss of or damage to cabin luggage arose from or in connection with the shipwreck, collision, stranding, explosion or fire or defect in the ship ..."[134]

Like the Montreal Convention the Athens regime is exclusive,[135] but there are several important distinctions between this and article 17 of the Montreal Convention and its predecessors.

- Liability is for *personal injury* as opposed to bodily injury. This, it is submitted, clearly includes psychiatric injury or other impairment of mental faculties.

- The use of the word "incident" as opposed to "accident"[136] may well be intended to extend the scope of liability modestly beyond that contemplated by the Montreal Convention and probably avoids some of the more arcane difficulties that have arisen in construing the meaning of the word "accident" under the Montreal and formerly the Warsaw-Hague regimes. However, it is likely that injury resulting from some internal factor specific to the passenger (*e.g.* a pre-existing physical weakness) are not likely to be covered by the Athens compensation regime any more than they give rise to compensation under the Montreal Convention.

The incident must occur in the course of the carriage. This is more comprehensively defined in Article 1.8. It includes travel by tender to a ship if the transfer is included in the fare or the tender is provided by the carrier, and it also covers the passenger in the course of embarkation and disembarkation. Lessons having been learned from the rules relating to carriage by air, "carriage" specifically *excludes* any period when the passenger is in a port installation or on the quay.

"carriage" covers the following periods:

(a) with regard to the passenger and his cabin luggage, the period during which the passenger and/or his cabin luggage

---

[134] In respect of loss or damage to other luggage fault is presumed irrespective of the cause of the incident.

[135] *No action for damages ... shall be brought against a carrier ... otherwise than in accordance with this Convention.*

[136] Or "occurrence" which was also deployed in the Warsaw-Hague regime.

are on board the ship or in the course of disembarkation, and the period during which the passenger and his cabin luggage are transported by water from land to the ship or vice-versa, if the cost of such transport is included in the fare or if the vessel used for this purpose of auxiliary transport has been put at the disposal of the passenger by the carrier. However, with regard to the passenger, carriage does not include the period during which he is in a marine terminal or station or on a quay or in or on any other port installation;

(b) with regard to cabin luggage, also the period during which the passenger is in a marine terminal or station or on a quay or in or on any other port installation if that luggage has been taken over by the carrier or his servant or agent and has not been re-delivered to the passenger;

(c) with regard to other luggage which is not cabin luggage, the period from the time of its taking over by the carrier or his servant or agent on shore or on board until the time of its re-delivery by the carrier or his servant or agent;

Liability is explicitly fault or neglect based, although there are circumstances in which fault or neglect is to be *presumed.*[137] Such presumptions are rebuttable and the onus of proving the absence of fault or neglect is on the carrier.

It is always for the passenger to prove that the incident which caused the damage occurred in the course of carriage, and the passenger must prove the extent of the damage in respect of which the claim is made. Fault or neglect on the part of the carrier or a servant or agent in the course of their employment is presumed in cases of injury or damage to *cabin luggage* where it arises from or in connection with:

- shipwreck;
- collision;
- stranding;
- explosion or fire;
- defect in the ship.

Where the loss or damage is to *stored* luggage, the presumption of fault and neglect arises in every case. In cases of injury and damage to cabin baggage claims falling outside the above five instances within the scope of Article 3(3), it is for the passenger to prove that the carrier is at fault. Where the

---

[137] As set out in article 1.3.

presumption of fault or neglect arises, the carrier may rebut the presumption, for example, by proving that the incident responsible for the damage was, say, a collision caused by the fault of another vessel. However, where the carrier *and* another vessel are both implicated in fault causing an incident to which the Convention applies, the liability of the carrier and the other vessel will be joint and several. A carrier's liability can be reduced in accordance with domestic laws of contributory negligence.[138]

Limits on liability

Article 7
Limit of liability for personal injury

The liability of the carrier for the death of or personal injury to a passenger shall in no case exceed 700,000 francs (for carriers other than UK carriers) and 100,000 special drawing rights (for UK carriers) per carriage. Where in accordance with the law of the court seized of the case damages are awarded in the form of periodical income payments, the equivalent capital value of those payments shall not exceed the said limit.

Article 8
Limit of liability for loss of or damage to luggage
1 The liability of the carrier for the loss of or damage to cabin luggage shall in no case exceed 833 special drawing rights per passenger, per carriage.

2 The liability of the carrier for the loss of or damage to vehicles including all luggage carried in or on the vehicle shall in no case exceed 3,333 special drawing rights per vehicle, per carriage.

3 The liability of the carrier for the loss of or damage to luggage other than that mentioned in paragraphs 1 and 2 of this Article shall in no case exceed 1,200 special drawing rights per passenger, per carriage.

By Article 7 the liability of the carrier for death or personal injury is limited to 46,666 units of account which has been increased to 300,000 units of account for carriers whose principal place of business is in the United Kingdom.[139] The unit of account is the Special Drawing Right as defined by the IMF, and the amount awarded to a passenger is calculated by taking the value of the domestic currency against the SDR at the date of the judgment.

---

[138] Article 6.
[139] The Carriage of Passengers and their Luggage by Sea (UK Carriers) Order 1998. SI 1998 No. 2917.

Under both Articles 7 and 8, interest and costs (governed by domestic law) are recoverable in addition to the Athens Convention limits. Article 8 provides that the limits for loss or damage to cabin luggage is 833 units of account and for non-cabin luggage 1,200 units of account per passenger, and for loss or damage to vehicles, 3,333 units of account per vehicle. The sterling equivalents of the limitations provided for in Articles 7 and 8 are approximately as follows:

- death or personal injury — £38,000.00 (or for UK based carriers approximately £240,000.00);
- cabin luggage — £140.00;
- other luggage — £228.00;
- vehicles — £2,750.00.

The Convention does not cover the loss of valuables as defined in article 5 (*e.g.* gold, negotiable instruments, works of art or jewellery) unless the valuables have been deposited with the carrier for the *agreed* purpose of safe keeping. Where safe keeping is agreed between passenger and carrier, the limits on the carrier's liability ("other luggage") still apply unless a higher figure is agreed between the parties or imposed by law.[140]

Higher liability limits

National governments may impose higher limits on liability for death and personal injury than those provided for in Article 7. However, any clause which purports to disapply, exclude or dilute the provisions of the Athens Convention[141] is a nullity.

The 1976 Limitation Convention

The Convention on Limitation of Liability for Maritime Claims now has the force of law in the United Kingdom by Schedule 7 of the Merchant Shipping Act 1995[142]. This Convention came into force in 1986. By the 1976 Convention carriers are allowed to limit their overall or global liability for loss and damage arising out of incidents at sea. This includes liability for death, injuries and loss or damage to luggage. The 1976 Convention[143] envisages the establishment of Limitation Funds to enable detained vessels to

---

[140] It is implicit that the carrier will make safe deposit facilities available as a result of article 5 and if facilities are not available it has been held that the passenger is not prevented from claiming for lost valuables. See Saggerson: *Lee & Lee v Airtours Limited* [2002] ITLJ 198.

[141] Article 18 – without affecting the validity of the contract of carriage.

[142] As amended by the Merchant Shipping (Convention on Limitation of Liability for Maritime Claims)(Amendment) Orders 1998 SI 1258 and a draft Order of 13 May 2004.

[143] Article 11.

be released and its scope goes well beyond loss and injury caused to passengers.[144] The size of the fund is measured by multiplying the number of passengers the ship is authorised to carry by 175,000 units of account (about £140,000.00). Total liability is capped by reference to the tonnage of the vessel[145]. The distribution of any fund established is determined by the laws of the country where the fund is established, but reliance may be placed on the limitations irrespective of whether such a fund is established.

The right to rely on the limits provided for in the 1976 Convention or by a Limitation Fund is lost in circumstances where the loss or damage has been caused by the person responsible either with intent to cause such loss or recklessly with knowledge that that such loss would probably result. This sort of conduct which bars the right to rely on the 1976 Convention limits[146] is a familiar regime and applies also under the Athens Convention.[147]

Loss of right to limit damages

Article 13(1) of the Athens Convention deprives the carrier of the right to limit its exposure to damages:

> ...if it is proved that the damage resulted from an act or omission of the carrier done with the intent to cause such damage, or recklessly and with knowledge that such damage would probably result.

It is the acts or omissions of the carrier itself which must be done intentionally or recklessly in order for the limits on liability to be disregarded. This appears to require proof that there has been a systematic or managerial failure of an intentional or reckless character, as opposed to intentional or reckless conduct by an employee in the course of his employment. The Athens Convention seems to assume that where an employee has caused injury or damage, action will be taken against that employee directly. If it is, the employee is subject to the same regime and also loses the right to limit his liability for intentional or reckless conduct. As with the Warsaw Convention it is for the *passenger* to prove intention or recklessness in order to overcome the Athens Convention limits. It is thought likely that any court concerned with allegations of recklessness would apply the same test as that which is applied under the Warsaw Convention.[148]

---

[144] It includes damage caused by pollution (including nuclear damage) and docks for example.
[145] 2 million units of account for a vessel not exceeding 2,000 tons; with incremental increases of 2,001 units up to 30,000 tons; 600 units up to 70,000 tons and 400 units for any weight beyond that – the Merchant Shipping (Convention on Limitation of Liability for Maritime Claims)(Amendment) Order 1998 SI 1258.
[146] Article 4 of the 1976 Convention.
[147] And see also the Warsaw Convention.
[148] As to which see the first section of this Chapter.

Ticketing errors by the carrier do *not* result in the loss of the carrier's right to rely on the limits of liability activated by the Athens Convention.

Limitation periods and procedural bars

Time-bar

> **Article 16**
>
> 1. Any action for damages arising out of the death of or personal injury to a passenger or for the loss of or damage to luggage shall be time-barred after a period of two years.
>
> 2. The limitation period shall be calculated as follows:
>
> (a) in the case of personal injury, from the date of disembarkation of the passenger;
> (b) in the case of death occurring during carriage, from the date when the passenger should have disembarked, and in the case of personal injury occurring during carriage and resulting in the death of the passenger after disembarkation, from the date of death, provided that this period shall not exceed three years from the date of disembarkation.;
> (c) in the case of loss of or damage to luggage, from the date of disembarkation or from the date when disembarkation should have taken place, whichever is later.
>
> 3. The law of the court seized of the case shall govern the grounds of suspension and interruption of limitation periods, but in no case shall an action under this Convention be brought after the expiration of a period of three years from the date of disembarkation should have taken place, whichever is later.
>
> 4. Notwithstanding paragraph 1, 2 and 3 of this Article, the period of limitation may be extended by a declaration of the carrier or by agreement of the parties after the cause of action has arisen. The declaration or agreement shall be in writing.

There is a two-tier system governing the limitation period under the Athens Convention. By article 16 any action for death, personal injury or loss or damage of luggage must be brought within *two years* of the contractual date of disembarkation[149]. However, the measurement of this two-year period is subject to any domestic rules allowing for the *suspension or interruption* of the limitation period. If domestic rules of the court seised of the action permit the suspension or interruption of limitation periods those domestic

---

[149] This applies to package holiday claims too where the other party to the contract is also the carrier. *Norfolk v Mytravel* – above.

rules can be applied subject to an *absolute* bar[150] after three years. Therefore, if the domestic law of the court seised of the action allows for the suspension of the limitation period when an admission of liability is made,[151] or where the claimant falls victim to a disability, and such suspension only has the effect of extending the limitation period to a maximum of three years from the contractual date of disembarkation. The short extension of the limitation period to the long-stop 3 years in such circumstances does not apply to England and Wales.[152]

Procedural bar

Article 15
Notice of loss or damage to luggage
1. The passenger shall give written notice to the carrier or his agent:

(a) in the case of apparent damage to luggage:
(i) for cabin luggage, before or at the time of disembarkation of the passenger;
(ii) for all other luggage, before or at the time of its re-delivery;

(b) in the case of damage to luggage which is not apparent, or loss of luggage, within fifteen days from the date of disembarkation or re-delivery or from the time when such re-delivery should have taken place.

2. If the passenger fails to comply with this Article, he shall be presumed, unless the contrary is proved, to have received the luggage undamaged.

The passenger must give written notice to the carrier in respect of any apparent damage to luggage.[153]

- in cases of cabin luggage this notice must be given before or at the time of disembarkation;

- in all other luggage case notice must be given at the time of its redelivery to the passenger.

Where the damage is not apparent, and in cases of *lost* luggage, the passenger must give written notice within 15 days of the contractual date of disembarkation or redelivery whichever is later. Where a passenger fails to

---

[150] A long-stop.
[151] This is likely to apply in some continental jurisdictions like Spain.
[152] That is section 33 of the Limitation Act 1980 and special rules of limitation for minors or others under a disability do not permit the extension of the 2 year limitation period under the Convention.
[153] Article 15.

give written notice in accordance with article 15, it is presumed that the luggage was redelivered undamaged, but this presumption is rebuttable.[154]

Domestic carriage by sea

The Athens Convention is applied with some modification to carriage by sea within the British Islands by section 184 and Schedule 6 of the Merchant Shipping Act 1995 and by Order in Council. The modified Athens regime, therefore, applies to carriage by sea between ports within the British Islands that does not involve an intermediate port of call in the territory of another State Party. Journeys by sea from England to the Channel Islands or the Isle of Man, for example, are covered by the Athens Convention regime as a result.

Anticipated reforms

The International Conference on the Revision of the Athens Convention took place in London in 2002. The agreed revisions in the form of the 2002 Protocol are not yet in force and will not come into force until 12 months after such time as 10 State Parties signify their acceptance. Only 4 had done so as of September 2007. The 2002 Protocol introduces compulsory insurance to cover passengers on ships and raises the limits of liability. It also introduces other mechanisms to assist passengers in obtaining compensation, based on well-accepted principles applied in existing liability and compensation regimes dealing with environmental pollution. These include replacing the fault-based liability system with a liability system for shipping related incidents firmly based on the principle that the burden of establishing absence of fault should be on the carrier, backed by the requirement that the carrier take out compulsory insurance to cover these potential claims. The limits contained in the Protocol set a maximum limit, empowering - but not obliging - national courts to compensate for death, injury or damage up to these limits. The Protocol also includes an "opt-out" clause, enabling State Parties to retain or introduce higher limits of liability (or unlimited liability) in the case of carriers who are subject to the jurisdiction of their courts. The limit of the compulsory insurance or other financial security shall not be less than 250,000 Special Drawing Rights (SDRs) per passenger on each distinct occasion. Ships are to be issued with a certificate attesting that insurance or other financial security is in force and a model certificate is attached to the Protocol in an Annex.

The revisions make some important changes to the regime as a whole the most important being:

---

[154] Article 15(2).

- Provision for direct claims against shipping insurers (insurance being made compulsory to cover passengers' injuries) in respect of "shipping incident"[155] claims up to 250,000 SDRs such claims being subject only to the defence that the incident was caused by war, terrorism or some natural phenomenon of an exceptional, inevitable and irresistible character.

- Liability up to 400,000 SDRs, or liability in respect of the carriage of passengers not arising out of a "shipping incident" remains subject to the carrier proving that the incident causing the loss occurred without fault or neglect on the carrier's part (or that of its employees).

The Berne Convention

International Carriage by Rail

The United Kingdom is a party to the *Convention Relative aux Transports Internationaux Ferroviaires* (COTIF) signed at Berne in 1980.[156] This convention contains international uniform rules for the carriage of passengers and their luggage by rail[157] These rules came into force in the United Kingdom on 1 May 1985 by Order in Council[158] and they represent a consolidation and rationalisation of previous rules. The Convention applies to rail journeys between or through the territories of state parties to the convention. Rail operators are not permitted to contract out of the regime.[159]

Liability for death and injury

Article 26
Basis of liability

§ 1. The railway shall be liable for the loss or damage resulting from the death of, personal injuries to, or any other bodily or mental harm to, a passenger, caused by an accident arising out of the operation of the railway and happening while the passenger is in, entering or alighting from railway

---

[155] I.e. shipwreck; collision or stranding of the ship; explosion, fire or defect (malfunction in the technical operation) in the ship or its equipment.
[156] Appendix A to the Convention concerning International Carriage by Rail (COTIF) of 9 May 1980 Uniform Rules concerning the contract for international carriage of passengers and luggage by rail (civ).
[157] The Uniform Rules references are given as "UR" below.
[158] Pursuant to the International Transport Conventions Act 1983 and by reference to the Rules set out in Command Paper 8535
[159] Article 26

vehicles. The railway shall also be liable for the loss or damage resulting from the total or partial loss of, or damage to, any articles which the passenger, victim of such an accident, had on him or with him as hand luggage, including any animals.

§ 2. The railway shall be relieved of liability:

(a) if the accident has been caused by circumstances not connected with the operation of the railway and which the railway, in spite of having taken the care required in the particular circumstances of the case, could not avoid and the consequences of which it was unable to prevent;

(b) wholly or partly, to the extent that the accident is due to the passenger's fault or to behaviour on his part not in conformity with the normal conduct of passengers;

(c) if the accident is due to a third party's behaviour which the railway, in spite of having taken the care required in the particular circumstances of the case, could not avoid and the consequences of which it was unable to prevent; if the railway is not thereby relieved of liability, it shall be wholly liable up to the limits laid down in the Uniform Rules but without prejudice to any right of recourse which the railway may have against the third party.

§ 3. The Uniform Rules shall not affect any liability which may be incurred by the railway in cases not provided for in § 1.

§ 4. For the purposes of this chapter. the railway that is liable shall be that which, according to the list of lines or services provided for in Articles 3 and 10 of the Convention, operates the line on which the accident occurred. If, according to that list there is joint operation of the line by two railways, each of them shall be liable.

Actions for death or personal injury (which here includes mental injury[160]) should be brought against the responsible railway; that is, the railway on whose system the accident occurred. The courts of the State in whose territory the responsible railway manages the system have jurisdiction over most claims.

There must be an *"accident"* and the accident must arise:

- out of the operation of the railway;

- whilst the passenger is on board a train;

- or whilst the passenger is entering or alighting from the train.

---

[160] The types of damage recoverable are listed in the Uniform Rules but in addition the UR reserve for the national law of the place where the action is brought the question of what (if any) additional types of loss may be recovered.

The word "accident" is not defined by the convention and it may be assumed that the courts would construe "accident" in the same way as under the Montreal Convention. Accordingly, a frail passenger who falls when alighting from a train as a result of their frailty is unlikely to have suffered an accident within the meaning of the convention. Alternatively, it could be argued that such an event was not caused by the operation of the railway and for this reason the event is outside the scope of the convention.

The Convention is concerned with *accidents* affecting passengers and has no application to persons injured or affected as a result of their having been in the vicinity of a railway accident. In order to sue, the passenger ticket or some other proof of the right to commence proceedings must be produced. Witnesses, bystanders, rescuers or other persons who have suffered damage as a result of a railway accident must look to the domestic law of the country where the accident occurred for a remedy.

Subject to the above qualifications the liability of the railway is a *qualified strict liability*. That is, the railway is relieved from liability only if it is able to establish one of the defences set out in paragraph 26(2) above. The two most important defences are based on the fault of the passenger for the death or injury, or the fault of some third party the consequences of which could not have been prevented despite the exercise of reasonable care.

Damages for death and injury

Article 27
Damages in case of death
§ 1. In the case of the death of the passenger the damages shall include:

(a) any necessary costs following on the death, in particular those of transport of the body, burial and cremation;

(b) if death does not occur at once, the damages provided for in Article 28.

§ 2. If, through the death of the passenger, persons whom he had, or would have had in the future, a legal duty to maintain are deprived of their support, such persons shall also be indemnified for their loss. Rights of action for damages by persons whom the passenger was maintaining without being legally bound to do so shall be governed by national law.

Article 28
Damages in case of personal injury
In the case of personal injury or any other bodily or mental harm to the passenger the damages shall include:

(a) any necessary costs, in particular those of treatment and transport;

(b) compensation for financial loss due to total or partial incapacity to work, or to increased needs.

Article 29
Compensation for other injuries

National law shall determine whether and to what extent the railway shall pay damages for injuries other than that for which there is provision in Articles 27 and 28, in particular for mental or physical pain and suffering (pretium doloris) and for disfigurement.

Article 30
Form and limit of damages in case of death or personal injury

§ 1 . The damages under Article 27, § 2 and Article 28(b) shall be awarded in the form of a lump sum. However, if national law permits payment of an annuity, damages shall be awarded in that form if so requested by the injured passenger or by the persons entitled referred to in Article 27, § 2.

§ 2. The amount of damages to be awarded under § 1 shall be determined in accordance with national law. However, for the purposes of the Uniform Rules, the upper limit per passenger shall be set at 70,000 units of account in the form of a lump sum or an annuity corresponding to that sum, where national law provides for an upper limit of less than that amount.

Damages for death include repatriation and funeral expenses, together with [pain and suffering damages for any period between injury and death. Dependants are also entitled to claim for their loss of dependency which will be calculated in accordance with the principals laid down by the Fatal Accidents Act 1976. Damages are to be calculated in accordance with the law of the jurisdiction seised of the claim. The upper limit placed on the recovery of damages is, however, 70,000 SDRs.

Carriers' defences

The carrier is relieved of liability[161] if it proves that the accident was caused by:

* circumstances unconnected with the operation of the railway;

* behaviour on the part of the passenger that did not conform to the normal conduct of passengers;

---

[161] UR 26(2) see Article 26 above.

- the conduct of a third party which could not have been avoided even with the exercise of such care as was required in all the circumstances and where the consequences could not be prevented.

These defences can be deployed by a carrier to relieve it from liability either in whole or in part and clearly covers acts of contributory negligence on the part of a passenger.

The carrier will, therefore, avoid liability where injury results from an incident caused by a passenger's own drunkenness, violent or other antisocial behaviour. Indeed the convention allows the railway to refuse carriage to any person behaving improperly, or who may by their behaviour or condition cause inconvenience to other passengers. Liability for incidents occasioned by acts of vandalism by third parties, for example, will give rise to liability under the convention unless the railway can show that the incident could not have been avoided even if reasonable care in all the circumstances had been exercised *and* the consequences of the incident could not be prevented. It follows that where an accident occurs as a result of some vandalism or other outside interference with the operation of the railway, the carrier will have to show that it had deployed reasonable security measures to prevent or minimise trespassing *and* to secure the safety of trains in case their other security measures failed — on the basis that no security system is fool-proof. So it could be that a railway fails in its defence despite taking sturdy measures to prevent trespassers getting to the track if due to slack procedures elsewhere in the system, the trespasser has easy access to tools or equipment with which damage is then caused.

Luggage

The railway is liable for *articles* that an injured person has in their possession that have been lost or damaged in an accident up to 700 SDRs per passenger.[162]

The carrier is also liable to passengers for total or partial loss or damage to luggage on board the train,[163] and for registered luggage in the custody of the carrier if the loss or damage arises out of an accident such as would give rise to liability for personal injury. The same defences are available to the carrier in luggage cases as are available in injury cases.

Compensation for the *loss* of registered luggage is limited to 40 SDRs per kilo, or 600 SDRs per item of luggage plus the refund of carriage charges, customs duties and other sums incurred in respect of the carriage of the lost

---

[162] Article 31.
[163] UR 26.

item.[164] Compensation for *damage* is limited to the amount that would have been awarded had that damaged part of the luggage been lost.[165]

Delay

The Convention does not cover losses sustained by delay to passengers. These claims are subject to the domestic law of the contract of carriage. Loss arising out of delayed registered luggage[166] *is* covered by the convention.[167] A missing article is deemed to be lost if not delivered within 14 days of a request for delivery The contractual time for delivery should be set out in the luggage voucher completed at or before the time goods are placed into the custody of the carrier.

Limits on liability

The right to limit the amount of recovery is lost in the circumstances covered by Article 42 below.

Article 42
Loss of the right to invoke the limits of liability

The provisions of Articles 30, 31 and 38 to 41 of the Uniform Rules or those of national law, limiting compensation to a fixed amount. shall not apply if it is proved that the loss or damage resulted from an act or omission, on the part of the railway, done with intent to cause such loss or damage, or recklessly and with knowledge that such loss or damage will probably result.

Limitation and procedural bars

Claims for personal injury and in respect of luggage must be made three years from the day *after* the accident. In fatal accidents cases, the time limit is three years from the date of death or five years from the day after the accident, whichever is earlier.[168] The limitation period is suspended where a claim is submitted to the railway within three months of the accident and time only begins to run again once the railway rejects the claim in writing.

Article 55
Limitation of actions

---

[164] Article 38(2)

[165] Article 39.

[166] Detailed provisions are set out in Article 40 available to download on the COTIF website.

[167] 0.40 units of account per kilogram (32p) or 7 units (£5.60) per item *provided* an actual loss can be established. Where a loss cannot be established the limits are reduced to 0.07 (6p) and 1.40 (£1.12) units of account respectively.

[168] UR 55.

§ 1. The period of limitation for actions for damages based on the liability of the railway in case of death of, or personal injury to, passengers shall be:

(a) in the case of a passenger, three years from the day after the accident;

(b) in the case of other persons entitled, three years from the day after the death of the passenger, subject to a maximum of five years from the day after the accident.

§ 2. The period of limitation for other actions arising from the contract of carriage shall be one year. Nevertheless, the period of limitation shall be two years in the case of an action for loss or damage resulting from an act or omission done with intent to cause such loss or damage, or recklessly and with knowledge that such loss or damage would probably result.

§ 3. The period of limitation provided for in § 2 shall run:

(a) in actions for compensation for total loss, from the fourteenth day after the expiry of the period of time referred to in Article 23, § 3;

(b) in actions for compensation or partial loss, for damage or for delay in delivery, from the day when delivery took place;

(c) in actions for payment or refund of carriage charges, supplementary charges or surcharges, or for correction of charges in the event of a tariff being wrongly applied or of an error in calculation or collection: from the day of payment or. if payment has not been made, from the day when payment should have been made;

(d) in actions to recover additional duty demanded by Customs or other administrative authorities, from the day of the demand made by such authorities;

(e) in all other cases involving the carriage of passengers, from the day of expiry of validity of the ticket. The day indicated for the commencement of the period of limitation shall not be included in the period.

§ 4. When a claim is presented to a railway in accordance with Article 49 together with the necessary supporting documents, the period of limitation shall be suspended until the day that the railway rejects the claim by notification in writing and returns the documents. If part of the claim is admitted, the period of limitation shall recommence in respect of that part of the claim still in dispute. The burden of proof of receipt of the claim or of the reply and of the return of the documents shall rest on the party who relies on those facts. The period of limitation shall not be suspended by further claims having the same object.

§ 5. A right of action which has become time barred may not be exercised by way of counterclaim or relied upon by way of exception.

§ 6. Subject to the foregoing provisions, the suspension and interruption of periods of limitation shall be governed by national law.

However, a claimant is barred from proceeding *altogether* if he fails to give notice of the accident within three months of becoming aware of any damage (where the passenger is the claimant this is likely to be within 6 months of the accident itself). The claimant's loss of a right of action in these circumstances does *not* occur if:

- the failure to give notice or the lateness of the notice was due to circumstances for which the claimant is not responsible (for example, a claimant seriously affected by significant injuries or otherwise under a disability); or

- the railway responsible for the accident knows of the accident within three months of its occurrence in any event (that is by other means or from other passengers); or

- the claimant proves that the accident was caused by the fault of the carrier.

Domestic Carriage by Rail

Unlike the Conventions relating to international carriage by air and sea the Berne Convention is not applied by a form of modified regime to domestic carriage by rail which is governed by domestic law. For the conditions applicable to domestic carriage by rail reference should be made to the National Conditions of Carriage.[169] For domestic carriage by rail, no limits are placed on the recovery of damages for personal injury or death. Compensation for delays of one hour or more, is limited to 10% of the face value of the ticket and is payable in travel vouchers. A claim must be submitted within two working days of completing the journey in question.

Compensation for loss or damage to luggage is fault based and is limited to £1,000.00 per item or the value of the item whichever is the lower. Recovering damages for such loss or delay depends on the passenger proving that the loss has been occasioned by the train company's neglect or default.

Common Carriers

" *The common carrier of passengers is he who holds himself out as willing to carry members of the public generally*" or "*one who exercises the public*

---

[169] Available from the Office of the Rail Regulator at 1, Waterhouse Square, Holborn Bars, 138-142 Holborn, London EC1N 2ST.

profession of carrying ... passengers whoever they may be".[170] A carrier may be a common carrier of goods or passengers or both. Any person who provides regular passenger services to those who are in a fit condition to travel and who are willing to pay the fare required, is likely to be a common carrier of passengers.[171] A common carrier may be a carrier by land, sea or air[172] The private (as opposed to common) carrier is one who may pick and choose who or what he might carry.[173]

Passengers

The duty of the common carrier towards passengers is to exercise reasonable care to carry the passengers safely. In the case of passengers this duty is the same as that of a private carrier. The carrier does not *warrant* the safety of passengers, neither does it warrant the safety of their vehicles but the standard of care required of the carrier in respect of both passengers and vehicles is a high one.[174] The carrier's duty to exercise reasonable care extends to anticipating possible dangers presented by outside sources or third parties and either taking steps to minimise any threatened risk, or warn passengers of the danger[175]. A carrier is likely to be an "*occupier*" of any vehicle, vessel or aircraft for the purposes of the Occupiers' Liability Acts 1957[176] and 1984 so the duties owed by a carrier includes the statutory common duty of care and extends to all those on board whether fare payers or otherwise.

The carrier's liability is fault based Proving of fault may not always be difficult for the passenger involved in a transport accident. The high standard of service, vehicles and equipment required of the Common or private carrier has caused the courts to infer negligence from the primary facts in transport

---

[170] *Halsbury* 5(1) – paragraph 402.
[171] Railway service operators In Great Britain have not been common carriers at least since the Transport Act 1962 – the position is unchanged since privatisation – Railways Act 1993.
[172] Although there does not appear to have been a case in which an air carrier has been liable as such.
[173] Subject now to unlawful discrimination legislation.
[174] In *Readhead v Midland Railway Co* [1869] 4 LR QB 379, a passenger failed to recover personal injury damages following a derailment on the grounds that the cause had been a latent defect in the wheel of the train which could not have been discovered by the exercise of due care. The common carrier of goods on the other hand is more in the position of an insurer. See *e.g.* Montague Smith J at 382 by which time the distinction between the common carrier of passengers and goods was already regarded as "well settled". The standard of public service transport vehicles for the carriage of passengers may be taken as a very high one. The principle was applied more recently in *O'Connor v British Transport Commission* [1958] 1 WLR 346 where a child fell from a guard's van in circumstances where the handle was found to be appropriate for ordinary use by passengers. As to standard of maintenance for vehicles see *Barkway v South Wales Transport* [1950] 1 All ER 392 — due diligence required for tyre inspection system.
[175] *Lewis v Burnett* [1945] 2 All ER 555.
[176] Section 1(3)(a).

cases perhaps more readily than any other class of case.[177] Similar general duties apply to carriers in respect of their stations, ports and depots.

The carrier is liable in contract to his passengers even where the negligence giving rise to the damage is that of an independent contractor engaged by the carrier. This is because at common law the carrier's *contractual* duty[178] was to the effect that due care *would be exercised* in the provision of the carriage services irrespective of who actually delivers the service in question.

Statutory provisions of general application should not be ignored. Section 2 of UCTA 1977 for example renders ineffective any attempt on the part of the carrier to exclude liability for personal injury or death resulting from negligence.[179] However, where a common carrier is offering international carriage services to which an international convention applies, the provisions of the relevant convention prevail over those of UCTA[180]. The carrier's liability may be excluded or limited or an action may become procedurally or time barred in accordance with the provisions of the relevant convention.

Luggage

Luggage is:

> "ordinary, personal luggage, that is to say luggage for personal use or convenience according to the habits or wants of the particular class to which the passenger belongs, with reference to either the immediate necessities or the ultimate purpose of his journey"[181]

Where the carrier is a common carrier and takes charge of a passenger's luggage, the carrier's liability is that of an *insurer* — and the carrier is absolutely bound to deliver the goods in the condition in which they were originally to be found.[182] The liability framework in respect of the passenger and the luggage is, therefore, different. Liability to passengers is fault based and the burden of proving fault lies on the claimant but with regard to *luggage*, the carrier's liability is based on a form of modified strict liability.

---

[177] *Ng Chun Pui v Lee Cheun Tat* [1988] RTR 298 (car crashed over central reservation); *Ayles v South Eastern Railway Company* [1867–9] 3–4 LRExch 146 (2 trains colliding, claim succeeded on very slight evidence of fault in the absence of any evidence to the contrary); *Fosbroke-Hobbes v Airwork Ltd* [1937] 1 All ER 108 (aircraft crashing on take-off enough in itself to make out a case).

[178] One that could not be delegated.

[179] As does section 1 of the Public Transport Vehicles Act 1981 in respect of the carriage of persons in public service vehicles.

[180] UCTA 1977 section 29.

[181] *Macrow v Great Western Railway* [1871] LR 6 QB 612 and see also *Casswell v Cheshire Lines Committee* [1907] 2 KB at page 503.

[182] See *Macrow* and *Casswell* above.

The carrier's liability for luggage also extends to hand baggage retained by the passenger unless the carrier proves:

- the luggage was taken under the passenger's sole charge; *and*

- the passenger's negligence was the cause of the loss or damage (due to bad packing, inexpert storage in an overhead compartment or interference with it during the course of the journey.)[183]

The carrier's liability for luggage begins and ends with the passenger's transit. This includes mounting and alighting from the transport provided and includes a reasonable period within which the passenger can be expected to collect any luggage consigned to a separate compartment.[184] The carrier is also liable for luggage handed over a reasonable and proper time before the commencement of the journey.[185]

Special contracts

The common carrier has always been able to limit or exclude his liabilities by means of a special contract. The common carrier's duties may, therefore, be regarded as duties imposed in default of any special contract. The default duties are nonetheless important because they will prevail in those situations where the carrier either fails to prove that any special contract terms have been incorporated into the carriage contract or where any special terms are struck down as a result of the statutory requirement of reasonableness. Whether incorporation has been achieved depends on the application of the ordinary principles of contract law.

> "... where a contract is made by the delivery, by one of the contracting parties to the other, of a document in a common form stating the terms upon which the person delivering it will enter into the proposed contract, such a form constitutes the offer of the party who tenders it, and if the form is accepted without objection by the person to whom it is tendered this person is as a general rule bound by its contents and his act amounts to an acceptance of the offer to him whether he reads the document or otherwise informs himself of its contents or not, and the conditions contained in the document are binding on him".[186]

It makes no difference apparently that the person to whom the document is delivered cannot read.[187] Unless the terms are now considered unreasonable,

---

[183] *Great Western Railway Company v Bunch* [1888] 13 App Cases at 48 (Lord Watson).
[184] *Patschieder v Great Western Railway Company* [1878] 3 LR Exch 153. – e.g. luggage in a special coach on a train or in the boot of a motor coach.
[185] *GWR v Bunch* – above.
[186] *Numan v Southern Railway* [1923] 2 KB 703.
[187] *Thompson v LM & S Railway* [1930] 1 KB 41.

the only issue is whether the offering carrier took reasonable steps to bring the terms to the attention of the intending passenger.

> This is a class of case in which of citing of authorities there is no end, and yet it is I think, quite possible to say 'hear the conclusion of the whole matter.[188]

The intervention of statutory, regulatory and international controls have limited the extent to which carriers can now exclude restrict their liability by special contract.

The Carriers Act 1830

This Act is still in force. Today it applies mainly to passengers being carried by road. It only applies to carriage by land. The purpose of the Act is to relieve carriers from the worst excesses of their potential liability as *insurers* for the carriage of luggage and items of special value[189] (that is to say over £10.00) that are not declared in advance or for which an additional carriage charge is not levied. Passengers may on occasions carry with them or consign to the custody of the carrier packages or parcels containing items of great value which it is impossible to discern from the nature of the packing.

The passenger must declare the nature and value of the goods in question and pay an increased charge. No particular form of declaration is prescribed but it must be in clear terms[190] and with the intention of making a declaration under the Act and so that the carrier may know that the passenger intends to hold him responsible for the goods of special value. Whether adequate notice under the Act has been given by the passenger will in all cases be a matter of fact. Where an adequate declaration has been made the carrier is liable as an insurer in the ordinary way for the carriage of goods. Where no adequate declaration has been made the carrier may avail himself of the £10.00 limit irrespective of whether it is the negligence of the carrier or his employees which causes the loss.[191]

---

[188] *Hood v Anchor Line* [1918] AC 837 at 846.
[189] Gold, silver, precious stones, bank notes, stamps, furs, hand-made lace and "trinkets" amongst other things.
[190] To enable a suitable extra charge to be levied no doubt.
[191] Unless the loss is caused by wilful deviation from the contract of carriage or conversion.

Chapter 11

SECURITY AND INSOLVENCY

Introduction

As in so many other respects the PTR 1992 have (at least on the surface) transformed the security requirements within the package travel business. In this chapter consideration will be given in some detail to the security provisions of the PTR 1992 in addition to other voluntary and statutory security schemes in so far as they may be relevant now that the Regulations are in force.

For many years the travel industry in general, and the package travel part of that industry in particular, have been beset by very public scandals, usually involving the collapse of tour operators, resulting in the loss to consumers of their hard-earned holiday money. In the worst cases, consumers have been stranded abroad with no means of financing their return home following the collapse of their tour operator. The first the holiday-maker knows of such difficulties is usually news from an angry hotelier demanding payment for meals and rooms that should have been paid for months before, and for which the tourist has already made payment to the tour operator.[1] Those waiting to embark on their holidays usually discover a problem when the tickets do not arrive, and telephone enquiries are dealt with by an anonymous answering service — a perfunctorily apologetic notice being sellotaped to the tour operator's office door. The fact that such scandals represent the exception rather than the rule,[2] and that throughout the relatively short history of package travel, infinitely more consumers have enjoyed holidays that only a few decades ago would have been the preserve of the wealthy undertaking a "Grand Tour", seems to get lost in the welter of recrimination that follows the insolvency of any tour company, be it large or small. On a smaller scale, scanning the more scandalous parts of the press,

---

[1] Precisely what happened to Austrian holidaymakers stranded on Crete – see *Verein Fur Konsumenteninformation v Austria* – ECJ 364/96.
[2] Although Austria appears to have had a glut of such failures in recent years – see above and also *Rechburger* C-140/97.

reports of holiday and tour "organisers" running off with funds that should have been appropriated to some annual trip or tour, are not as rare as they should be. Clarksons, Court Line and Laker are amongst the bigger names to have faltered within living memory. These are but a few headline-making examples which have led many consumers to hold tour operators in low esteem. Such a bad public image was probably never entirely justified — not least because in each of the examples cited above, sophisticated voluntary security arrangements were in place to protect the consumer; but nonetheless, it has taken many years for the travel industry to live down the reputation imposed on it by a disreputable, disorganised or unlucky few. That the industry has, in large measure, lived down this poor reputation is mostly due to self-regulation and voluntary financial control. Notwithstanding this self-regulation at the reputable end of the industry — the larger part of it — the PTR 1992 impose obligations in respect of the security of consumers' money on every person (corporate or individual) who contracts to supply consumers with package holidays. This is a laudable ambition. However, there can be no doubt that the effectiveness of the PTR 1992 in this regard will only be as good as the enforcement of the regulations. The disreputable, disorganised, dishonest and the plain ignorant will, no doubt, still offer packages without putting in place security arrangements demanded of them by the regulations; and when they do, the enforcement authorities are not likely to encounter them until a problem has arisen, or an insolvency has occurred. Prosecuting such defaulters after the event may be sufficient to send a message of warning to others minded to behave in the same way and ignore the statutory regime, but trading standards prosecutions will achieve very little for the consumers victimised by the failure of their tour operator to employ regulated security measures specifically designed for their protection.

A Cautionary Tale

D, a man with no experience in the travel industry, entered into a partnership with a Spanish company to promote what was billed as "The Dance Event of the Year" in Marbella for a week in September 1994. The target audience for this event were young adults between the ages of 18 and 30, and the package (involving air travel accommodation and entry to a number of disco-style dance events) was advertised in popular music magazines. The cost was of the order of £350.00 per person. Because of the way the package was marketed (as raves), large numbers of unemployed and low-paid youngsters signed-up for the trip — often comprising large groups of friends. D, the organiser of the project at the British end, collected thousands of pounds from the would- be party-goers. He had never heard of the PTR 1992, until a few months before the commencement of the package, when he was alerted to them by a neighbour. Seeking advice from a solicitor,

D opened a "trust" account[3] of which the trustees were solicitors from the firm whose advice he had sought. Many more thousands of pounds were collected, but regrettably not paid into the trust account. Instead, all the money collected was sent to Spain with the intention (not unreasonable to D, the inexperienced entrepreneur) that the money should be used to pay for the accommodation and the services of the discos and DJs that were to be employed during the course of the *"Dance Event of 1994"*. Two weeks before the event was due to begin, it was cancelled from the Spanish end, due to insufficient bookings. Any money that might have been left was in Spain. None of the intending package tourists received any compensation. D was prosecuted and convicted of an offence (*inter alia*) contrary to regulation 16 of the PTR 1992 for failing to have in force security arrangements for clients' money of the type envisaged by the regulators. D was broke — at least in this jurisdiction. The consumers are still waiting for their money back.

The point of this cautionary tale, taken from the facts of a real case, is not to belittle the efforts of the regulators but to point out that whatever statutory obligations are imposed, there are still (in this area as in so many others) likely to be instances where consumers are done out of their hard-earned cash, and their well-earned holiday. Without being unduly pessimistic, it is unlikely in the extreme that the conviction in the above case will have had a salutary effect on other would-be "entrepreneurs"; the only hope is that it has sufficiently deflated D, and pointed him in the direction of some other business, thus saving future unsuspecting tourists from a similar fate. Perhaps the security provisions in the Regulations will only have prospective force when *consumers* themselves realise that they are entitled to security, and demand to have security arrangements explained and information supplied *before a package contract is made.* As if the point needed emphasising, it should be noted that the PTR 1992 apply only to *packages as defined by the regulations.* For non-regulated packages, and arrangements that cannot be described even as unregulated packages, the consumer must look to the voluntary schemes or the general law for salvation.

Before turning to the detailed provisions of the PTR 1992 relating to security it is worth pausing to revise some of the basic problems that arise in the event of a tour operator's or travel agent's insolvency, and to consider briefly the statutory and voluntary security arrangements that exist outside the PTR 1992.

---

[3] PTR regulation 20.

Insolvency — Tour Operators

It is small consolation to the consumer to be informed that the ordinary principles of contract are not displaced simply by reason of the fact that his tour operator has gone into liquidation. The consumer, may in theory, have a perfectly enforceable contract against the company in liquidation - but this will mean very little in practice where service providers have not been paid, airline seats not reserved, and where inevitably, there is no money left to pay for the services or from which the consumer can be compensated, or his advance payments refunded. The fate of the consumer stranded at home before his travel commences, is as nothing in comparison to the problems faced by those who have embarked on their travel only to be stranded by a defaulting tour operator. Theirs is the additional problem of seeking and paying for transportation home — as well as interim accommodation. The repayment of deposits and expenses incurred is unlikely; the payment of compensation for loss of enjoyment and disappointment is unthinkable. Before the PTR 1992 the consumer would have had a number of possible avenues to explore.

He could look to the travel agent in respect of any money paid which the travel agent was holding as an agent of the consumer — this would include those instances where money was paid to the agent before any contract with the tour operator had been concluded or confirmed as a general rule. It is also possible that the agent would have offered an independent "money-back" guarantee as consideration for the consumer booking through his agency. Looking to recover money held by a travel agent should almost always be feasible where the travel agent was acting as a mere booking agent for the consumer in non-package cases.

If the consumer had paid for the travel services by credit card, he may have a claim against the credit company by reason of section 75 of the Consumer Credit Act of 1974. Such a claim would almost certainly exist where the credit card had been accepted directly by the tour operator. The position has proved more controversial where the travel agent has accepted the credit card as payment for package services offered by a tour operator.

Consumer Credit Act 1974

Section 75 and the tour operator

It seems to be universally accepted that where a consumer pays a tour operator directly (whether the payment is a deposit, a down payment or in full) by credit card (as opposed to a charge card), the credit card company, being jointly liable to the consumer for any breach of contract by the supplier by reason of section 75, must satisfy the consumer's claim. Section 75 provides:

> If the debtor [the consumer] under a debtor-creditor-supplier agreement falling within section 12(b) or (c) has, in relation to a transaction financed by the agreement, any claim against the supplier in respect of a misrepresentation of breach of contract, he shall have a like claim against the creditor [credit card company], who with the supplier [the tour operator], shall accordingly be jointly and severally liable to the debtor.

The consumer has a "like claim" against the card company, as he would against the tour operator (the "supplier") of the travel services.

Consumers often appreciate that credit card use carries the advantage of a potential right of recourse against the card issuer should the supplier breach his obligations relating to the supply contract.[4] The question that arose in *Office of Fair Trading v Lloyds TSB Bank plc and others* was whether this right against the credit card company extends to the use of credit cards in *foreign transactions*. The Office of Fair Trading ("OFT"), acting in the interests of consumers, maintains that it does. Lloyds TSB Bank plc and Tesco Personal Finance Ltd, credit card issuers and representatives of the UK credit card industry, maintain the contrary.

Lord Mance in the course of his Opinion stated that there was nothing in sections 11, 12 or 75(1) purporting to legislate extra•territorially in relation to the supplier or the supply transaction financed by the credit agreement. To impose on United Kingdom card issuers a liability to United Kingdom card holders by reference to liabilities arising under a foreign supply transaction was not, he said, axiomatically to legislate extra•territorially. However, the card issuing appellants in the case contended for, and Gloster J. at first instance accepted, a limitation excluding from section 75(1) supply transactions with the following characteristics:

> (1) the contract [between the debtor and the supplier] was made wholly outside the United Kingdom, or (if not) the acts of offer and acceptance were done partly within and partly outside the United Kingdom; and
> (2) the contract was governed by a foreign law; and
> (3) the goods were delivered, or services supplied outside the United Kingdom, or the goods were despatched outside the United Kingdom for delivery within the United Kingdom.

---

[4] Provided always the amount spent is more than £100 and less than £30,000.- the financial boundaries of the Consumer Credit Act 1974.

The credit card companies submitted that the implications, if section 75(1) applies to overseas transactions, are "startling and readily apparent", in that it would make United Kingdom card issuers the potential guarantors of some 29 million foreign suppliers, with whom they would not have any direct contractual relations. Gloster J accepted this argument. The House of Lords did not because it was one that depended on today's market whereas The 1974 Act had to be construed against the background of the market as it existed and was understood and foreseen at the time of the *Crowther* Report and the passing of the Act in 1974. The House of Lord concluded that the factors which led the Crowther Committee to recommend the imposition on card issuers of a liability reflecting suppliers' liability to debtors, all apply as much to overseas as to domestic supply transactions • if not more so. In relation to overseas transactions, there would be likely to be an even greater discrepancy between the card holder's ability to pursue suppliers on the one hand and the ease with which card issuers could obtain redress through the contractual and commercial ties which Crowther contemplated would link them and suppliers. Card issuers' ability to bear irrecoverable losses and so "spread the burden" exists in relation to both overseas and domestic transactions.

The conclusion of the House of Lords was that there was nothing in the 1974 Act to introduce or require any further limitation in the territorial scope of section 75(1), other than that the credit agreement must be a United Kingdom credit agreement. The argument that section 75(1) was limited in application to domestic supply transactions and so inapplicable to overseas supply transactions was rejected.

The same conclusion was reached in the personal injury case of *Grove v Amex Europe Ltd.*[5] Mr. Grove paid for his French hotel accommodation with his American Express (credit) Card. Whilst staying at the hotel in France he had an accident and was injured which he attributed to the failure on the part of the Hotel to exercise reasonable skill and care in the provision of the Hotel facilities and services. He sued Amex who in turn joined the Hotel company as a third party. A preliminary issue was tried as to whether section 75(1) extended to the supply of services overseas and the judge ruled that it *did* – which ruling has now 4 years later been underpinned by the House of Lords.

Section 75 may also come to the rescue of some consumers engaged in the purchase of timeshare interests in holiday property. Claims against bank creditors were made by consumers pursuant to section 75 in several linked actions as long ago as 1996. In *Jarrett and others v Barclays Bank plc and*

---

[5] 28 April 2003 HHJ Behar Wandsworth County Court (Unreported).

others[6] consumers claimed damages against the credit suppliers when it emerged that they had variously purchased timeshare interests on the strength of misrepresentations made to them. On this occasion the banks argued that only the courts of the country where the timeshare property was situated had jurisdiction over the actions given the then applicable Article 16 of the Brussels Convention.

Article 16 stated:

> The following courts shall have exclusive jurisdiction, regardless of domicile:
> *(a)* In proceedings which have as their object rights in rem in immoveable property or tenancies of immoveable property, the Courts of the Contracting State in which the property is situated.

The following text is edited from the detailed judgment of Millett LJ.

> The reference to the like claim in s.75 Consumer Credit Act 1974 must refer to the like cause of action. Plainly the remedies cannot be the same, for the remedies available to the debtor against the supplier may include injunctions or orders for specific performance which could not lie against the creditor. Further the use of the words "the like" presupposes some differences. I can see no reason at all for supposing that Parliament intended to enact in relation to the statutory cause of action conferred by s.75 (or s.56) any jurisdictional requirement to be observed in proceedings against the supplier. But I do not think that the answer to the question lies in a consideration of the statute rather than the Brussels Convention and in the principles established by the European Court of Justice in the interpretation of the words "proceedings which have as their object." In my view, in the light of those statements of principle, these actions do not have as their object tenancies of immovable property. In each action the foundation for the claim against the Bank under s.75 is the debtor-creditor-supplier agreement. That contract has attached to it the personal statutory rights conferred by the Consumer Credit Act 1974 on the debtor. Of course the enforcement of those statutory rights is connected to or linked with the claims of the consumer against the supplier under the timeshare agreements but it is based on the debtor-creditor-supplier agreement not the timeshare agreement. The consumer does not seek the resolution of any of the disputes [which have as their object rights in rem]. There is no reason to suppose that it was the intention of the signatories to the Brussels Convention that rights conferred by the legislation in one contracting state for the protection of the consumer should, if those rights are linked to a dispute between the

---

[6] 31st October 1996 (CA)

consumer and a third party concerning rights in rem or a tenancy, only be enforced in the courts of another contracting state.

Section 75 and the travel agent

Why should section 75 not also work where the payment by credit card has been made to the travel agent who in turn passes it on to the tour operator? When the tour operator goes bust should it make any material difference whether the consumer's credit card payment has been made directly to the tour operator or indirectly through the travel agent? It *should* make no difference at all, and the only reason this scenario has excited more controversy than the situation where the tour operator is paid direct, is because the credit card companies have fought a strident rearguard action to persuade all concerned that section 75 does not apply where payment has been to the travel agent. The reasoning is that section 75 only applies where the consumer has a claim for misrepresentation or breach of contract against the "supplier" in relation to a "transaction" financed by the debtor-creditor-supplier agreement. The key words are "supplier" and "transaction". The credit card companies have argued that where the consumer pays his travel agent the "transaction" is the payment by the consumer for the travel agent's services as facilitator, co-ordinator or "middleman". The travel agent is the "supplier" of travel agency services, not the supplier of the travel arrangements. So when the tour operator goes into liquidation, and breaches a travel contract as a result, the travel agent is unaffected. He has discharged his obligations to provide the services of a travel agency, and the consumer has no claim for misrepresentation or breach of contract against the travel agent, and no "like claim" to make against, or pass on to, the credit card company.

The view of the credit card companies has a good deal of (reluctant) support amongst commentators.

It is not a view that finds favour with the Office of Fair Trading, and but for the fact that the companies' argument has found academic support it would be tempting to treat it as a desperate gamble on their part to avoid a potentially wide form of hitherto largely untapped liability. When consumers victimised by the collapse of Laker, applied for compensation to Barclaycard and Access they were refused in appropriate cases on the grounds that they had paid their travel agents who were not in breach of contract — no "like" claim could be raised against the creditors accordingly. The dispute was compromised, but the credit card companies never accepted that they had a section 75 liability in those circumstances.

The better view it is submitted is that the creditor is liable to the debtor (consumer) where credit card payment has been made to the travel agent — be it by way of deposit or payment in full. The "transaction" that the debtor pays for is the travel contract. Consumers would be flabbergasted if told that they were paying on credit for the use of the travel agents services as a *facilitator*. Clearly they are not. The price that is required of them (albeit by the travel agent) is the price of the package or other contract to be provided by the tour operator. That is the only reason the consumer is using his credit card. The "supplier" of the services, for which the consumer is paying on credit, is the tour operator. The consumer uses the travel agent as a mere conduit for the passage of the money. Accordingly, where the tour operator goes under, the "supplier" in the "transaction" will be in breach of contract, and the debtor (consumer) will have a "like" claim in breach of contract against the creditor in relation to the travel contract as he would have had against the tour operator — even though the parties used the travel agent as an *agent for the passage of* the travel contract price to the tour operator. It does not matter whose agent the travel agent was when the credit card money was transmitted to the tour operator. Whether he was the agent of the consumer or the tour operator, the "transaction" financed was still that of the provision by the tour operator of the travel services.

By far the most common recourse for the pre-Regulation consumer was one of the many "voluntary" security schemes run by tour operators' and travel agents' professional and trade associations, or the statutory scheme run by the Civil Aviation Authority (CAA) pursuant to the Civil Aviation (Air Travel Organiser's Licensing) Regulations 1995, the ATOL. Many of these remain in force alongside the PTR 1992, and indeed compliance with such an "official" security scheme will often be sufficient compliance for the purposes of the PTR 1992.

The Air Travel Organiser's Licence[7]

All tour operators selling flights and air holidays must hold a licence from the CAA. The present arrangements, which are now being reformed, are that before it gets a licence each operator is examined to ensure it is properly managed and financially sound and it must lodge a bond - a financial guarantee provided by a bank or insurance company. If it fails, the CAA then uses the money to pay for people abroad to continue their holidays and to travel home as planned, and to make refunds to those who have paid but not travelled. If the bond is not enough, any shortfall is met by the Air Travel Trust Fund, which is managed by the CAA and backs up the individual bonds. ATOL (short for Air Travel Organisers' Licensing) is managed by the CAA and gives protection from losing money or being stranded abroad to 27 million people in the UK who buy air holidays and flights from tour operators each year. In the year to March 2007, ATOL enabled 4,706

---

[7] 1995 SI 1054.

customers of failed tour operators to complete their holidays and return to the UK and 54,116 received a refund of advance payments. For the year, total expenditure on claims and repatriations was £14.2 million. The Government decided to proceed with a reform of the ATOL Scheme and introduce a £1 per person per journey ATOL Protection Contribution (APC) to replenish the Air Travel Trust Fund and reform bonding arrangements. The ATOL system was first established on a statutory basis in the UK with the ATOL Regulations, made under the Civil Aviation Act 1971. Europe-wide protection for all package holidays was introduced in 1990 with the Package Travel Directive (PTR 1992 in the UK). ATOL also covers flight-only sales by companies other than an airline or an agent that supplies the ticket immediately. Budget airlines are, therefore, not required to subscribe to the ATOL system.

Companies, and those selling package holidays that include a flight, are required to hold an ATOL. In 2006, this comprised some 2,500 businesses, providing 27 million air holidays and flights. The CAA issues these licences and the ATOL holders pay the costs incurred by CAA in administering the ATOL system through annual charges, estimated at £5.5m in total in 2005, or around 16p per passenger. A requirement of a licence being granted is that the licence holder puts in place financial arrangements in case of insolvency. The great majority of businesses, including all the largest operators, do this by providing a bond of between 10% and 15% of their forecast annual licensable turnover. ATOL holders incur costs in obtaining ATOL licences and complying with the requirements of the system. A part of this includes the costs of obtaining bonds. Estimates of the cost of bonding vary. ATOL holders estimate an average cost of £2 per passenger, with lower rates for large companies and higher for smaller ones. The Travel Bonding Working Group of the Association of British Insurers estimates costs of between £1.00 and £1.20. Bonding requirements are based on an ATOL holder's projected business. If the amount of business carried out is likely to exceed the initial projections, an ATOL holder must vary the licence and obtain additional bonding. The extra burden of obtaining this additional bonding, both in terms of financial cost and management time, creates an incentive for firms to overestimate passenger figures at their annual renewal and therefore 'over bond'. This represents an additional cost of bonding, as when these additional seats are included in calculations the price of bonding increases further. In addition, ATOL holders face compliance costs related to bonding in terms of management time and effort, an issue of particular concern to small firms. The bond is available to meet refund and repatriation expenses should the firm become insolvent. If the refund and repatriation expenditure is greater than funds available from the bond, the Air Travel Trust Fund (ATTF) provides funding to meet any excess.

The ATTF is managed by a Board of Trustees made up of CAA Board members and officials and is a separate legal entity to the CAA. Its forerunner was established in 1972 and a sizeable fund was built up through a statutory levy on ATOL holders, collected from 1975 to 1977. This was set at 2% of the average price of a holiday for the majority the collection period. Interest earned on the amount held meant that the fund continued to grow until the failure of the tour operator ILG in 1991, the second largest ATOL holder at the time, which depleted the funds to such an extent that investment income was no longer high enough to offset claims. The CAA's power to levy the industry had lapsed in 1986 and the ATTF went into deficit in 1996. Costs falling to the fund were then met through a bank overdraft guaranteed by Government. At the beginning of 2007, the ATTF overdraft was £18.4 million with monthly interest charges of around £83,000. The overdraft is currently supported by a Government guarantee of £31 million. The Civil Aviation Act 2006 gives fresh powers to the Secretary of State and CAA to make regulations requiring ATOL holders to contribute to the ATTF.

In 2005-6, 25 ATOL holders became insolvent. The proceeds of insolvent licence holders' bonds and the ATTF provided refunds to 21,858 passengers and repatriated 1,754 passengers, the total cost of which was £8.8 million. Expenditure on refunds and repatriation varies from year to year. Over the past 10 years the average annual expenditure has been around £6 million. The increasing popularity of scheduled low cost carriers, which sell directly to the public and are not required to hold an ATOL licence for seat only sales, has led tour operators to argue that the requirement to have an ATOL (in particular the additional costs this imposes on them by having to obtain bonds) and the liability that falls to them under the PTD creates a market distortion that puts them at an unfair disadvantage. The fact that bonding costs must be paid up front places a further burden on ATOL holders. In an industry where margins are tight, bonding has a direct effect on the cash flow and working capital of a tour operator as well as limiting access to credit that could otherwise be used for investment purposes.

On 1 April 2008 the law will change. Companies will still be required to hold an Air Travel Organiser's Licence (ATOL), however, for most companies, the CAA is replacing the existing ATOL Bonds with the new £1 contribution. Under the new arrangements, licence holders will make regular ATOL Protection Contributions (or APC) to the CAA that will be held by the Air Travel Trust Fund (ATTF).

The changes have not been unanimously applauded. The British Insurance Brokers' Association has warned that the new ATOL APC (ATOL Protection Contribution) system offers insufficient protection for the modern independent traveller. The massive growth of internet sales has resulted in many millions of consumers booking their own flights and hotels separately and not through a travel "organiser". However, the new APC system will not cover losses for these travellers as it only compensates customers in the event of their travel organiser becoming insolvent.

97 per cent of holidaymakers had ATOL protection in 1997, according to the Civil Aviation Authority. This figure fell to 61 per cent in 2006, leaving 18 million holidaymakers without ATOL protection (or APC Protection).

Nonetheless, the regulators felt that the provision of bonds was less consistent with better regulation principles than other financial protection mechanisms. The requirement for every ATOL holder to make arrangements for its potential failure every year appeared to be disproportionate to the risk being addressed, as there are approximately 2,500 ATOL holders and on average 20 failures a year. Bonding also imposes a significant compliance burden on licensed firms, from both the bond providers and the CAA, a burden that is not faced by other operators in the air travel market for example low cost airlines.

It is considered by politicians that ATOL holders should meet the full costs of providing the financial protection required by EU and domestic legislation for those booking air package holidays, including that funded by the ATTF since the fund has been in deficit. In the absence of intervention, the ATTF deficit would increase with no prospect of it being repaid by industry. The deficit would eventually have to be borne by the taxpayer. The uniform £1 levy has been considered the most appropriate, the most proportionate and the most efficient mechanism to improve the level of funds available as part of a compensation scheme in the event of tour operator failures.

Distribution of bond money

The administrators of bonds usually have a wide discretion as to how their funds will be distributed in the event of the insolvency of a tour operator. Nonetheless, the general rule of thumb is that the money will be applied in the following order of priorities:

- repatriation of those consumers stranded abroad;
- repayment of repatriation expenses of those consumers who were compelled to pay for their own arrangements due to lack of knowledge of a rescue scheme;
- refunding the money paid by consumers in respect of travel arrangements they were unable to undertake due to the operator's collapse (this will include partial refunds to the repatriated where only a proportion of the holiday was taken);

- indemnifying the credit card companies who have made payments pursuant to section 75 of the Consumer Credit Act of 1974.

Insolvency — Travel Agents

The ABTA Travel Agent's Fund will often compensate consumers and tour operators who sustain losses as a result of the collapse of a member travel agent. Whether a consumer is prejudiced by the failure of a travel agent will often depend on the time at which the collapse occurs, and the status by which the travel agent holds any interim payments made by the consumer.

In most cases, the consumer's travel contract is with the tour operator. Accordingly, wherever a contract has been concluded, the insolvency of a travel agent will matter very little to the consumer — despite the administrative inconveniences that might occur. The fact that a travel agent becomes insolvent whilst holding money as an agent for the tour operator should not interfere with the direct contractual relationship the consumer has with the operator. Whether or not the travel agent has transmitted the money to the operator, the consumer will be entitled to full performance (without penalty) from the tour operator. The operator will have to take his chances by proving the travel agent's insolvency. Where the travel contract is covered by an ATOL, the ATOL rules provide that any money held by the travel agent are held *as an agent* of the tour operator[8] — and this will almost always be the case in any event by reason of the fact that no money will be paid until a contract between consumer and operator has been concluded.

However, there will undoubtedly be instances where the travel agent holds money *before* a contract with the tour operator has been concluded, and at a time when it is determined that the travel agent was not acting as an agent of the tour operator but perhaps as a booking agent for the consumer instead. In such a situation the tour operator would be within his rights to demand a further payment (probably only the deposit or some other modest down payment) in return for accepting the booking, and the consumer would have to prove in the liquidation of the travel agent for the recovery of any such preliminary sum paid. It has been faintly suggested[3] that in such circumstances a consumer may argue that he had already concluded a collateral contract with the tour operator where, in return and consideration for booking the holiday through the relevant travel agent, the tour operator warranted that a deposit could *safely* be paid to the travel agent. This

---

[8] But see *Minhas v Imperial Travel Limited* [2003] CL February 263.

ingenious solution is unlikely to be tested in the courts, and, it is submitted, is not likely to succeed even if tested. The amounts involved — given that, *ipso facto*, no contract has been concluded with the tour operator — are going to be relatively small (except perhaps in isolated cases of "late bookings" where the full price is paid "up-front" to the travel agent). Even if the matter were to be litigated, it is thought to be something of a "leap in the dark" for the consumer to prove that the tour operator intended to warrant the security of monies paid to another business organisation over whom the operator would have little financial influence and less control. The collateral contract approach would be wholly dependent on a finding by the court that the tour operator had entered or would enter into the travel contract with the consumer *on condition* that a certain travel agent was used. It is thought that such a finding is unlikely.

Readers are referred to Chapter 8 on travel agents for a discussion on the issue of whether the travel agent is indeed to be regarded as the agent of the consumer at all times until the travel contract is concluded. It is submitted that the consumer's approach, where no contract has been concluded at the time of the agent's insolvency, would be better focused on challenging the contention that the money was held by the travel agent as agent for the consumer, rather than raising the spectre of collateral contracts. It remains arguable that in holding deposit monies or rather down payments, or even the full price pending conclusion of the contract with the operator, the travel agent is acting as the agent of the tour operator *not the consumer* which would give the consumer good reason to insist that his bookings be confirmed by the operator on pain of action for the recovery of the price and damages for failing to perform the contract.

It is thought in some quarters that travel agents themselves should make security arrangements in accordance with the PTR 1992. Whether they should or not will depend on whether travel agents fall within the definition of the other party to the contract — "the contract" being *the agreement linking the consumer to the organiser or to the retailer, or to both as the case may be.*[9]

If an extended meaning is given to the term "linking", it is possible that the courts could interpret the dealings between consumer, travel agent and tour operator as one "agreement" linking them all together — which would require the travel agent to provide security under the PTR 1992 regardless of whether they were the party with whom the consumer contracted (in the conventional sense) for the provision of the package services, and regardless

---

[9] PTR 1992 regulation 2 – see Chapter 2.

of whether the agent-retailer was an organiser of a regulated package or not. It is highly improbable that the courts would strain the definitions in regulation 2 to impose statutory security arrangements on a travel agent who was not also the "*other party*" to the package contract in the narrow sense[10]. Security provisions of the 1992 Regulations.

The PTR 1992 impose the obligation to provide security on "*the other party to the contract*".[11] This will usually be the tour operator in standard package cases — but the expression, it will be recalled, extends to *organisers* and *retailers* or *both* — whoever is the party to the package contract (agrees that the package services will be supplied), other than the consumer.

The security provisions of the PTR 1992 apply to regulated packages only. They have no application where a consumer is booking independent travel components. However, the regulations apply to all engaged in the supply of packages, however big or small; and whether operating in the course of a business or otherwise.

Evidence of compliance

Regulation 16 provides:

> (1) The other party to the contract shall at all times be able to provide sufficient evidence of security for the refund of money paid over and for the repatriation of the consumer in the event of insolvency.

The requirement is that evidence of compliance with the security provisions shall at all times be available. Enforcement officers (where they have reasonable grounds for suspecting that an offence may have been committed[12]), are entitled to call for the inspection of such evidence.

The security must remain in place until the package contract has been "fully performed" or "completed".[13] It is not necessary for the security to remain in place until such time as all disputes on the *proper performance* of the contract have been resolved. Accordingly, once the consumer has returned home the contract has been fully performed — even if *improperly performed*. There is no security for pending actions.

Unless the package is protected by the security measures in force in another Member State of the European Union; or the package is one in respect in which an ATOL is in force (which will be all the air travel packages supplied

---

[10] See *Hone v Going Places Leisure Travel Limited* discussed in Chapters 2 and 4 at first instance.
[11] E.g. PTR 1992 regulation 16(1).
[12] Schedule 3.
[13] Regulation 16(5).

by tour operators in this country), the "*other party*" must ensure that security is provided in one of the ways permitted by regulations 17, 18, 19 or 20. Clearly then, the regulations in this country will largely affect:

- non-air travel packages;
- those smaller or informal organisers and voluntary organisations offering packages to consumers.

It is a criminal offence to fail to have approved security "in force" or to fail to provide sufficient evidence that one is in force.[14] "*In force*" plainly means operational. The offences are triable either way, and subject to the same penalty regime as imposed throughout the regulations. The offences are offences of strict liability — subject to the statutory defences discussed in Chapter 12.

Approved security

Regulations 17–21 permit the following types of security arrangements:

- bonding — regulation 17;
- combined bonding and insurance — regulation 18;
- insurance — regulation 19;
- monies in trust (businesses) — regulation 20;
- monies in trust (those acting otherwise than in the course of a business) — regulation 21.

It is interesting to note that apart from regulation 16 and throughout the remaining security provisions of the PTR 1992, nothing is said about *repatriation*. There is no guidance in the regulations as to how security money should be deployed in the event that repatriation becomes necessary. It is almost as if the regulators forgot that they had imposed the need for security for *two* reasons: first to provide a reserve fund for *refunds* and secondly for *repatriation*. It is also difficult to see how repatriation can be organised with any funds held on security. Regulation 16(1) states that security money is for repatriation; but regulation 16(5) requires the maintenance of the security fund until the contract has been "fully performed". Given the obligations imposed by regulation 14,[15] for example, it is difficult to see how full performance can be achieved until the consumer is returned home, or to his place of departure. A defendant would have to attempt reliance on the statutory defences in the event that he used security money in order to effect repatriation. Alternatively,

---

[14] Regulation 16(3).
[15] Returning consumers to their place of departure in the event that the package cannot be performed.

perhaps regulation 16 would be the victim of the kind of "purposive" interpretation European Regulations are notorious for — and as a result it may be decided that no offence has been committed where the fund has been deployed for one of the very reasons it was required to be established. Otherwise repatriation will have to be funded from other resources despite the existence of a fund for this very purpose.

Bonding

Where a body is approved by the Secretary of State, and has a reserve fund or *insurance* covering consumers in respect of the matters set out in regulation 16(1), then regulation 18 may be used for the purpose of providing a bond. The reason is, that where a reserve fund or insurance exists, the bond required may be smaller than the bond required under regulation 17. In the absence of a reserve fund or insurance, for example, the bond may represent 25%

> of all the payments which the other party to the contract estimates that he will receive under or in contemplation of contracts for relevant packages in the twelve month period from the date of entry into force of the bond...[16]

On the other hand the relevant percentage where insurance cover is held by an approved body, need be only 10%.[17]

ABTA and AITO are "approved" by the Secretary of State. Their members, accordingly, supply security — other than through the ATOL scheme — by way of regulation 18. These organisations cover a large proportion of the industry in this country and each applied sophisticated bonding schemes to their members long before required to do so by statutory regulation. Very small tour operators operators, and the voluntary "organiser" are not likely to find "bonding" a viable option.

Insurance

Regulation 19 addresses the problem of a small or voluntary organiser by allowing security to be provided by means of insurance. Rather like third-party motor insurance, the regulators insist that any policy should not be voidable on technical grounds.[18] The principle drawback of this apparently attractive solution for the smaller or voluntary organiser, is that it is not easy to find an appropriate insurance policy. Indeed, it may not be possible to get such a policy *at all*. What was an attractive solution for the regulators has obviously proved less attractive to the insurance industry.

---

[16] PTR 1992 Regulation 17(4).
[17] Regulation 18(4).
[18] Regulation 19(3).

Trusts

Regulations 20 and 21 allow for security monies to be held on trust:[19] regulation 20 in respect of those who are engaged in the business of supplying package travel services, and regulation 21 for those acting *other than in the course of business.*

Regulation 20 provides that: *"all monies paid over by a consumer under or in contemplation of a contract for a relevant package are held in the United Kingdom by a person as trustee for the consumer until the contract has been fully performed ... "*

The costs of the trust are to be paid by the "*other party*" not out of the trust fund. Interest on the trust accrues to the *other party.*[20] The money can be released to the *other party* where there is produced to the *trustee* a signed statement to the effect that the contract has been fully performed but as it is the *other party* that furnishes this evidence the utility of such a safeguard may be open to question. The trustee administers the trust in the event of the "other party's" insolvency.

It follows that with the exception of any interest on the trust fund, the *other party* is prohibited from using the money paid by his consumers to defray the expenses of putting together or organising the relevant package. This should be the cause of substantial cashflow problems, particularly as the "trust" solution is most likely to be used by smaller organisers — perhaps those without the funds to pay for a bond under other regulations.

Regulation 21

The main differences between regulations 20 and 21 are that those who are not acting in the course of a business can pay for the cost of the trust out of the trust funds, and the money can be used to defray the cost of a component of the package.[21]

Trusts in practice

Those honest and well-administered organisations which implement regulation 20 will endeavour to the best of their abilities to comply with the statutory requirements. These organisations will include the likes of local authorities and boards of school governors (not usually at the top of anybody's list of potential

---

[19] As the "cautionary tale" told above illustrates, the communal "raspberry" blown in the direction of the Trust provisions seems to have been justified.
[20] See generally regulations 20(2) and (3).
[21] PTR regulation 21(3)(a).

insolvents). Churches, charities and similar voluntary organisations — who more than occasionally supply or "organise" packages defined by the PTR 1992 — are also likely to stick rigidly to the terms required of them. These users of regulation 20 could enlist the support of the "Travel Trust Association", but even so may occasionally fall victim of mismanagement or incompetence, and to that extent, regulation 20 serves a valuable purpose.

However, it is submitted that in practice the trust system will only work by self-regulation. It is highly improbable that local enforcement agencies[22] will be able to monitor the administration of these trusts in order to prevent the misuse of funds. The only principle effect of the provisions will, therefore, be to enable *prosecutions* to take place, inevitably after something has gone badly wrong. Those interested in retribution may find this consoling but is small consolation for the victimised consumer whose money is lost. It will be borne in mind that there is nothing in either regulation 20 or 21 to require a *written* trust document.

Trustees

Any Tom, Dick or Harry can be a trustee. No experience or expertise is required; yet the trustee is supposed to administer and monitor the trust in accordance with regulation 20. Most non-professional trustees are unlikely to read regulation 20, and it is a moot point whether any who did would find it accessible. How is the trustee supposed to know whether the money is all being paid *into* the trust? If it is not, what is the trustee supposed to do about it, (other than inform a trading standards department) in order to protect consumers?

Signed statements

Trust funds can be released to the *other party* when the trustee receives a signed statement to the effect that the packages have been fully performed. What is the trustee supposed to do on receipt of such a statement, other than release the money? There is no obligation on him to investigate the truth of the statement within the PTR 1992. The same applies where, under regulation 21, a signed statement is produced to the effect that money is needed to pay for a package component. Even if the assiduous trustee calls for evidence[23] (invoices, receipts or contracts) to verify the claims made in the "signed statements", is the trustee going to have the knowledge, experience or expertise to spot occasions on which he is being "conned" along with the consumers? Is the trustee likely to be very assiduous, or capable of asserting his authority if he is

---

[22] Local authority trading standards departments.
[23] Regulation 20(5).

a relative or friend of the "other party" — a solution that is not only permitted by the regulations, but one that is likely to be adopted by many organisers at the smaller end of the market?

Professionals

Is the appointment of an expensive, professional trustee (an accountant, a banker or solicitor) going to remove all these problems? One would like to think so — but the "cautionary tale" which opened this chapter involved a solicitor-trustee who knew less about the Regulations than the organiser.[24]

Regulation 22 creates further criminal offences: the making of *false statements* to a trustee, and *applying monies* obtained by statements for purposes other than those mentioned in the statement. The penalties are the same as those throughout the PTR 1992. These offences are offences of strict liability. There is no requirement that the maker of the statement should be dishonest, or have an intention to deceive or defraud. Proof of falsity as a matter of fact will suffice; as will proof that the money was applied for a different reason to that contained in the relevant statement. However, the statutory defences in regulation 24 apply.

The reality of the "trust" provisions in the Regulations is that they will almost always be used in circumstances where, by prosecution, the enforcement authority is attempting to "shut the stable door after the horse has bolted". For those with a self-sufficient reason for abiding by the trust rules, regulations 20 and 21 impose a measure of self-discipline. In other cases however, it is submitted that their effect could be positively dangerous and counter-productive. Some consumers who might otherwise have been sceptical about a particular organiser, or suspicious of his integrity or ability in the package market, *might just have their fears allayed by reassurances that all is well because a form of trust security has been implemented.* The requirement that a brochure include particulars of the security arrangements that have been made[25], may give an aura of unjustified credibility to some organisers purporting to rely on the Trusts provisions.

The culture of security was already well established by voluntary self-regulation before the 1992 Regulations. Apart from creating criminal penalties for those disreputable organisers who are found wanting in their implementation of the trust rules, the Regulations will achieve little in this context, it is submitted, unless and until insurance is readily available.

---

[24] See further *Brown: Trust Me I'm a Tour Operator* [1994] ITLJ 11.
[25] Schedule 1 of the PTR 1992.

Chapter 12

CRIMINAL OFFENCES

Introduction

The law imposing criminal liability in the context of consumer protection is undergoing a dramatic overhaul. The Consumer Protection from Unfair Trading Regulations 2007 came into force on 26th May 2008. Now that the Regulations are in force the Trade Descriptions Act 1968 will, in large measure, cease to have effect, and sections 20 to 26 of the Consumer Protection Act 1987 will also be repealed. Nevertheless, offences committed prior to 26th May 2008 will fall within the previous regime, and for the sake of completeness both legislative frameworks are examined in the following two chapters.

The offences dealt with below fall into the category often known as "regulatory crime" — and it may be small consolation for those liable to conviction for such offences that in the eyes of many, the offences are not in any real sense "criminal" at all. The view has often been expressed, particularly in the context of consumer protection legislation, that the imposition of regulatory penalties through the criminal courts is merely intended to reinforce the extent of the supplier's positive obligations to the general public to ensure maximum consumer safeguards. This attitude is clearly discernible, for example, from the speeches of Lords Hailsham and Scarman in *Wings Ltd v Ellis*[1] (a case under the Trade Descriptions Act 1968) and the judgment of Lord Widgery CJ in *MFI Warehouses Ltd v Nattrass*[2] (also with regard to trade descriptions).

Regulatory or consumer protection crimes follow a common statutory pattern:

- The offences are frequently offences of strict liability.

---

[1] [1985] AC 272.
[2] [1973] 1 WLR 30.

- Strict liability offences are subject to specific statutory defences, the burden of proving which lies on the defendant. Broadly speaking, the defendant must show that due diligence has been exercised to avoid the commission of the offence. In practice this is a high threshold to cross.

- The combination of strict liability and statutory defences erects a framework of qualified strict liability.

- Where an element of *mens rea* is included in the offence (e.g. s.14(1)(b) of the Trade Descriptions Act 1968) the element of *mens rea* (e.g. recklessness) often carries its own statutory definition which is different — and more onerous — than that imposed by the general criminal law.

- This framework of qualified strict liability has the effect of imposing on organisers and retailers alike a mutual and self-policing role. Every party along the chain of supply before the product or service reaches the consumer has a measure of responsibility to ensure that what is offered to the general public is and is promoted in a way that is "decent, honest and true", and this will invariably involve an obligation on the likes of the retailer to institute a system of checks and double-checks to ensure that those further up the line of supply[3] are not guilty of, for example, any misdescriptions relating to the facilities or services offered.

- Where corporate bodies are guilty of regulatory offences, directors and managers who can be shown to have "connived" at an offence, or to whom the offence is "attributable" can be pursued in the criminal courts as well as the guilty corporation. Bad, or even complaisant, managers and directors cannot, therefore, hide behind their respective corporate veils.

This outline will be enlarged upon in what follows in the context of a number of specific criminal offences, first under the PTR 1992, then the Trade Descriptions Act 1968, Consumer Protection Act 1987, Denied Boarding Regulations and Disability Discrimination Regulations. Consideration will then be given to the forthcoming regime under the Consumer Protection from Unfair Trading Regulations 2007. The statutory defences to these regulatory regimes are dealt with in Chapter 13. A brief examination of the Health and Safety at Work Act 1974 and of various other criminal offences will conclude this chapter.

The PTR 1992

- All offences created by the PTR 1992[4] are triable either way. In accordance with general principles the prosecution may invite trial on

---

[3] Invariably the tour operators.
[4] Regulations 5,7,8,16 and 22.

indictment (though the invitation may be declined by magistrates and summary trial offered), and the defendant has an absolute right to elect trial at the Crown Court if this is deemed desirable.

- Each offence carries a fine of up to £5,000.00 (currently level 5 on the standard scale[5]) on summary conviction, and an *unlimited* fine following conviction on indictment.

- The Regulations are enforced by Local Weights and Measures Authorities.[6]

- The time limit for prosecution is three years from the commission of the offence, or one year from the discovery of the offence by the prosecutor — whichever is the earlier — and a certificate from the prosecutor as to when he became aware of the commission of the offence is conclusive of the date of discovery (unless the contrary is proved).[7]

- With the exception of the offences under Regulation 5(2) — relating to retailers only — all the offences under the 1992 Regulations are offences of strict liability, subject to the statutory defences set out later in the Regulations themselves.

- The statutory due diligence defence is contained in Regulation 24. Regulation 25 makes provision for the prosecution of persons other than the principal offender (*e.g.* directors, secretaries and managers of companies and others whose act or default has led to the commission of an offence by a principal offender).

- A defence of "innocent publication" is included in regulation 25(5) in respect of the making available of misleading brochures.

General Observations

These offences relate only to those dealing with regulated packages. It is important, therefore, that any prosecuting authority proves that the alleged offender is dealing with a regulated package in the context of the offence alleged (and see also in this regard the discussion of the decision in *Association of British Travel Agents v Civil Aviation Authority*[8]).

For criminal matters of strict liability, where the onus of proving a defence rests on a defendant, some of the offences created by the PTR 1992 are of an alarmingly general nature. For example, tour operators (and other

---

[5] The statutory maximum.
[6] Schedule 3.
[7] Regulation 26.
[8] (2006) EWCA Civ 1299 – discussed in detail in Chapter 1.

"organisers") are subject to criminal sanctions[9] for any failure to provide "adequate information" in their brochures about the matters set out in Schedule 1. Schedule 1 itself requires "adequate information" to be given in respect of "general information about passport and visa requirements which apply to British Citizens for the journey". The PTR 1992 provide no assistance as to what may constitute either "adequate" or "general" information.

Under regulation 8 it is an offence for "*the other party to the contract*" not to provide specified information to the consumer "*in good time before the start of the journey in writing or in some other appropriate form*". One may look in vain for any guidance as to what constitutes *good time* or an *appropriate form.*

Prosecution for offences of this general type are likely to be limited in practice to those who have failed to provide the specified information at all, or at least to cases where the information supplied is so uninformative as to be manifestly useless to the consumer. Clearly, judges of fact (magistrates or juries) are intended to adjudicate upon the adequacy or otherwise of the information supplied if it is supplied, but this is a rather haphazard and uncertain approach. It may be that the breadth and generality of these offences is designed to provide organisers with a terrorising inducement to ensure that if there is any room for doubt whatsoever in respect of any information provided to the consumer, further details should be included to remove such lingering doubts.

Regulation 8 (pursuant to which further information must be given to the consumer about the administrative arrangements for the package such as one usually encounters in the "traveller's wallet" provided by many tour operators shortly before a package commences) gives no assistance as to what constitutes "good time before the start of the journey". ABTA tour operators will comply with the recommendation to give at least 14 days notice of the required information under regulation 8. ABTA and DBERR guidance are helpful indicators of what enforcement authorities will probably demand of tour operators — but they are not in themselves the law, and it is perfectly possible for a tour operator to be found guilty of an offence even though it has followed all available guidance. On the other hand, it is equally possible that a tour operator would be acquitted of an offence notwithstanding failure to comply with relevant guidance; all cases will turn on their own facts.

---

[9] Regulations 5(1) and (3).

Requirements Relating to Brochures: Organisers

Regulation 5(1) provides:

> Subject to paragraph (4) below, no organiser shall make available a brochure to a possible consumer unless it indicates in a legible, comprehensible and accurate manner the price and adequate information about the matters specified in Schedule 1 to these Regulations in respect of the packages offered for sale in the brochure to the extent that those matters are relevant to the packages offered.

Organisers of regulated packages are strictly liable under Regulation 5 (1), subject to the statutory defences. The ingredients of the offence are that no organiser shall:

- make available
- a brochure
- to a *possible* consumer
- unless it indicates in a legible, comprehensible and accurate manner
- the price and adequate information about the matters specified in Schedule 1.

Make available

This is a broad concept and imposes a continuing obligation. Any brochure that is distributed to travel agents, circulated within the trade, despatched to consumers directly or is otherwise disseminated or stored in a way that renders it likely to come into the hands of any person, is a brochure that the organiser "*makes available*". It could be said that as soon as a brochure is printed, it is made available. The fact that one edition of a brochure may be replaced by an update does not mean that the first edition is no longer "available" — on the contrary, unless extreme care is taken to recall all earlier editions, they are still very much "available", having been made available before changed circumstances led to the production of the subsequent edition. Recalling all examples of a previous edition is usually a hopeless prospect. Brochures already in the hands of a consumer are unlikely to be successfully recalled, and should any such consumer pass the brochure to a friend, it remains a brochure that has been made available by the organiser. However, it is unlikely that an organiser makes available a "Summer '07" brochure once the season covered by the brochure has passed. In such a situation the "availability" of the brochure is likely to be limited to the period of time for which its use was intended.

The organiser does not make a brochure available once and for all. He continues to make it available and repeatedly makes it available as long as any example remains in circulation. So, where an accurate brochure has been made available, but is replaced due to a change in the facilities at a resort half way through the season, the "innocent" organiser will continue to commit an offence due to the fact that the first brochure has become inaccurate, and continues to be something he "makes available" — even though heroic efforts might be made to track down all the inaccurate copies. The principle under strict liability must be: "once available always available" (subject to proof of total recall), and the organiser must rely, if he can, on the statutory defences to excuse an offence.

A brochure

As has been seen in Chapter 1, the PTR 1992 define a brochure as "*any brochure in which packages are offered for sale.*"[10] This is singularly unhelpful. Perhaps it does underline the fact, however, that to qualify as a brochure for the purposes of the PTR 1992, the publication does not have to be entirely made up of arrangements that are regulated packages, or even entirely made up of travel or holiday particulars (whether packages or not). A booklet containing a range of services on offer, including, for example, concerts and concert tickets, lectures, sports facilities and the odd combination of the foregoing to make up a regulated package, could still be a *brochure* within the definition. However, the PTR 1992 are limited to such publications where *more than one package* is offered.

Most of the literature displayed by the travel agent will be a "brochure". Apart from the standard glossy publications lined up on the shelves, the expression probably includes booklets and pamphlets with more than one double-sided page, as well as folded leaflets. The fact that an organiser chooses to call his literature something other than a "brochure" is irrelevant. Accordingly, where supplementary promotional literature is published, or extracts made for publicity and advertising reasons, reference should always be made to the principle brochure, and clear information given as to where and how the principle brochure can be obtained. The protestation that "this is not a brochure" may then carry a little more weight. A hand-out or single-page information sheet is probably not a brochure, and it is suggested that advertisements in newspapers and magazines also fall outside the scope of regulated brochures.

Unfortunately, the position of the newspapers and magazines *themselves*[11] may not be so clear cut. If a Sunday supplement offers a couple of regulated packages to readers (of which the newspaper is the organiser — *e.g.* trips for members of the wine club, or for collectors of the newspaper's tokens),

---

[10] Regulation 2(1).
[11] As opposed to advertisements.

escaping the clutches of regulation 5 would involve the newspaper distinguishing its supplement from a brochure (or a booklet or pamphlet as the dictionary defines "brochure"). One would like to think that any suggestion that *The Sunday Chronicle Magazine* was a regulated "brochure" would be met with some scepticism, but the position is not at all clear.

Possible consumer

Everybody is a "*possible consumer*". The employees of the organiser are possible consumers. The proof readers of the brochure are possible consumers. The travel agent is a possible consumer. This ingredient of the offence could not have been drafted in wider terms. The offence is clearly directed at the making available of brochures, not the consumer's reliance on them. The breadth of this particular ingredient is obviously intended to cope with those few important occasions where an enforcing authority might identify inaccuracies or other criminal flaws in a brochure as soon as, or even before it "hits the streets". Prosecution could be contemplated in cases of serious flaws even though no actual consumer has suffered any disadvantage, and the threat of prosecution should be more than sufficient to persuade even the most recalcitrant organiser with the glossiest and most expensively produced (but flawed) brochures, to recall and reprint.

Legible, comprehensible and accurate

As a general guideline the following is suggested:

- "legible" means "clearly readable" by the reasonable person exercising reasonable care;
- "comprehensible" means "understandable and intelligible" by the reasonable person exercising reasonable care;
- "accurate" means that the specified information must be absolutely correct (as opposed to a reasonable approximation, however honestly intended).

As has already been seen, the problem with legibility, comprehensibility and accuracy under Regulation 5 is that, with the exception of the *price* (which is an unambiguous example of information that must comply), what it is intended should be legible, comprehensible and accurate is only "*adequate information*" in respect of the matters specified in Schedule 1. So it is best to approach this part of Regulation 5 back to front.

- Does the information fall within Schedule 1?
- If so, is it *adequate*?
- If so, is it *legible, comprehensible and accurate*?

To some extent *adequacy* and *accuracy* are mutually supportive. A half-truth may be *accurate* as far as it goes, but may make the information as a whole *inadequate* because it paints but part of a picture. To say of the transport for one leg of the journey that it will be "by elephant" may be accurate up to a point. Its accuracy may be called into question when it emerges that there is only one elephant to transport a group of 30 people, most of whom will have to wait for several hours to get their turn, whilst those who go first will have to endure hours of boredom at the other end waiting for the stragglers. Implicit in the suggestion that elephant transport will be provided is the suggestion that there will be enough elephants to cater for a group such as that which the consumer is to join. It is the *inadequate* nature of the information given that casts doubt on its accuracy. Only when it has been decided that the information given is adequate can a proper determination of its accuracy be made.

Schedule 1

Schedule 1 sets out nine categories of information that must be legibly, comprehensibly and accurately included in a brochure *where any of the categories are relevant* to the package offered. So, for example, it is thought that a regulated package that did not include "transport" would not have to say anything about transport,[12] and a package that did not include any meals would not have to say anything about meals.[13]

Reference must be made to the nine categories in the Schedule itself.[14] A broad outline is given here only for convenience:

1. Destination and transport.

2. Accommodation — location, category, comfort and main features.[15]

3. Meals.[16]

---

[12] Schedule 1 paragraph 1.
[13] Schedule 1 paragraph 3.
[14] See Appendix 2.
[15] In *Inspirations East Limited v Dudley Metropolitan BC* [1998] ITLJ 16 the Divisional Court held that magistrates were entitled to convict where a brochure contained inaccuracies about the suitability of a hotel for the disabled where the hotel carried the tour operator's disabled symbol because in promoting the hotel as disabled friendly the tour operator had made the disabled facilities "main features" in the context of a disabled consumer's booking.
[16] Note - *Bellinger v TUI UK Ltd* 21st August 2006 CLCC (Unreported), DJ Price: C booked a package holiday over the telephone with D, a tour operator. At C's request D levied a half board supplement to the booking. D stated only that breakfast along with lunch or dinner would be provided. On arrival C was informed by the hotel that she would be given just a main course. After D's representative intervened, the hotel offered to provide a starter in addition. C refused the offer, electing to eat only breakfast at the hotel. C sued for breach of contract claiming the cost of her meals outside of the hotel. Held: as a matter of contractual construction, unless the

4. Itinerary.

5. Passport, visa and health requirements.

6. Payment timetable.

7. Whether a minimum number of travellers is required for the package.

8. Arrangements (if any) for delay at outward or homeward points of departure.

9. Security arrangements for purchase money.

There has been some debate as to whether it is necessary for an organiser to state in the brochure that there are *no* arrangements of the respective types dealt with in Schedule 1. This has arisen particularly in the context of paragraph 8 which provides for " *The arrangements (if any) which apply*" in the event of outward or homebound delay. The inclusion of the words "if any" in brackets in this paragraph (and they do not appear in any other) may indicate that an organiser should specifically state when there are no such arrangements. On the other hand it is difficult to see how "the arrangements" can be "relevant to the packages offered" if there are no such arrangements.

It is suggested that the organiser need only state the arrangements in respect of each category relevant to the holiday in question. The only other solution would be for organisers to deal with each paragraph in the schedule for every package, stating "none" or "not applicable" where the information was actually irrelevant to the particular package in question, which seems both absurd and unnecessary.

Requirements relating to brochures: retailers

Regulation 5(2) provides:

> Subject to paragraph (4) below, no retailer shall make available to a possible consumer a brochure which he knows or has reasonable cause to believe does not comply with the requirements of paragraph (1).

Regulation 5(2) applies to retailers in the same way as sub-paragraph 5(1) applies to *organisers* — with one important difference. Regulation 5(2) is *not an offence of strict liability*. A retailer is guilty of an offence only if the retailer "*make(s) available to a possible consumer a brochure which he knows or has reasonable cause to believe does not comply with the requirements of* "sub-paragraph 5 (1)". Although Regulation 5 (2) imports an element of *mens rea* into the offence as far as retailers are concerned, it

---

contrary was stated in D's brochure, C was entitled under the half board supplement to a starter, a main course and a dessert.

nonetheless imposes considerable burdens on the likes of travel agents, if other regulatory regimes are anything to go by.

Knowledge

Plainly, where a retailer deliberately makes brochures available in circumstances where there is actual knowledge that the brochure is flawed in some relevant respect, an offence is committed. Many retailers, however, will be companies or partnerships. All will employ staff. Who has to possess the actual knowledge of a relevant flaw in a brochure before the business can be said to be in possession of "knowledge" for the purposes of Regulation 5(2)? An application of the ordinary principles of the law of agency would suggest that the knowledge coming to the attention of an agent is imputed to the principal. Accordingly, it would appear that once any member of staff employed by a retailer comes by "knowledge" of a relevant flaw in a brochure in the course of his employment, that knowledge will be imputed to the principal-employer. No other conclusion is possible following Lord Scarman's observations in *Wings Ltd v Ellis.*[17] Reference should be made to the standard works on agency for a detailed discussion of this proposition.

The knowledge of the agent is imputed to the principal because it is presumed that the agent will pass on relevant knowledge to his principal. For retailers, this highlights the importance of devising and implementing procedures whereby all staff are aware of the significance of any brochure errors that are drawn to their attention. In larger retailing organisations the problems may be colossal. Large and multiple retailers may have hundreds of branches across the country. Knowledge of a brochure error coming to the attention of one branch can be imputed to the organisation as a whole, whereafter the continued availability of the offending brochure at another branch, perhaps at the opposite end of the country, will constitute a criminal offence (albeit one meriting a very modest penalty). The proving of a statutory defence of due diligence will be entirely dependent on the efficiency of the system employed by the retailer for:

• identifying brochure errors;

• ensuring such errors are communicated throughout the organisation as soon as is practicably feasible;

• acting on such notifications to ensure that the offending material is withdrawn or corrected as soon as notification is circulated.

The existence of modern data-viewing equipment in almost all multiple travel agencies should make the communication of discovered flaws

---

[17] See further the Trade Descriptions Act 1968 – below.

relatively easy. However, communication will only occur if staff are made aware of the need to pass on the information they receive and the reasons why communication is so important. Equally, those in receipt of the information must be trained to react to its receipt in a way that does not undermine the defence of due diligence. It is all very well getting information about brochure errors from the other end of the country, but the system must invoke some activity.

Reasonable cause to believe

This obviously covers the situation where the retailer is given reliable or potentially reliable information from consumers, service providers, or the organiser or tour operator of the package, but does nothing about it. A retailer may also have reasonable cause to believe (well short of knowledge) that a brochure does not comply with the requirements of Regulation 5(1) in other situations. For example:

- where a retailer agrees to stock a brochure from an organiser who is known to have fallen foul of the regulations on previous occasions;

- where a brochure is stocked from a new organiser about which the retailer knows nothing;

- where there is something about the get-up of the brochure itself that is out of the ordinary — perhaps it is printed on second rate paper, or is prone to disintegrate on handling, or the ink rubs off and smudges the particulars, or perhaps it is riddled with errata — all of which may put a reasonable retailer on notice that a batch of brochures intended for the incinerator has mistakenly found its way to his shop doorstep.

It may well be that Regulation 5(2) imposes positive obligations on a retailer to institute a system of reasonable, random checks on the brochures that pass through his hands. On the face of the regulation itself, one might think that in the absence of knowledge or something to give the retailer grounds for suspicion about the accuracy of a brochure, the retailer could remain passive. Effectively, the retailer might want to say: "I did not know of the inaccuracy, and there was nothing that would have alerted a reasonable person to such an inaccuracy".

This would be a dangerous position for any retailer to adopt in the face of any piece of consumer protection legislation, and the Divisional Court in an unreported case[18] has decided that such a passive approach is not good enough. In the context of similar provisions in section 10(4) of the Consumer Protection Act 1987, Butler-Sloss LJ concluded that it was incumbent on a

---

[18] *Old Barn Nurseries v West Sussex County Council* 5 December 1994.

retailer to institute a system of random checks, falling short of due diligence, in order to be kept reasonably informed about the safety of the products on sale in the retailer's shop. In the absence of such random checks a retailer could not be heard to say that he had no reasonable grounds for suspecting that a particular product fell foul of the general safety requirement imposed by section 10 of the Consumer Protection Act.

The most important procedural difference between section 10(4) of the Consumer Protection Act 1987 and Regulation 5(2) of the PTR 1992 is that under the 1987 Act the *retailer* has the burden of proving that there were no reasonable grounds for suspecting that the goods did not comply with the general safety requirement; whereas under Regulation 5(2), the prosecution must prove that the retailer *had* reasonable cause to believe that the brochure did not comply with the Regulations. But the difference may be more apparent than real. In the case cited, the retailer's evidence was admitted and accepted. If Butler-Sloss LJ's judgment is followed, by analogy, all the prosecution must prove is that the travel agent or retailer did not institute a random system of checks to see if the brochures made available at his outlet complied with the regulations, and in the absence of such a system, cannot complain about the absence of reasonable cause. If this harsh interpretation of Regulation 5(2) gains currency, the *reasonable cause* will be the shutting of the retailer's eyes to the possibility of error in the brochures, by his failure to institute a system of random checks. It would not matter that the chances of any such system identifying the relevant flaw might be negligible.

Information to be Provided Before the Contract is Concluded

Regulation 7 provides:

> 7(1) Before a contract is concluded the other party to the contract shall provide the intending consumer with the information specified in paragraph (2) below in writing or in some other appropriate form.

> (2) The information referred to in paragraph (1) above is: -

> > (a) general information about passport and visa requirements which apply to United Kingdom nationals who purchase the package in question, including information about the length of time it is likely to take to obtain the appropriate passports and visa;

> > (b) information about health formalities required for the journey and the stay; and

> > (c) the arrangements for security for the money paid over and (where applicable) for the repatriation of the consumer in the event of insolvency.

Regulation 7 applies to "*the other party to the contract*" — even though its effect is designed to take place before a contract is concluded. The "other party", therefore, must be the other party to the contract that is ultimately concluded. In most cases this will be the tour operator.

There is some degree of overlap between what is required of a brochure[19] and what is required from the "other party" before contract. This is undoubtedly because not every regulated package is purchased in reliance on a brochure. However, the regulation does not cover the breadth of information covered by Schedule 1 under Regulation 5. No doubt this is because those who seek information about transport, meals or categories of accommodation (and other matters covered by the Schedule but not by Regulation 7) can be sent away to look at a brochure (if there is one) or other promotional or explanatory information; or will be taken to have agreed to suffer the risk of booking the wrong type of trip if they have not bothered to inform themselves of the contents of the package they are buying.

As with Regulation 5, it is a little puzzling to see a failure to provide undefined "general information" classified as an offence carrying the risk of criminal conviction and penalty, and as with certain parts of Regulation 5, the probability in practice is that prosecutions will be restricted to cases where there has been a complete failure to provide this pre-contract information, or the inadequacy of it is so manifestly plain as to brook no argument.

Again, in order to avoid one possible administrative absurdity, the words "if any" might silently be read into Regulation 7(2)(a). In the case of a regulated package which consists of a coach tour round Wales, it would be rather pointless emphasising before the contract was concluded with a consumer that passports and visas were not required of UK nationals. The words "*if applicable*" are inserted in Regulation 7(2)(c) with regard to arrangements for repatriation — it is a trifle mystifying why the same was not done in Regulation 7(2)(a).

The information must be supplied "*in writing or in some other appropriate form*". Woe betide any "*other party*" who sells a package over the telephone as a result of a newspaper advertisement, or in some other way that does not involve the use or adoption of a brochure. A criminal offence will have been committed — unless an oral description of the information qualifies as "*some other appropriate form*". If it does, it is difficult to see why the regulators found it necessary to provide for the giving of information in writing at all.

Information to be Provided Before Departure

Regulation 8 provides:

---

[19] Regulation 5.

8(1)The other party to the contract shall in good time before the start of the journey provide the consumer with the information specified in paragraph (2) below in writing or in some other appropriate form.

(2) The information referred to in paragraph (1) is the following: -

(a) the times and places of intermediate stops and transport connections and particulars of the place to be occupied by the traveller (for example, cabin or berth on ship, sleeper compartment on train;

(b) the name and address and telephone number -

(i) of the representative of the other party to the contract in the locality where the consumer is to stay; or if there is no such representative,

(ii) of any agency in that locality on whose assistance a consumer in difficulty would be able to call, or, if there is no such representative or agency, a telephone number or other information which will enable the consumer to contact the other party to the contract during the stay; and

(c) [information regarding travelling arrangements for persons under 16]

(d) [information about insurance if the consumer has not been obliged by the contract to take out his own insurance].

As has already been seen, there is no definition, and no means of defining the term "*in good time*", though DTI good practice recommends 14 days before the journey commences. Less than this is inevitable where a last-minute bargain is purchased by the consumer. Once again it is difficult to envisage a criminal prosecution in the event that only seven days' notice is given (the DTI minimum period), or five days or even four.

This timetable seems to be reasonable enough in broad terms as the information now required of the "*other party*" relates mainly to travel arrangements and representative contact details. One does pause to wonder whether 14 days is not a rather long period for the sort of travel and contact details Regulation 8 requires to be provided.

Under Regulation 8(2) the tour operator (or "other party") must give:

• The personal name, address and a number for *the human representative* in the locality where the consumer is to stay.

• *Only if there is no human representative* (NB not if the tour operator does not know who it is to be at the time the information is given) will particulars of any suitable *agency* suffice.

• *If there is neither representative nor agency* then a contact telephone number or other information must be provided enabling the consumer to contact the tour operator during the stay (by which is meant during the course of the package).

"Other information" as an alternative to the tour operator's telephone number, will include a fax, e-mail or telex number. It is unlikely that any other sort of information would be a reasonably suitable alternative to a telephone number. This part of Regulation 8 is manifestly intended to require the provision of a "hotline" service, in the event that there is no local representative or agency. The proviso to Regulation 8 (2)(b)(ii) which manifests this intention, does not, however, purport to regulate the manner in which such a "hotline" service should be administered.

It is worth noting in the context of Regulation 8 (2)(c) — the provision of information which enables a child or "*the person responsible*" for the child to be contacted at the place where the child is to stay — is of universal application outside the United Kingdom, even where a child is travelling with its parents.

Security

Regulations 16 and 22 create criminal offences in respect of the "security" provisions, and are dealt with separately in Chapter 11.

Liability of those other than the principal offender

PTR 1992 regulation 25 provides:

> (1) Where the commission by a person of an offence under [these Regulations] is due to an act or default committed by some other person in the course of any business of his, the other person shall be guilty of the offence whether or not proceedings are taken against the first-mentioned person.

> (2) Where a body corporate is guilty of an offence in respect of any act or default which is shown to have been committed with the consent or connivance of, or to be attributable to any neglect on the part of, any director, manager, secretary or other similar officer or any person who was purporting to act in such capacity he, as well as the body corporate, shall be guilty of an offence

> (3) Where the affairs of a body corporate are managed by its members, paragraph (2) above shall apply in relation to the acts and defaults of a member in connection with his functions of management as if he were a director of the body corporate.

These are common regulatory provisions designed to permit proceedings against those individuals who are actually to blame or partly to blame for the commission of an offence by a principal offender. The clearest example of secondary offenders are culpable directors who are responsible for the offences committed by their corporations,[20] although Regulation 25(1) contemplates a secondary defendant where the principal offender is himself an individual.

A prosecutor may choose whether to prosecute *both* principal and "secondary" offender, or whether to pursue only the person whose fault has led to the commission of the offence by the principal offender. Whether or not the principal offender is prosecuted, the prosecution must prove that:

- a principal offender has committed an offence under the PTR 1992;

- the defendant under Regulation 25(1) was acting in the course of any "business of his" (not necessarily a travel business);

- in the course of that business the defendant committed an act or default that caused the commission of the offence by the principal offender.

The fact that the principal offender may have a statutory defence (whether as found at trial or whether the probability of such a defence inclines the authorities against a prosecution) is irrelevant. That is to say, where the principal offender is acquitted by reason of his exercise of all due diligence, it by no means follows that the secondary offender will also be acquitted *unless he too can establish one of the statutory defences in his own right.* This is simply because the offence has been committed whether or not the principal offender is relieved of the consequences of its commission (*i.e.* conviction and penalty) by reason of a statutory defence. The statutory defences arise under Regulation 24 only when that person (*i.e.* the one undertaking the burden of proving the statutory defence) can show "*that he took all reasonable steps and exercised all due diligence to avoid committing the offence*". It is plain from these last words that "the offence" has been committed — and that one person's statutory defence cannot come to the aid of another. That is not to say that a number of people (*e.g.* company directors or employees) might not individually be able to rely on identical factors and evidence in proving a common statutory defence.

An example would be where false information was included in a travel brochure due to failure on the part of a hotel to disclose important information to the tour operator about its facilities and services, or their availability at certain times. Perhaps the accurate details were urgently transmitted to the tour operator by courier before the brochure went to print, but never arrived due to incompetence on the part of the courier company. The courier company (in the course of its non-travel business) could be held criminally to account under Regulation 25(1) whether or not the tour operator had exercised due diligence.

---

[20] Regulation 25(2).

One special situation is covered by Regulation 25(5). A retailer, or organiser, may produce an inaccurate brochure. The publisher of the brochure "makes it available" in publishing it, and certainly in distributing it. The publisher may be prosecuted as a culpable party under Regulation 25(1) on the grounds that the retailer or organiser has committed the offence of making an inaccurate brochure available to possible consumers due, in part, to the act of the publisher in publishing the brochure — whether or not the retailer or organiser is also charged. A special defence of "innocent publication" is provided for which will be considered in Chapter 13.

The Trade Descriptions Act 1968 ('the TDA')

As indicated above, when the Consumer Protection from Unfair Trading Regulations 2007 come into force, the TDA will be rendered largely irrelevant as far as the industry is concerned. However, for a short time offences committed prior to 6th April 2008 will continue to be prosecuted under the TDA, and one supposes that case law decided under the TDA will continue to be of relevance in informing the interpretation of the new Regulations.

False statements — section 14

Section 14 of the Trade Descriptions Act[21] so far as is relevant for present purposes, provides as follows:

14(1) It shall be an offence for any person in the course of any trade or business -

(a) to make a statement which he knows to be false; or

(b) recklessly to make a statement which is false; as to any of the following matters, that is to say -

(i) the provision in the course of a business of any services, accommodation or facilities;

(ii) the nature of any services

(iii) the manner in which any services, accommodation or facilities are so provided; or

(iv) the examination, approval or evaluation by any person of any services, accommodation or facilities so provided; or

(v) the location or amenities of any accommodation so provided.

(2) For the purposes of this section -

---

[21] Referred to here as the TDA.

(a) anything (whether or not a statement as to any of the matters specified in the preceding subsection) likely to be taken for such a statement shall be deemed to be a false statement; and

(b) a statement made regardless of whether it is true or false shall be deemed to made recklessly, whether or not the person making it had reasons for believing that it might be false.

Further, by subsection 14(4), a statement is "false" where it is false "to a material degree".

The offences are triable either way. On summary conviction a defendant is liable to a fine of up to £5,000.00 (level 5 on the standard scale — the "prescribed sum"; and on indictment to an unlimited fine or imprisonment for up to 2 years. The provision for punishment by imprisonment makes these offences potentially more serious than those under the PTR 1992, where the option to impose a sentence of imprisonment is not available to the courts even following trial on indictment. Imprisonment is, in practice, reserved for those who *dishonestly* contravene the TDA — usually on a grand scale (the best example being those who deliberately, and with intent to defraud, alter the odometer readings on motor vehicles, as in *R* v *Davies*[22] where the Court of Appeal thought nine months imprisonment for a total of 28 "clocking" offences was not a day too long).

In bringing a case pursuant to section 14(1) of TDA, the prosecution must prove that:

* in the course of *any* trade or business;

* a statement was made;

* the statement was made *knowingly* or *recklessly*;

* in respect of any of the matters specified in subsections 14(1)(i)-(v); or would be likely to be taken as a statement in respect of one of the specified matters;

* the statement was false (to a material degree).

In the course of any trade or business

Unlike the offences created by the PTR 1992 a defendant must be acting in the course of any trade or business when the false statement is made in order to be caught by the TDA. The PTR 1992 apply generally to "*the other party to the contract*", whether or not they are acting in the course of a business — though in order to be the "*other party to the contract*" within the meaning

---

[22] [1991] 13 CrAppR(S) 459.

of the Regulations it will be remembered that the person concerned must be either a retailer, or organiser, "*otherwise than occasionally*".

The TDA applies to those who are "occasional" organisers, provided that they are acting in the course of any trade or business, and, it is thought, more often, to those who are clearly selling travel services by way of business, but whose arrangements fall outside the scope of regulated packages as defined by the PTR 1992.

Can an "occasional" organiser be acting in the course of any trade or business, and thus be outside the PTR 1992, but caught by the TDA? The answer is probably — not often, but sometimes. If the organiser is intending to profit from the travel arrangements, then his organisation of the arrangements is arguably in the nature of "trade", even though it may be a one-off arrangement. This may be so even if the organiser — in the event — only breaks even, or makes a loss (see *Davies v Sumner*[23]). The company that puts together conference and leisure services for its employees from which a profit is anticipated will be caught by section 14 of the TDA, even though the trade or business of the company is accountancy rather than travel services. In *Davies* Lord Keith posited that another way of falling foul of the "trade or business" requirement of the TDA, was where there was some *regularity* in the type of transaction under investigation (be it selling cars or holidays). It is suggested that what Lord Keith meant by "regularity" was *frequency. Intended profit* and/or *frequency* in the sales, are the two keys which open up "any trade or business" under section 14 of the TDA.

Statements

A statement under section 14(1) of the TDA can be made in writing, orally (face to face or over the telephone), or in some other descriptive fashion (such as by photographs, artists' impressions and videos). The writing can be a brochure, letter, or any advertising or promotional literature. A statement can be made by the abbreviations commonly found in travel brochures denoting the facilities offered by a hotel (*e.g.* the "AC" for air-conditioning in *Wings Ltd v Ellis*). There is no requirement of *reliance.* Accordingly, it is not necessary for a prosecutor to prove that a consumer read, saw or heard the statement and made his travel arrangements on the strength of it. Neither does the misstatement have to give rise to a breach of contract — the consumer may already have made a contract at a time when the statement is furnished.

Yugotours v Wadsley[24] is a good example of what can constitute a "statement". The appellants produced a brochure offering on one page a

---

[23] [1984] 1 WLR 1301 per Lord Keith of Kinkel.
[24] [1989] Crim LR 623.

number of island-hopping and Adriatic cruises. On the facing page was a picture of a three-masted schooner in full sail, splintering the azure blue ocean. The cruise the consumers purchased was advertised as taking place "on board this majestic schooner". Regrettably, it did not. The consumers were assigned to a vessel that was little more than a motor cruiser. Parker LJ (with whom Simon Brown J agreed) held that the *picture* was a statement (the contrary being but faintly argued) within the meaning of section 14(1). The only issues were whether it was false when made, and whether there was evidence of any *mens rea* on the part of the offending company. On the facts of that case the picture was expressly associated with the consumer's cruise. It is unlikely that the decision would have been any different had the cruise's association with "this majestic schooner" been merely implicit from the fact that the picture was printed on the page facing the particulars of the cruise the consumers purchased. Had there been no direct or explicit reference to "this schooner", the statement contained in the picture might have been of a more general character, such as, "this is the *type* or *class* of vessel you may expect on your cruise" — but as the consumers in *Yugotours* v *Wadsley* were provided with a motor boat the point did not divert the court for long. In cases where there is some ambiguity as to what the "statement" refers, or precisely what it might mean, the meaning has to be resolved by the court as an objective matter of fact. If a disco is offered, it is a matter of fact for the court to determine whether a disco (as sensibly understood by the reasonable person) was provided.

Anything likely to be taken for a statement

Even though "statement" is a broad concept, covering spoken and written words and indications[25] as well as pictures, its meaning is further extended by section 14(2)(a).

The test in this last respect is whether what was published or said is "*likely to be taken*" as a statement in respect of one of the specified matters covered by the Act. It is submitted that particular care should be exercised in the publication of pictures in this context. Where a brochure is peppered with pictures, it is quite likely that such pictures are "*likely to be taken*" by some perfectly reasonable consumers, as attributable to the resorts or locations where they are to travel. Where a resort, hotel or even town is some distance from the pictures of an area included in a brochure, it would be wise to include approximate distances and travel times in the particulars of the travel arrangements provided. At the end of the day, it is a matter of fact as to

---

[25] E.g. *R v Piper* [1995] CA Unreported – a case in which a trader was convicted under section 14 TDA for displaying the crest of the Guild of Master Craftsmen (of which he was not a member) on his letterhead.

whether the interpretation of an ambiguous statement suggested by the prosecution is one "*likely to be taken*" by the reasonable consumer.

The extension of the meaning of "statement" by section 14(2)(a) allows the court to look at the information with which consumers are provided in a broad and overall sense. If the information — however it is transmitted — is "*likely to be taken*" by the reasonable consumer, as a statement of the services or facilities within section 14(1), then the transmission of that information is deemed to be a statement (whether it actually is a statement about the services or not). This is intended to cover the possibilities that:

- the information might not be a statement at all; or

- the statement that is made is not literally applied by the organiser to the services offered to the consumer.

For example, a badly or ambiguously placed five-star symbol might be intended for hotel "X", but because of the presentation of a number of hotels on one page of a brochure it is "*likely to be taken*" as a statement referring to hotel "Y" by an ordinary reader. Alternatively, adopting the facts of *Yugotours* v *Wadsley* purchasers of another cruise holiday might simply have been told that they were to enjoy a cruise aboard "one of the company's pleasure boats". It may well be that whilst the facing page's A4 picture of the majestic schooner under full sail was intended to apply, and was described as applying to *another* cruise in the relevant part of the text, the picture was nevertheless "*likely to be taken*" by reasonable consumers as a statement to the effect that the company's ships were all of the pictured or similar type or class and thus attributable to the "pleasure boat" cruise as well.

In practice, the occasions on which it will be necessary to resort to section 14(2)(a) will be few, as it will almost always be possible to rely on a positive inaccuracy in the information provided to the consumer rather than having to rely on implications from silence. However, where an "original" statement:

- was accurate when first made, but is rendered false by a change of circumstances; or

- was false in the first place but not made knowingly or recklessly originally; or

- the person making the original statement has a valid statutory defence; or

- was not a statement of present fact, but merely an expression of future intention;

then the real culpability of a defendant may lie in telling only half the story when he attempts to correct the inaccuracy. In such circumstances silence may be the real crime.

However, even where an accurate statement is rendered inaccurate by changing circumstances, it will often be more efficient to prosecute the maker of the statement on the basis that he *repeatedly* makes the statement (which has become false) every time a possible consumer reads or sees the information, and in many other cases, the half-truth itself will be a "false statement" in its own right. Where the resort beach has been closed following an oil spillage, and the organiser writes to his customers stating that "parts of the beach are temporarily inaccessible", one would normally expect to see a prosecution for the "false-positive", rather than rely on the silent assumption that other parts of the beach are open and accessible.

One final use to which 14(2)(a) can be put arose in *R v Clarksons Holidays Ltd.*[26] Clarksons published artists' impressions of a hotel that was not complete in their brochure. The pictures did not have a caption saying that the hotel was incomplete. However, in the small print at the back of the brochure, Clarksons included a lengthy explanatory note about artists impressions — which in effect said that, whilst they did the best they could to provide an artist's impression where a hotel was not complete, some details might vary when the construction was completed. A consumer found the hotel to be unfinished, and complained to his local trading standards authority. Clarksons sought to defend the subsequent prosecution on the grounds that the lengthy explanatory note at the end of their brochure indicated that the hotel was incomplete, and that its final construction might differ in certain respects from the particulars in the main body of the brochure. Accordingly, they maintained, the particulars in the brochure relating to the unfinished hotel were not statements of existing fact at the time the consumer read it, but merely indicative of the facilities that would be made available in the future — when the hotel was finished. Effectively, Clarksons said that the particulars and the artist's impression for the unfinished hotel were not "statements" because the explanatory note indicated that they were not statements. Neither the jury nor the Court of Appeal had any truck with this reasoning, not least of all (amongst other reasons) because the particulars and the impression were "*likely to be taken*" as statements by the consumer, especially since the explanatory note was tucked away at the end of the brochure.

So, the "anything" in section 14(2)(a) can be an expression of future intention *likely to be taken* as a statement of existing fact by a reasonable consumer. The "anything" can also be a statement which the organiser insists, whether by explanatory notes or otherwise, is *not* a statement.

[26] [1972] 57 CrAppR 38.

Existing fact and future intention

Section 14 of the TDA does not cover *promises*. To be caught by the TDA the statement that is made must be in respect of an existing fact.

The classic application of this distinction in a travel context come from McKenna J in *R v Sunair*.[27] It was noted by the judge that in order to be a false statement within the section, what was communicated to the consumer had to be true or false at the time it was made. This could never be so of a promise. *"A promise to do something in the future may be kept or it may be broken. But neither the prediction nor the promise can be said to have been true or false at the time when it was made".*[28]

Sunair was prosecuted because its brochure stated that certain facilities and services would be available for consumers. When the consumers arrived the promised children's pushchairs were broken, and children's meals and English menu were unavailable. Although convicted by a jury, the conviction was quashed on appeal due to the fact that the judge had failed to direct the jury as to the difference between a statement of existing fact and a promise of future performance.

It is important to note that the quashing of the conviction was due to a material misdirection on the part of the trial judge. The case does *not* decide that brochure particulars cannot be statements within the meaning of the section. Of course they can be, and usually are. English lawyers will be familiar with the expression that the state of a man's mind is as much a matter of fact as the state of his digestion. So it is that if a promise is made in respect of the provision of facilities and services, but the travel organiser does not have a genuine intention of providing those facilities or services, and has made no arrangements for the fulfilment of his contractual promise with the consumer — then he may be guilty of an offence, not for breaking his promise, but for making a false statement of existing fact — albeit an implicit one — in respect of his ability or intention to provide the promised services. The falsity lies in the presumption underlying the promise, namely that the organiser has the will or power to keep its promise. In all probability, then, had the jury in *Sunair* been adequately directed, the result would have been the same.

In *Yugotours* v *Wadsley* the tour operator made a promise as to the future performance of the contract "on board this majestic schooner" and made a statement of existing fact as to its ability to bring this promise to fruition. However, the tour operator had not made any arrangements for hiring or

---

[27] [1973] 1 WLR 1105.
[28] Above at page 1109G.

buying any kind of three-masted schooner like that in the picture — on the contrary, it had contracts for the hire of two sub-standard, two-masted ships. More to the point, the pictured schooner had nothing whatsoever to do with the provision of the Yugotours holidays. The false statement at the heart of the Yugotours case was, therefore, that at the time the brochure was read by the consumer, the company could not have had any intention of providing the pictured schooner or any colourable version of it.

In another Sunair case[29] the company *promised* twin-bedded rooms with private facilities and a terrace, to its customers. On arrival at the hotel the consumers discovered that their rooms did not have terraces. The Divisional Court overturned the company's conviction under section 14 TDA, on the grounds that Sunair had a contract with the hotel whereby only terraced twin rooms would be supplied to Sunair customers. The hotel's incompetence may have put Sunair in breach of contract — it had broken a *promise* — but at all material times the company thought it had the wherewithal to comply with the promise it had made. Accordingly, there was no implicit false statement with regard to the company's ability or intention to provide what had been promised.

So it is that in many cases it will be possible to make out of a promise at least an implicit statement as to present intention or ability to keep that promise. Whether that implicit statement is false will be a matter of fact. However, over-enthusiastic prosecutors should take note of the warning of Lord Wilberforce in *British Airways Board* v *Taylor:*[30]

> There may be inherent in a promise an implied statement as to a fact, and where this is really the case, the court can attach appropriate consequences to any falsity in, or recklessness in the making of, that statement ... But this proposition should not be used as a general solvent to transform the one type of assurance with another: the distinction is a real one and requires to be respected ... As Lord Widgery CJ said in *Beckett* v *Cohen* it was never intended that the 1968 Act should be used so as to make a criminal statement out of what is in reality a breach of warranty.

Repeated statements

Once published in a brochure or similar literature, a statement is made repeatedly:

- when it is posted in bulk to agents or consumers;

- when it is read by its ultimate recipient;

- when its contents are repeated or described in conversation;

---

[29] *Sunair Holidays v Dodd* [1970] 1 WLR 1037.
[30] [1976] 1 WLR 13.

- at every stage of a chain of distribution.

(See *Wings Ltd* v *Ellis*[31])

The statement is repeatedly made every time it is read or considered by any person. Repeated statements of this character are commonly referred to as "continuing statements". So, if a statement is false, it is made not only when the consumer picks a brochure from the agent's shelf to read for himself, but on each occasion the original reader passes it to his family, friends and colleagues for them to look at.

Once a brochure is in the public domain circumstances may change, rendering previously accurate statements false. The swimming pool may close; the beach may become polluted. Short of recalling every example of the circulating brochure, there is nothing that can then be done to prevent the making of a false statement. If the pool or the beach have been included in the list of resort facilities, but access to them becomes restricted after the circulation of the brochure, the list of facilities in the brochure — once accurate — has been rendered false by chance. Such a transformation of a truthful statement into a false one can cause acute problems for tour operators and travel agents who are notified of the changed circumstances that have, effectively, made "liars" out of them and their brochures; or who do not have adequate administrative systems to keep themselves informed of any changes of circumstances, because then, what has become a false statement continues to be made, and it will be made either with knowledge that the statement is false, or recklessly by those responsible for its earlier, innocent dissemination. Tour operators might try to limit the worst effects of this sort of situation by circulating "correction slips" or letters explaining the change of circumstances. However, whilst every paid-up customer may get an "errata" it is impossible to target every possible member of the public who has or is likely to read the relevant brochure, and those who are not in receipt of a clear and unambiguous correction will be victims of the continuing false statement. It is highly debatable in any event, whether a "correction" deprives the false statement of its inaccuracy, or whether the correction merely gives rise to arguable grounds for a statutory defence. There are at least two different situations.

First, where a consumer receives a written correction to the effect that the promised beach is now closed, it could not be said in any real sense that the statement in the brochure concerning the hotel's private beach (now false) was *continuing* at least as far the recipient of the correction was concerned. This must also be the case where brochures in agencies have clear errata details stapled or glued to the front page, or where shelf markers are used to

---

[31] [1985] AC 272 per Lord Hailsham.

identify brochures where further assistance should be sought, or where they are subject to additional information sheets. Provided the correction (or reference to further information) is clear and bold enough to subsume the statement it is designed to correct, and provided the correction reaches the readers of the original statement — then corrections can negative the effect of what is discovered to be a false statement. (This would apply both to those false statements that have become so due to changed circumstances and to those that have always been false, but may have only recently been discovered.) Support for the proposition that one should look at the whole of the circumstances comes from a Crown Court case — *R* v *McMillan Aviation Ltd.*[32] The case concerned the exposure for sale of a car with a false odometer reading. The car was supplied to a purchaser, and the vendor was charged with "offering to supply" a car to which a false description as to mileage had been applied. The vendor was acquitted on the grounds that when the car had been sold to the purchaser, the sales note signed by the purchaser contained a clear disclaimer in respect of the mileage. This disclaimer was sufficient (taking all the circumstances as a whole) to "trump" the false odometer reading. The defendant in *McMillan* might consider himself to have been rather fortunate on those facts.

Secondly, however, a consumer or possible consumer may come across a brochure informally. There may be no correction in sight, and the tour operator would not know where to send a correction anyway. This consumer visits a travel agent on the strength of the brochure to book the hotel with its nice beach. The consumer misses the "errata" sheet on display near the brochure rack. Happily, the agent's information system is such that when the customer goes to the desk, he is immediately told orally that the brochure is out of date, and the beach closed. In this situation, the particulars in the brochure about the beach will still constitute a false statement. The agent's administrative system prevents the client from *relying* on the false statement — but there can be no doubt that the particulars about the beach are and remain false. Here an offence is committed despite a good corrections policy in operation at the travel agent's office. To avoid conviction for "making a false statement", the defendant would have to prove one of the statutory defences.

False to a material degree

Section 14(4) of the TDA does not concern itself with trifles. In order for there to be an offence the false statement or "thing" that is likely to be taken for a statement must be "false to a material degree". What is and is not "false to a material degree" must always be a question of fact — though some examples are no doubt more self-evident than others. One would like

---

[32] [1981] Crim LR 785.

to think that no prosecuting authority would concern itself with prosecutions in respect of trivial matters. However, this highlights the fact that the *materiality* in subsection 14(4) relates to the *falsity* or inaccuracy — it does not relate to the service or facility in respect of which the statement has been made. Reverting to the facts of one of the *Sunair* cases, it would be inconsequential for many people that no pushchairs were available at the hotel, contrary to what may have been stated in the brochure — an unimportant factor for those consumers not travelling with toddlers for instance. A complaint by an adult family, therefore, that no pushchairs were on hand could legitimately be regarded as trivial. However, the falsity of the statement would not be trivial in itself. The statement that pushchairs were available for those who wished to use them would have been a statement that was "false to a material degree", indeed it would have been completely untrue on the facts of that case.

Conversely, a brochure may state that all rooms have en suite, luxury, marble bathrooms. In truth, it may emerge that the bathrooms are luxurious, but the decor is a marble "effect", not real marble. The statement would be false, but, it is suggested, not false to a *material degree.*

Specified categories of statement

To fall foul of section 14 TDA the false statement must be "*as to any of the matters*" specified in subsection 14(1) (b). The specified matters relate largely to services of one type or another and are particularly relevant to those providing travel arrangements for the consumer.

Adopting the sub-paragraph numbering of section 14(1)(b), the specified matters in respect of which the false statement must be made in order to fall within the provisions of the TDA are:

(i) "the provision of any services, accommodation or facilities" — for example, a statement as to the provision of pushchairs, children's meals and an English menu in the Sunair case;

(ii) "the nature of any services, accommodation or facilities" — for example, a qualitative statement with regard to services offered, such as "Business Class" travel;

(iii) "the time at which, manner in which or persons by whom any services, accommodation or facilities are so provided" — for example "a nightly discotheque with leading local entertainers";

(iv) "the examination, approval or evaluation by any person of any services, accommodation or facilities" — for example, star or symbol ratings, or more general statements to the effect that all facilities and services have

been checked by the tour operator's staff and found to be of a high
standard;

(v) "the location or amenities of any accommodation" — for example,
"beachside hotel, five minutes from ancient town centre".

Mens rea — knowledge and recklessness

Unlike the offences created by the PTR 1992, section 14(1) of the TDA[33]
carries a mental element. The prosecution must prove that a false statement
was made which the maker "*knows to be false*" or was made "*recklessly*".

However, as will be seen there have been times when the offences created by
section 14 of the TDA have come perilously close to being interpreted by the
courts as offences of "strict" or at least "semi-strict" liability, so diluted has
the mental element become.

Knowledge — Wings v Ellis

Wings Limited were convicted of making a false statement as to the nature of
accommodation at a hotel in Sri Lanka, which they knew to be false,
contrary to section 14(1)(ii) of the TDA. They published a brochure early in
1981 and used the code "AC" to indicate that the rooms in the Seashells
Hotel were air conditioned. The company discovered that this description of
the accommodation was inaccurate, and in June 1981, issued an instruction
to staff and travel agents to correct the error. They also wrote to those
consumers who had already booked informing them of the mistake. One
consumer — Mr Wade — booked in January 1982, but he was not informed
of the error. He went to Sri Lanka expecting air conditioning. There was
none. He complained to his local trading standards officers. The company
was convicted of making a false statement that it *knew to be false*. Its appeal
to the Divisional Court was allowed, but the conviction under section
14(1)(a)(ii) was restored by the House of Lords. At the time the brochure
was printed and first circulated, the company had no knowledge that the
statement about air conditioning was false. However, the statement was
repeatedly made every time a person read the uncorrected brochure. By the
time Mr Wade read it, the company knew that the statement was false.
Accordingly, it had made a statement knowing the same to be false. Lord
Brandon put the position most succinctly in posing his own version of the
certified question for the opinion of the High Court:[34]

> Whether a defendant may properly be convicted of an offence under section
> 14(1)(a) of the Trade Descriptions Act 1968 where he has made a continuing

---

[33] But not section 1 TDA.
[34] Above at page 298E.

false statement, which he did not know was false when he first made it, but which, having come to know of its falsity at some later time, he has thereafter continued to make.

The answer to this question, in Lord Brandon's opinion, was undoubtedly, "Yes". Lord Scarman noted: *"The subsection says not that it is an offence knowingly to make the statement but that it is an offence to make the statement."*

The company's case to the effect that it only made one statement — on the publication of the brochure — was roundly rejected by the court.

Whose knowledge?

In the divisional court in *Wings*, Mann J said that[35]: *"A company cannot be guilty of an offence unless the specified state of mind was a state of mind of a person who is or forms part of the directing mind and will of the company"*.

This proposition — based fairly and squarely on the decision in *Tesco Supermarkets* v *Nattrass*[36] — has also been the subject of some revision by the House of Lords.

Lord Scarman:

> The Act, of course, to be of any value at all in modern conditions has to cover trades and businesses conducted on a large scale by individual proprietors, by firms, and by bodies corporate. The day to day business activities of large enterprises, whatever their legal structure, are necessarily conducted by their employees, and particularly by their sales staff. It follows that many of the acts prohibited by the Act will be the acts of employees done in the course of the trade or business and without the knowledge at the time of those who direct the business. It will become clear that the Act does cover such acts...

Given, therefore, that it is not necessary to know of the falsity of a statement at the time it is *first* made, and that knowledge of the falsity may come about through the agency of an employee, who may not pass on his knowledge with the alacrity his employer would have wished, the degree of culpability required under section 14(1) TDA seems to be very low indeed. So low, in fact, that one can well understand Lord Scarman's reference to the offences as ones of "semi-strict" liability.

Reckless and regardless

Recklessness is defined by section 14(2)(b) of the TDA: *"a statement made regardless of whether it is true or false shall be deemed to be made*

---

[35] [1984] 1 WLR 731.
[36] [1972] AC 153.

recklessly, whether or not the person making it had reason for believing that it might be false."

This definition of recklessness is very wide indeed. It covers everything from what would be considered "reckless" within the general criminal law, to acts of pure carelessness. In *MFI Warehouses Ltd* v *Nattrass*[37] Lord Widgery CJ refused to apply or consider authorities from other areas on the meaning of recklessness, and applied the simple deeming provisions of section 14(2)(b). There is little doubt that to be "reckless" within the meaning of this section one needs to be little more than "thoughtless". If one simply does not apply one's mind to whether a given statement is true or false, then one has made it "regardless of whether it is true or false". The breadth of this meaning ascribed to "recklessness" is justified by Lord Widgery on the grounds that the TDA is a regulatory statute enforced through the criminal courts by penalty, rather than a statute creating criminal offences in any real sense of the term.

One of the problems created by the emphasis the courts have placed on the regulatory, rather than criminal, nature of the statute (which finds its clearest expression in *Wings Ltd* v *Ellis*), is that the threshold of proof required to convict a defendant is a relatively modest one; but after conviction it will be necessary to sentence a defendant by determining whereabouts on the scale of culpability the offence falls. This is not unique to the TDA, but the problem, it is submitted, is particularly acute, where culpability can extend across a range encompassing "innocent" but convicted defendants (as per Hailsham in *Wings*), or the thoughtlessly careless under section 14(1)(b); to those who have set out on a course of conduct designed to cheat and defraud the public (as in *Davies*). The problem is that a defendant may be easily convicted without proof of fraud or deliberate recklessness, and then sentenced on the basis of a culpability the prosecution did not need to prove to establish the commission of the offence. It will be incumbent on defendants, therefore, to ensure that they have some material of their own available to impress the court at the sentencing stage that the offence was one of inadvertence, error or carelessness rather than one of cheat, fraud or dishonesty — even where these more culpable elements are not part of the prosecution case.

Whose recklessness?

The requirement of recklessness has had something of a chequered history in the context of travel cases. Mann J's proposition in the Divisional Court in *Wings* to the effect that a corporation could only been convicted of an offence under section 14 if the required state of mind was proved to be the state of mind of someone who was part of the controlling mind or will of the corporation, was a proposition made in the context of recklessness (the second charge faced by

---

[37] See above.

Wings Ltd, the conviction being overturned by the Divisional Court and not restored by the House of Lords). However, in *Yugotours* v *Wadsley*,[38] Parker LJ appeared to make serious inroads into Mann J's unexceptional proposition. Parker LJ accepted that there was no evidence that any person who formed part of the directing mind of the company had considered the truth or falsity of the relevant statement in the brochure. Nonetheless he felt able to conclude that where a company failed to call any evidence in respect of the circumstances in which the statement in the brochure came to be made and which persons at the company were responsible for allowing the statement to go uncorrected, there was a clear *inference* to be drawn from all the circumstances that some individual representative of the directing mind of the corporation must have had the relevant state of mind, even though that person could not be identified:

> the state of mind envisaged by section 14(1)(b) is inevitably a matter which can in almost all circumstances only be a matter of inference. There was ample evidence here in my judgment from which such an inference could be drawn, and the result follows that, there being no explanation, that inference can stand.

The effect of Parker LJ's decision may be regarded as a subtle reversal of the burden of proof. Parker LJ appears to have sanctioned an approach that in the absence of an explanation by the company, there is a presumption to be made that a person who forms part of the directing mind of the corporation must have been reckless in allowing a false statement to be made, or continued. Such a presumption or inference arose in *Yugotours* — from "ample evidence" which seems to have been no more than the fact that a brochure was printed for the company, which one would presume had the approval of some directing mind within the organisation. In the absence of an explanation from the company, it is to be inferred from the fact that a false statement was made in a "company" document such as a brochure, that some directing mind must have authorised the brochure "regardless of whether [the statements in it] were true or false". It is thought unlikely that many large organisations would be able to produce evidence to the effect that an appropriately senior officer of the company considered each and every statement in the brochure — applying his mind to whether those statements were true or false. Nevertheless, it would appear from the *Yugotours* case that:

- in every case where a company produces a brochure, or some similar publication, an inference is to be drawn that the publication must have had the authorisation of an officer of the company;

- in every case a further inference is to be drawn that in respect of any individual false statement in the publication the relevant officer must

---

[38] [1989] Crim LR 623.

have failed to have regard to the truth or falsity of that statement —
otherwise, it is presumed, it would not have been made;

- the offence under section 14(1)(b) is then made out, unless the company
  can prove that every effort was made to check the accuracy of what was
  published, thus rebutting the above presumption.

The wafer-thin difference between this and strict liability feeds the
conclusion that *mens rea* was abolished in the *Yugotours* case.

McCowan LJ restored some equilibrium in *Airtours* v *Shipley*.[39] Here the
tour operator described a hotel in its brochure as having a swimming pool. It
did not. The error had been included in the brochure by a process the
company was unable to explain. The company was, however, able to prove
the existence and operation of a checking and corrections policy,
implemented by the "directing minds" of the company through its
employees. The Divisional Court overturned the conviction under section
14(1)(b) TDA. McCowan LJ expressly approved the dictum of Mann J in
Wings v *Ellis*, and expressed reservations about the decision in *Yugotours*,
whilst accepting that there would be cases where *evidence* of recklessness by
the directing minds of a company would be a matter of inference. Airtours
was found not to be reckless within section 14(1)(b) because its directing
minds had devised and implemented a proper and adequate system for the
production of brochures that involved having regard to the truth or falsity of
the statements contained in it.

It would appear, therefore, following the *Yugotours* and *Airtours* cases, that:

- *"... a corporate defendant is not guilty unless the requisite intent was a
  state of mind of one or more of those natural persons who constitute the
  directing mind and will of the company"* (per Mann J in *Wings Ltd* v
  Ellis);

- however, a court is entitled to *infer*, and will *readily infer*, that the
  relevant state of mind exists in one of those natural persons (and thus
  the company) where a false statement is made in a corporate document
  or publication (or in other circumstances where the irresistible
  conclusion is that officers of the company must have authorised its
  making) *and there is no evidence of any system within the organisation
  by which regard is given to the truth or falsity of the statement made*;

- where such a corporate system has been devised, implemented and
  supervised by the directing minds, they will not be taken as having made
  any false statement *regardless* of whether it was true or false — the

---

[39] 1994 Divisional Court – Unreported but digested *Butterworths: Trading & Consumer Law Vol 1.*

creation, design and guidance of the system is capable of providing the necessary regard as far as the directing minds are concerned;

- Airtours were able to persuade the court that they had in place an "excellent" system — and their conviction was overturned. Yugotours had no such evidence to call; their conviction was upheld. The conclusion is that whilst Parker LJ may have lowered the threshold of proof required under section 14(1)(b) for "reckless" offences, McCowan LJ has reinforced the general rule of law as enunciated by Mann J in *Wings*;

- the observation of Lord Hailsham in Wings is, therefore, still apposite. The offences under section 14 of the TDA are emphatically not offences of absolute or strict liability.

The Consumer Protection Act 1987 ('the CPA')

Again, when the Consumer Protection from Unfair Trading Regulations 2007 come into force, the CPA will be rendered irrelevant as far as the industry is concerned. Nevertheless, as with the TDA, for a short time offences committed prior to 6th April 2008 will continue to be prosecuted under the CPA, and caselaw decided under the Act will continue to be relevant in the context of the Regulations.

The price of a regulated package is one of the matters which must be specified in the package brochure under regulation 5 of the PTR 1992. The Consumer Protection Act 1987 (Part 111)[40] is concerned with *price indications* generally, and in particular *misleading price indications*. The most important provisions for present purposes are sections 20–22 CPA. The provisions are enforced by local authority trading standards departments, and are subject to the same penalty regime as imposed by the PTR 1992. There is no penalty of imprisonment similar to that provided for by the TDA.

Two offences are created.

The first, under section 20(1) is the giving of "*an indication which is misleading as to the price at which [services] are available*".

The prosecution must prove:

- a person in the course of a business of his,

- has given a misleading indication about the price (or the method of calculating the price)

- of goods, services accommodation or facilities to a consumer.

---

[40] Referred to as the CPA.

The second (section 20(2)) is, where a price indication has been given it "*has become misleading*" and the defendant has failed to take all such steps as are reasonable to "prevent consumers from relying on the indication". The prosecution must prove:

- a person in the course of a business of *his*,

- has given an indication of a price (or its method of calculation) which has subsequently become misleading,

- that some consumers might still be relying on the indication; and

- the person has not taken reasonable steps to correct the indication.

Whilst a defendant must have given the indication in the course of a *business of his* (c.f. Trade Descriptions Act), section 20(3) makes it clear that the indication can be given either as a principal or agent: "*... it shall be immaterial ... whether the person who gives ... the indication is ... acting on his own behalf or on behalf of another.*" So whilst employees are safe from prosecution under the CPA, the travel agent most definitely is not. Any price indication issued on behalf of a tour operator will be caught by section 20(3). The travel agent is acting in the course of a business of *his*, albeit he is acting at the tour operator's request in displaying the price indication. Naturally, a travel agent who is making indications by price lists, posters or promotions on his own account, is liable.

What is a price?

This is defined by section 20(6) of the CPA as "*the aggregate of the sums required to be paid by a consumer for the supply of the goods or the provision of services, accommodation or facilities.*"

What is an indication?

This not defined by the CPA, but an indication can be given "*by any means whatsoever*". "*Indication*" clearly includes price lists; price panels; vouchers; notices; advertisements and VDU displays. It would also include an oral statement of the price, which in turn would also include oral promises of discounts and savings.

What is misleading?

Section 21(1)CPA provides a definition of "*misleading*". An indication given to consumers is misleading if:

> what is conveyed by the indication, or what those consumers might reasonably be expected to infer from the indication or any omission from it include any of the following, that is to say:
>
> (a) that the price is less than in fact it is; or

(b) that the applicability of the price does not depend on facts or circumstances on which it does in fact depend; or

(c) that the price covers matters in respect of which an additional charge is in fact made; or

(d) that a person who in fact has no such expectation -

    (i) expects the price to be increased or reduced or

    (ii) expects the price to be maintained or;

(e) that the facts or circumstances by reference to which the consumers might reasonably be expected to judge the validity of any relevant comparison made or implied by the indication are not what in fact they are.

It is immaterial[41] that the indication is not misleading to all consumers, provided it is capable of misleading some. There is no requirement that a consumer has actually relied upon the misleading indication. Prosecutions may be brought on the basis that an enforcement officer discovering a misleading indication may prove that the indication was objectively *capable* of misleading some consumers to whom it was directed. By section 20(6)(b) CPA a "consumer" is "any person who might wish to be supplied with the services or facilities otherwise than for the purposes of any business of his". There is no reason for the enforcing authority to wait for a complaint from a member of public before entertaining a prosecution.

The list of possible ways[42] in which the price indication may be misleading is exhaustive. The list provided under CPA section 21(2) relating to indications in respect of the *method* of calculating a price, is very similar in effect to the list provided above in respect of indications relating to the *price itself.*

In a travel context the list of possible ways in which a price indication might be misleading is relatively straightforward to interpret.

- The first category is probably the most obvious. It is a flat understatement of the real price. A package may be offered for £500.00, whereas its actual price is £600.00. Thus, any error in the printing of a price or its communication to the consumer can lead to a criminal prosecution. This is exactly what happened in *Berkshire County Council v Olympic Holidays.*[43]. Due to a computer "blip" a price was displayed on a VDU to a consumer that was, in fact, £182.00 less than the true price. Regrettably, instead of allowing the consumer to have the holiday at the lower and mistaken price, the tour operator stood its ground and insisted on the true price. Ultimately, the company was acquitted on the grounds that it had

---

[41] Section 20(3)(c).
[42] Section 21(1).
[43] [1994] ITLJ 5.

made out a statutory defence. It did not recover its costs, and in the blinding light of hindsight, it may have been much more economical to allow the consumer to have the holiday at the cheaper price.

- The second category concerns situations where some information is held back from the consumer. For example, a price indication may be given without reference to the fact that its availability is restricted to a certain period, or a certain location, or by taking a flight by an indirect route. Children's rates may be advertised which do not make it clear that the reduction is dependent on the child travelling with two full-fare paying adults — and is not available to single parents. Apartment and villa holidays are often prone to misleading price indications if it is not made crystal clear how much the accommodation as a whole will cost over a given period — consumers may not always appreciate that price depends on occupancy. £200.00 per week may become £400.00 if only two rather than four persons are sharing.

- The third category is straightforward. No impression must be given that "supplementary" or "extras" charges are included in the advertised price.[44] Where supplements apply, they should be clearly marked — this would include single supplements, extra excursion costs, meal supplements, and charges that may arise in respect of things like airport departure taxes.

- The fourth category catches those who attempt to persuade a consumer to purchase a service on the grounds that the price will soon increase, or that there will definitely be no "cut-price" offers later in the season. It clearly includes those examples of pricing which involve bogus suggestions that a service is being offered cut-price for a limited period.

- The final category applies to misleading comparisons with other services. The classic example is a comparison between one tour operator's cheapest price and another's most expensive, where the two packages offered are not reasonably similar. It would include an offer by an airline of tickets to Hong Kong at £300.00 "compared to our rival's price of £900.00"; where the rival's flight was nonstop and direct, and the offeror's flight involved changing planes at four places en route.

---

[44] This category has been the subject of heated controversy in the airline industry during the course of 2007. The Office of Fair Trading has taken action against a large number of airlines who were not including all fixed, non-optional costs on their web site price lists (taxes being the classic example of excluded compulsory "extras"). In this successful campaign the OFT has been joined by ABTA who have taken a similarly aggressive stand against prevaricating members in this regard. See: [2007] ITLJ Bulletin page xxviii.

Section 20(2) makes it plain that where a price becomes misleading after it was given, the person giving the indication must take all such steps as are reasonable to prevent consumers from relying on the indication. So, where a second-edition brochure is produced which makes price changes, the tour operator and travel agent must take all reasonable steps to ensure that nobody thereafter relies on the first edition. The CPA applies in similar circumstances, therefore, to the TDA as applied in *Wings Ltd* v *Ellis*[45] (as to which see above under the TDA); it might be said the CPA gives statutory effect to the House of Lord decision in *Wings*.

Companies and managers

The CPA includes provisions analogous to those under the TDA in that where an offence is committed with the "consent or connivance" of any director, manager, secretary or other similar officer of a body corporate — that other person shall be guilty of an offence as well as the body corporate (s 40(2) CPA).

Prices — Code of Practice

Section 25 of the CPA makes provision for the approval of a price indications Code of Practice. A Code of Practice has been issued. Contravention of the Code is not itself a criminal offence, but broadly speaking, non-compliance with the Code can be used as *evidence* against a defendant for an alleged offence contrary to the Act. Conversely, compliance with the Code can be used by a defendant to illustrate either that no offence has been committed, or that he has exercised all due diligence to avoid committing the offence in question. Codes of Practice are also regularly issued by the Health and Safety Executive under the Health and Safety At Work Act 1974, (H&SAWA) which enjoy the same evidential status. Even though the regime applicable to Codes of Practice under regulatory statutes is the same, it is worth emphasising that even though a breach of a Code is never in itself a criminal offence, where a breach or non-compliance with a code can be demonstrated, a conviction almost inevitably follows. Accordingly, tour operators and travel agents would be well advised to acquaint themselves with the CPA Code of Practice, which actually includes a number of specific suggestions relating to "good practice" in the context of pricing indications in the travel industry.

---

[45] See above.

The Consumer Protection from Unfair Trading Regulations 2007

The Regulations, which come into force on 6th April 2008, and which implement the Unfair Commercial Practices Directive[46] will supersede the statutory regime under the Trade Descriptions Act 1968 and the Consumer Protection Act 1987, and it is anticipated that in the years to come most prosecutions involving tour operators and retailers will fall within this new regime. The new regime conforms to an increasingly familiar pattern in circumstances where the generating legislation comes from the European Commission. Broad, sweeping *criminal* offences are created, accompanied by a dearth of detailed categorisation or definition. Much is left to the perceived good sense of prosecuting authorities and the practical application of undefined standards by tribunals of fact (i.e. magistrates and juries). It is likely that as these regulations are applied on a case by case basis it will be the English courts that assume the responsibility for laying down the substance of what is required in order to justify a successful prosecution. At the same time, the ambition seems to be to create a generally applicable and overarching scheme of offences (on a one-size-fits-all basis) rather than the creation of specific offences tailored to deter specific examples of commercially unfair behaviour.

Prohibited practices

The Regulations apply to commercial practices before, during and after a contract is formed, and introduce a general obligation on traders not to treat consumers unfairly, whether by acts or omissions, or to subject them to aggressive commercial practices such as high pressure selling techniques. Regulation 3 sets out the basic premise:

(1) Unfair commercial practices are prohibited.

(2) Paragraphs (3) to (5) set out the circumstances when a commercial practice is unfair.

(3) A commercial practice is unfair if –

(a) it contravenes the requirements of professional diligence; and

(b) it materially distorts or is likely to materially distort the economic behaviour of the typical consumer with regard to the product.

(4) In paragraph (3)(b) "to materially distort the economic behaviour of the typical consumer" means appreciably to impair the typical consumer's

---

[46] (2005/29/EC).

ability to make an informed decision thereby causing him to take a transactional *decision that he would not have taken otherwise.*"

The prosecutor must show that:

- The practice contravenes the requirements of professional diligence;

- It materially distorts or is likely to materially distort;

- The economic behaviour of the typical consumer with regard to the product.

A practice is unfair if it is a misleading action[47] or omission,[48] is aggressive[49] or falls within Schedule 1 to the Regulations, which lists 31 commercial practices which are in themselves prohibited. For a practice to be a breach of any other prohibition, it must have had, or be likely to have, an effect on the typical consumer.

Professional diligence

Professional diligence is defined in Regulation 2 as:

> ...the standard of special skill and care which a trader may reasonably be expected to exercise towards consumers which is commensurate with either –
>
> (a) honest market practice in the trader's field of activity, or
>
> (b) the general principle of good faith in the trader's field of activity; or both.

Compliance with relevant Codes of Conduct or DBERR or FTO Guidelines may well be relevant here; but, as always, compliance will not always be necessary, or sufficient, for a trader to be found to have been professionally diligent. The very vagueness of the concept is potentially a trap for the unwary; where a trader follows a practice which he himself considers to accord with standard professional practice, but which a court considers not to have accorded with *honest* market practice, he will be guilty of an offence. It is to be hoped that prosecutors will bring proceedings only in the clearest of cases; but it is thought that the meaning of this subsection will prove to be analogous to the definition of an elephant: you can't describe it, but you know a dishonest practice when you see it.

Misleading actions and omissions

An action is misleading if it contains false information or if it, or its overall presentation, in any way deceives or is likely to deceive the typical consumer, even if the information is factually correct; and if it causes or is likely to

---

[47] Regulation 5.
[48] Regulation 6.
[49] Regulation 7.

cause the typical consumer to take a transactional decision he would not otherwise have taken. The information in question must relate to a number of listed matters,[50] including the main characteristics of the product, the price or the manner in which the price is calculated, and the consumer's rights or the risks he may face. The main characteristics of the produce include the benefits, fitness for purpose and specification of the product.[51]

Clearly the Regulations are intended to catch the *Yugotours* situation, in which a photograph is misleading in that the typical consumer is likely to draw the conclusion that the subject of the photograph has a relevance to the holiday advertised. It is no excuse that the information provided is factually correct; the context may render it misleading because, although the picture is indeed of a schooner, such a vessel is not to be used for the holiday in question.

The Code of Practice for Traders on Price Indications provides guidance as regards the information to be provided to consumers regarding pricing. The Code is currently being rewritten to reflect the requirements of the Regulations, and it is anticipated that a revised Code will be made available shortly after the Regulations come into force. Compliance with the Code is likely to be accepted as good evidence that the information given is not misleading (or at least to assist in any defence of due diligence under Regulation 17 – of which more in chapter 13).

An omission is misleading if, in context, it omits or hides material information or provides such information in a manner which is unclear, unintelligible, ambiguous or untimely, and as a result causes or is likely to cause the typical consumer to take a transactional decision he would not otherwise have taken[52]. Information is material if it is required, for example, by the PTR 1992, or if it relates to the main characteristics of the product. A good example is that of low cost air fares, which are commonly advertised exclusive of taxes. Even if the small print at the bottom of the advertisement warns consumers that the price quoted is exclusive of duty, it is suggested that such an advertisement would fall foul of the Regulations; the incidence and amount of chargeable taxes is material information, the omission of which might cause a typical consumer to decide to purchase a flight he might not otherwise have bought.

Aggressive practices

A commercial practice is aggressive if it either significantly impairs or is likely to significantly impair the typical consumer's freedom of choice or

---

[50] Regulation 5(4).
[51] Regulation 5(5).
[52] Regulation 6(1).

conduct in relation to the product concerned through the use of harassment, coercion or undue influence, and either causes or is likely to cause the consumer to take a transactional decision he would not otherwise have taken. It is hoped that such practices are unusual in a travel context; but high-pressure sales techniques will be caught by the provision.

Schedule 1 prohibited practices

The list of 31 prohibited practices which are in all circumstances deemed unfair contains a number which are of interest to the industry, including:

(1) Claiming to be a signatory to a code of conduct when the trader is not;

(5) Making an invitation to purchase products at a specified price without disclosing the existence of any reasonable grounds the trader may have for believing that he will not be able to offer for supply, or to procure another trader to supply, those products or equivalent products at that price for a period that is, and in quantities that are, reasonable having regard to the product, the scale of advertising of the product and the price offered (bait advertising);

(7) Falsely stating that a product will only be available for a very limited time, or that it will only be available on particular terms for a very limited time, in order to elicit an immediate decision and deprive consumers of sufficient opportunity or time to make an informed choice;

(10) Presenting rights given to consumers in law as a distinctive feature of the trader's offer;

(11) Using editorial content in the media to promote a product where a trader has paid for the promotion without making that clear in the content or by images or sounds clearly identifiable by the consumer (advertorials).

With regard to category (5) of the prohibited practices, it is noteworthy that the concept of an "invitation to purchase" is *not* the same as the common law "invitation to treat". The phrase encompasses communications which provide enough information to enable a consumer to make a purchase, so that, for example, advertisements which do not specify price are not invitations to purchase for these purposes. Conversely, pages on a website or advertisements in a newspaper which allow consumers to fill out a booking form *will* amount to invitations to purchase.

Category (7) is a particular danger; it is an offence to place pressure on a consumer by falsely overstating the limited availability of a product, and retailers must be careful not to fall foul of Schedule 1 in attempting to secure immediate bookings, rather than allowing customers to walk away and consider their options before booking. On the other hand, few customers would thank a travel agent for failing to warn them that the last few low-cost packages available might be snapped up before they made up their minds to book. Once again, because of the breadth of the Regulations the trader is left to walk a tight-rope, and to rely on the prosecuting authorities to take a sensible approach to prosecuting these offences.

Offences under the Regulations

It is an offence knowingly or recklessly to engage in a commercial practice which contravenes the requirements of professional diligence and either materially distorts or is likely to materially distort the economic behaviour of the typical consumer with regard to the product.[53] Further offences relate to engaging in misleading actions,[54] misleading omissions,[55] aggressive commercial practices,[56] and the prohibited practices contained within Schedule 1.[57] All offences, with the exception of contravention of the general prohibition on unfair practice, are strict liability offences. In respect of the general prohibition, it is suggested that the wider definitions of knowledge and recklessness set out above are likely to be applied in this context, in the light of the rationale behind the Regulations, namely to maximise consumer protection.

Offences will be triable either way and will attract fines (with the maximum fine set at £5,000 at time of writing) and/or terms of imprisonment of up to two years.[58] Prosecutions must be brought within three years of the date of the offence or within one year of the prosecutor discovering the offence, whichever is earlier.[59]

The Regulations provide enforcement authorities with draconian powers to investigate compliance, including the power to make test purchases[60] and to enter premises with[61] and without[62] a warrant.

General observations

The Regulations are so widely drawn that they are likely to render most other regulatory crimes in this area otiose. In particular, all information provided to consumers must be entirely accurate, and must include all relevant matters. The brochure advertising a luxurious five star hotel, for example, must also inform holidaymakers that the premises is next door to a

---

[53] Regulation 8.
[54] Regulation 9.
[55] Regulation 10.
[56] Regulation 11.
[57] Regulation 12.
[58] Regulation 13.
[59] Regulation 14.
[60] Regulation 21.
[61] Regulation 23.
[62] Regulation 22.

noisy building site, if the tour operator is not to risk prosecution under Regulation 6. Increased openness will also be necessary in relation to pricing, particularly in respect of air fares; advertisements for flights notoriously often quote fares exclusive of tax and other duties, but under Regulation 6 such ambiguity will cease to be lawful.

It is suggested that all potentially misleading actions and omissions are likely to be found likely to affect the behaviour of the typical consumer; if it were not likely to do so, the court will reason, why would the trader have found it worthwhile to mislead the consumer? And it is worth noting that the characteristics to be attributed to the typical consumer are a moveable feast. To take an obvious example, the type of consumer likely to venture on a Club 18–30 holiday might be very different to the type of consumer likely to be interested in a Saga cruise. The information to be provided to each category of consumer will therefore be different according to their anticipated needs. Further, some consumers will require more information than others, for example those with disabilities or with particular dietary requirements. Misleading information regarding the width of doorways or the food likely to be served in the hotel restaurant, respectively, might not have an affect on most consumers, but might well cause a typical disabled consumer or a typical consumer with religious convictions to alter his or her decision on whether to book the holiday.

Again, how this issue will fall to be decided once the Regulations come into force is anyone's guess: and a degree of age, gender, religious and even racial stereotyping is likely to creep into the analysis. It is suggested that magistrates and judges take particular care in describing, for example, the 'typical' consumer of cruises, or the 'typical' Muslim consumer in the context of Haj pilgrimage packages. Those in the industry will be aware that it is rare that a holidaymaker turns out to be entirely 'typical'.

The Denied Boarding Regulations

The Denied Boarding Regulations[63] impose criminal liability for breach of Articles 4 to 6, 10, 11 and 14 of EC Regulation No. 261/2004.[64] Conviction carries a maximum fine of £5,000.[65] It is a defence for an operating air carrier to show that it took all reasonable steps and exercised all due diligence to avoid committing the offence.[66]

---

[63] The Civil Aviation (Denied Boarding, Compensation and Assistance) Regulations 2005 (SI 2005/975).
[64] Regulation 3(1).
[65] Regulation 3(2).
[66] Regulation 4(1).

The Disability Discrimination Regulations

The Disability Discrimination Regulations[67] impose a complex regime of criminal liability. Essentially, different entities are liable for breach of the various different Regulations. The following entities are liable for breach of the following Articles of EC Regulation No. 1107/2006:[68]

- Air carriers, agents of air carriers, tour operators: Articles 3, 4, 6(1) to 6(3) and 12;

- Air carriers only: Articles 10 and 11;

- Operating air carriers only: Article 6(4);

- Managing bodies of airports: Articles 5, 7(1), 7(2), 7(3), 7(5), 7(6), 8(1), 8(2), 8(5), 8(6), 9(1), 9(3), 11 and 13.

Offences under Article 8(2) carry a maximum penalty of £1,000; offences under Articles 4(3), 5(2), 7(1), 7(2), 7(3), 7(5), 7(6), 8(6), 9(1), 9(3), 10 and 11 carry a maximum penalty of £5,000; offences under Articles 3, 4(1), 4(4), 5(1), 8(1), 8(5) or 13 carry an unlimited fine[69] (following trial on indictment; the latter offence is triable either way). It is a defence to show that the Defendant took all reasonable steps to avoid committing the offence, but he cannot defend the prosecution on the basis of his reliance on information given to him, unless he shows that it was reasonable for him to have relied on that information.[70]

The Health and Safety at Work Act 1974

It is not possible in a book of this nature to discuss the full implications of the "H&SAWA". Nonetheless, for those offering transport, accommodation and leisure services generally, it is important to remember that the provisions of the H&SAWA apply as much to them as they do to any other "employer". The principle criminal law duties are imposed by sections 2 and 3.

Section 2(1) of H&SAW provides that *"It shall be the duty of every employer to ensure so far as is reasonably practicable the health, safety and welfare of all his employees"*. This duty clearly extends, for example, to the provision of safe equipment to instructors employed in the leisure industry. Equally important is section 3(1) which states:

---

[67] The Civil Aviation (Access to Air Travel for Disabled Persons and Persons with Reduced Mobility) Regulations 2007.
[68] Regulation 3.
[69] Regulation 4.
[70] Regulation 5.

> It shall be the duty of every employer to conduct his undertaking in such a way as to ensure so far as is reasonably practicable, that persons not in his employment who may be affected thereby are not thereby exposed to risks to their health and safety.

The employer's duty thus extends to persons who are not employed by him if they may be affected by the undertaking the employer is carrying out. This provision is plainly capable of covering those employers in the leisure industry whose undertakings will affect members of the public — and the section has been deployed against, for example, those running outward-bound schools, theme parks and fairgrounds whose undertakings can compromise members of the public. The onus of proving the limits of what is reasonably practicable rests firmly on the employer-defendant. There are no statutory or "due diligence" defences, so the offences can accurately be described as truly "strict".

Breaches of the H&SAWA itself are not actionable in the civil courts[71] but breaches of statutory regulations made pursuant to the Act are.[72] Codes of Practice made pursuant to the Act are admissible in evidence.

The criminal penalties are laid out in section 33, and it should be noted that although offences under sections 2 and 3 of the H&SAWA are triable either way, magistrates have the power to impose summary fines of up to £20,000.00 in some circumstances. For failure to comply with orders of the court, or prohibition and improvement notices served in respect of an undertaking, there is also a power of imprisonment — up to six months following summary trial, and two years after trial on indictment. Enforcement of the H&SAWA is through local authority inspectors and the Health and Safety Executive.

The *extra-territorial* effect of the H&SAWA 1974 is, however, very limited. Outside Great Britain the reach of the Act is restricted to offshore installations and pipelines and activities in territorial waters.[73]

Timeshare

The Timeshare Act 1992 (as amended) is largely concerned with the imposition of criminal sanctions.[74] Chapter 9 is devoted to these and other timeshare related issues.

---

[71] Section 47(1)
[72] Section 47(2).
[73] HSWA 1974 (Application Outside GB) Order 2001 SI 2127.
[74] But not entirely –see section 10A.

Manslaughter

In the light of several now notorious "leisure" related and transportation disasters, there has been much debate about the scope of the common law offence of manslaughter, both in respect of individuals and corporations. In short, company directors, officers, and those to whom powers have been lawfully delegated are at risk under the common law of manslaughter (as indeed for other criminal offences) *both* as natural persons or individuals (due to their personal unlawful acts or gross negligence), and as embodiments of the corporation. In theory both corporation and individual can be indicted.

In *R* v *Great Western Trains Co. Ltd*[75] (proceedings arising out of the Southall rail crash of 1997) Scott Baker J. doubted the application of a direct corporate liability to common law offences as opposed to those offences created by statute where a "controlling mind" of the company could not also be identified as a guilty party. The unwillingness of the courts to adopt the concept of accretion or aggregation of guilt — that is, a sequence of management and operational failures [none of which are themselves sufficient to amount to gross negligence] when taken together show gross failures on the part of the company when looked at as a whole – was confirmed in further proceedings arising out of the crash[76]. In that case the Court of Appeal expressed the view that a company could be convicted of manslaughter only if an individual could be identified with the company could be should to have been guilty of the offence; his or her guilt could then be attributed to the company.

The Corporate Manslaughter and Corporate Homicide Act 2007

This is due to come into force in April 2008, abolishes the common law offence of corporate manslaughter[77] and replaces it with a statute-based offence, triable by indictment only and only with the consent of the Director of Public Prosecutions. The impact of an offence of corporate killing has been the subject of almost frenzied concern in the travel industry for some years given the potential that exists in the provision of holidays for fatal accidents – whether on an individual or multiple basis.

---

[75] 30 June 1990 – Central Criminal Court – Unreported.
[76] *A-G's Ref (No. 2 of 1999)* [2000] QB 796.
[77] Section 20.

Territorial Limitation

The concerns that have been expressed are largely allayed by the territorial limitations on the application of the offence of corporate manslaughter. Section 28 of the Act provides that section 1 of the Act (i.e. the offence of corporate manslaughter) only applies if the harm resulting in death was sustained in the UK, its territorial waters or in a number of other specifically identified circumstances such as on an off-shore installation. This territorial limitation is of the utmost significance for the travel industry. Fatalities in hotel fires or coach crashes abroad will not give rise to a charge under the new Act because the harm resulting in the death or deaths will not have been sustained in the UK.

Under s.1 of the Act:

(1) An organisation to which this section applies is guilty of an offence if the way in which its activities are managed or organised—

(a) causes a person's death, and

(b) amounts to a gross breach of a relevant duty of care owed by the organisation to the deceased.

(2) The organisations to which this section applies are—

(a) a corporation;

(b) a department or other body listed in Schedule 1;

(c) a police force;

(d) a partnership, or a trade union or employers' association, that is an employer.

(3) An organisation is guilty of an offence under this section only if the way in which its activities are managed or organised by its senior management is a substantial element in the breach referred to in subsection (1).

It is clear, then, that the organisation must have breached its duty of care in a manner which is not only "gross" but causative of the death of the deceased. This might be proven in a drowning case in circumstances in which a property audit was so grossly negligently performed that a swimming pool was not identified as being hazardous; but only if, had the audit been properly performed, the pool would have been closed. Otherwise the breach of duty could not be said to have caused the death[78].

Section 2 defines "relevant duty of care" as follows:

---

[78] See Butler: *The Travel Industry and the Corporate Manslaughter and Corporate Homicide Act 2007* 2007 [ITLJ] 197.

(1) A "relevant duty of care", in relation to an organisation, means any of the following duties owed by it under the law of negligence—

(a) a duty owed to its employees or to other persons working for the organisation or performing services for it;

(b) a duty owed as occupier of premises;

(c) a duty owed in connection with—

(i) the supply by the organisation of goods or services (whether for consideration or not),

(ii) the carrying on by the organisation of any construction or maintenance operations,

(iii) the carrying on by the organisation of any other activity on a commercial basis, or

(iv) the use or keeping by the organisation of any plant, vehicle or other thing;

(d) a duty owed to a person who, by reason of being a person within subsection (2), is someone for whose safety the organisation is responsible...

(4) A reference in subsection (1) to a duty owed under the law of negligence includes a reference to a duty that would be owed under the law of negligence but for any statutory provision under which liability is imposed in place of liability under that law.

(5) For the purposes of this Act, whether a particular organisation owes a duty of care to a particular individual is a question of law.

The judge must make any findings of fact necessary to decide that question.

(6) For the purposes of this Act there is to be disregarded—

(a) any rule of the common law that has the effect of preventing a duty of care from being owed by one person to another by reason of the fact that they are jointly engaged in unlawful conduct;

(b) any such rule that has the effect of preventing a duty of care from being owed to a person by reason of his acceptance of a risk of harm.

For the most part, then, tour operators (and, in certain circumstances, retailers) will owe a relevant duty of care to holidaymakers in respect of the constituent elements of the holiday. Those tour operators supplying "extreme" or adventure holidays should beware: this is so even where the holidaymaker has accepted a risk of harm, although the prosecutor would still have to show a causative instance of gross negligence.

Section 8 provides guidance as to the issue of whether or not the organisation has been guilty of a gross breach of duty:

(1) This section applies where—

(a) it is established that an organisation owed a relevant duty of care to a person, and

(b) it falls to the jury to decide whether there was a gross breach of that duty.

(2) The jury must consider whether the evidence shows that the organisation failed to comply with any health and safety legislation that relates to the alleged breach, and if so—

(a) how serious that failure was;

(b) how much of a risk of death it posed.

(3) The jury may also—

(a) consider the extent to which the evidence shows that there were attitudes, policies, systems or accepted practices within the organisation that were likely to have encouraged any such failure as is mentioned in subsection (2), or to have produced tolerance of it;

(b) have regard to any health and safety guidance that relates to the alleged breach.

(4) This section does not prevent the jury from having regard to any other matters they consider relevant.

(5) In this section "health and safety guidance" means any code, guidance, manual or similar publication that is concerned with health and safety matters and is made or issued (under a statutory provision or otherwise) by an authority responsible for the enforcement of any health and safety legislation.

It seems, then, that in considering whether a corporate body is guilty of manslaughter the jury must take into account the degree to which the body is guilty of institutionalised lack of care. It is suggested that if a defendant is able to show that at the relevant time it had in place a system of checks, including health and safety audits, and that those checks were implemented properly, it should escape conviction.

It remains to be seen whether the prosecuting authorities obtain any more convictions under the new legislation than they did under the common law offence, under which only two corporations were ever successfully prosecuted.

Sex Crimes

Section 72 of the Sexual Offences Act 2003 extends the jurisdiction of the courts of the United Kingdom in respect of certain sexual offences committed by British citizens or residents whilst abroad. The 2003 Act invokes a type of double-actionability. Where a listed sexual offence is committed abroad which is an offence both in the territory where the unlawful act took place and in the United Kingdom, that offence is an offence in the United Kingdom and can be prosecuted and punished in this country. The relevant offences relate to offences against children under 13 and under 16, including possession of indecent photographs of children. Schedule 2 of the Act makes it an offence to conspire to commit offences of this nature. In practice, the provisions of the Act are little-used, with no reported authority in relation to a successful section 72 prosecution. However, this is likely to be due both to difficulties in proving such crimes (difficulties which are not specific to extra-jurisdictional prosecutions), and to an increasing will on the part of "sex tourism" destinations to prosecute British holidaymakers within the local jurisdiction.

Air Rage

Travellers should be aware of the specific criminal offences created in respect of conduct aboard aircraft as now set out in the Air Navigation Order 2000.[79] Those offences[80] include prohibitions against:

- behaviour recklessly or negligently endangering an aircraft or persons on an aircraft;

- drunkenness on board on aircraft;

- smoking when smoking is by notice prohibited;

- using threatening, abusive or insulting words or behaviour towards the crew;

- intentionally interfering with the duties of a crew member.

Endangering an aircraft carries a maximum penalty of imprisonment for five years,[81] and other offences under the Order carry penalties of up to two years' imprisonment. The very substantial anti-social element of these offences, as well as the significant risk of harm to fellow travellers, have inclined the courts to treat seriously any offences on board aircraft; and the imposition of prison sentences for these offences is routine. Mr Ayodeji, for example, in *R v Ayodeji*,[82] was sentenced to eight months' imprisonment after pleading guilty to being drunk on an aircraft during a 6½ hour flight from Lagos to London. His sentence was upheld by the Court of Appeal as being perfectly reasonable in the circumstances, particularly given that he appeared to have set out to get drunk and behave obnoxiously. Stag parties travelling to and from their destinations should beware.

---

[79] SI 2000 1562.
[80] See sections 63-68.
[81] Aviation Offences Act 2003.
[82] (2001) 1 Cr App R 106.

Chapter 13

CRIMINAL STATUTORY DEFENCES

Introduction

The PTR 1992

Regulation 24 of the PTR 1992 is headed "Due diligence defence" and states:

> 24(1) Subject to the provisions of this regulation, in proceedings against any person for an offence under regulations 5, 7, 8, 16 or 22 of the Regulations, it shall be a defence for that person to show that he took all reasonable steps and exercised all due diligence to avoid committing the offence.
>
> (2) Where in any proceedings against any person for such an offence the defence provided by paragraph (1) above involves an allegation that the commission of the offence was due —
>
>> (a) to the act or default of another or
>>
>> (b) to reliance on information given by another, that person shall not, without the leave of the court, be entitled to rely on the defence unless, not less than seven clear days before the hearing of the pro ceedings, ... he has served a notice under paragraph (3) below on the person bringing the proceedings.
>
> (3) — [Notice provisions]
>
> (4) It is hereby declared that a person shall not be entitled to rely on the defence provided by paragraph 91) above by reason of his reliance on information supplied by another, unless he shows that it was reasonable in all the circumstances for him to have relied on the information, having regard in particular —
>
>> (a) to steps which he took, and those which might reasonably have been taken for the purposes of verifying the information; and
>>
>> (b) to whether he had reason to disbelieve the information.

Trade Descriptions Act 1968

Section 24 of the TDA states:

24(1) In any proceedings for an offence under this Act it shall ... be a defence for the person charged to prove: —

(a) that the commission of the offence was sue to a mistake or to reliance on information supplied to him or to the act or default of another person, an accident or some other cause beyond his control, and

(b) that he took all reasonable precautions and exercised all due diligence to avoid the commission of such an offence by himself or any other person under his control.

(The section goes on to make similar provision with regard to the giving of notice to the prosecution before a hearing to those provisions to be found in Regulation 24(3) of the PTR 1992 and section 39(3) of the CPA.)

Consumer Protection Act 1987

The statutory defence provided by section 39 of the Consumer Protection Act 1987 is in precisely the same terms as that in Regulation 24 of the 1992 Regulations.

The Consumer Protection from Unfair Trading Regulations 2007

The statutory defence contained within Regulation 17 of the Regulations is more difficult to establish that that set out in the PTR and CPA, and is more analogous to section 24 of the TDA. It states:

In any proceedings for an offence under regulation 9 (misleading actions), 10 (misleading omissions), 11 (aggressive commercial practices) or 12 (specific unfair commercial practices) it shall be a defence for a person to prove –

(a) that the commission of the offence was due to -

(i) a mistake;

(ii) reliance on information supplied to him by another person;

(iii) the act or default of another person;

(iv) an accident; or,

(v) another cause beyond his control;

and

(b) that he took all reasonable precautions and exercised all due diligence to avoid the commission of such an offence by himself or any person under his control.

Notice of the Defendant's intention to rely on the defence, if it relates to the default of another person or to reliance on information provided by another person, must be given in writing to the prosecutor at least seven days before the date of the hearing.

The Denied Boarding Regulations

It is a defence under the Regulations for an operating air carrier to show that it took all reasonable steps and exercised all due diligence to avoid committing an offence.[1]

The Disability Discrimination Regulations

It is a defence under the Regulations to show that the Defendant took all reasonable steps to avoid committing the offence, but he cannot rely on his reliance on information given to him unless he shows that it was reasonable for him to have relied on that information.[2]

Health and Safety at Work Act 1974

There are no equivalent statutory defences in the H&SAWA. The offences created by sections 2 and 3 thereof are subject to the test of what is "reasonably practicable". However, the onus of proving what is reasonably practicable in the circumstances rests on the defendant.[3]

Onus of proof

In all regulatory statutes providing for due diligence and like defences, the onus of proving the defence lies on the defendant.

All reasonable steps (or precautions) and all due diligence

This is the common phrase. Given the civil standard of proof,[4] defendants often underestimate the task facing them. It is not at all the same thing as a defendant pleading that he did the best he could; or tried very hard in difficult commercial circumstances; or did not have the necessary economic resources to fund, or enough staff to conduct, any more checks; or even that his supplier, or source of information, was a brand-name whose credentials seemed to be impeccable. Furthermore, it will almost never be sufficient for a defendant to rely on an oral explanation from the witness box as to the steps he maintains had been taken to comply with the relevant regulations. In practice the production of a documented system of due diligence is essential in order for a defendant to step over this high threshold. Furthermore, the

---

[1] Regulation 4(1).
[2] Regulation 5.
[3] Section 40.
[4] The balance of probabilities.

production of a system on paper — though often necessary — is seldom sufficient. In addition it must be shown that the paper system had been *implemented*; and proving implementation often in itself involves the production of further documentary proof that the basic system had been adequately monitored. In practice, the courts are stern task masters in judging whether *all* reasonable steps have been taken, and *all* due diligence exercised to avoid the commission of an offence.

The taking of *all* steps and exercising *all* due diligence are strong words, and "diligence" is itself a word that conveys the need for real and positive effort on the part of the defendant to avoid the commission of an offence — the defendant bears the burden of "ferreting-out" possible offences being committed in the course of carrying on his undertaking.

One of the reasons why the statutory defences sometimes seem to impose almost impossibly high standards on defendants is the unavoidable conclusion that if a system of due diligence had been in place, the offence would not have been committed. Such logic is beguiling at first glance, but is not entirely justified. The very fact that parliament has made provision for the statutory defences is recognition of the fact that, even in the best managed organisations, mistakes are likely to occur from time to time. The due diligence defence is supposed to make allowances for this inevitability. Statutory offences and regulations which are subject to the due diligence defence do not counsel perfection in the ability of an organisation to prevent errors, but the way in which the courts apply the defence does get very close to counselling perfection in the manner in which the organisation attempts to minimise or eradicate the risk of errors occurring. Of course, in the context of the H&SAWA even such limited room for manoeuvre is constrained. The H&SAWA *does* counsel perfection — subject to the test of reasonable practicability, it brooks no excuses at all.

All reasonable steps (or precautions)

If the prosecution can point to any step — which is not fanciful - which might have been taken but was not taken by a defendant, it is unlikely that the defence will be made out. Taking all reasonable steps includes sampling and testing products delivered, supplied or offered even by reputable organisations — even though random testing, checking or sampling might not have identified the problem ultimately complained of. If a misdescription in a travel brochure resulting from a printing error may get through a tight net of random checking on the part of a tour operator for example, the defence may still be usefully deployed. The operator might demonstrate that he had taken all reasonable steps, but that notwithstanding, the error about which a consumer complains was not spotted in the course of extensive checks made in the course of the brochure's production. The key in respect of tour operators checking their brochures or misprints is that the net must be provably as tight as is reasonably imaginable — even thought the standard required in so proving is "only" on the balance of probabilities.

In a case such as *Wings Limited V Ellis,*[5] which involved a prosecution under the Trade Descriptions Act — in circumstances where a statement in a brochure was not *known* to be false at the time the brochure was first circulated, but where the falsity became known at a later date, whereafter the defendant did not realise that the statement continued to be *made* — theoretically it would be open to the tour operator to demonstrate that all reasonable steps were taken to prevent the continued "making" of the false statement once the error had been identified: by the removal or withdrawal of all known examples of the original brochure; by issuing strong warnings and continued reminders to travel agents to discontinue use of the brochure, and to warn any consumer relying (or who might be relying) on the same that its use had been discontinued; by the implementation of arrangements for the recovery and destruction of all known circulating copies of the brochure; and by dispatching written notices to all recorded consumers known to be, or to have been, in possession of a brochure. Even having taken all these steps, the tour operator might reasonably be taken to know that recovering all the original brochures was not practicably feasible. The tour operator could still then be accused of "knowingly" making a false statement. However, by proving the above reasonable steps, he may show that he had essentially done everything in his power to stop making the false statement.

The defendant in *Wings* did not run the statutory defence. This may have been in recognition of the fact that the *oral* corrections the operator relied upon the travel agent to make when faced with an intending customer, could not have crossed the high statutory threshold (see Lord Templeman in particular who said; "*By relying on an oral correction being made by the sales agent and transmitted to the travel agent, the respondent [defendant] accepted the risk of committing an offence ... ").*

Here one gets to the real crux of a defendant's difficulties when trying to prove any of the statutory defences. The economic consequences of undertaking the colossal burden of taking *all* reasonable steps, and the equally colossal burden of *proving* that such steps have been taken, may incline many, as Lord Templeman suggested, to take the risk of committing an offence. Balancing the comparative cost of implementing all reasonable steps, against the financial penalty likely to be imposed by the magistrates, may lead many to the conclusion that the cost of avoiding the penalty, and the effort of proving the effectiveness of the system, is too great The risk of

---

[5] Discussed in Chapter 12.

committing the offence is a risk worth taking in financial terms. Furthermore, if the cost of taking all reasonable steps is incurred, the defendant still runs the risk that the prosecutor or the magistrate will think of some additional step that might have been taken which the system does not cover, or cannot be shown to cover. So, having incurred the vast expense, as well as having undertaken the administrative burden, the risk of conviction remains. Small wonder that many organisations take the risk that they will not be caught out, or that if they are, the penalty will be sufficiently modest to bear. After all, in *mitigation* of penalty following a plea of guilty (especially in courts of summary jurisdiction) the threshold to be crossed in maintaining that all reasonable steps "were very nearly, but not quite, taken" is a good deal lower than that imposed by the statutory defences.

All due diligence

In one sense, the taking of all reasonable steps would seen to imply that the defendant had exercised "*all due diligence*". What else can diligence require other than that all reasonably imaginable steps have been taken? The coupling of due diligence with reasonable steps may be intended to do no more than reinforce the intended high threshold imposed by these statutory defences . However, it may be that if "all reasonable steps" describes *what* needs to be done, "all due diligence" describes *how* it must be done. "All reasonable steps" describes the *system*, whilst "all due diligence" describes the *implementation* of the system. The steps that are to be taken must be diligently enforced. They should be taken as soon as is practicable; and whatever steps are necessary should be vigorously pursued. If a paper system is enforced languidly, without enthusiasm, or the employees of the defendant are allowed simply to "go through the paper motions" it is unlikely that a court would be persuaded that the steps had been undertaken with all due diligence — although undeniably the court could also find that in reality the steps that were taken were not all reasonable steps.

A subjective element?

In an unreported case in 1980,[6] Lord Lane CJ said: " ... *I scarcely need to say that every case will vary in facts; but what might be reasonable for a large retailer might not be reasonable for a village shop*".

Defendants will take note of this dictum. However, it is difficult to see why this should be the case. The requirement of the statutory defence is that all reasonable steps are taken; not that all steps reasonable *for the defendant in question* should be taken. Does a reasonable step become not reasonable because the smaller retailer may not have the economic or other resources to

---

[6] *Garrett v Boots the Chemist.*

carry it through? In the context of tour operators and travel agents, it is respectfully suggested that too much store should not be placed on this passing dictum from the then Lord Chief Justice. It is thought improbable that many courts could be persuaded that a small, independent tour operator, would be entitled to undertake fewer checks on the information he was supplied by his agents and contractors than a larger conglomerate. The checks might have to be undertaken in a different way — by the pooling of resources with other independent operators — but there is no apparent reason why, in an area that the courts have repeatedly emphasised is one where the protection of the consumer is paramount, the degree of protection offered should be diluted simply by reference to the size of the undertaking in the dock. There is even less reason to suppose that the duties imposed on the smaller operator to check the accuracy of its printed material against the risk of printing or communications error were any less than those imposed on its bigger brothers.

Perhaps the point to note an underline in Lord Lane's remarks, is that the statutory defences ultimately turn on questions of fact, and that facts will vary from case to case.

The additional burdens under the TDA and Consumer Protection Regulations

The defendant relying on these defences has an additional burden to discharge. Under the TDA and Consumer Protection Regulations it is necessary for a defendant to prove not only that he took all reasonable steps and exercised all due diligence, but that *in addition*, the commission of the offence was due to one of the qualifying reasons set out in the relevant section or regulation. Before proving that 'due diligence' defence, the defendant must prove that the commission of the offence was due to one of the following events:

- a mistake;
- reliance on information supplied to him;
- the act or default of some other person;
- an accident;
- some other cause beyond his control.

These qualifying events are widely drawn, and most defendants who are in a position to establish 'due diligence' will probably be able to attach themselves to one or other of them — even if only the last catch-all event. Even so, under the TDA and Regulations the defendant is charged with responsibility for identifying the event on which he relies — though there is no reason why he cannot choose several, in the hope that one will stick.

Towards a System of Due Diligence

Every organisation must develop a 'due diligence' system to suit its own requirements. There can be no hard and fast rules that would be applicable to every corporation in every situation. What amounts to 'due diligence' is a question of fact to be decided in each case. Having said that, there are certain principles that can be noted with a view to implementation in accordance with the facts pertaining to given individual organisations. The framework employed here relates particularly to tour operators.

The framework must include:

(i)   Procedures or systems for ensuring that what is advertised or offered by a tour operator is accurate.

(ii) Procedures which extend to monitoring the implementation of (i) above.

(iii) Written records of (i) and (ii) above — without which it is unlikely that the tour operator will be able to prove that a system is operational and effective.

Proving due diligence

(a) The tour operator should have written contracts covering the supply to him of all advertised accommodation, transport and other tourist services included in a package to be offered to consumers.

(b) The contract for accommodation (for example) should include provision to the operator's clients of the type and standard and offering the facilities to be advertised in the brochure.

(c) Where any national approval standards are applicable to accommodation (*e.g.* star ratings in respect of a hotel), the tour operator should see and retain a copy of the certificate or other documentary evidence proving the award of the relevant rating.

(d) Certification or other documentary evidence should be copied in respect of any local safety or hygiene regulations — particularly those relating to kitchens and restaurants in the case of hygiene, and sports activities in respect of safety (which latter would include certificates of competence for instructors or supervisors).

(e) Brochure particulars for any accommodation should be approved and signed and dated by local management as well as by a representative of the tour operator who has visited the accommodation in question.

(f) Any photographs proposed for use in conjunction with other brochure particulars should similarly be signed and dated. The use of photographs more than 12 months old at the date of publication should be avoided, unless it can be positively confirmed by a representative of the operator that the picture is still accurate.

(g) No accommodation should be included in a brochure unless it has been inspected by a representative of the tour operator. Inspections should be on both 'announced' and 'unannounced' bases. The announced visit may be necessary to gain access to kitchens and other areas usually off-limits to the casual visitor. Unannounced visits should be used to test the nature and quality of services on offer where the hotel or other serviced accommodation is not in a state of readiness for formal inspection. Inspections should be carried out by staff at various different levels within the organisation, and where conducted by junior or inexperienced staff the inspections themselves must be subject to cross-checking.

(h) All visits should be recorded on a standard form listing all elements of the accommodation to be inspected. Where action or attention to any descriptive or substantive problem is required this should not only be noted, but standard procedures should be devised to notify the management of the action that is required, and in order that the required action may be followed up. Such procedures should include methods of recording what needs to be done, and what has been done to correct the perceived problem.

(i) Local representatives should be required to complete accuracy reports in respect of any accommodation offered, and these reports should take the form of or include answers to standardised questions in order that all aspects of the brochure particulars are covered. Similar updating reports should be required of local representatives on a regular basis.

(j) Written consumer complaints procedures should be devised, as should a mechanism to collect and collate consumer 'comments', whether or not those comments amount to complaints. Local staff and agents should be informed in writing in comprehensible terms *why* the accurate and prompt transmission of complaints or any other changes in circumstances affecting the accommodation or destination are necessary.

(k) Brochure and other promotional literature, including all price charts, should be meticulously proofed and checked again on publication — the checking process should be documented.

(l) A written 'corrections' policy should be in place, capable of responding to reports from local representatives and from the consumer complaints and report forms. The 'corrections' policy should be capable of inducing an immediate response to perceived brochure or advertising errors, which response should be effective. Effectiveness involves the immediate notification in writing of all existing consumers affected by the change of circumstances or the error, as well as all travel agents (which latter

notification should include a step-by-step instruction as to what the
travel agent should do by way of correcting any incorrect brochure or
promotional information). In reality, the only safe (but expensive) course
in respect of any error (however small) is to remove the brochure from
display, recall the entire stock — and start again.

(m) All computer software used by the operator should be regularly serviced
and tested. Any problems or 'blips' should be noted, and the corrective
action documented. All staff and agents likely to use the software should
be notified of the problem (even if it is solved), and be alerted to the risk
of repetition. They should be informed as to how best to check against
the risk of such error recurring. Documenting this software checking
process is vital if due care and diligence is to be proved.

(n) It should be possible to access the entire 'due diligence' procedure, from
substantive action instructions to monitoring instructions from one
standard manual. Similarly it should be possible to access all records
documenting the implementation of the procedure from one place.
Implementation documents are useless unless they are signed and dated,
and note the particular task or action taken by the given employee or
officer. Even the 'checks' should be randomly cross-checked.

Corrections and disclaimers

There is no doubt that any 'due diligence' system will be most effective when
implemented 'at source'. That is to say in circumstances where errors do not
arise in the first place. It is far better to avoid errors than to spend time,
money and energy trying to correct them. Two classes of possible
prosecution need to be considered in the context of brochures and VDU
displays — and for present purposes it matters not whether the prosecution
is pursuant to regulation 5 of the 1992 Regulations or the misleading price
indication provisions of the CPA. Firstly, those where the error has been
made in the original production of the brochure or other promotional
material; and secondly, those cases where the brochure, though originally
accurate, has by some change of circumstances been rendered inaccurate.

In the first category, it is theoretically too late to invoke 'due diligence' by
implementing a sophisticated 'corrections' policy. However good the policy is,
the offence alleged will already have been committed. If due diligence is to
work in this category of case, it has to be made to work at the stage when the
information was first compiled. That is, despite the taking of all reasonable
steps and exercising all due diligence the error slipped through a tight net at
the time the material was originated. If this doesn't work it is technically far
too late to say that everything humanly possible was done to correct an error
that should not have been made. The defence either works on an examination
of the system at the time production of the literature, or it fails altogether. One

cannot, it is submitted, exercise due diligence to avoid the commission of an offence after the offence has been committed. An inexact analogy would be that the dishonest 'borrower' of money from the travel agent's till, cannot defend himself on a charge of theft by saying that he went to inordinate lengths to try to replace the money at a later date. However, even though an offence may have been committed, the deployment of a 'corrections' policy in respect of original errors may persuade many prosecuting authorities that criminal proceedings were not in the public interest.[7]

In the second category, the defendant, having proved that the error had arisen by reason of a change of circumstances since initial production and circulation, *can* proceed to show that by means of his 'corrections' policy he made superhuman efforts to prevent the repeated 'making' of the statement by giving prominence to a disclaimer or correction (for intending future consumers) and notifying all those likely to have been effected by the problem already. Care must be taken that the disclaimer or correction 'trumps' the error, that is to say, is bold and clear enough to deprive the error of any force in the mind of any reasonable customer — but where such care is taken, it can successfully be argued that due diligence has been exercised in avoiding the commission of offences on a continuing or repeated basis by the continued circulation of the brochure that contains the error. For example, a price may have become misleading in a brochure, which is then unambiguously marked with a sticker or a shelf-edge marker stating 'THE PRICES ON PAGE 20 ARE MISLEADING — please seek counter assistance' — or something of the sort. The price panel inside the brochure may still constitute a 'misleading indication', but the correction or disclaimer, together with a notification policy for those known to have the brochure in their possession may open the door to a statutory defence. (It may even be possible to argue that in such circumstances the 'panel' has been 'deprived' of its misleading quality in respect of the brochures to which a disclaimer or correction is attached or to which one is unambiguously associated.)

Considerable care needs to be exercised if one is relying on disclaimers. An example from rogue car dealer illustrates the common reaction of the Courts. Where a motor trader knew or had reasonable grounds for believing that the mileage travelled by a vehicle substantially exceeded that shown on the odometer he could not effectively disclaim the odometer reading merely by stating that it was incorrect if he did not go on to reveal the truth as he knew it.[8]

---

[7] A correction at any stage must always be as bold and "compelling" as the original error – *Norman v Bennett* [1974] 3 All ER 351.
[8] *Howard Farrand v Lyndy Lazarus & ors* [2002] EWHC 226 (Admin).

Act of default of another or information supplied by another

Another common feature of the statutory defence of "due diligence" enables a defendant to state that the offence that has been committed has been due to the act or default of another, or has been the result of information supplied by another. *This still forms part of the "due diligence" defence.* That is to say, *in exercising due diligence and taking all reasonable steps*, information was supplied on which reliance was placed, or another person was at fault for the breakdown of the 'due diligence system' in place.

Where "*another*" is blamed, notice to the effect that another is to be blamed (including particulars of the person responsible) must be served on the party bringing the prosecution seven clear days before the hearing. So seven days must elapse between the date of receipt by the prosecutor and the return date on any summons. This period allows the prosecutor time to consider joinder of additional parties, or the substitution of parties to the intended proceedings under, for example regulation 25 of the 1992 Regulations (by reason of which provision and similar provisions in other regulatory statutes, the person whose fault the offence is can be proceeded against instead of, or in addition to the 'principal offencer', at least where that other person has been acting in the course of a *business of his.*[9]

If the defendant relies on the fact that he relied on information supplied by another, the defendant must also prove that it was reasonable in all the circumstances for him to have relied on that information, and the court is directed to have particular regard in judging the question of reasonableness:

- to the steps that were taken, or might reasonably have been taken to verify the information relied on;

- whether the defendant had any reason to disbelieve the information.

It is, therefore, manifestly insufficient for a defendant simply to point the finger of blame in the direction of anyone supplying him with information (such as hoteliers, airlines, local agents or representatives), unless it can be shown, on the balance of probabilities, that reliance on the information was reasonable.

As far as tour operators are concerned, certain elements in the outline of the 'due diligence' requirements illustrate the circumstances in which it would be reasonable for them to rely on information supplied by others; notably, the implementation of a system of cross-checking information supplied by representatives, hoteliers and consumers, and a two-tier system of inspections. Other factors might include, the historical reliability of the

---

[9] see also CPA section 39.

source of the information, the reputation of the source within the industry, and the experience of the source.

Travel agents will also have cause to rely heavily on information supplied by tour operators — not only in respect of brochure descriptions, but for price indications. For travel agents it is of particular importance to note that the 'information supplied' element forms but part of the 'due diligence' defence. The reasonableness of the travel agent's reliance on the information supplied by the tour operator has to be judged in the context of *all the circumstances* — which circumstances will include a wider 'due diligence' system. It is seldom likely to be persuasive for a defendant travel agent to say by way of statutory defence that he took 'all reasonable steps' to avoid the commission of an offence simply by relying on information supplied by a nationally known tour operator. However, if such reliance is coupled with other steps — such as a system of random cross-checks on the information the tour operators supply, then the beginnings of a statutory defence may emerge.

Employees as other persons

There is no reason why a defendant cannot say that the act or default complained of was the result of an act or omission of an employee. An employee, who is not part of the directing mind or will of the company, and who can- not be described as the embodiment of the company, is 'another person'. This has been clear since at least *Tesco v Nattrass*[10]. It may well be, therefore, that despite an impeccable 'due diligence' system, an employee causes the employer to commit an offence. *Provided* the general effectiveness of the 'due diligence' system can be proved, there is no reason why the blame cannot be placed on the shoulders of the employee. The employee's failure to implement a clear and well-monitored system led to the offence it would be said.

If this is done, the 'blameworthy' employee is not at risk of prosecution himself under the 1992 Regulations or the CPA, despite the fact that regulation 25 and section 40 allow for the prosecution of the 'blameworthy' party in addition to, or in place of the employer. This is because regulation 25 and section 40 limit the power to prosecute 'some other person' to such a person who has been acting 'in the course of a business of his'. However lamentably an employee has failed to implement the employer's 'due diligence' system, he is not at fault in the course of a business *of his*, however much he may be at fault in the course of his *employer's business*.

---

[10] See Chapter 12.

In *R v Warwickshire County Council ex p Johnson*[11] the Divisional court held in the context of section 40 CPA that '*business of his*' meant no more than in the course of a trade, business or profession — and that accordingly the expression was wide enough to encompass employees — as was always the position under the Trade Descriptions Act. The House of Lords, however[12] overturned the employee's conviction for giving a false indication as to price, holding, with some expressed reluctance, that giving the words in section 40 CPA their ordinary meaning, and given the policy behind the section debated by the minister responsible for the Act's passage through the House of Lords, employees were not covered by section 40. There is no reason to suppose that the position is any different under regulations 25 of the 1992 Regulations.

So, whilst an employee may be 'another' person for the purposes of section 39(2)(a) CPA or regulation 24(2)(a) of the 1992 Regulations — whose 'act or default' has caused the commission of an offence, and whose particulars should be supplied to the prosecution seven clear days before the hearing — an employee *cannot* be a person 'other than the principal offender' who might be prosecuted as a result of the act or default by reason of which the employer's offence was committed. Lord Roskill in *Warwickshire* thought this a curious result — but one that was justified on the plain words in section 40 of the CPA.

Lord Beaverbrook, the responsible minister, said in debate[13]

> It is of course for employers to institute systems and staff training to ensure that their employees do not give misleading price indications. If, in spite of all these precautions, a rogue employee nevertheless gives a misleading price indication, then the defence of due diligence, as set out in [section] 39, is likely to be available to his employer. But I have to say that I see little point in prosecuting individual employees in these circumstances.

The emphasis in the minister's speech must be on the words 'rogue employee'. Corporate defendants will have to be very careful in pointing the finger of blame towards an employee who is immune from prosecution. Where employers do, they are likely to have their systems of training and monitoring rigorously investigated, because if training and supervision is alleged to be so good, the commission of an offence will be hard to explain. The commission of an offence due to the default of an employee is some evidence that the system itself is inadequate — at least in its supervisory and monitoring elements. However, if the offence is the result of a 'rogue' employee, then it may not matter how effective the training and supervision

---

[11] 156 JP 577.
[12] [1993] AC 583.
[13] *Hansard* Volume 485 column 1140.

is for the honest and conscientious employee. The determined 'rogue' employee is not likely to follow the system of 'due diligence' in which he has been so well trained. Accordingly, the employer must be in a position to show that his 'due diligence' systems cater for the employee who may be slower, or more stupid or careless than his colleagues. It is submitted that 'due diligence' is only likely to be available to the employer who blames an offence on the act or default of his employee, where it can also be shown that the employer's 'due diligence' system *intricately* covers the possibility of employee error.

If only the actions of 'rogue employees' were contemplated as the repositories of 'blame' under section 39 or regulation 24 in conjunction with a successful plea of 'due diligence', one wonders why the minister felt that there was little point in prosecuting such 'rogues'. One might be justified in thinking that they were *exactly* the individuals who should find themselves in the dock — whether under the CPA or the PTR 1992.

Policy & Abuse of Process

The fact that regulatory regimes create so many offences of strict liability imposes an important public policy burden on prosecuting authorities. It is submitted that such a burden is all the more critical in the context of the broader range of more loosely defined criminal activities contained in The Consumer Protection from Unfair Trading Regulations 2007.[14] It seems that the courts are quick to hold prosecuting authorities to their own internal policy documents whereby prosecutions are only sanctioned in the event that an offence has been committed dishonestly or persistently.[15] This is a curious state of affairs because had Parliament intended prosecutions to be so limited it would no doubt have drafted the offences in such a way as to brook proceedings only for persistent or dishonest offenders. *R v Glen Adaway*[16] is a good illustration of the point. The Divisional Court noted that before criminal proceedings were instituted by a local authority, acting in relation to strict liability offences under the Trade Descriptions Act 1968, consideration had to be given to the terms of the *authority's own policy guidelines* on the prosecution of offences. The criterion to be satisfied before the relevant local authority prosecuted an offence were that a defendant had to have either engaged in *fraudulent* activity or *deliberately* or *persistently* breached his legal obligations. As the appeal had progressed it was clear, beyond peradventure, that neither criterion was capable of substantiation. The judge

---

[14] See Chapter 12

[15] But the importance of prosecutions on this basis is undeniable, *viz* the punishment of a Leicester businessman by the imposition of a £20,000 fine for "leaving customers in the lurch" when their Haji pilgrimages to Mecca were improperly organised. See [2007] ITLJ Bulletin.

[16] [2004] EWCA Crim 2831.

should at first instance have reached the conclusion that the prosecution was oppressive and stayed the proceedings. The conviction was quashed. The court went on to observe that it could not be emphasised too strongly that before criminal proceedings were instituted by a local authority, acting in relation to *strict liability* offences under the TDA, they had to consider, with care, the terms of their own prosecuting policy. Where they failed to do so, or reached a conclusion wholly unsupported, it was unlikely the courts would be sympathetic to attempts to justify such prosecutions given the other demands on time at Crown Court and appellate level. Plainly, local authorities should not publish such generous policy guidelines if their enforcement officers are to retain a free hand in deciding whose behaviour is appropriately worthy of prosecution. Equally plainly, local authority guidance will differ from borough to borough.

Chapter 14

LITIGATION: MISCELLANEOUS POINTS OF PROCEDURE

Introduction

It is outside the scope of this work to consider in detail the provisions of the Civil Procedure Rules (CPR), their scope and impact but some general material is included in this chapter that may prove of particular interest to those engaged in travel law litigation, in particular pre-action disclosure; admissions and their withdrawal; costs capping and Part 36 offers of settlement.

The small claims track

CPR Part 27 applies to any claim which has a financial value of not more than £5,000.00 or claims which include a claim for personal injuries where the value of the personal injury is not more than £1,000.00. The much criticised description 'county court arbitration' is no longer to be employed. The small claims track is another attempt by the rule-makers to introduce a cost-effective procedural mechanism for dealing with modestly valued actions.[1] There is no longer any automatic referral to 'arbitration' in the county court. Small track claims will be allocated by the court at the appropriate time. Many travel (particularly holiday) claims will be allocated to the small claims track, even those in which there is a modest element of personal injury.[2] Upon allocation the court will give directions — where possible without the attendance of the parties.[3] The court may treat any preliminary hearing as the final hearing if the parties agree.[4] The much trumpeted informality of the old style county court 'arbitration' is rejuvenated and hearings are to be informal — but at least nominally in

---

[1] This was the reason underlying the establishment of the County Courts themselves in 1846 when jurisdiction in contract and tort was limited to £20.00.
[2] Miner cuts and bruises of no long-standing significance.
[3] CPR 27.6.
[4] CPR 27.6(4).

public.[5] It is envisaged that standard directions will be forwarded to the parties in most cases.[6]

The fast track

Allocation to this track[7] is the general rule for claims valued at between £5,000.00 and £15,000.00 *where the court considers that the trial is likely to last for no more than one day*. There are three principle ambitions for fast track cases. The first is that an action should be listed for trial as expeditiously as possible — and timetables are set out in the rules to achieve this end. The second is that the time allowed for the trial itself should be limited. The third ambition is that the costs of the trial should be kept in proportion to the value of the action. The directions the court is presumptively to make on allocation are intended to drive the litigation forward to a trial within 30 weeks of directions being given.

Where a travel related case escapes the small claims track, it is overwhelmingly likely in the absence of significant personal injury or multi-claimant participation, to be allocated to the fast track.

The multi track

Cases valued at more than £15,000.00, or of lower value which are considered likely by reason of their complexity to take more than a day to hear, are to be assigned to the multi-track. Whilst the case management culture developed by the new rules applies with as much vigour to the multi-track as it does to the small claims and fast track tracks [*sic*] one suspects that it is in the multi-track that most established litigators will feel most at home. In travel claims this track is likely to be the preserve of serious injury cases, multi-party litigation, or those cases whose representatives make the best case on the allocation questionnaire.[8]

CPR Part 29

Cases commenced in the High Court with an estimated value of less than £15,000.00 will usually be transferred to a county court unless involving a fatal accident.[9] Any that remain will be multi-track cases.

---

[5] CPRE 27.8 and 27PD4.1.
[6] See Appendices.
[7] CPR Part 28.
[8] The recoverable costs differences being very significant.
[9] CPR 29.2(4).

Jurisdiction

Since the High Court and County Courts Jurisdiction Order 1991 (the Jurisdiction Order), the county court has enjoyed unlimited jurisdiction in matters of contract and tort pursuant to section 15 of the County Courts Act 1984. Accordingly, where a travel claim does not involve a claim in respect of personal injuries, the jurisdiction of the High Court and county court is now *the same*. In theory any action for breach of contract arising out of, for example, the PTR 1992 may be commenced either in the High Court or in the county court. In practice, the overwhelming majority of such actions should be commenced in the county court, particularly as current interlocutory practice in the High Court involves the transfer of most actions valued at less than £50,000.00 (sometimes even more) to a suitable county court of the High Court's own motion — pursuant to section 40(2) of the County Courts Act 1984.

Paragraph 7 of the Jurisdiction Order provides general rules to the effect that any action valued at less £25,000.00 *shall* be tried in the county court, and one valued at £50,000.00 or more *shall* be tried in the High Court, unless:

- actions valued at less than £25,000.00 are commenced in the High Court, and the High Court considers any such action to be one of substance or complexity judged in accordance with criteria laid down in the Jurisdiction Order;

- actions valued at £50,000.00 or more are commenced in the county court, and that court does not consider the matter to be one of substance or complexity when judged against the same criteria.

The value of an action

The value of an action is that which the claimant *reasonably* expects to recover by way of damages and/or by way of the money's worth of any relief other than damages.[10] Interest and costs are to be disregarded in the estimation of the value of any action. The claimant's reasonable expectations are to be judged objectively at the time the proceedings are commenced, and such expectations should be based on evidence and carefully distinguished from pious hopes and euphoric optimism. In actions where the claim is for general damages rather than the recovery of specific sums of money, it is important to assess with care the likely level of such damages in line with other cases, and the value should often be in proportion to the value of the contract on which the action is based. Where there is more than one claimant, the value of the action is to be judged by reference to the *aggregate*

---

[10] Jurisdiction order paragraph 9.

of their legitimate expectations. The risk of any deduction for contributory fault is to be ignored.

The transfer criteria

Paragraph 7(5) of the Jurisdiction Order contains an exhaustive list of the criteria the High Court and county courts are to bear in mind when determining whether an action should be transferred either up or down. They are as follows:

- the financial substance of the action — *including the value attributable to any counterclaim;*

- whether the action is one involving issues likely to be of some public importance;

- the complexity of the facts, legal issues, remedies and procedures involved in the action;

- whether transfer of the action one way or the other is likely to result in a speedier trial (although this factor alone will not justify transfer).

In most travel-related claims where personal injuries are not involved the financial substance of the action is unlikely to justify maintaining the case in, or transferring it to, the High Court. Where an action involves the resolution of disputed points of interpretation under the PTR 1992, it could be argued that points of public importance and legal issues of some complexity arise. However, it is tentatively suggested that most High Court Masters would be slow to accept that the issues of interpretation were of such importance as to compel a listing before a High Court judge. Furthermore, any party would have to consider very carefully the high costs implications of litigating in the High Court merely in order to obtain a more authoritative regulatory interpretation for the benefit of humanity at large.

Therefore, unless the case is one of exceptionally high value, or inordinate complexity, travel litigation is most likely to be commenced and tried in the county court.

Personal injuries

A slightly modified regime exists in respect of proceedings *which include a claim for damages in respect of personal injuries.* "Personal injuries" includes disease, impairment of physical or mental condition, and death.[11] For actions valued at less than £50,000.00 commencement in the county court is *compulsory.* In commencing an action in the High Court where the claim

---

[11] Jurisdiction Order paragraph 5.

includes a claim for personal injury damages, the writ should carry an endorsed certificate of value to the effect that the action's estimated value is £50,000.00 or more. Issuing from the central office of the High Court without such a certificate is well nigh impossible, and this practical bar prevents many unwitting errors in the choice of court — albeit rather late in the day. Where errors of jurisdiction are made, the court has a discretion *either* to transfer the proceedings to the proper court or *to strike the proceedings out*[12]. Striking out is not only an expensive experience, but can be potentially fatal in respect of any action that has been commenced towards the end of the relevant limitation period. The court is only likely to exercise its discretion to strike out an action wrongly commenced in the High Court where the action should *plainly* have been commenced in the county court, and the failure to do so was not due to a bona fide mistake — but in any action that carries a certificate of value, the party responsible for the certification had better be in a position to justify the valuation, on reasonable grounds existing at the time of commencement, if allegations and suspicions of bad faith are to be avoided.

These are important provisions affecting many travel and holiday cases where damages are often claimed which would fall within the definition under paragraph 5(2) of the Jurisdiction Order. Where the claim concerns, for example, broken bones, the fact that it includes a claim in respect of personal injuries is almost too obvious to be worthy of emphasis. However, *impairment of physical or mental condition* (which need only be temporary, or even transient), includes all claims where damages for anxiety and mental distress form part of the relief sought. (Physical discomfort is, however, probably not impairment of one's *condition*.) So in many travel cases, commencement in the county court for actions valued at less than £50,000.00 will actually be *compulsory*. This extended definition of "personal injuries" may also have the effect of keeping many holiday claims within the Fast Track. The extended definition of personal injuries also has implications with respect to the appropriate limitation period.

Limitation Periods

Section 38 of the Limitation Act 1980 contains a similarly broad definition of "personal injuries". The special time limit for actions in respect of personal injuries in section 11 of the Act applies to:

> any action for damages for negligence ... or breach of duty (whether the duty exists by virtue of contract or of any provision made by statute...) ...

---

[12] County Courts Act section 40(1) – *Restick v Crickmore* [1994] 1 WLR 420.

where the damages claimed by the plaintiff ... consist of or include damages
in respect of personal injuries to the plaintiff or any other person.

Where a travel claim involves claims for mental anguish and distress
therefore, practitioners should work with the *three-year* primary limitation
period in mind.[13]

Small claims

Where personal injuries are not involved a small claim includes anything that
has a financial value of not more than £5,000.00. Where personal injuries are
involved the small claims track remains appropriate where the value of injury
is not more than £1,000.00. Standard directions have been issued with regard
to small claims travel cases.[14] In a change from the previous practice rules,
there is no automatic reference to the small claims track. Cases are allocated as
part of the case management procedure. Where a claim involves complex
issues of fact or law there is no reason why representations cannot be made in
the allocation questionnaire as to the allocation of the claim to a different
track. In another change from previous practice, there is no prohibition on
making applications for summary judgment in the small claims track —
although such applications should be made before or at the time of allocation.
The underlying objective behind trial on the small claims track is summarised
in the six points itemised in the rules[15]. Representation may be in person, by
lawyer or by lay representative. Hearings should be in public.

• the court may adopt any method of proceeding at a hearing that it
  considers to be fair;[16]

• the strict rules of evidence do not apply;

• the court need not take evidence on oath;

• the court may limit cross-examination;

• however, the court must give reasons for its decision.

Appeals against decision made on the small claims track are subject to
restriction similar to those that existed previously — but the court may
dispose of an appeal without a hearing if it considers it appropriate. The
grounds are:

---

[13] This is a little curious in so far as a small claim for a few hundred pounds arising from an
alleged failure to provide a holiday facility will be subject to the conventional 6 year contractual
limitation whereas the invariably more serious personal injury action is subject to the shorter 3
year period.
[14] See Appendices.
[15] CPR 27.8
[16] This includes dealing with the matter on paper if the parties agree.

- error of law;

- serious irregularity affecting the proceedings.

Issues

In approaching a travel-related claim as in any other the parties should concentrate on the *issues* from the time the letter of claim is written or received. It is the determination of the issues that will be the function of the court. This "front-loading" of case preparation should help to determine what evidence is required.

- Are there issues of fact — if so what are they[17]?

- Are there issues of English law — what did the contract say or imply?

- Are there any issues of foreign *law* — is it for example an accident to which local rules of the road apply?

- If the contract is subject to English law, what *standards* of safety or hygiene does English law demand for this contract — local standards or British standards?

- Is there a likely to be the need for expert evidence?

- Is there an issue on the causation of damages — such as may arise if the claimant had a pre-existing injury?

- What issues on quantum are there — such as whether an injury or illness has caused loss of future earnings or whether in a quality complaint case the claimant alleges or is likely to allege consequential loss or expense?

In respect of each of the *issues* the parties should proactively ask themselves what *evidence* is likely to be required to meet each of the issues identified.

Pre-Action Disclosure

The power to require pre-action disclosure arises pursuant to CPR 31.16, which implements s.33 of the Supreme Court Act 1981 and s.52 of the County Courts Act 1984. The Court has power to make a pre-action disclosure order pursuant to CPR 31.16(3) *only if:*

> (a) the respondent is likely to be a party to subsequent proceedings;
> (b) the applicant is also likely to be a party to those proceedings;

---

[17] For defendants: what factual allegations are made that we dispute positively and what are we not in a position to challenge?

(c) if proceedings had started, the respondent's duty by way of standard disclosure, set out in rule 31.6, would extend to the documents or classes of documents of which the applicant seeks disclosure; and
(d) disclosure before proceedings have started is desirable in order to—
    (i) dispose fairly of the anticipated proceedings;
    (ii) assist the dispute to be resolved without proceedings; or
    (iii) save costs.

The Applicant and Respondent being likely to be parties to any subsequent proceedings does not mean that the Applicant must show that it is likely that proceedings will be issued. The court must ask itself whether, if proceedings *were* issued, it is likely that the Applicant and Respondent would be parties. As for the *second* limb of the test – that the documents would be covered by standard disclosure[18] – the court can only be satisfied of this if it is reasonably clear what the issues in the litigation are likely to be, that is, the nature of the claim and the defence, to make sure that the documents sought are ones which are likely to adversely affect or support the parties' prospective cases.

The *third* limb of the test was discussed in the case of *Nikitin v Butler.*[19] This is an unusual case on its facts, in which Langley J. held that pre-action disclosure was not "desirable" within 31.16(d) for the following reasons:

• The proceedings could fairly be brought without the disclosure sought, and the Applicant had "quite sufficient" information to take proceedings;
• It was unlikely (indeed "fanciful") that the disclosure would assist out-of-court resolution of the proceedings;
• The application had served to *increase* costs, not to save them.

The discretion to order pre-action disclosure

If the criteria in 31.16(3) are met, then and only then, does the court have the *power* to make an order. Whether the court makes an order if these criteria are met remains a matter for the court's discretion. It is probably fair to say that the third limb of the test merges easily into a test of discretion. But a court should be guided to keep the jurisdictional and discretionary issues separate. In *Black v Sumitomo* the Court of Appeal emphasised that the jurisdictional test is not a high one. The real test is one of discretion, looking at all of the surrounding circumstances. There is however little

---

[18] See also: *Hutchison 3g UK Ltd v Orange Personal Communications Services Ltd and others* [2008] EWHC 55 (Comm).
[19] [2007] EWHC 173 (QB).

guidance from the higher courts as to how this discretion ought to be exercised, save to say that it is unfettered.

The most useful guidance as to the exercise of discretion can be derived from the case of *Black v Sumitomo*[20] itself. The Court of Appeal noted that the nature of the injury or loss complained of; the clarity and identification of the issues raised by the complaint; the nature of the documents requested; the relevance of any protocol or pre-action inquiries; and the opportunity which the complainant has to make his case without pre-action disclosure were all relevant considerations. In that particular case the Court of Appeal considered that there should be no pre-action disclosure, for the following reasons:

- the loss allegedly sustained, as well as the factual and legal issues, were speculative;
- the claim had emerged out of the blue four years after the relevant events;
- there was real doubt that any of the documents requested would actually provide evidence in support of the case, rather than a mere "train of inquiry". The documents sought would allow a "roving inquisition" rather than a "focussed allegation";
- it would be difficult for the Respondent to retrieve the documents;
- the Applicant was determined to pursue the litigation and would not be deterred by the absence of the disclosure sought;
- there was a real likelihood that disclosure of the magnitude sought would be oppressive.

The key factors to consider are the nature of the claim (whether speculative or otherwise), how focused or defined the requested disclosure is and how onerous the request will be to comply with. There have been pre-action disclosure applications where the application has omitted to say which documents are sought! Any such application is wholly misguided. In *Access to Justice*, discussing pre-action disclosure Lord Woolf made clear that:

> (I)t must be remembered ... that any such application would have to be in respect of specific documents which will have to be shown to be in the possession of the respondent.[21]

In *Cheshire Building Society v Dunlop Haywards (DHL) Limited*[22] the High Court refused to grant pre-action disclosure where the Claimant had failed to

---

[20] [2002] EWCA Civ 1819.
[21] Lord Woolf's final report on Access to Justice, July 1996, at paragraph 50.
[22] [2007] EWHC 403 (QB).

formulate its case sufficiently so as to demonstrate that the documents sought were discloseable at all.

Costs

The costs of a pre action disclosure application are specifically covered (much to the surprise of many) in CPR 48.1:

> (2) The general rule is that the court will award the person against whom the order is sought his costs—
> > (a) of the application; and
> > (b) of complying with any order made on the application.
>
> (3) The court may however make a different order, having regard to all the circumstances, including—
> > (a) the extent to which it was reasonable for the person against whom the order was sought to oppose the application; and
> > (b) whether the parties to the application have complied with any relevant pre-action protocols.

There are few reported decisions on the question of the costs of a pre-action disclosure application. The most revealing case is *Bermuda International Securities v KPMG*,[23] in which an order for disclosure was made as against KPMG. However the court, following CPR 48.1, ordered Bermuda to pay the costs of the application. Bermuda appealed this order. The Court of Appeal held:

- The starting point is that the costs will be payable to the Respondent.
- The court has a power to make a different order.
- In this case the Respondent had resisted the application root and branch and had dug their heels in to do so.
- In those circumstances the appropriate order on the application was no order as to costs (*not* Respondent to pay the Applicant's costs).
- Furthermore no matter that the Respondent had acted unreasonably the costs of *complying* with the order for disclosure should be payable by the Applicant in any event.

Therefore even in a case where the Respondent has been wholly unreasonable in resisting the application the appropriate order is no order as to costs, and not costs payable to the Applicant. There is no reported decision of a higher court ordering that the Respondent should pay the costs of the Applicant regardless of their behaviour. This is of course contrary to the practice of District Judges round the country.

---

[23] [2001] EWCA Civ 269.

The Pre-Action Protocol

The Pre-Action Protocol for Personal Injuries states at paragraph 3.10 that if a Defendant denies liability he should enclose with his letter of reply documents in his possession which are material to the issues between the parties and which would be likely to be ordered to be disclosed by the court either on an application for pre-action disclosure or on disclosure in the proceedings. It is important to note that the documents caught by this section are not the same documents that fall within standard disclosure. The section only applies to documents in the *possession*[24] of the Defendant, not documents that were or have been in his control (standard disclosure). However, the Pre-Action Protocol has no internal enforcement provisions. The usual way Claimant's enforce a breach of the Pre-Action Protocol is to issue the substantive proceedings. The court can then take account of breaches of the Protocol once the claim has been issued. The alternative remedy that is often used is to issue a pre-action disclosure application for the documents that were not disclosed under the Protocol. If this is the course taken then it is highly arguable that the failure of the Defendant to disclose the documents under Protocol was unreasonable. This may justify the court in making an adverse costs order as against the Defendant. There is no reported decision on this point, but it is almost invariably the practice of District Judges to do so.

Responding to requests for pre-action disclosure

It is prudent in all cases to attempt, as much as possible, to comply with the Protocol; and where this is not possible, to keep the Claimant informed of any progress and any difficulties (for example, with regard to closed seasons, language and, say, cultural problems). However, it is always worth bearing in mind that pre-action disclosure is only available in respect of documents which are relevant to the Claimant's claim, and where the Claimant has failed to set out his case sufficiently in the letter of claim, any application should fail. Further, the decision in *Black v Sumitomo* makes it clear that the difficulty of retrieving the documents is relevant; where a Claimant is fishing for information and is requesting all accident report forms for the year of the accident, for example, pre-action disclosure may not be appropriate.

---

[24] This is of particular interest to tour operators who are not conventionally in possession of hotel documents such as hygiene control data.

Admissions

The CPR Prior to 6ᵗʰ April 2007

Making an admission

Pursuant to CPR Part 14.1:

> (1) A party may admit the truth of the whole or any part of another party's case.
>
> (2) He may do this by giving notice in writing (such as in a statement of case or by letter).
>
> (3) Where the only remedy which the claimant is seeking is the payment of money, the defendant may also make an admission in accordance with—
>
>> (a) rule 14.4 (admission of whole claim for specified amount of money);
>>
>> (b) rule 14.5 (admission of part of claim for specified amount of money);
>>
>> (c) rule 14.6 (admission of liability to pay whole of claim for unspecified amount of money); or
>>
>> (d) rule 14.7 (admission of liability to pay claim for unspecified amount of money where defendant offers a sum in satisfaction of the claim).
>
> (4) Where the defendant makes an admission as mentioned in paragraph (3), the claimant has a right to enter judgment except where—
>
>> (a) the defendant is a child or patient; or
>>
>> (b) the claimant is a child or patient and the admission is made under rule 14.5 or14.7.
>
> (Rule 21.10 provides that, where a claim is made by or on behalf of a child or patient or against a child or patient, no settlement, compromise or payment shall be valid, so far as it relates to that person's claim, without the approval of the court.)
>
> (5) The court may allow a party to amend or withdraw an admission.
>
> (Rule 3.1(3) provides that the court may attach conditions when it makes an order.)

An admission may be express or implied, but it must be clear.[25] An admission which is not clear, either as to subject matter or extent, is not considered by the courts to be an admission at all, and if in doubt, those acting for Claimants should seek clarification of any admission on which they wish to rely.

---

[25] *Ellis v Allen* [1914] 1 Ch. 904 at 909; *Ash v Hutchinson & Co. (Publishers) Ltd* [1936] Ch. 489 at 503; *Technistudy v Kelland* [1976] 1 W.L.R. 1042; *Murphy v Culhane* [1977] Q.B. 94).

Entering judgment on an admission

The Claimant's right to enter judgment on an admission pursuant to r.14.1(3) is subject only to the usual requirement, pursuant to r.21.10, where the Defendant is a child or patient, or the Claimant is a child or patient, and the admission is under r.14.5 or r.14.7 (but note, not if the admission is under r.14.4 or r.14.6). In these cases, involving a child or patient, an application to the court is necessary. Otherwise, in the vast majority of cases, the Claimant has a right to enter judgment. Pursuant to CPR Part 14.3:

> (1) Where a party makes an admission under rule 14.1(2) (admission by notice in writing), any other party may apply for judgment on the admission.
> (2) Judgment shall be such judgment as it appears to the court that the applicant is entitled to on the admission.

If the Defendant in a damages action admits the claim, the Claimant can obtain judgment for "*an amount to be decided by the court*" (and one good reason for doing so is to enable the Claimant to obtain an order for an interim payment: see r.25.7(1)(b) and CPR Part 25). As where a judgment in default is entered, a judgment entered on an admission for an amount to be decided by the court does not preclude the Defendant from raising an issue as to any particular head of loss or damage provided that to do so is not inconsistent with the judgment. For example, in certain cases, but not others, it may be possible to raise an issue regarding contributory negligence where liability has been admitted. However, for the Claimant to obtain judgment in a negligence action the Defendant must have admitted *both* that he was negligent *and* that the Claimant thereby suffered damage; an admission of the negligence only is not sufficient.[26] The reason is that an admission of negligence without an admission that the Claimant suffered injury thereby is not an admission of liability. The Claimant, therefore, cannot obtain judgment on an application under r.14.3 but may be able to obtain, in an appropriate case, summary judgment under Part 24.[27]

Resiling from admissions

In cases decided before the implementation of the CPR in April 1999, the Court of Appeal accepted that a party needed the permission of the court to withdraw an admission, whether it had been made before or after the commencement of the proceedings. The leading case was *Gale v Superdrug*

---

[26] *Blundell v Rimmer* [1971] 1 W.L.R. 123, approved in *Rankine v Garton Sons & Co.* [1979] 2 All E.R. 1185 and *Parrott v Jackson* [1996] P.I.Q.R. P394.
[27] *Dummer v Brown* [1953] 1 Q.B. 710.

Stores Plc.[28] In that case liability was admitted pre-action and an interim payment was made. When proceedings were issued the Defendant filed a full defence to the claim. The Judge upheld the decision of the District Judge in refusing to allow the Defendant to resile, and focused on the Defendant's explanation, which he considered inadequate. As to prejudice on the part of the Claimant he pointed to "*the inevitable prejudice*" which resulted from delay, the interim payment which had raised the Claimant's expectations and the Claimant's disappointment. In the Court of Appeal Waite L.J. rejected the submission that the sufficiency of the excuse by the party seeking to resile was the starting point - and indeed the finishing point if no sufficient excuse was offered. Excuse was simply part of the overall picture. The court had a wide discretion and had to look at prejudice on both sides. In the absence of evidence of actual prejudice he considered that the appeal should be allowed. In relation to disappointment he commented:

> Litigation is, however, a field in which disappointments are liable to occur in the nature of the process, and it cannot be fairly conducted if undue regard is paid to the feelings of the protagonists.

In Millet L.J.'s judgment, permission should be granted if the application (1) was made in good faith (as opposed to tactical manoeuvring), (2) raised a triable issue with a reasonable prospect of success; and (3) would not prejudice the Claimant in a manner which could not be adequately compensated. He took the view that it was not normally necessary to justify the decision to resile and it was enough if a Defendant wished to do so. In relation to disappointment he said that: "*Of course, the unexpected nature of the defence must have been a disappointment to the Plaintiff; but I cannot think that this should count for anything. The sounder the defence sought to be raised by amendment, the greater the disappointment to the Plaintiff if it is allowed and the greater the injustice to the Defendant if it is not. What the court must strive to avoid is injustice, not disappointment.*"

The pre-CPR position, therefore, seemed to be that in most cases the Defendant would be allowed to resile from pre- and post-action admissions if it could show that it had an arguable case. It may be felt that this is consistent with the furtherance of the overriding objective of the CPR to do justice between the parties.

The CPR and pre-action protocols

Lord Woolf put forward the idea of Pre-Action Protocols in Chapter 10 of his report "Access to Justice" 1996. He suggested that they were to "*build*

---

[28] [1996] 1 W.L.R. 1089.

on and increase the benefits of early but well informed settlements which genuinely satisfy both parties to disputes." The objectives of the Pre-Action Protocols are set out at Practice Direction 1.4:

- to encourage the exchange of early and full information about the prospective legal claim;
- to enable parties to avoid litigation by agreeing a settlement of the claim before the commencement of proceedings;
- to support the efficient management of proceedings where litigation cannot be avoided.

The Personal Injury Pre-Action Protocol is designed for fast track cases with a value of less than £15,000, but the spirit of the protocol is to be complied with in multi-track cases. We are now very familiar with the procedure: the Claimant sends a letter of claim, and the Defendant has three months from the date of acknowledgement of the claim to investigate. He or she must then respond stating whether or not liability is denied. And then there is paragraph 3.9:

> Where liability is admitted, the presumption is that the defendant will be bound by this admission for all claims with a total value of up to £15,000.

The Clinical Negligence Protocol, in contrast, contains the usual provisions as to letters of claim and responses. But it states at paragraph 3.25 that within three months of the letters of claim the healthcare provider should provide a reasoned answer:

> if the claim is admitted the healthcare provider should say so in clear terms;
> if only part of the claim is admitted the healthcare provider should make clear which issues of breach of duty and/or causation are admitted and which are denied if it is intended that any admissions will be binding....

This suggests that no admission is to be regarded as binding unless the healthcare provider specifically states that that is the case. Other protocols, such as the Professional Negligence Pre-Action Protocol, are silent as to the status of admissions. For a time, it seemed that, under the CPR and in pursuance of the objectives of the protocols, pre-action admissions would be binding in fast track personal injury cases but not in clinical negligence cases (many of which are of course themselves personal injury cases). The leading case on admissions under the CPR is now that of the Court of Appeal in *Sowerby v Charlton*[29] in which Brooke L.J. held that r.14.1(5) does not apply to pre action admissions, and indicated that the authorities decided

---

[29] [2006] 1 WLR 568.

under RSC Order 27 should now be approached with caution, particularly the decision in *Gale v Superdrug Stores Ltd.* The facts in *Sowerby* may be summarised as follows:

- On 26th April 2003 the Claimant was rendered paraplegic when she fell about 8' over the edge of a flight of stone steps leading from the pavement up to the front door of a private residential property. One side of the steps was unguarded.
- On 23rd October 2003 her solicitors wrote a letter of claim.
- Eventually, on 10th May 2004 the Defendant's solicitors stated in a 'without prejudice' letter: "Having investigated this claim the Defendant is prepared to admit a breach of duty." They then made a proposal for settlement of the contributory negligence issue.
- The Claimant's solicitors responded on 13th May, asking that the position in relation to liability be confirmed in open correspondence, and seeking a substantial interim payment. In a later letter they rejected the settlement proposal and asked that the breach of duty be openly admitted.
- On 30th June the Defendant's solicitors re-dated their letter of 10th May and re-sent it to the Claimant's solicitors, this time as an open letter.
- Proceedings were then issued and served, and the defence was filed and served on 24th September 2004. To the Claimant's solicitors' surprise, primary liability was put in issue (on the advice of Counsel).
- On 20th December 2004 the Claimant successfully applied to Master Tennant for the paragraphs of the defence denying liability to be struck out. Judge Playford QC upheld the Master's decision on appeal.
- The Defendant appealed to the Court of Appeal, and was granted permission to appeal on the basis that the scope of CPR Part 14.1 raised an important point of practice on which there was no post-CPR authority, and some debate at first instance.

The Court of Appeal considered the scope and interaction of Part 14.1 and of the Personal Injury Pre-Action Protocol, and found as follows:

- The old pre-CPR provisions had been held to be capable of embracing admissions made before as well as after the action commenced. Accordingly, the courts did have the power under the old rules to give leave to a Defendant to withdraw an admission made in pre-action correspondence.
- However, the CPR was an entirely new procedural code and was principally concerned with the regulation of cases after an action has been started. The pre-CPR cases should therefore be approached with caution.

- CPR Part 14.1 did not apply to pre-action admissions.
- Accordingly, CPR 14.1(5) did not apply to pre-action admissions, and it is therefore unnecessary for a Defendant to obtain the court's permission to resile from an admission *made prior to the commencement of proceedings.*

As a consequence, in multi-track cases a Defendant may resile from a pre-action admission of liability without applying for the court's permission to do so; in fast track cases to which the Personal Injury Pre-Action Protocol applies, there is a presumption that such an admission will be binding, but it remained unclear whether that presumption was rebuttable or whether it was necessary for a Defendant to apply for the court's permission to resile from such an admission. As regards admissions made after the issue of proceedings, the Court of Appeal approved the guidance provided by Sumner J. in *Braybrook v Basildon & Thurrock University NHS Trust*[30] where it was held that:

> 1. In exercising its discretion the court will consider all the circumstances of the case and seek to give effect to the overriding objective.
> 2. Amongst the matters to be considered will be:
> (a) the reasons and justification for the application which must be made in good faith;
> (b) the balance of prejudice to the parties;
> (c) whether any party has been the author of any prejudice they may suffer;
> (d) the prospects of success of any issue arising from the withdrawal of an admission;
> (e) the public interest, in avoiding where possible satellite litigation, disproportionate use of court resources and the impact of any strategic manoeuvring.
> 3. The nearer any application is to a final hearing the less chance of success it will have even if the party making the application can establish clear prejudice. This may be decisive if the application is shortly before the hearing.

The appeal in *Sowerby* itself was dismissed; the Court of Appeal held that there was no real prospect of the Defendant resisting a finding of primary liability, and allowed summary judgment on this issue and upheld the Master's order that the issue of contributory negligence should be

---

[30] October 7th 2004.

determined by way of preliminary hearing. Further guidance was given by the Court of Appeal in *Stoke on Trent City Council v Walley*,[31] in which:

- The Claimant was a refuse collector employed by the Defendant. He injured his knee in the course of his employment on 28th August 2001.
- The Defendant's loss adjustors admitted liability for the accident on 13th June 2003.
- In the fullness of time the file was reviewed by another loss adjustor, and on 12th May 2004 he wrote to the Claimant's solicitors resiling from the admission.
- Proceedings were issued and served, and the Defendant entered a defence denying liability for the accident.
- The Claimant issued an application seeking to strike out the defence on the grounds that it was an abuse of the process of the court or was otherwise likely to obstruct the just disposal of the proceedings. The Defendant cross-applied to resile from the admission.
- The Deputy District Judge, and then the Circuit Judge, held that the Defendant was bound by its admission.

The court held that in circumstances such as this it was appropriate for the Claimant to make an application under CPR Part 3.4(2) to strike out the defence or part of it as being an abuse of process or as being otherwise likely to obstruct the just disposal of the case. However,

> ...in order to rely on an abuse of process, it would usually be necessary for the claimant to show that the defendant had acted in bad faith...in order to show that withdrawal of the admission would be likely to obstruct the just disposal of the proceedings, the claimant would have to show that he would suffer real prejudice if the admission were withdrawn...

It seems that 'real prejudice' can be demonstrated by the destruction of evidence, the death of a witness or additional difficulty in obtaining funding; but cannot be demonstrated by feelings of '*uncertainty, turmoil, even despair*'. The Claimant in *Walley* failed to demonstrate relevant prejudice and the Defendant was not bound by its admission. It remains to be seen precisely what the practical effect of these decisions will be. In cases which are likely to be allocated to the multi-track when issued, it is likely that Defendants will be allowed to resile from any pre-action admissions. Although this *seems* to be good news from a Defendant's standpoint, however, if Claimants cannot rely on pre-action admissions with any confidence, their representatives may well decide that they are obliged to

[31] [2007] 1 WLR 352.

continue to prepare a case on liability, even where an admission is made, until proceedings are issued and a defence formally admitting liability is filed. Conditional fee agreement uplifts will have to reflect this uncertainty. The corollary of this is that it may be difficult for Defendants to object to these costs, and the unintended result may be an overall increase in costs, both in terms of base costs and uplift. Neither *Sowerby* nor *Walley* concerned or gave guidance regarding claims likely to be listed on the fast track. In such cases, where the Personal Injury Pre-Action Protocol applies, it seems likely that the courts will operate a rebuttable presumption that a Defendant will be bound by a pre-action admission, unless it applies to the court for permission to resile from it. The courts are likely to allow a Defendant to resile from an admission unless the Claimant can show that this would cause him to suffer prejudice.

Admissions and Compromise Agreements

One way around all of this confusion and uncertainty is for parties to enter into compromise agreements. In *Burden v Harrods Limited*[32] the Defendant conceded primary liability but stated in correspondence: " *We would argue for a 25 per cent deduction in respect of contributory negligence.*" The Claimant's solicitors' response was: " *We confirm that our client is prepared to accept your offer to deal with her claim on a 75 per cent basis in her favour...*" The Defendant's solicitors replied: " *We note your client accepts 25 per cent contribution.*" The Defendant successfully argued before the Judge that this was an admission, and he allowed the Defendant to withdraw it. Calvert-Smith J. allowed the Claimant's appeal and held that there had been a valid compromise, and the Court of Appeal refused permission for a second appeal. It was argued before them at the permission hearing that there was no intention to create legal relations unless there was full and final settlement, and this would certainly be consistent with the Clinical Negligence Pre-Action Protocol, which requires a Defendant to indicate whether or not an admission is binding. However, the Court of Appeal rejected this argument; a compromise effected as a result of pre-action negotiations was binding. Accordingly, Part 14 was irrelevant. May L.J. took the view that Part 14.1 was concerned with formal admissions after proceedings were started, and also commented that paragraph 3.9 of the Personal Injury Pre-Action Protocol was "less than entirely clear", and he was not sure of what the effect of the presumption would be if the paragraph did apply in any particular case. This suggests that any 'carving' of liability will result in a binding compromise from which it is not possible to resile. Nevertheless, questions remain. Could this argument be run in a case where there has been an admission of liability in full? The problem may be

---

[32] [2005] P.I.Q.R. P17.

identifying the consideration – but it is nonetheless arguable. It seems odd that as the law stands under *Sowerby* and *Burden* a Defendant would be in a better position if it admitted liability in full.

Admissions Made on or after 6th April 2007

Admissions made on or after 6th April 2007 are governed by the Civil Procedure (Amendment No.3) Rules 2006, which come into force on that date. The new rules, insofar as they are relevant in this context, state:

> 4. In Part 14 –
>   (a) for the heading in rule 14.1, substitute 'Admissions made after commencement of proceedings';
>   (b) for rule 14.1(5), substitute 'The permission of the court is required to amend or withdraw an admission.'; and
>
>   (a) after rule 14.1, insert—
>
> **'Admissions made before commencement of proceedings**
>
> 14.1A – (1) A person may, by giving notice in writing, admit the truth of the whole or any part of another party's case before commencement of proceedings (a "pre-action admission").
>
> (2) Paragraphs (3) to (5) of this rule apply to a pre-action admission made in the types of proceedings listed at paragraph 1.1(2) of the Practice Direction to this Part (ie in personal injury claims, resolution of clinical disputes and disease and illness claims) if one of the following conditions is met –
>
>   (a) it is made after the party making it has received a letter of claim in accordance with the relevant pre-action protocol; or
>
>   (b) it is made before such letter of claim has been received, but it is stated to be made under Part 14.
>
> (3) A person may, by giving notice in writing, withdraw a pre-action admission –
>
>   (a) before commencement of proceedings, if the person to whom the admission was made agrees;
>
>   (b) after commencement of proceedings, if all parties to the proceedings consent or with the permission of the court.
>
> (4) After commencement of proceedings—

(a) any party may apply for judgment on the pre-action admission; and

(b) the party who made the pre-action admission may apply to withdraw it.

(5) An application to withdraw a pre-action admission or to enter judgment on such an admission—

(a) must be made in accordance with Part 23;

(b) may be made as a cross-application.

This amendment to the CPR is intended to simplify the position; there is now no distinction between pre-action admissions in claims likely to be allocated to the fast track and claims likely to be allocated to the multi-track. In either case, where a party makes a pre-action admission, it may withdraw it if the other party agrees, or with the permission of the court. Nevertheless, the law of unintended consequences continues to apply: the amendment is silent on the factors to be taken into account in deciding whether to allow a party to resile from an admission, and there is sure to be plenty of litigation on this issue. Furthermore, the amendment has not resolved the Claimant's solicitor's dilemma; if the Defendant is to be allowed to resile from a pre-action admission (albeit with the permission of the court), can those representing the Claimant afford to stop investigating the issue of liability in the months or years before proceedings are issued? It would appear that the safest course is for Claimant's solicitors to investigate the issue of liability thoroughly even before sending the letter of claim. It would be harsh indeed for a costs judge to disallow the costs of doing so in the current climate, since at present it seems unlikely that any pre-action admission of liability is worth the paper it is written on. On the other hand, it seems unfair that the Defendant should be burdened with the costs of all this investigation in circumstances in which it admits liability at the first opportunity. It is anticipated that balancing this unfairness will be one of the most important considerations of the Court of Appeal when it first considers the amendment and issues guidance as to its interpretation.

Costs Capping

What is Cost Capping?

Cost capping is the process whereby one party (invariably a Defendant in travel cases) applies to the Court at an *early* stage of proceedings for an order limiting *in advance* the amount of fees and expenditure recoverable by the other side (usually the Claimants) at the conclusion of the action. Where an order is made the Court prospectively limits the extent to which the parties incur litigation costs. The "cap" however then becomes the presumptive amount the capped party is able to claim in costs in the absence of a change of circumstances. Thus it is said:

- costs are prevented from spiraling out of control;
- the parties know in advance the likely level of costs recovery if successful or the costs risk if unsuccessful;
- the litigation can be managed by each party proportionately in the context of the limit placed on costs;
- the "capped" party's ability to behave oppressively by wracking up enormous bills with which to threaten the opposition is reduced;
- lengthy satellite litigation about costs after the event (itself expensive) may thereby be minimized;
- parties will litigate on a more equal footing and in the context of greater costs certainty.

In *Various Ledward Claimants v Kent & Medway HA*[33] in which the chief costs judge was sitting with her as an assessor Hallett J. said:

> "10 ... I am very concerned that without my intervention the costs in this particular case will spiral out of control, if they have not done so already. I intend to do what I can in the time remaining to ensure that they remain proportionate ...
>
> 11 I am satisfied that this case is a classic example of litigation, driven by the lawyer acting for the claimants, in which there is a real risk that costs have been and will be incurred unnecessarily and unreasonably ...
>
> 12 ... In summary, I fear that [the claimants' solicitor] is, at the very least, over generous with her time and with the time of her staff in planning the preparation of these actions for trial."

In *Southam and Others v JMC Holidays (otherwise known as the non-Aguamar case)*[34] the judge noted:

> This case only goes to reinforce my view that it is becoming ever more necessary for the courts to control the expenditure of costs before they are incurred. How can it be that two firms of solicitors, respected professional men and women, can have so widely differing views about what is the proper cost of undertaking the relevant work? £500,000 on one view, or £50,000 on the other. It is difficult to comprehend. The sooner the rules provide for budget costs, or authorised costs, or some form of predictable

---

[33] [2003] EWHC 2551 (QB).
[34] (March 2003, Birmingham CC unreported) HHJ MacDuff QC.

costs, to do away with after the event assessments, the better it will be for all concerned, particularly those whom the lawyers are supposed to serve, namely their clients. The sooner rules are put in place to avoid unbecoming satellite litigation, concerned only with lawyers' remuneration, the better.

Why Travel Litigation?

Costs capping is by no means restricted to holiday litigation (defamation cases are another rich source of this newly exercised procedural power) but capping has featured recently and largely in holiday cases. It is not difficult to see why.

- Group or multi-Claimant actions are increasingly common (whether subject to formal Group Litigation Orders or not) - such actions can involve anything between 6 and 6,000 individual claims.
- These groups are rampant in holiday litigation, particularly (but not limited to) mass illness outbreaks.
- Cruise, plane and coach passengers will often effectively pool their claims where they arise out of single incidents and hotel (sometime even resort) guests will do the same where their complaints arise out of shared quality complaints. In many cases the large number of Claimants is compounded by the joinder of several different tour operators or service providers concerned with same alleged holiday shortcomings (more often than not shortcomings arising out of food and hygiene standards). More often than not each individual claim (even where injury or illness is involved) would be hopelessly uneconomic to contest as a distinct claim. There is both safety and strength in numbers.
- The uneconomic nature of individual claims coupled with the absence of legal aid even for personal injury cases (and the questionable availability of after the event insurance where the cost-benefit of litigation is at best marginal) would lead to appreciable numbers of Claimants with valid or at least arguable claims being left without a viable remedy. Such would not be consistent with modern concepts of access to justice.
- As a result, Defendants could be the ones capable of behaving oppressively in the knowledge that many arguably justifiable consumer complaints would have to be abandoned before they ever effectively started.

This explains why holiday litigation has spawned a particular brand of group action. Such a development has, however, resulted in escalating costs. Without the most careful administrative control it is easy to see how in coordinating (or failing to coordinate) a large number of relatively tiny claims can give rise to unnecessary duplication of time and effort, unfocused and thus wasteful time management, inadequate identification of relevant group issues and a failure (whether in the context of the costs common to all

Claimants, or individual Claimant's costs) to behave in a proportionate manner; all compounded by a proliferation of expert witnesses across several disciplines, endless medical condition and prognosis reports and lengthy, untargeted ("cut-and-paste") Schedules of Loss and Damage. It would not be unusual to have an action brought by 200 Claimants, the claims averaging a value of £2,500 (a potential total of £500,000) in which the predicted costs of the Claimants amount to £2.5 million *before* conditional fee uplift). The evidence of any economies of scale in this realistic example is slight. It seems, therefore, that at least in terms of costs the tables have been turned against Defendants. When part of a group, it is the *Claimants,* under the threat of an enormous exposure to costs, who can potentially intimidate Defendants into submission – it being radically cheaper to capitulate than to contest. The fact that under the protection of conditional fee agreements the Claimants are able to litigate entirely risk free only makes matters worse. The costs risks to Defendants are enhanced by after-the-event insurance premiums and worse the costs will be subject to a success fee or "uplift" which will not unusually be 100%. Small wonder then that Defendants facing such actions have balked at the costs implications and often felt it safer and cheaper to give in. This in turn feeds a *suspicion* on the Defendants' side of the court that group actions include appreciable numbers of band-wagon jumpers who have climbed aboard in the knowledge that the group action will compromise to their advantage.

A Balancing Exercise

Cost capping in holiday claims (and others) can be seen as one of the best examples of the *overriding objective* in action. It is not a punishment to be meted out to the advantage of one party over the other and should not hinder access to justice as proportionately understood. It is an attempt to balance the interests of those with genuine grievances (however modestly valued) with the interests of those targeted by such modest grievances bearing in mind that some such grievances will be unjustified. This is the "level playing field" of conventional modern parlance.

In *Dawson v First Choice Holidays & Flights Ltd*[35] the judge said:

> I have to confess to a certain irritation at the suggestion that a costs cap might somehow impede the Claimants' rights of access to justice. On any view these are little cases. There may be one or two which are somewhat larger. These are cases which would never have been pursued in the days before "no win no fee" arrangements could be made. Would someone with a day or two of diarrhoea on holiday and a claim of a value of £158 (the

---

[35] 2007 12 March 5BM 150976 HHJ MacDuff QC – at paragraph 35.

average settlement to date) have gone to his solicitor on the High Street and asked them to pursue the holiday company for damages? Would he have done so if he had known that his potential costs liability to his own solicitor (never mind the opposition if he lost) would be £7,500 (1/200th of £1.5 millions)? Would even the Claimant with more severe symptoms (value £15,000 or even more) have done so if he had been told that he was required to pay money on account of costs which would mount to £7500 and costs to the other side if he lost? There seems to be a feeling in some quarters that even the smallest claim requires "access to justice" at whatever the cost. Where is the justice for the defendant who, faced with a conditional fee agreement, may end up with a costs bill of £1,500,000 plus success fee (likely to be 100% I judge), when the claims against it total only a fraction of that sum; where 90% of the claims will be valued well within the fast track limit, and many within the small claims limit? Access to justice does not mean that any claimant must be allowed to bring his claim, however small, at whatever cost, regardless of all sensible economic argument, and with no personal costs exposure. He can, of course bring it on the small claims track with very limited entitlement to costs.

The point, it seems, is this. Those with modest claims will not be denied access to a remedy in the courts (as part of a large group) merely because their costs are regulated in advance by the Court. *On the contrary*, the availability of group actions provides the mechanism by which such Claimants have access to justice – it is just not justice *at any price and without any risk* – particularly where the price is being paid by someone else. In his *Access to Justice Final Report*, July 1996, Lord Woolf noted:

> Fear of costs deters some litigants from litigating when they would otherwise be entitled to do so and compels other litigants to settle their claim when they have no wish to do so. It enables a more powerful litigant to take unfair advantage of the weaker litigant …

On the other hand at paragraph 83 of the judgment in *Dawson* we read:

> I acknowledge and understand the worry on the part of the Claimants' lawyers that an unscrupulous opposing party could take advantage of the existence of a cap to introduce diversionary or other tactics to cause extra work to the Claimants and their lawyers, designed to drive them towards the limit of the costs cap and to stifle the claims or induce irrecoverable expenditure. This is something which this particular judge (or indeed any judge) will not condone. It is always open to the parties to apply back for an adjustment to the capping level. The costs of that application would lie outside the capping order, and would be dealt with on their merits. If, on such an application, the applicant was able to demonstrate such behaviour, I would have no hesitation in lifting the cap and making an appropriate costs order against the guilty party. I would also have no hesitation in allowing the parties the necessary amount of time to enable the question to

be fully investigated and fairly determined. It is not something which I envisage will happen in this case. I am confident that the parties will cooperate to make this order work. There must be provision to either party to apply to vary (up or down) the level of the cap in the event that circumstances change, for whatever reason.

Furthermore, any public perception or suspicion that lawyers are generating cases and costs for the purposes of lining their own pockets must be *seen* to be misplaced. It is unseemly – it disfigures the civil justice system - for lawyers to concentrate more of their resources upon squabbling about costs than upon their clients' damages. Equally, Claimants who carry no costs risks under conditional fee agreements should not be treated to *"Rolls Royce"* levels of attention at which they would justifiably flinch if likely to have to pay a bill for such luxuries at the conclusion of the case. As Brooke LJ said in *King v Telegraph Group Ltd.*[36]

> ... it would be very much better for the court to exercise control over costs in advance, rather than to wait reactively until after the case is over and the costs are being assessed.

Similar sentiments have recently been expressed by Dyson LJ in *Leigh v Michelin Tyres plc*[37] and by (for a second time) Hallett J. in *Sheppard v Mid Essex Health Authority.*[38]

The source of cost capping

The power to impose a costs cap on one party or both is now taken for granted. Express provision for it in procedural rules is, however, not easy to find. In *AB v Leeds Teaching Hospitals NHS Trust*[39] Gage J held that the court's general powers of case management were sufficiently wide to encompass the making of a costs capping order both in group litigation (with which he was then concerned) and in other actions. It is, after all, an important feature of the overriding objective that the court must be enabled to save expense and deal with a case in ways which are proportionate to the amount of money involved, the importance of the case, the complexity of the issues and the financial position of each party (CPR 1.1), and the parties are required to help the court to further the overriding objective (CPR 1.3) – as said Brooke LJ: *King v Telegraph Group plc.*[40] Such a power (according to

---

[36] [2005] 1 WLR 2282.
[37] [2004] 1 WLR 846.
[38] [2006] 1 Costs LR 8.
[39] [2003] EWHC 1034 (QB).
[40] See above.

Brooke LJ) is most probably derived from CPR 3.2(m) which confers a power to

> take any other step or make any other order for the purpose of managing the case and furthering the overriding objective.

The Court of Appeal drafted a comprehensive set of principles to be applied in respect of costs capping (relating to personal injury claims) before handing down judgment in *Willis v Nicolson*[41] (a single Claimant action). The principles, however, were not published as part of the judgment or indeed at all. Buxton LJ having considered the matter further concluded that it was inappropriate for the Court to undertake this role – which accordingly, has been consigned to the Civil Procedure Rules Committee from whom after extensive consultation we can expect to receive further detailed guidance. However, it is already tolerably clear from the proliferation of costs capping orders in the last 3 years (many of which have arisen in holiday claims) that where the issues in an action are straightforward the court can and will exercise its pre-emptive case management powers to limit costs expenditure generally or a particular *type* of costs expenditure as, for example in *Tierney v News Group Newspapers Ltd*[42] where the parties were restricted to junior counsel. This is done, not punitively, but in the interests of proportionality and to ensure so far as practicable a level playing field in order to minimize fiscal oppression by one side or the other. Application for such an order should be made at as early a stage in the litigation as feasible but the Court *can* act on its own initiative if the projected costs appear to present a potential affront to the administration of justice. Such orders are not limited to "exceptional cases". By way of counter-balance, should it emerge that as a result of the behaviour of the opposition a "capped" party is materially disadvantaged in its case management and preparation, the level and even the imposition of the costs cap can and in appropriate cases will be reviewed. The capping process will often entail an order being made in principle with the level of any cap being set at a hearing before a costs judge – itself a potentially expensive and time-consuming business. No doubt the underlying and unstated ambition of both Courts and Rule makers is that suitably judged implementation of early costs limits will exert more proportionate costs discipline on those managing particularly large group litigation which self-regulation in turn will obviate the need for such applications, cap hearings and orders in the futures.

---

[41] [2007] EWCA Civ 199.
[42] [2006] EWHC 50.

Part 36 Offers

Introduction

The rules about Part 36 offers have changed with effect from 6th April 2007.[43] Nonetheless it is predictable that in many hands the rules of this procedural game will continue to be misunderstood. It is all too common to find that the Part 36 procedure is used by Claimants and Defendants alike as a mechanism by which an auction is introduced into the proceedings. The objective of having a system in which costs penalties flow from a failure to do better than a formal offer put forward by the other side is surely to try and induce each side to put it best offer forward at the earliest moment. Thus, Defendants should think they are offering modestly over the odds and Claimants should believe they are signalling a willingness to settle for rather less than the claim is objectively worth. In other words, surely the purpose underlying this system is that any party making a Part 36 offer should be able more or less to *guarantee* that it will do better if successful at trial. In travel litigation the Part 36 process is seldom used in this way. Rather, the parties tend to make offers at extremes of the range of possibilities in terms of damages awards and then proceed to meet somewhere in the middle. This process is in many instances reasonably effective in bringing about compromises, but one wonders why the process, so deployed, needs the imprint of Part 36. The same could be said of offers made in respect of liability where percentage deductions – whether for contributory negligence and/or litigation risk – are routinely negotiated under the banner of CPR Part 36.

The Formalities

The formalities of Part 36 offers and payments are set out in CPR Part 36.5 and CPR Part 36.6 respectively. A Part 36 offer must be in writing and must state:

- whether it relates to the whole of the claim or to part of it or to an issue that arises in it and if so to which part or issue;
- whether it takes into account any counterclaim; and
- if it is expressed not to be inclusive of interest, give the details relating to interest set out in rule 36.22(2).

A Part 36 offer made not less than 21 days before the start of the trial must:

- be expressed to remain open for acceptance for 21 days from the date it is made; and

---

[43] As to which see further below.

- provide that after 21 days the offeree may only accept it if:
  (i) the parties agree the liability for costs; or
  (ii) the court gives permission.

A Part 36 offer made less than 21 days before the start of the trial must state that the offeree may only accept it if:

- the parties agree the liability for costs; or
- the court gives permission.

Part 36.2A governs offers to settle personal injury claims which include a claim for future pecuniary loss. Any such offer must state:

- The amount of any offer to pay the whole or part of any damages in the form of a lump sum.
- What part of the offer relates to damages for future pecuniary loss to be paid or accepted in the form of periodical payments and must specify—
  (i) the amount and duration of the periodical payments,
  (ii) the amount of any payments for substantial capital purchases and when they are to be made, and
  (iii) that each amount is to vary by reference to the retail prices index (or to some other named index, or that it is not to vary by reference to any index).
- Either that any damages which take the form of periodical payments will be funded in a way which ensures that the continuity of payment is reasonably secure in accordance with section 2(4) of the Damages Act 1996 or how such damages are to be paid and how the continuity of their payment is to be secured:

and *may* state:

- What part of the offer relates to damages for future pecuniary loss to be accepted in the form of a lump sum.
- Where part of the offer relates to other damages to be accepted in the form of a lump sum, what amounts are attributable to those other damages.

A Part 36 payment may relate either to the whole claim, or to part of it, or to a particular issue. Notice of the payment must be made in the prescribed form, which must state:

- The amount of the payment.
- Whether the payment relates to the whole claim or to part of it or to any issue that arises in it and if so to which part or issue.

- Whether it takes into account any counterclaim.
- If an interim payment has been made, that the Defendant has taken into account the interim payment; and
- If it is expressed not to be inclusive of interest, the details relating to interest set out in rule 36.22(2).

Pursuant to Part 36.9, an offeree may request an offeror to clarify an offer or payment notice, within 7 days of the offer or payment being made. If no clarification is forthcoming with 7 days of the request, the offeree may apply under Part 23 for an order for clarification and in *Ford v GKR Construction Ltd*[44] the Court of Appeal endorsed the requirement for the parties to make full and prompt disclosure of all relevant matters when conducting litigation.

Withdrawing or Reducing Part 36 Offers and Payments

A Part 36 offer may be withdrawn at any time, and need not remain open for 21 days (for example *Scammell v Dicker*[45]). If a Part 36 offer *is* withdrawn, it will not have the consequences set out in Part 36, but it may still have effect in relation to the judge's general discretion as to costs – see *Trustees of Stokes Pension Fund v Western Power Distribution (South -West) Plc.*[46] A Part 36 payment may be withdrawn or reduced only with the permission of the court. Any such application should be made in accordance with Part 23. In *Capital Bank Plc v Stickland*[47] the Court of Appeal held that under the present rules the fact that there has been a change of circumstance following the payment in is certainly relevant and may well be the most important factor to be taken into account in deciding whether or not to allow withdrawal or reduction of a Part 36 payment into court in a particular case. In *Flynn v Scougall*[48] it was held that an application within time for acceptance to reduce or withdraw a payment in does not constitute an automatic suspension or stay of time for acceptance pending disposal of application, although the court retains a jurisdiction to entertain the application after notice of acceptance has been given.

On 20th September 1999 Mr Flynn, a fireman, was injured when the Defendant's car collided with the fire engine in which he was travelling. Initially his medical expert suggested that the accident had accelerated Mr Flynn's retirement by a period of 5 years. Proceedings were issued. Accordingly, on 14th March 2003 the Defendant made a payment into court

---

[44] [2000] 1 W.L.R. 1397.
[45] [2001] 1 W.L.R. 631.
[46] [2005] 1 WLR 3595.
[47] [2005] 1 W.L.R. 3914.
[48] [2004] 1 W.L.R. 3069.

of £24,500. Shortly thereafter, on 20th March 2003, her representatives obtained their own medical evidence, which suggested an acceleration period of only 3 months. An application was made to reduce the payment in to £10,000, and the Claimant was notified of this. In the meantime, and before the 21 day period for acceptance had expired, the Claimant accepted the payment in. At first instance the judge allowed the Defendant's application to withdraw part of the payment into court, saying that it would be unjust to allow the Claimant to take advantage of the situation which had arisen. He further held that when the application was made, it had the effect of staying or freezing the time period for acceptance. The Court of Appeal reversed the judge's decision. It held that there was a difference between Part 36 offers and payments; contractual principles applied to the former but not to the latter. A payment in is governed by the procedural machinery under Part 36, and the judge was therefore wrong to conclude that an application to withdraw monies in court had the effect of staying the time for acceptance. The Court of Appeal went on to say that whilst a Defendant can apply to reduce or withdraw money in court within the 21 days period of acceptance, the Claimant has an unfettered right to accept a payment in within the 21 day period. The judge had not attached sufficient weight to this last factor, which was a very important element to the application. Further the Defendant had not shown that there was a change in circumstances so as to justify the withdrawal of such a sum. They had taken the risk of making an early payment in before receiving their own medical evidence. In the circumstances, it was right to allow the Claimant to accept the money.

The repercussions of this decision are self-evident; where those acting for Defendants are foolish enough to pay money into court before obtaining their own medical reports, the Claimant has an unfettered right to accept the payment within 21 days. It is not clear what circumstances would override the Claimant's right to accept the payment within 21 days, but certainly the discovery of fraud would be a valid reason.

Disclosing Part 36 Offers or Payments

Pursuant to Part 36.19, a Part 36 offer is to be treated as being without prejudice except as to costs, and the fact that a Part 36 payment has been made may not be communicated to the trial judge until the costs phase of the trial has been reached (unless the Defendant raises a defence of tender before claim). It may, however, be necessary or desirable to communicate the fact that an offer or payment has been made at an interlocutory stage, and this is permissible as in *Williams v Boag*,[49] although care should be taken when the designated civil judge is dealing with case management, as he is also likely to

---

[49] [1941] 1 K.B. 1.

be the trial judge. It is probably best when informing a judge that a Part 36 offer or payment has been made to keep the details of the offer or payment vague.

Where the trial judge is informed of the existence of a Part 36 offer or payment, he will have a discretion regarding whether to continue to hear the trial or to recuse himself, but in the interests of furthering the overriding objective (and in particular of saving court time and the parties' costs) will usually continue with the trial unless to do so would cause injustice.[50]

The Effect of Accepting a Part 36 Offer or Payment

Where either a Part 36 offer or a Part 36 payment is accepted, the claim (or that part of it to which the offer or payment relates) is stayed (Part 36.15). The stay does not affect the power of the court to deal with either enforcement or costs. The costs consequences of accepting a Defendant's Part 36 offer or payment are governed by Part 36.13:

- Where a Part 36 offer or a Part 36 payment is accepted without needing the permission of the court the Claimant will be entitled to his costs of the proceedings up to the date of serving notice of acceptance.
- Where a Part 36 offer or a Part 36 payment relates to part only of the claim, and at the time of serving notice of acceptance the Claimant abandons the balance of the claim, the Claimant will be entitled to his costs of the proceedings up to the date of serving notice of acceptance, unless the court orders otherwise. The court retains complete discretion regarding the costs of the whole action, and is able to deal not only with the abandoned parts of the claim but with the parts of the claim to which the offer or payment refers[51]. Where the Claimant's costs include any costs attributable to the Defendant's counterclaim if the Part 36 offer or the Part 36 payment notice states that it takes into account the counterclaim. Costs will be payable on the standard basis.

Where a Claimant's Part 36 offer is accepted without needing the permission of the court, the Claimant will be entitled to his costs of the proceedings up to the date upon which the Defendant serves notice of acceptance (Part 36.14).

---

[50] *Millensted v Grosvenor House (Park Lane) Ltd* [1937] 1 K.B. 717, *Garratt v Saxby* [2004] 1 W.L.R. 2152.
[51] *E. Ivor Hughes Educational Foundation v Leach* [2005] EWHC 1317 (Ch).

The Effect of Rejecting a Part 36 Offer or Payment

Where a Claimant fails to do better than a Part 36 offer or payment unless it considers it unjust to do so, the court will order the Claimant to pay any costs incurred by the Defendant after the latest date on which the payment or offer could have been accepted without needing the permission of the court.

Although Part 36.20 is silent on whether indemnity costs could be awarded where the Claimant fails to better a Defendant's Part 36 offer or payment, and although normally standard basis costs would follow, indemnity costs could be awarded if the circumstances of the case justified indemnity costs.[52]

In *Factortame v Secretary of State*[53] (a case involving the acceptance by a Claimant of a Part 36 offer following its significant amendment by the Defendant to whom the relevant information had always been available) Walker L.J. commented:

> Each case will turn on its own circumstances. It seems to me that so far as possible the judge should be trying to assess who in reality is the unsuccessful party and who has been responsible for the fact that costs have been incurred which should not have been. It is plainly right that a full-scale trial examining privileged material, and listening to ex post facto justification should be avoided. It furthermore does not seem to me to be right to seek to lay down rules as to where the onus will lie where a defendant is allowed to amend his case. As I have already said straightjackets in this area should be avoided. The starting point is that a claimant who fails to beat a payment in will *prima facie* be liable for the costs. An amendment may be of such a character that a judge will feel that the onus should be firmly placed on the defendant to persuade him that the prima facie rule should continue to apply; on the other hand the judge may be quite clear by reference to his feel of the case that the amendment is being used as an excuse to take money out of court that should have been accepted when originally made. Some cases will lie between the two extremes, and the judge will have to adjust his assessment to give effect to possibilities which it would be inappropriate to try out and thus by reference to his overall view of the case.

In *Blackham v Entrepose UK*,[54] the Court of Appeal scrutinised the interpretation of the expression 'beating the offer made' in the context of determining the effect of interest in the making of a Part 36 offer or payment in. The court held that courts must consider like with like and that,

---

[52] *Excelsior Commercial Holdings v Salisbury Hamer Aspden & Johnson* [2002] EWCA Civ 879.
[53] [2002] 1 W.L.R. 2438.
[54] The Times 28th September 2004.

accordingly, the Part 36 offer should be examined from the point of view of that which it represented at the time it was made, as against what the judgment represented. The Defendants made a payment into court of £40,000 on 12th November 2001. The notice requirements under CPR 36 were complied with and the payment in included interest payable up to the last date of acceptance. It was not accepted. At trial on 3rd February 2004 judgment was entered for £40,854.03, including interest that had continued to accrue after the Claimant rejected the offer. On the last day on which the payment could have been accepted in December 2001, the award made at the trial inclusive of interest would have been only £39,644.71. The Defendants unsurprisingly argued that the Claimant had not done better than the offer. This argument was rejected by the trial judge but upheld by the Court of Appeal, who agreed that when looking at whether an offer or payment has been beaten, it must be considered at the time at which it was made. In considering the issue of costs the judge must take the damages awarded and calculate the interest that would have been payable up to the last date of acceptance of the payment into court, and then compare the resulting figure to the amount in court: like for like. The trial judge had said that this opened up more issues than it resolved. Allowances would have to be made for inflation in respect of the capital sum of damages awarded between payment in and trial, as well as discounts for the period between the date that the payment was made and the last day on which it could be accepted. The Court of Appeal disagreed. The decision clearly favours Defendants over Claimants (since a Claimant cannot rely on the accumulated interest to beat a payment in), and it is not free of practical difficulties. For example, in a claim where there are a number of heads of loss that attract different rates of interest, accruing from different periods of time, the calculation will be difficult and may lead to a disproportionate amount of time being spent on deciding whether or not the payment was beaten. Anyone representing a party at the end of a trial where there is a longstanding payment in should make sure that they have their calculator poised to do some arithmetic on interest.

The Effect of Beating a Part 36 Offer

Where a Claimant beats his Part 36 offer, the court may order that the Defendant should pay:

- interest on the whole or part of any sum of money (excluding interest) awarded to the Claimant at a rate not exceeding 10% above base rate for some or all of the period starting with the latest date on which the Defendant could have accepted the offer without needing the permission of the court.

- costs on the indemnity basis from the latest date when the Defendant could have accepted the offer without needing the permission of the court.
- interest on costs at a rate not exceeding 10% above base rate.

The court will make these orders unless it considers it unjust to do so (Part 36.21(4)).

An order for indemnity costs under Part 36.21(3) is not penal and carries no stigma or implied disapproval of the Defendant's conduct, so moral lack of probity or conduct deserving of moral condemnation is not a prerequisite of jurisdiction to award indemnity costs.[55]

It is not always clear whether a Claimant has beaten a Part 36 offer, particularly where the Claimant obtains judgment for a sum equal to an offer. This situation arose in *Read v Edmed*,[56] the facts of which were as follows:

- On 24th November 2000 the 80 year old Claimant was knocked off her bicycle by the Defendant, who was travelling at some speed with his head out of the driver's side window because the windscreen was misted over.
- On 28th July 2003 the Claimant's solicitors offered to accept an apportionment of liability of 50:50 (the Claimant had ridden her bicycle into the path of the Defendant's car).
- This offer was rejected.
- At trial the judge apportioned liability on the basis of a 50:50 split.
- The Claimant argued that the offer should be treated as though she had bettered her offer; the Defendant argued that because she had not beaten her offer, no consequences flowed from it.

Bell J. held that, applying the spirit of Part 36.21 and of the other costs rules, as a matter of general principle, where in a relatively uncomplicated claim for damages for personal injury a Claimant made a valid Part 36 offer to settle an issue of liability at a given proportion of his or her claim, and the Defendant refused that offer, and the court gave judgment for precisely that proportion of the claim, the Claimant should be entitled to the benefit of an award of indemnity costs from the time of the expiry of the offer and interest on those costs as if Part 36.21 applied to the matter, in order to ensure that he or she was not out of pocket. This was subject to the usual caveat that the court is to take all the circumstances into account including any

---

[55] *Reid Minty v Taylor* [2002] 1 W.L.R. 2800.
[56] [2005] P.I.Q.R. P16.

unreasonable conduct by a Claimant such as to make such an order unfair. Accordingly, the Claimant was treated as though she had bettered her offer. Conversely, in *Painting v Oxford University Press*[57] the Claimant beat the Defendant's Part 36 payment into court, but was treated as though she had not. In *Painting*:

- The Claimant claimed damages in the region of £400,000.
- On 4th February 2004 the Defendant paid into court about £184,000.
- The Defendant then recalled that it had in its possession video surveillance evidence of the Claimant doing various things that she would not be expected to do, on account of her injuries. This evidence had been available prior to the payment into court, but seems to have been overlooked.
- Consequently, on 13th February 2004 the Defendant asked permission to withdraw all but £10,000 of the monies in court, and permission was granted.
- At trial the Claimant was found to be exaggerating her symptoms, but was awarded about £23,000.
- The judge ordered that the Defendant should pay her costs, as she had beaten the residual sum left in court.
- The Defendant appealed on the basis that the substantive issue in the case was whether or not the Claimant was exaggerating, and it had succeeded on this issue.

The Court of Appeal allowed the appeal on the basis that but for the main issue (i.e. whether the Claimant was exaggerating her symptoms) the matter would probably have settled. The judge had not taken into account that the Defendant was successful on this issue and that the Claimant had not taken any steps to negotiate settlement of the claim when deciding how to exercise his discretion on costs. These were factors that should be taken into account pursuant to Part 44. Accordingly, the Court of Appeal ordered that the Defendant should pay the Claimant's costs up to the final date for acceptance of the monies in court, and that the Claimant should pay the Defendant's costs thereafter. This is one of the most Defendant friendly decisions for a long time. It is also rather surprising, because although the decision turned on the issue of conduct, the Court of Appeal treated it as though the Claimant had failed to beat a Part 36 payment into court. It is likely that the decision in *Painting* will increasingly be marginalised as being decided on its own facts.

---

[57] [2005] P.I.Q.R. Q5.

Other Offers to Settle

Pursuant to Part 36.1(2),

> Nothing in this Part prevents a party making an offer to settle in whatever way he chooses, but if that offer is not made in accordance with this Part, it will only have the consequences specified in this Part if the court so orders.

Part 44.3(4)(c) provides that the court must have regard to any payment into court or admissible offer to settle made by a party which is drawn to its attention, whether or not it is made in accordance with Part 36. However, it is to be noted that although the existence of a non-conforming offer may be a very important consideration in the exercise of the court's discretion with regard to costs, it should not be equated precisely to a payment into court or Part 36 offer. The court retains its discretion, and the existence of such an offer should influence, but not govern, the exercise of the discretion.[58] In *Crouch v King's Healthcare N.H.S. Trust,*[59] where no payment in was made, the court held that the non-conforming offer made "was as sound as a payment in", and that it should have been treated in the same way as an offer made by way of a Part 36 payment. In the leading case of *The Trustees of Stokes Pension Fund v Western Power Distribution (South West) Plc*[60] Dyson L.J. gave guidance as to the exercise of the court's discretion in cases in which a non-conforming offer had been made. He said:

> How should the discretion accorded by CPR 36.1(2) and 44.3(4)(c) be exercised in relation to an offer made to settle a money claim where the claimant recovers less than the amount of the offer? In the absence of any guidance in the rules, it falls to the courts to provide it. I emphasise that it is a matter for the discretion of the court. It is clear from CPR 36.3(1) that the offer cannot automatically have the costs consequences specified in Part 36. The question, therefore, is what weight should be given to an offer made to settle a money claim. In my judgment, an offer should usually be treated as having the same effect as a payment into court if the following conditions are satisfied...
>
> First, the offer must be expressed in clear terms so that there is no doubt as to what is being offered. It should state whether it relates to the whole of the claim or to part of it or to an issue that arises in it, and if so to which part or issue; whether it takes into account any counterclaim; and if it is expressed not to be inclusive of interest, giving details relating to interest equivalent to those set out in CPR 36.22(2). This condition does no more

---

[58] *McDonnell v McDonnell* [1977] 1 W.L.R. 34).
[59] [2005] 1 W.L.R. 2015.
[60] [2005] 1 W.L.R. 3595.

that reflect the requirements specified in CPR 36.5(2) in relation to payments into court.

Secondly, the offer should be open for acceptance for at least 21 days and otherwise accord with the substance of a Calderbank offer.

Thirdly, the offer should be genuine and, not to use the words of Waller LJ 'sham or non-serious in some way'.

Fourthly, the defendant should clearly have been good for the money at the time when the offer was made.

To the extent that any of these conditions is not satisfied, the offer should be given less weight than a payment into court for the purposes of a decision, as to the incidence of costs. Where none of the conditions is satisfied, it is likely that the court will hold that offer affords the defendant no costs protection at all. But if all of the conditions to which I have referred are met, then I can see no reason in principle why the effect of an offer should differ from that of a payment into court. Simon Brown LJ mentioned the need to promote clarity and certainty, I agree. That is why an offer which is unclear and uncertain will usually not carry the same weight as a payment made into court. But an offer which satisfies the four conditions should by definition be no less clear or certain than a payment into court. It is important to emphasise that the purpose of a payment into court is not to provide the claimant with security for his judgment if he succeeds at trial. It is to encourage settlement.

In reality, it would be difficult for a claimant who refused an offer to contend after a trial that the offer was not genuine or that the defendant was not good for the money, unless he said that this was why he was refusing the offer at the time. In the absence of such a statement at that time, the court would be likely to infer that the reason for the refusal of the offer was simply that the claimant considered it to be too low. The best way for a claimant to test the genuineness of an offer and the defendant's ability to pay is to accept the offer (or at least to do so conditionally on payment being forthcoming) and see what happens. If this does not occur, it will be a rare case where a claimant will have any prospects of showing that the offer was not genuine or would not have been honoured.

There may be circumstances where the existence of a good practical reason for not making a payment into court would be considered to be a sufficient reason for holding that an offer should have the same costs consequences as a payment into court. But the existence of such a reason is certainly not a necessary condition for treating an offer as having such consequences. In my judgment, however, the substance and effect of the offer are more important than the reasons why the defendant did not make a payment into court.

After *Stokes Pension Fund,* therefore, non-conforming offers from reputable Defendants (such as government bodies and most insurers) will usually be treated in much the same way as Part 36 offers and payments into court, unless there is some compelling reason to the contrary. If there *is* such a reason, the Claimant must make it clear when rejecting an offer why he does so.

Part 36 Offers and Payments Made on or after 6th April 2007

The Civil Procedure (Amendment No.3) Rules 2006, which came into force on 6th April 2007, substituted a new Part 36 for the rules referred to above. The transitional arrangements are as follows:

- Where a Part 36 offer or payment was made before 6th April 2007, if it would have had the consequences set out in the old regime, it will have the consequences set out in the new regime after that date.
- Where a Part 36 offer or payment was made before 6th April 2007, the permission of the court is required to accept that offer or payment, if permission would have been required under the old regime.
- Where a Part 36 offer or payment was made less than 21 days before 6th April 2007, it will have the consequences set out in the old regime until the expiry of 21 days from the date of the offer or payment.

Offers and payments made on or after 6th April 2007 are subject to the new Part 36 contained within Schedule 1 of the 2006 Rules. The main differences between the two regimes are as follows (this list is not intended to be exhaustive):

- Most importantly, a Defendant may now make a Part 36 offer after the issue of proceedings, and need not make a Part 36 payment into court. Such an offer will have the effect of a Part 36 payment under the old rules.
- Accepted offers must be paid within 14 days, failing which the Claimant will be able to apply for judgment on the compromise and the Defendant will lose costs protection.
- A Part 36 offer must now be stated to be made pursuant to Part 36.
- A Part 36 offer must now specify a period of not less than 21 days within which the Defendant will be liable for the Claimant's costs if the offer is accepted (unless the offer is made within 21 days of trial).
- Before expiry of that period the offer may be withdrawn or reduced only if the court gives permission.
- A Part 36 offer may be accepted at any time, whether or not the offeree has subsequently made a counteroffer, unless the offeror serves notice of withdrawal on the offeree.
- A Part 36 offer or payment may be communicated to the trial judge if the offeror and offeree so agree in writing.

The amendment enshrines the ratio in *Stokes Pension Fund*, in that it is no longer necessary for Defendants to effect payments into court in order to obtain the protection of the provisions of Part 36 relating to costs. In addition, parties will need to be alert to the possibility of acceptance of an offer even after further offers and counteroffers have been made. It might, perhaps, be wise to keep a separate 'offer clip' on file so that it is clear which offers have been made, rejected and withdrawn and which remain outstanding and, therefore, capable of acceptance. In the final analysis, each costs case turns on its own facts, and more often than not there will be a decision which favours a Claimant for every decision which favours a Defendant. But the key seems to be to comply with the provisions of Part 36, whilst always taking a sensible overview in accordance with the overriding objective. Having said that, there will always be certain judges who exercise their discretion in wholly unexpected ways – and some of the cases quoted above show that when they do, they can and should be appealed.

Witnesses — court proceedings

The attendance of witnesses at court proceedings is still very important[61]. The early identification of all relevant witnesses and the taking of comprehensive witness statements is absolutely essential. Mutual exchange of witness statements is now the rule rather than the exception, and the witness statements that are exchanged will almost always stand as evidence-in-chief. Practice varies from court to court and indeed from judge to judge, but it should not be assumed that a trial judge will always grant a party the indulgence of asking "just a few supplementary questions" before surrendering the witness for cross-examination. Where such an indulgence *is* granted, courts and opponents soon tire if the "few supplementary questions" extend over more than a few minutes or trespass on matters that could quite easily have been canvassed in the original witness statement. Even where a judge prefers a witness to deal with the central issues in the case by direct, oral evidence, the exchanged witness statement provides an additional tool on which the opposition can cross-examine should any inconsistencies or omissions emerge.

Because so many witness statements will stand as evidence-in-chief, the importance of making them, *independent*, comprehensive and accurate is

---

[61] The second edition of this work suggested that the introduction of the CPR and the principle of proportionality would reduce the significance of the attendance of foreign witnesses – but old judicial habits have proved hard to displace. There remains no substitute for having the witnesses present irrespective of the cost where the witness deals with anything other than uncontroversial matters.

self-evident. *Wreford-Smith v Airtours Holidays Plc*[62] is a case that went badly wrong for the Claimants because their witness statements all had a familiar ring about them. The claimants appealed the dismissal of their claim against the defendant for personal injuries sustained in a road traffic accident. The accident occurred on a dual carriageway in Turkey. The claimants were holiday-makers returning from a package holiday booked though D, and were travelling on a coach contracted by D. The carriageway was divided from the opposite carriageway by a central reservation made up of bushes. The coach was struck by a taxi travelling in the opposite direction which, for an unexplained reason, veered across the central reservation and into the coach. As a consequence the coach veered off down an embankment and turned over many times before colliding with a pylon. There was no dispute that the driver of the taxi had been predominantly to blame for the accident. However, by these proceedings C alleged that the driver of the coach had to some extent been to blame for failing to have been sufficiently alert to the road in front and the dangers upon it, for driving the coach at a speed in excess of that permitted on the highway, and for failing to take any action in order to avoid the taxi. The judge preferred the evidence of two witnesses called on behalf of D to the extent that whilst the coach had been exceeding the speed limit, the driver had had no chance to avoid the accident since it had occurred too quickly. The trial judge was entitled to find on the evidence of two reliable witnesses that the coach driver contracted by the defendant had not been to blame for failing to take any action in order to avoid an oncoming car that had veered into his carriageway and collided with his coach. The judge took into account the fact that the burden of proving the case had rested upon C and that their evidence, contained in a number of witness statements, had been compiled five years after the event and, mostly, in very similar standard terms. It was the judge's broad conclusion that C's evidence had been a process of reconstruction and that he had preferred the evidence of the two witnesses for D to the extent that X simply had no time to react to the danger. The judge's findings were findings that had been plainly open to him to reach in light of his acceptance of D's evidence. He was entirely justified to dismiss the claim and find that despite X's speed he had not been negligent.

It is equally important to make them *accessible*. Where possible the statements should follow the path laid out in the particulars of claim, so that a judge can follow the complaints in the claim in tandem with the statement. Separate issues and complaints should be dealt with and identified separately. Documents and photographs used in the course of a witness statement should be clearly identifiable — and if there is any room for doubt in respect of their identification there is no harm in annexing copies of the

---

[62] 5th. April 2004 Court of Appeal.

central documents to the witness statement itself — even if this leads to some trifling duplication of documents in the trial bundle.

Although statements will invariably be drafted by lawyers or clerks, where possible, the actual words of the witness should be utilised. Where more than one witness speaks to the same events (*e.g.* a husband and wife in a holiday claim), they should *both* make statements from their own viewpoints. The lazy practice of one "adopting" the complaints of the other should be avoided. Witness statements should not be taken on the telephone whatever the costs considerations.[63] Where two statements are produced in such circumstances the importance of utilising the actual words of the witness becomes even more acute. It is pointless preparing two statements if one is merely a revised version of the word-processing adopted for the other. Each statement should tell its own self-contained story. Where the evidence is to come from witnesses abroad whose first language is not English, the statement should be written *in their language* of choice[64] and if necessary translated into English by an accredited translator.[65]

Claimants still often fall into the understandable trap of describing their complaints in terms of generalities that have little meaning to anyone but themselves. Holiday complaints often provide good examples of this. It is unproductive to describe anything as "appalling" or "dreadful" or even "filthy" without then going on to describe in precisely what way the facility in question was "appalling" or "filthy". To complain that an organiser's representative was "unhelpful" is itself unhelpful. To say that food was "unappetizing" may not even amount to a breach of contract. These or similar expressions may provide a useful starting point for further detailed descriptions of the individual complaints, but each must be explained in turn for the benefit of an audience who will not have any independent insight into the problems complained of.

Defendants should take care to follow a similarly rational path. The claimant's complaints should be addressed individually, and where possible, in the same order as they appear in the particulars of claim. If the particulars are not tidy enough to identify related complaints together, then there is no reason why the defendants should not inject a little rational order for themselves — for example by dealing with all the accommodation complaints together or in sequence; followed by the transportation

---

[63] See e.g. Saggerson: *A Slip in the Shower* [2003] ITLJ 74
[64] There is a proper procedure for foreign language witness statements in CPR Part 32 PD 23.1 – the original should be filed along with the translation. This process is very often ignored, but the practice of informal translation of statements and their filing only in English is much to be deplored – and the resulting evidence is surely worthless.
[65] The translator will then also have to make a statement setting out his or her qualifications and the process by which the translation was undertaken.

complaints and so on. If a statutory defence is to be relied upon, it must be remembered that it is the defendant who will have the burden of proving it, so that each element in the relevant defence is dealt with. There is nothing to be lost and everything to be gained by dealing with the statutory defence requirements under specific headings — this not only alerts the court to the main points of the defence, but helps to concentrate the minds of litigants and advisers alike as to what *actually needs to be proved*. Where it is averred, for example, that all due care was taken, the steps that amount to the taking of due care should be comprehensively recited in the statements together with clear references to any supporting documentation.

Tour operators who have devised and implemented a system of travellers' reports should be at a distinct advantage. The recording of the precise nature of complaints at the time they are made by the consumer is vital; as is *immediate* verification, and a contemporaneously noted comment by the tour operator's representative or agent. If the defendant's evidence is later consistent with what a local representative noted at the time of the complaint, the defendant's position can be immeasurably enhanced.[66] If an *independent* bystander is prepared to chaperone the defendant's representative and co-sign the contemporaneous notes then made — so much the better. Even where no complaints have been received from the consumer at the destination, a voluntarily completed questionnaire by all travellers can prove invaluable — not only as a tool to limit the scope of a claimant's complaints, but also as a means of identifying those travellers who might provide evidential support for the tour operator should the need arise.

Consumers need to take care in completing voluntary or complaints questionnaires. A complaint later pursued can be undermined if it has not been mentioned at an earlier opportunity. Legal advisers need to be made aware at the outset whether such questionnaires have been completed at any stage by the consumer. Often, a consumer will be well advised to state expressly on any forms or questionnaires, that *a full and detailed* resumé will be submitted on the consumer's return home. The pressures and anxieties of travel may otherwise lead a consumer to miss out some important aspects of his claim. He may feel harassed or pressurised to complete his forms quickly, he may not be good at written self-expression. A court would listen to any such explanation with sympathy, and it is by no means the case that any omissions would inevitably be held against the consumer. Nonetheless, where a proviso of the type suggested above is included on anything filled in

---

[66] Local representatives should always be alert to ensure that they distinguish between what they are being told by a consumer and what the representative has seen for themselves. Local "reps" also benefit from being kept informed as to *why* evidence is important and what it is for.

by the potential claimant, it is much less likely that a court would be inclined to place undue emphasis on matters not raised on the spot.[67]

The identity of those witnesses on whose evidence a party will rely will obviously depend on availability in individual cases. However, where a claimant has supporting material from fellow travellers, care should be taken to separate those matters on which the supporting witnesses can give *direct* corroborative support, and those where the picture they paint is supportive but *incidental.* For example, evidence from a fellow traveller to the effect that a tour operator's representative was drunk on one occasion is only indirectly supportive of the claimant's contention that the same representative was rude and unhelpful on other occasions. This is not to say that claimants should not use indirectly supporting evidence. On the contrary, it may be very helpful in colouring a general impression of the holiday and the representative's attitude towards his customers. Similarly, the *defendant* may wish to use supporting evidence from other travellers to provide a general impression of the facilities offered in the course of the package, or to corroborate a suggestion that the plaintiff was unreasonably demanding, or is exaggerating difficulties, that may have been more apparent than real.

It will be remembered that with compulsory mutual exchange of witness statements, the greatest tactical advantage is gained by having *more* rather than *fewer* witnesses whose evidence has been exchanged — even if one is less than optimistic that all will be able to attend a subsequent hearing (*e.g.* defendants' witnesses working abroad). No party can be forced to call a witness whose evidence has been exchanged, it is better to have prepared for the possibility of attendance, than to be left seeking permission to call additional evidence at the trial. Apart from anything else, a strong case on paper at the stage where evidence is exchanged will be tactically beneficial with regard to settlement negotiations before the matter reaches a courtroom — the opposition are not going to know who is, and who is not going to be present at the trial, and must assume that those witnesses whose evidence has been exchanged will attend to give live evidence. Claimants will need to be aware of the possibility of a defendant calling a number of witnesses from abroad. This plainly increases the costs of the litigation, and for hearings in open court, the claimant will be liable for those costs (or a significant proportion of them) in the event that his claim is unsuccessful.

---

[67] See also PTR 1992 regulation 15(9).

Foreign language witnesses

It is surprising how often witnesses whose first language is not English provide witness statements that are not only in English, but in idiomatic *legal* English. Hardly surprisingly, when this occurs, their evidence is virtually worthless. Here a few rules of thumb.

a. If an overseas witness is not English but speaks fluent English (fluent enough that is to cope with the stresses and strains of cross-examination in a foreign [English] courtroom[68]) then this should be stated in the opening and introductory part of any witness statement. This is important for all witnesses, but particularly those whose evidence is to be admitted pursuant to the Civil Evidence Act 1995 as hearsay.

b. If there is any doubt about the witnesses fluency in English (in the sense described above) then that witness should first make a statement in their *native* language. The reason it is important to do it this way round (rather than have an original English statement translated into the foreign language) is that someone else is bound to be the author of the original English statement and it is all the more likely, therefore, that it will; not be the actual words of the witness and even worse, it is likely to contain English language expressions and nuances that are quite literally "foreign" to the witness.

c. Once a foreign language statement has been taken it should then be translated into English by an accredited translator and the translation together with a verifying certificate of accuracy filed with the original foreign language statement.

d. Permission should be obtained from the Court at the earliest available Directions hearing for the foreign language statement to be filed in this way. The process is explained in CPR Part 32 PD 23.2.

It is *not* appropriate to have someone simultaneously translate an English language statement into the foreign language and use the evidential provisions for blind or illiterate witnesses to certify that the statement has been read over, understood and verified. One cannot deny that this process is expensive but unfortunately it is necessary and the incidental costs inevitable where litigation involves overseas witnesses. It goes without saying that any witness whose written evidence is taken in a foreign language will need a court accredited interpreter in the event that they attend to give "live" evidence at any trial or hearing.

---

[68] It cannot be over-emphasised that a witness whose English is perfectly adequate – even admirable – in the context of offering tourist services to holidaymakers abroad may genuinely struggle with courtroom and legal English and in doing so may unjustly appear to be prevaricating.

Taking "live" evidence through an interpreter is a much undervalued and under-practised skill. It is even more vital than usual that questions are short and direct – and that issues are divided up into very small pieces for the witness to address in a logical sequence. Questions based on assumed propositions (disputed facts), counter-factual and conditional questions are to be avoided if the questioning (and thus inevitably the evidence) is not to descend into unhelpful confusion. Interpreters should always speak in the first person when answering questions – that is, as the voice of the witness, never in reported speech.

"Real evidence"

A tour operator (now defunct) once defended a claim brought by a holiday claimant whose main contention was that the food — particularly the daily packed lunches — provided during the currency of the package holiday were unfit for human consumption. The tour operator robustly contended that the claims were exaggerated, and that the claimant's real problem was that she was unaccustomed to foreign food. After considerable cross-examination on this basis, the claimant announced triumphantly that she could *prove* the tour operator wrong because she had *brought an example of a packed lunch with her.* Reaching into a plastic carrier bag she pulled out a foil-wrapped bundle containing an example of a packed lunch. Given that the holiday had taken place nearly two years previously, nobody was very keen to permit the claimant to open the lunch in the courtroom until it emerged that the lunch in question had been prepared by the claimant *that morning* only as an example of what she had been provided whilst on holiday. There could be no doubt that if her mock-up lunch bore any passing resemblance to the standard of food offered by the tour operator, the holiday food was manifestly unfit for human consumption. The claimant won her case.[69]

The production of the example, in reality, was no better than the claimant's oral description of her holiday lunches (this was in the days before exchange of witness statements). The *impact* of the production of the mock-up would, however, be difficult to exaggerate — particularly as the claimant waited (whether by accident or design) until the conclusion of her cross-examination before producing it. Indeed, until the production of the mock-up her complaints seemed rather trivial and overstated. It should not be necessary to go to the extremes encountered in another case, this time about food poisoning, where the claimant's doctor stated in his medical report *"I have enclosed a copy of Mrs Smith's stool for reference"*. Happily, he meant a copy of the laboratory analysis.

---

[69] See Grant & Mason: *Holiday Law* 3rd. edition page 469 for some other eye-opening examples of "real evidence".

In most cases the production of "real evidence" of this type will not be possible. However, examples of real evidence can and should be deployed where it is feasible by both claimants and defendants. It *will* often be feasible to produce examples of materials in issue in an action and the impact of such production is invariably considerable.[70]

The use of photographs and videos should certainly be maximised. In the case of claimants this will usually entail looking at their holiday "snaps", and in many cases a claimant may have taken pictures of those aspects of a package that have been the cause of concern or complaint. Additionally, however, closer examination of the "snaps" may disclose helpful pictures *in the background* even where the primary purpose of the photograph may not have been to illustrate a complaint at all. Claimants should not hesitate to get such pictures enlarged in order to focus on the relevant background. Photographs or videos taken by fellow travellers are also worth following up. If a claimant launches a complaint on his return to this country armed with a list of willing supporters from amongst his holiday friends and acquaintances, one of the first things that might be done is to see if any of these other travellers is in possession of photographs or videos capable of lending "real" support to any aspect of the claimant's claim. Even if rounding up supportive witnesses from all parts of the country and abroad is unrealistic in any given case, the production of photographs under cover of a Civil Evidence Act notice may be just as good.

Defendants may also take advantage of this. A video of a resort, or part of a resort or hotel, facility or service, following complaint by a consumer, may help to put the consumer's complaints into some sort of proper perspective. If the video (or photograph) is taken specifically in response to a given complaint, then the pictures can specifically address the complaints made. General promotional videos and pictures are unlikely to be of much assistance. If the video or pictures are "self-dated" then so much the better. If a video is shot in response to a consumer complaint, its value will depend on its *integrity*. If the pictures are clearly restricted or selective, the evidence could be counter-productive. Similarly, if certain aspects of the consumer's complaints are left out, an inference may arise that they have been left out because the video would be unfavourable to the defendant. Plainly, the sooner after receipt of a complaint any pictorial evidence can be secured, the better.

As with all types of evidence, it is important for both Claimants and Defendants to consider photographs and videos *as a whole*. Where reliance is to be placed on holiday "snaps", *all* such "snaps" will have to be disclosed. Claimants should bear in mind when making complaints and particularly

---

[70] For example: small samples of non-slip flooring or floor-coverings.

when drafting witness statements, that their evidence about the travel arrangements in question is consistent with the whole *body* of photographic evidence. A Claimant complaining about a filthy swimming pool may be undermined if photographic evidence shows him to be having a whale of a time in that very pool. The fact that a consumer used a particular pool does not mean necessarily that it was clean and fresh — but it certainly reduces the level at which the claimant can claim his enjoyment and expectations were affected. This is true even if the Claimant does not seek to rely on any photographs himself. The defendant is perfectly entitled to call for inspection of the claimant's holiday pictures — as relevant documents — whenever a claimant maintains that his enjoyment was reduced by reason of the matters complained of. The photographs may only show that the consumer's enjoyment of the holiday was not reduced *by that much*, but this may be a significant issue nonetheless, both in terms of liability and quantum.

Real evidence and the CPR

The production of photographs and videos by either side in a travel-related claim, together with plans, maps and relevant extracts from accidents books, maintenance records will enhance the prospects of an application for a peremptory judgement — either by way of summary judgement under CPR Part 24 of by way of striking out under CPR Part 3.4. The remedy of summary judgement is new for defendants and it represents a useful tool for attempting to dispose of feeble claims that may be arguable but where there is no real prospects of succeeding on the claim. Defendants in particular may need to use these new opportunities in order to test the approach of local courts so as to determine the extent to which such hearings will take the form of brisk, peremptory trials, or whether in fact *any* prospect of success is regarded by the court in question as a "real" prospect. Nonetheless, the early availability and presentation of "real" evidence may enhance the prospects of either side at this summary stage and the watering — down of the summary judgement test for both claimants, and now Defendants, in the Civil Procedure Rules — justifying the principle of "front-loading" case preparation which underlies so much of the CPR thinking. Naturally, defendants are not well placed to take advantage of this if their staff are not equipped by training and facilities to obtain the information that is necessary — be this photographs, samples, or copies of maintenance records.

Medical evidence

For classic personal injury cases the need for medical evidence is not likely to be overlooked — especially as court rules require the filing of a medical report with the particulars of claim[71] — if medical evidence is to be relied upon at all. In very minor cases, it may well be that no medical evidence is needed — (*e.g.* cases involving short-term gastric illness or modest whiplash).

The same is true of travel cases. Medical evidence is not compulsory even where the claim involves allegations of physical distress, anxiety or other forms of mental anguish, or minor physical ailments. In cases of minor physical or mental distress following breach of a travel contract, it may well be that evidence from relatives and friends can support the claimant's claims. Very often the claimant's evidence alone will suffice. However, whatever the nature of the personal injury or illness that is alleged, be it mental or physical, long term or transient, there is no doubt that a court is unlikely to consider the injury of much significance in the absence of medical evidence. If the ailment, whatever it may be, has not been considered sufficiently serious by a claimant to warrant medical intervention — even for the purposes of a report — then the court is not usually inclined to award sums in damages on other than a fairly nominal basis. The reporting doctor may not be able to bear witness to the fact that the claimant *is* ill, but he may well be able to provide supporting evidence of the likely consequences and effects of an illness the claimant says he has suffered, and identify some of those after effects (which is no more than many medical reports in standard personal injury cases can do in any event). Even better, if medical attention is sought at a relatively early stage, the doctor may well be able to verify from what he can then establish or see with his own eyes, that the claimant has plainly *been* ill in the manner alleged. So, even in relatively minor cases, the provision of medical evidence can be useful. Seldom is a claimant disbelieved or doubted when a doctor gives the evidence — even if all the doctor is doing is reciting what the claimant said for himself in the course of a medical interview. Medical records from a local doctor or hospital, or even copies of prescriptions issued abroad may also help to support any travel case with an injury element.

Other experts

The need for experts on foreign law, practice and foreign standards should be considered. This will be relevant in at least two important situations. The first is where (outside the PTR 1992) action is contemplated in England in respect of an accident abroad where it is necessary to prove fault in accordance with the law of the place where the accident occurred.[72] This calls for legal expert evidence to prove as a fact what the foreign applicable law states.

---

[71] CPR 16PD4.3.
[72] Private International Law (Miscellaneous Provisions) Act 1995 - section 11.

The second situation is where pursuant to the PTR 1992 a tour operator is sued for breach of an English contract but arising out of the default of a supplier of package services causing an accident due to questionable local safety standards. Most tour operators will be careful to ensure that they agree as part of the package contract to comply with safety standards of the locality where the package holiday takes place. Before it can successfully be alleged that there has been a failure in, or improper performance of,[73] the package, it will be necessary to prove what the local safety standards are[74] and to what extent (if any) the standard has been breached. It is incumbent on the consumer or claimant to show that by failing to comply with local safety standards the "*other party to the contract*" or his agent has failed in the proper performance of the package holiday contract in question.[75] Until such a "failure" on the part of the tour operator or his agents can be proved, there will be no case for the tour operator to answer in respect of the questionable safety standards.[76] It cannot be assumed, in cases where foreign safety standards are in issue, that the accident itself will raise a presumption that local safety requirements have been breached.

[73] PTR 1992 regulation 15(1) and (2).
[74] And whether it is a regulatory standard or a general law standard – see further Chapter 4.
[75] See Chapter 4. The onus of proof that a breach of contract has occurred does not shift to the defendant simply because the defendant is an organiser of foreign holidays.
[76] But refer also to Chapter 4 for examples where tour operators sometimes prove the Claimant's case for him in this regard by maintaining that standards were higher than they in fact were – e.g. *Wren v Unijet*.

Chapter 15

STATEMENTS OF CASE AND DOCUMENTS

Introduction

In this final chapter a number of sample documents and statements of case have been produced. They are described as samples rather than precedents. It can be dangerous to copy a given example without making appropriate and sometimes radical changes to suit the particulars and facts of a given case, and without giving consideration in individual case to the reasons why certain causes of action, allegations and now *evidence* should be referred to. Whilst the title as well as the language of many court documents has recently changed it remains to be seen whether the substance of litigants' statements of case will be significantly altered from what should always have represented good practice before the rule changes. Few model documents have been prepared and little guidance given as to how statements of case should now be prepared and presented. The absence of such guidance is no doubt deliberately designed to emphasise that the statement of case should set out the litigant's case on the facts, the law and the evidence in a format which is most suitable and proportionate to the dispute in hand without undue formality and without slavish adherence to any prescribed model. The purpose of any statement of case is to communicate to the other side and to the court the factual, evidential and legal *issues* which need to be resolved between the parties. The clear identification of issues should help concentrate the mind on what *evidence* is required to prove each party's case in respect of the identified issues.

Statements of Case

Claimants

A number of different examples are given in the specimen documents that follow. Claim forms for quality and injury cases are attempted, together with a variety of Particulars of Claim. The Particulars of Claim do not stray far from what might have been expected previously, although it is perfectly acceptable to annex to such Particulars any documents relied on or referred to in the body of the document. As before, in the interests of clarity, headings and sub-headings with clear paragraph and sub-paragraph numbering cannot be over-used in order to identify the points being made.

Defences

A defence must provide a comprehensive response to the Particulars of Claim. Denials must be accompanied with an explanation for the denial or an alternative version of facts on which the Defendant relies and whilst it is still permissible to "not admit" an allegation, or rather to require that the allegation be proved by the Claimant, it is thought that some reason must be given as to why the Defendant is unable to address the point more specifically. There is no general rule which requires a defendant to state the basis of any legal defence, to refer to or annex any documents, or to name witnesses on whose evidence reliance will be placed, but it is likely to be better if matters of law and evidence can be addressed in the Defence with the same particularity as they receive in the Particulars of Claim.

Statements of truth

All statements of case should include a statement of truth. The purpose of the statement of truth, it is submitted, is principally evidential and generated by a drive for efficiency. If a party has verified the statement of case there should be no need in straightforward cases for further affidavits or sworn witness statements for the purposes of pre-trial hearings or applications. It remains to be seen whether such statements of truth are taken any more seriously than the oath or affirmation behind the *jurat* of an affidavit. It is a contempt of court to make such a statement falsely, though not perjury as the statement of truth is not sworn. It is the *facts* in the statement of truth that the claimant declares to be true, but there is no apparent reason why such a statement of truth cannot honestly and properly be made where the facts verified are secondary facts or matters which appear to flow as a matter of reasonable inference from primary facts within the claimant's or defendant's own personal knowledge. The statement of truth on a case statement is, however, likely to be used as a vehicle through which to cross-examine any party whose case evolves in a manner inconsistent with the statement of case.

Further information

The Request for Further Information replaces the Request for Further and Better Particulars and Interrogatories. It can be either an informal process, or formalised by order of the court. Whether preparing documents for the court or for the opposition, the best rule of thumb is never to assume that the reader knows what you are talking about.

Preliminary applications

Applications for summary judgment on either side or to strike out a case statement should be made before or with the filing of the allocation questionnaire.

Allocation

It is not only the value of the action that is important in terms of allocation to the appropriate track under the CPR. A number of other factors should play an important role in allocation. Many of these additional factors may be of particular relevance to travel claims — including holiday cases. The notes for completing the allocation questionnaire printed on the document itself create the impression without further reference to the rules that *value* is all-important. Whilst the value of an action is unquestionably a significant — if not the most significant factor — conscientious completion of the questionnaire may result in the allocation of many travel and holiday claims to a "higher" level than value alone might imply. The factors that ought to be taken into account when completing the allocation questionnaire which might have a particular bearing on travel claims are:

- the likely complexity of the facts, law and evidence;

- the number of parties;

- the amount of oral evidence;

- the importance of the claim to those who are not parties to the litigation (test cases);

- whether in the light of the above the trial is likely to last for more than one day;

- the views of the parties as to appropriate allocation.

Cases of public importance or test cases can be allocated to the multi-track in the High Court where appropriate. However, unless the procedural judge is alerted to the factors additional to value that might have an impact on the allocation of the case, the headline value placed on the action by the parties is likely to dominate allocation considerations. One counter-veiling factor which may keep a travel case in the small claims track or fast track is the *circumstances of the parties* particularly when this is weighed in conjunction with the overriding objective provisions, especially the first that exhorts to courts to keep the parties on an equal footing where practicable.

Nonetheless, even in cases of relatively modest value travel cases are likely to disclose some of the following issues:

- conflicts of law;

- evidence of (and disputes concerning) foreign law;

- conflicts of national health and safety standards (with conflicting expert evidence);

- factual evidence that may be more efficiently taken orally (at least as regards primary issues such as quality standards, complaints and accidents);

- factual evidence from a travel service organiser is likely to be of an extended nature as in order to demonstrate past good practice, and exercise of reasonable care in respect of the services supplied to the claimants, several witnesses at different levels of the organiser's administration may be required to illustrate how good practice has been implemented;

- the number of factual witnesses can be many, even in the context of a family holiday — particularly where friends and supporters are acting as corroborative witnesses;

- some factual witnesses may be coming from abroad, and some (from the direct local service supplier) may have to give their evidence through an interpreter;

- even cases of modest value can be of major public importance or at least of significance to other travellers on the same package or trip [who may be waiting for the result of the lead case] — and this factor is just as important to the defending tour operator or organiser whose liability exposure is potentially far greater than the value of the case being allocated;

- as seen repeatedly throughout the course of this book there are many issues on the interpretation of the 1992 Regulations and the general law affecting travel case which have yet to be the subject of any authoritative decisions.

Where a Part 20 claim is anticipated, and this involves the introduction of a foreign service provider or joint tortfeasor, the above potential complexities are likely to be multiplied accordingly.

It is thought that there will be many travel-related claims — involving packages and other causes of action — which justify allocation above the headline value attributed to the claim by the parties.

Identifying Issues

It is, therefore, of crucial importance that issues in the action are identified clearly in the defence case statement, and further outlined in the appropriate boxes provided in the allocation questionnaire. The early identification of the issues that are likely to occupy the court's time was, perhaps, always the purpose of pleadings. The rule changes introduced in April 1999 are, more than anything else, designed to remind practitioners and reinforce this element of best practice in pre-trial documents.

Protocols

As yet there is no travel or holiday claims pre-action protocol and a multiparty protocol (though expected) is not yet published. Plainly, where there is a personal injury element within the scope of the fast track by reason of its value, the personal injury protocol should be followed. In cases where there is no personal injury element, the parties are nonetheless, exhorted to follow the "cards on the table" spirit of the protocol and compliance with the recommendation for early and frank communication between the parties should be followed wherever possible in injury cases outside the fast track and, it is suggested, for smaller quality complaint cases as well. The advantage for claimants in providing early pre-action information to the organiser, is that such candour is likely to reduce the scope for references in the defence case statement to an insufficiency of time within which to identify and obtain foreign evidence or factual evidence from foreign sources or obtain records from foreign administrative offices. Both sides should be ready and willing to disclose relevant documentation to each other at an early stage of the pre-action communications. This not only reduces the need for additional disclosure at a later stage, but helps both sides identify what are likely to be the real issues for the court ultimately to decide — and this process should be seen simply as part of the renewed importance of *issue identification* in the statements of case filed for both claimants and defendants. The fact that a defendant may often be constrained at an early stage to admit certain unpalatable facts[21] that would formerly have been "not admitted":

- this does not mean that claimants cannot be required to prove facts of which the defendant has no knowledge and no means of obtaining such knowledge where this is appropriate;

- candour should not be seen as a sign of weakness — rather the opportunity should be taken by defendants in pre-action communication and in the statement of case and allocation procedures, to concentrate on the issues of fact and law that represent their strongest points, and in the process of this concentration of effort the impression may rightly be given that the defence case is a strong one, or a strongly arguable one at an early stage. In turn this may incline the court more readily to exercise its new and more vigorous powers to strike out the claimant's case or grant summary judgment to the *defendant* where the claimant's case appears to have no reasonable prospects of success. For defendants, highlighting the good cases and arguable issues may pay dividends over hiding everything (good, bad or indifferent) in a sequence of bare denials and non-admissions.

Overriding objective

Cases must be dealt with justly, and in a manner likely to keep the parties on an equal footing whilst where practicable saving expense. Costs and time must be proportionate to the importance of the case and the amount of money involved and should be dealt with expeditiously.

In many routine travel-related cases the implementation of the overriding objective will place real constraints on the time, effort and money that can be devoted to litigation. It is all the more important, therefore, wherever possible in these routine claims to litigate them in accordance with administrative or office systems designed to maximise efficiency. Accordingly, using standard form statements of case and maximising the use of annexes or appendices is likely to be encouraged and cost-effective.

What follows is a sequence of documents which can be adopted and *adapted* to suit a number of eventualities.

Customer Questionnaire

1. What company supplied your holiday?

2. Which travel agent did you use?

3. When did you book?

4. When did you pay your deposit?

5. When did you pay your final instalment?

6. Do you still have the invoices/receipts? (Please send copies)

7. How many people in your party (that is covered by your invoice)?

8. Where did you go on holiday? Was it given a descriptive name *e.g.* "Mystical East"?

9. Date of departure and date of return?

10. How did you choose your holiday — brochure/advert/recommendation/travel agent?

11. Were there any special reasons for your holiday — wedding/honeymoon/retirement/redundancy/inheritance?

12. Was there any one special facility you were looking forward to — sports/tours/tuition/a particular sight?

13. Did you tell anyone about 11 or 12 above on the booking form or at the travel agent?

14. Overall (despite your complaints) would you rate your holiday as — very good/good/satisfactory/very satisfactory/miserable/appalling/worse than not having a holiday at all?

15. Do your complaints concern one factor in particular or a combination of factors?

16. Have you completed any complaints or comments form before now? If so where, when and at whose request did you complete such a form?

17. Please complete the "Summary of Complaints" in your own words.

Summary of Complaints

Please state briefly the nature of your complaint under each heading.

1.   ADVANCE INFORMATION

      (itineraries, ticketing, travel advice etc)   (a)

                                                                               (b)

2.   POINT OF DEPARTURE

                                                                               (a)

      (reception at airport, seaport or other departure point)   (b)

3.   ARRIVAL AT DESTINATION   (a)

      (airport, seaport etc)

                                                                               (b)

4.   HOTEL/RESORT RECEPTION   (a)

      (transfer/readiness of rooms)   (b)

5.   HOTEL QUALITY   (a)

      (i) rooms/bathrooms

      (ii) bars and restaurants   (b)

      (iii) reception/portering

      (iv) location   (c)

      (v) other services

6.   COURIER SERVICES

      (i) arrival/departure   (a)

      (ii) during stay

    (iii) helpfulness   (b)

    (iv) knowledgability

    (v) problem solving   (c)

7.   OTHER FACILITIES

    (i) sports   (a)

    (ii) health/fitness

    (iii) night life   (b)

    (iv) activities

    (v) tours/trips   (c)

8.   SPECIAL NEEDS

    Did you have any special needs that were not met?   (a)

    (b)

Claim Form	In the County Court
	Claim No:

Package Holiday Claim   SEAL

1.
2.
3.
Claimant(s)

1.
2.
3.
Defendant(s)

Brief details of Claim:
The Claimant(s) claim is for damages for breach of a package holiday contract pursuant to regulation 15 of the Package Travel (Etc.) Regulations 1992 and for interest on damages pursuant to section 69 of the County Courts Act 1984. Full particulars are given overleaf, in respect of an accident on 15 July 2002 in Paphos, Greece.

The value of this action will not exceed £15,000.00

Defendant(s) name & address:	Court Fee	
	Solicitor's Costs	To be assessed.
	Issue Date:	

Claim No:........................

Does, or will your claim include any issues under the Human Rights Act 1998?

Yes •   No •

Particulars of Claim:

1.   **The Defendant(s) supplied a package holiday to the Claimant(s).**

    1.1   Between   *State the dates*

> Outbound date:
> Return date:

    1.2   At   *Name the hotel or accommodation*

> Name:
> Rating in brochure:

    1.3   In   *Identify the country, region and/or resort*

    1.4   For a price of   *State the inclusive price paid for holiday*

> £

    1.5   The price included   *Specify what was included in the holiday price paid before departure*

> **Delete** Any *Inappropriate* Components
>
> (a) Accommodation
> (b) Return transport by air / sea / rail
> (c) Airport transfers by coach / car / other
> (d) Pre-paid excursion(s) called.....................................
> ....
> ....
> (e) Other features:
> Ski-packs/equipment hire
> Tours
> Leisure Park Entry
> Car Hire
> Shuttle transport
> *Others/specify*.............................
> ....
> ....

2.   **By reason of regulation 15 of the Package Travel (Etc.) Regulations 1992 the Defendant(s) is liable for the proper performance of the holiday contract and for any damage caused by any failure to perform**

or improper performance of the contract (whether the contract was performed by the Defendant(s) or agents, suppliers or subcontractors..

3. The holiday contract included the following express or implied terms.

    3.1 The holiday would be provided as described in the holiday brochure and/or promotional material.
    3.2 The facilities and services comprising the holiday would be of a reasonable standard and commensurate with the holiday description.
    3.3 The services and facilities comprising the holiday would be delivered with reasonable skill and care.

4. In breach of contract the holiday was not supplied as described and/or failed to reach a reasonable standard and/or the services and facilities were not supplied with reasonable skill and care.

PARTICULARS

Complaints about Accommodation:	(a) (b) (c)
Complaints about Food/Drink:	(a) (b) (c)
Facilities/services promised but not provided or provided badly (say why):	(a) (b) (c)
Complaints about transport:	(a) (b) (c)
Complaints about staff:	(a) (b) (c)
Other complaints – give brief details:	(a) (b) (c)

5. **Because of the above the holiday was worthless or worth significantly less than the price paid and the Claimant(s) who suffered loss of enjoyment, anxiety and distress. The claim includes claims for damages for:**

    5.1   Diminution in the value of the holiday

    5.2   Loss of enjoyment

Special Feature	Tick	Comment (optional)
(a) Wedding		
(b) "Honeymoon" or second "honeymoon"		
(c) Special Birthday		
(d) Anniversary		
(e) Retirement		
(f) Sports and recreation		
(g) Once in a lifetime holiday		
(h) Others – give brief details:		

    5.3   Expenses incurred as a result of the breaches of contract.

Item	Amount	Comment
Taxis	£	
Other transport	£	Details:
Food	£	Give reason why cost incurred:

Drink	£	
Clothing	£	Specify what:
Cleaning materials	£	Explain what:
Alternative accommodation	£	Specify where:
Alternative activities	£	Specify what:
Other Expenses:	£	*Give brief details:*

6. **Interest is claimed pursuant to section 69 of the County Courts Act 1984:**

    6.1 On damages for diminution in value at 6% from the date the holiday was paid for [*date:*   ] and on expenses at 6% from the date the holiday ended [*date:*   ];

    6.2 On damages for loss of enjoyment at 2% from the date the holiday ended as stated above.

    6.3 All interest is claimed to the date of judgment or sooner payment.

7. **The following copies of documents are attached to this Claim Form and Particulars of Claim.**

COPY DOCUMENT	TICK
Confirmation Invoice	
Payment receipt	
Photocopy of relevant brochure page(s) [Number..........]	
Itinerary	
Letter of Complaint [dated........................]	
Reply from Defendant [dated....................]	
Photograph(s) [State how many................]	

> Other(s)
> [*specify*...
> ....

Statement of Truth [delete as appropriate]
I believe [the Claimant believes] that **the facts stated in this Claim Form are true.**
[I am duly authorized by the Claimant to sign this statement].

Signed... [Claimant or Litigation Friend if the Claimant is a minor or patient] [Claimant's solicitor].

Full name..

Name of Claimant's solicitor's firm...

Position or office held [if signing for a company].

Claimant's or Claimant's solicitor's address to which documents should be sent including [if appropriate] details of fax, DX or e-mail.

IN THE MANCHESTER COUNTY COURT

CLAIM NO:

BETWEEN:

RACEY CARR

Claimant

-and-

THIRD CHOICE HOLIDAYS LIMITED

Defendant

PARTICULARS OF CLAIM
Slippers and Trippers

---

1. By a contract evidenced in the Defendant's confirmation invoice booking reference 129171/501, the Defendant supplied to the Claimant and her family a package holiday between 15 and 26 May 2001 comprising international flights and accommodation at the Lagotel Hotel, Alcudia, Majorca ("the Hotel") for the price of £1,405.00.

2. The Package Travel [Etc.] Regulations 1992 applied to the package holiday supplied to the Claimant by virtue of which the Defendant is liable to the Claimant for any damage sustained as a result of the improper performance of the services comprising part of the package irrespective of whether those services were provided by the Defendant or one of it suppliers.

3. There was an implied term of the package holiday contract to the effect that the facilities and services forming part of the accommodation at the Hotel provided as part of the package holiday would be provided with reasonable care and skill.

4. The owners or managers of the Hotel and their employees were suppliers of the Defendant.

5. The Hotel was served by lifts including lifts leading to the Reception area of the Hotel close to the entrance of the swimming pool area and the Hotel bar.

6. On 20 May 2001 the Claimant was descending in the lift to collect her son from the children's club. As she entered the lift the Claimant noticed a pool of water on the lift floor. As she attempted to exit the lift on the ground floor a crush of other guests entered the lift, and in attempting to get out of the lift the Claimant slipped in the puddle of water, did the "splits" and injured her knee.

7. The accident was caused by the negligence and/or fault of the managers or proprietors of the Hotel for whom the Defendant is liable by virtue of the said Regulations and/or by reason of the improper performance of the holiday contract.

PARTICULARS

7.1 The lift was used routinely by those who had used the hotel swimming pool and was known as such by the Hotel because of its proximity to the pool area and because of the existence of a notice warning of the likely slipperiness of the floor in the area outside the lift (which notice had not been seen by the Claimant before the accident).

7.2 It was at all material times known to the Hotel due to the above that wet persons or persons with wet feet were foreseeably likely to use the lift and that as a result the lift floor would become wet.

7.3 Despite the ease with which such precautions might have been taken the Hotel failed to carpet the lift floor or otherwise protect it in such a way as was likely to absorb water deposited by Hotel guests.

7.4 The hotel failed to provide any absorbent surface or matting outside the lift or in the foyer to reduce the risk of the lift floor becoming and remaining wet.

7.5 The hotel caused or permitted the floor of the lifts to become and remain hazardous for guests using the same in the ordinary course of their visit.

8. As a result of the accident the Claimant has suffered injury, loss and damage.

PARTICULARS OF INJURY

The Claimant was born on 27 October 1973.

She suffered torn ligaments to the right knee from which she has made a reasonable recovery.

Full particulars of the injuries are set out in the medical report of Mr. Brown FRCS dated 29 July 2008 which is served with this Particulars of Claim.

PARTICULARS OF SPECIAL DAMAGE

A schedule of loss is served with this Particulars of Claim.

In addition the Claimant claims –

Damages for the loss of enjoyment of the second half of the Claimant's holiday and that of her family and damages from diminution in value thereof.

9.   The Claimant's claim is for damages within the meaning of section 69 of the County Courts Act 1984 pursuant to which she claims interest at 2% on general damages and 3% on special damage accrued at the date of trial or settlement or interest at such rates and for such periods as the court shall think fit.

10. The estimated value of this action will exceed £1,000.00 but not £15,000.00.

AND THE CLAIMANT CLAIMS:

1.   DAMAGES
2.   INTEREST by virtue of paragraph 9 above – to be assessed.

A BARRISTER

STATEMENT OF TRUTH

I believe that the facts set out in this Particulars of Claim are true.

Etc.

IN THE RELEVANT COUNTY COURT

CLAIM NO:

BETWEEN:

GEORGE CROSS

Claimant

-and-

(1)   MARK SPENCER
(2)   MARY SPENCER

Defendants

PARTICULARS OF CLAIM
Holiday Let

---

1.   By a contract evidenced in an exchange of emails culminating with that dated 24 September 2003 from the Second Defendant to the Claimant, the First and Second Defendant agreed to let to the Claimant and his family for the purposes of a holiday, the Villa Splendida, Mallorca, ("the Villa") between the 12 and 28 August 2007 for which the Claimant paid a deposit of £200 and a balance of €2,115.00.

2.   There were implied terms of the said holiday let, implied in order to give effect to the presumed common intention of the parties and/or by virtue of section 13 of the Supply of Good and Services Act 1982 to the following effect namely that:

(a)   The facilities at the Villa would be of a reasonable standard.
(b)   Reasonable skill and care would be exercised in the provision of the facilities and services at the Villa.
(c)   The Villa would be equipped with lighting to a reasonable standard, such standard being that to which ordinary visitors might reasonably expect to find in their own homes.
(d)   The Villa would be reasonably maintained and/or in reasonable condition in all relevant respects at the time the Claimant and his family arrived for their holiday on 14 August 2004.

3.   The Claimant and his family arrived on 12 August 2004.

4.   During the course of that first night, on or about 13 August 2004, the Claimant had occasion to use the main bathroom.

5.   Having risen barefoot from his bed and having switched on the hall light the Claimant went to the main bathroom in the Villa in order to use the toilet. As he

entered the main bathroom (which was his first visit there) he reached for the light switch to operate the bathroom lights, tried two such switches on the wall by the bathroom door but the lights did not work.

6. The Claimant was constrained to feel his way around the bathroom and in particular behind the door to find the toilet as he could not see where he was going and as he proceeded his left foot made contact with a glass toilet brush holder which fractured on contact and the Claimant stood on the splintered glass injuring his left foot.

7. The accident was caused as a result of the breach of contract of the Defendants and/or the negligence of the Defendant and/or their servants or agents.

PARTICULARS

(a) Failing to provide a main bathroom with lights that worked from the switches near the entrance door as any reasonable visitor would have expected.
(b) Providing a desk lamp perched on top of a bathroom cabinet to provide lighting to the main bathroom without making it clear to visitors that this was the main source of light for the main bathroom.
(c) Failing to provide a bathroom facility to a reasonable standard and/or with reasonable skill and care.
(d) Failing to ensure that the bathroom lights were workable from their light switches before the Claimant took up occupancy of the Villa.
(e) Failing to warn the Claimant and his family of the danger presented by the absence of working light switches in the main bathroom.
(f) Failing to devise or implement any or any adequate system of inspection and/or maintenance in respect of the premises.
(g) Providing a dangerous glass brush-holder rather than a shatter-proof or metal or plastic one.
(h) Subjecting and exposing the Claimant to the foreseeable risk of injury.

8. The Claimant relies on the fact that there was a desk lamp positioned in the bathroom as evidence that the Defendants and/or their servants or agents knew that there was a fault with the bathroom light switches.

9. The Claimant also relies on the proposition that the facts speak for themselves.

10. As a result of the accident the Claimant suffered injury, loss and damage.

PARTICULARS OF INJURY

The Claimant was born on 29 March 1973. He sustained a severe laceration to the left foot that required hospitalisation and repair of severed tendons. The medical report of [____] dated [___] is filed and served with this Particulars of Claim.

PARTICULARS OF LOSS AND DAMAGE

A Schedule of Loss and Damage is filed and served with this Particulars of Claim. Furthermore, the accident occurred on the first night of the Claimant's holiday and as a result he and his family lost any benefit from the holiday. The Claimant claims a refund of the cost of the family holiday plus damages for loss of enjoyment (at large).

11. The Claimant's claim is for damages within the meaning of section 69 of the County Courts Act 1984 pursuant to which he claims interest at such rates and for such periods as the court shall think fit.

12. The estimated value of this action will not exceed £15,000.00, but the value of damages for pain and suffering will exceed £1,000.00.

A COUNSELLOR

STATEMENT OF TRUTH

I declare that the contents of this Particulars of Claim are true.

Signed

Dated

TO THE DISTRICT JUDGE AND TO THE DEFENDANTS

Dated this [___] day of [___] 2007.

IN THE HIGH COURT OF JUSTICE

QUEEN'S BENCH DIVISION

1999 - Z - NO: 001

BETWEEN:

ZELDA ZOOM & OTHERS

Claimants

-and-

HOLIDAYS LIMITED

Defendant

PARTICULARS OF CLAIM

(Food Poisoning & Quality Complaints)

1. The Defendant carries on business as an organiser and supplier of package holidays. Each of the Claimants specified in the Schedule to the was a consumer within the meaning of the Package Travel, Package Holidays and Package Tours Regulations 1992 ["the 1992 Regulations"] to whom the Defendant supplied a package holiday at the Hotel Splendid, in Zenda, Ruritania.

2. (a) The dates of the Claimants' respective holidays were as follows:

(i) Zenda Zoom — 29 June to 13 July 1999

(ii) Zachary Zoom — 29 June to 13 July 1999

(iii) John Brown — 17 to 30 September 1999

(iv) Audrey Brown — 17 to 30 September 1999

(v) Julie Joop — 30 September to 13 October 1999

(b) Each of the holidays supplied was evidenced by a Confirmation Invoice respectively numbered: S12345 (Zoom); S54321 (Brown) and S13245 (Joop).

3. There were express and/or implied terms or warranties in the contracts by which the Defendant supplied the package holidays to each of the Claimants by reason of the contents of the Defendant's Ruritania '99 brochure, the Defendant's standard terms and conditions set out therein, and/or by reason of regulation 6 of the Regulations to the following effect, namely that the Hotel Splendid:

(i) was of a 5-star standard (that is to say of a first class or alternatively a high and/or better than average standard);

(ii) had kitchen, food preparation, cleanliness, hygiene and accommodation standards commensurate with its 5-star rating;

(iii) had such standards of cleanliness and hygiene as to keep the Claimants reasonably free from the risk of illness;

(iv) was air conditioned;

(v) had a gymnasium, a strip club and 15 bars on the premises;

(vi) offered an environment for a luxurious and/or relaxing holiday.

4. Further by reason of clause 15 of the Defendant's standard terms and conditions the Defendant expressly accepted responsibility for ensuring that all the components of the Claimants' holidays were supplied to a reasonable standard and further expressly accepted liability for any negligence on the part of their agents and/or suppliers in respect of claims for bodily injury or illness.

5. The 1992 Regulations and in particular regulations 4 and 15 applied to each of the package holidays supplied by the Defendant to the Claimants.

6. Further or alternatively, there was an implied term of each of the package holiday contracts for the supply of holidays to each of the Claimants pursuant to section 13 of the Supply of Goods and Services Act 1982 to the effect that the Defendant would exercise the reasonable care and skill of an experienced tour operator in the selection and monitoring of accommodation allocated to the Claimants.

7. (a) The Defendant is in breach of the said express and/or implied terms or warranties of the holiday contracts as set out in paragraphs 3, 4 and 6 above.

(b) Further or alternatively, the Defendant supplied to the Plaintiffs misleading information contrary to regulation 4 of the 1992 Regulations.

(c) Further or alternatively the proprietors and/or managers of the Hotel Splendid who were agents or suppliers within the meaning of the Defendants' standard terms and conditions and/or within the meaning of regulation 15 of the 1992 Regulations were negligent and/or caused the failure of or improper performance of the holiday contracts for whose acts and/or omissions the Defendant is liable.

PARTICULARS COMMON TO ALL CLAIMANTS

A. *Breach of Contract & Improper Performance*

General

(i) The hotel itself was not of a 5-star, first class, better than average or reasonable standard.

(ii) The hotel services supplied to the Claimants were not of a reasonable standard.

(iii) The water supply was contaminated by legionella bacteria.

Food Hygiene

(iv) Food was offered from an open-air buffet regardless of weather conditions.

(v) Tables, chairs, cloths, cutlery and crockery were invariably stained and dirty.

(vi) The buffet tables had containers of uncovered hot and cold food and was invariably infested by flies and other insects.

(vii) Cats and birds were allowed to prowl around the buffet and dining areas.

(viii) Customers were expected to handle bread from uncut loaves.

(ix) Water provided for tea and coffee was not hot.

(x) Hotel staff were scruffy and dirty in appearance with stained clothes on which they often wiped cutlery.

Accommodation

(xi) The bedrooms smelt of sewage.

(xii) There was no or no reliable air conditioning, and where air conditioning units could be made to function they were intolerably noisy and/or blew out warm air and leaked dirty and foul smelling water.

(xiii) Water in rooms was discoloured (brown) and foul smelling.

(xiv) Furniture gave the appearance of disrepair (beds had legs missing, wardrobes had no doors, and table wobbled).

(xv) Electrical wires were exposed, and "sparked".

(xvi) Bed sheets gave the appearance of being grubby and unwashed.

(xvii) Sinks and baths contained flaking rust and toilets were affected by dirt, stains and lime scale.

Resort Facilities

(xviii) The swimming pool gave off an offensive smell of chlorine and the water was constantly murky.

(xix) The pool water made users eyes sting.

(xx) There was no strip club.

(xxi) There were only 2 bars.

(xxii) There was no gymnasium.

B. *Breach of Section 13 Duty*

(i) The Defendant and/or its servants or agents failed to devise and/or implement any system of inspection, supervision or monitoring of the standards and services offered at the Hotel Splendid during 1999 either with regard to the original selection of the hotel as accommodation for its customers or in respect of correcting the flaws identified in A above.

(ii) The Defendant failed to devise or implement any or any adequate system for keeping itself and its customers informed of deteriorating conditions at the hotel, and/or of previous health scares at the hotel in 1998 or earlier in 1999 — in particular 2 reported cases of Legionnaires disease in July and October 1998; and 6 cases of Legionnaires disease reported between June and August 1999.

(iii) The Defendant failed to devise and/or implement any system for keeping itself and its customers informed of any health alerts issued to the Association of British Travel Agents (ABTA) in respect of health scares at the hotel, in particular the alert that was issued on 20 July 1999.

(iv) The Defendant allowed the Claimants to take up residence in the hotel notwithstanding the said health scares in 1998 and 1999 and the poor condition of the accommodation and services offered at the hotel.

The Defendant subjected the Claimants to the foreseeable risk of illness and/or bodily injury by reason of the condition of the hotel.

C. *Negligence of Hotel Proprietors or Managers*

[For which the Defendant is liable by reason of its standard terms and conditions and/or pursuant to regulation 15 of the 1992 Regulations.]

(i) causing or permitting the contamination of the hotel water supply with Legionella bacteria;

(ii) failing to keep the Claimants informed of the health scares a the hotel in 1998 and 1999;

(iii) allowing the hotel to remain open for business despite knowing from July 1999 (at the latest) that the water supply was contaminated by Legionella bacteria.

(iv) causing or permitting the condition of the hotel and its services to fall below a reasonable standard as particularised in A above.

D. *Misleading Information*

Contrary to regulation 4 of the 1992 Regulations the Defendant advertised the hotel in its brochures as having the following standards and facilities when it did not enjoy such standards or facilities:

(i) a first class hotel of official 5-star rating;

(ii) having 15 bars, a strip club, and a gymnasium.

8. By reason of the matters aforesaid each of the Claimants has suffered injury, loss and damage.

PARTICULARS OF INJURY

(i) Zelda Zoom

(dob 18 January 1948)

She experienced severe symptoms of gastroenteritis with severe vomiting and diarrhoea in excess of 20 times a day. She lost 4.5 stones in weight. She suffered abdominal pains throughout her holiday. She had an infection of giardia. She is more susceptible to future food poisoning. The report of Dr Exray dated 9.6.00 is served herewith.

(ii) Zachary Zoom

(dob 30 September 1936)

Severe vomiting and diarrhoea for 4 days over which period he lost 2.5 stones in weight. On the 4th. day of his holiday he developed a severe fever and flu-like symptoms. He presented at hospital on his return home with a high temperature diagnosed pneumonia in the left lung and infection with Legionella bacteria.

He has been continuously debilitated and suffers from chronic fatigue syndrome, depression and mood swings.

The report of Dr Exray dated 1.12.00 is served herewith.

(iii) John Brown

(dob 12 June 1965)

He suffered chronic diarrhoea, nausea and abdominal pain over several days. On his return home he was diagnosed as having contracted legionella infection, from he was debilitated for 6 months, unable to work and confined to his home. He has made a full recovery.

(iv) Audrey Brown

(dob 1 January 1967)

She suffered acute gastroenteritis from the 3rd day of her holiday until 6 weeks after her return home. She lost 2lbs in weight, and suffered continuous nauseating headaches. Although physically recovered, she continues to suffer from Post Traumatic Stress Disorder.

The report of Dr Exray dated 1.1.00 is served herewith, together with the report of Dr Quack [psychiatrist] dated 29.1.00.

(v) Julie Joop

(dob 6 June 1970)

She suffered an acute onset of diarrhoea [10–15 times a day], nausea, abdominal pain and fever. She lost a stone in weight She had drenching night sweats for 2 weeks. Associated with the above she developed chest pains and flu or cold-like symptoms together with severe headaches and aching joints. She was investigated for legionella infection which was the cause of considerable distress and anxiety.

Since returning home she has continued to suffer the symptoms of irritable bowel syndrome. The prognosis for this is uncertain, but the condition may be permanent. She has been depressed and has a phobic reluctance to go on holidays in the future.

The report of Dr Exray dated 20 June 2000 is served herewith.

PARTICULARS OF SPECIAL DAMAGE

Schedules in respect of each Claimant are served herewith.

9. Each of the Claimants suffered distress and anxiety for themselves and in respect of the illnesses of other members of their families, and lost the enjoyment of their respective holidays. Furthermore, on 30 September 1999 the Claimants were evacuated from the Hotel Splendid due to the contamination of the hotel water system with Legionella bacteria which caused each of the Claimants further anxiety and distress as to the risk of contracting legionnaires disease against which risk each if the Claimants was given prophylactic medication.

10. By reason of the foregoing each of the Claimant's holidays (costing approximately £500.00 per person) was worthless, or substantially diminished in value.

11. The Claimants' claims are for damages and fall within the provisions of section 35A of the Supreme Court Act 1981 by reason of which each claims interest on general damages for personal injury and loss of enjoyment at the rate of 3% per annum from the date the Claim Form was issued, and on special damages and loss of bargain at the rate of 8% from 30 September 1995 or otherwise for such periods and at such rates as the court shall think fit.

AND EACH OF THE CLAIMANTS CLAIMS:

1. DAMAGES;

2. INTEREST thereon pursuant to paragraph 11 above — to be assessed.

Signed:

A LAWYER

Statement of Truth. Etc.

IN THE OBVIOUS COUNTY COURT

CLAIM NO:

B E T W E E N :

SUZANNE DOCKSON

Claimant

-and-

(1)   **KEVIN BOYLAND**
(2)   **ETHNIKI INSURANCE**
[A Company incorporated by the laws of Greece]

Defendants

PARTICULARS OF CLAIM
Overseas Accident – Direct Action Against Insurer

1.   On Friday 29 September 2007 the Claimant was a front seat passenger in a motor vehicle registration number XAB 9248 ("the vehicle") driven by the First Defendant.

2.   The Second Defendant ("the insurer") was at all material times the insurer of the said vehicle and of the First Defendant and an insurer which issued the policy of insurance relating to the said vehicle within the meaning of the fourth motor insurance directive [the Directive of the European Parliament and Council of 16 May 2000 on the approximation of the laws of the Member States relating to insurance against civil liability in respect of the use of motor vehicles number 2000/26/EC ("Directive").

3.   On Friday 29 September 2007 the First Defendant was driving the vehicle up a mountain road in Zante, Greece in the direction of the Blue Caves at Skinari when he drove into collision with a motor vehicle driven by one Frangoyannis down the mountain in the opposite direction.

4.   The collision was caused by the negligence of the First Defendant.

PARTICULARS OF NEGLIGENCE

The First Defendant was negligent in that he:

4.1 Drove into collision with the on-coming vehicle at a point marked "••" on the police accident report sketch plan. Vehicle debris was found by the police on the other side of the central carriage line.

4.2 Caused or permitted his vehicle to stray across the centre line of the road which was 5.9 metres wide.

4.3 Failed to concentrate on what he was doing.

4.4 Failed to look where he was going.

4.5 Failed to stop, slow down or otherwise manage and control his vehicle to avoid the collision.

5. As a result of the accident the vehicle was caused to slide backwards down the mountainside and the Claimant suffered injury, loss and damage.

PARTICULARS OF INJURY

The Claimant was born on 19 March 1979.

She suffered a laceration of the dorsum of the left hand associated with damage to the tendon serving the index and middle fingers; lacerations to the left shoulder and a laceration to the right shoulder. Her left hand was surgically explored and sutured and was subsequently splintered for 6 weeks.

The left hand is scarred (as are her shoulders) and recovery of dexterity in the fingers and hand has been slow and incomplete.

The report of Mr. H.B. Casserly dated 29 October 2003 is filed and served with this Particulars of Claim.

PARTICULARS OF SPECIAL DAMAGE

Such particulars as are available to date are set out in the Schedule filed and served with this Particulars of Claim.

6. Greek law applies to the accident. By article 926 of the Greek Civil Code the driver of a motor vehicle is liable to any passenger irrespective of whose fault caused the accident.

7. Furthermore, by Greek law the insurer is jointly and severally liable for the accident and the Claimant has a direct right of action against the insurer in respect of her claim for damages.

8. Further or alternatively, by reason of the said Directive, and/or by reason of section III Article 9 of Council Regulation 44/2001 the Claimant is an entitled party and has a right to issue proceedings against the insurer and the insurer is directly liable to the Claimant in respect of her injury, loss and damage.

9. The court has jurisdiction in respect of this action by reason of the fact that:

9.1 The First Defendant is domiciled in England and Wales;

9.2   The Second Defendant is subject to Section 2, article 6(1) and/or Section 3, articles 9(1)(b) and/or 11 of Council Regulation 44/2001 (The Jurisdiction Regulation).

9.3   No other proceedings in any other jurisdiction are pending in respect of the index accident.

10.   The Claimant's claim is for damages within the meaning of section 69 of the County Courts Act 1984 pursuant to which the Claimant claims interest:

10.1   On general damage for pain, suffering and loss of amenity at the rate of 2% from the date of issue until judgment or sooner payment.

10.2   On special damage at the rate of 6% from the 13 September 2001 until judgment or sooner payment.

10.3   Alternatively, for such periods and at such rates as the Court shall think fit.

11.   This Court has power under the Civil Jurisdiction and Judgments Act 1982 to hear this claim there being no pending proceedings between the parties in any other Convention territory of any Member State as defined by section 1(3) of the Act[1].

12.   The Claimant's claim includes a claim for personal injury damages that will exceed £1,000.00.

AND THE CLAIMANT CLAIMS:

1.   DAMAGES.

2.   INTEREST pursuant to paragraph 10 above – to be assessed.

A OPTIMISTIC

STATEMENT OF TRUTH Etc.

IN THE ORDINARY COUNTY COURT

---

[1] And see CPR 6BPD.2 for various forms of certification relating to jurisdiction for different types of claim.

CLAIM NO:

B E T W E E N :

ESME THRUGKETTLE

-and-

SPACEAGE AIRWAYS LIMITED

Claimant

Defendant

PARTICULARS OF CLAIM
Montreal Convention – Simple Form

1.   At all material times on 20 January 2002 the Claimant was an intending passenger on the Defendant's flight SP1122B from Alicante to Leeds-Bradford ["the flight"] being the return flight at the conclusion of the Claimant's family's package holiday.

2.   The Defendant is, and was at all material times, an airline and a "*carrier*" within the meaning of the Montreal Convention, incorporated into English law by the Carriage By Air Act 1961 (as amended by the Carriage by Air Acts (Implementation of the Montreal Convention 1999) Order 2002).

3.   The said flight constituted "*international carriage*" within the meaning of Article 1(2) of the Montreal Convention and the said Convention applied to the flight. The Claimant was provided with a "*document of carriage*" within the meaning of Article 3 of the Convention.

4.   The Claimant and her family checked-in for the flight before 10.00 am and were given boarding passes, after which they proceeded through passport control and waited in the departure lounge of the airport.

5.   The flight was called and passengers began queuing at the embarkation gate, numbered A4.

6.   The Claimant's husband was at all material times in a wheelchair. The Claimant and her family did not join the embarkation queue at the gate but the Claimant herself went to check to see if the queue had started moving.

7.   As she checked the state of the queue at the entrance to gate A4 the queue began to surge forward and as a result the Claimant fell on the black, speckled granite floor surface due to a small [approximately 2.5cm] step or drop in the floor which was unclear and unmarked as a result of which fall she sustained injury.

8.   The Claimant had an accident within the meaning of Article 17 of the Convention which accident caused her bodily injury.

9.   The said accident occurred in the course of one of the operations of embarking on international flight SP1122B

10.   Accordingly, the Defendant, as carrier, is liable to the Claimant for damage in the event of her bodily injury sustained in any of the operations of embarking on the Defendant's flight.

11.   The Claimant suffered the following injuries:

11.1 She was rendered unconscious and now is at significantly increased (25%) risk of epilepsy;
11.2 She broke her glasses and suffered lacerations to the face and nose as a result of which she is permanently disfigured;
11.3 She suffered intense pain in the dominant right shoulder and elbow and was subsequently diagnosed as having a fracture of the right (dominant) elbow which fracture has not united – further surgery is anticipated;
11.4 She aggravated pre-existing back pain and sciatica was triggered as a result of the fall.

11.5 Medical evidence will be produced.

12. The Claimant suffered loss and damage.

12.1 Pain, suffering and loss of amenity.

12.2 She was unable to care properly for her disabled husband and additional domestic care and assistance was required.

12.3 She incurred incidental expenses which included the cost of physiotherapy, none-prescription drugs and the cost of replacement glasses.

12.4 A Schedule of Special Damage will be produced.

13. The Claimant's claim is for damages within the meaning of section 69 of the County Courts Act 1984 pursuant to which the Claimant claims interest:

13.1 On damages for pain and suffering at 2% from the date of issue of proceedings;

13.2 On special damage at the rate of 7% from 28 December 2000 to 28 February 2002 and thereafter at 6%.

13.3 Alternatively, such interest at such rates and periods as the court shall think fit.

14. The value of this action is currently estimated to exceed £15,000.00 but not £50,000.00.

AND THE CLAIMANT CLAIMS:

1. DAMAGES

2. INTEREST pursuant to paragraph 11 above – to be assessed.

A. LAWYER

STATEMENT OF TRUTH

I, Esme Thrugkettle, declare that the facts set out in this Particulars of Claim are true.

Etc.

IN THE SAME OLD COUNTY COURT   Claim No [...]
BETWEEN

DOLORES McSPREADER

CLAIMANT

and

CHOCKS AWAY AIRLINES UK LIMITED,

DEFENDANT

PARTICULARS OF CLAIM
Montreal Convention – Strict Liability & Negligence

1.   The Claimant was, at all material times, a passenger on flight TCX278L from Tenerife, Spain to Newcastle, UK departing Tenerife on 22 October 2004 at 2359 (local time) and scheduled to arrive at Newcastle at 0525 on 23 October 2004.

2.   The Defendant is, and was at all material times, an airline and a "*carrier*" within the meaning of the Montreal Convention, incorporated into English law by the Carriage By Air Act 1961 (as amended by the Carriage by Air Acts (Implementation of the Montreal Convention 1999) Order 2002).

3.   The said flight constituted "*international carriage*" within the meaning of Article 1(2) of the Montreal Convention and the said Convention applied to the flight. The Claimant was provided with a "*document of carriage*" within the meaning of Article 3 of the Convention.

4.   On 23 October 2004, shortly after the aircraft had arrived at Newcastle at around 0500 (local time), the Claimant disembarked the aircraft by means of a set of disembarkation steps. She was wearing flat shoes. It was raining and was still dark. A handrail ran alongside the steps, but the handrail stopped around 2 steps short of the apron at ground level. The handrail and the steps were both wet and slippery. The Claimant descended the last 2 steps without the assistance of any handrail and, as she did so, slipped and fell to the ground. By reason of this incident the Claimant sustained bodily injury which is more fully described below.

5.   A Swissport Occurrence Report dated 23 October 2004 from a Mr Andrew Smith to a Mr David Rivers states, among other things, as follows, "*A passenger fell down the bottom two steps of the front set of stairs while disembarking. I was standing just next to the passenger, where I immediately went to assist her and called for 222 over the radio.*"

6.   The said incident was an accident which took place during an operation of disembarkation and which caused bodily injury to the Claimant by reason of which the Defendant is liable to compensate the Claimant in accordance with Article 17(1) of the Montreal Convention.

7. By reason of the said accident, the Claimant suffered personal injury and has sustained losses and expenses.

PARTICULARS OF INJURY

The Claimant was born on 15 October 1926.

By reason of her accident the Claimant suffered a laceration over her left eyebrow and subconjunctival haemorrhage in the left eye which led to diplopia and blurred vision. The Claimant also experienced headaches. The Claimant also sustained a soft tissue injury to her left shoulder and to her left hip. A Medical report from Mr Anukul Kumar Deb Goswami, Consultant Orthopaedic Surgeon, dated 3 August 2006, is attached hereto. The Claimant reserves the right to serve further medico-legal evidence in due course if so advised.

PARTICULARS OF LOSS AND EXPENSE

A Schedule is attached hereto.

8. The Claimant's primary case is that the Defendant was a carrier and that, accordingly, its liability arises under Article 17(1) of the Montreal Convention, as stated above.

9. Further or alternatively, the Claimant states that the said accident and the resultant injury, loss and damage was caused by the negligence of the Defendant, its servants and/or agents.

PARTICULARS OF NEGLIGENCE

The Defendant, its servants and/or agents, were negligent in:

a. Failing to ensure that the disembarkation steps were covered with a non-slip material;

b. Failing to ensure that the handrail ran the full length of the disembarkation steps;

c. Failing to ensure that there was a cover over the disembarkation steps in the light of the prevailing weather conditions;

d. Exposing the Claimant to a reasonably foreseeable and easily avoided risk of injury;

e. Failing, in all the circumstances, to exercise reasonable care and skill so as to avoid causing foreseeable injury to the Claimant.

10. Further, the Claimant claims interest on such sums as may be awarded to her at such rate and for such period as the Court thinks fit pursuant to section 69 of the County Courts Act 1984.

11. The Claimant's claim is presently estimated to exceed £1,000 in damages for personal injury, but is not estimated to exceed £15,000 in total and, accordingly, is suitable for allocation to the Fast track jurisdiction of the County Court.

AND the Claimant claims:

1. Damages; and,

2. Interest thereon pursuant to statute to be assessed.

MATHIEU PARGITER

I believe that the facts stated in these Particulars of Claim are true. Etc.

IN THE HIGH COURT OF JUSTICE   Claim No HQ0
QUEEN'S BENCH DIVISION
BETWEEN

HONOUR BLACKETT
(*on her own behalf and as widow and executrix of* DAVID HURLBUTT
BLACKETT, *deceased*)

Claimant

and

INTERNATIONAL TRAVEL LIMITED

Defendant

PARTICULARS OF CLAIM
Fatal Accident

---

1. The date of birth of the deceased was 17 September 1947. He is alleged herein to have died as a result of an accident caused by the negligence of the Defendant's employees, agents, suppliers and/or sub-contractors, their servants or agents. The deceased died in Yangshuo, People's Republic of China on 20 August 2002. The Consular Mortuary Certificate dated 23 August 2002 records that the cause of death was given as accidental death by drowning.

2. The Claimant brings these proceedings on her own behalf in respect of injury, losses and expenses sustained by her as a result of the accident on 20 August 2002 which is described more fully below.

3. Further, the Claimant was the wife of the deceased and is the executrix of his estate. She brings these proceedings on behalf of his estate under the Law Reform (Miscellaneous Provisions) Act 1934 and for her benefit as wife and dependant of the deceased under the Fatal Accidents Act 1976.

4. The Defendant is, and was at all material times, a company incorporated in Australia with limited liability (but which has a registered branch in England and Wales). The Defendant is a tour operator engaged, among other things, in the sale and supply of package holidays to members of the general public.

5. By a contract evidenced in writing by an Itinerary (Booking Reference 936635) the Defendant agreed to provide the Claimant and the deceased with a package touring holiday to the People's Republic of China between 3 August 2002 and 25 August 2002. The tour was described in the Defendant's brochure under the title, "*Essence of China Southbound – 21 Days Beijing to Hong Kong*". The total cost of the touring holiday was £3,536 for the Claimant and the deceased.

6. The said holiday was a "*package*" within the meaning of regulation 2(1) of the Package Travel etc. Regulations 1992 and the accommodation, facilities and services provided pursuant to the parties' contract were regulated in accordance with the said 1992 Regulations.

7.　Further, the Defendant's Booking Conditions were incorporated as express or, alternatively, as implied terms of the parties' package holiday contract and materially provided, as follows:

"[under clause 1 headed, "*Your Contract with Intrepid Travel*"] *The contract, including all matters arising from it, is subject to English law and the exclusive jurisdiction of the English courts.*" ...

[under clause 13 headed, "*Our Responsibilities*"] *Where the Client suffers death or personal injury as a result of an activity forming part of the tour arrangements booked with Intrepid, Intrepid accepts responsibility unless there has been no fault on Intrepid's part or its suppliers and the cause was the Client's fault, the actions of someone unconnected with the tour arrangements or one which neither Intrepid nor its suppliers could have anticipated or avoided even if all due care had been exercised.*" [Insofar as is necessary the Claimant will rely at trial on the Defendant's Booking Conditions for the full meaning and effect of the same.]

8.　Further or alternatively, it was an implied term of the parties' contract that the Defendant would exercise reasonable care and skill so as to ensure the reasonable safety of the Claimant and the deceased. The said term falls to be implied by reason of section 13 of the Supply of Goods and Services Act 1982.

9.　On 20 August 2002 the Claimant and deceased arrived with their tour party in Yangshuo. Included within the advertized brochure itinerary, and paid for in advance and pre-arranged as part of the package tour, was a bicycle ride and boat trip on the Li River.　The day trip commenced with a bicycle ride through countryside. The part arrived at the Li River at around 3.30 pm on 20 August 2002. There were 14 travellers in the party and the group was paired off to take a trip along the river on bamboo rafts (the Claimant and deceased occupied one raft). The rafts had a bamboo floor, a couple of deck chairs which were tied (side by side) loosely to the floor and a canopy over the chairs. The travellers sat on the chairs and a boatman stood at the back of the raft to "*power*" and steer the raft with a long pole/oar.

10.　Most of the travellers wore sandals, shorts, T-shirts and the like. There was a shortage of life vests. There were sufficient life vests for the travellers, but an insufficient supply for all of the boatmen; the boatmen for the raft occupied by the Claimant and deceased did not wear a life vest. The boatman for the Claimant and deceased's raft spoke no English.

11.　The party set off down the river. The river level was high. The boatman for the raft occupied by the Claimant and deceased appeared nervous and did not appear to know how to negotiate the river and the weirs on the river. The boatman had to obtain instructions from a local person in negotiating the first weir on the river. Other boatmen had difficulty negotiating the river and the weirs.

12.　The accident happened while the raft was negotiating a weir. As the Claimant and deceased approached a particularly large and fast flowing weir they saw other rafts waiting by the bank. Their boatman steered the raft straight into the weir. The boatman was unable to steer the raft at the correct angle and the raft capsized. The deceased fell off first. The loose deck chairs, the canopy, the boatman and the Claimant all fell into the water. There was a current in the water. It did not appear that the boatman could swim and he clung onto the capsized raft (he was not wearing a life vest).

13. There were no safety boats and there was no-one in an official or other capacity on the river bank who was able to assist.

14. The deceased was wearing a life vest and was a good swimmer. However, the Claimant next saw the deceased floating face down in the water. The deceased was lifted out of the water and attempts were made to resuscitate him. An ambulance (with a doctor and nurse) attended the scene where resuscitation attempts continued and further continued on the way to a local hospital. The deceased was found to be dead on arrival at the hospital.

15. The accident was caused by the negligence of the Defendant, its employees, agents, suppliers and/or sub-contractors, their servants and/or agents in the performance of their duty of care to the Claimant and the deceased.

PARTICULARS OF NEGLIGENCE

The Defendant, its employees, agents, suppliers and/or sub-contractors, their servants and/or agents were negligent in:

a.   Steering the raft into a large weir with fast-flowing water and then losing control of it;

b.   Failing to wait at the side of the index weir and to check that it was safe to proceed before attempting to negotiate the weir;

c.   Causing, permitting or allowing the Claimant and deceased to be carried on a raft which was insufficiently robust and secure to provide a safe means of transport on the index river;

d.   Failing to provide sufficiently safe and secure seating on the raft;

e.   Failing to ensure that the canopy was sufficiently safe and secure;

f.   Failing to ensure that the raft was robust, properly stabilized and capable of safely negotiating the weirs on the river in the conditions which prevailed on 20 August 2002;

g.   Failing to carry out any or any adequate inspection of the equipment, river and prevailing conditions prior to the day trip on 20 August 2002 and so to ensure that it was safe to proceed and that appropriate instruction and supervision was provided to the boat trip supplier and boatmen;

h.   Failing to ensure that the index boatman was properly trained and instructed in safe rafting techniques on the index river;

i.   Failing to ensure that the boatman was capable of swimming;

j.   Failing to supply the boatman with a life vest;

k.   Failing to ensure that the boatman could speak English to the level required to be capable of providing any appropriate safety instructions to the Claimant and deceased;

l.   Failing to ensure that the river rafting trip and the boatmen providing it were properly organized and properly supervised both on the river and from the riverbank;

m. Failing to warn the Claimant and deceased that the river rafting trip would involve the negotiation of fast flowing weirs, with a risk of capsizing, rather than being a sedate river trip;

n. Failing to provide any or any appropriate back up team to deal with capsize and other emergencies (both on the river and/or on the riverbank);

o. Failing to put into place protocols for the prompt provision of local medical assistance and to ensure that such protocols were observed;

p. Failing to select an appropriate local excursion supplier with properly trained and competent staff;

q. Failing, in all the circumstances, to ensure that the Claimant and deceased were reasonably safe during the trip on 20 August 2002.

Insofar as may be necessary, the Claimant will rely on the maxim, the thing speaks for itself.

16. The Defendant has not yet provided any factual witness evidence and disclosure has been limited. The Claimant reserves the right, if so advised, to seek to amend these Particulars of Negligence once factual evidence has been disclosed.

17. The Defendant is liable for the negligence pleaded at paragraph 15 above by reason of the Booking Conditions pleaded at paragraph 7 above. In particular, and without prejudice to the generality of the Claimant's reliance on the said Booking Conditions, the Claimant states that clause 13 of the same (**"Our Responsibilities"**) makes it clear that the Defendant accepts liability for death and personal injury, unless there is no fault on the part of the Defendant and/or its suppliers.

18. Further or alternatively, the Defendant is, by reason of the facts and matters pleaded at paragraph 15 above, in breach of the implied term pleaded at paragraph 8 above and is, accordingly, liable to the Claimant by reason of regulation 15 of the Package Travel etc. Regulations 1992.

19. By reason of the facts and matters set out above, the Claimant has suffered personal injury and has sustained losses and expenses.

PARTICULARS OF INJURY TO THE CLAIMANT

The Claimant was born on 18 October 1963. By reason of the accident the Claimant sustained abrasion injuries to her hand, arm, knee and shin. In addition, the Claimant has suffered from distressing dreams and flashbacks. She has developed avoidance behaviour. The Claimant has been diagnosed as suffering from post-traumatic stress disorder and further treatment has been recommended. The Claimant attaches hereto medico-legal reports from [various doctors].

PARTICULARS OF CLAIMANT'S LOSS AND EXPENSE

A schedule is attached hereto. The Claimant also seeks general damages for loss of enjoyment and special damages for diminution in value of the holiday, such damages to be assessed.

20. Further, by reason of the facts and matters set out above, the Defendant, its employees, agents, suppliers and/or sub-contractors, their servants and/or agents caused or materially contributed to the death of the deceased and to injury, losses and expenses.

PARTICULARS

The deceased was born on 17 September 1947. He was aged 54 years at the time of his death. His life expectancy was normal. He was in work at the time of his death and would have continued in work. The Claimant and the deceased were both involved in the accident in which the deceased drowned. He will have suffered for several minutes struggling for his life and, in that time, will have had a sense of imminent death and a shortened life.

21. As a result of the deceased's death, his estate and dependant have sustained losses and expenses as are set out below.

PARTICULARS OF CLAIM BY THE DECEASED'S ESTATE

The Claimant serves herewith the death certificate and post mortem report. Please see attached schedule.

PARTICULARS OF LOSSES AND EXPENSES CLAIMED BY CLAIMANT AS DEPENDANT

A schedule setting out the value of the claim for the statutory bereavement award and the value of the dependency is attached hereto.

22. Further, the Claimant claims interest pursuant to section 35A of the Supreme Court Act 1981 on general damages at 2% *per annum* from the date of service of the proceedings to the date of settlement or trial, on past financial expense or where the deceased's estate has been kept out of money at the full prevailing special investment account rate from the date of loss to the date of settlement or trial, on any other financial loss at half this rate; alternatively, on the amounts found to be due to the Claimant at such rate and for such period as the Court thinks fit.

23. The Claimant expects to recover more than £300,000 in total.

AND the Claimant claims:

a.   Damages on her own behalf and interest thereon;

b.   Damages on behalf of the deceased's estate under the Law Reform (Miscellaneous Provisions) Act 1934;

c.   Damages for dependency under the Fatal Accidents Act 1976;

d.   Interest thereon.

                                                              SARA SIDDENS

I believe that the facts stated in these Particulars of Claim are true. Etc.

IN THE WARRINGTON COUNTY COURT

Claim No:

BETWEEN

LESLEY ANN

CLAIMANT

and

GREAT HOLIDAYS LIMITED

DEFENDANT

PARTICULARS OF CLAIM
Excursion

---

1.   The Defendant is, and was at all material times, a limited company engaged, among other things, in the sale and supply of package holidays to members of the general public.

2.   On or before 7 January 2005 and by a contract evidenced in writing by a Co-Op Travel Receipt (Ref No 76973) the Defendant agreed to supply to the Claimant and her partner, Mr J Brown, a 14 night package holiday at the Cennet Hotel, Side, Turkey. The commencement date of the holiday was 1 July 2001. The total price of the holiday was £1,496.

3.   The said holiday was a "*package holiday*", regulated as such under the Package Travel etc. Regulations 1992, which applied at all material times to the package holiday contract and all of the facilities provided thereunder.

4.   The Defendant's Booking Conditions were incorporated as express or, alternatively, as implied terms of the parties' contract and provided, among other things, as follows:[the Claimant reserves the right to rely at trial on the Defendant's Booking Conditions in their entirety, as an aid to the construction of what appears below, should this be necessary]

"*If any member of your party is killed or injured as a result of an activity forming part of your holiday arrangements booked before your departure from the UK, we will accept responsibility if the death or injury is due to a fault on our part or that of our agents or suppliers.*"

5.   Further or alternatively, it was an implied term of the parties' contract that the accommodation, facilities and services (including any excursions) arranged by the

Defendant be of a satisfactory standard so that they be safe (a strict duty derived from subsection 4(2) of the Supply of Goods and Services Act 1982).

6.   Further or alternatively, it was an implied term of the parties' contract that the accommodation, facilities and services which formed part of the parties' contract and/or which formed part of any service arranged by the Defendant be provided with reasonable care and skill so that the Claimant would be reasonably safe. The said term is to be implied by reason of section 13 of the Supply of Goods and Services Act 1982.

7.   Further, it was an implied term of the parties' contract that the Defendant would exercise reasonable care and skill in the selection of all suppliers and agents responsible for the provision of services (including the provision of excursions).

8.   At a meeting organized by the Defendant during the course of the holiday the Defendant's uniformed local representative, Ms Julie Boreham, recommended a boat trip excursion to Kekova and Myra. The Claimant and her partner paid £44 for the said excursion. The Claimant paid Ms Boreham directly for the said excursion in pounds sterling. The said excursion was advertized in a leaflet bearing the Defendant's logo.

9.   The boat trip excursion took place on 12 July 2001. At the end of the trip the boat moored in the harbour and the Claimant was the third person to disembark. As she advanced towards the gangplank to leave the boat the Claimant slipped in a pool of water and grease that had formed on the deck of the boat and slipped and fell backwards. As she fell the Claimant instinctively put out her arm to break her fall or to try and retain her balance. A member of the crew of the boat had left a hot barbecue griddle at the side of the boat next to the gang plank. As the Claimant fell her left arm impacted with the very hot griddle. As a result of the accident the Claimant suffered personal injury described more fully below.

10.   The said accident was caused by the negligence of the Defendant, its suppliers, their servants and/or agents.

PARTICULARS OF NEGLIGENCE

The Defendant, its suppliers, their servants and/or agents were negligent in:

a.   Failing to keep the deck of the boat clean;

b.   Failing to detect the greasy residue on the deck of the boat whether by a system of reasonable inspection or otherwise;

c.   Failing to warn the Claimant whether verbally, by a sign or otherwise of the risk of slipping presented by the greasy residue on the deck of the boat;

d.   Leaving a very hot griddle in a place where it might foreseeably come into conflict with persons leaving the boat;

e.   Failing to warn the Claimant whether verbally, by a sign or otherwise of the presence of the griddle;

f. Failing properly or at all to supervise disembarkation and/or to assist the Claimant in disembarkation;

g. Exposing the Claimant to a reasonably foreseeable risk of injury;

h. Failing, in all the circumstances, to exercise reasonable care and skill to ensure the reasonable safety of the Claimant during excursion while using the services arranged by the Defendant.

11. The Defendant has accepted contractual liability for the negligence of its suppliers pleaded at paragraph 10 above, by reason of its booking conditions pleaded at paragraph 4 above.

12. Further or alternatively, the Defendant is in breach of the implied terms, set out in paragraphs 5 and/or 6 above, and is, accordingly, liable to the Claimant by reason of regulation 15 of the Package Travel etc. Regulations 1992.

13. Further or alternatively, the Claimant contracted separately with the Defendant, through its local representative, for the provision of the boat trip excursion. The said contract was subject to the same implied terms pleaded at paragraphs 5 and/or 6 above. By reason of the negligence pleaded at paragraph 10 above the Defendant is in breach of the said implied terms in the excursion contract and is, accordingly, liable to compensate the Claimant. In this context, the Claimant will rely, among other things, on the fact that the excursions were:

a. advertized in a *Great!* leaflet headed, "*Great! Book with Confidence*";

b. advertized by the "Great" local representative;

c. booked and paid for through the Defendant's local representative.

14. Further, the Defendant is in breach of the implied term pleaded at paragraph 7 above and is, accordingly, liable to compensate the Claimant.

15. By reason of the accident the Claimant has suffered personal injury and has sustained losses and expenses.

PARTICULARS OF INJURY

The Claimant was born on 29 April 1970. By reason of the accident she suffered a suspected occult scaphoid fracture of her left (non-dominant) wrist. This was treated with a scaphoid cast. The Claimant also suffered a burn injury to her left hand, wrist and forearm. The Claimant's injuries and symptoms are more fully described in the medico-legal report of Dr. Ipswich dated 25 June 2006, a copy of which is attached hereto.

PARTICULARS OF LOSSES AND EXPENSES

A Schedule is attached hereto.

The Claimant states, further to her claim for diminution in value, that herself and her partner lost the enjoyment of their holiday as a result of the Claimant's injury. She claims damages for the diminution in value of the holiday and for loss of enjoyment to be assessed.

16. Further to her claim for damages in respect of the accident on 12 July 2001, the Claimant also alleges that the Defendant, its servants and/or agents, acted or failed to act in breach of its contractual duty to provide holiday services of a reasonable standard.

PARTICULARS OF BREACH OF CONTRACT

The Defendant is in breach of contract in:

a. Failing to provide free water sports and sauna (in breach of the promise contained at page 140 of the Defendant's brochure for Turkey 2001 which promise had the status of an implied warranty by reason of regulation 6 of the Package Travel etc. Regulations 1992);

b. Failing to provide any or any adequate air conditioning in the Claimant's room (in breach of the promise contained at page 140 of the Defendant's brochure which promise had the status of an implied warranty by reason of regulation 6 of the Package Travel etc. Regulations 1992);

c. Failing to provide food of a reasonable standard at the Claimant's Hotel.

17. Further, the Claimant claims interest pursuant to section 69 of the County Courts Act 1984 on the amount found to be due to her at such rate and for such period as the Court thinks fit.

18. For jurisdictional purposes the Claimant's claim for general damages for pain, suffering and loss of amenity is estimated to exceed £1,000, but her claim is not estimated to exceed £15,000 in total and, accordingly, this claim is suitable for allocation to the Fast Track jurisdiction of the County Court.

AND the Claimant claims:

1. Damages to be assessed;

2. Interest thereon pursuant to statute to be assessed.

JACK HORNER

Dated this the   day of   200X

I believe that the facts stated in these Particulars of Claim are true. Etc.

IN THE HIGH COURT OF JUSTICE

QUEEN'S BENCH DIVISION   Claim no.

B E T W E E N

BILLY DAINTY

Claimant

-and-

TRAVEL LIMITED

Defendant

PARTICULARS OF CLAIM

Swimming Pool – Local Standards

1.   By a contract ["the Holiday Contract"] the Defendant tour operator supplied to the Claimant and a party of his friends a package holiday at the Royal Beach self-catering apartments ["the apartments"] in the resort of Kavos in Corfu, Greece between the 16th and 24th August 2002.

2.   The Holiday was one to which the Package Travel [Etc.] Regulations 1992 ["the 1992 Regulations"] applied and the holiday comprised inclusive international flights, airport transfers in Corfu and accommodation at the apartments with use of all its facilities, including in particular the swimming pool ["the pool"] and surrounding terrace.

3.   The proprietors and managers of the apartments were suppliers and/or subcontractors of the Defendant within the meaning of the 1992 Regulations.

4.   There were implied terms of the Contract, implied by law or alternatively to give effect to the presumed common intention of the parties, to the following effect namely:

4.1 The facilities at the apartments and in particular the swimming pool and its surrounds would comply with local regulations and safety standards applicable in Corfu, Greece in 2002.
4.2 Reasonable skill and care would be exercised in the provision of facilities and services at the apartments and in particular at the swimming pool and its surrounds.
4.3 The facilities at the apartments would be of a reasonable standard by complying with recommended minimum standards laid down by the Federation of Tour Operators.

5.   A failure to provide facilities and services which comply with local regulations and safety standards, or to exercise reasonable skill and care in the provision of the

aforementioned facilities and services, each constitutes improper performance of the Holiday Contract within the meaning of the 1992 Regulations.

6.   The apartments had a swimming pool.

7.   The Greek Swimming Pool Regulations 1973 ["the Greek Regulations"] applied to the pool. In particular:

7.1 By clause 21.2 trained supervisors shall be on duty during the entire period of the pool's operation.
7.2 By clause 23.1 notices should be posted in conspicuous places with rules for the correct use of the pool as well as applicable safety regulations.
7.3 By clause 23.2 the operation of the pool must be such as to minimise the risks of drowning or injury to bathers.
7.4 By clause 13.1 all swimming pool areas operating at night should have a comprehensive system of lighting in operation so that all points of the pool and the water in the pool should be well lit.
7.5 By clause 23.3(h) night-time bathing should only be permitted in fully lit and suitably supervised locations.

8.   The Defendant and/or the apartments set standards in respect of the pool and its operation and management including:

8.1 A requirement that there be visible "No Diving" signs in the vicinity of the pool.
8.2 A requirement that each unit of accommodation should have written instructions in respect of the use of the pool and its hours of operation.
8.3 A requirement that visitors such as the Claimant who visited the Defendant's "Welcome meeting" were informed about pool safety and pool opening hours.

9.   On 22nd August at approximately 3:30 or 4:00am the Claimant walked to the swimming pool, in which other people were swimming at the time. He dived into what was unbeknown to him the shallow end of the pool and as a result he hit his head on the bottom of the pool and sustained a C5 fracture of the spine which rendered him an incomplete tetraplegic.

9.1 The Claimant had used the pool on only one previous occasion throughout his holiday.

9.2 On first arriving at the apartments on or about 17 August 2002 at about 03.20hours the pool was in use and the Claimant asked the bar manager whether the pool was available for night bathing. The bar manager confirmed that the pool was there and could be used whenever required.

10. The accident was caused by:

10.1 The failure of the Defendant and the proprietors and/or managers of the apartments to ensure that the swimming pool and ancillary facilities and services [such as signage and supervision] complied with the Greek Standards; and

10.2 The breach by the Defendant and/or its agents and employees of the implied terms of the Holiday Contract set out in paragraph 4 above and their own standards as set out in paragraph 9 above.

10.3 The improper performance of the Holiday Contract by the proprietors and/or managers of the apartments for which the Defendant is liable by virtue of the 1992 Regulations.

PARTICULARS

Improper performance by the proprietors and/or managers of the apartments

i)   In breach of Clause 21.2 of the Greek Regulations failing to ensure that a trained or any supervisor was present at the swimming pool at the time of the accident, at which point the pool was in operation.

ii)   In breach of Clause 23.1 of the Greek Regulations failing to post any or any adequate notices in conspicuous places and with rules for the correct use of the pool and applicable safety regulations, and in particular failing to post any or any adequate notices:

  a)   stating that the pool should not be used after dark;
  b)   stating that pool should not be used under the influence of alcohol;
  c)   stating that the pool should not be used except under the supervision of a trained supervisor;
  d)   warning of the importance of checking the depth of the pool before diving;
  e)   prohibiting diving at all or alternatively in the shallow end of the pool;

iii)   In breach of Clause 23.3(h) of the Greek Regulations causing or permitting the Claimant to use the pool without a trained or any supervisor being present;

iv)   In breach of Clause 23.3(h) of the Greek Regulations causing or permitting the Claimant to use the pool when it was not fully, or at all, lit externally or internally so that users might see the configuration and depth of the pool;

v)   In breach of Clause 23.2 of the Greek Regulations failing in all the circumstances to take such steps as to minimise the risk of injury to the Claimant;

vi)   Failing to have in place any adequate depth or "no diving" markings or signs until the day after the Claimant's accident.

The Defendant or its agents or employees

vii)   Failing to ensure that the swimming pool and its surrounds complied with the Greek Regulations (as per 11.3 i) and ii) above);

iii)   Permitting or condoning diving in the swimming pool generally and in particular in the shallow end and near the bar.

iv)   Permitting or condoning the use of the swimming pool at night time in the absence of a trained or any supervisor and/or adequate pool lighting.

v)   Failing in all the circumstances to exercise reasonable skill and care in the provision of facilities and services at the apartments and in particular at the swimming pool and its surrounds.

vi) In breach of the Defendant's own standards failing to issue any advice, guidance or warnings about the use and configuration of the pool at the "welcome meeting" attended by the Claimant; failing to issue written notices for display in the Claimant's unit of accommodation and failing to ensure the conspicuous display of depth and diving markings and warnings.

11. As a result of the accident the Claimant has suffered injury, loss and damage.

PARTICULARS OF INJURY

The Claimant was born on the 4 May 1987.
He sustained a C5 fracture of the spine as a result of which he is an incomplete tetraplegic.

PARTICULARS OF LOSS AND DAMAGE

12. The Claimant's claim is for damages within the meaning of section 35A of the Supreme Court Act 1981 pursuant to which the Claimant claims interest at:

    12.1   2% on general damages from the date the proceedings were issued until judgment or sooner payment;

    12.2   6% on special damages from the date of the accident until judgment or sooner payment in respect of those items of loss already accrued;

    12.3   3% on continuing losses;

    12.4   Such other alternative interest as the court shall think fit.

13. The estimated value of this action will exceed £50,000.00.

AND THE CLAIMANT CLAIMS:

    1.   DAMAGES
    2.   INTEREST pursuant to paragraph 13 above – to be assessed.

JOHN DOE

STATEMENT OF TRUTH Etc.

IN THE NEAREST COUNTY COURT

CLAIM NO:

B E T W E E N :

(1)   COLIN FIDDLER
(2)   KATRINA FIDDLER

Claimants

-and-

SPA HOLIDAYS LIMITED

Defendant

D E F E N C E
General Quality

1.   The Claimants booked and the Defendant company supplied to them a 14 night holiday based at the Sandos Caracol Beach and Spa Resort at Playa Del Carmen in Mexico for the sum of £3,043.50 as evidenced by the Defendant's Confirmation Invoice.

2.   The Defendant's website description of the Hotel and Resort make clear that Playa Del Carmen is located south of Cancun on the Yucatan Peninsula.

3.   Furthermore, the website description of the Hotel expressly states that the accommodation will have a private bathroom with shower (not bath) and further lists the various facilities available at the resort.

4.   The Claimants were supplied precisely what they booked.

5.   It is apparent that the Claimants did not like the resort or the facilities to be found there, but it is denied that there has been any breach of contract or improper performance of the holiday contract.

(a) The Claimants were provided with Premium Class air travel; it never having been asserted that there was any special check-in facility and it was not a term of the contract that the air travel would have any particular form of entertainment.

(b) It is admitted that the Claimants on arrival at the Resort Hotel wanted to upgrade their accommodation and did so, in effect on 2 occasions (the second occasion being to a suite offered by the goodwill of the resort management). However, this is because they wanted to enjoy facilities and services which they had not originally booked. They had originally booked and were supplied with "standard" room accommodation.

(c) The Defendant has no knowledge of any problems with a jacuzzi, but even assuming such problems are proved, mechanical and electrical equipment regrettably breaks down from time to time and this happened without there being any negligence or breach of contract. Such things can be fixed.

6. It is clear that the Second Claimant became ill with a viral illness and also suffered from mosquito bites whilst on holiday and it is averred that this has unfortunately coloured the Claimants' view of the facilities and services at the Resort Hotel.

7. The fact that the Claimants refer to the Resort Hotel as "Colditz" and like a public convenience or one of Hitler's death camps, and being situated in a swamp, demonstrates that they are prone to exaggeration and hyperbole and are not reliable.

8. Accordingly, this claim is denied in its entirety. Such allegations as the Claimants have in respect of breach of contract must be strictly proved.

9. This action will require the gathering of evidence from Mexico and is likely to have a value over £5,000.00 and should accordingly, be allocated to the Fast Track.

B BULLIER

STATEMENT OF TRUTH
The Defendant believes that the facts set out in this Defence are true. Etc.

IN THE BLEEDING COUNTY COURT

CLAIM NO:

B E T W E E N :

EMILY AUSTEN

Claimant

-and-

CAMPING HOLIDAYS LIMITED

Defendant

D E F E N C E
General Safety – Local Standards

---

1.   Paragraphs 1 and 2 of the Particulars of Claim are admitted.

2.   Paragraph 3 (setting out alleged implied contract terms) of the Particulars of Claim is denied. It is denied that the Defendant owed the Claimant a separate duty in tort. It is not necessary to impose such a duty on the Defendant.

3.   It is admitted that there was an implied term of the holiday contract to the effect that the services and facilities comprising the package holiday would be provided with reasonable skill and care.

4.   The standard of reasonable skill and care falls to be assessed by reference to the general standard of reasonableness applicable in all the circumstances in Hungary.

(a) It is for the Claimant to establish and prove by admissible evidence what the standard of reasonableness was in France and the extent to which the Claimant's holiday facilities fell short of that standard in a manner causative of such loss and damage as the Claimant is able to establish.

(b) It is not for the Defendant to prove the contrary.

(c)   The Defendant will rely on the binding authority of Goldring J in *Holden v First Choice Holidays & Flights Ltd* [QBD 10 May 2006]; *Wilson v Best Travel* [1993] 1 All ER 353 and *Codd v Thomson Tour Operations Ltd* [2000 CA].

(d)   For the avoidance of doubt it is further denied that the common duty of care applies in this action because the Occupiers' Liability Act 1957 does not apply in France.

5.   Paragraph 4 of the Particulars of Claim is admitted.

6.   The Defendant has no knowledge of the matters alleged in paragraph 5 of the Particulars of Claim which must be proved. It is noted that the Claimant had been accommodate dint he relevant caravan for 3 days without apparently noticing anything wrong with the steps. It is, therefore, more probable than not that any accident she had was simply the result of her missing her footing.

7.   Breach of contract and/or negligence is denied whether as alleged in paragraph 6 of the Particulars of Claim or otherwise.

8.   Without prejudice to the generality of the foregoing denial that Defendant states as follows:

(a)   It is for the Claimant to prove that any of the precautions itemized in the particulars under paragraph 6 of the Particulars of Claim would have made any difference to the outcome.

(b)   The caravan had been used throughout the summer season before the Claimant's arrival without incident and without any problem with the steps being reported or identified.

(c)   The Claimant had used the steps for 3 days without incident.

(d)   The steps are manufactured by Kinnersley & Co., and tested under EN Standard 1645-1:2002.

(e)   After the Claimant's alleged accident some rivets were replaced in the steps but the presence or absence of these rivets would not have caused the step to slip sideways as the Claimant alleges and the absence of such rivets would not have altered the integrity or the stability of the step structure.

9.   Further or alternatively the accident was caused in whole or in part by the negligence of the Claimant.

PARTICULARS OF CONTRIBUTORY NEGLIGENCE

(a)   Falling on the steps when nobody else had fallen there.

(b)   Failing to concentrate on what she was doing.

(c)   Failing to look where she was going.

(d)   Failing to take that additional degree of care for her own safety as descending such a set of steps demands.

(e)   Being intoxicated.

10.   The injuries described in the medical evidence filed with the Particulars of Claim are noted but the extent and consequences of those injuries are neither admitted nor denied and must be proved.

11.   In the interests of proportionality the Defendant admits (without prejudice to liability) to £56.21 in expenses claimed.

12.   A contingent right to interest is admitted at such rates and for such periods as the court shall think fit.

A PUPIL

STATEMENT OF TRUTH

The Defendant believes that the facts set out in this Defence are true. Etc.

IN THE LIVERPOOL COUNTY COURT

CLAIM NO: LG305486

B E T W E E N :

ALICE BARLOW

Claimant

-and-

THOMSON HOLIDAYS LIMITED

Defendant

DEFENDANT'S SKELETON ARGUMENT
PACKAGE HOLIDAY SPECIMEN
Defective Hotel Equipment

Page references are references to the trial bundle.
Authorities referred to will be produced.

Introduction

1.   The Claimant claims damages from the Defendant (a tour operator) as a result of suffering injuries caused by an apparently malfunctioning automatic sliding door at her package holiday hotel (Hotel Venus in Benidorm) on 9 November 2002. As she walked through the door which had opened for her, it closed on her knocking her to the ground. She fractured her right wrist and suffered various other associated injuries. Photographs starting at *page 245* show the doors and set the scene.

The Legal Framework

2.   The legal issue might be distilled into this question: Can the Claimant prove that the Defendant or its hotel supplier has failed to exercise reasonable skill and care in a way causative of the incident or injury? It arises in the following way.

3.   D is subject to the Package Travel [Etc.] Regulations 1992. There is no dispute that these regulations apply. In particular regulation 15 provides (emphasis added - so far as is relevant for present purposes):

> **15 Liability of other party to the contract for proper performance of obligations under contract**
> (1)   *The other party to the contract*[2] *is liable* to the consumer[3] *for the proper performance of the obligations under the contract*, irrespective of whether such

---

[2] The Defendant

obligations are to be performed by that other party or by other suppliers of services but this shall not affect any remedy or right of action which that other party may have against those other suppliers of services.

(2) *The other party to the contract is liable* to the consumer *for* any damage caused to him by the failure to perform the contract or *the improper performance of the contract* unless the failure or the improper performance is due neither to any fault of that other party nor to that of another supplier of services, because— *(and certain exceptions are then set out)...*

4.   The application and interpretation of this regulation has been to the courts before and is dealt with by Longmore LJ in *Hone v Going Places Leisure Travel Limited* [2001] EWCA Civ 947 at paragraph 15 (emphasis added):

15. Regulation 15(2) provides for the other party to the contract to be liable for any damage caused to the consumer by failure to perform the contract or by the improper performance of the contract. The present case is not a case of failure to perform. It can only be a case of improper performance. *It is only possible to determine whether it is a case of improper performance by reference to the terms of the contract which is being performed. To my mind, regulation 15(2) does not give the answer to the question, "What is improper performance?" Rather it is a requirement of the application of regulation 15(2) that there should be improper performance.* That can only be determined by reference to the terms of the contract. There may be absolute obligations, e.g. as to the existence of a swimming-pool or any other matter, but, *in the absence of the assumption of an absolute obligation, the implication will be that reasonable skill and care will be used in the rendering of the relevant service.* There will thus be no improper performance of the air carriage unless there is an absence of reasonable skill and care in the provision of that service. If, as here, it is the claimant who seeks to rely on regulation 15(2), then he has to show that there has been improper performance.

5.   In short, D is liable for any improper performance of the contract on the part of itself *or* hoteliers providing accommodation facilities and an improper performance arises where there is a failure to exercise reasonable skill on the part of D or its suppliers.

6.   This liability is expressly accepted in the D's booking conditions (*Page 191 clause 7 "Personal Injury"*) where D accepts liability effectively for the "negligence" of its suppliers.

The Claimant's Pleaded Case

7.   The fault that is alleged against the Defendant (or for which the Defendant is responsible) is set out at *page 4* [Particulars of Claim].

   (a)   D *knew or ought to have known* that the door was liable to close suddenly.
   (b)   Failure to *inspect or repair* the automatic sensors controlling the door.
   (c)   Failed to have sufficient *number* of *sensors.*
   (d)   Failed to *warn* the Claimant of a risk of the doors closing suddenly.

---

¹ The Claimant.

8. If these pleaded allegations of fault are made out against either D or the Hotel, then D is liable for breach of the holiday contract.

9. The facts as described by the Claimant are not significantly in dispute. [See *page 47 paragraph 3*]. It also appears that some days *later* the doors did the same thing again [*page 48 paragraph 10*] – this was on 16 November and affected a Mrs. Russell holidaying with "JMC" at the Hotel[4].

The Defendant's Case

10. An intermittent fault had developed that could not reasonably have been identified prior to the Claimant's accident.

11. There had been no pre-existing problem with these doors. Clearly they went wrong, but automatic equipment *does* from time to time without there being any fault on the part of a hotelier or tour operator. The problem was not known about and there was no reason to think that there might be a problem.

> 11.1 The Claimant and her husband had been in residence for 4 days – and presumably used the doors before without incident, as had all other residents during that period.
> 11.2 The doors were installed in about 1995 (*page 142*) – about 7 years before the accident – and there are no known reported incidents of a similar nature (whether causing injury or otherwise) – even if there had been minor non-injury incidents that went unreported, these doors are part of a main thoroughfare in the Hotel and such incidents would not have gone unnoticed by staff.
> 11.3 The Defendant's staff conducted "unscientific" testing after the Claimant's accident [*page 70 para. 7* & *page 85 para. 5* & *pages 73* & *88*]. They could not identify any problems[5] with the doors in the immediate aftermath of the accident.
> 11.4 The above strongly points to an intermittent fault having developed. [See also – <u>expert engineer's</u> report *page 120 para. 3.42* which considers an installation problem unlikely and *page 123 - 1(b)* & *page* 129 para. 11].
> 11.5 The likelihood of an intermittent fault is further supported by the *Claimant's* evidence as she sat and waited for the ambulance – *page 48 para. 6*].
> 11.6 An expert engineer has reported [from *page 91*] and he sets out in the documentary background [*page 97*] the declaration of compliance in respect of the doors.
>
> • It is not possible to see in the photographs all the design components of the doors [*pages 107-110*].
> • The assumed motion of the Claimant was within the parameters at which the doors would have been expected to operate properly [*page 11 para. 3.16*] – assuming correct set-up.

---

[4] There are customer report forms describing the Claimant's accident at pages 197 & 198 – Mrs. Russell's appears at page 211.
[5] Although the Claimant maintains otherwise – at page 49 para. 13.

- The accident does not necessarily mean there was anything wrong with the installation [*page 113 para. 3.20*].
- He considers within the limits pf his information 2 applicable European standards – The EC Low Voltage Directive & The EC Machinery Directive. [*Pages 117 & 118*]. The doors appeared to conform [*page 3.41* para. 3.41].
- He states:

"Faults in these types of systems tend to occur without prior warning or manifestation of the condition. Where there is an intermittent fault, these are difficult to detect due to the lack of regular repeatability ... "

"Incidental" Issues

12. Even if the recollection of C & her husband is correct about the doors closing on people such as the reps. after the accident, it does not alter the fact that *before* the Claimant had her accident there was no apparent problem and no reason according to the engineer why a problem should have been picked up.

13. Mrs. Goggs states that the doors seemed to her to open and close "much more quickly" than would normally be expected. [*Page 60*]. This is at best impressionistic. The point being, however, that they were nonetheless opening and closing at appropriate times whatever the witness' impression was.

14. The hotel did put in an extra sensor after the event – but this is not evidence that they were at fault beforehand. They were reacting to the unexpected as a reasonable occupier should. There is no material from which one could infer that this would have made any difference to the outcome.

15. The Defendant is also entitled to rely on regulation 15(2)(c) of the Package Travel Regulations 1992 – an "event" that could not have been foreseen or forestalled – but this presupposes that the Claimant first proves breach of contract.

Spanish Law?

16. A Spanish lawyer has produced an "Advice" at the request of the Claimant. [*Page 152*].

17. The Defendant does not entirely understand why – but it is anticipated that it is intended to form the basis of an argument that the burden of proof is reversed in this case and/or that "reasonable care" means "diligence" in Spain.

18. The correct position has been set out by Swinton Thomas LJ in *Codd v Thomson Tour Operations Limited* B2/1999/1321 and by Philips J. in *Wilson v Best Travel* [1993] 1 All ER 353. *Codd* is authority for the proposition that the burden of proof does *not* shift in English proceedings of this sort – and is binding.

"This is not a case in which, in my view, it is appropriate to say that the hotel or the tour operator is liable for this accident without proof of negligence. In order to succeed <u>the claimant must prove that the hotel management was negligent</u> either in relation to the lift or in relation to the safety procedures." [emphasis added: Swinton Thomas LJ para. 24].

19. *This* action is brought pursuant to an English contract and British Statutory regulation. These demand that reasonable care is exercised to bring about a proper performance of the holiday contract. What *constitutes* reasonable care is informed by the prevailing local standard of how premises are managed in any given country – but this has nothing to do with Spanish procedural rules such as the reversal of the burden of proof or so-called "quasi-strict liability" (whatever that is).

20. The cases referred to in the "Advice" have not been produced and no doubt they all turn on their own facts and the evidence available.

21. However, even if applying a "diligence" test there is a limit to what diligence can do when faced with an intermittent fault of the sort that is likely to have occurred in the present case.

Quantum

22. The doctor reported on 1 August 2003. There is no doubt it was a nasty wrist injury. At *page 268* the doctor concludes that full restoration of finger and wrist movement should have been restored (say 21 months post accident). There are small risks of carpal tunnel problems (10%) and secondary rupture of the thumb (5%) although happily neither has occurred as yet.

23. Unfortunately she has also become troubled by associated loss of confidence and anxiety (always having been of an anxious personality type) according to the psychiatrist (*page 276 para. 32).*

24. The combination of wrist and finger problems makes the injury difficult to place in the JSB Guidelines – but "moderate hand injury" (page 41 of the 7th. edition) would suggest a figure in the region of £4,000.00 for the orthopaedic elements.

25. Without wanting to belittle the generalised anxiety from which she suffers, it is not seriously disabling and fits into the "minor" category of psychiatric injury at page 12 of the 7th edition. £2,500.00 is suggested.

26. The Defendant's position on Special Damage and Future Loss is set out in the Counter Schedule at *page 16.* It is not known whether the claimant is going to produce an updated Schedule.

Alan Saggerson
29 September 2005

Travel Law and Litigation

IN THE MANCHESTER COUNTY COURT

CLAIM NO: 5MA 07012

B E T W E E N :

(1)   CHRISTINE PEMBERTON
(2)   KEITH PEMBERTON

Claimants

-and-

FIRST CHOICE HOLIDAYS AND FLIGHTS LIMITED

Defendant

CLAIMANTS' SKELETON ARGUMENT
PACKAGE HOLIDAY SPECIMEN
Injury - Hurricane

Introduction

1.   The Defendant ["First Choice"] supplied to the Claimants (the First Claimant, her husband and her parents) a package holiday between 15 and 29 October 2002 based at the all-inclusive Las Palmas Hotel, Puerto Vallatara in Mexico ["the Hotel"].

2.   There were express terms of the holiday contract by virtue of the Defendants' standard terms and conditions to the effect that:

2.1   *"Our Responsibility. We accept responsibility for ensuring that you receive the holiday you have booked regardless of whether parts of the holiday are to be provided directly by us, or other suppliers ... "*
2.2   *"We accept responsibility for ... bodily injury caused to you as a result of any failure to perform or improper performance of the services we have agreed to supply to you* (except as provided for in regulation 15(2) of the Package Travel [Etc.] Regulations 1992)[6].

3.   There was an implied term of the contract (Supply of Goods and Services Act 1982 section 13) to the effect that all services forming part of the package holiday would be provided to a reasonable standard and with reasonable skill and care, which services included the services of First Choice local representatives and the management and staff of the Hotel.

---

[6] The Package Travel Regulations regime is annotated in Appendix 2. This is not likely to be controversial.

Hurricane "Kenna"
4.   On or about Friday 25 October 2002 hurricane "Kenna" struck the coast of Mexico in the vicinity of the Hotel. Vallatara (the location of the Hotel) did not receive a "direct hit" in meteorological terms, but the Hotel was devastated in the path of the hurricane. The First Claimant (Christine Pemberton) was trapped in the beach-side breakfast restaurant at about 9.00am as a result of inundation by an enormous wave (which came crashing through the restaurant roof) as a result of which she sustained an undisplaced fracture of her left fibula and other injuries. The other Claimants in the breakfast restaurant fled from the inundation.

5.   As a result of the wave and accompanying storm the rest of the day was one of chaos, uncertainty and anxiety for all the Claimants causing the loss of personal belongings and terrorising all concerned as they were pushed from pillar–to-post in an effort to keep them away so far as was then practicable from the sea and the worst effects of the storm.

6.   The Claimants do not allege that the Defendant or the Hotel was responsible for the hurricane!

Claimants' Claim
7.   There are two central points.

(a)   The beach side breakfast restaurant should have been evacuated (long) before the inundation.
(b)   The Claimants should have been alerted to the *potential seriousness* of the weather conditions in advance – thus they would have been better prepared and saved much unnecessary discomfort and anxiety as well as damage to their property.

Evidential Basis
8.   The evidential basis of the Claimant's claim cannot be put better than it has been by the manager of the Hotel. He says that internet reports that he monitors gave an indication of "rough weather" the night before the 25 October and goes on:

"...From 8am I called the Hotel several times from my home to check that everything was OK. I could see the sea from my house and later the waves became bigger and hitting my home. This must be before the wave hit the Hotel as I called again ... In any event I told the catering manager to ask all the clients who were in the restaurant ... to go upstairs ..."

If this had been done as the manager directed the First Claimant would not have sustained her fractured leg.

9.   In fact something ought to have been done much earlier. Severe weather was on the cards and this was likely to affect the safety and comfort of people in beachside resort hotels. The representative at the Decamaron Hotel (it is thought about 9 miles way on the same bay) says this:

"... nothing particular was done[7] ... on the day of 24 November (she means October) ... apart from tying down loose furniture and so forth as all the restaurants at the Hotel are very open and exposed. Guests were also asked to place things on bed (sic) as I think the manager expected some degree of flooding. At around 5.00am ... the Manager got in touch ...as he wanted guests to move to the rear block of the Hotel.

10. We know that the Hotel was on hurricane watch from 24 October & that the Hotel is situated in a part of the bay where big waves are likely due to the sudden deep-shallow changes in depth (see evidence of Stuart Thompson – who also tells us that even the Hotel Las Palmas took furniture inside and tied down loose items).

11. Whilst all this was going on the Claimants' case is that they were simply allowed to use the beachside restaurant as normal.

Liability
12. The failure to evacuate the restaurant that morning was a failure to exercise reasonable skill and care on the part of the Defendant and the operators of the Hotel for whom they are liable.

13. The failure to take the precautions taken at the Hotel Decamaron the day before was also a breach that caused unnecessary anxiety and distress and damage to personal property.

Damages
14. Damages remain in issue but continued efforts will be made to try and agree pain and suffering; loss of enjoyment; loss of bargain and special damage before trial.

JOHN DORY

---

[7] This must be one of the greatest understatements imaginable in the light of the balance of her evidence.

IN THE USUAL COUNTY COURT

CLAIM NO:

BETWEEN:

JOHN BROWN

Claimant

-and-

MY HOLIDAYS LIMITED

Defendant/Part 20 Claimant

-and-

HOTELES ZARAGOTHAS ESPANAS SL
(A company incorporated in Spain)
Part 20 Defendant/Third Party

PART 20 (Third Party) PARTICULARS OF CLAIM
Specimen

---

1.   In this action the Claimant claims damages against the Defendant for injury, loss and damage together with interest and costs arising out of alleged breaches of contract, negligence and/or improper performance of a holiday contract pursuant to regulation 15 of the Package Travel [Etc.] Regulations 1992 relating to a road accident on 14 January 2005.

2.   The Claimant's claim is set out in the Particulars of Claim a copy of which is served with this Part 20 Claim in which he alleges he suffered injury die to an accident cause by the supply to him of a defective motorised buggy by the said Hotel.

3.   The Defendant has denied liability to the Claimant as set out in the Defence, a copy of which is served with this Part 20 Claim.

4.   The Part 20 Defendant at all material times owned and/or operated and/or managed the Hotel El Gorgo, Sevilla, Spain at the time of the Claimant's accident and was at all material times responsible for operational control of the Hotel and the facilities, services and equipment made available to visitors such as the Claimant whilst he was staying there.

5.   By a written contract dated 12 February 2004 Part 20 Defendant agreed to provide holiday hotel accommodation to the Defendant's (and its associated

companies') customers for a period including the day of the Claimant's accident being 14 January 2005.

6.   There were express terms of the said written contract and of the agreement to the following effect namely that:

6.1 By clause 99 thereof, English law would apply to the contract;

6.2 By clause 98 the Part 20 Defendant guaranteed that the facilities and services of the Hotel would be commensurate with its rating and that the Part 20 Defendant would be liable for any justified complaints submitted by the Defendant due to *inter alia* inferior standards of service and/or negligence on the part of the Part 20 Defendant or its staff;

6.3 By clause 97 the Part 20 Defendant agreed that it would comply with all relevant local and national laws, decrees, regulations and codes of recommended practice relating to *(inter alia)* general safety;

6.4 Further by clause 96 the Part 20 Defendant would indemnify the Defendant against all losses, liabilities, claims or expenses for or in respect of injury loss or damage to persons or property which may arise from any cause whatsoever out of or in connection with the supply of services at the Hotel.

7.   Further or alternatively there were implied terms of the contract between the Defendant and the Part 20 Defendant to the effect that:

7.1 The services and facilities provided to the Defendant's customers as part of their holiday accommodation including the inclusive provision of bicycles would be of a reasonable standard.

7.2 The Part 20 Defendant and its servants or agents including staff at the Hotel would exercise reasonable care to ensure that guests staying at the Hotel were protected from the foreseeable risk of illness caused by the use of hotel facilities or equipment such as bicycles.

8.   The Defendant is by reason of paragraph 7 above, entitled to an indemnity in respect of all damages, interest and costs payable or already paid to the Claimant, or alternatively the Defendant is entitled to a contribution in respect of such claims and payments.

9.   In breach of the aforesaid implied terms set out above:

9.1 The Part 20 Defendant failed (in the event that the Claimant's case is made out) to provide services and facilities (namely buggies) to a reasonable standard.

9.2 The Part 20 Defendant or their servants or agents failed to exercise such care as was reasonable in all the circumstances to ensure that the Defendant's customers were protected from the foreseeable risk of illness (by appropriate maintenance and repair of the buggies).

10. The Defendant repeats and adopts and relies on the Particulars given in the Particulars of Claim as Particulars of breach of contract against the Part 20 Defendant.

11. The Part 20 Defendant owed to the Claimant a duty (whether contractual or non-contractual) arising out of its supply to the Claimant of a buggy that duty being to the effect that the buggy would be of a reasonable standard, reasonably safe and maintained to a reasonable level.

12. As a result of the Part 20 Defendant's breach of contract the Claimant suffered injury, loss and damage such as he alleges (subject to proof) in the Particulars of Claim.

13. Further or alternatively, the Defendant claims for an indemnity or alternatively a contribution by virtue of:

> 13.1 Sections 1 and 2 of the Civil Liability (Contribution) Act 1978 in respect of which the Defendant claim the Part 20 Defendant should be entirely responsible for the Claimants' claims because the Part 20 Defendant was the provider of holiday facilities and services (the bicycle) in question;
> 13.2 In respect of the Claimant's claim the Defendant avers that the Part 20 Defendant is entirely responsible for the Claimant's various complaints.

14. Accordingly the Defendant is entitled to the relief set out in the Prayer for Relief (below) together with interest thereon pursuant to section 69 of the County Courts Act 1984 for such periods and at such rates as the court shall think fit.

15. The Court has jurisdiction over this Part 20 Claim by virtue of the express terms of the contract between the parties and by reason of CPR Part 6.20(3)(b) and/0r (5)(c) and further by virtue of article 6 of Council Regulation (EC) 44/2001 there being no other proceedings in respect of this claim in any other jurisdiction.

AND THE DEFENDANT/PART 20 CLAIMANT CLAIMS:

1. A contractual or statutory Indemnity in respect of any sums ordered to be paid to the Claimants by the Defendant.
2. Alternatively, a contractual or statutory Contribution towards such sums.
3. Similar Indemnity or Contribution in respect of the sums paid to the additional customers.
4. Alternatively, Damages for breach of contract.
5. Interest at the rate of 6% or otherwise as the Court shall direct pursuant to paragraph 13 above – to be assessed.

A GENIUS

STATEMENT OF TRUTH
Etc.

SAMPLE WITNESS STATEMENT

TITLE AS IN ACTION

I, Andrew John Smith, of 23, Acacia Avenue, Suburbia, London SW93 XL5 will say:

Background

1. (a) I am the first claimant in this action. I was born on 25 December 1960 and am now 34 years old. I am a sprocket-twister by profession, having worked at Engineers & Sons in London SW93 since I left school. On 1 January 1993 I became engaged to marry the second claimant in this action, Brenda Brown. I did not relish the prospect of a traditional English wedding and I disliked the idea of a civil ceremony at the local civic centre. My fianceé and I decided that we would greatly enjoy a quiet, private and exotic wedding in the Caribbean.

(b) From about October 1992 (before our engagement), until 1 September 1993 we scoured holiday brochures looking for our ideal setting. We spent hours every evening and at weekends trying to find the perfect location. Over the August bank holiday of 1993 we looked at the defendant's "Summer Spectaculars" brochure for 1994. On page 63 particulars of the "Le Weddings" all-inclusive holiday resort were given. As soon as we saw the particulars we both realised that it was precisely what we had been looking for over the preceding year.

(c) A copy of the brochure will be available to the court. The resort seemed perfect. It was specifically designed to cater for weddings and "honeymoons", and its use was restricted to newly-weds or about-to-be-weds. It clearly described itself as a luxury resort, and I remember having to look up in the dictionary the meaning of the word "sybaritic" and being delighted to see that it meant "luxurious and pleasurable".

(d) More pointedly, the particulars also explained that all the arrangements for the wedding would be put in place by the resort. All we had to do was to select the date, the time and the part of the resort in which we would like the wedding to be held. A licensed registrar was promised, as was an appropriate marriage licence. All we had to do was to turn up at the appointed time and place. Even witnesses would be provided for us.

(e) Other than the wedding arrangements, the brochure enthused about the luxury rooms. All were advertised as having air-conditioning; we were informed that all had king-size double beds and that all had a sea-facing balcony or patio. An a la carte menu was promised at all meal times, which was important because I feared that at any all-inclusive resort that the menus might be very restricted (a bit canteen style), but I was reassured by the promise of the a la carte menu. Finally, an enticing array of water sports and court sports were promised (with what I assumed would be qualified) tuition. I was particularly looking forward to water-skiing, and to scuba diving which I had not done before, but which I hoped to learn whilst on holiday. Had there been time, I would have enjoyed using the tennis courts and brushing up my ground strokes with the help of a tennis professional.

The booking

2. (a) On 1 September 1993 at 9.00am I was waiting outside the High Street travel agent for it to open. When it opened I immediately filled in the forms to book our holiday for the fortnight between 1 and 15 September 1994. The wedding was booked for noon on 5 September 1994. I paid a deposit of £400.00 by Access card and the booking was immediately held by the travel agent's computer. I received the final invoice and booking confirmation from the defendants on 2 June 1994 (it was dated 1 June 1994 and numbered XYZ123), and wrote the defendant a letter dated 3 June enclosing a cheque for the balance of the price (£3,600.00). I wrote directly to the defendant rather than paying at the travel agent because I wanted to take the opportunity of confirming the exact details of the holiday and wedding so that there would be no hitches. These documents will be available to the court.

(b) In mid-August 1994 I received a package from the defendant containing a guide to the resort and the island of St Lucia, a map, and a bundle of money-off coupons to spend whilst I was away. I also received with this package a letter from the defendant wishing me and my fianceé an enjoyable holiday, and extending the company's congratulations on our forthcoming marriage.

(c) By this time I had been greatly looking forward to the holiday and the wedding for nearly a year. It would be fair to say that I was thinking of little else, and could hardly wait for the departure date to arrive. I had not had a holiday (apart from a few days off at home) since the summer of 1991 when I visited Butlins at Bognor Regis for a week, and given the expense of the wedding holiday, and the costs associated with setting up home as a married couple, I did not anticipate having another holiday abroad and certainly not another luxury holiday for some considerable time to come.

Travel and arrival

3. (a) Finally, the day of departure arrived. The second plaintiff and I, having spent almost the entire previous week making the necessary arrangements, duly embarked upon our journey to St Lucia, flying from Gatwick Airport at 0930 hours on 1 September 1994, flight number BA/050. Naturally, we were somewhat anxious to ensure all would transpire satisfactorily and were greatly relieved when we finally arrived at "Le Weddings" resort without any difficulties.

(b) Upon entering our room (no 100), we were dismayed to find an array of faults and disappointments. When we first opened the door to our room, we were greeted with an overwhelming smell of damp: the carpet was soaking wet, pools of water having gathered around the refrigerator and the air-conditioning unit. Furthermore, and contrary to what we had been led to believe in the defendant's brochure, we had only been allocated a single room with a single bed. The room was quite simply filthy, as were the windows (which I could barely see out of). In a vain attempt to allow some fresh air into the room, I attempted to open the windows; unfortunately, I failed in my endeavours, the windows were jammed shut.

(c) Matters worsened as I proceeded to inspect the room in greater detail. The sheets provided for our bed were so worn out that holes had appeared in them, were damp and appeared not to have been washed for some months. The second plaintiff inspected the bathroom, and pointed out that most of the tiles therein were either cracked or had fallen off. At this point, the second plaintiff commented how warm the room was: remembering that all rooms in "Le Weddings" were supposed to be air-conditioned, I checked the unit and found it to be making no noise whatsoever, and judging by the pool of water beneath, something clearly appeared to be wrong with it. In desperation, I checked the balcony, only to find it so small that only one person could stand on it at a time, and the view from it was essentially comprised of the hotel kitchens. Only by leaning around the wall adjacent to our balcony could I actually see the sea.

(d) I was so appalled by the actual state of the room when compared to the assurances in the defendant's brochure that I rushed to see the resort manager, despite my fatigue after a relatively long journey. After a number of hours complaining to various members of staff, I finally managed to speak to him, indicating the level of my dissatisfaction with the room. He assured me that, although no alternative room was available, the room would be cleaned, the air-conditioning unit fixed and a double bed provided. I was extremely unhappy with his apparent lack of sympathy for our predicament, but simply had no choice but to accept his comments for the meantime.

"Le Weddings": 2–11 September 1994

4. (a) The Room

On the morning of 1 September 1994, it transpired that the en-suite bathroom was in fact in a far worse condition than we had initially thought. The plastic toilet seat had sheared on one side, leaving dangerous jagged edges protruding in an upwards direction: consequently, both the second plaintiff and I had to use the lavatory in the downstairs restaurant. On the one occasion that the toilet in the en-suite bathroom was used, the flushing mechanism failed to work, necessitating the pouring of a bucket of bath water into the cistern. Furthermore, the surface of the bath was cracked, rendering the bath virtually useless, no plug provided fitted the bath or sink plug holes, and the towels were so filthy and tattered that they were beyond any use other than as rags.

(b) Repairs

At approximately 6.30am on 2 September 1994 we were rudely awoken by a group of repair men, who simply walked past us in bed across to the balcony laughing to themselves, before making a horrific amount of noise in re-tiling the balcony. At no time did anybody ask either the second plaintiff's permission or mine for this intrusion. This disgracefully embarrassing incident continued at the same time each morning until 10 September 1994.

(c) Meals

Contrary to being presented with an a la carte menu at all meal times, we were only offered a set meal in the downstairs restaurant each evening. As the food was of such a poor quality, we were forced to dine elsewhere (necessitating a taxi journey each time) on six separate occasions at a total cost of £240.00.

(d) Running water

On our return to our room after a day on the beach on 3 September 1994, we discovered that the resort had no running water available whatsoever. This disgraceful predicament continued through until the late hours of 10 September 1994. Throughout this period, all the management managed to do to alleviate our problems was to leave buckets of cold and rather dirty water at the bottom of our staircase, some three flights of stairs beneath our room. Although I initially made this journey on a number of occasions, in the end I simply gave up, and we were forced to use the cold shower provided on the beach in order to wash.

(e) Air-conditioning

During the beginning of our second week at "Le Weddings", a man finally arrived to repair our failed air-conditioning system which was continuing to leak. Despite many noisy attempts, he eventually gave up, leaving an extraordinary amount of dirt and dust all over our floor. At no time was this mess ever cleaned up.

(f) The Wedding

Based upon the appalling standard of the resort following our arrival, we were dreading something would go wrong with our wedding. On 5 September 1994, we arrived at the arranged location at 11.30am only to find that nobody else was there; we waited around becoming more and more anxious, until in desperation we contacted the resort manager, only to be told that no registrar was available. However, we were assured one would be available on 6 September 1994, and that our wedding would take place then. In fact, this turned out to be untrue, no registrar being available on that date or any other for the remainder of our stay in St Lucia. We were told (on 6 September) by the resort manager that there was a civil servants' strike and that he could not foresee when a registrar would become available. This struck me as curious because it was apparent that other weddings were being conducted at neighbouring resorts. This, the manager explained, was the result of other couples being married by religious ministers. We were not offered the alternative of a minister to conduct our marriage service.

(g) Sports

The enticing array of sports promised in the defendant's brochure also failed to materialise. I never in fact managed to get onto the tennis courts, let alone play a game of tennis, the court being in such a poor condition that it was "closed for repairs". Furthermore, the water sports provided only took place on Tuesdays and Fridays of each week. Accordingly, I went along to the first available session with the second plaintiff, only to discover than the man in charge of the activities was in fact an English accountant (who confessed to me that he had taken the job after being barred from practice), who knew as little as I did about scuba-diving and water-skiing. Consequently, I only ever ventured into the water to swim (which in itself was beyond the skill of the said "instructor"), to my great disappointment. Consequently, I had to go by taxi to the nearest resort (called "Le Sport") which offered the sports facilities with qualified tuition that I was so looking forward to: in total I had four lessons in scuba diving at £25.00 each. I never managed to go water-skiing.

(h) Meals out

On three separate evenings we decided that we had to escape from the horrors of "Le Weddings" (despite the "all inclusive" package supposedly provided), venturing into neighbouring resorts in order to at least feel as if we were on holiday at a total cost of £150.00. When we "escaped" in this fashion we were able to enjoy some temporary relaxation for a few hours, and tried to forget all the horrors of our hotel.

(i) Room service

At no stage was our room actually "cleaned". A chamber maid popped in whenever she felt like it to empty out bins and swap one filthy set of sheets for another. The manager's assurances never came to fruition.

"Le Sport": 12–15 September 1994

5. (a) In the evening of 11 September 1994, we sat in our room at "Le Weddings", wondering if we could do anything to salvage our supposed holiday. Our room was in an absolutely disgusting condition, and we had barely had any sleep at all for the last ten nights. Our first real holiday together had been ruined. In desperation we decided to book into the nearby "Le Sport" resort, hoping to get some satisfaction from our last few days in St Lucia. As a result we had to pay a further £450.00 for a three-night stay in "Le Sport" from 12 to 15 September 1994. Unfortunately, even this attempt achieved little success: our holiday had already been ruined, and even at "Le Sport" it was very difficult to put out of our minds the disasters of the preceding weeks.

(b) We caught flight BA/051 back to England on 15 September 1994. I could hardly wait to get home. On our return we were absolutely exhausted, having gained no benefit whatsoever from our supposed "luxury" holiday. The defendant's claims in their brochure relating to "Le Weddings" were simply untrue.

The wedding

6. On our return to England, having failed to marry in St Lucia (which was really the whole point of the trip to St Lucia), we were forced to arrange our wedding at the Civic Centre, Suburbia, to our great disappointment. Our wedding took place on 8 January 1995 and cost £1,200.

This statement is true to the best of my information and belief.

Signed

Dated

COUNCIL DIRECTIVE 90/314 O F13 JUNE 13 1990 ON PACKAGE TRAVEL, PACKAGE HOLIDAYS AND PACKAGE TOURS[1]

THE COUNCIL OF THE EUROPEAN COMMUNITIES,

Having regard to the Treaty establishing the European Economic Community, and in particular Article 100a thereof,

Having regard to the proposal from the Commission (1),

In cooperation with the European Parliament (2),

Having regard to the opinion of the Economic and Social Committee (3),

Whereas one of the main objectives of the Community is to complete the internal market, of which the tourist sector is an essential part;

Whereas the national laws of Member States concerning package travel, package holidays and package tours, hereinafter referred to as 'packages', show many disparities and national practices in this field are markedly different, which gives rise to obstacles to the freedom to provide services in respect of packages and distortions of competition amongst operators established in different Member States;

Whereas the establishment of common rules on packages will contribute to the elimination of these obstacles and thereby to the achievement of a common market in services, thus enabling operators established in one Member State to offer their services in other Member States and Community consumers to benefit from comparable conditions when buying a package in any Member State;

Whereas paragraph 36 (b) of the Annex to the Council resolution of 19 May 1981 on a second programme of the European Economic Community for a consumer protection and information policy (4) invites the Commission to study, inter alia, tourism and, if appropriate, to put forward suitable proposals, with due regard for their significance for consumer protection and the effects of differences in Member States' legislation on the proper functioning of the common market;

---

[1] OJ 1990 L158/59.

Whereas in the resolution on a Community policy on tourism on 10 April 1984 (5) the Council welcomed the Commission's initiative in drawing attention to the importance of tourism and took note of the Commission's initial guidelines for a Community policy on tourism;

Whereas the Commission communication to the Council entitled 'A New Impetus for Consumer Protection Policy', which was approved by resolution of the Council on 6 May 1986 (6), lists in paragraph 37, among the measures proposed by the Commission, the harmonization of legislation on packages;

Whereas tourism plays an increasingly important role in the economies of the Member States; whereas the package system is a fundamental part of tourism; whereas the package travel industry in Member States would be stimulated to greater growth and productivity if at least a minimum of common rules were adopted in order to give it a Community dimension; whereas this would not only produce benefits for Community citizens buying packages organized on the basis of those rules, but would attract tourists from outside the Community seeking the advantages of guaranteed standards in packages;

Whereas disparities in the rules protecting consumers in different Member States are a disincentive to consumers in one Member State from buying packages in another Member State;

. Whereas this disincentive is particularly effective in deterring consumers from buying packages outside their own Member State, and more effective than it would be in relation to the acquisition of other services, having regard to the special nature of the services supplied in a package which generally involve the expenditure of substantial amounts of money in advance and the supply of the services in a State other than that in which the consumer is resident;

Whereas the consumer should have the benefit of the protection introduced by this Directive irrespective of whether he is a direct contracting party, a transferee or a member of a group on whose behalf another person has concluded a contract in respect of a package;

Whereas the organizer of the package and/or the retailer of it should be under obligation to ensure that in descriptive matter relating to packages which they respectively

organize and sell, the information which is given is not misleading and brochures made available to consumers contain information which is comprehensible and accurate;

Whereas the consumer needs to have a record of the terms of contract applicable to the package; whereas this can conveniently be achieved by requiring that all the terms of the contract be stated in writing of such other documentary form as shall be comprehensible and accessible to him, and that he be given a copy thereof;

Whereas the consumer should be at liberty in certain circumstances to transfer to a willing third person a booking made by him for a package;

Whereas the price established under the contract should not in principle be subject to revision except where the possibility of upward or downward revision is expressly provided for in the contract; whereas that possibility should nonetheless be subject to certain conditions;

Whereas the consumer should in certain circumstances be free to withdraw before departure from a package travel contract;

Whereas there should be a clear definition of the rights available to the the consumer in circumstances where the organizer of the package cancels it before the agreed date of departure;

Whereas if, after the consumer has departed, there occurs a significant failure of performance of the services for which he has contracted or the organizer perceives that he will be unable to procure a significant part of the services to be provided; the organizer should have certain obligations towards the consumer;

Whereas the organizer and/or retailer party to the contract should be liable to the consumer for the proper performance of the obligations arising from the contract; whereas, moreover, the organizer and/or retailer should be liable for the damage resulting for the consumer from failure to perform or improper performance of the contract unless the defects in the performance of the contract are attributable neither to any fault of theirs nor to that of another supplier of services;

Whereas in cases where the organizer and/or retailer is liable for failure to perform or improper performance of the services involved in the package, such liability should be limited in accordance with the international conventions governing such services, in particular the Warsaw Convention of 1929 in International Carriage by Air, the Berne Convention of 1961 on Carriage by Rail, the Athens Convention of 1974 on Carriage by Sea and the Paris Convention of 1962 on the Liability of Hotel-keepers; whereas, moreover, with regard to damage other than personal injury, it should be possible for liability also to be limited under the package contract provided, however, that such limits are not unreasonable;

Whereas certain arrangements should be made for the information of consumers and the handling of complaints;

Whereas both the consumer and the package travel industry would benefit if organizers and/or retailers were placed under an obligation to provide sufficient evidence of security in the event of insolvency;

Whereas Member States should be at liberty to adopt, or retain, more stringent provisions relating to package travel for the purpose of protecting the consumer,

HAS ADOPTED THIS DIRECTIVE:

Article 1

The purpose of this Directive is to approximate the laws, regulations and administrative provisions of the Member States relating to packages sold or offered for sale in the territory of the Community.

Article 2

For the purposes of this Directive:

1. 'package' means the pre-arranged combination of not fewer than two of the following when sold or offered for sale at an inclusive price and when the service covers a period of more than twenty-four hours or includes overnight accommodation:

(a) transport;

(b) accommodation;

(c) other tourist services not ancillary to transport or accommodation and accounting for a significant proportion of the package.

The separate billing of various components of the same package shall not absolve the organizer or retailer from the obligations under this Directive;

2. 'organizer' means the person who, other than occasionally, organizes packages and sells or offers them for sale, whether directly or through a retailer;

3. 'retailer' means the person who sells or offers for sale the package put together by the organizer;

4. 'consumer' means the person who takes or agrees to take the package ('the principal contractor'), or any person on whose behalf the principal contractor agrees to purchase the package ('the other beneficiaries') or any person to whom the principal contractor or any of the other beneficiaries transfers the package ('the transferee');

5. 'contract' means the agreement linking the consumer to the organizer and/or the retailer.

Article 3

1. Any descriptive matter concerning a package and supplied by the organizer or the retailer to the consumer, the price of the package and any other conditions applying to the contract must not contain any misleading information. 2. When a brochure is made available to the consumer, it shall indicate in a legible, comprehensible and accurate manner both the price and adequate information concerning:

(a) the destination and the means, characteristics and categories of transport used;

(b) the type of accommodation, its location, category or degree of comfort and its main features, its approval and tourist classification under the rules of the host Member State concerned;

(c) the meal plan;

(d) the itinerary;

(e) general information on passport and visa requirements for nationals of the Member State or States concerned and health formalities required for the journey and the stay;

(f) either the monetary amount or the percentage of the price which is to be paid on account, and the timetable for payment of the balance;

(g) whether a minimum number of persons is required for the package to take place and, if so, the deadline for informing the consumer in the event of cancellation.

The particulars contained in the brochure are binding on the organizer or retailer, unless:

- changes in such particulars have been clearly communicated to the consumer before conclusion of the contract, in which case the brochure shall expressly state so,

- changes are made later following an agreement between the parties to the contract.

Article 4

1. (a) The organizer and/or the retailer shall provide the consumer, in writing or any other appropriate form, before the contract is concluded, with general information on passport and visa requirements applicable to nationals of the Member State or States concerned and in particular on the periods for obtaining them, as well as with information on the health formalities required for the journey and the stay;

(b) The organizer and/or retailer shall also provide the consumer, in writing or any other appropriate form, with the following information in good time before the start of the journey:

(i) the times and places of intermediate stops and transport connections as well as details of the place to be occupied by the traveller, e.g. cabin or berth on ship, sleeper compartment on train;

(ii) the name, address and telephone number of the organizer's and/or retailer's local representative or, failing that, of local agencies on whose assistance a consumer in difficulty could call.

Where no such representatives or agencies exist, the consumer must in any case be provided with an emergency telephone number or any other information that will enable him to contract the organizer and/or the retailer;

(iii) in the case of journeys or stays abroad by minors, information enabling direct contact to be established with the child or the person responsible at the child's place of stay;

(iv) information on the optional conclusion of an insurance policy to cover the cost of cancellation by the consumer or the cost of assistance, including repatriation, in the event of accident or illness.

2. Member States shall ensure that in relation to the contract the following principles apply:

(a) depending on the particular package, the contract shall contain at least the elements listed in the Annex;

(b) all the terms of the contract are set out in writing or such other form as is comprehensible and accessible to the consumer and must be communicated to him before the conclusion of the contract; the consumer is given a copy of these terms;

(c) the provision under (b) shall not preclude the belated conclusion of last-minute reservations or contracts.

3. Where the consumer is prevented from proceeding with the package, he may transfer his booking, having first given the organizer or the retailer reasonable notice of his intention before departure, to a person who satisfies all the conditions applicable to the package. The transferor of the package and the transferee shall be jointly and severally liable to the organizer or retailer party to the contract for payment of the balance due and for any additional costs arising from such transfer.

4. (a) The prices laid down in the contract shall not be subject to revision unless the contract expressly provides for the possibility of upward or downward revision and states precisely how the revised price is to be calculated, and solely to allow for variations in:

- transportation costs, including the cost of fuel,

- dues, taxes or fees chargeable for certain services, such as landing taxes or embarkation or disembarkation fees at ports and airports,

- the exchange rates applied to the particular package.

(b) During the twenty days prior to the departure date stipulated, the price stated in the contract shall not be increased.

5. If the organizer finds that before the departure he is constrained to alter significantly any of the essential terms, such as the price, he shall notify the consumer as quickly as possible in order to enable him to take appropriate decisions and in particular:

- either to withdraw from the contract without penalty,

- or to accept a rider to the contract specifying the alterations made and their impact on the price.

The consumer shall inform the organizer or the retailer of his decision as soon as possible.

6. If the consumer withdraws from the contract pursuant to paragraph 5, or if, for whatever cause, other than the fault of the consumer, the organizer cancels the package before the agreed date of departure, the consumer shall be entitled:

(a) either to take a substitute package of equivalent or higher quality where the organizer and/or retailer is able to offer him such a substitute. If the replacement package offered is of lower quality, the organizer shall refund the difference in price to the consumer;

(b) or to be repaid as soon as possible all sums paid by him under the contract.

In such a case, he shall be entitled, if appropriate, to be compensated by either the organizer or the retailer, whichever the relevant Member State's law requires, for non-performance of the contract, except where:

(i) cancellation is on the grounds that the number of persons enrolled for the package is less than the minimum number required and the consumer is informed of the cancellation, in writing, within the period indicated in the package description; or

(ii) cancellation, excluding overbooking, is for reasons of force majeure, i.e. unusual and unforeseeable circumstances beyond the control of the party by whom it is pleaded, the consequences of which could not have been avoided even if all due care had been exercised.

7. Where, after departure, a significant proportion of the services contracted for is not provided or the organizer perceives that he will be unable to procure a significant proportion of the services to be provided, the organizer shall make suitable alternative arrangements, at no extra cost to the consumer, for the continuation of the package, and where appropriate compensate the consumer for the difference between the services offered and those supplied.

If it is impossible to make such arrangements or these are not accepted by the consumer for good reasons, the organizer shall, where appropriate, provide the consumer, at no extra cost, with equivalent transport back to the place of departure, or to another return-point to which the consumer has agreed and shall, where appropriate, compensate the consumer.

Article 5

1. Member States shall take the necessary steps to ensure that the organizer and/or retailer party to the contract is liable to the consumer for the proper performance of the obligations arising from the contract, irrespective of whether such obligations are to be performed by that organizer and/or retailer or by other suppliers of services without prejudice to the right of the organizer and/or retailer to pursue those other suppliers of services.

2. With regard to the damage resulting for the consumer from the failure to perform or the improper performance of the contract, Member States shall take the necessary steps to ensure that the organizer and/or retailer is/are liable unless such failure to perform or improper performance is attributable neither to any fault of theirs nor to that of another supplier of services, because:

- the failures which occur in the performance of the contract are attributable to the consumer,

- such failures are attributable to a third party unconnected with the provision of the services contracted for, and are unforeseeable or unavoidable,

- such failures are due to a case of force majeure such as that defined in Article 4 (6), second subparagraph (ii), or to an event which the organizer and/or retailer or the supplier of services, even with all due care, could not foresee or forestall.

In the cases referred to in the second and third indents, the organizer and/or retailer party to the contract shall be required to give prompt assistance to a consumer in difficulty.

In the matter of damages arising from the non-performance or improper performance of the services involved in the package, the Member States may allow compensation to be limited in accordance with the international conventions governing such services.

In the matter of damage other than personal injury resulting from the non-performance or improper performance of the services involved in the package, the Member States may allow compensation to be limited under the contract. Such limitation shall not be unreasonable.

3. Without prejudice to the fourth subparagraph of paragraph 2, there may be no exclusion by means of a contractual clause from the provisions of paragraphs 1 and 2.

4. The consumer must communicate any failure in the performance of a contract which he perceives on the spot to the supplier of the services concerned and to the organizer and/or retailer in writing or any other appropriate form at the earliest opportunity.

This obligation must be stated clearly and explicitly in the contract. Article 6

In cases of complaint, the organizer and/or retailer or his local representative, if there is one, must make prompt efforts to find appropriate solutions.

Article 7

The organizer and/or retailer party to the contract shall provide sufficient evidence of security for the refund of money paid over and for the repatriation of the consumer in the event of insolvency.

Article 8

Member States may adopt or return more stringent provisions in the field covered by this Directive to protect the consumer.

Article 9

1. Member States shall bring into force the measures necessary to comply with this Directive before 31 December 1992. They shall forthwith inform the Commission thereof.

2. Member States shall communicate to the Commission the texts of the main provisions of national law which they adopt in the field governed by this Directive. The Commission shall inform the other Member States thereof.

Article 10

This Directive is addressed to the Member States.   ...

ANNEX

Elements to be included in the contract if relevant to the particular package;

(a) the travel destination(s) and, where periods of stay are involved, the relevant periods, with dates;

(b) the means, characteristics and categories of transport to be used, the dates, times and points of departure and return;

(c) where the package includes accommodation, its location, its tourist category or degree of comfort, its main features, its compliance with the rules of the host Member State concerned and the meal plan;

(d) whether a minimum number of persons is required for the package to take place and, if so, the deadline for informing the consumer in the event of cancellation;

(e) the itinerary;

(f) visits, excursions or other services which are included in the total price agreed for the package;

(g) the name and address of the organizer, the retailer and, where appropriate, the insurer;

(h) the price of the package, an indication of the possibility of price revisions under Article 4 (4) and an indication of any dues, taxes or fees chargeable for certain services (landing, embarkation or disembarkation fees at ports and airports, tourist taxes) where such costs are not included in the package;

(i) the payment schedule and method of payment;

(j) special requirements which the consumer has communicated to the organizer or retailer when making the booking, and which both have accepted;

(k) periods within which the consumer must make any complaint concerning failure to perform or improper performance of the contract.

Appendix 2

THE PACKAGE TRAVEL, PACKAGE HOLIDAYS AND PACKAGE TOURS REGULATIONS 1992[1]

Made --- 22nd December 1992

Whereas the Secretary of State is a Minister designated for the purposes of section 2(2) of the European Communities Act 1972 in relation to measures relating to consumer protection as regards package travel, package holidays and package tours;

And whereas a draft of these Regulations has been approved by a resolution of each House of Parliament pursuant to section 2(2) of and paragraph 2(2) of Schedule 2 to that Act;

Now, therefore the Secretary of State in exercise of the powers conferred on him by section 2(2) of that Act hereby makes the following Regulations

1 CITATION AND COMMENCEMENT

These Regulations may be cited as the Package Travel, Package Holidays and Package Tours Regulations 1992 and shall come into force on the day after the day on which they are made.

2 INTERPRETATION

(1) In these Regulations—

"brochure" means any brochure in which packages are offered for sale;

"contract" means the agreement linking the consumer to the organiser or to the retailer, or to both, as the case may be;

"the Directive" means Council Directive 90/314/EEC on package travel, package holidays and package tours;

---

[1] SI 1992 No 3288.

["member State" means a member State of the European Community or another State in the European Economic Area;]

"offer" includes an invitation to treat whether by means of advertising or otherwise, and cognate expressions shall be construed accordingly;

"organiser" means the person who, otherwise than occasionally, organises packages and sells or offers them for sale, whether directly or through a retailer;

"the other party to the contract" means the party, other than the consumer, to the contract, that is, the organiser or the retailer, or both, as the case may be;

"package" means the pre-arranged combination of at least two of the following components when sold or offered for sale at an inclusive price and when the service covers a period of more than twenty-four hours or includes overnight accommodation:—

    (a) transport;

    (b) accommodation;

    (c) other tourist services not ancillary to transport or accommodation and accounting for a significant proportion of the package,

        and

        (i)   the submission of separate accounts for different components shall not cause the arrangements to be other than a package;

        (ii)   the fact that a combination is arranged at the request of the consumer and in accordance with his specific instructions (whether modified or not) shall not of itself cause it to be treated as other than pre-arranged;

and

"retailer" means the person who sells or offers for sale the package put together by the organiser.

(2) In the definition of "contract" in paragraph (1) above, "consumer" means the person who takes or agrees to take the package ("the principal contractor") and elsewhere in these Regulations "consumer" means, as the context requires, the principal contractor, any person on whose behalf the principal contractor agrees to purchase the package ("the other beneficiaries") or any person to whom the principal contractor or any of the other beneficiaries transfers the package ("the transferee").

NOTES Amendment Para (1): definition "member State" inserted by SI 1995/1648, reg 2(a).

3 APPLICATION OF REGULATIONS

(1)   These Regulations apply to packages sold or offered for sale in the territory of the United Kingdom.

(2)   Regulations 4 to 15 apply to packages so sold or offered for sale on or after 31st December 1992.

(3)   Regulations 16 to 22 apply to contracts which, in whole or part, remain to be performed on 31st December 1992.

4 DESCRIPTIVE MATTER RELATING TO PACKAGES MUST NOT BE MISLEADING

(1)   No organiser or retailer shall supply to a consumer any descriptive matter concerning a package, the price of a package or any other conditions applying to the contract which contains any misleading information.

(2)   If an organiser or retailer is in breach of paragraph (1) he shall be liable to compensate the consumer for any loss which the consumer suffers in consequence.

5 REQUIREMENTS AS TO BROCHURES

(1)   Subject to paragraph (4) below, no organiser shall make available a brochure to a possible consumer unless it indicates in a legible, comprehensible and accurate manner the price and adequate information about the matters specified in Schedule 1 to these Regulations in respect of the packages offered for sale in the brochure to the extent that those matters are relevant to the packages so offered.

(2)   Subject to paragraph (4) below, no retailer shall make available to a possible consumer a brochure which he knows or has reasonable cause to believe does not comply with the requirements of paragraph (1).

(3)   An organiser who contravenes paragraph (1) of this regulation and a retailer who contravenes paragraph (2) thereof shall be guilty of an offence and liable:—

(a)   on summary conviction, to a fine not exceeding level 5 on the standard scale; and

(b)   on conviction on indictment, to a fine.

(4)   Where a brochure was first made available to consumers generally before 31st December 1992 no liability shall arise under this regulation in respect of an identical brochure being made available to a consumer at any time.

6 CIRCUMSTANCES IN WHICH PARTICULARS IN BROCHURE ARE TO BE BINDING

(1)   Subject to paragraphs (2) and (3) of this regulation, the particulars in the brochure (whether or not they are required by regulation 5(1) above to be included in the brochure) shall constitute implied warranties (or, as regards Scotland, implied terms) for the purposes of any contract to which the particulars relate.

(2)   Paragraph (1) of this regulation does not apply—

> (a)   in relation to information required to be included by virtue of paragraph 9 of Schedule 1 to these Regulations; or

> (b)   where the brochure contains an express statement that changes may be made in the particulars contained in it before a contract is concluded and changes in the particulars so contained are clearly communicated to the consumer before a contract is concluded.

(3)   Paragraph (1) of this regulation does not apply when the consumer and the other party to the contract agree after the contract has been made that the particulars in the brochure, or some of those particulars, should not form part of the contract.

7 INFORMATION TO BE PROVIDED BEFORE CONTRACT IS CONCLUDED

(1)   Before a contract is concluded, the other party to the contract shall provide the intending consumer with the information specified in paragraph (2) below in writing or in some other appropriate form.

(2)   The information referred to in paragraph (1) is:—

> (a)   general information about passport and visa requirements which apply to [nationals of the member State or States concerned] who purchase the package in question, including information about the length of time it is likely to take to obtain the appropriate passports and visas;

> (b)   information about health formalities required for the journey and the stay; and

> (c)   the arrangements for security for the money paid over and (where applicable) for the repatriation of the consumer in the event of insolvency.

(3)   If the intending consumer is not provided with the information required by paragraph (1) in accordance with that paragraph the other party to the contract shall be guilty of an offence and liable:—

(a)   on summary conviction, to a fine not exceeding level 5 on the standard scale; and

(b)   on conviction on indictment, to a fine.

NOTES

Amendment
Para (2): in sub-para (a) words "nationals of the member State or States concerned"
in square brackets substituted by SI 1998/1208, reg 5.
Date in force: 30 June 1998: see SI 1998/1208, reg 1.

8 INFORMATION TO BE PROVIDED IN GOOD TIME

(1)   The other party to the contract shall in good time before the start of the journey provide the consumer with the information specified in paragraph (2) below in writing or in some other appropriate form.

(2)   The information referred to in paragraph (1) is the following:—

     (a)   the times and places of intermediate stops and transport connections and particulars of the place to be occupied by the traveller (for example, cabin or berth on ship, sleeper compartment on train);

     (b)   the name, address and telephone number—

          (i)   of the representative of the other party to the contract in the locality where the consumer is to stay,

          or, if there is no such representative,

          (ii)   of an agency in that locality on whose assistance a consumer in difficulty would be able to call,

or, if there is no such representative or agency, a telephone number or other information which will enable the consumer to contact the other party to the contract during the stay; and

(c)   in the case of a journey or stay abroad by a child under the age of 16 on the day when the journey or stay is due to start, information enabling direct contact to be made with the child or the person responsible at the place where he is to stay; and

(d)   except where the consumer is required as a term of the contract to take out an insurance policy in order to cover the cost of cancellation by the consumer or the cost of assistance, including repatriation, in the event of accident or illness, information about an insurance policy which the consumer may, if he wishes, take out in respect of the risk of those costs being incurred.

(3) If the consumer is not provided with the information required by paragraph (1) in accordance with that paragraph the other party to the contract shall be guilty of an offence and liable:—

(a)   on summary conviction, to a fine not exceeding level 5 on the standard scale; and

(b)   on conviction on indictment, to a fine.

9 CONTENTS AND FORM OF CONTRACT

(1) The other party to the contract shall ensure that—

(a)   depending on the nature of the package being purchased, the contract contains at least the elements specified in Schedule 2 to these Regulations;

(b)   subject to paragraph (2) below, all the terms of the contract are set out in writing or such other form as is comprehensible and accessible to the consumer and are communicated to the consumer before the contract is made; and

(c)   a written copy of these terms is supplied to the consumer.

(2) Paragraph (1)(b) above does not apply when the interval between the time when the consumer approaches the other party to the contract with a view to entering into a contract and the time of departure under the proposed contract is so short that it is impracticable to comply with the sub-paragraph.

(3) It is an implied condition (or, as regards Scotland, an implied term) of the contract that the other party to the contract complies with the provisions of paragraph (1).

(4) In Scotland, any breach of the condition implied by paragraph (3) above shall be deemed to be a material breach justifying rescission of the contract.

10 TRANSFER OF BOOKINGS

(1) In every contract there is an implied term that where the consumer is prevented from proceeding with the package the consumer may transfer his booking to a person who satisfies all the conditions applicable to the package, provided that the consumer gives reasonable notice to the other party to the contract of his intention to transfer before the date when departure is due to take place.

(2)   Where a transfer is made in accordance with the implied term set out in paragraph (1) above, the transferor and the transferee shall be jointly and severally liable to the other party to the contract for payment of the price of the package (or, if

part of the price has been paid, for payment of the balance) and for any additional costs arising from such transfer.

11 PRICE REVISION

(1) Any term in a contract to the effect that the prices laid down in the contract may be revised shall be void and of no effect unless the contract provides for the possibility of upward or downward revision and satisfies the conditions laid down in paragraph (2) below.

(2) The conditions mentioned in paragraph (1) are that—

> (a) the contract states precisely how the revised price is to be calculated;

> (b) the contract provides that price revisions are to be made solely to allow for variations in:—

>> (i) transportation costs, including the cost of fuel,

>> (ii) dues, taxes or fees chargeable for services such as landing taxes or embarkation or disembarkation fees at ports and airports, or

>> (iii) the exchange rates applied to the particular package; and

(3) Notwithstanding any terms of a contract,

> (i) no price increase may be made in a specified period which may not be less than 30 days before the departure date stipulated; and

> (ii) as against an individual consumer liable under the contract, no price increase may be made in respect of variations which would produce an increase of less than 2 per cent, or such greater percentage as the contract may specify,("non-eligible variations") and that the non-eligible variations shall be left out of account in the calculation.

12 SIGNIFICANT ALTERATIONS TO ESSENTIAL TERMS

In every contract there are implied terms to the effect that—

> (a) where the organiser is constrained before the departure to alter significantly an essential term of the contract, such as the price (so far as regulation 11 permits him to do so), he will notify the consumer as quickly as possible in order to enable him to take appropriate decisions and in particular to withdraw from the contract without penalty or to accept a

rider to the contract specifying the alterations made and their impact on the price; and

(b)		the consumer will inform the organiser or the retailer of his decision as soon as possible.

13 WITHDRAWAL BY CONSUMER PURSUANT TO REGULATION 12 AND CANCELLATION BY ORGANISER

(1)	The terms set out in paragraphs (2) and (3) below are implied in every contract and apply where the consumer withdraws from the contract pursuant to the term in it implied by virtue of regulation 12(a), or where the organiser, for any reason other than the fault of the consumer, cancels the package before the agreed date of departure.

(2)	The consumer is entitled—

(a)		to take a substitute package of equivalent or superior quality if the other party to the contract is able to offer him such a substitute; or

(b)		to take a substitute package of lower quality if the other party to the contract is able to offer him one and to recover from the organiser the difference in price between the price of the package purchased and that of the substitute package; or

(c)		to have repaid to him as soon as possible all the monies paid by him under the contract.

(3)	The consumer is entitled, if appropriate, to be compensated by the organiser for non-performance of the contract except where—

(a)		the package is cancelled because the number of persons who agree to take it is less than the minimum number required and the consumer is informed of the cancellation, in writing, within the period indicated in the description of the package; or

(b)		the package is cancelled by reason of unusual and unforeseeable circumstances beyond the control of the party by whom this exception is pleaded, the consequences of which could not have been avoided even if all due care had been exercised.

(4)		Overbooking shall not be regarded as a circumstance falling within the provisions of sub-paragraph (b) of paragraph (3) above.

14 SIGNIFICANT PROPORTION OF SERVICES NOT PROVIDED

(1)	The terms set out in paragraphs (2) and (3) below are implied in every contract and apply where, after departure, a significant proportion of the services contracted for is not provided or the organiser becomes aware that he will be unable to procure a significant proportion of the services to be provided.

(2) The organiser will make suitable alternative arrangements, at no extra cost to the consumer, for the continuation of the package and will, where appropriate, compensate the consumer for the difference between the services to be supplied under the contract and those supplied.

(3) If it is impossible to make arrangements as described in paragraph (2), or these are not accepted by the consumer for good reasons, the organiser will, where appropriate, provide the consumer with equivalent transport back to the place of departure or to another place to which the consumer has agreed and will, where appropriate, compensate the consumer.

15 LIABILITY OF OTHER PARTY TO THE CONTRACT FOR PROPER PERFORMANCE OF OBLIGATIONS UNDER CONTRACT

(1)   The other party to the contract is liable to the consumer for the proper performance of the obligations under the contract, irrespective of whether such obligations are to be performed by that other party or by other suppliers of services but this shall not affect any remedy or right of action which that other party may have against those other suppliers of services.

(2)   The other party to the contract is liable to the consumer for any damage caused to him by the failure to perform the contract or the improper performance of the contract unless the failure or the improper performance is due neither to any fault of that other party nor to that of another supplier of services, because—

> (a)   the failures which occur in the performance of the contract are attributable to the consumer;
>
> (b)   such failures are attributable to a third party unconnected with the provision of the services contracted for, and are unforeseeable or unavoidable; or
>
> (c)   such failures are due to—
>
>> (i)   unusual and unforeseeable circumstances beyond the control of the party by whom this exception is pleaded, the consequences of which could not have been avoided even if all due care had been exercised; or
>>
>> (ii)   an event which the other party to the contract or the supplier of services, even with all due care, could not foresee or forestall.

(3)   In the case of damage arising from the non-performance or improper performance of the services involved in the package, the contract may provide for compensation to be limited in accordance with the international conventions which govern such services.

(4)   In the case of damage other than personal injury resulting from the non-performance or improper performance of the services involved in the package, the contract may include a term limiting the amount of compensation which will be paid to the consumer, provided that the limitation is not unreasonable.

(5)   Without prejudice to paragraph (3) and paragraph (4) above, liability under paragraphs (1) and (2) above cannot be excluded by any contractual term.

(6)   The terms set out in paragraphs (7) and (8) below are implied in every contract.

(7)   In the circumstances described in paragraph (2)(b) and (c) of this regulation, the other party to the contract will give prompt assistance to a consumer in difficulty.

(8)   If the consumer complains about a defect in the performance of the contract, the other party to the contract, or his local representative, if there is one, will make prompt efforts to find appropriate solutions.

(9)   The contract must clearly and explicitly oblige the consumer to communicate at the earliest opportunity, in writing or any other appropriate form, to the supplier of the services concerned and to the other party to the contract any failure which he perceives at the place where the services concerned are supplied.

16 SECURITY IN EVENT OF INSOLVENCY—REQUIREMENTS AND OFFENCES

(1)   The other party to the contract shall at all times be able to provide sufficient evidence of security for the refund of money paid over and for the repatriation of the consumer in the event of insolvency.

(2)   Without prejudice to paragraph (1) above, and subject to paragraph (4) below, save to the extent that—

> (a)   the package is covered by measures adopted or retained by the member State where he is established for the purpose of implementing Article 7 of the Directive; or

> (b)   the package is one in respect of which he is required to hold a licence under the Civil Aviation (Air Travel Organisers' Licensing) Regulations 1972 or the package is one that is covered by the arrangements he has entered into for the purposes of those Regulations,

the other party to the contract shall at least ensure that there are in force arrangements as described in regulations 17,18, 19 or 20 or, if that party is acting otherwise than in the course of business, as described in any of those regulations or in regulation 21.

(3)   Any person who contravenes paragraph (1) or (2) of this regulation shall be guilty of an offence and liable:—

(a)   on summary conviction to a fine not exceeding level 5 on the standard scale; and

(b)   on conviction on indictment, to a fine.

(4)   A person shall not be guilty of an offence under paragraph (3) above by reason only of the fact that arrangements such as are mentioned in paragraph (2) above are not in force in respect of any period before 1 April 1993 unless money paid over is not refunded when it is due or the consumer is not repatriated in the event of insolvency.

(5)   For the purposes of regulations 17 to 21 below a contract shall be treated as having been fully performed if the package or, as the case may be, the part of the package has been completed irrespective of whether the obligations under the contract have been properly performed for the purposes of regulation 15.

17 BONDING

(1)   The other party to the contract shall ensure that a bond is entered into by an authorised institution under which the institution binds itself to pay to an approved body of which that other party is a member a sum calculated in accordance with paragraph (3) below in the event of the insolvency of that other party.

(2)   Any bond entered into pursuant to paragraph (1) above shall not be expressed to be in force for a period exceeding eighteen months.

(3)   The sum referred to in paragraph (1) above shall be such sum as may reasonably be expected to enable all monies paid over by consumers under or in contemplation of contracts for relevant packages which have not been fully performed to be repaid and shall not in any event be a sum which is less than the minimum sum calculated in accordance with paragraph (4) below.

(4)   The minimum sum for the purposes of paragraph (3) above shall be a sum which represents:—

(a)   not less than 25 per cent of all the payments which the other party to the contract estimates that he will receive under or in contemplation of contracts for relevant packages in the twelve month period from the date of entry into force of the bond referred to in paragraph (1) above; or

(b)   the maximum amount of all the payments which the other party to the contract expects to hold at any one time, in respect of contracts which have not been fully performed,

whichever sum is the smaller.

(5)   Before a bond is entered into pursuant to paragraph (1) above, the other party to the contract shall inform the approved body of which he is a member of the minimum sum which he proposes for the purposes of paragraphs (3) and (4) above and it shall be the duty of the approved body to consider whether such sum is sufficient for the purpose mentioned in paragraph (3) and, if it does not consider that this is the case, it shall be the duty of the approved body so to inform the other party to the contract and to inform him of the sum which, in the opinion of the approved body, is sufficient for that purpose.

(6)   Where an approved body has informed the other party to the contract of a sum pursuant to paragraph (5) above, the minimum sum for the purposes of paragraphs (3) and (4) above shall be that sum.

(7)   In this regulation—

"approved body" means a body which is for the time being approved by the Secretary of State for the purposes of this regulation;

"authorised institution" means a person authorised under the law of a member State[, of the Channel Islands or of the Isle of Man] to carry on the business of entering into bonds of the kind required by this regulation.

NOTES
Amendment
Para (7): in definition "authorised institution" words in square brackets inserted by SI 1995/1648, reg 2(b).

18 BONDING WHERE APPROVED BODY HAS RESERVE FUND OR INSURANCE

(1)   The other party to the contract shall ensure that a bond is entered into by an authorised institution, under which the institution agrees to pay to an approved body of which that other party is a member a sum calculated in accordance with paragraph (3) below in the event of the insolvency of that other party.

(2)   Any bond entered into pursuant to paragraph (1) above shall not be expressed to be in force for a period exceeding eighteen months.

(3)   The sum referred to in paragraph (1) above shall be such sum as may be specified by the approved body as representing the lesser of—

>   (a)   the maximum amount of all the payments which the other party to the contract expects to hold at any one time in respect of contracts which have not been fully performed; or

>   (b)   the minimum sum calculated in accordance with paragraph (4) below.

(4) The minimum sum for the purposes of paragraph (3) above shall be a sum which represents not less than 10 per cent of all the payments which the other party to the contract estimates that he will receive under or in contemplation of contracts for relevant packages in the twelve month period from the date of entry referred to in paragraph (1) above.

(5) In this regulation "approved body" means a body which is for the time being approved by the Secretary of State for the purposes of this regulation and no such approval shall be given unless the conditions mentioned in paragraph (6) below are satisfied in relation to it.

(6) A body may not be approved for the purposes of this regulation unless—

> (a)   it has a reserve fund or insurance cover with an insurer authorised in respect of such business in a member State[, the Channel Islands or the Isle of Man] of an amount in each case which is designed to enable all monies paid over to a member of the body of consumers under or in contemplation of contracts for relevant packages which have not been fully performed to be repaid to those consumers in the event of the insolvency of the member; and

> (b)   where it has a reserve fund, it agrees that the fund will be held by persons and in a manner approved by the Secretary of State.

(7) In this regulation, authorised institution has the meaning given to that expression by paragraph (7) of regulation 17.

NOTES
Amendment
Para (6): in sub-para (a) words in square brackets inserted by SI 1995/1648, reg 2(c).

19 INSURANCE

(1)   The other party to the contract shall have insurance under one or more appropriate policies with an insurer authorised in respect of such business in a member State under which the insurer agrees to indemnify consumers, who shall be insured persons under the policy, against the loss of money paid over by them under or in contemplation of contracts for packages in the event of the insolvency of the contractor.

(2)   The other party to the contract shall ensure that it is a term of every contract with a consumer that the consumer acquires the benefit of a policy of a kind mentioned in paragraph (1) above in the event of the insolvency of the other party to the contract.

(3) In this regulation:

"appropriate policy" means one which does not contain a condition which provides (in whatever terms) that no liability shall arise under the policy, or that any liability so arising shall cease:—

(i)   in the event of some specified thing being done or omitted to be done after the happening of the event giving rise to a claim under the policy;

(ii)   in the event of the policy holder not making payments under or in connection with other policies; or

(iii)   unless the policy holder keeps specified records or provides the insurer with or makes available to him information therefrom.

20 MONIES IN TRUST

(1)   The other party to the contract shall ensure that all monies paid over by a consumer under or in contemplation of a contract for a relevant package are held in the United Kingdom by a person as trustee for the consumer until the contract has been fully performed or any sum of money paid by the consumer in respect of the contract has been repaid to him or has been forfeited on cancellation by the consumer.

(2)   The costs of administering the trust mentioned in paragraph (1) above shall be paid for by the other party to the contract.

(3)   Any interest which is earned on the monies held by the trustee pursuant to paragraph (1) shall be held for the other party to the contract and shall be payable to him on demand.

(4)   Where there is produced to the trustee a statement signed by the other party to the contract to the effect that—

(a)   a contract for a package the price of which is specified in that statement has been fully performed;

(b)   the other party to the contract has repaid to the consumer a sum of money specified in that statement which the consumer had paid in respect of a contract for a package; or

(c)   the consumer has on cancellation forfeited a sum of money specified in that statement which he had paid in respect of a contract for a relevant package,

the trustee shall (subject to paragraph (5) below) release to the other party to the contract the sum specified in the statement.

(5)   Where the trustee considers it appropriate to do so, he may require the other party to the contract to provide further information or evidence of the matters

mentioned in sub-paragraph (a),(b) or (c) of paragraph (4) above before he releases any sum to that other party pursuant to that paragraph.

(6)   Subject to paragraph (7) below, in the event of the insolvency of the other party to the contract the monies held in trust by the trustee pursuant to paragraph (1) of this regulation shall be applied to meet the claims of consumers who are creditors of that other party in respect of contracts for packages in respect of which the arrangements were established and which have not been fully performed and, if there is a surplus after those claims have been met, it shall form part of the estate of that insolvent other party for the purposes of insolvency law.

(7)   If the monies held in trust by the trustee pursuant to paragraph (1) of this regulation are insufficient to meet the claims of consumers as described in paragraph (6), payments to those consumers shall be made by the trustee on a pari passu basis.

21 MONIES IN TRUST WHERE OTHER PARTY TO CONTRACT IS ACTING OTHERWISE THAN IN THE COURSE OF BUSINESS

(1)   The other party to the contract shall ensure that all monies paid over by a consumer under or in contemplation of a contract for a relevant package are held in the United Kingdom by a person as trustee for the consumer for the purpose of paying for the consumer's package.

(2)   The costs of administering the trust mentioned in paragraph (1) shall be paid for out of the monies held in trust and the interest earned on those monies.

(3)   Where there is produced to the trustee a statement signed by the other party to the contract to the effect that—

>   (a)   the consumer has previously paid over a sum of money specified in that statement in respect of a contract for a package and that sum is required for the purpose of paying for a component (or part of a component) of the package;

>   (b)   the consumer has previously paid over a sum of money specified in that statement in respect of a contract for a package and the other party to the contract has paid that sum in respect of a component (or part of a component) of the package;

>   (c)   the consumer requires the repayment to him of a sum of money specified in that statement which was previously paid over by the consumer in respect of a contract for a package; or

>   (d)   the consumer has on cancellation forfeited a sum of money specified in that statement which he had paid in respect of a contract for a package,

the trustee shall (subject to paragraph (4) below) release to the other party to the contract the sum specified in the statement.

(4)   Where the trustee considers it appropriate to do so, he may require the other party to the contract to provide further information or evidence of the matters mentioned in sub-paragraph (a),(b),(c) or (d) of paragraph (3) above before he releases to that other party any sum from the monies held in trust for the consumer.

(5)   Subject to paragraph (6) below, in the event of the insolvency of the other party to the contract and of contracts for packages not being fully performed (whether before or after the insolvency) the monies held in trust by the trustee pursuant to paragraph (1) of this regulation shall be applied to meet the claims of consumers who are creditors of that other party in respect of amounts paid over by them and remaining in the trust fund after deductions have been made in respect of amounts released to that other party pursuant to paragraph (3) and, if there is a surplus after those claims have been met, it shall be divided amongst those consumers pro rata.

(6)   If the monies held in trust by the trustee pursuant to paragraph (1) of this regulation are insufficient to meet the claims of consumers as described in paragraph (5) above, payments to those consumers shall be made by the trustee on a pari passu basis.

(7)   Any sums remaining after all the packages in respect of which the arrangements were established have been fully performed shall be dealt with as provided in the arrangements or, in default of such provision, may be paid to the other party to the contract.

22 OFFENCES ARISING FROM BREACH OF REGULATIONS 20 AND 21

(1)   If the other party to the contract makes a false statement under paragraph (4) of regulation 20 or paragraph (3) of regulation 21 he shall be guilty of an offence.

(2)   If the other party to the contract applies monies released to him on the basis of a statement made by him under regulation 21(3)(a) or (c) for a purpose other than that mentioned in the statement he shall be guilty of an offence.

(3)   If the other party to the contract is guilty of an offence under paragraph (1) or (2) of this regulation shall be liable—

(a)   on summary conviction to a fine not exceeding level 5 on the standard scale; and

(b)   on conviction on indictment, to a fine.

23 ENFORCEMENT

Schedule 3 to these Regulations (which makes provision about the enforcement of regulations 5, 7, 8, 16 and 22 of these Regulations) shall have effect.

24 DUE DILIGENCE DEFENCE

(1)   Subject to the following provisions of this regulation, in proceedings against any person for an offence under regulation 5, 7, 8, 16 or 22 of these Regulations, it shall be a defence for that person to show that he took all reasonable steps and exercised all due diligence to avoid committing the offence.

(2)   Where in any proceedings against any person for such an offence the defence provided by paragraph (1) above involves an allegation that the commission of the offence was due—

(a)   to the act or default of another; or

(b)   to reliance on information given by another,

that person shall not, without the leave of the court, be entitled to rely on the defence unless, not less than seven clear days before the hearing of the proceedings, or, in Scotland, the trial diet, he has served a notice under paragraph (3) below on the person bringing the proceedings.

(3)   A notice under this paragraph shall give such information identifying or assisting in the identification of the person who committed the act or default or gave the information as is in the possession of the person serving the notice at the time he serves it.

(4)   It is hereby declared that a person shall not be entitled to rely on the defence provided by paragraph (1) above by reason of his reliance on information supplied by another, unless he shows that it was reasonable in all the circumstances for him to have relied on the information, having regard in particular—

(a)   to the steps which he took, and those which might reasonably have been taken, for the purpose of verifying the information; and

(b)   to whether he had any reason to disbelieve the information.

25 LIABILITY OF PERSONS OTHER THAN PRINCIPAL OFFENDER

(1)   Where the commission by any person of an offence under regulation 5, 7, 8, 16 or 22 of these Regulations is due to an act or default committed by some other person in the course of any business of his, the other person shall be guilty of the offence and may be proceeded against and punished by virtue of this paragraph whether or not proceedings are taken against the first-mentioned person.

(2)   Where a body corporate is guilty of an offence under any of the provisions mentioned in paragraph (1) above (including where it is so guilty by virtue of the said paragraph (1)) in respect of any act or default which is shown to have been

committed with the consent or connivance of, or to be attributable to any neglect on the part of, any director, manager, secretary or other similar officer of the body corporate or any person who was purporting to act in any such capacity he, as well as the body corporate, shall be guilty of that offence and shall be liable to be proceeded against and punished accordingly.

(3)   Where the affairs of a body corporate are managed by its members, paragraph (2) above shall apply in relation to the acts and defaults of a member in connection with his functions of management as if he were a director of the body corporate.

(4)   Where an offence under any of the provisions mentioned in paragraph (1) above committed in Scotland by a Scottish partnership is proved to have been committed with the consent or connivance of, or to be attributable to neglect on the part of, a partner, he (as well as the partnership) is guilty of the offence and liable to be proceeded against and punished accordingly.

(5)   On proceedings for an offence under regulation 5 by virtue of paragraph (1) above committed by the making available of a brochure it shall be a defence for the person charged to prove that he is a person whose business it is to publish or arrange for the publication of brochures and that he received the brochure for publication in the ordinary course of business and did not know and had no reason to suspect that its publication would amount to an offence under these Regulations.

26 PROSECUTION TIME LIMIT

(1)   No proceedings for an offence under regulation 5, 7, 8, 16 or 22 of these Regulations or under paragraphs 5(3), 6 or 7 of Schedule 3 thereto shall be commenced after—

> (a)   the end of the period of three years beginning within the date of the commission of the offence; or

> (b)   the end of the period of one year beginning with the date of the discovery of the offence by the prosecutor,

whichever is the earlier.

(2)   For the purposes of this regulation a certificate signed by or on behalf of the prosecutor and stating the date on which the offence was discovered by him shall be conclusive evidence of that fact; and a certificate stating that matter and purporting to be so signed shall be treated as so signed unless the contrary is proved.

(3)   In relation to proceedings in Scotland, subsection (3) of section 331 of the Criminal Procedure (Scotland) Act 1975 (date of commencement of proceedings) shall apply for the purposes of this regulation as it applies for the purposes of that section.

27 SAVING FOR CIVIL CONSEQUENCES

No contract shall be void or unenforceable, and no right of action in civil proceedings in respect of any loss shall arise, by reason only of the commission of an offence under regulations 5, 7, 8, 16 or 22 of these Regulations.

28 TERMS IMPLIED IN CONTRACT

Where it is provided in these Regulations that a term (whether so described or whether described as a condition or warranty) is implied in the contract it is so implied irrespective of the law which governs the contract.

SCHEDULE 1 INFORMATION TO BE INCLUDED (IN ADDITION TO THE PRICE) IN BROCHURES WHERE RELEVANT TO PACKAGES OFFERED

Regulation 5

1 The destination and the means, characteristics and categories of transport used.

2 The type of accommodation, its location, category or degree of comfort and its main features and, where the accommodation is to be provided in a member State, its approval or tourist classification under the rules of that member State.

3 The meals which are included in the package.

4 The itinerary.

5 General information about passport and visa requirements which apply for [nationals of the member State or States in which the brochure is made available] and health formalities required for the journey and the stay.

6 Either the monetary amount or the percentage of the price which is to be paid on account and the timetable for payment of the balance.

7 Whether a minimum number of persons is required for the package to take place and, if so, the deadline for informing the consumer in the event of cancellation.

8 The arrangements (if any) which apply if consumers are delayed at the outward or homeward points of departure.

9 The arrangements for security for money paid over and for the repatriation of the consumer in the event of insolvency.

NOTES
Amendment
Para 5: words "nationals of the member State or States in which the brochure is made available" in square brackets substituted by SI 1998/1208, reg 4.
Date in force: 30 June 1998: see SI 1998/1208, reg 1.

SCHEDULE 2 ELEMENTS TO BE INCLUDED IN THE CONTRACT IF RELEVANT TO THE PARTICULAR PACKAGE

REGULATION 9

1 The travel destination(s) and, where periods of stay are involved, the relevant periods, with dates.

2 The means, characteristics and categories of transport to be used and the dates, times and points of departure and return.

3 Where the package includes accommodation, its location, its tourist category or degree of comfort, its main features and, where the accommodation is to be provided in a member State, its compliance with the rules of that member State.

4 The meals which are included in the package.

5 Whether a minimum number of persons is required for the package to take place and, if so, the deadline for informing the consumer in the event of cancellation.

6 The itinerary.

7 Visits, excursions or other services which are included in the total price agreed for the package.

8 The name and address of the organiser, the retailer and, where appropriate, the insurer.

9 The price of the package, if the price may be revised in accordance with the term which may be included in the contract under regulation 11, an indication of the possibility of such price revisions, and an indication of any dues, taxes or fees chargeable for certain services (landing, embarkation or disembarkation fees at ports and airports and tourist taxes) where such costs are not included in the package.

10 The payment schedule and method of payment.

11 Special requirements which the consumer has communicated to the organiser or retailer when making the booking and which both have accepted.

12 The periods within which the consumer must make any complaint about the failure to perform or the inadequate performance of the contract.

SCHEDULE 3 ENFORCEMENT

REGULATION 23

ENFORCEMENT AUTHORITY

1(1)   Every local weights and measures authority in Great Britain shall be an enforcement authority for the purposes of regulations 5, 7, 8, 16 and 22 of these

Regulations ("the relevant regulations"), and it shall be the duty of each such authority to enforce those provisions within their area.

(2) The Department of Economic Development in Northern Ireland shall be an enforcement authority for the purposes of the relevant regulations, and it shall be the duty of the Department to enforce those provisions within Northern Ireland.

PROSECUTIONS

2(1) Where an enforcement authority in England or Wales proposes to institute proceedings for an offence under any of the relevant regulations, it shall as between the enforcement authority and the Director General of Fair Trading be the duty of the enforcement authority to give to the Director General of Fair Trading notice of the intended proceedings, together with a summary of the facts on which the charges are to be founded, and to postpone institution of the proceedings until either—

(a) twenty-eight days have elapsed since the giving of that notice; or

(b) the Director General of Fair Trading has notified the enforcement authority that he has received the notice and the summary of the facts.

(2) Nothing in paragraph 1 above shall authorise a local weights and measures authority to bring proceedings in Scotland for an offence.

POWERS OF OFFICERS OF ENFORCEMENT AUTHORITY

3(1) If a duly authorised officer of an enforcement authority has reasonable grounds for suspecting that an offence has been committed under any of the relevant regulations, he may—

(a) require a person whom he believes on reasonable grounds to be engaged in the organisation or retailing of packages to produce any book or document relating to the activity and take copies of it or any entry in it, or

(b) require such a person to produce in a visible and legible documentary form any information so relating which is contained in a computer, and take copies of it,

for the purpose of ascertaining whether such an offence has been committed.

(2) Such an officer may inspect any goods for the purpose of ascertaining whether such an offence has been committed.

(3) If such an officer has reasonable grounds for believing that any documents or goods may be required as evidence in proceedings for such an offence, he may seize and detain them.

(4) An officer seizing any documents or goods in the exercise of his power under sub-paragraph (3) above shall inform the person from whom they are seized.

(5)   The powers of an officer under this paragraph may be exercised by him only at a reasonable hour and on production (if required) of his credentials.

(6)   Nothing in this paragraph—

(a)   requires a person to produce a document if he would be entitled to refuse to produce it in proceedings in a court on the ground that it is the subject of legal professional privilege or, in Scotland, that it contains a confidential communication made by or to an advocate or a solicitor in that capacity; or

(b)   authorises the taking possession of a document which is in the possession of a person who would be so entitled.

4(1)   A duly authorised officer of an enforcement authority may, at a reasonable hour and on production (if required) of his credentials, enter any premises for the purpose of ascertaining whether an offence under any of the relevant regulations has been committed.

(2)   If a justice of the peace, or in Scotland a justice of the peace or a sheriff, is satisfied—

(a)   that any relevant books, documents or goods are on, or that any relevant information contained in a computer is available from, any premises, and that production or inspection is likely to disclose the commission of an offence under the relevant regulations; or

(b)   that any such an offence has been, is being or is about to be committed on any premises.

and that any of the conditions specified in sub-paragraph (3) below is met, he may by warrant under his hand authorise an officer of an enforcement authority to enter the premises, if need be by force.

(3)   The conditions referred to in sub-paragraph (2) above are—

(a)   that admission to the premises has been or is likely to be refused and that notice of intention to apply for a warrant under that sub-paragraph has been given to the occupier;

(b)   that an application for admission, or the giving of such a notice, would defeat the object of the entry;

(c)   that the premises are unoccupied; and

(d)   that the occupier is temporarily absent and it might defeat the object of the entry to await his return.

(4)   In sub-paragraph (2) above "relevant", in relation to books, documents, goods or information, means books, documents, goods or information which, under

paragraph 3 above, a duly authorised officer may require to be produced or may inspect.

(5) A warrant under sub-paragraph (2) above may be issued only if—

(a)   in England and Wales, the justice of the peace is satisfied as required by that sub-paragraph by written information on oath;

(b)   in Scotland, the justice of the peace or sheriff is so satisfied by evidence on oath; or

(c)   in Northern Ireland, the justice of the peace is so satisfied by complaint on oath.

(6) A warrant under sub-paragraph (2) above shall continue in force for a period of one month.

(7) An officer entering any premises by virtue of this paragraph may take with him such other persons as may appear to him necessary.

(8) On leaving premises which he has entered by virtue of a warrant under sub-paragraph (2) above, an officer shall, if the premises are unoccupied or the occupier is temporarily absent, leave the premises as effectively secured against trespassers as he found them.

(9) In this paragraph "premises" includes any place (including any vehicle, ship or aircraft) except premises used only as a dwelling.

OBSTRUCTION OF OFFICERS
5(1) A person who—

(a)   intentionally obstructs an officer of an enforcement authority acting in pursuance of this Schedule;

(b)   without reasonable excuse fails to comply with a requirement made of him by such an officer under paragraph 3(1) above; or

(c)   without reasonable excuse fails to give an officer of an enforcement authority acting in pursuance of this Schedule any other assistance or information which the officer may reasonably require of him for the purpose of the performance of the officer's functions under this Schedule,

shall be guilty of an offence.

(2) A person guilty of an offence under sub-paragraph (1) above shall be liable on summary conviction to a fine not exceeding level 5 on the standard scale.

(3)   If a person, in giving any such information as is mentioned in sub-paragraph (1)(c) above,—

(a)   makes a statement which he knows is false in a material particular; or

(b)   recklessly makes a statement which is false in a material particular,

he shall be guilty of an offence.

(4)   A person guilty of an offence under sub-paragraph (3) above shall be liable—

(a)   on summary conviction, to a fine not exceeding level 5 on the standard scale; and

(b)   on conviction on indictment, to a fine.

IMPERSONATION OF OFFICERS

6(1)   If a person who is not a duly authorised officer of an enforcement authority purports to act as such under this Schedule he shall be guilty of an offence.

(2)   A person guilty of an offence under sub-paragraph (1) above shall be liable—

(a)   on summary conviction, to a fine not exceeding level 5 on the standard scale; and

(b)   on conviction on indictment, to a fine.

DISCLOSURE OF INFORMATION

7(1)   If a person discloses to another any information obtained by him by virtue of this Schedule he shall be guilty of an offence unless the disclosure was made—

(a)   in or for the purpose of the performance by him or any other person of any function under the relevant regulations; or

(b)   for a purpose specified in section 38(2)(a),(b) or (c) of the Consumer Protection Act 1987.

(2)   A person guilty of an offence under sub-paragraph (1) above shall be liable—

(a)   on summary conviction, to a fine not exceeding level 5 on the standard scale; and

(b)   on conviction on indictment, to a fine.

PRIVILEGE AGAINST SELF-INCRIMINATION

8 Nothing in this Schedule requires a person to answer any question or give any information if to do so might incriminate him.

Index

Lightning Source UK Ltd.
Milton Keynes UK
19 March 2010

151590UK00001B/2/P